A READER FOR

WRITERS

A READER FOR

WRITERS

A CRITICAL ANTHOLOGY OF PROSE READINGS

THIRD EDITION

JEROME W. ARCHER
Arizona State University

JOSEPH SCHWARTZ
Marquette University

McGRAW-HILL BOOK COMPANY

New York St. Louis San Francisco Düsseldorf Kuala Lumpur London
Mexico Montreal New Delhi Panama Rio de Janeiro Singapore Sydney Toronto

This book was set in News Gothic by Monotype Composition Company, Inc., and printed on permanent paper and bound by The Maple Press Company. The designer was J. E. O'Connor. The editors were Cheryl Kupper, Susan Gamer, and Robert Fry. Les Kaplan supervised production.

A READER FOR WRITERS

Library of Congress Catalog Card Number
77–141914

07–002193–7

2 3 4 5 6 7 8 9   MAMM   7 9 8 7 6 5 4 3 2 1

ACKNOWLEDGMENTS

Mortimer J. Adler, "How to Mark a Book," from *Saturday Review* (July 6, 1940).

James Agee, "Knoxville: Summer 1915," from *A Death in the Family*, by James Agee. Copyright © 1957 by James Agee Trust. First published in *The Partisan Review*. Reprinted by permission of the publisher, Grosset & Dunlap, Inc.

Hervey Allen, "Genesis," from *The Forest and the Fort*, by Hervey Allen. Copyright © 1971 by Ann Andrews Allen. Reprinted by permission of Holt, Rinehart and Winston, Inc.

W. H. Auden, "Concerning the Unpredictable," from *The New Yorker* (February 21, 1970). Copyright 1970, New Yorker Magazine, Inc.

James Baldwin, "Stranger in the Village," from *Notes of a Native Son*, by James Baldwin. Copyright © 1953, 1955 by James Baldwin. Reprinted by permission of the Beacon Press.

Robert Benchley, "Throwing Back the European Offensive," by Robert Benchley, from *The Benchley Roundup* selected by Nathaniel Benchley. Copyright 1927 by Harper & Row, Publishers, Inc.

Daniel J. Boorstin, "The New Barbarians," condensed from "The New Barbarians," copyright © 1968 by Daniel J. Boorstin. Reprinted by permission of Random House, Inc. This article appears, in somewhat different form, in *The Decline of Radicalism*, by Daniel J. Boorstin. Originally appeared in *Esquire*.

Elizabeth Bowen, "The Incoming Tide," from *The Heat of the Day*. Copyright 1948, 1949 by Elizabeth Bowen. Reprinted by permission of Alfred A. Knopf, Inc.

J. Bronowski, "Science and Sensibility," from *The Common Sense of Science*, by J. Bronowski. Cambridge, Mass.: Harvard University Press, 1953, London: Heinemann Educational Books, Ltd. Reprinted by permission.

Raymond Leopold Bruckberger, "An Assignment for Intellectuals," *Harper's*

Magazine (February 1956). Copyright by Harper & Brothers, New York. Reprinted by permission of Harold Matson Co.

Alexander Calandra, "Angels on a Pin," from *Saturday Review* (December 21, 1968).

George F. Carter, "The American Civilization Puzzle," from *The Johns Hopkins Magazine* (February 1957).

John Ciardi, "What Every Writer Must Learn," from *Saturday Review* (December 15, 1956).

Kenneth B. Clark, "Intelligence, the University and Society." Reprinted from *The American Scholar* (Winter 1966–1967). Copyright © 1966 by the United Chapters of Phi Beta Kappa. By permission of the publishers.

Joseph Conrad, "The Landing of the *Narcissus*," from *The Nigger of the Narcissus*, J. M. Dent & Sons, Ltd., London.

Aaron Copland, "What to Listen for in Music," from the book of that title by Aaron Copland, revised edition. Copyright 1939 and 1957 by McGraw-Hill Book Company, New York.

Tobias Dantzig, "The Empty Column," from *Number: The Language of Science*, by Tobias Dantzig. New York: The Macmillan Company, 1954. Copyright 1930, 1933, 1939, 1954 by The Macmillan Company.

Bernal Diaz del Castillo, "The Storming of the Great Temple: A Soldier's View," from *The Discovery and Conquest of Mexico* by Bernal Diaz del Castillo. Copyright 1956 by Farrar, Straus & Cudahy, Inc., New York. Reprinted by permission of the publisher.

Joan Didion, "On Self-Respect," from *Slouching Towards Bethlehem*, by Joan Didion, copyright © 1961, 1968 by Joan Didion. Reprinted with the permission of Farrar, Straus & Giroux, Inc.

Peter F. Drucker, "The Romantic Generation," from the forthcoming book Men, Ideas & Society. Copyright © 1966 by Peter F. Drucker. Reprinted by permission of Harper & Row, Publishers, Inc.

Rene Dubos, "Rebels in Search of a Cause," from *So Human an Animal*, pages 3–9. Copyright © 1968 by Rene Dubos. Reprinted by permission of Charles Scribner's Sons.

Loren Eiseley, "The Innocent Fox." Excerpted from the chapter "The Innocent Fox." Copyright © 1969 by Loren Eiseley. Reprinted from Loren Eiseley, *The Unexpected Universe*, by permission of Harcourt Brace Jovanovich, Inc.

George P. Elliott, "Poetry Makes Nothing Happen." Copyright © 1968 by George P. Elliott. This essay first appeared in the *New York Times Book Review*.

Ralph Ellison, "Blues People," from *Shadow and Act*, by Ralph Ellison. Copyright © 1964 by Ralph Ellison. By permission of Random House, Inc.

James Fremantle, "The Battle of Gettysburg: The Observer," from *The Fremantle Diary*, ed. Walter Lord. Copyright 1954 by Walter Lord. Reprinted by permission of Little, Brown and Co.

Milton Friedman, "The Market v. the Bureaucrat," *National Review* (May 19, 1970). Used by permission of *National Review*, 1950 E. 35th Street, New York 10016.

Christopher Fry, "Enjoying the Accidental," from *Vogue* (October 15, 1957). Copyright © 1957 by Christopher Fry. Reprinted by permission of the author.

Walker Gibson, "A Note on Style and the Limits of Language," from *The Limits of Language*, ed. (with introduction) by Walker Gibson. Reprinted by permission of Hill and Wang, Inc.

Albert Goldman, "The Emergence of Rock," from *New American Review* No. 3 (1968). Copyright © 1968 by Albert Goldman. Reprinted by permission of The Sterling Lord Agency.

Ulf Hannerz, "The Rhetoric of Soul: Identification in Negro Society," from *Race,* Vol. IX, no. 4 (1968).

Frank A. Haskell, "The Battle of Gettysburg: The Participant," from *The Battle of Gettysburg,* by Frank A. Haskell, ed. Bruce Catton. Boston: Houghton Mifflin Company, 1958. Reprinted by permission.

Ernest Hemingway, "Camping Out," in *The Wild Years,* ed. Gene Z. Hanrahan, Dell Publishing Co., Inc. Copyright by Mary Hemingway.

Irving Howe, "A Review of *Mr. Sammler's Planet,"* from *Harper's Magazine* (February 1970).

Aldous Huxley, "Who Are You?" from *Harper's Magazine* (November 1944). Copyright 1944 by Harper & Brothers, New York. Reprinted by permission of the publishers and the author.

Johannes Jörgensen, "All Riddles Solved," from *Jörgensen: An Autobiography,* Vol. I, pp. 79–91. New York and London: Longmans, Green & Company, Inc., 1929. Used by permission of David McKay Company, Inc.

Pauline Kael, "Lolita," from *I Lost It at the Movies,* by Pauline Kael, by permission of Atlantic, Little, Brown and Co. Copyright © 1954, 1955, 1961, 1962, 1963, 1964, 1965 by Pauline Kael.

John F. Kennedy, "Inaugural Address," from *To Turn the Tide* by John F. Kennedy, ed. J. W. Gardner. Copyright 1962 by John F. Kennedy. New York: Harper & Brothers, 1962. Reprinted by permission of Harper & Row, Publishers, Inc.

Martin Luther King, Jr., "Letter from Birmingham Jail, April 16, 1963," from *Why We Can't Wait,* by Martin Luther King, Jr. Copyright © 1963 by Martin Luther King, Jr. Reprinted by permission of Harper & Row, Publishers, Inc.

Russell Kirk, "A Preliminary Delineation: Conservative and Radical," from *The Conservative Mind.* Copyright 1953 by Henry Regnery Company, Chicago.

Seymour Krim, "Literature Makes Plenty Happen," from *The New York Times* (April 14, 1968). Copyright © 1968 by *The New York Times Company.*

Joseph Wood Krutch, "Is Our Common Man Too Common?" from *Saturday Review* (January 10, 1953). "What Is a Good Review?" from *The Nation* (April 17, 1937).

Katharine Kuh, "Place, Time, and Painter," from *Saturday Review* (September 6, 1969).

John LaFarge, "The Web of Confidence," from *An American Amen,* by John LaFarge. Copyright 1958 by John LaFarge. Reprinted by permission of the publisher, Farrar, Straus & Cudahy, Inc., New York.

Dorothy Lee, "Suburbia Reconsidered: Diversity and the Creative Life," from *Man and the Modern City,* ed. Elizabeth Geen. University of Pittsburgh Press, 1963.

Walter Lippmann, "The Indispensable Opposition," from *The Atlantic Monthly* (August 1939). Copyright 1939 by The Atlantic Monthly Company.

Della Lutes, "Are Neighbors Necessary?" from *American Mercury* (November 1936). Reprinted by permission of the publisher and Mrs. Cecily L. Dodd.

Archibald MacLeish, "The Revolt of the Diminished Man," from *Saturday Review* (June 7, 1969).

Phyllis McGinley, "Suburbia: Of Thee I Sing," from *A Short Walk From the*

Station, by Phyllis McGinley. Copyright 1949 and 1951 by Phyllis McGinley. Reprinted by permission of The Viking Press, Inc., New York.

W. Somerset Maugham, "Three Characteristics of Style," from *The Summing Up*, by W. Somerset Maugham. Reprinted by permission of Doubleday & Company, Inc., New York, the author, and William Heinemann, Ltd., London.

William Maxwell, "The Desert," from *The Folded Leaf*, Vintage Press. Copyright 1945 by William Maxwell.

Rollo May, "The Man Who Was Put in a Cage," from *Psychology and the Human Dilemma*, by Rollo May. Copyright © 1967 by Litton Educational Publishing, Inc., by permission of Van Nostrand Reinhold Company.

Ved Mehta, "The Poorest of the Poor," from *A Portrait of India*, by Ved Mehta. Copyright © 1967, 1968, 1969, 1970 by Ved Mehta. Reprinted with the permission of Farrar, Straus & Giroux, Inc. This material originally appeared in *The New Yorker*.

Thomas Merton, "I Fall in Love," from *The Seven Story Mountain*, copyright 1948 by Thomas Merton. Reprinted by permission of Harcourt, Brace & World, Inc.

Jessica Mitford, "The Story of Service," from *The American Way of Death*, by Jessica Mitford. Copyright © 1963 by Jessica Mitford. Reprinted by permission of Simon and Schuster, Inc.

Daniel P. Moynihan, "Nirvana Now," from *The American Scholar* (Autumn 1967). Copyright © 1967 by the United Chapters of Phi Beta Kappa. By permission of the publishers.

Malcolm Muggeridge, "My True Love Hath My Heart," from *Jesus Rediscovered*, by Malcolm Muggeridge. Copyright © 1969 by Malcolm Muggeridge. Reprinted by permission of Doubleday & Company, Inc.

Herbert J. Muller, "What Science Is," from *Science and Criticism*, by Herbert J. Muller. New Haven, Conn.: Yale University Press, 1943. Reprinted by permission.

Katherine Anne Porter, "Portrait: Old South," from *The Days Before*, by Katherine Anne Porter. Copyright © 1944 by Katherine Anne Porter. Reprinted by permission of the author.

J. F. Powers, "The Valiant Woman," from *Prince of Darkness and Other Stories*, by J. F. Powers. Copyright 1947 by J. F. Powers. Reprinted by permission of Doubleday & Company, Inc., New York.

William H. Prescott, "The Storming of a Great Temple: A Historian's View," from *The Conquest of Mexico*, 1843.

Agnes Repplier, "Small Tragedies," from the book of that title by Agnes Repplier. Copyright 1938 by Atlantic Monthly Press, Boston. Reprinted by permission of Fidelity-Philadelphia Trust Company.

David Riesman, "Tootle: A Modern Cautionary Tale," from *The Lonely Crowd*. New Haven, Conn.: Yale University Press, 1950; rev. ed., 1953.

Arthur M. Schlesinger, "What Do the Terms Mean?" from *New Viewpoints in American History*. Copyright 1922 by The Macmillan Company, New York. Used by permission of the publisher.

Wilfred Sheed, "My Passport Was at Shortstop," from *Sports Illustrated* (November 11, 1968). Copyright © 1968 by Time, Inc. Reprinted by permission of Robert Lantz-Candida Donadio Literary Agency, Inc.

James Thurber, "The Night the Ghost Got In," from *My Life and Hard Times*, published by Harper & Row. Copyright © 1933, 1961 by James Thurber. Originally printed in *The New Yorker*.

Leopold Tyrmand, "American Century," from *Notebooks of a Dilettante*, by Leopold Tyrmand. Copyright © 1967, 1968, 1969, 1970 by Leopold Tyrmand. Reprinted with permission of The Macmillan Company. This material originally appeared in *The New Yorker*.

Peter van Dresser, "The Modern Retreat from Function," from *Landscape*, Vol. 10, no. 3 (Spring 1961).

Barbara Ward, "Real Religion—and False," from *The New York Times* (December 9, 1954). Reprinted by permission of the publisher and the author.

Robert Penn Warren, "Malcolm X: Mission and Meaning." New Haven, Conn.: *The Yale Review* no. 56 (December 1966). Copyright © 1967 by Robert Penn Warren. Reprinted by permission of William Morris Agency, Inc., on behalf of the author.

Robert Warshow, "The Gangster as Tragic Hero," from *The Immediate Experience*, by Robert Warshow. New York: Doubleday and Company, Inc., 1962. Copyright by Joseph Goldberg, Trustee of the Estate. Reprinted by permission.

Richard M. Weaver, "The Image of Culture," from *Modern Age: A Quarterly Review*, Vol. 8, no. 2 (Spring 1964).

Eudora Welty, "A Visit of Charity," from *A Curtain of Green and Other Stories*, by Eudora Welty. Copyright 1941 by Eudora Welty. Reprinted by permission of Harcourt, Brace & World, Inc., New York.

Harold Zyskind, "A Rhetorical Analysis of the Gettysburg Address," from the *Journal of General Education*, 3 (1950).

CONTENTS

3 THE GREEKS HAD A WORD FOR IT: **ARGUMENT**   367

7 THE THREE NECESSARIES: **STYLE**   623

As its title suggests, *A Reader for Writers* is a book of readings for students of writing. We have prepared this textbook because in our own teaching we want to use a book of readings organized essentially within a rhetorical framework and employing the technique of extensive questioning. No one has yet found a better way to teach composition than by the use of prose models, with exercises and suggestions for writing based on the models. The organization of this anthology of reading remains traditional in that the bulk of the book is concerned with an examination of the major forms of discourse— exposition, argument, description, and narration. But the special requirements of general classroom experience have not been ignored to favor firm, unpliant organization for its own sake. A section on personal narrative, which presents the student with topics he is most equipped to deal with immediately, acts as an introduction. Concluding the text are two sections of readings customarily used in the composition course: a section on specific patterns of writing— the familiar essay, and reviews—and a section on style that gives direct practical advice to the student. These two sections can be manipulated within any course organization to be used wherever the instructor finds them to be of most value. A glossary of terms used in this anthology is supplied for the convenience of the student.

The principal method of this text assumes that extensive questioning about selections is both desirable and necessary. Two kinds of questions are employed for a relatively intensive analysis of the essays. Footnote questions, appearing at the bottom of the page and referring to specific paragraphs, are used to enable the student to give prompt attention to certain details (grammatical, rhetorical, thematical) within the text of the essay that seem to demand immediate attention. This punctual reference to the text will keep the student continually aware while he reads. We hope by this device to forestall the look of open-mouthed wonder that so often crosses the face of the composition student when the instructor poses a question in class. We hope also to reduce drastically the fruitless waiting period as the student attempts both to comprehend and to answer the question. The footnote questions become less extensive and gradually disappear in the latter part of the text, on the assumption that the student by then will have learned to pay close attention to what he reads. The questions on the whole selection which follow the essay appear in almost all anthologies of this kind. In this book they serve their traditional purpose: to alert the student to writing and reading problems which are best dealt with by looking at the essay as a whole. We believe that it would be best for the instructor to select from both kinds of questions in conducting a class discussion. The experienced teacher is encouraged, however, to use the editorial matter as best fits his specific situation. It may be turned to account, passed by, modified, or supplemented as necessity and inclination may decide.

We have questioned almost all the essays to elicit from the student discussion that is especially relevant to the rhetorical category to which we are specifically directing his attention. We have, however, made a distinct effort also to provide questions which emphasize the totality of a given selection. Thus, questions on sentence structure, rhetorical strategy, punctuation, and metaphor may appear side by side. Some questions also look backward to help the student review what he has already studied. Robert Louis Stevenson's apt comparison of the writer to a juggler keeping a number of balls in the air simultaneously should never be forgotten. And though the instructor is forced to select in order to concentrate, too much emphasis in this direction may encourage students to think of writing (and reading) as an artificial bringing together of mutually exclusive parts. Both to analyze and to synthesize may appear, indeed, an impossibility; but teachers of composition do the impossible in their best hours in the classroom.

Two selections in each section except the first and the last have no questions of any kind. These appear for the benefit of the instructor who prefers at times to prepare his own questions and aids for study or who prefers the free association method of questioning which grows out of class discussion. These essays may also be used for reviewing or for testing student achievement.

The essays selected for study are in the tradition of good prose in English. Although most of them are by contemporary writers, we have not been so parochial as to exclude prose of the past when it might serve our purposes. All the readings can aid the student in solving his own writing problems, since each provides him with a model in which he may discover the application of rhetorical practice. The essays are not rigid *exempla* of the forms of writing that they illustrate, and they were not intended to be. Only a Procrustean violence would permit the selection of an essay that illustrated only one rhetorical strategy. Perhaps this can be done with pieces and parts of essays, a paragraph here or there; but the totality of a prose selection makes it impossible to categorize any finished piece so neatly.

If this anthology of readings succeeds in teaching the student to concentrate with some diligence on the *manner* in which ideas, moods, feelings, or observations are expressed, it will have accomplished its purpose. The competent kind of literate expression expected of the college graduate can be learned; and it can be learned best, we are convinced, by asking the student to become aware of the way in which things can be expressed. All writing involves making choices among many possibilities. Within the traditional forms of discourse, these possibilities may well be innumerable. We have tried to select essays which suggest that a variety of possibilities is available. By imitation and by the invention which grows from imitation, the student writer should have enough knowledge and practice from his study of the essays in this anthology to make his choices wisely for his own writing.

The third edition retains the structure and intent of the earlier editions. We have profited greatly from the advice of users of those editions; their comments, together with our own continued experience with the text, have resulted in the replacement of an extensive number of readings. We feel that the newly included essays—representing almost half of the selections in the text—reflect a greater range of interests and techniques, provide stronger models, and present added opportunities for fruitful classroom discussion. We hope that the effectiveness of the book as a flexible teaching instrument has been materially enhanced.

Jerome W. Archer
Joseph Schwartz

A READER FOR

WRITERS

1

FIRST PERSON SINGULAR_____

PERSONAL NARRATIVE

I began these pages for myself, in order to think out my own particular pattern of living, my own individual balance of life, work and human relationships. And since I think best with a pencil in my hand, I started naturally to write.   Anne Morrow Lindbergh

A writer's "own particular pattern of living" often provides him with one of his most interesting subjects—himself. In telling his own story, a writer constructs a personal narrative, a kind of autobiography. In considering the events of his life, certain incidents stand out as self-contained, having a beginning, a middle, and an end. Each one might be regarded as a "chapter" of his life. We have included five such incidents in this section, each self-contained enough to be complete in itself. From an analysis of these "chapters," certain principles of writing personal narrative emerge. In each of these selections, the author himself is the center of the experience: he is the focal point of the event. His prominence is essential. Obviously, personal narrative differs from other factual narrative in that it finds its source in, and centers its interest on, the personal history of the writer.

A writer begins to find a limited subject by thinking about the "individual balance" of his own "life, work and human relationships." He has discovered a true subject when he finds something apparently self-contained which he thinks is interesting enough to re-create, for to be interested yourself is the first condition of interesting others. An author does not review his life indiscriminately: he knows that it is not the experience itself but the meaningful evaluation and skillful presentation of it that is important. A true subject may be something which appears to be unusual, something with inherent dramatic qualities, such as a brush with death, but it may also be something which seems commonplace and ordinary. Both kinds of experience, however, must be charged with significance by the writer, who must take care to avoid indolence in presenting the unusual and indifference in projecting the commonplace. True subjects are as various as the experience of authors. Thomas Merton describes the "devouring, emotional, passionate love of adolescence" which, he insists, no one can go through twice. Agnes Repplier presents the complexities of the moral problem of a young schoolgirl. James Baldwin tells us how his experience as the only black man in a remote Swiss village demonstrated that "people are trapped in history and history is trapped in them," and that, through "no element of intentional unkindness," the villagers regarded him as "an exotic rarity," and not as a fellow human being. Wilfrid Sheed describes how, transplanted from England to the United States as a young boy, he was initiated into American culture through his interest and participation in American sports. None of these authors is like the sailors Cardinal Newman described: men who "range from one end of the earth to the other; but the multiplicity of external objects, which they have encountered, forms no symmetrical and consistent picture upon their imaginations; they see the tapestry of human life, as it were, on the wrong side, and it tells no story." What all our writers have in common is the quality of perception, the ability to see the tapestry of life on the right side as it tells a story. Experience, when it is viewed and understood, acquires value. It gains significance—a significance which depends, however, not upon the experience itself but upon the writer. Willa Cather said that any corner of the world will do for a writer. It follows, we believe, that any "chapter" of a life will do as a starting point for a personal narrative. Any event, unusual or ordinary, simple or complex, is a proper subject if it is limited enough to be self-contained.

Like all good writing, personal narrative must have a central purpose which dominates and guides the development of the subject. The central purpose may be to reveal character through situation, to show how a situation has influenced character, or to present the facts of an experience for its own sake. If Merton's central purpose is to communicate the impact of love upon an adolescent, the details he selects for inclusion in his narrative can be tested by that purpose. He presents himself as a particular kind of adolescent by including details such as his calculated aloofness from the other passengers. Appropriate hints about the lady's past, such as her experience in a "famous" night club, which would excite the ardor of this kind of young man, are incorporated. These details and others grow from the central purpose in a natural and necessary sequence.

The careful writer of personal narrative presents the details informed by the central purpose in a concrete manner, emphasizing the specific and particular, making a real effort to avoid the vague and general. By avoiding the commonplace in expression, Merton interestingly presents an incident so universal it might be called commonplace. He recalls accurately and in detail his own reactions and presents them in a concrete fashion. For example, he does not simply say that he was attracted to a beautiful woman: he presents those details which make that kind of statement meaningful. She is small, as delicate as if made of porcelain, with "big wide-open California eyes" and a voice that has "some suggestion of weariness about it as if she habitually stayed up too late at night." In her essay, Miss Repplier describes the head of the convent school as "cold, severe, sardonic"; she does not merely tell us that the convent girls disliked the head. In his description of the little Swiss village, Baldwin suggests its remoteness by citing specific features: it had "no movie house, no bank, no library, no theater." In his first experiences with baseball, Sheed observes that, as in cricket, there are many moments of inaction, of what he calls "pregnant pauses," but he verifies that observation by giving us specific evidence: "The pitcher peering in to get the sign, the ritual chant of the infield, the whispered consultations. . . ."

All personal narrative is based upon the accurate observation and intimate remembrance of a self-contained incident. Little more is required for a suitable beginning. After sufficient examination and contemplation, the writer discovers the central purpose which gives meaning to the details. If he has a manner of expression which makes the details meaningful to the reader, he will be read.

I FALL IN LOVE

THOMAS MERTON

In three months, the summer of 1931, I suddenly matured like a weed. 1

I cannot tell which is the more humiliating: the memory of the half-baked adolescent I was in June or the glib and hard-boiled specimen I was in October when I came back to Oakham full of a thorough and deep-rooted sophistication of which I was both conscious and proud.* 2

The beginning was like this: Pop wrote to me to come to America. I got a brand-new suit made. I said to myself, "On the boat I am going to meet a beautiful girl, and I am going to fall in love." 3

So I got on the boat. The first day I sat in a deck chair and read the correspondence of Goethe and Schiller which had been imposed on me as a duty, in preparation for the scholarship examinations at the university. What is worse, I not only tolerated this imposition but actually convinced myself that it was interesting. 4

The second day I had more or less found out who was on the boat. The third day I was no longer interested in the Goethe and Schiller. The fourth day I was up to my neck in the trouble that I was looking for. 5

It was a ten-day boat.† 6

I would rather spend two years in a hospital than go through that anguish again! That devouring, emotional, passionate love of adolescence that sinks its claws into you and consumes you day and night and eats into the vitals of your soul! All the self-tortures of doubt and anxiety and imagination and hope and despair that you go through when you are a child, trying to break out of your shell, only to find yourself in the middle of a legion of full-armed emotions against which you have no defense! It is like being flayed alive. No one can go through it twice. This kind of a love affair can really happen only once in a man's life. After that he is calloused. He is no longer capable of so many torments. He can suffer, but not from so many matters of no account. After one such crisis he has experience and the possibility of a second time no longer exists, because the secret of the anguish was his own utter guilelessness. He is no longer capable of such complete and absurd surprises. No matter how simple a man may be, the obvious cannot go on astonishing him forever.‡ 7

---

* Paragraph 2: How does the initial contrast in attitude show what development will take place in the essay?

† Paragraph 6: What is the justification for using a one-sentence paragraph in this instance?

‡ Paragraph 7: How is the suffering of a first experience of adolescent love distinguished from other, later sufferings? Why does the author generalize about the character of the anguish *before* he presents the situation which caused it? Define "guilelessness" as used here.

I was introduced to this particular girl by a Catholic priest who came from Cleveland and played shuffleboard in his shirt sleeves without a Roman collar on. He knew everybody on the boat in the first day, and as for me, two days had gone by before I even realized that she was on board. She was traveling with a couple of aunts and the three of them did not mix in with the other passengers very much. They kept to themselves in their three deck chairs and had nothing to do with the gentlemen in tweed caps and glasses who went breezing around and around the promenade deck.   8

When I first met her I got the impression that she was no older than I was. As a matter of fact she was about twice my age: but you could be twice sixteen without being old, as I now realize, sixteen years after the event. She was small and delicate and looked as if she were made out of porcelain. But she had big wide-open California eyes and was not afraid to talk in a voice that was at once ingenuous and independent and had some suggestion of weariness about it as if she habitually stayed up too late at night.   9

To my dazzled eyes she immediately became the heroine of every novel and I all but flung myself face down on the deck at her feet. She could have put a collar on my neck and led me around from that time forth on the end of a chain. Instead of that I spent my time telling her and her aunts all about my ideals and my ambitions and she in her turn attempted to teach me how to play bridge. And that is the surest proof of her conquest, for I never allowed anyone else to try such a thing as that on me, never! But even she could not succeed in such an enterprise.   10

We talked. The insatiable wound inside me bled and grew, and I was doing everything I could to make it bleed more. Her perfume and the peculiar smell of the denicotinized cigarettes she smoked followed me everywhere and tortured me in my cabin.*   11

She told me how once she was in a famous night club in a famous city when a famous person, a prince of the royal blood, had stared very intently at her for a long time and had finally got up and started to lurch in the direction of her table when his friends had made him sit down and behave himself.†   12

I could see that all the counts and dukes who liked to marry people like Constance Bennett would want also to marry her. But the counts and dukes were not here on board this glorified cargo boat that was carrying us all peacefully across the mild dark waves of the North Atlantic. The thing that crushed me was that I had never learned to dance.‡   13

---

* Paragraph 11: Why does he call the wound "insatiable"?

† Paragraph 12: Why would the story of the incident in the night club increase the boy's ardor?

‡ Paragraph 13: Is the final sentence of this paragraph irrelevant?

We made Nantucket Light on Sunday afternoon and had to anchor in quarantine that night. So the ship rode in the Narrows on the silent waters, and the lights of Brooklyn glittered in the harbor like jewels. The boat was astir with music and with a warm glowing life that pulsated within the dark hull and poured out into the July night through every porthole. There were parties in all the cabins. Everywhere you went, especially on deck where it was quiet, you were placed in the middle of movie scenery——the setting for the last reel of the picture.   14

I made a declaration of my undying love. I would not, could not, ever love anyone else but her. It was impossible, unthinkable. If she went to the ends of the earth, destiny would bring us together again. The stars in their courses from the beginning of the world had plotted this meeting which was the central fact in the whole history of the universe. Love like this was immortal. It conquered time and outlasted the futility of human history. And so forth.*   15

She talked to me, in her turn, gently and sweetly. What it sounded like was: "You do not know what you are saying. This can never be. We shall never meet again." What it meant was: "You are a nice kid. But for heaven's sake grow up before someone makes a fool of you." I went to my cabin and sobbed over my diary for a while and then, against all the laws of romance, went peacefully to sleep.   16

However, I could not sleep for long. At five o'clock I was up again, and walking restlessly around the deck. It was hot. A grey mist lay on the Narrows. But when it became light, other anchored ships began to appear as shapes in the mist. One of them was a Red Star liner on which, as I learned from the papers when I got on shore, a passenger was at that precise moment engaged in hanging himself.   17

At the last minute before landing I took a snapshot of her which, to my intense sorrow, came out blurred. I was so avid for a picture of her that I got too close with the camera and it was out of focus. It was a piece of poetic justice that filled me with woe for months.†   18

Of course the whole family was there on the dock. But the change was devastating. With my heart ready to explode with immature emotions I suddenly found myself surrounded by all the cheerful and peaceful and comfortable solicitudes of home. Everybody wanted to talk. Their voices were full of questions and information. They took me for a drive on Long Island and showed me where Mrs. Hearst lived and everything. But I only hung my head out of the window of the car and watched the green trees go swirling by, and wished that I were dead.   19

* Paragraph 15: What makes us aware that the author is commenting on this experience from a point of view different from that which he had at the time of the event?

† Paragraph 18: Why is this incident referred to as "a piece of poetic justice"?

The Whole Selection

1 Is the essay written from the point of view of an adolescent or that of an adult looking back on the experience? Cite evidence for your opinion.

2 What specific details (e.g., "a Catholic priest who came from Cleveland" and "big wide-open California eyes") contribute to the reality of the experience?

3 As compared with the narrative by Agnes Repplier (pages 9–12), this selection uses relatively little dialogue. Should the author have used more? If not, why not?

4 Notice how simple and often how colloquial the diction is and how straightforward the presentation. What words in this selection did you have to look up in a dictionary?

SMALL TRAGEDIES

AGNES REPPLIER

I was twelve years old, and very happy in my convent school. I did not particularly mind studying my lessons, and I sometimes persuaded the less experienced nuns to accept a retentive memory as a substitute for intelligent understanding, with which it has nothing to do. I "got along" with other children, and I enjoyed my friends; and of such simple things is the life of a child composed.   1

Then came a disturbing letter from my mother, a letter which threatened the heart of my content. It was sensible and reasonable, and it said very plainly and very kindly that I had better not make an especial friend of Lilly Milton; "not an exclusive friend," wrote my mother, "not one whom you would expect to see intimately after you leave school."*   2

I knew what all that meant. I was as innocent as a kitten; but divorces were not common in those conservative years, and Mrs. Milton had as many to her credit as if she were living—a highly esteemed and popular lady— today. I regretted my mother's tendency to confuse issues with unimportant details (a mistake which grown-up people often made), and I felt that if she knew Lilly—who was also as innocent as a kitten, and was blessed with the sweetest temper that God ever gave a little girl—she would be delighted that I had such an excellent friend. So I went on happily enough until ten days later, when Madame Rayburn, a nun for whom I cherished a very warm affection, was talking to me upon a familiar theme—the diverse ways in which I might improve my classwork and my general behavior. The subject did not interest me deeply,—repetition had staled its vivacity,—until my companion said the one thing that had plainly been uppermost in her mind: "And Agnes, how did you come to tell Lilly Milton that your mother did not want you to go with her? I never thought you could have been so deliberately unkind."   3

This brought me to my feet with a bound. "Tell Lilly!" I cried. "You could not have believed such a thing. It was Madame Bouron who told her."†   4

A silence followed this revelation. The convent discipline was as strict for the nuns as for the pupils, and it was not their custom to criticize their superiors. Madame Bouron was mistress general, ranking next to the august head, and of infinitely more importance to us. She was a cold, severe, sardonic woman, and the general dislike felt for her had shaped itself into a cult. I had accepted this cult in simple good faith, having no

---

* Paragraph 2: Classify the grammatical structure of the first and second sentences.

† Paragraph 4: Why didn't the author attach this paragraph to the end of paragraph 3?

personal grudge until she did this dreadful thing; and I may add that it was the eminently unwise custom of reading all the letters written to or by the pupils which stood responsible for the trouble. The order of nuns was a French one, and the habit of surveillance, which did not seem amiss in France, was ill-adapted to America. I had never before wasted a thought upon it. My weekly home letter and the less frequent communicative epistles from my mother might have been read in the market place for all I cared, until this miserable episode proved that a bad usage may be trusted to produce, sooner or later, bad results.   5

It was with visible reluctance that Madame Rayburn said after a long pause: "That alters the case. If Madame Bouron told Lilly, she must have had some good reason for doing so."   6

"There was no good reason," I protested. "There couldn't have been. But it doesn't matter. I told Lilly it wasn't so, and she believed me."   7

Madame Rayburn stared at me aghast. "You told Lilly it was not so?" she repeated.   8

I nodded. "I could not find out for two days what was the matter," I explained; "but I got it out of her at last, and I told her that my mother had never written a line to me about her. And she believed me."   9

"But my dear child," said the nun, "you have told a very grievous lie. What is more, you have borne false witness against your neighbor. When you said to Lilly that your mother had not written that letter, you made her believe that Madame Bouron had lied to her."   10

"She didn't mind believing that," I observed cheerfully, "and there was nothing else that I could say to make her feel all right."   11

"But a lie is a lie," protested the nun. "You will have to tell Lilly the truth."   12

I said nothing, but my silence was not the silence of acquiescence. Madame Rayburn must have recognized this fact, for she took another line of attack. When she spoke next, it was in a low voice and very earnestly. "Listen to me," she said. "Friday is the first of May. You are going to confession on Thursday. You will tell Father O'Harra the whole story just as you have told it to me, and whatever he bids you do, you must do it. Remember that if you go to confession and do not tell this you will commit the very great sin of sacrilege; and if you do not obey your confessor you will commit the sin of open disobedience to the Church."   13

I was more than a little frightened. It seemed to me that for the first time in my life I was confronted by grown-up iniquities to which I had been a stranger. The thought sobered me for two days. On the third I went to confession, and when I had finished my customary offenses—which, as they seldom varied, were probably as familiar to the priest as they were to me—I told my serious tale. The silence with which it was received bore witness to its seriousness. No question was asked me; I had been too explicit to render questions needful. But after two minutes (which seemed like two hours) of thinking my confessor said: "A lie is a lie. It must be retracted. Tomorrow you will do one of two things. You will tell your friend the truth, or you will tell Madame Bouron the whole story just as you told me. Do you understand?"*   14

"Yes," I said in a faint little voice, no louder than a sigh.   15

"And you will do as I bid you?"   16

"Yes," I breathed again.   17

"Then I will give you absolution, and you may go to Communion. But remember, no later than tomorrow. Believe me, it will get no easier by delay."   18

Of that I felt tolerably sure, and it was with the courage of desperation that I knocked the next morning at the door of Madame Bouron's office. She gave me a glance of wonderment (I had never before paid her a voluntary call), and without pause or preamble I told my tale, told it with such bald uncompromising verity that it sounded worse than ever. She listened at first in amazement, then in anger. "So Lilly thinks I lied to her," she said at last.   19

"Yes," I answered.   20

"And suppose I send for her now and undeceive her."   21

"You can't do that," I said. "I should tell her again my mother did not write the letter, and she would believe me."   22

"If you told another lie, you would be sent from the school."   23

"If I were sent home, Lilly would believe me. She would believe me all the more."   24

The anger died out of Madame Bouron's eyes, and a look of bewilderment came into them. I am disposed to think that, despite her wide experience as nun and teacher, she had never before encountered an *idée fixe,* and found out that the pyramids are flexible compared to it. "You know," she said uncertainly, "that sooner or later you will have to do as your mother desires."   25

I made no answer. The "sooner or later" did not interest me at all. I was living now.   26

There was another long pause. When Madame Bouron spoke again it was in a grave and low voice. "I wish I had said nothing about your mother's letter," she said. "I thought I could settle matters quickly that way, but I was mistaken, and I must take the consequences of my error. You may go now. I will not speak to Lilly, or to anyone else about this affair."†   27

---

* Paragraph 14: Explain the meaning of the second sentence.

† Paragraphs 25 through 27: Why does the author use three paragraphs here instead of one?

I did not go. I sat stunned, and asking myself if she knew all that her silence would imply. Children seldom give adults credit for intelligence. "But," I began feebly——   28

"But me no buts," she interrupted, rising to her feet. "I know what you are going to say; but I have not been the head of a school for years without bearing more than one injustice."   29

Now when I heard these words sadly spoken something broke up inside of me. It did not break gently, like the dissolving of a cloud; it broke like the bursting of a dam. Sobs shook my lean little body as though they would have torn it apart. Tears blinded me. With difficulty I gasped out three words. "You are good," I said.*   30

Madame Bouron propelled me gently to the door, which I could not see because of my tears. "I wish I could say as much for you," she answered, "but I cannot. You have been very bad. You have been false to your mother, to whom you owe respect and obedience; you have been false to me; and you have been false to God. But you have been true to your friend."   31

She put me out of the door, but I stood in the corridor facing the clock. I was still shaken by sobs, but my heart was light as a bird. And, believe it or not, the supreme reason for my happiness was—not that my difficulties were over, though I was glad of that; and not that Lilly was safe from hurt, though I was glad of that; but that Madame Bouron, whom I had thought bad, had proved herself to be, according to the standards of childhood, as good as gold. My joy was like the joy of the blessed saints in Paradise.   32

* Paragraph 30: Why didn't the author present sentences 3, 4, and 5 in this paragraph as one sentence?

The Whole Selection

1 How does paragraph 1 relate to the central purpose of the essay?
2 What elements in the diction and sentence structure are in accord with the experience of a young girl, on the one hand, and, on the other hand, with the maturity of the author when she wrote this essay?
3 Whose character—the author's or Madame Bouron's—has been more influenced by the development of the events in this essay?

STRANGER IN THE VILLAGE

JAMES BALDWIN

From all available evidence no black man had ever set foot in this tiny Swiss village before I came. I was told before arriving that I would probably be a "sight" for the village; I took this to mean that people of my complexion were rarely seen in Switzerland, and also that city people are always something of a "sight" outside of the city. It did not occur to me—possibly because I am an American—that there could be people anywhere who had never seen a Negro. 1

It is a fact that cannot be explained on the basis of the inaccessibility of the village. The village is very high, but it is only four hours from Milan and three hours from Lausanne. It is true that it is virtually unknown. Few people making plans for a holiday would elect to come here. On the other hand, the villagers are able, presumably, to come and go as they please— which they do: to another town at the foot of the mountain, with a population of approximately five thousand, the nearest place to see a movie or go to the bank. In the village there is no movie house, no bank, no library, no theater; very few radios, one jeep, one station wagon; and, at the moment, one typewriter, mine, an invention which the woman next door to me here had never seen. There are about six hundred people living here, all Catholic —I conclude this from the fact that the Catholic church is open all year round, whereas the Protestant chapel, set off on a hill a little removed from the village, is open only in the summertime when the tourists arrive. There are four or five hotels, all closed now, and four or five *bistros,* of which, however, only two do any business during the winter. These two do not do a great deal, for life in the village seems to end around nine or ten o'clock. There are a few stores, butcher, baker, *épicerie,* a hardware store, and a money-changer—who cannot change travelers' checks, but must send them down to the bank, an operation which takes two or three days. There is something called the *Ballet Haus,* closed in the winter and used for God knows what, certainly not ballet, during the summer. There seems to be only one schoolhouse in the village, and this for the quite young children; I suppose this to mean that their older brothers and sisters at some point descend from these mountains in order to complete their education— possibly, again, to the town just below. The landscape is absolutely forbidding, mountains towering on all four sides, ice and snow as far as the eye can reach. In this white wilderness, men and women and children move all day, carrying washing, wood, buckets of milk or water, sometimes skiing on Sunday afternoons. All week long boys and young men are to be seen shoveling snow off the rooftops, or dragging wood down from the forest in sleds.* 2

* Paragraph 2: What is the transitional relationship between paragraph 1 and paragraph 2?

The village's only real attraction, which explains the tourist season, is the hot spring water. A disquietingly high proportion of these tourists are cripples, or semicripples, who come year after year—from other parts of Switzerland, usually—to take the waters. This lends the village, at the height of the season, a rather terrifying air of sanctity, as though it were a lesser Lourdes. There is often something beautiful, there is always something awful, in the spectacle of a person who has lost one of his faculties, a faculty he never questioned until it was gone, and who struggles to recover it. Yet people remain people, on crutches or indeed on deathbeds; and wherever I passed, the first summer I was here, among the native villagers or among the lame, a wind passed with me—of astonishment, curiosity, amusement, and outrage. That first summer I stayed two weeks and never intended to return. But I did return in the winter, to work; the village offers, obviously, no distractions whatever and has the further advantage of being extremely cheap. Now it is winter again, a year later, and I am here again. Everyone in the village knows my name, though they scarcely ever use it, knows that I come from America—though, this, apparently, they will never really believe: black men come from Africa—and everyone knows that I am the friend of the son of a woman who was born here, and that I am staying in their chalet. But I remain as much a stranger today as I was the first day I arrived, and the children shout *Neger! Neger!* as I walk along the streets.*   3

It must be admitted that in the beginning I was far too shocked to have any real reaction. In so far as I reacted at all, I reacted by trying to be pleasant—it being a great part of the American Negro's education (long before he goes to school) that he must make people "like" him. This smile-and-the-world-smiles-with-you routine worked about as well in this situation as it had in the situation for which it was designed, which is to say that it did not work at all. No one, after all, can be liked whose human weight and complexity cannot be, or has not been, admitted. My smile was simply another unheard-of phenomenon which allowed them to see my teeth —they did not, really, see my smile and I began to think that, should I take to snarling, no one would notice any difference. All of the physical characteristics of the Negro which had caused me, in America, a very different and almost forgotten pain were nothing less than miraculous—or infernal —in the eyes of the village people. Some thought my hair was the color of tar, that it had the texture of wire, or the texture of cotton. It was jocularly suggested that I might let it all grow long and make myself a winter coat. If I sat in the sun for more than five minutes some daring creature was certain to come along and gingerly put his fingers on my hair, as though he were afraid of an electric shock, or put his hand on my hand, astonished

* Paragraph 3: In the second to last sentence, what does "black men come from Africa" mean in the context?

that the color did not rub off. In all of this, in which it must be conceded there was the charm of genuine wonder and in which there was certainly no element of intentional unkindness, there was yet no suggestion that I was human: I was simply a living wonder.*   4

I knew that they did not mean to be unkind, and I know it now; it is necessary, nevertheless, for me to repeat this to myself each time that I walk out of the chalet. The children who shout *Neger!* have no way of knowing the echoes this sound raises in me. They are brimming with good humor and the more daring swell with pride when I stop to speak with them. Just the same, there are days when I cannot pause and smile, when I have no heart to play with them; when, indeed, I mutter sourly to myself, exactly as I muttered on the streets of a city these children have never seen, when I was no bigger than these children are now: *Your* mother *was a nigger.* Joyce is right about history being a nightmare—but it may be the nightmare from which no one *can* awaken. People are trapped in history and history is trapped in them.†   5

There is a custom in the village—I am told it is repeated in many villages—of "buying" African natives for the purpose of converting them to Christianity. There stands in the church all year around a small box with a slot for money, decorated with a black figurine, and into this box the villagers drop their francs. During the *carnaval* which precedes Lent, two village children have their faces blackened—out of which bloodless darkness their blue eyes shine like ice—and fantastic horsehair wigs are placed on their blond heads; thus disguised, they solicit among the villagers for money for the missionaries in Africa. Between the box in the church and the blackened children, the village "bought" last year six or eight African natives. This was reported to me with pride by the wife of one of the *bistro* owners and I was careful to express astonishment and pleasure at the solicitude shown by the village for the souls of black folk. The *bistro* owner's wife beamed with a pleasure far more genuine than my own and seemed to feel that I might now breathe more easily concerning the souls of at least six of my kinsmen.   6

I tried not to think of these so lately baptized kinsmen, of the price paid for them, or the peculiar price they themselves would pay, and said nothing about my father, who having taken his own conversion too literally never, at bottom, forgave the white world (which he described as heathen) for having saddled him with a Christ in whom, to judge at least from their treatment of him, they themselves no longer believed. I thought of white men arriving for the first time in an African village, strangers there, as I am a stranger here, and tried to imagine the astounded populace touching

* Paragraph 4: In the second sentence, why is "like" placed in quotation marks?
† Paragraph 5: Classify the grammatical structure of the fourth sentence.

their hair and marveling at the color of their skin. But there is a great difference between being the first white man to be seen by Africans and being
the first black man to be seen by whites. The white man takes the astonishment as tribute, for he arrives to conquer and to convert the natives, whose
inferiority in relation to himself is not even to be questioned; whereas I,
without a thought of conquest, find myself among a people whose culture
controls me, has even, in a sense, created me, people who have cost me
more in anguish and rage than they will ever know, who yet do not even
know of my existence. The astonishment with which I might have greeted
them, should they have stumbled into my African village a few hundred
years ago, might have rejoiced their hearts. But the astonishment with
which they greet me today can only poison mine.*   7

And this is so despite everything I may do to feel differently, despite
my friendly conversations with the *bistro* owner's wife, despite their three-
year-old son who has at last become my friend, despite the *saluts* and
bonsoirs which I exchange with people as I walk, despite the fact that I
know that no individual can be taken to task for what history is doing, or
has done. I say that the culture of these people controls me—but they can
scarcely be held responsible for European culture. America comes out of
Europe, but these people have never seen America, nor have most of them
seen more of Europe than the hamlet at the foot of their mountain. Yet
they move with an authority which I shall never have; and they regard me,
quite rightly, not only as a stranger in their village but as a suspect late-
comer, bearing no credentials, to everything they have—however unconsciously—inherited.†   8

For this village, even were it incomparably more remote and incred-
ibly more primitive, is the West, the West onto which I have been so
strangely grafted. These people cannot be, from the point of view of power,
strangers anywhere in the world; they have made the modern world, in
effect, even if they do not know it. The most illiterate among them is
related, in a way that I am not, to Dante, Shakespeare, Michelangelo,
Aeschylus, Da Vinci, Rembrandt, and Racine; the cathedral at Chartres says
something to them which it cannot say to me, as indeed would New York's
Empire State Building, should anyone here ever see it. Out of their hymns
and dances come Beethoven and Bach. Go back a few centuries and they
are in their full glory—but I am in Africa, watching the conquerors arrive. 9

The rage of the disesteemed is personally fruitless, but it is also
absolutely inevitable; this rage, so generally discounted, so little understood even among the people whose daily bread it is, is one of the things

---

* Paragraph 7: In the first sentence, what does the author say about his father?

† Paragraph 8: In place of the dashes in this paragraph, the author might have used
commas. Why did he use dashes?

that makes history. Rage can only with difficulty, and never entirely, be brought under the domination of the intelligence and is therefore not susceptible to any arguments whatever. This is a fact which ordinary representatives of the *Herrenvolk,* having never felt this rage and being unable to imagine it, quite fail to understand. Also, rage cannot be hidden, it can only be dissembled. This dissembling deludes the thoughtless, and strengthens rage and adds, to rage, contempt. There are, no doubt, as many ways of coping with the resulting complex of tensions as there are black men in the world, but no black man can hope ever to be entirely liberated from this internal warfare—rage, dissembling, and contempt having inevitably accompanied his first realization of the power of white men. What is crucial here is that, since white men represent in the black man's world so heavy a weight, white men have for black men a reality which is far from being reciprocal; and hence all black men have toward all white men an attitude which is designed, really, either to rob the white man of the jewel of his naïveté, or else to make it cost him dear.   10

The black man insists, by whatever means he finds at his disposal, that the white man cease to regard him as an exotic rarity and recognize him as a human being. This is a very charged and difficult moment, for there is a great deal of will power involved in the white man's naïveté. Most people are not naturally reflective any more than they are naturally malicious, and the white man prefers to keep the black man at a certain human remove because it is easier for him thus to preserve his simplicity and avoid being called to account for crimes committed by his forefathers, or his neighbors. He is inescapably aware, nevertheless, that he is in a better position in the world than black men are, nor can he quite put to death the suspicion that he is hated by black men therefore. He does not wish to be hated, neither does he wish to change places, and at this point in his uneasiness he can scarcely avoid having recourse to those legends which white men have created about black men, the most usual effect of which is that the white man finds himself enmeshed, so to speak, in his own language which describes hell, as well as the attributes which lead one to hell, as being as black as night.   11

Every legend, moreover, contains its residuum of truth, and the root function of language is to control the universe by describing it. It is of quite considerable significance that black men remain, in the imagination, and in overwhelming numbers in fact, beyond the disciplines of salvation; and this despite the fact that the West has been "buying" African natives for centuries. There is, I should hazard, an instantaneous necessity to be divorced from this so visibly unsaved stranger, in whose heart, moreover, one cannot guess what dreams of vengeance are being nourished; and, at the same time, there are few things on earth more attractive than the idea of the unspeakable liberty which is allowed the unredeemed. When, beneath the black mask, a human being begins to make himself felt one cannot escape a certain awful wonder as to what kind of human being it is. What one's imagination makes of other people is dictated, of course, by the laws of one's own personality and it is one of the ironies of black-white relations that, by means of what the white man imagines the black man to be, the black man is enabled to know who the white man is.   12

The Whole Selection

1 Irony is often employed in effective writing. What irony is implicit in the relationship of Baldwin's central experience in this essay to his remark in paragraph 3: "Yet people remain people, on crutches or indeed on deathbeds"? What irony is found in the phrase, " 'buying' African natives," in paragraphs 6 and 12, particularly the latter?

2 In paragraph 3, the writer says, "... Wherever I passed ... a wind passed with me—of astonishment, curiosity, amusement, and outrage." These four elements constitute the subject of much of the rest of the essay. Does the author present them as elements of his own experience in the village or as elements of the experience of the villagers?

3 In the fourth sentence of paragraph 5, observe the rhythm effected by the use of parallelism. Where else in the essay does the author use parallelism?

MY PASSPORT WAS AT SHORTSTOP

WILFRID SHEED

They took away my cricket bat at the age of 9 and told me I wouldn't be needing it anymore. Out of kindness they didn't tell me I wouldn't need my soccer ball, either. Otherwise, I don't think I would have come to America at all. I would have lied about my age and joined the horse marines.   1

Exile is an ugly business at any age. Harold Pinter, the playwright, carted his bat with him all over England to remind him of the past (he must have been 8 when he started out). I was forced to hand over mine at the frontier, and with it the long summer evenings, the boys with the dangling suspenders, the whole Fanny-by-gaslight world of cricket; my life for the next few years would be a hunt for fresh symbols, a bat and ball I could believe in.   2

Baseball dismayed me at first blush almost as much as the big cars and the big faces in the street. In the dictionary of the senses *cricket* stood for twilight, silence, flutter. (See also *Swans*.) *Baseball* equaled noonday, harsh, noise, clatter. (See *Geese*.) That was how it looked at first—boys milling around dusty lots jabbering and hitching at their pants. But as I kept craning from train windows and car windows in my first days in America, I noticed something promising: that nothing ever seemed to be happening at that particular moment—the same basic principle as cricket. The pitcher peering in to get the sign, the ritual chant of the infield, the whispered consultations and then, if you were very lucky, a foul tip (before you were whisked out of range). Baseball was not as busy as it seemed but lived, like the mother game, on pregnant pauses. This, plus the fact that it happened to be in season and you played it with a bat and ball, made it look like my best bet.   3

Unfortunately, the place where we first lived was an almost deserted village, so there was no one to play with. There was one boy about a mile down the road. He straightened out my batting stance and filled me in on the First World War, too, but he was five years older than I, with his own life to live, so I couldn't bother him too often.   4

Instead, I became perhaps the outstanding solitary baseball player of my generation, whaling fungoes down the long, narrow garden and plodding after them, chattering to myself and whaling them back again. Anything pulled or sliced got lost, so my first encounter with American botany was staring sightlessly through it, hunting the tawny baseball. When that palled, I would chalk a strike zone on the garage door and lob a tennis ball at it. Already I had the style, though God knows where it came from: the mock aggression and inscrutable loneliness. Gary Cooper high on a hill, twitching

his cap, shaking off the sign: nodding, rearing, firing. Clunk, against the
old garage door. The manner came with my first glove.   5

Another thing that stoked my love affair was the statistics. I like a
game that has plenty of statistics, the more inconsequential the better, and
I began soaking up baseball records like a sea sponge before I even knew
what they meant. I liked the way you could read *around* baseball, without
ever getting to the game at all. I devoured a long piece in the old *Sateve-
post* about Hank Greenberg, baseball's most eligible bachelor, and another
about young Ted Williams, who only shaved twice a week. Official baseball
sneaked up on me through its trivia. My learned friend up the road took
me, at last, to an actual game at Shibe Park, and I was hooked for fair. It
was the St. Louis Browns vs. the Philadelphia Athletics, hardly an offering
to stir the blood, but more than enough to stir mine. The Brownies built
up a big lead, but the A's, led by Wally Moses and Bob Johnson, staged
one of their rare comebacks and pulled it out of the fire. The sandlot games
I had seen so far had not been beautiful to look at, only intellectually interesting (I used phrases like that occasionally, a real little snot in some
ways); but here we had something as elegant as the Radio City Rockettes
—explosively elegant and almost as fussily stylish as cricket.   6

Baseball became my constant, obsessive companion after that. Up
and down the garden, faster and faster, first as Dick Siebert, the A's first
baseman, then as Arky Vaughan, whose name and dour appearance I
fancied, then right-handed as Jimmy Foxx. And at night I played out whole
games in my head, in which I was always the quiet, unobtrusive professional (I detested showboating) who hit the penultimate single or made a
key play in the *eighth* inning. It was as if I'd brought my cricket bat with
me, after all.   7

The point about this was that it was all what D. H. Lawrence would
have called "baseball in the head." When I came to play with other boys in
the next few years, I continued my solipsistic ways, trotting out quietly to
my position, chewing all the gum that my mouth would hold and gazing
around with mild, shrewd eyes; or, for a time, grinning like Stan Hack, the
Cub third baseman—a steady player on a steady club, the way I wanted to
spend eternity.   8

A sociologist might (and I would probably agree with him, having just
made him up) explain my choice of this particular type of athlete quite
simply. Baseball was my social passport, and a slight averageness is good
on a passport. It means that the officials look at you less closely. Who is
that guy over there? Maybe he'd like to play. Say—he's quietly efficient,
isn't he? I remember standing around picnic sites and county fairs, wist-
fully, with my glove half concealed under my arm as if I didn't mean anything by it. I was slightly ashamed of my accent and bitterly ashamed of

my first name; but baseball did not judge you by those things. The Statue of Liberty, bat in hand, said, "Try this, kid."   9

Sometimes, magically, it happened. I was rather light for a ballplayer in spite of weighing myself a lot. I knew the names of all the light ball-players (the Waner brothers were a special comfort), but still, 80 pounds was 80 pounds, and even with the most graceful swing in town I could rarely nudge the ball past second base. However, I waited out numerous walks, if there happened to be an umpire, fielded as well as the pebbles allowed and always looked a little better than the clumsy lout they had buried in right field. Afterwards they went their way, into houses I knew nothing about, to a life that contained other things besides baseball; and I went mine.   10

In the fall of '41 I left for boarding school. Although the baseball season was still raging, I found that it was all over as far as my new school was concerned. I felt as if I had lost a friend. My companion of the long, silent summer was replaced by a harsh, grunting affair, where people shouted like drill sergeants and made a big thing of getting in shape, being in shape, staying in shape. Suck in your gut, get those knees up.   11

I saw right away that football was the enemy. If 80 pounds was of dubious value in summer, it was downright ludicrous in fall. Beyond that I distrusted the atmosphere of the game, all that crouching and barking. It was a side of America that might have appealed to a little German boy, but hardly to me. The essential solitude of baseball gave way to the false heartiness, the just-feel-that-stomach toughness. We only played touch football that year, but even so managed to make a military thing of it.   12

God knows how, I came to love football anyway. The finished product, the game itself, transcended all the midweek drivel. I had seen the previous winter one game, in which Whizzer (now Sir Whizzer) White scored two touchdowns against the woebegone Eagles of Philadelphia, and I guess I liked it all right. I drew some crayon pictures of it, anyway, showing little Davey O'Brien being smothered by Lions.   13

But there was an actuality to the game as played that was quite different from the game as watched or the game as planned. I became second-string quarterback in our rather peculiar school and got to run back a kick-off in a quasi-real game. Huddled in the lee of a gland case, a 250-pound eighth-grader, I made our only considerable gain of the day. I relished the swooping, shifting patterns that had to be diagnosed instantly, the hilarity of each yard gained, the pleasure of doing something you've practiced and getting it right.   14

It was quite different from my dreamy, poetic, half-mad relationship with baseball. This was crisp and outgoing, hep-two-three-four, and based on the realities of the game, not on some dream of it. Yet it filled the same social purpose. It became a shortcut, or substitute, for mastering the local culture. I still didn't know how to talk to these people but while I was play-ing I didn't have to. The soundless pat on the back, the "nice going, Sheed"—you could be any manner of clod, or even an English boy, and it didn't matter. I remember blocking a punt with my stomach and writhing in agony and feeling it was worth it for the brief respect I commanded.   15

This was canceled on another occasion, which is still almost too pain-ful to describe, and which I write here only that it may be of help to others: that is, to any 80-pound English refugees who happen to be reading this. The setting was a pickup game played in semidarkness. The agreed-on goal line was a fuzzy patch of trees off in the middle distance, I'm still not sure where. My team was losing 12–0, and it was understood that the next play would be the last one: hence meaningless, a lame-duck exercise. Their man threw a long pass. I intercepted it and stepped backward, someplace in the area of the goal line.   16

Triumphant hands were clapped on me, and I was told that I had just handed two points to the enemy. Would (and I have woulded this would often since) that Zeus had smitten my tongue at that moment. The game would have been forgotten—12–0, 14–0, who cared—and I would have been spared three lousy years. As it was, I said in fruitiest Cockney, "How was I supposed to know where the goal line was?"   17

Wrong thing to say. I heard no more about it that day. The saying went underground for a while, and when it emerged the context had been garbled slightly. I was now alleged to have run the wrong way, like in the Rose Bowl, and to have capped it, in what was now a horrible whine, " 'ow was Aye suppowsed to know which why the gowl was!" Well, O.K., I was used to that by now, in an Irish school. But this legend so grabbed the popular imagination that I was still hearing it three years later from boys who had just entered the school.   18

The moral of this tragedy is that sport as a Julien Sorel passport has its treacherous side. It can bestow curses as carelessly as blessings, and the curses stick. However, those first two years would have been grim with-out sports, which played an unnaturally large part in my life, and still do in my mind, because they were, at times, all I had.   19

As to my life as a fan, that, too, was a social passport, and therefore doctored slightly. "Hey, how come you know so much about baseball?" could be a friendly question or it could be weighted with menace. Like the not-so-dumb blonde, I found there were circles where it paid to keep my knowledge to myself, even though it burned in the mouth and even though some fat fool was deluding the crowd with wrong statistics.   20

It was, though, an acceptable subject, and there weren't too many of those. I did not understand cars, had not been camping last summer, had a noncooking mother: subject after subject broke in my hands. Only sports could be trusted. Fate had presented me with three frowsy teams to talk about: the Phillies, A's and Eagles, all usually cemented into their respective last places. (I was foolishly pleased when a friend said, "Don't the A's usually finish around sixth?" The A's never finished anywhere near sixth.) Pennsylvania University was some small consolation—I saw it beat Army, Harvard, Cornell on various weekends—but hardly enough. My own social position was too sensitive to burden with three risible teams, so I decided to diversify. I took on board the Brooklyn Dodgers and the Washington Redskins. Sammy Baugh was a man I could identify with. Lean and steel-eyed, my winter self.   21

On balance, I would say that playing games didn't do much for my character. It gives one a highly specialized confidence and a highly qualified cooperativeness, but in return it makes one incurably childish. Intellectually, it teaches you that you can't argue with a fact, a mixed blessing. However, being a Brooklyn fan was useful. It taught me to suffer. The Dodgers immediately and definitively broke my heart. I had barely become a fan when Mickey Owen dropped the third strike and gave a World Series game away. Then the next season, 1942, Peter Reiser banged his head on the wall and they blew a 10-game lead over the Cardinals. The Dodgers came to Philadelphia on July 4th strutting like gods and pasted the local scarecrows 14–0 and 5–4. Reiser hit the neatest, mellowest little home run you ever saw. Medwick, Camilli—players twice as big, twice as regal as any since.   22

On the Sunday after Labor Day the Cardinals came in. They had beaten the Dodgers the day previous, on Whitey Kurowski's home run, to reach first place for the first time. The Dodgers were playing two with Cincinnati. There was strangling doom in the air. I knew, everyone knew, what was going to happen. All afternoon I watched the scoreboard. The Phillies were managing to split with the Cards, an unlikely reprieve, but the Dodgers went down slowly, inexorably to total defeat.   23

I was insane with grief. It was worse than the fall of France, and the feelings were not dissimilar: the same sense of irreversible momentum and crushed dreams. It seemed strange even then that a misfortune suffered by a random collection of strangers could hurt so much. Yet for days I was sick with sorrow and actually tried to forget about baseball: a trick I wasn't to master for another 20 years. I recovered in time to root lustily for the Cardinals in the World Series. A defeat for the Yankees was already sweeter than a victory for anyone else. Hence there was an element of vindictive nihilism in my baseball thinking, which was to run riot when Walter O'Malley took his team from Brooklyn to L.A. some 16 years later, and which has dominated since that time.   24

In the fall of '43 we moved to New York. The Philadelphia hermitage was over. No more mowing lawns and hoeing vegetable beds in our victory garden to pay my way to Shibe Park, no more early-morning trolley rides to Frankford and long subway rides from there in order to get the whole of batting practice and two games for my buck and a quarter. I had not realized what a grueling regimen this was until I took a friend with a medium interest in baseball along for company. Even though we saw Ted Williams strike out three times on the knuckleball and then hit a home run in the 10th, my friend never once mentioned baseball again.   25

But now I was in New York, the capital of baseball, and my appetite raged wantonly, like some Thomas Wolfe character in Europe, prowling the streets and roaring. In those days every barber shop had a radio, every butcher shop—the whole block was a symphony of baseball.   26

To be young in Paris, to be coming up for 13 in New York! Unfortunately, the game itself was not in such hot shape right then. The stars were wafting, or drafting, away and being replaced by squinting, shambling defectives like the ones I had left behind in Philadelphia. The Dodgers tried out a 16-year-old shortshop. The lordly Yankees were reduced to the likes of Joe Buzas and Ossie Grimes. The St. Louis Browns actually had a one-armed centerfielder. The hottest player in town was an aging retread called Phil Weintraub. You had to love baseball to survive those years.   27

But I liked going to the parks anyway. They offered the cultural continuity of churches. You could slip into one in a strange city and pick up the ceremony right away. College football stadiums made me nervous with their brutal cliquishness, and professional football stadiums always gave me rotten seats—the same one, it seemed like, high up and to the left, in back of the goal line. But ball parks were home and still are, a place where I understand what my neighbors are up to, even after a year abroad.   28

The football scene was a slight improvement over Godforsaken Philadelphia. The wartime Giants must have been one of the dullest teams in history, with their off-tackle smashes and their defensive genius. But they were usually able to make a game of it. I saw Don Hutson *throw* a touchdown pass off an end-around reverse, and my hero, Sammy Baugh, quick-kick 66 yards to the Giants' four. You didn't seem to see things like that in Philadelphia.   29

My own playing career mooned along all this while, striking me, at least, as promising. I had become a spottily effective left end, running solemn little down-and-outs and tackling with bravura (I found I wasn't afraid of head-on tackles, which put one in the elite automatically). I discovered that basketball yielded to humorless determination better than most games and I once succeeded in sinking 17 foul shots in a row. But the game had no great emotional interest; it was more like a bar game of skill that whiles away the evenings. I liked the hot gymnasiums and the feel of the floor underfoot, and it was fun fretting about the score, but the game

left no resonance afterwards. Fast breaks and the swishing of the strings—
a thin collection of memories.   30

Baseball continued to intoxicate, worse than ever; tossing the ball
among snowdrifts at the beginning of spring, the sweet feeling in the hands
when you connected and sent it scudding over the winter grass, the satisfaction of turning your back on a fly and turning round in more or less the
right place to catch it. I had grown off my 80-pound base and was now a
gawky fanatic of 105 or so; willing to field for hours, taking my glove everywhere, pounding an endless pocket into it, scavenging for a game.   31

This sport, which I had needed so badly on arrival, was now making
me pay for its favors. I was enslaved to it, like Emil Jannings to Marlene
Dietrich. My life had become seriously lopsided. I refused to go swimming
because it interfered with my career—tightened the skin on the chest and
all that. I looked at the countryside with blank eyes. My father admonished
me to throw away my baseball magazines after one reading, but I hid them
like an addict. I don't recall reading anything else at all. Nothing, not even
the war, interested me anymore.   32

In my new neighborhood my passport was honored handsomely. I was
the best shortstop, in an admittedly skimpy field, and I was always sure of
a game. I didn't bother to make friends in any other context, seeing myself
as an aloof professional who never mixed business with pleasure. I took an
ascetic view of people who goofed off and had a mortal horror of games
degenerating into horseplay. "Come on, let's play ball," I would say aus-
terely, like some Dominican friar behind on his *autos-da-fé*. My father, who
spent half the war in each country, took me to see a cricket match in Van
Cortlandt Park, and it struck me as a vague, ramshackle game. We got into
a discussion over the concept "not cricket." It seemed to me ridiculous not
to take every advantage you could in a game. The slyness and bluff of baseball were as beautiful to me as the winging ball.   33

How long this would have lasted, I have no way of knowing. I might
have snapped out of it in a year or two, under pressure of girls and such,
or followed it glumly until some awakening in a Class A minor league. I
contracted polio at the age of 14, and my career was over just like that.
I ran a fever and for the first couple of nights I could see nothing in it but
sports images: football highlights, baseball highlights, boxing (I was the
only boy in school who had rooted for Louis over Conn, so I had the films
of the fight in my repertoire), all rushing through my head like the Gadarene
swine on their way to the sea. I was allowed to switch sports, but not the
main subject. My obsession had to play itself out.   34

When calmness returned, I found my interest in sports had fixated,
frozen, at that particular point. I was to remain a 14-year-old fan for the
next 20 years. I continued thinking that the life of a professional ballplayer

was attractive long after a sensible man would have abandoned the notion. I returned to England for a while and became a cricket nut all over again. 35

Yet it wasn't really the same. I knew now that my bat had been taken for good and I had better find something else to do. Sports still raged, but in one lobe only. The other was liberated, free to grow up if it could. And my interest in sport was more house-trained and philosophical: no more wrist-slashing over defeat, no more hero worship, an occasional thin smile while losing at pool—all in all, about as much maturity as you can expect from a hardened sports addict. 36

But when I see some Negro or Puerto Rican kid making basket catches or running like an arrow, breaking the language barrier and waving his passport, I feel like saying O.K., but don't take it too seriously, don't let this be all. Sports are socially useful, up to a strictly limited point. I stopped being a foreigner the moment I blocked that kick, and a moment is sometimes all it takes. But blocking kicks or whacking baseballs only gets you so far. (Don't bring those muddy boots in the living room.) The mockery starts up again the minute you leave the park. 37

I thought sports had made me an American but in some ways they actually retarded the process. I played them like an English colonial officer, exhausting himself with some amusing native game and missing too many other things. Having said that, let me double back on it: if you had to limit yourself to one aspect of American life, the showdowns between pitcher and hitter, quarterback and defense, hustler and fish, would tell you more about politics, manners, style in this country than any one other thing. Sports constitute a code, a language of the emotions, and a tourist who skips the stadiums will not recoup his losses at Lincoln Center and Grant's Tomb. 38

ALL RIDDLES SOLVED

JOHANNES JÖRGENSEN

At the age of eighteen it is still a long way to the quiet garden of Persephone and endless reprose in its fields of asphodel. It was in that year that Adda Ravnkilde committed suicide. She was a talented young authoress, a volume of whose stories was published posthumously, with a preface by no less a sponsor than Georg Brandes. But she had at least left something behind by which to be remembered before she went into the great darkness. I had achieved nothing yet, nothing whatever.   1

And so I remained alive. I went on studying as well as I could—in the autumn of 1885 I began learning Sanskrit—while at the same time continuing my "recreative reading"—a list of books from that period contains names so desperately far apart as Bettina, Shelley, Goncourt, Turgenieff, Arthur Fitger, Coleridge, Rossetti, Swinburne, Morris. At the same time I was ploughing my way through Taine's *De l'Intelligence*, Renan's *Origines du Christianisme*, Strauss : *Der alte und der neue Glaube*, Darwin, too, of course, in a translation by J. P. Jacobsen.[1] "How do you get time to read all that?" a fellow-student asked me one day when I was talking about my omnivorous reading. Nor can it be denied that it entirely lacked any plan. I allowed myself to be led by my *daemon* and by my oppressed state of mind, which demanded forgetfulness. At Svendborg they were quite unaware of the high-handed way in which I was employing my time. Besides, I had taken my intermediate degree in philosophy with honours and had been able to inform my anxious mother and my questioning uncle that "in all essentials I had the same philosophical point of view as the lecturer, Mr. Höffding." With this the new "Erasmus Montanus"[2] obtained his Imprimatur and his free-thinking was given the official stamp.   2

---

[1] Jacobsen (Jens Peter) was born in Jutland in 1847 and died in 1885. Chief of the Danish writers of the second half of the nineteenth century. Made special studies of natural history, chiefly of botany and translated Darwin's works. His first novel *Mogens* was published in 1872 and was followed in 1875 by *A Shot in the Mist* which contains his conception of Nature. It shows the influence of Sainte Beuve, of Flaubert, of Merimée and of Brandes, who encouraged him to give to Danish literature that which was still unknown to it, the prose poem. His historical novel, *Marie Grubbe* (1876), is wholly modern in the psychology of its characters and in the naturalism of its descriptions, which, though they may not be said to present a bygone period based on serious study, are not lacking in accuracy. The style is characteristic, very elaborate, and as required by the subject, slightly archaic. The hero of Jacobsen's other major novel, *Niels Lyhne*, is a romantic atheist. The writer's prose reaches perfection in this melancholy work; it is at the same time rhythmic and varied in colour. Other works by Jacobsen are *Fru Fönss*, *The Plague of Bergamo*, *There ought to have been Roses*. *Marie Grubbe* has been translated into French. Jacobsen has been said to have much in common with George Meredith.

[2] Hero of one of the comedies of Holberg, the Danish Molière. He is a student and the son of a peasant, who is puffed up with pride by his newly-acquired knowledge. The play can be read in a French translation in the volume devoted to Holberg of *One Hundred Foreign Masterpieces* (*Renaissance du Livre*). [Jörgensen's note.]

Meanwhile my studies were not regulated by any plan, any more than my life. I had surrendered myself to Nature and now she dominated me; I was at the mercy of great forces. In vain did I long for peace in the cool arms of Persephone; another goddess was compelling me to my knees. Swinburne too, has sung of her—he calls her "O mystic and sombre Dolores, our Lady of Pain"   3

The adversaries whom a young freethinker had to face in those days were fond of maintaining that freethought necessarily led to what is usually called immorality, that is, transgression of the sixth commandment. We emphatically denied this and pointed out J.P. Jacobsen as one who in practice had proved the contrary and whose life, on a foundation of pure atheism, was irreproachable, regarded also from the standpoint of Christian morality. But when this principle had been established it cannot be denied that we recovered our spirits and asked, "But, by the way, why is so-called immorality immoral?"   4

Human ethics gave no answer. The problem was left unsolved—and literature made it a subject of discussion together with all the other problems. At the new year in 1886 I had left the small circle of Liberals in the Students' Association and become a member of the recently founded Students' Society.[3] Here I was in the storm centre of the discussion of problems. How many an afternoon, which ought to have been devoted to the University, was not wasted in the low-ceiled, democratically plain rooms of the "Society" in endless discussions and revolutionary forecasts of the future!   5

The problem of problems was the question of sex. It occurs as No. 3 on the list of "social problems" which I had made at the time and which gives an idea of what engaged the minds of young radicals forty years ago:

1. The emancipation of women.
2. Education of both sexes in common. Teaching of physiology, gymnastics, handicrafts.
3. Sex relations.
4. Superculture. Nervousness. Over-working of the middle classes.
5. Prostitution.
6. Illegitimate children.
7. Total abstinence.
8. Social morals and the liberty of art.
9. Instruction for working men.
10. Free legal advice.
11. Militia.
12. Adult suffrage from the age of 22. Representation of minorities.
13. Progressive taxation.
14. Co-operation. Trades Unions and Consumers' Associations.
15. Separation of Church and State. Official Atheism.   6

[3] A group which had left the Students' Association to form an opposition to the Conservative government then in power.

All these questions were of course more or less made the subject of debate in the Society's rooms, but it cannot be denied that No. 3 was discussed with more heat than the others. Nor is this any wonder: of late years it has also been necessary to discuss it from a Christian point of view. It is by no means an easy matter for a young man continually to repress one of the most powerful appetites in Nature. He must have strong motives if he is to persevere in it year after year. And we young free-thinkers could not find these motives. Höffding's handbooks on morals did not provide them. When the great strife over morality broke out between Björnson and Brandes,[4] most of us were on the side of the latter. In any case we could not be scandalised at the famous, oft quoted words about the "worthless prejudice" to which young girls of the better classes sacrificed themselves in joyless celibacy. We also found celibacy joyless and wished for nothing better than the destruction of that prejudice.   7

There was nothing remarkable, nothing illogical, and granted the point of view, nothing immoral in this. If the human moralist is right, if morals are really autonomous, then each one is free to do with himself as he pleases. That others disapprove of his conduct does not prove that it is wrong. Not even a disapproval expressed by entire humanity would be any proof against it, for the right of the individual to act autonomously can never be abolished. Modern ethics have no sanction and their last word will therefore necessarily be, as Nietzsche has rightly said, and no professor can make unsaid, that "nothing is true and everything is permitted."   8

A couple of years were still to pass before Nietzsche became known to Denmark (and through Denmark to the world). But Strindberg had already presaged an approaching "transmutation of values"; a Russian nihilist, Tschernyschewski, had struck the same note in his novel, *Que faire?* which was much read by young radicals of the day.   9

To tell the truth, the Students' Society was not altogether inspired by this spirit of anarchy. The general moral level was that of the "morals of happiness," "the greatest possible happiness for the greatest number." Officially we adhered to Höffding's ethics.   10

But, as everywhere else, the exoteric doctrine differed from the esoteric; the kernel was one thing, the shell another. Involuntarily I went whither the words seemed the most sincere, where people said what they meant, and where one did not shrink from any thought or expression, if only the truth could be brought to light, naked and bleeding like a newborn infant. I sat down at the Socratic table, at first as a listener, afterwards contributing my share as a speaker. Here my shyness disappeared altogether, as did also my feeling of being a stranger, as much as it could dis-

---

[4] On the question of A *Gauntlet,* a play published and performed in 1883, in which Björnson had maintained that the moral demands made on young girls should equally be made on young men.

appear at all, for here I felt that I was amongst my own kin. We were all of
the tribe of Cain.   11

All over the world it looked as though the victory were to be ours.
With the deep-set eyes under the furrowed brow, and the famous raven's
wings above it, our great, admired and idolised leader looked out from his
desk upon Europe. "Watchman, what of the night?" the English poet had
asked in *Songs before Sunrise*. Home again from his travels in Europe,
Georg Brandes could report that the dawn was near, and that a galaxy of
brilliant stars of the morning were heralding the new day: Victor Hugo and
Swinburne, Carducci and Paul Heyse and Gottfried Keller, Zola and Flaubert, Taine and Renan, Darwin, Spencer and Mill; Turgenieff, Strindberg,
Ibsen, Björnson and Drachmann; and was he not amongst them too, he,
Lucifer, the red star of the dawn?   12

There was really a joy of assault in our souls. We believed that all
riddles were now to be solved, all fetters to be struck off. We hoped for the
end of Christianity, for the coming of the social republic, the resurrection
of the pagan body and the happiness, attained at last, of a liberated
humanity.   13

This was our faith, and Hans Jæger's[5] *The Bohemia of Christiania*
was our Bible.   14

For those who have not had the experience of the coming of that book
it is difficult to imagine the effect that it produced. In stronger words than
even those of Strindberg's *Red Room* and Garborg's novels it stated everything, described everything, even to the deepest degradation. Such were
our aspirations, our desires, our sufferings—and what was the remedy,
what did Society offer us to quench our thirst in the flames? The bought
woman or the immoral relationship. First the harlot, then the church
wedding—that was the conservative solution of the problem of sex.   15

Against this solution the Norwegian writer rose in all his strong and
deep man's longing for the love of a woman. In a book of a thousand pages
he cursed the society that only allowed a choice between police-regulated
degradation and life outside the pale of the law—between prostitution and
Bohemia. Yet he did not find any solution either of the problem—not yet at
least, he said. This "not yet" became the bridge which led from personal
revolt to social revolution, from romanticism to socialism. In Hans Jæger's
opinion, with which we young Danes agreed, the ideal relationship between
the sexes was that of perfect freedom. A temporary alliance—we had no

[5] Jæger (Hans), b. 1854—d. 1910. A Norwegian writer who treated the most daring subjects in the most naturalistic manner. His *Bohemia of Christiania* was published in 1885
and was denounced in the courts, the author receiving a penalty of sixty days imprisonment in Norway and fifty days in Sweden. He blamed Society for the vices which he
described with complaisance and preached anarchy. To the younger generation he
appeared in the rôle of reformer. He greatly influenced contemporary writers, some of
whom exceeded him in immorality. Knut Hamsun was one of those who came under his
influence.

objection to its lasting for life—but free. In order to realise this freedom, however, the economic independence of both partners was necessary. In existing marriage the woman was still bought by the man, she looked upon him as "the bread-winner"; he looked upon her as his wedded mistress—in other words, marriage was another form of prostitution. For love between man and woman really to become what it ought to be it would have to be set free from marriage, and this could be achieved only if the capitalistic form of production were abolished, and men and women given an equal position as working citizens in the Socialist State. "And the children?" we were asked. "Will be brought up by the State," was the prompt answer. Thus it was not hate, but love, that drove us into Socialism.   16

In order to give a public manifestation of our adherence to Socialistic principles the small circle to which I belonged decided to join in the working men's festival procession on the anniversary of the day when Denmark obtained her Constitution.   17

Thus it was that we formed part of the procession on that bright afternoon of the 5th of June, 1886, our gaze fixed upon the red banner fluttering in the summer breeze. We were only few in numbers, a mere couple of rows, but we wore our students' caps, and we wore them purposely; we wanted to bring them under the banner of revolt. As we swung into the old street leading into the centre of the city, we received the first "Bravo" from the thick wall of spectators—but also a shout from an old conservative who cried, "Shame! Danish students to walk under that red rag!" Proudly we marched on, the brass band in front playing the Socialist march, and now, what was that? It came like the flapping of a flag in the wind, *Allons, enfants de la patrie*—the Marseillaise!   18

The old, ever young, immortal Marseillaise! The Marseillaise, tearing asunder, overthrowing everything. The Marseillaise, the battle-song of the Revolution, its song of triumph, its *Te Deum!* The Marseillaise, to the ringing notes of which thousands and tens of thousands have stormed to the hero's death, and tens of thousands drawn their last breath under the sweep of its eagle's wings. The Marseillaise, the Marseillaise! I have only to hear the first notes of it and I feel myself growing pale, and the tears welling up, the irresistible tears—the Marseillaise, the Marseillaise—the tears are blinding me—I do not see where I am—the pale-green newly-opened leaves on the lime-trees are about me, overhead the red banners are stretched like sails in the wind; the June sun is shining, and beside me a strong man's voice is fervently singing:

Aux armes, citoyens,
Formez vos bataillons,
Marchons, marchons, qu'un sang impur
Abreuve nos sillons.   19

And so we celebrate on this day, this afternoon, this evening, this night, the fête of our youth, of our liberty. With the people, in the midst of the people, like the people. All barriers have been broken down, all bonds loosened, all chains snapped. We do not listen much to the speeches, keeping more to the outer borders of the fête, amongst the families sitting on the ground with their picnic baskets. There is a pleasant smell from the down-trodden juicy grass. Amongst the pretty young daughters of artisans, who have no objection to a chat with a newly joined academic comrade—in all the tents refreshments can be bought, and democratic beer is drunk at rough-hewn tables, where one sits amongst masons on a bench which is only a plank.   20

Then the evening in Tivoli[6]—crowds, friends and acquaintances of whom one catches a glimpse in the current, when the same current sweeps them away again. In the Bodega one suddenly finds oneself in the midst of a circle drinking port wine around a barrel. Suddenly, too, one sees the fireworks in the company of a girl in a light summer frock, with one's arm around her waist, which does not seem to annoy her; she remains until her mother or someone else calls her from the surge of the passing crowd and she disappears as she came.   21

One passes on, again some friends turn up—another drink—Tivoli closes—one is out again in the brightly lit streets, crowded with people in summer attire on this summer night—a string of young girls approaches— one is surrounded, others too in the midst of them—there is shouting and laughing—a tavern in Vesterbro, a swarm of people both inside and out, all the tables engaged, a place at the corner of a table—a drink—a glass is upset—"On your dress?" "Oh, but let us go!" "Where to?" "Home to my place!"   22

The next morning you stand outside the door of the house in which you live, you have forgotten the key of the door or lost it; you go in through the door of the next house, the door of which is always open, and climb the palings—and when at last you have slipped into your room, thankful not to have been seen, and feeling no shame over the experiences of the night—your glance falls on a little cardboard box standing on the table—a box wrapped in paper, clumsily tied with a piece of cotton by an unpractised hand; you recognise the writing, you guess what the little box contains, flowers from home. In the white dawn of a June morning the enemy of society, the Socialist, the Bohemian, opens the box and carefully removes the damp moss from the narcissi and auriculas. Tucked in at the side he finds a letter, which he reads, sitting at the open window: 23

---

[6] A pleasure garden centrally situated in Copenhagen, in which may be found all kinds of entertainments.

Dear Brother,

I cannot endure it any longer, I have been and still am longing for you, for a walk with you, seeing you and hearing you speak. For I don't quite understand your letters, I don't know—perhaps I am mistaken, but it seems to me that it is not my own "old man" who has written them. Now you will be cross, of course, and wonder whether I am writing to worry you, but I can't help it; you seem to me to have disappeared. Ah, well, I had better not speak of it, after all I shall never be able to explain so that you will understand.—Well, the woods are green now, and they did not seem to wait for the rain they needed to make the buds unfold, as the newspapers said. It always annoys me to read that stuff, year in, year out, so I was amused when the woods made haste before the rain came. But then it did come, with a storm after it, so that now the woods are almost dark, yet lovely, lovely. A fort-night ago to-morrow Bertha and I were at the Grass Eyots. The beeches had just come into leaf the two last nights, I do not think I ever saw anything so beautiful, but then I say that every time—just pale green wherever you looked, and then the branches hang, you know, bent downwards a little, and they sway so very softly, oh, so softly, and the birds fly, oh, so quietly, as only birds in the Grass Eyots can fly; and then the sunlight, an abundance everywhere, quantities of gleams, rays, then, suddenly, heaps of sunshine pouring down on an old tree-stump, only because the branches of a tree were blown aside. But out in the bog, the big marsh, you know, oh, how I wish you where there and could see all its glories—tree-stumps quite smothered in moss, meadowsweet, anemones, wild violets, dandelions and all those things that you can find in a bog. But here I am, filling the whole page without thinking; that was not what I meant to do. Thank you for the cards and the letter, was pleased to get both. Enclosed with this is a box of flowers. Bertha and I were out at half-past five this morning to gather them at Kristians-minde. The lillies-of-the-valley are from Bertha's garden, then there are apple-blossoms, wild ones, from the walk near the beach at Kris-tiansminde, and wild violets. Have you ever really looked at wild violets? Look at these and then tell me whether they aren't much prettier than March violets. People have got it into their heads that violets, to be really pretty, must be "deep blue!" How stupid! Then there is bennet and wood-ruff, and look carefully at a delicate white one, I don't know what it is called, but you can see for yourself. This is my spring greeting—I am longing for a letter from you. Do not misunderstand me and think you are obliged to write. I can wait a long time. Go for a very beautiful walk and write if you feel inclined, not otherwise.   24

My examination last week passed off to the satisfaction of every-one concerned. Pastor Prip said he could not understand how I could teach so many children of different ages so well. I am just beginning to be really fond of my work and that is of course what helps me to get on. I believe, too, that I have succeeded in making the children like most of the subjects, I think that is most important. I have been having holidays Thursday, Friday and Saturday and begin again on Monday.   25

I like your *Sleepless Nights* in *Nutiden* better than the first poem; the words are placed better. Have much more to write about, but am afraid I must stop.   Hosts of love from,

Your sister, S.   26

The letter was from the eldest of my sisters. Although two years younger than I, she had already begun to teach in a local school. Accompanied by her best friend, she had been out early on a cool, June morning to gather flowers and send me this greeting of spring. What had I to send her? Discontented, despairing verses, like those she had read of mine, and which ended in this edifying manner:

> The night's black grains of sand are running
> Soundlessly down through space,
> They have bolted all the doors,
> They have stopped all the paths,
> Every fruitless prayer for happiness
> Has long since grown mute in the soul,
> Slain and dead is every longing,
> Hope is a legend, darkened is the sun.   27

This was I—and that was my sister. This was Copenhagen—and that was Svendborg. These were the new thoughts—that was the old faith.   28

I turned the letter over; there was a little postscript, written in a childish hand, from the other of my sisters:

> "The cross-flower with the grey, ugly leaves is a night-violet, it has no scent until after sunset. Sofie says I am to tell you this.
> Much love from
> Elisabeth.   29
> At this moment we are in the wash-house packing the flowers.
> Elisabeth.
> 14 years old.   30

Suggestions for Writing

1 An essay in which you are the principal character need not be based upon an esoteric experience. Write a personal narrative dealing with an event quite normal or ordinary in character. You may try to point out how this thing of ordinary interest brought out an essential part of your personality.

2 "He that increaseth knowledge increaseth sorrow" (*Ecclesiastes* 1:18). Increased knowledge may lead to small tragedies or to great ones, but most people have probably experienced small ones in their childhood. Remembering such an incident, construct a personal narrative in which an increase of knowledge brought an increase of sorrow or an increase of sorrow brought an increase of knowledge.

3 First romance or young romance has encouraged many excellent writers to evoke warm or humorous memories of the past. Somewhat in the style

of Thomas Merton, try to recapture your own feelings in the first brush with romance. Perhaps you were six or sixteen; whatever your age, try to create the feeling of the time and the event.

4 In trying to discover something about ourselves in order to write a personal narrative, we may have reached the conclusion Oliver Wendell Holmes did: "There are three Johns: 1. the real John, known only to his maker; 2. John's ideal John, never the real one, and often very unlike him; 3. Thomas's ideal John, never the real John, nor John's John, but often very unlike either." Sometimes, however, we can ascertain something about the "real John" if we remember how we felt at the moment of a decision of some kind. This may be a significant decision about an important matter, or it may be relatively unimportant. Schopenhauer says that "it is in trifles, and when he is off his guard, that a man best shows his character." Write a personal narrative concerning a decision you made, important or trivial; make this meaningful for the reader by carefully selecting colorful details.

EXPLAINING THE FACTS_____

EXPOSITION

*It is true, as Plato said, that most men are blind to the fact of their
ignorance of the essential character of each individual thing. They do
not see in each thing that which distinguishes it from every other; they
do not see what, if the thing were freed from all but its own
characteristic, would remain, and would be the point of it, and would
define its existence in the midst of a multitude of things like and
unlike. What men are least apt to do is to see the point.*

Stark Young (The Flower in Drama and Glamour,
Charles Scribner's Sons, New York, 1955)

In analyzing any piece of writing, the reader must make a significant attempt to discover the writer's main intention. The writer's obligation is to provide enough clues to enable the reader to make a judgment as to what purpose he had in mind. Obviously, he wishes to communicate something to the reader; and he does it in a *particular way,* in a way that is larger and more informing than the subject of the composition itself—a way which, in fact, makes the subject meaningful within a form of expression. All purposeful writing, therefore, can be analyzed by a reader as a response to a question he asks himself in order to discover the writer's *primary intention.* Did he wish to give information, clarify meaning, or explain an idea? Did he wish to influence the reader to accept a certain point of view or a particular attitude, or to assent to one possibility among many? Did he wish to give the reader a word picture, a verbal representation, to capture direct experience through sense impressions? Did he wish to tell what happened as a result of a sequence of events? As we answer each of these questions affirmatively, we discover a different primary intention. Each intention corresponds with one of the traditional forms of discourse—exposition, argument, description, and narration.

Exposition, the most commonly used form, informs the reader or explains something to him. For example, in this book, Mortimer Adler tells us how to read a book and Albert Goldman defines the origins and nature of rock music. Argument convinces or persuades a reader. Phyllis McGinley attempts to persuade us to see the good values in suburban living, and Daniel Boorstin argues that the disrupters and dissenters in America today are "not radicals at all, but a new species of barbarian." Description communicates the experience of observations directly through sense impressions. Elizabeth Bowen and William Maxwell give us descriptions of some aspects of nature, and James Agee evokes the mood and atmosphere of a city neighborhood on a warm summer evening. Katharine Anne Porter describes a character. Narration captures the movement of events in time. Robert Penn Warren tells us of the career of Malcolm X while he also analyzes it; Ved Mehta brings to life for us the work of a group of nuns caring for lepers in Calcutta; William Prescott re-creates the storming of the great Aztec temple.

In most writing, intentions are mixed; seldom do we find a pure form. But in any mixture brewed by a responsible writer, the reader can discover a primary intention or purpose. Each fulfills for the writer some fundamental need in his desire to communicate. Also, although a mixture of forms ordinarily is found in any piece of writing, each form is best studied in isolation. An analysis of the individual examples in the various sections of this anthology will lead to closer observation and clearer understanding of each of the forms. Our first concern will be with exposition.

"Exposition" means simply "a setting forth of facts," "writing or speaking that sets forth or explains." The word *exposition* often appears in a variety of disguises. The biologist who "describes" the life cycle of the mosquito, the historian who "discusses" the causes of the French Revolution, and the economist who "reports" on the present value of the dollar are all writing exposition. It informs, explains, interprets, analyzes, elucidates, or instructs. These suggestions make it clear that exposition is directed at helping the reader to "see the point." Its purpose is to make the reader understand. Unlike argument, it does not intend to convince or persuade. Unlike description, it does not present a verbal representation for its own sake. Exposition *states directly* that this is the nature of a person or thing, that this is the way something works, that this is the meaning of an idea.

The exposition or explanation of a subject can be developed in many ways, probably in as many ways as there are expository essays. Some of the ways of developing a subject in an expository manner are so common, however, that they can be isolated and studied separately. These are: definition, example, comparison and contrast, process analysis, classification and division, cause and effect. We shall be concerned here with these often-used, common methods of expository analysis, emphasizing how one method of analysis and then another is especially evident in a selected group of essays. Of course, the methods of analysis are generally found in combination, just as the forms of discourse are. The reason for concentration on one method at a time we have already noted: this allows closer observation and clearer understanding. The study of exposition is, in short, the study of the methods of analysis which develop any subject in an expository fashion.

THE NATURE OF THE SUBJECT: DEFINITION

Definition is a good place to begin our discussion of the methods
of analysis, because explanation—the aim of exposition—so
often requires definition. John Crowe Ransom insists that definition
is one of the best possible practices for the writer because "it
requires control of thought and language." Definition is the method
of analysis that answers the question, "What is it?" It tells what a
thing is; but giving a name or supplying synonyms is only a
beginning step in a complicated process. Our word "definition"
comes ultimately from the Latin de and finire, meaning "to set a
limit" or "to bound." This is the essence of definition—to set
up boundaries. These boundaries must have some relationship to
common usage, logic, or reality—the three areas of definition
to be considered in this introduction.

The problem created by ignoring common usage is well
dramatized by the story of Alice in Wonderland. When Alice stepped
through the looking glass, the astounding and unexpected
happened with habitual regularity. She had every reason to be
puzzled, for instance, by her conversation with Humpty Dumpty.

> "I don't know what you mean by 'glory,'" Alice said.
> Humpty Dumpty smiled contemptuously. "Of course
> you don't—till I tell you. I meant 'there's a nice knockdown
> argument for you,'"
> "But 'glory' doesn't mean 'A nice knockdown argument,'"
> Alice objected.
> "When I use a word," Humpty Dumpty said in a
> rather scornful tone, "it means just what I choose it to mean—
> neither more nor less."

Although Humpty Dumpty is careful enough to define his term,
he defines it so personally, so privately, that it ceases to have any
exchange value. Because of his contemptuous dismissal of
common usage, Alice objects to his definition. She had expected
"glory" to mean what it means for most people. If a good desk
dictionary had been handy, she probably would have appealed to it to
enforce her objection.

Probably our own commonest notion of definition has to
do with the meanings listed after words in a dictionary. This, surely,
is a kind of definition, for the dictionary does set up boundaries,
defining a word as most people use it or have used it. This kind of
definition, however, is not necessarily logical or rhetorical, for
the editors of dictionaries are concerned with the history and
progress of the word itself or with its present conventional usage.
They are not concerned with the reality which the word names.

In an acceptable desk dictionary, for instance, "democracy" is defined in one instance as "lack of snobbery," because the word is used in this context frequently: "There is real *democracy* in this school." This would, however, be an inadequate logical (that is, formal) definition as a starting point for an essay on political democracy.

But dictionaries also record logical definitions if these are used or have been used by a sufficient number of people. Thus, in the same dictionary "democracy" is defined in another instance as a government by the people, either directly or through elected representatives. Despite its limitations, this is a logical definition because it has the two required parts of a logical definition. The thing to be defined is put in a class, a genus, or a category grouping things together because of their likenesses or common traits. The genus of "democracy" is government. The second part of a logical definition specifies the characteristics of the thing to be defined in order to distinguish it from other members of the same class. These characteristics are referred to as the "species" or "differentiae." Thus, "democracy" is distinguished from other kinds of government because the people do the governing, either directly or through elected representatives. At least one such differentia, or distinguishing attribute, must be expressed in any logical definition. Because a logical definition defines reality and not just the name given to a real thing, the combination of genus and species as a rigid formula can be applied to any definition offered as logical.

Although most logical definitions express the established meaning of a term in the manner described above, some are stipulative, constructed by an individual writer for some particular purpose. A character in one of Robert Frost's poems, for example, defines "home" as "the place where, when you have to go there, they have to take you in." This is not the dictionary definition of home; but it is a striking logical definition, including the concepts of a genus and a species. And G. K. Chesterton's definition of a sentimentalist as a man who "seeks to enjoy every idea without its sequence, and every pleasure without its consequence" cannot be found in a dictionary; yet many people prefer this witty paradox that is also logical. Each of these definitions has the two essential parts: a class to which the term can be referred and at least one distinguishing attribute that differentiates it from the other members of that class.

The writer must be on his guard against certain common errors which are sometimes made in framing a logical definition.

A definition should ordinarily avoid being circular: that is, the defining part should not include the term being defined. No real boundaries are established when a Puritan is defined as a believer in Puritanism. Also, the genus should not be too small to include the thing to be defined. If Arnold Bennett's famous definition of a classic read, "A classic is a *novel* that gives pleasure to the minority which is intensely and permanently interested in literature," the genus "novel" would have omitted, for example, all poetry. What Bennett did write was, "A classic is a *work* that gives pleasure to the minority which is intensely and permanently interested in literature." A more general fault, however, is to make the genus so large that it fails to serve any useful purpose. If a pen is defined as something to write with, the genus is so large that it has no value.

Since logical definitions are satisfied with the minimal statement of an equation, good writing often requires what are called "rhetorical" (or "extended" or "informal") definitions. They may be a paragraph long or an essay long; yet they too must preserve the formula of the logical definition—genus and species—which makes an equation possible. Rhetorical definitions are often used because of the complex nature of some terms—"justice," for instance. Sometimes a writer wishes to express what *he* feels is the true meaning of a term; how often, for example, has "liberty" been defined? Often, too, the general, conventional meaning of a term is clear enough, but the writer feels there is a need for a fuller and deeper understanding of it, as may be the case with a concept such as "patriotism." A writer may also object to a stereotyped definition, or write his own definition to correct a wrong notion.

Rhetorical definitions are, therefore, always written with a particular purpose in mind; they are what Richard Weaver has called "*ad hoc* definitions." When St. John de Crèvecœur, for example, published his famous *Letters from an American Farmer* in 1782, he had a European audience in mind, one very much aware of America's revolutionary newness. This is evident from his often-quoted definition of an American, especially in the conclusion of his extended definition:

> The American is a new man, who acts upon new principles;
> he must therefore entertain new ideas, and form new opinions.
> From voluntary idleness, servile dependence, penury, and useless
> labor, he has passed to toils of a very different nature.

In this text, both Russell Kirk and Arthur Schlesinger write rhetorical definitions of "conservative," which each feels limits the

term better than does the ordinary definition associated with it.
The special quality of a rhetorical definition becomes evident if we
keep in mind its *ad hoc* character, its use for a particular occasion.

A rhetorical definition will also generally concern itself
with the development of the species or distinguishing attributes of a
logical definition rather than with the genus. Thus, a rhetorical
definition of "democracy" would probably not extend the meaning
of "government" (the genus); but it would concern itself with
a further explanation of what distinguishes "democracy" from other
forms of government (the species). When Albert Goldman (page 45)
develops his definitions of rock and soul music, he does not develop
the class "music"; rather he concentrates on the particular
features or phenomena of what is to be defined. It would be of little
value for Schlesinger to discuss at length the class of which
radical and conservative are a part; what counts for him are the
specific differences.

Logical definitions can be extended—made rhetorical—in a
wide variety of ways. In fact, in the construction of such definitions,
which is itself a method of analysis, the writer will often find
himself employing many of the other methods of analysis, such as
example or comparison and contrast. Similarly, in the
construction of an essay having a central purpose other than
or wider than definition, the writer may employ definition. The
essays for this section illustrate this fact. Some, like Goldman's, are
primarily definition—they reveal certain ways of *extending* a
definition—and some, like Joan Didion's (page 51) and Ralph
Ellison's (page 63), use rhetorical definition for a wider purpose—
they reveal certain ways of *using* extended definition.

THE EMERGENCE OF ROCK

ALBERT GOLDMAN

. . . There is no simple way of comprehending the extraordinarily rapid and complex development of the rock sound and culture. But perhaps the clearest way is to begin at the beginning and try to follow the principal trends of the music, along with their respective cultural ambiences and meanings, both in the Negro and in the white world.   1

Rock was born in a flashback, a celluloid loop doubled back inside a time machine. The date was 1954; the place was Cleveland, Ohio; the occasion, the first broadcast of Negro race records to an audience of white teen-agers. Alan Freed, a local disk jockey, made the experiment. Almost immediately, it became apparent that he had struck a nerve that was ready to vibrate. The records he played were known in the trade as "rhythm and blues." Ground out by tiny Negro record companies in the South, they were aimed at the black ghettos of the North. What they contained was a particularly potent strain of the same urban blues that had swept over the country in the late thirties during the vogue of the big bands. Indeed, if one can imagine an old Kansas City blues band crushed like a tin can so that nothing remains of it but top, bottom, and lots of rusty ragged edges, he will have a fair idea of how the early r&b combos sounded. Concentrating on essentials, these groups used a disproportionate number of instruments (electric rhythm and bass guitars, plus piano and drums) to hammer out the beat, while the solo performers, vocal or instrumental, worked way out in front, using a primitive style compounded of honks and cries and words bawled out like curses.*   2

It was, therefore, an old and radically racial sound that Freed offered to his listeners in the Midwest, and later in New York: a sound that told of dirt and fear and pain and lust. But the white kids loved it; and soon, as if to signify that the music had been adopted by a new public, Freed changed its name to "rock 'n' roll," though even this new name came from an old blues, "My baby rocks me with a steady roll." The success of rock attracted white performers: the first r&b song recorded by a white singer was "Rock Around the Clock" by Bill Haley and the Comets. Haley initiated that process of white assimilation of Negro style that for many years has been a basic feature of the movement; but the tendency of early rock was to pull away from the heavy racial sound in favor of the lighter, swifter beat of hillbilly music, which was to be one of rock's more durable elements, and a subject matter (cars, Cokes, and heartaches) more suitable to white teen-

---

* Paragraph 2: Which sentences in this paragraph clarify what the "flashback" consisted of?

agers. On this new wave of country blues, Chuck Berry and then Elvis
Presley rode to fame. When Presley entered the army at the end of the
decade, one expected the fad to recede and vanish. But the culture
remained firmly rock-bound.*   3

While rock was enjoying this first surge of popularity, Negro music
was undergoing a series of changes among the most profound in its history.
The music of the ghetto was being revived and recharged by powerful new
performers bent on outdoing their white imitators, while its basic genres—
blues and gospel—were coalescing to produce a new style of enormous
strength and popularity.   4

The greatest of these singers—indeed, the greatest of all the basic
rock performers—was Little Richard. Richard's records all sounded as if
they were made in the Saturday night uproar of a turpentine logging camp.
His raw strident voice was torn from his throat in a bawling, shouting tor-
rent that battered and scattered the words until they sounded like raving.
Behind this desperately naked voice worked a boogie-woogie rhythm section
tightened to vise-like rigidity. The furious energy of the singing caught in
the iron cage of the rhythm produced an almost unbearable tension. Instead
of illustrating the words, which often spoke of pleasure ("I'm gonna ball
tonight!"), the music conveyed the agonizing effort to break through to joy.
(Or just to break through: Richard usually ended his chorus with the blood-
curdling scream of a man hurling himself over a precipice.) What Little
Richard was saying musically—and the Negro ghetto with him—was not
that he was having a good time, but that he had the right to one and would
"cut" anyone who got in his way. His note was erotic defiance. As such,
Little Richard represented a new type of Negro youth. Reckless and rebellious, he gave us the first taste of the voice that was later to holler, "Burn,
baby, burn!"   5

Oddly enough, the other great performer who emerged in this period
expressed a character of precisely the opposite sort. Ray Charles was the
eternal Negro, a poor blind man crying out of his darkness, singing to
assuage his pain. Yet as a musician he was far from being a traditionalist;
in fact, in undertaking to mix gospel and blues he violated one of the
strictest taboos of Negro music. Throughout modern times, gospel and
blues had always been rigidly segregated expressions of the sacred and
the profane. Blues worked cathartically, urging that everything painful be
confronted, named, lamented, and exorcised in a lonely, impersonal, almost
aloof style. Gospel had functioned in a completely opposite manner, one
that overwhelmed unhappiness by a swelling evocation of the joys of life
beyond the present world. Just as the blues was traditionally depressed,
understated, ironic, and resigned, gospel was typically ebullient, extrava-

---

* Paragraph 3: In the first sentence, what does "radically" mean? In the same sentence,
why does the author use "and" instead of commas after "dirt" and "fear"?

gant, even at times orgiastic in its affirmation. The Negro community had preserved the solace of each of these traditions by maintaining a total separation between them. The singing of blues in church was forbidden, while the blues singer steadfastly confronted his troubles without ever looking heavenward.*   6

That is, until Ray Charles and his followers stepped boldly over the boundary and ended the prohibition. One of the first effects of this revolution was an inversion of traditional modes. Not only did these singers perform minor blues in the style of plaintive dirges, such as one might hear in church; they also added blues lyrics to the hand-clapping, foot-stamping, tambourine-banging gospel shouts. On stage they adopted many of the mannerisms, practices, and rituals of the storefront Negro church. They testified, danced ecstatically, called for witnesses, appeared to be led from above, tore off their clothes, and fell and rose again like men in the grip of a religious revelation.†   7

Charles's own manner was often that of the preacher: the voice deliberately crude, cracked, thickened with Southern Negro pronunciations; the style figured with cantorial embellishments. The effect was that of a man seized by emotion, spilling out his feelings with absolute candor. Typical of the original gospel-blues mix was "Yes, Indeed," one of Charles's most successful early numbers. The piece opens with soft church chords played on a harmonium; next, Charles gives out the text in his deep deacon's voice, a word or two—then the gospel beat, heavy and lurching, comes crashing in with a chorus of "Amen girls" hypnotically chanting after every phrase, "Yaas, indeed!" As the piece stomps through its traditional 16-bar course, the confidently rising intervals generate an aura of optimism that reaches its climax in a moment of pure "salvation." The horns riff joyously, the chord changes signal that we are coming home, and the lead voice sings: "Well, I know when it gets ya, you get a feelin' deep down in your soul, every time you hear that good old rock 'n' roll. Yaas, indeed." The lyrics tumble here to a dreadful anticlimax, just at the point where the music becomes most transcendent, for what would have been in the original a religious affirmation has been rubbed out and a pop music cliché scribbled in its place.‡   8

Once the barrier was down between gospel and blues, the distinctions between other Negro musical traditions also began to disappear. Singers, composers, instrumentalists, and arrangers began to take what they wanted

---

* Paragraph 6: Where do you find parallelism used in this paragraph? What are the basic differences between blues and gospel music as defined here?

† Paragraph 7: In the third sentence, why did the author use a semicolon instead of a comma or period?

‡ Paragraph 8: Present the thought of the last sentence in your own words.

from a racial ragbag of Delta blues, hillbilly strumming, gutbucket jazz, boogie-woogie piano, pop lyricism, and storefront shouting. The result— less a new genre than a mélange of musical materials—was called "soul."*   9

When one thinks of soul today, the image that presents itself is of a monotonously revolving kaleidoscope loaded with dozens of factory-stamped, smoky-colored bits of gospel, rock, blues, jazz, pop, folk, rock, pop, blues, and so on in endlessly shifting combinations of this week's, last month's, tomorrow's "sound." The agency most responsible for this commercialization of Negro music is Motown, the General Motors of rock. Its founder, owner, and manager is Berry Gordy, Jr., a one-time assembly-line worker, who since the early sixties has been turning out hit tunes produced by teams of composers, arrangers, and performers, all working closely to the specifications of the Motown formula.   10

The basic ingredient of the formula is the beat. Pushing beyond the traditional "and *two* and *four*" style of drumming, Berry's arrangers trained the drums to bark on every beat. Then they strengthened and enlarged the new beat by overamplification and by doubling it with tambourine, tom-tom, cymbals, bass, and, eventually, anything that would bounce. Today, Motown rocks with a driving, slogging rhythm that rumbles up through the floor of a discothèque like an earthquake.   11

The other active ingredient of the formula is the "shout," a short, arresting phrase that flashes the song's message. This is underscored and embellished with every resource provided by Negro tradition and the Hollywood sound stage. The most primitive types of plantation music—the sounds of Jew's harps, tambourines, pipes, and quills—have been unearthed to fill the formula's demand for a "funky" core. Around this core have been wrapped some fairly complicated arrangements, entailing the integration of strings, symphonic percusssion sections, choirs, and soloists.†   12

Motown's effort to concentrate all the sounds of Negro tradition into a super-soul has often produced the opposite of the intended effect—a typically commercial dilution of the Negro essence. But sometimes Detroit's stylists, especially the gifted team of Eddie and Bryant Holland and Lamont Dozier, have updated tradition so skillfully that they succeed in adding a genuinely contemporary voice to Negro music. Not content to paste pop lyrics over old church tunes, this team has approached gospel in a sophisticated spirit, seeking to exploit its ritual of salvation without sacrificing

---

* Paragraph 9: Why does the author make this a separate paragraph instead of attaching it to the next paragraph?

† Paragraph 12: The order of the last sentence might have been: subject first, main verb next, and introductory prepositional phrase last. Why is the order the author used more effective as regards emphasis within the sentence and coherence between this sentence and the preceding sentence?

the love story indispensable to the pop ballad. In their best work they can telescope into three relentless minutes the events of a whole evening in a storefront church without dislodging the conventional facade of the ballad.* 13

"I'll Be There," the most admired song of Motown's The Four Tops, opens on a characteristically exotic note: pipes and slap bass evoking a movie image of Genghis Khan and his men trotting across the steppes of Central Asia. Then this mirage is suddenly blown away and we are down to the bedrock of soul: the drums pounding, the tambourines jingling, and the anguished voice of Levi Stubbs exhorting his sweetheart in the manner of an evangelist preacher:

> *If you feel that you can't go on,*
> *Because all of your hope is gone,*
> *And your life is filled with much confusion,*
> *Until happiness is just an illusion:*

"Reach out!" cry the wraithlike voices that have been trailing and echoing Stubbs. "Reach out for *me!*" he adds, distending the word with a flourish of emotion. Then for one suspenseful moment, all the voices cease, and we gaze into a void in which there is nothing but the nakedly writhing beat. Suddenly the emptiness is filled with the solemn sound of the "shout," "I'll be there," sung in unison by leader and chorus and accompanied by the exotic pipes of the introduction, which now assume their proper place as a kind of stained-glass window behind the singers. The final touch of religious excitement was added during the recording session: when the break in the melody opened for the last time, Levi shouted to the girl, "Look over your shoulder!" For a Negro audience this phrase summons up one of the most intense moments at a gospel service: the sight of some believer pointing wildly toward a corner of the church where he has caught a glimpse of the Holy Spirit. 14

Motown does a dizzying business with its exploitation of classic Negro styles, and most of this business is done in the Negro ghettos (where nobody pays any attention to The Beatles). Generally, the success of the style is attributed to Negro pride, to the joy with which Negroes respond to the basic expressions of their culture. But the regressive, almost caricatured Negritude of soul, and even more importantly, the desperately naked avowal of suffering made in the more seriously expressive songs, suggest that this music celebrates blackness less for its beauty than for its strength as a revived resource against the white terror. 15

Soul's revival of gospel music has been accompanied by a return to archaic patterns of body movement which combine gestures of incantation

---

* Paragraph 13: In the last sentence, to what do the "three relentless minutes" refer? Why are they "relentless"?

and exorcism. In the currently popular boogaloo, for example, there is a complete pantomime of terror. The dancer's neck is twisted spasmodically as if by a lynch rope, his eyes roll up into his head, his hands shoot out past his face as if to avert a blow, and his whole body tips as though he were about to collapse. The imagery of anxiety in such a performance accords perfectly with the character of the words and music which excite it, and all three qualify drastically the notion that rock is simply the revelry of orgy.   16

The Whole Selection

1 In paragraph 5, what phenomena or ingredients of rock music are specified by the author?
2 Is soul music, as defined in paragraphs 9 through 16, simply a merging of two different kinds of rock music, as defined in paragraphs 5 through 8?
3 What function does paragraph 4 serve in relation to the structure of the rest of the essay?
4 Good writing depends upon the use of precise, specific verbs. Make a list of such verbs as you find them in paragraphs 8 through 12.

Word Study *ambience, ebullient, dirge, wraithlike, exorcism*

ON SELF-RESPECT

JOAN DIDION

Once, in a dry season, I wrote in large letters across two pages of a note-book that innocence ends when one is stripped of the delusion that one likes oneself. Although now, some years later, I marvel that a mind on the outs with itself should have nonetheless made painstaking record of its every tremor, I recall with embarrassing clarity the flavor of those particu-lar ashes. It was a matter of misplaced self-respect.*

    1

    I had not been elected to Phi Beta Kappa. This failure could scarcely have been more predictable or less ambiguous (I simply did not have the grades), but I was unnerved by it; I had somehow thought myself a kind of academic Raskolnikov, curiously exempt from the cause-effect relationships which hampered others. Although even the humorless nineteen-year-old that I was must have recognized that the situation lacked real tragic stature, the day that I did not make Phi Beta Kappa nonetheless marked the end of some-thing, and innocence may well be the word for it. I lost the conviction that lights would always turn green for me, the pleasant certainty that those rather passive virtues which had won me approval as a child automatically guaranteed me not only Phi Beta Kappa keys but happiness, honor, and the love of a good man; lost a certain touching faith in the totem power of good manners, clean hair, and proven competence on the Stanford-Binet scale. To such doubtful amulets had my self-respect been pinned, and I faced myself that day with the nonplused apprehension of someone who has come across a vampire and has no crucifix at hand.†

    2

    Although to be driven back upon oneself is an uneasy affair at best, rather like trying to cross a border with borrowed credentials, it seems to me now the one condition necessary to the beginnings of real self-respect. Most of our platitudes notwithstanding, self-deception remains the most difficult deception. The tricks that work on others count for nothing in that very well-lit back alley where one keeps assignations with oneself: no winning smiles will do here, no prettily drawn lists of good intentions. One shuffles flashily but in vain through one's marked cards—the kindness done for the wrong reason, the apparent triumph which involved no real effort, the seemingly heroic act into which one had been shamed. The dis-mal fact is that self-respect has nothing to do with the approval of others —who are, after all, deceived easily enough; has nothing to do with reputa-tion, which, as Rhett Butler told Scarlett O'Hara, is something people with courage can do without.

    3

* Paragraph 1: What are the "particular ashes"?

† Paragraph 2: In the last sentence, to what do the "doubtful amulets" refer? Why are they called "doubtful"?

To do without self-respect, on the other hand, is to be an unwilling audience of one to an interminable documentary that details one's failings, both real and imagined, with fresh footage spliced in for every screening. *There's the glass you broke in anger, there's the hurt on X's face; watch now, this next scene, the night Y came back from Houston, see how you muff this one.* To live without self-respect is to lie awake some night, beyond the reach of warm milk, phenobarbital, and the sleeping hand on the coverlet, counting up the sins of commission and omission, the trusts betrayed, the promises subtly broken, the gifts irrevocably wasted through sloth or cowardice or carelessness. However long we postpone it, we eventually lie down alone in that notoriously uncomfortable bed, the one we make ourselves. Whether or not we sleep in it depends, of course, on whether or not we respect ourselves.*   4

To protest that some fairly improbable people, some people who *could not possibly respect themselves,* seem to sleep easily enough is to miss the point entirely, as surely as those people miss it who think that self-respect has necessarily to do with not having safety pins in one's underwear. There is a common superstition that "self-respect" is a kind of charm against snakes, something that keeps those who have it locked in some unblighted Eden, out of strange beds, ambivalent conversations, and trouble in general. It does not at all. It has nothing to do with the face of things, but concerns instead a separate peace, a private reconciliation. Although the careless, suicidal Julian English in *Appointment in Samarra* and the careless, incurably dishonest Jordan Baker in *The Great Gatsby* seem equally improbable candidates for self-respect, Jordan Baker had it, Julian English did not. With that genius for accommodation more often seen in women than in men, Jordan took her own measure, made her own peace, avoided threats to that peace: "I hate careless people," she told Nick Carraway. "It takes two to make an accident."†   5

Like Jordan Baker, people with self-respect have the courage of their mistakes. They know the price of things. If they choose to commit adultery, they do not then go running, in an access of bad conscience, to receive absolution from the wronged parties; nor do they complain unduly of the unfairness, the undeserved embarrassment, of being named co-respondent. In brief, people with self-respect exhibit a certain toughness, a kind of moral nerve; they display what was once called *character,* a quality which, although approved in the abstract, sometimes loses ground to other, more instantly negotiable virtues. The measure of its slipping prestige is that one tends to think of it only in connection with homely children and United States senators who have been defeated, preferably in the primary, for

* Paragraph 4: Whose is "the sleeping hand on the coverlet"?

† Paragraph 5: What sense do you make out of Jordan Baker's statement to Nick Carraway in view of Miss Didion's describing Jordan as being herself careless?

reelection. Nonetheless, character—the willingness to accept responsibility for one's own life—is the source from which self-respect springs.   6

Self-respect is something that our grandparents, whether or not they had it, knew all about. They had instilled in them, young, a certain discipline, the sense that one lives by doing things one does not particularly want to do, by putting fears and doubts to one side, by weighing immediate comforts against the possibility of larger, even intangible, comforts. It seemed to the nineteenth century admirable, but not remarkable, that Chinese Gordon put on a clean white suit and held Khartoum against the Mahdi; it did not seem unjust that the way to free land in California involved death and difficulty and dirt. In a diary kept during the winter of 1846, an emigrating twelve-year-old named Narcissa Cornwall noted coolly: "Father was busy reading and did not notice that the house was being filled with strange Indians until Mother spoke about it." Even lacking any clue as to what Mother said, one can scarcely fail to be impressed by the entire incident: the father reading, the Indians filing in, the mother choosing the words that would not alarm, the child duly recording the event and noting further that those particular Indians were not, "fortunately for us," hostile. Indians were simply part of the *donnée*.   7

In one guise or another, Indians always are. Again, it is a question of recognizing that anything worth having has its price. People who respect themselves are willing to accept the risk that the Indians will be hostile, that the venture will go bankrupt, that the liaison may not turn out to be one in which *every day is a holiday because you're married to me.* They are willing to invest something of themselves; they may not play at all, but when they do play, they know the odds.*   8

That kind of self-respect is a discipline, a habit of mind that can never be faked but can be developed, trained, coaxed forth. It was once suggested to me that, as an antidote to crying, I put my head in a paper bag. As it happens, there is a sound physiological reason, something to do with oxygen, for doing exactly that, but the psychological effect alone is incalculable: it is difficult in the extreme to continue fancying oneself Cathy in *Wuthering Heights* with one's head in a Food Fair bag. There is a similar case for all the small disciplines, unimportant in themselves; imagine maintaining any kind of swoon, commiserative or carnal, in a cold shower.   9

But those small disciplines are valuable only insofar as they represent larger ones. To say that Waterloo was won on the playing fields of Eton is not to say that Napoleon might have been saved by a crash program in cricket, to give formal dinners in the rain forest would be pointless did not the candlelight flickering on the liana call forth deeper, stronger

---

* Paragraph 8: What does "Indians always are" mean?

disciplines, values instilled long before. It is a kind of ritual, helping us to
remember who and what we are. In order to remember it, one must have
known it.   10

To have that sense of one's intrinsic worth which constitutes self-
respect is potentially to have everything: the ability to discriminate, to love
and to remain indifferent. To lack it is to be locked within oneself, paradoxically incapable of either love or indifference. If we do not respect ourselves, we are on the one hand forced to despise those who have so few
resources as to consort with us, so little perception as to remain blind to
our fatal weaknesses. On the other, we are peculiarly in thrall to everyone
we see, curiously determined to live out—since our self-image is untenable
—their false notions of us. We flatter ourselves by thinking this compulsion to please others an attractive trait: a gist for imaginative empathy,
evidence of our willingness to give. *Of course* I will play Francesca to your
Paolo, Helen Keller to anyone's Annie Sullivan: no expectation is too misplaced, no role too ludicrous. At the mercy of those we cannot but hold in
contempt, we play roles doomed to failure before they are begun, each
defeat generating fresh despair at the urgency of divining and meeting the
next demand made upon us.*   11

It is the phenomenon sometimes called "alienation from self." In its
advanced stages, we no longer answer the telephone, because someone
might want something; that we could say *no* without drowning in self-
reproach is an idea alien to this game. Every encounter demands too much,
tears the nerves, drains the will, and the specter of something as small as
an unanswered letter arouses such disproportionate guilt that answering it
becomes out of the question. To assign unanswered letters their proper
weight, to free us from the expectations of others, to give us back to ourselves—there lies the great, the singular power of self-respect. Without it,
one eventually discovers the final turn of the screw: one runs away to find
oneself, and finds no one at home.   12

* Paragraph 11: What kinds of "demand" has the author been referring to?

The Whole Selection

1 In much of paragraphs 1 through 5, the author defines self-respect
   negatively by telling what it is not—certainly an effective device in
   extended definition. Where does she begin to define positively?
2 In paragraph 7, the author effectively uses parallelism. What other uses
   of this device can you find in the essay?
3 To be sure that you understand the last paragraph of the essay, try to
   restate the substance of it in your own words.

Word Study *amulets, platitudes, ambivalent, donnée, untenable, empathy*

A PRELIMINARY DELINEATION: CONSERVATIVE AND RADICAL

RUSSELL KIRK

Any informed conservative is reluctant to condense profound and intricate intellectual systems to a few pretentious phrases; he prefers to leave that technique to the enthusiasm of radicals. Conservatism is not a fixed and immutable body of dogma, and conservatives inherit from Burke a talent for re-expressing their convictions to fit the time. As a working premise, nevertheless, one can observe here that the essence of social conservatism is preservation of the ancient moral traditions of humanity. Conservatives respect the wisdom of their ancestors (this phrase was Strafford's, and Hooker's, before Burke illuminated it); they are dubious of wholesale alteration. They think society is a spiritual reality, possessing an eternal life but a delicate constitution: it cannot be scrapped and recast as if it were a machine. "What is conservatism?" Abraham Lincoln inquired once. "Is it not adherence to the old and tried, against the new and untried?" It is that, but it is more. Professor Hearnshaw, in his *Conservatism in England*, lists a dozen principles of conservatives, but possibly these may be comprehended in a briefer catalogue. I think that there are six canons of conservative thought——*   1

   Belief that a divine intent rules society as well as conscience, forging an eternal chain of right and duty which links great and obscure, living and dead. Political problems, at bottom, are religious and moral problems. A narrow rationality, what Coleridge calls the Understanding, cannot of itself satisfy human needs. "Every Tory is a realist," says Keith Feiling: "he knows that there are great forces in heaven and earth that man's philosophy cannot plumb or fathom. We do wrong to deny it, when we are told that we do not trust human reason: we do not and we may not. Human reason set up a cross on Calvary, human reason set up the cup of hemlock, human reason was canonised in Notre Dame." Politics is the art of apprehending and applying the Justice which is above nature.   2

   Affection for the proliferating variety and mystery of traditional life, as distinguished from the narrowing uniformity and equalitarianism and utilitarian aims of most radical systems. This is why Quintin Hogg (Lord Hailsham) and R. J. White describe conservatism as "enjoyment." It is this buoyant view of life which Walter Bagehot called "the proper source of an animated Conservatism."   3

   Conviction that civilized society requires orders and classes. The only true equality is moral equality; all other attempts at levelling lead to

---

* Paragraph 1: Does the first sentence of this paragraph indicate in any way that Kirk considers himself a radical or a conservative?

despair, if enforced by positive legislation. Society longs for leadership, and if a people destroy natural distinctions among men, presently Buonaparte fills the vacuum.   4

Persuasion that property and freedom are inseparably connected, and that economic levelling is not economic progress. Separate property from private possession, and liberty is erased.   5

Faith in prescription and distrust of "sophisters and calculators." Man must put a control upon his will and his appetite, for conservatives know man to be governed more by emotion than by reason. Tradition and sound prejudice provide checks upon man's anarchic impulse.*   6

Recognition that change and reform are not identical, and that innovation is a devouring conflagration more often than it is a torch of progress. Society must alter, for slow change is the means of its conservation, like the human body's perpetual renewal; but Providence is the proper instrument for change, and the test of a statesman is his cognizance of the real tendency of Providential social forces.   7

Various deviations from this system of ideas have occurred, and there are numerous appendages to it; but in general conservatives have adhered to these articles of belief with a consistency rare in political history. To catalogue the principles of their opponents is more difficult. At least five major schools of radical thought have competed for public favor since Burke entered politics: the rationalism of the *philosophes* and Hume, the romantic emancipation of Rousseau and his allies, the utilitarianism of the Benthamites, the positivism of Comte's school, and the collectivistic materialism of Marx and other socialists. This list leaves out of account those scientific doctrines, Darwinism chief among them, which have done so much to undermine the first principles of a conservative order. To express these several radicalisms in terms of a common denominator probably is presumptuous, foreign to the philosophical tenets of conservatism. All the same, in a hastily generalizing fashion one may say that radicalism since 1790 has tended to attack the prescriptive arrangement of society on the following grounds——   8

The perfectibility of man and the illimitable progress of society; meliorism. Radicals believe that education, positive legislation, and alteration of environment can produce men like gods; they deny that humanity has a natural proclivity toward violence and sin.†   9

Contempt for tradition. Reason, impulse, and materialistic determinism are severally preferred as guides to social welfare, trustier than the

* Paragraph 6: Does the phrase "sound prejudice" appear ambiguous to you? Consult your dictionary for the etymology and various meanings of "prejudice."

† Paragraph 9: Does Kirk expect you to know the definition of "meliorism" or does he define it?

wisdom of our ancestors. Formal religion is rejected and a variety of anti-
Christian systems are offered as substitutes.   10

Political levelling. Order and privilege are condemned; total democracy, as direct as practicable, is the professed radical ideal. Allied with this
spirit, generally, is a dislike of old parliamentary arrangements and an
eagerness for centralization and consolidation.   11

Economic levelling. The ancient rights of property, especially property
in land, are suspect to almost all radicals; and collectivistic reformers hack
at the institution of private property root and branch.   12

As a fifth point, one might try to define a common radical view of the
state's function; but here the chasm of opinion between the chief schools
of innovation is too deep for any satisfactory generalization. One can only
remark that radicals unite in detesting Burke's description of the state as a
divinely ordained moral essence, a spiritual union of the dead, the living,
and those yet unborn.   13

So much for preliminary delineation. The radical, when all is said, is
a neoterist, in love with change; the conservative, a man who says with
Joubert, *Ce sont les crampons qui unissent une génération à une autre—*
these ancient institutions of politics and religion. *Conservez ce qu'ont vu
vos pères.* If one seeks by way of definition more than this, the sooner he
turns to particular thinkers, the safer ground he is on.*   14

* Paragraph 14: What is the function of the second sentence of this paragraph? What is the
meaning of the final sentence? Can you relate it to Kirk's reluctance to generalize?

The Whole Selection

1 In how many ways is "conservative" or "conservatism" defined? Cite
specific sentences and phrases. Does this repetition serve some function?
2 In what instances does Kirk use authority to define his terms?
3 In order to define, Kirk uses contrast. Why is that especially appropriate
for this definition?
4 Can you distinguish the genus and the specific difference in Kirk's
definition?
5 Without consulting a dictionary, try to indicate what Kirk's definitions
are of "neoterist," "political levelling," "politics," and "society."

WHAT DO THE TERMS MEAN?

ARTHUR M. SCHLESINGER

The heated discussion conducted in recent years by press and platform on the merits and demerits of radicalism and conservatism causes the student of American history to search his mind concerning the effects of these opposing types of thought on the past history of the United States. In such an inquiry, an initial difficulty presents itself: what do the terms, "conservative" and "radical," mean? Popular usage has tended to rob these expressions of exact meaning and to convert them into epithets of opprobrium and adulation which are used as the bias or interest of the person may dictate. The conservative, having mapped out the confines of truth to his own satisfaction, judges the depravity and errors of the radical by the extent of his departure from the boundaries thus established. Likewise the radical, from his vantage-point of truth, measures the knavery and infirmities of his opponents by the distance they have yet to travel to reach his goal. Neither conservative nor radical regards the other with judicial calm or "sweet reasonableness." Neither is willing to admit that the other has a useful function to perform in the progress of society. Each regards the other with deep feeling as the enemy of everything that is fundamentally good in government and society.*   1

    In seeking a workable definition of these terms, the philosophic insight of Thomas Jefferson is a beacon light to the inquirer. When Jefferson withdrew from active political life at the close of his presidency in 1809, he left behind him the heat and smoke of partisan strife and retired to a contemplative life on his Virginia estate, where his fellow-countrymen learned to revere him as the "Sage of Monticello." The voluminous correspondence of these twilight years of his life is full of instruction for the student of history and politics. His tremendous curiosity caused him to find an unfailing source of speculation in the proclivity of mankind to separate into contrasting schools of opinion. In one luminous passage, representative of the bent of his thought, he declared: "Men, according to their constitutions, and the circumstances in which they are placed, differ honestly in opinion. Some are Whigs, Liberals, Democrats, call them what you please. Others are Tories, Serviles, Aristocrats, etc. The latter fear the people, and wish to transfer all power to the higher classes of society; the former consider the people as the safest depository of power in the last resort; they cherish them, therefore, and wish to leave in them all the powers to the exercise of which they are competent."†   2

* Paragraph 1: Why has popular usage made a definition of the terms difficult?

† Paragraph 2: Just before quoting Jefferson, why does Schlesinger add the phrase "representative of the bent of his thought"?

In this passage, Jefferson does not use the expressions "conservative" and "radical"—indeed, those words had no place in the American political vocabulary until Civil War times—but his penetrating analysis throws a flood of light on the significance of those terms nevertheless. The Tory who fears the people and the Whig who trusts them are equivalent to our own categories of "conservative" and "radical." Thus Jefferson finds the vital distinction between the two schools of opinion in their respective attitudes toward popular government.   3

But before accepting Jefferson's classification as correct, what shall we do with the common notion that the conservative is a person who opposes change and that the ear-mark of the radical is his liking for innovation? This does not seem to be a fundamental distinction. If a difference of opinion concerning the need of change were the basic difference between the two, then Americans who advocate a limitation of the suffrage to male property-owners may properly be regarded as radicals, for they advocate an alteration in the established order; and the French patriots of today opposing the re-establishment of the Orleanist monarchy are to be classed as conservatives, for they would keep things unchanged. Few people would be willing to follow the logic of their premises to such conclusions. On the other hand, it cannot be denied that history has generally shown the radical in the role of an active proponent of change and has cast the conservative for the part of the stalwart defender of things as they are. Is such evidence to be dismissed as a coincidence oft-repeated, or has there been behind the actions of both radical and conservative some self-interested purpose which has determined their respective attitudes toward the established order?*   4

The very question perhaps suggests the answer. Broadly speaking, all history has been an intermittent contest on the part of the more numerous section of society to wrest power and privilege from the minority which had hitherto possessed it. The group which at any period favored broader popular rights and liberties was therefore likely to find itself a contender for the new and untried, leaving to its antagonists the comfortable repute of being the conservators of the *status quo* and the foes of change. But, though the historical conditions influenced the character of the contest, such conditions were, after all, merely the stage setting of the struggle. Advocacy of change should, under such circumstances, be regarded merely as the means employed to attain an end and, in no sense, as an end in itself. Recurring now to Jefferson's definition, the goal sought by each group— whether it be in the direction of greater or less democracy—would appear to constitute the real difference between the two.†   5

* Paragraph 4: In what way is the idea of this paragraph connected with that of the previous one, and by what specific phrases and sentences?

† Paragraph 5: What is the *status quo*?

It should be clear, then, that the radical is a person who, in contrast to the conservative, favors a larger participation of the people in the control of government and society and in the benefits accruing from such control. To attain his ideal the radical may become a protagonist of change; he usually has been one, as a matter of history, but this fact is a mere incident to, and not the touchstone of, his radicalism. The temperament of the radical is sanguine. He can say with Jefferson: "I steer my bark with Hope in the head, leaving fear astern. My hopes, indeed, sometimes fail; but not oftener than the forebodings of the gloomy." The conservative, on the other hand, is skeptical of the capacity of the mass of the people to protect their own interests intelligently; and believing that social progress in the past has always come from the leadership of wealth and ability, he is the consistent opponent of the unsettling plans of the radical. If the old saw is true that a pessimist is the wife of an optimist, perhaps the cynicism of the conservative is amply accounted for by his enforced association with the radical. The radical regards himself as a man of vision; but the conservative sees him only as a visionary. The radical as a type is likely to be broad-minded and shallow-minded; the disinterested conservative is inclined to be high-minded and narrow-minded.*   6

Of course, the expressions "radical" and "conservative" are relative terms, for at any given time the lines are drawn by the opposing forces upon the basis of the circumstances then existing. It is a truism that the radical of today may become the conservative of tomorrow. This does not necessarily argue inconsistency. It may indicate rather that, when the specific measures which the radical has advocated have been adopted, he believes that the supreme aim of public policy has been attained and he becomes a defender of the new *status quo* against any further extension of popular rights. This is perhaps the same as saying that the conservative of today, had he held the same opinions on political and social questions a generation ago, would have been looked upon then as a radical. The movement of history has been from radicalism to conservatism as far as the attitude of individuals is concerned, but from conservatism to radicalism so far as the trend of public policy is concerned.†   7

Not only are the terms relative in the sense just indicated, but they are comparative as applied to variations of opinion that exist within each school of thought. In the conservative camp are to be found different degrees of distrust of popular rule, varying from the purblind reactionaries on the extreme right to the moderates on the extreme left. Similarly the

* Paragraph 6: Are the definitions presented here logical or rhetorical? Where in this paragraph can you find an example of a balanced sentence?

† Paragraph 7: Would Russell Kirk agree that the expressions "radical" and "conservative" are relative terms? What does Schlesinger mean by "relative" in this instance? See paragraph 6 and note the conclusion of this paragraph. What is a "truism"?

radical camp has its subdivisions, comprising all grades of confidence in popular government from a left wing of ultra-radicals to a wing at the opposite extreme composed of progressives or liberals. The apostles of lawlessness—those who would accomplish their ends through a defiance of, or assault on, the law—are to be found in the exterior wings of both camps. In this sense the reactionaries who seek to gain their purposes through the corruption or intimidation of the courts are to be regarded as much the enemies of law and order as the followers of Daniel Shays in 1786 when they tried to disperse the courts with violence. On the other hand, the moderates of the conservative camp tend to fraternize with the liberals of the radical camp without, however, completely merging their identity because of deep-grained prepossessions and habits of thought. It is in this middle zone or "No Man's Land" between the camps that there occurs the only true meeting of minds; and in democratic countries, advances can be made, under legal forms and proper safeguards, only through the temporary union of these groups for common purposes.* 8

No attempt need be made here to idealize or glorify either the radical or the conservative. Adherents of each are constantly engaged in constructing traditions which would ascribe superhuman attributes to the great leaders and spokesmen of their respective schools of opinion in the past. In this myth-making process the radicals inevitably suffer a serious handicap, for the audacious reformer of a century ago is likely to appear today as a man of orthodox ideas, and latter-day conservatives, without any appreciation of the earlier clash of ideas, are likely to claim him as their very own. For example, the average American citizen who values property rights as superior to human rights easily imagines himself in the forefront of the riot that led to the Boston Massacre, for through the mellow haze of time he forgets the real character of that street brawl with its raucous mob of blatant, missile-hurling roughs and halfbreeds. 9

Whatever may be said in praise of either the conservative or the radical, both find themselves in bad company, for each made his appeal to some of the basest as well as to some of the most ennobling qualities of human nature. The thinking conservative finds his chief allies in the self-complacency of comfortable mediocrity, in the apathy and stupidity of toil-worn multitudes, and in the aggressive self-interest of the privileged classes. All those who dread uncertainty either because of timidity or from conventional-mindedness or for fear of material loss are enlisted under the conservative standard. The honest radical draws much of his support from self-seeking demagogues and reckless experimenters, from people who want the world changed because they cannot get along in it as it is, from poseurs and dilettanti, and from malcontents who love disturbance for its

* Paragraph 8: What is the structure of the last sentence in this paragraph?

own sake. The two schools have more in common than either would admit;
both have their doctrinaires and dogmatists; both tend toward a stiffening
of intellectual creeds; and who can deny that each has its share of mental
defectives and the criminal-minded?   10

The Whole Selection

1 State the central idea of this essay in one sentence.
2 Where does the introductory matter of the essay end? Is it effective?
3 What qualifying ideas are added to the terms in paragraphs 7 and 8?
4 List at least five words or phrases used for transitions between paragraphs.

Word Study *opprobrium, proclivity, accruing, protagonist, sanguine, cynicism,
              purblind, reactionary, apathy, poseurs, dilettanti, malcontent,
              prepossessions, orthodox*

BLUES PEOPLE

RALPH ELLISON

In his Introduction to *Blues People* LeRoi Jones advises us to approach the work as

> . . . a strictly theoretical endeavor. Theoretical, in that none of the questions it poses can be said to have been answered definitely or for all time (sic!), etc. In fact, the whole book proposes more questions than it will answer. The only questions it will properly move to answer have, I think, been answered already within the patterns of American life. We need only give these patterns serious scrutiny and draw certain permissible conclusions.

It is a useful warning and one hopes that it will be regarded by those jazz publicists who have the quite irresponsible habit of sweeping up any novel pronouncement written about jazz and slapping it upon the first available record liner as the latest insight into the mysteries of American Negro expression.   1

Jones would take his subject seriously—as the best of jazz critics have always done—and he himself should be so taken. He has attempted to place the blues within the context of a total culture and to see this native art form through the disciplines of sociology, anthropology and (though he seriously underrates its importance in the creating of a viable theory) history, and he spells out explicitly his assumptions concerning the relation between the blues, the people who created them and the larger American culture. Although I find several of his assumptions questionable, this is valuable in itself. It would be well if all jazz critics did likewise; not only would it expose those who have no business in the field, but it would sharpen the thinking of the few who have something enlightening to contribute. *Blues People,* like much that is written by Negro Americans at the present moment, takes on an inevitable resonance from the Freedom Movement, but it is in itself characterized by a straining for a note of militancy which is, to say the least, distracting. Its introductory mood of scholarly analysis frequently shatters into a dissonance of accusation, and one gets the impression that while Jones wants to perform a crucial task which he feels *someone* should take on—as indeed someone should—he is frustrated by the restraint demanded of the critical pen and would like to pick up a club.   2

Perhaps this explains why Jones, who is also a poet and editor of a poetry magazine, gives little attention to the blues as lyric, as a form of poetry. He appears to be attracted to the blues for what he believes they tell us of the sociology of Negro American identity and attitude. Thus,

after beginning with the circumstances in which he sees their origin, he
considers the ultimate values of American society:

> The Negro as slave is one thing. The Negro as American is quite an-
> other. But the *path* the slave took to "citizenship" is what I want to
> look at. And I make my analogy through the slave citizen's music—
> through the music that is most closely associated with him: blues and
> a later, but parallel, development, jazz. And it seems to me that if the
> Negro represents, or is symbolic of, something in and about the nature
> of American culture, this certainly should be revealed by his character-
> istic music. . . . I am saying that if the music of the Negro in America,
> in all its permutations, is subjected to a socio-anthropological as well as
> musical scrutiny, something about the essential nature of the Negro's
> existence in this country ought to be revealed, as well as something
> about the essential nature of this country, i.e., society as a whole. . . . 3

The tremendous burden of sociology which Jones would place upon
this body of music is enough to give even the blues the blues. At one
point he tells us that "the one peculiar reference to the drastic change in
the Negro from slavery to 'citizenship' is in his music." And later with
more precision, he states:

> . . . The point I want to make most evident here is that I cite the
> beginning of the blues as one beginning of American Negroes. Or, let
> me say, the reaction and subsequent relation of the Negro's experience
> in this country in *his* English is one beginning of the Negro's conscious
> appearance on the American scene.   4

No one could quarrel with Mr. Jones's stress upon beginnings. In
1833, two hundred and fourteen years after the first Africans were brought
to these shores as slaves, a certain Mrs. Lydia Maria Child, a leading member of the American Anti-Slavery Society, published a paper entitled: *An
Appeal in Favor of that Class of Americans Called Africans*. I am uncertain
to what extent it actually reveals Mrs. Child's ideas concerning the complex
relationship between time, place, cultural and/or national identity and race,
but her title sounds like a fine bit of contemporary ironic *signifying*—
"signifying" here meaning, in the unwritten dictionary of American Negro
usage, "rhetorical understatements." It tells us much of the thinking of
her opposition, and it reminds us that as late as the 1890s, a time when
Negro composers, singers, dancers and comedians dominated the American musical stage, popular Negro songs (including James Weldon Johnson's "Under the Bamboo Tree," now immortalized by T. S. Eliot) were
commonly referred to as "Ethiopian Airs."   5

Perhaps more than any other people, Americans have been locked in
a deadly struggle with time, with history. We've fled the past and trained

ourselves to suppress, if not forget, troublesome details of the national memory, and a great part of our optimism, like our progress, has been bought at the cost of ignoring the processes through which we've arrived at any given moment in our national existence. We've fought continuously with one another over who and what we are, and, with the exception of the Negro, over who and what is American. Jones is aware of this and, although he embarrasses his own argument, his emphasis is to the point.   6

For it would seem that while Negroes have been undergoing a process of "Americanization" from a time preceding the birth of this nation—including the fusing of their blood lines with other non-African strains, there has persisted a stubborn confusion as to their American identity. Somehow it was assumed that the Negroes, of all the diverse American peoples, would remain unaffected by the climate, the weather, the political circumstances—from which not even slaves were exempt—the social structures, the national manners, the modes of production and the tides of the market, the national ideals, the conflicts of values, the rising and falling of national morale, or the complex give and take of acculturalization which was undergone by all others who found their existence within the American democracy. This confusion still persists and it is Mr. Jones's concern with it which gives *Blues People* a claim upon our attention.   7

Mr. Jones sees the American Negro as the product of a series of transformations, starting with the enslaved African, who became Afro-American slave, who became the American slave, who became, in turn, the highly qualified "citizen" whom we know today. The slave began by regarding himself as enslaved African, during the time when he still spoke his native language, or remembered it, practiced such aspects of his native religion as were possible and expressed himself musically in modes which were essentially African. These cultural traits became transmuted as the African lost consciousness of his African background, and his music, his religion, his language and his speech gradually became that of the American Negro. His sacred music became the spirituals, his work songs and dance music became the blues and primitive jazz, and his religion became a form of Afro-American Christianity. With the end of slavery Jones sees the development of jazz and the blues as results of the more varied forms of experience made available to the freedman. By the twentieth century the blues divided and became, on the one hand, a professionalized form of entertainment, while remaining, on the other, a form of folklore.   8

By which I suppose he means that some Negroes remained in the country and sang a crude form of the blues, while others went to the city, became more sophisticated, and paid to hear Ma Rainey, Bessie, or some of the other Smith girls sing them in night clubs or theatres. Jones gets this mixed up with ideas of social class—middle-class Negroes, whatever that term actually means, and light-skinned Negroes, or those Negroes corrupted by what Jones calls "White" culture—preferring the "classic" blues, and black, uncorrupted, country Negroes preferring "country blues." 9

For as with his music, so with the Negro. As Negroes became "middle-class" they rejected their tradition and themselves. ". . . they wanted any self which the mainstream dictated, and the mainstream *always* dictated. And this black middle class, in turn, tried always to dictate that self, or this image of a whiter Negro, to the poorer, blacker Negroes." 10

One would get the impression that there was a rigid correlation between color, education, income and the Negro's preference in music. But what are we to say of a white-skinned Negro with brown freckles who owns sixteen oil wells sunk in a piece of Texas land once farmed by his ex-slave parents who were a blue-eyed, white-skinned, red-headed (kinky) Negro woman from Virginia and a blue-gummed, black-skinned, curly-haired Negro male from Mississippi, and who not only sang bass in a Holy Roller church, played the market and voted Republican but collected blues recordings and was a walking depository of blues tradition? Jones's theory no more allows for the existence of such a Negro than it allows for himself; but that "concord of sensibilities" which has been defined as the meaning of culture, allows for much more variety than Jones would admit. 11

Much the same could be said of Jones's treatment of the jazz during the thirties, when he claims its broader acceptance (i.e., its economic "success" as entertainment) led to a dilution, to the loss of much of its "black" character which caused a certain group of rebellious Negro musicians to create the "anti-mainstream" jazz style called bebop. 12

Jones sees bop as a conscious gesture of separatism, ignoring the fact that the creators of the style were seeking, whatever their musical intentions—and they were the least political of men—a fresh form of entertainment which would allow them their fair share of the entertainment market, which had been dominated by whites during the swing era. And although the boppers were reacting, at least in part, to the high artistic achievement of Armstrong, Hawkins, Basie and Ellington (all Negroes, all masters of the blues-jazz tradition), Jones sees their music as a recognition of his contention "that when you are black in a society where black is an extreme liability [it] is one thing, but to understand that it is the society which is lacking and is impossibly deformed because of this lack, and not *yourself*, isolates you even more from that society." 13

Perhaps. But today nothing succeeds like rebellion (which Jones as a "beat" poet should know) and while a few boppers went to Europe to escape, or became Muslims, others took the usual tours for the State Department. Whether this makes *them* "middle class" in Jones's eyes I can't say, but his assertions—which are fine as personal statement—are not in keeping with the facts; his theory flounders before that complex of human motives which makes human history, and which is so characteristic of the American Negro.   14

Read as a record of an earnest young man's attempt to come to grips with his predicament as Negro American during a most turbulent period of our history, *Blues People* may be worth the reader's time. Taken as a theory of American Negro culture, it can only contribute more confusion than clarity. For Jones has stumbled over that ironic obstacle which lies in the path of any who would fashion a theory of American Negro culture while ignoring the intricate network of connections which binds Negroes to the larger society. To do so is to attempt a delicate brain surgery with a switch-blade. And it is possible that any viable theory of Negro American culture obligates us to fashion a more adequate theory of American culture as a whole. The heel bone is, after all, connected, through its various linkages, to the head bone. Attempt a serious evaluation of our national morality and up jumps the so-called Negro problem. Attempt to discuss jazz as a hermetic expression of Negro sensibility and immediately we must consider what the "mainstream" of American music really is.   15

Here political categories are apt to confuse, for while Negro slaves were socially, politically and economically separate (but only in a special sense even here), they were, in a cultural sense, much closer than Jones's theory allows him to admit.   16

"A slave," writes Jones, "cannot be a man." But what, one might ask, of those moments when he feels his metabolism aroused by the rising of the sap in spring? What of his identity among other slaves? With his wife? And isn't it closer to the truth that far from considering themselves only in terms of that abstraction, "a slave," the enslaved really thought of themselves as *men* who had been unjustly enslaved? And isn't the true answer to Mr. Jones's question, "What are you going to be when you grow up?" not, as he gives it, "a slave" but most probably a coachman, a teamster, a cook, the best damned steward on the Mississippi, the best jockey in Kentucky, a butler, a farmer, a stud, or, hopefully, a free man! Slavery was a most vicious system and those who endured and survived it a tough people, but it was *not* (and this is important for Negroes to remember for the sake of their own sense of who and what their grandparents were) a state of absolute repression.   17

A slave was, to the extent that he was a *musician*, one who expressed himself in music, a man who realized himself in the world of sound. Thus, while he might stand in awe before the superior technical ability of a white musician, and while he was forced to recognize a superior social status, he would never feel awed before the music which the technique of the white musician made available. His attitude as "musician" would lead him to seek to possess the music expressed through the technique, but until he could do so he would hum, whistle, sing or play the tunes to the best of his ability on any available instrument. And it was, indeed, out of the tension between desire and ability that the techniques of jazz emerged. This was likewise true of American Negro choral singing. For this, no literary explanation, no cultural analyses, no political slogans—indeed, not even a high degree of social or political freedom—was required. For the art—the blues, the spirituals, the jazz, the dance—was what we had in place of freedom.   18

Technique was then, as today, the key to creative freedom, but before this came a will toward expression. Thus, Jones's theory to the contrary. Negro musicians have never, as a group, felt alienated from any music sounded within their hearing, and it is my theory that it would be impossible to pinpoint the time when they were not shaping what Jones calls the mainstream of American music. Indeed, what group of musicians has made more of the sound of the American experience? Nor am I confining my statement to the sound of the slave experience, but am saying that the most authoritative rendering of America in music is that of American Negroes.   19

For as I see it, from the days of their introduction into the colonies, Negroes have taken, with the ruthlessness of those without articulate investments in cultural styles, whatever they could of European music, making of it that which would, when blended with the cultural tendencies inherited from Africa, express their own sense of life—while rejecting the rest. Perhaps this is only another way of saying that whatever the degree of injustice and inequality sustained by the slaves, American culture was, even before the official founding of the nation, pluralistic; and it was the African's origin in cultures in which art was highly functional which gave him an edge in shaping the music and dance of this nation.   20

The question of social and cultural snobbery is important here. The effectiveness of Negro music and dance is first recorded in the journals and letters of travelers but it is important to remember that they saw and understood only that which they were prepared to accept. Thus a Negro dancing a courtly dance appeared comic from the outside simply because the dancer was a slave. But to the Negro dancing it—and there is ample evidence that he danced it well—burlesque or satire might have been the point, which might have been difficult for a white observer to even imagine. During the 1870s Lafcadio Hearn reports that the best singers of Irish songs, in Irish dialect, were Negro dock workers in Cincinnati, and advertisements from slavery days described escaped slaves who spoke in Scottish dialect. The master artisans of the South were slaves, and white Americans have been walking Negro walks, talking Negro flavored talk (and prizing it when spoken by Southern belles), dancing Negro dances and singing Negro melodies far too long to talk of a "mainstream" of American culture to which they're alien.   21

Jones attempts to impose an ideology upon this cultural complexity, and this might be useful if he knew enough of the related subjects to make it interesting. But his version of the blues lacks a sense of the excitement and surprise of men living in the world—of enslaved and politically weak men successfully imposing their values upon a powerful society through song and dance.   22

The blues speak to us simultaneously of the tragic and the comic aspects of the human condition and they express a profound sense of life shared by many Negro Americans precisely because their lives have combined these modes. This has been the heritage of a people who for hundreds of years could not celebrate birth or dignify death and whose need to live despite the dehumanizing pressures of slavery developed an endless capacity for laughing at their painful experiences. This is a group experience shared by many Negroes, and any effective study of the blues would treat them first as poetry and as ritual. Jones makes a distinction between classic and country blues, the one being entertainment and the other folklore. But the distinction is false. Classic blues were both entertainment *and* a form of folklore. When they were sung professionally in theatres, they were entertainment; when danced to in the form of recordings or used as a means of transmitting the traditional verses and their wisdom, they were folklore. There are levels of time and function involved here, and the blues which might be used in one place as entertainment (as gospel music is now being used in night clubs and on theatre stages) might be put to a ritual use in another. Bessie Smith might have been a "blues queen" to the society at large, but within the tighter Negro community where the blues were part of a total way of life, and a major expression of an attitude toward life, she was a priestess, a celebrant who affirmed the values of the group and man's ability to deal with chaos.   23

It is unfortunate that Jones thought it necessary to ignore the aesthetic nature of the blues in order to make his ideological point, for he might have come much closer had he considered the blues not as politics but as art. This would have still required the disciplines of anthropology and sociology—but as practiced by Constance Rourke, who was well aware of how much of American cultural expression is Negro. And he could learn much from the Cambridge School's discoveries of the connection between poetry, drama and ritual as a means of analyzing how the blues function in their proper environment. Simple taste should have led Jones to Stanley Edgar Hyman's work on the blues instead of Paul Oliver's sadly misdirected effort.   24

For the blues are not primarily concerned with civil rights or obvious political protest; they are an art form and thus a transcendence of those conditions created within the Negro community by the denial of social justice. As such they are one of the techniques through which Negroes have survived and kept their courage during that long period when many whites assumed, as some still assume, they were afraid.   25

Much has been made of the fact that *Blues People* is one of the few books by a Negro to treat the subject. Unfortunately for those who expect that Negroes would have a special insight into this mysterious art, this is not enough. Here, too, the critical intelligence must perform the difficult task which only it can perform.   26

WHAT SCIENCE IS

HERBERT J. MULLER

Roughly stated, the scientific method is to go and look, and then look again. The most elaborate experiments and abstruse equations are designed to answer the simple question, "What are the facts?" Today this question seems so natural and obviously sensible that it is hard to understand how for centuries men could repeat Pliny's statement, that the blood of a goat would shatter a diamond, when a simple test would have disproved it. Yet it seems that they did not perform the test; and the explanation is that the basis of their thought was not empirical but "rational." Although Aristotle went to nature, he returned for authority to pure reason. He simply asserted that heavy bodies must fall faster than light ones, just as he asserted that planets move in circles because the circle is the only perfect figure. Hence Galileo's Pisa experiment marked a real revolution in thought. It marked, Dewey summarizes:

> a change from the qualitative to the quantitative or metric; from the heterogeneous to the homogeneous; from intrinsic form to relations; from esthetic harmonies to mathematical formulae; from contemplative enjoyment to active manipulation and control; from rest to change; from eternal objects to temporal sequence. 1

In this summary, science already begins to look strange to the plain man; and of course it is strange. Even as roughly stated, its method is still not generally applied to moral, political, or other problems. For science is not, strictly, "organized common sense." Common sense is not only much vaguer and more cocksure but in a way, curiously, more practical. It deals with the total concrete situation, takes life as it comes. Science always abstracts for a very limited purpose, makes up fictions. Especially in late years, it has left common sense far behind. When scientists try to speak the plain man's language, they tell him that the quantum theory may be understood by the analogy of a clock whose mechanism had vanished, leaving only the ticks, and that if he still doesn't understand, the point is that the universe is "not only queerer than we suppose, but queerer than we *can* suppose." 2

Yet science does remain simply a form of organized intelligence; to become oriented to it, we again do well to begin with the obvious. Although men talk as if the object of intelligence were the discovery and contemplation of eternal truths, actually they employ it chiefly to handle the new situations that are always arising even in a routine life. In daily experience they are continually experimenting, reconstructing, adjusting themselves to a continually changing environment; otherwise there could be no consciousness, no real experience at all. The scientific method is a systematic extension of this behavior. George H. Mead therefore described it as "only the evolutionary process grown self-conscious." Biologically, it is an advance in the natural direction: more differentiation, finer adaptation to environment, greater control over environment.   3

Similarly the basic interests of science, the concern with the "material" world, are not actually newfangled or alien. Men often feel that nature is hostile to them, at best very careless, at worst unfathomably cruel; in their philosophies they have represented it as a show of illusory or accidental appearances, in their religions as a mess of devil's pottage. Nevertheless they also feel a deep and constant kinship. They naturally personify the world about them and draw from it their metaphors for human life: they bud and bloom in youth, they ripen like fruit on the bough, they fall into the sere, the yellow leaf. The rhythms of nature are in their blood. Like poetry, science explores and articulates these relations; it realizes our rich heritage as children of this earth. Like Christian theology, moreover, it assumes that the heritage is lawful. Science grew out of the medieval faith that the world is orderly and rational, and that all happenings in it could be explained. Scientists now consider this a postulate, not a fact, and their explanations are usually offensive to orthodox theologians; nevertheless they have the same working faith as the theologians. Thus Newton could lay the foundations of the mechanistic universe in a spirit of extreme piety, and be applauded by other devout Christians; he was simply clarifying the ways of God to man. Thus agnostic scientists still admire all the evidence of uniformity, regularity, harmony in the universe. They admire the most wonderful of mircles, that there are not incessant miracles.   4

In other words, they are not really so inhuman as they are reputed to be. Whereas the man on the street sees only the gadgetry of science, intellectuals are prone to the other extreme of viewing it always in the abstract. They dwell upon its remorseless impersonality, the coldness of its truth; they forget its personal satisfactions, the imaginative value of its truths. For to scientists truth is indeed beauty. Mathematicians exclaim over the "elegance" of their demonstrations, Einstein delights in the "preestablished harmonies" that physicists discover, J. W. N. Sullivan is struck by the "astonishing beauty and symmetry" that Minkowski gave the theory of relativity by adding the notion of a four-dimensional continuum. On the other hand, they are displeased by unsightly gaps or bulges in their theory-patterns, dislike the messiness of quantum physics even when its theories seem to fit the facts. Their effort is always to get all their facts to fall into a shape, and their preference among theories, when the experimental test has yet to decide, appears to be determined chiefly by the esthetic quality of the shape. Thus Sullivan notes the comments of Einstein and Eddington on each other's attempt to reduce the laws of electro-magnetism to geometry: Einstein said he simply did not "like" Eddington's theory, though he could not disprove it, and Eddington said Einstein's theory was a matter of "taste." Altogether, the generic motive of science is no doubt utilitarian—"service to mankind," if one likes more exalted terms; but the individual scientist, like the individual artist, does his work for the simple, unexalted reason that he likes it, and when it turns out right he feels a comparable lift and glow.   5

The simple answer to Ransom, then, is that science does "free the spirit." He has forced a narrow view of utility upon it, just as moralists and scientists often do upon art. Like thought itself, science has become a passion and a luxury. It follows the gleam, it stirs hopes too wildly dear. It is indeed often not utilitarian enough: science for science's sake is as much a cult as art for art's sake, and can carry one as far from the actualities of purposeful living. Yet this same passion calls out the plain answer to Roelofs. Science does produce saints. Not to go down the long list of heroes and martyrs, Mme. Curie will do as an example of simple, noble goodness. Such idealism is not itself scientific, to be sure, and may be called religious. Nevertheless the fact remains that science can inspire it without benefit of clergy.   6

This demonstration that even the scientist is human may seem incon-sequential. It finally leads, however, to the heart of the problem of what science is. The recent developments in its philosophy may be summed up in precisely this recognition of the "human element," the human "stand-point" that is literally involved in all statements. Scientific laws are not chips off the old block Reality; as interpretations of sense impressions, they take after the human mind as well. All knowledge is a joint enter-prise, an affair whose conditions are both inside and outside the organism. It is the offspring of the marriage of man and nature, a union in which the older partner may be expected to outlive the younger but which is indissoluble during the life of man.   7

This idea will concern us later on. Immediately, Einstein tells us how to understand the scientist's method: "Don't listen to his words, examine his achievements." Still better, watch him at work, examine the actual operations by which he gets his knowledge; and here an excellent guide is William H. George's *The Scientist in Action.* Whatever it may become in theory, George points out, a scientific fact is in practice an observation of coincidences. Although products of sensory impression, facts are im-personal in that they are independent of the judgment of any one man; they are statements of coincidences that can be observed under the same conditions by all men. The scientist can therefore gather and test them without bothering about such philosophical problems as whether there really is an external world; "real" is not an observable property. He does have to bother, however, with the problem of classifying and interpreting his facts, fitting them into patterns called theories and laws. The more comprehensive these are, the better he is pleased; but the most comprehensive is still tentative and does not "reduce by one the number of absolute truths to be discovered." Newton's great laws were patterns into which hitherto unconnected facts could be fitted; Einstein devised a different pattern that could accommodate all these and other facts; and we may expect that more inclusive but still different patterns will be devised by Zweistein, Dreistein, etc.   8

In other words, facts and figures do *not* speak for themselves. For all their stubbornness, they are accommodating enough to allow a number of different interpretations—and there are always enough of them around to support almost any theory. Moreover, the facts are not simply there, waiting in line to be discovered. The scientist selects from a host of possibilities, he looks *for* as well at *at*, he may accordingly *overlook*—as Grimaldi's experiments on the path of light were long neglected because they did not fit in with Newton's corpuscular theory. Hence the advance of science has not been automatic or really systematic, and it has not been in a straight line. Science is first of all the creation of scientists, who are also men with temperaments, special interests, predispositions. (Bertrand Russell has noted, for example, the divergent developments in animal psychology under Thorndike and Koehler: "Animals studied by Americans rush about frantically, with an incredible display of hustle and pep, and at last achieve the desired result by chance. Animals observed by Germans sit still and think, and at last evolve the solution out of their inner consciousness.") More significantly, science is the creation of a definite type of mentality, which has been interested in certain kinds of phenomena but notoriously indifferent to others, averse to the seeming "wild data." Most significantly, it is the creation of a culture, a society with special interests. Even physics, which seems wholly impersonal and autonomous, has been influenced by vested social interests. The concept of energy was developed to meet the manufacturers' need of a bookkeeping device, a way of measuring the efficiency of machines in units of work; in general there is an obvious correspondence between the long reign of classical mechanics and the needs of industry. Today, when science has developed a highly specialized technique, language, and subject matter of its own, it is still dependent upon the greater society for its privileges. It is the more profoundly a fashion of the times.   9

This view is not designed to humble or discredit the scientist. Rather it relieves him of the awful responsibility of speaking absolute truth. It stresses his continuity with the organic processes of evolution, the tremendous adventure of civilization, the vital needs and purposes of society; the scientist no more than the poet can afford the illusion that his activity is pure or priestly. It makes clearer the cultural pattern of science today: the concept itself of patterns, fields, organic wholes, which—as we shall see—has become important in all the sciences, and which parallels the collectivistic trend in the world of affairs. And it enables a more realistic approach, specifically, to the difficult issue of just where science properly begins and ends.   10

The popular notion is that science necessarily involves the use of instruments in a laboratory. Knowledge cannot be really scientific unless men have got it out of a test tube, taken an X-ray picture of it, or tried it out on some guinea pigs. Such methods are very well for dealings with sticks and stones, animal life, or the human body; but it follows that they cannot apply to the motions of mind or spirit. Laboratory workers themselves are often contemptuous of the social sciences, and of psychology when it leaves the laboratory and deals with such immeasurables as "consciousness" and "insight." They distrust any statement that cannot be put into an equation. And so the critic is warned off the sciences of man, which are naturally closest to his interests. He is left with the problem of determining just where, then, the sciences stop and the humanities begin, and just what use he can make of the power that has in any event so thoroughly made over the world in which the humanities have their being.   11

To begin with, there are important distinctions that should remain distinct. Some generous philosophers identify science with all disciplined thought, uniting all the humanities and the sciences in one big happy family. Thus Cassius J. Keyser defines science as any work that aims to establish by legitimate means a body of categorical propositions about the actual world; he therefore accepts as science the work of Plato and Aristotle—and blurs the fundamental difference between their thought and the thought of Galileo or Darwin. Moreover, there are important differences between the sciences. The physicist and the chemist have the adventitious advantage of large subsidies (capitalism has been a generous if not a disinterested patron) and now of relative freedom from personal prejudice or official interference; the psychologist and the sociologist are at any moment likely to tread on the corns of public opinion or get mixed up in some live social issue. But the former also have the intrinsic advantage of a subject matter that lends itself to the extremely helpful devices of mathematical measurement and controlled experiment. The experimental test is especially important, as the ultimate criterion for distinguishing scientific knowledge from philosophic speculation   12

Nevertheless most distinguished scientists appear to agree with Max Planck, that from physics to sociology there is a continuous chain; and I can see no practical or logical reason for choosing to break the chain. On practical grounds, it would seem desirable to give science as much scope as possible, and not to discourage important social inquiries by verbal quibbles or qualms about their scientific chastity; it would seem foolish to demand complete, positive knowledge or none. On logical grounds, any sharp break in the chain is not only arbitrary but inconsistent with the basic scientific assumption of natural continuity. That the physical sciences are more objective and more exact than the sciences of man makes them neither more fundamental nor fundamentally different. The differences are in degree, not in kind.   13

Ultimately the unity of science lies in the logic, not the materials or the specific techniques of its inquiry. As formulated by Dewey in his monumental work, this is a logic of discovery and invention. Its forms are not a priori but postulational and operational; they are not absolute modes of pure reason but generalizations drawn from previous inquiry and liable to modification by subsequent discoveries. Indeed, scientists object to any theory, such as vitalism in biology, which is complete and therefore offers no possibility of advance; their curious objection, J. H. Woodger observes, is that it is *too* successful, *too* perfect. They demand that all theories live dangerously. But this experimental logic does not absolutely require the specific technique of laboratory experiment. It requires primarily that theories be so formulated as to leave room for future discoveries and almost certain modifications. It thereby exposes, indeed, the essential weakness of the sciences of man today, which is not so much the jungle growth of theory as the attitude toward this theory. As scientists, psychologists and sociologists are still very young, and like youngsters much too cocky—few physicists speak with quite the assurance of John B. Watson or Pareto. More specifically, they are seldom content with mere postulates and approximates; they set up some explanatory principle as necessary and sufficient, the one positive truth by which all the other little truths must be sired or certified. Yet their attitude is quite gratuitous. This very criticism of it implies that an experimental logic can be applied to these problems too.   14

"Wherever there is the slightest possibility of the human mind to *know*," wrote Karl Pearson, "there is a legitimate problem of science." If men have "known" all sorts of absurdities, there can be no question about a fact, strictly defined, and such facts are available in all spheres of interest. Observation, not measurement of coincidences is their criterion. If it is clearly more difficult to classify and interpret them in the sciences of man, it is not clearly impossible; important relations have already been established and systematically formulated. Students of the humanities who deny that there are fundamental laws in their province necessarily think in a way that presupposes such laws—else their thought would be pointless. In sum, only by divorcing human affairs from natural processes can they be shut off from scientific inquiry; and this ancient expedient disposes of the problem by creating two more.   15

Suggestions for Writing

1 Define any one of the following items in no more than 300 words:
  a The typical tourist (bus driver, airline stewardess, automobile salesman, barber, rock or jazz drummer, symphony orchestra director, campus politician)
  b The ideal father (mother, brother, sister)
  c The scientific method (the cold war, parliamentary government)
2 After looking at the following definitions of "gentleman," write an extended definition of a gentleman, developing either Newman's or Fuller's. If you prefer to be more daring, write one of your own on the basis of these two suggestions.
  a "It is almost a definition of a gentleman to say he is one who never inflicts pain."—John Henry Newman
  b "Manners and money make a gentleman."—Thomas Fuller
3 Being able to define an abstraction economically is of great value to the progress of learning and for the clarification of one's own thought. Write a formal or extended definition of any one of the following abstractions. Do not hesitate to imitate the methods of Joan Didion, Russell Kirk, or Arthur Schlesinger. Use sources other than your dictionary to aid you.
  a Americanism
  b Communism
  c Activism
  d Totalitarianism
  e Tolerance
4 In the eighteenth century Crèvecoeur asked a famous question which writers are still trying to answer: "What, then, is the American?" What is your answer to this question?

THE USES OF ILLUSTRATION: EXAMPLE

Example as a method of analysis has the same aim as definition—to clarify the subject. The etymology of the word "example" suggests that it is a selection from a larger quantity. It is, indeed, a way of writing exposition that gives the reader an illustration in order to explain the whole—the whole idea, the whole central point, or any part or parts of the whole. It is, then, a sample or specimen that illustrates. Because of the nature of the thought process, readers are attracted to the concrete and particular; we learn more easily from the concrete. It is because of its concrete character that example appears to be such a natural method of analysis and is so naturally used.

In some of the essays in the section on definition we have already seen the uses of example. Albert Goldman in "The Emergence of Rock" enlivens his definitions by describing the performances of musicians who do (or do not) exemplify the elements which constitute his definition of authentic rock or soul music. Joan Didion develops her definition of self-respect by examples from her own life, from the life of another person, and from two characters in novels. The essays in the present section provide us with even more obvious illustrations of the use of example as a method of analysis.

In David Riesman's "Tootle: A Modern Cautionary Tale" (page 81) we see how an author makes use of a single extended example. He wishes to explain how smooth social or play techniques encourage children to accept an "other-directed mode of conformity." And he does this by using the story of *Tootle the Engine* as an example of the kind of book which encourages this form of behavior. Loren Eiseley, also using an extended example, in "The Innocent Fox" (page 88), demonstrates the oneness of man with all nature. The principal teaching device of Jesus was the "parable," the example. We have selected from the New Testament one of the most famous, "The Parable of the Good Samaritan" (page 84), to show another kind of extended example—the hypothetical example; the example of the good Samaritan is a concrete answer to the question, "Who is my neighbor?" The writer who uses a hypothetical example must be careful to construct it so that the underlying reasoning is valid. Della Lutes' "Are Neighbors Necessary?" (page 86) suggests yet another procedure for using extended examples. Instead of one, she selects two, and she compares and contrasts them in order to arrive at a particular demonstration of the meaning of "a good neighbor."

Providing a variety of examples to illustrate the meaning of the whole can be an excellent technique, but the examples should never be so numerous as to obscure the point of the whole (whether "the whole" is an essay or a part of one). The advice of an ancient rhetorician is still worth considering: "A single lamp is worth a thousand fireflies." In "Roarers, Whisperers, and Moderators" (page 95), Samuel Johnson gives us three examples to illustrate the envy and hostility which a man emerging into fame may expect to incur, but each example illustrates different modes in which calumniators of such a man may practice.

In all the essays in this section the point being explained is made clearer to the reader by the example used. This is the most important test of any example. It must act as a bridge from the idea to the reader. David Riesman explains his example sufficiently so that it is clear in its details to the reader who may not be familiar with the story of Tootle. Once we understand the story itself, we can follow Riesman as he relates it to the point being made. The examples should also be vivid, and most examples must be made vivid by the author's presentation of the specimen in very specific terms. Some examples are vivid by their very nature, as is Loren Eiseley's example of his encounter with the little fox, and Rollo May's example of the man in the cage (page 98); but each of these authors enhances the vividness of his example by presenting precise details.

Selecting a part to illustrate the whole, then, involves the writer in making a deliberate choice in order to make his central point clear to the reader. He chooses a representative example because it will clarify the point, because it is a valid sample, and because it is concrete and colorful. A good example will have a sense of immediacy in its appeal to and in its effect upon a reader. It is not difficult to understand, therefore, why Aristotle, the father of rhetoric, called example "the natural means of producing conviction."

TOOTLE: A MODERN CAUTIONARY TALE

DAVID RIESMAN

Parents are sometimes apt to assume that comic books and the radio, as the cheapest and most widespread media, are the principal vehicles of newer attitudes and values and that, in a home barricaded against Roy Rogers and Steve Canyon, these patterns of audience response would also be excluded. The fact is, however, that many important themes of other-direction are introduced into the socializing and informative books of the non-comic variety which middle- and upper-middle-class children are given —conversely, these "educative" books are probably not without influence on the more socially conscious radio and comic-book artists. A whole range of these media teaches children the lesson given parents and teachers in many recent works on child development. The slant of that lesson is suggested by a passage from a book in use by teachers and PTA groups:

> The usual and desirable developmental picture is one of increasing self-control on the part of the individual children, of increasingly smooth social or play technics, and of an emergence at adolescence or early adulthood of higher forms of cooperation. The adolescent should have learned better "to take it" in group activity, should have developed an improved, though not yet perfect, self-control, and should have real insight into the needs and wishes of others.[1]*

1

Tootle the Engine (text by Gertrude Crampton, pictures by Tibor Gergely) is a popular and in many ways charming volume in the "Little Golden Books" series. It is a cautionary tale even though it appears to be simply one of the many books about anthropomorphic vehicles—trucks, fire engines, taxicabs, tugboats, and so on—that are supposed to give a child a picture of real life. Tootle is a young engine who goes to engine school, where two main lessons are taught: stop at a red flag and "always stay on the track no matter what." Diligence in the lessons will result in the young engine's growing up to be a big streamliner. Tootle is obedient for a while and then one day discovers the delight of going off the tracks and finding flowers in the field. This violation of the rules cannot, however, be kept secret; there are telltale traces in the cowcatcher. Nevertheless, Tootle's play becomes more and more of a craving, and despite warnings he continues to go off the tracks and wander in the field. Finally the engine schoolmaster is desperate. He consults the mayor of the little

---

[1] M. E. Breckenridge and E. L. Vincent, *Child Development*, W. B. Saunders Company, Philadelphia, 1943, p. 456.

---

* Paragraph 1: Why does the author quote this passage instead of putting it in his own words? Summarize the quoted passage in your own words.

town of Engineville, in which the school is located; the mayor calls a town meeting, and Tootle's failings are discussed—of course Tootle knows nothing of this. The meeting decides on a course of action, and the next time Tootle goes out for a spin alone and goes off the track he runs into a red flag and halts. He turns in another direction only to encounter another red flag; still another—the result is the same. He turns and twists but can find no spot of grass in which a red flag does not spring up, for all the citizens of the town have cooperated in this lesson.*   2

Chastened and bewildered he looks toward the track, where the inviting green flag of his teacher gives him the signal to return. Confused by conditioned reflexes to stop signs, he is only too glad to use the track and tears happily up and down. He promises that he will never leave the track again, and he returns to the roundhouse to be rewarded by the cheers of the teachers and the citizenry and the assurance that he will indeed grow up to be a streamliner.†   3

The story would seem to be an appropriate one for bringing up children in an other-directed mode of conformity. They learn it is bad to go off the tracks and play with flowers and that, in the long run, there is not only success and approval but even freedom to be found in following the green lights.² The moral is a very different one from that of *Little Red Riding Hood*. She, too, gets off the track on her trip to the grandmother; she is taught by a wolf about the beauties of nature—a veiled symbol for sex. Then, to be sure, she is eaten—a terrifying fate—but in the end she and grandmother both are taken from the wolf's belly by the handsome woodchopper. The story, though it may be read as a cautionary tale, deals with real human passions, sexual and aggressive; it certainly does not present the rewards of virtue in any unambiguous form or show the adult world in any wholly benevolent light. It is, therefore, essentially realistic, underneath the cover of fantasy, or, more accurately, owing to the quality of the fantasy.‡   4

There is, perhaps, a streak of similar realism in *Tootle*. There the adults play the role we have described earlier: they manipulate the child into conformity with the peer-group and then reward him for the behavior

---

² It is not made clear in the story what happens to Tootle's schoolmates in engine school. The peer-group relations of Tootle, either to the other engines or the other citizens of Engineville, are entirely amiable, and Tootle's winning can hardly mean that others fail. Who can be sure that Tootle would want to be a streamliner if others were not to be streamliners too?

---

* Paragraph 2: Why is *Tootle* referred to as a "cautionary tale"? What does "anthropomorphic" mean? What are the "telltale traces" in the cowcatcher?

† Paragraph 3: What is meant by "conditioned reflexes"?

‡ Paragraph 4: In your own words contrast *Little Red Riding Hood* with *Tootle the Engine*. If both can be read as cautionary tales, in what ways are they different? What is the general function of this paragraph?

for which they have already set the stage. Moreover, the citizens of Engine-ville are tolerant of Tootle: they understand and do not get indignant. And while they gang up on him with red flags they do so for his benefit, and they reward him for his obedience as if they had played no hand in bringing it about. Yet with all that, there is something overvarnished in this tale. The adult world (the teachers) is *not* that benevolent, the citi-zenry (the peer-group) *not* that participative and cooperative, the signals are *not* that clear, nor the rewards of being a streamliner that great or that certain. Nevertheless, the child may be impressed because it is all so nice —there is none of the grimness of Red Riding Hood. There is, therefore, a swindle about the whole thing—a fake like that the citizens put on for Tootle's benefit. At the end Tootle has forgotten that he ever did like flowers anyway—how childish they are in comparison with the great big grown-up world of engines, signals, tracks, and meetings!*   5

* Paragraph 5: What justification can be offered for the ordering of the sentences in this paragraph? Describe the second sentence of this paragraph grammatically and rhetoric-ally. Point out the transitional words connecting the sentences in this paragraph.

The Whole Selection

1 Why is the example chosen an appropriate one for Riesman's purposes?
2 Point out two repetitions of the idea of conformity. Does this tend to unify the author's point?
3 Indicate which paragraphs are tied to the ones preceding by obvious connecting, or transitional, words. How is the transition effected from paragraph to paragraph where there are no such obvious transitional words?

Word Study manipulate, benevolent, conditioned response, chastened, antago-nistic, palpably

THE GOSPEL OF ST. LUKE, CHAPTER 10

25 And, behold, a certain lawyer stood up, and tempted him, saying, Master, what shall I do to inherit eternal life? 1

26 He said unto him, What is written in the law? how readest thou? 2

27 And he answering said, Thou shalt love the Lord thy God with all thy heart, and with all thy soul, and with all thy strength, and with all thy mind; and thy neighbour as thyself. 3

28 And he said unto him, Thou hast answered right: this do, and thou shalt live. 4

29 But he, willing to justify himself, said unto Jesus, And who is my neighbour? 5

30 And Jesus answering said, A certain man went down from Jerusalem to Jericho, and fell among thieves, which stripped him of his raiment, and wounded him, and departed, leaving him half dead. 6

31 And by chance there came down a certain priest that way: and when he saw him, he passed by on the other side. 7

32 And likewise a Levite, when he was at the place, came and looked on him, and passed by on the other side. 8

33 But a certain Samaritan, as he journeyed, came where he was: and when he saw him, he had compassion on him, 9

34 And went to him, and bound up his wounds, pouring in oil and wine, and set him on his own beast, and brought him to an inn, and took care of him. 10

35 And on the morrow when he departed, he took out two pence, and gave them to the host, and said unto him, Take care of him; and whatsoever thou spendest more, when I come again, I will repay thee. 11

36 Which now of these three, thinkest thou, was neighbour unto him that fell among the thieves? 12

37 And he said, He that shewed mercy on him. Then said Jesus unto him, Go, and do thou likewise. 13

The Whole Selection

1 Where, specifically, is the question which the example is meant to answer?

2 Three men have an opportunity to help the man fallen among thieves. How does the selection of these three enforce the lesson for the audience Jesus is addressing?

3 What, finally, is the test of a good neighbor according to the example?

4 Construct a single sentence which summarizes the meaning of the example.
5 There are few words in this selection which the average reader would not understand. Can you think of a historical reason for this verbal simplicity?

ARE NEIGHBORS NECESSARY?

DELLA LUTES

A good neighbor, as the term was understood in the days when as a little girl I lived on a farm in Southern Michigan, meant all that nowadays is combined in corner store, telephone, daily newspaper, and radio. But your neighbor was also your conscience. You had to behave yourself on account of what the neighbors would think.*   1

A good neighbor knew everything there was to know about you—and liked you anyway. He never let you down—as long as you deserved his good opinion. Even when you failed in that, if you were in trouble he would come to your rescue. If one of the family was taken sick in the night, you ran over to the neighbor's to get someone to sit up until the doctor arrived. Only instead of sending for the doctor, you went for him. Or one of the neighbors did.†   2

The Bouldrys were that kind of neighbors. Lem Bouldry was a good farmer and a good provider. Mis' Bouldry kept a hired girl and Lem had two men the year round. They even had a piano, while the most the other neighbors boasted was an organ or a melodeon. Mis' Bouldry changed her dress every afternoon (my mother did too; she said she thought more of herself when she did), and they kept the front yard mowed.‡   3

But the Covells were just the opposite—the most shiftless family the Lord ever let set foot on land. How they got along my father said he didn't know, unless it was by the grace of God. Covell himself was ten years younger than my father, yet everybody called him "Old Covell." His face and hands were like sole leather and if his hair had ever been washed, it was only when he got caught in a rainstorm. Father said Old Covell would borrow the shirt off your back, then bring it around to have it mended; Mother said, well, one thing certain, he wouldn't bring it around to be washed.§   4

Yet the time Mis' Covell almost died with her last baby—and the baby did die—Mis' Bouldry took care of her; took care of the rest of the children too—four of them. She stayed right there in the Covell house, just going home to catch a little sleep now and then. She had to do that, for there wasn't so much as an extra sheet in that house, much less an   ‹

* Paragraph 1: How is the original definition qualified? Why is this necessary?

† Paragraph 2: What seems to be the real test of a good neighbor?

‡ Paragraph 3: What details indicate that the Bouldrys were a solid, rather well-to-do family?

§ Paragraph 4: Why is Covell called "Old Covell"?

extra bed. And Mis' Bouldry wasn't afraid to use her hands even if she did
keep a hired girl—she did all the Covell's washing herself.*   5

But even Old Covell, despite his shiftlessness, was a good neighbor
in one way: he was a master hand at laying out the dead. Of course, he
wasn't worth a cent to sit up with the sick, for if it was Summer he'd go
outside to smoke his pipe and sleep; and if it was Winter he'd go into the
kitchen and stick his feet in the oven to warm them and go to sleep there.
But a dead man seemed to rouse some kind of pride and responsibility
in him. There was no real undertaker nearer than ten miles and often
the roads were impassable. Folks sent for my mother when a child or
woman died, but Old Covell handled all the men. Though he never wore
a necktie himself, he kept on hand a supply of celluloid collars and little
black bow ties for the dead. When he had a body to lay out, he'd call for
the deceased's best pants and object strenuously if he found a hole in the
socks. Next, he'd polish the boots and put on a white shirt, and fasten one
of his black ties to the collar button. All in all, he would do a masterly job.† 6

Of course, nobody paid Old Covell for this. Nobody ever thought of
paying for just being neighborly. If anybody ever offered to, they'd have
been snubbed for fair. It was just the way everybody did in those half-
forgotten times.‡   7

* Paragraph 5: Why does the author give us a specific example in this paragraph?

† Paragraph 6: What details show that Old Covell's pride and responsibility were aroused
  by the dead?

‡ Paragraph 7: What is the precise function of the final paragraph?

The Whole Selection

1 Why does the author select two families to illustrate the concept of the
  good neighbor? In what ways do the Bouldrys and the Covells differ?
  How are they alike? How does each family as a particular instance
  illustrate the concept?

2 To make the examples more realistic and interesting, Della Lutes includes some specific details, just as the writer of fiction would; e.g.,
  "and the baby did die." Point out several other instances of realistic
  and specific details.

3 Certain colloquial expressions are used in the essay, e.g., "He wasn't
  worth a cent to sit up with the sick." Find others used in the essay. Are
  they effective?

4 Miss Lutes defines a good neighbor before she illustrates the type. Pick
  out as many different definitions as you can find. How do these various
  definitions contribute to our understanding of the term?

5 In what ways is the definition exemplified in this essay like the definition
  of the good neighbor from the Bible? Are there any differences?

THE INNOCENT FOX

LOREN EISELEY

Only to a magician is the world forever fluid, infinitely mutable and eternally new. Only he knows the secret of change, only he knows truly that all things are crouched in eagerness to become something else, and it is from this universal tension that he draws his power. —Peter Beagle

Since man first saw an impossible visage staring upward from a still pool, he has been haunted by meanings—meanings felt even in the wood, where the trees leaned over him, manifesting a vast and living presence. The image in the pool vanished at the touch of his finger, but he went home and created a legend. The great trees never spoke, but man knew that dryads slipped among their boles. Since the red morning of time it has been so, and the compulsive reading of such manuscripts will continue to occupy man's attention long after the books that contain his inmost thoughts have been sealed away by the indefatigable spider.*   1

Some men are daylight readers, who peruse the ambiguous wording of clouds or the individual letter shapes of wandering birds. Some, like myself, are librarians of the night, whose ephemeral documents consist of root-inscribed bones or whatever rustles in thickets upon solitary walks. Man, for all his daylight activities, is, at best, an evening creature. Our very addiction to the day and our compulsion, manifest through the ages, to invent and use illuminating devices, to contest with midnight, to cast off sleep as we would death, suggest that we know more of the shadows than we are willing to recognize. We have come from the dark wood of the past, and our bodies carry the scars and unhealed wounds of that transition. Our minds are haunted by night terrors that arise from the subterranean domain of racial and private memories.†   2

Lastly, we inhabit a spiritual twilight on this planet. It is perhaps the most poignant of all the deprivations to which man has been exposed by nature. I have said *deprivation,* but perhaps I should, rather, maintain that this feeling of loss is an unrealized anticipation. We imagine we are day creatures, but we grope in a lawless and smoky realm toward an exit that eludes us. We appear to know instinctively that such an exit exists.‡   3

---

* Paragraph 1: What kind of "manuscripts" does the author refer to?

† Paragraph 2: What do the last two sentences mean?

‡ Paragraph 3: What is the central idea of this paragraph? By now, you undoubtedly recognize that the author of this essay, who happens to be an anthropologist and an archaeologist, is delving into some arcane (see your dictionary) regions of human experiences that come close to being inscrutable, though many of us, to some extent, have had similar experiences. If you have had difficulty in answering the questions on it up to this point, you should probably read the essay through rather quickly and then read it again very carefully, giving attention again to the footnote questions.

I am not the first man to have lost his way only to find, if not a
gate, a mysterious hole in a hedge that a child would know at once led to
some other dimension at the world's end. Such passageways exist, or man
would not be here. Not for nothing did Santayana once contend that life
is a movement from the forgotten into the unexpected.*   4

As adults, we are preoccupied with living. As a consequence, we see
little. At the approach of age some men look about them at last and discover the hole in the hedge leading to the unforeseen. By then, there is
frequently no child companion to lead them safely through. After one or
two experiences of getting impaled on thorns, the most persistent individual is apt to withdraw and to assert angrily that no such opening exists. 5

My experience has been quite the opposite, but I have been fortunate. After several unsuccessful but tantalizing trials, which I intend to
disclose, I had the help, not of a child, but of a creature—a creature who,
appropriately, came out of a quite unremarkable and prosaic den. There
was nothing, in retrospect, at all mysterious or unreal about him. Nevertheless, the creature was baffling, just as, I suppose, to animals, man
himself is baffling. . . .   6

The episode occurred upon an unengaging and unfrequented shore.
It began in the late afternoon of a day devoted at the start to ordinary
scientific purposes. There was the broken prow of a beached boat sub-
siding in heavy sand, left by the whim of ancient currents a long way
distant from the shifting coast. Somewhere on the horizon wavered the
tenuous outlines of a misplaced building, growing increasingly insubstantial in the autumn light.†   7

After my companions had taken their photographs and departed, their
persistent voices were immediately seized upon and absorbed by the extending immensity of an incoming fog. The fog trailed in wisps over the
upthrust ribs of the boat. For a time I could see it fingering the tracks of
some small animal, as though engaged in a belated dialogue with the
creature's mind. The tracks crisscrossed a dune, and there the fog hesitated, as though puzzled. Finally, it approached and enwrapped me, as
though to peer into my face. I was not frightened, but I also realized with
a slight shock that I was not intended immediately to leave.‡   8

I sat down then and rested with my back against the overturned
boat. All around me the stillness intensified and the wandering tendrils of the
fog continued their search. Nothing escaped them.   9

* Paragraph 4: In the last sentence, to what in the preceding paragraph does "the forgotten" refer?

† Paragraph 7: What details in this paragraph illustrate the "unengaging and unfrequented" nature of the shore?

‡ Paragraph 8: In the third sentence, why is the dialogue described as "belated"? In the
  last sentence, is the statement "I was not intended immediately to leave" to be taken
  literally—did the fog somehow "intend" not to let the author leave?

The broken cup of a wild bird's egg was touched tentatively, as if with meaning, for the first time. I saw a sand-colored ghost crab, hitherto hidden and immobile, begin to sidle amidst the beach grass as though imbued suddenly with a will derived ultimately from the fog. A gull passed high overhead, but its cry took on the plaint of something other than itself. 10

I began dimly to remember a primitive dialogue as to whether God is a mist or merely a mist maker. Since a great deal of my thought has been spent amidst such early human and, to my mind, not outworn speculations, the idea did not seem particularly irrational or blasphemous. How else would so great a being, assuming his existence, be able thoroughly to investigate his world, or, perhaps, merely a world that he had come upon, than as he was now proceeding to do?* 11

I closed my eyes and let the tiny diffused droplets of the fog gently palpate my face. At the same time, by some unexplained affinity, I felt my mind drawn inland, to pour, smoking and gigantic as the fog itself, through the gorges of a neighboring mountain range. 12

In a little shaft of falling light my consciousness swirled dimly over the tombstones of a fallen cemetery. Something within me touched half-obliterated names and dates before sliding imperceptibly onward toward an errand in the city. That errand, whatever its purpose, perhaps because I was mercifully guided away from the future, was denied me.† 13

As suddenly as I had been dispersed I found myself back among the boat timbers and the broken shell of something that had not achieved existence. "I am the thing that lives in the midst of the bones"—a line from the dead poet Charles Williams persisted obstinately in my head. It was true. I was merely condensed from that greater fog to a smaller congelation of droplets. Vague and smoky wisplets of thought were my extensions.‡ 14

From a rack of bone no more substantial than the broken boat ribs on the beach, I was moving like that larger, all-investigating fog through the doorways of the past. Somewhere far away in an inland city the fog was transformed into a blizzard. Nineteen twenty-nine was a meaningless date that whipped by upon a flying newspaper. The blizzard was beating upon a great gate marked St. Elizabeth's. I was no longer the blizzard. I was hurrying, a small dark shadow, up a stairway beyond which came a labored and importunate breathing.§ 15

The man lay back among the pillows, wracked, yellow, and cadaverous. Though I was his son he knew me only as one lamp is briefly lit from another in the windy night. He was beyond speech, but a question was

* Paragraph 11: Is the last sentence a rhetorical question or a simple question?
† Paragraph 13: Was the cemetery actually seen or was it imagined by the author?
‡ Paragraph 14: How had the author "been dispersed"?
§ Paragraph 15: What is the "rack of bone"?

there, occupying the dying mind, excluding the living, something before which all remaining thought had to be mustered. At the time I was too young to understand. Only now could the hurrying shadow drawn from the wrecked boat interpret and relive the question. The starving figure on the bed was held back from death only by a magnificent heart that would not die.*   16

I, the insubstantial substance of memory, the dispersed droplets of the ranging fog, saw the man lift his hands for the last time. Strangely, in all that ravished body, they alone had remained unchanged. They were strong hands, the hands of a craftsman who had played many roles in his life: actor, laborer, professional runner. They were the hands of a man, indirectly of all men, for such had been the nature of his life. Now, in a last lucid moment, he had lifted them up and, curiously, as though they belonged to another being, he had turned and flexed them, gazed upon them unbelievingly, and dropped them once more.   17

He, too, the shadow, the mist in the gaping bones, had seen these seemingly untouched deathless instruments rally as though with one last purpose before the demanding will. And I, also a shadow, come back across forty years, could hear the question at last. "Why are you, my hands, so separate from me at death, yet still to be commanded? Why have you served me, you who are alive and ingeniously clever?" For here he turned and contemplated them with his old superb steadiness. "What has been our partnership, for I, the shadow, am going, yet you of all of me are alive and persist?"   18

I could have sworn that his last thought was not of himself but of the fate of the instruments. He was outside, he was trying to look into the secret purposes of things, and the hands, the masterful hands, were the only purpose remaining, while he, increasingly without center, was vanishing. It was the hands that contained his last conscious act. They had been formidable in life. In death they had become strangers who had denied their master's last question.†   19

Suddenly I was back under the overhang of the foundered boat. I had sat there stiff with cold for many hours. I was no longer the extension of a blizzard beating against immovable gates. The year of the locusts was done. It was, instead, the year of the mist maker that some obscure Macusi witch doctor had chosen to call god. But the mist maker had gone over the long-abandoned beach, touching for his inscrutable purposes only the broken shell of the nonexistent, only the tracks of a wayward fox, only a man who, serving the mist maker, could be made to stream wispily through the interstices of time.   20

* Paragraph 16: What is the meaning of the second sentence?
† Paragraph 19: What was "their master's last question"?

I was a biologist, but I chose not to examine my hands. The fog and the night were lifting. I had been far away for hours. Crouched in my heavy sheepskin I waited without thought as the witch doctor might have waited for the morning dispersion of his god. Finally, the dawn began to touch the sea, and then the worn timbers of the hulk beside which I sheltered reddened just a little. It was then I began to glimpse the world from a different perspective.   21

I had watched for nights the great bolts leaping across the pane of an attic window, the bolts Emerson had dreamed in the first scientific days might be the force that hurled reptile into mammal. I had watched at midnight the mad scientists intent upon their own creation. But in the end, those fantastic flashes of the lightning had ceased without issue, at least for me. The pane, the inscrutable pane, had darkened at last; the scientists, if scientists they were, had departed, carrying their secret with them. I sighed, remembering. It was then I saw the miracle. I saw it because I was hunched at ground level, smelling rank of fox, and no longer gazing with upright human arrogance upon the things of this world.   22

I did not realize at first what it was that I looked upon. As my wandering attention centered, I saw nothing but two small projecting ears lit by the morning sun. Beneath them, a small neat face looked shyly up at me. The ears moved at every sound, drank in a gull's cry and the far horn of a ship. They crinkled, I began to realize, only with curiosity; they had not learned to fear. The creature was very young. He was alone in a dread universe. I crept on my knees around the prow and crouched beside him. It was a small fox pup from a den under the timbers who looked up at me. God knows what had become of his brothers and sisters. His parents must not have been home from hunting.   23

He innocently selected what I think was a chicken bone from an untidy pile of splintered rubbish and shook it at me invitingly. There was a vast and playful humor in his face. "If there was only one fox in the world and I could kill him, I would do." The words of a British poacher in a pub rasped in my ears. I dropped even further and painfully away from human stature. It has been said repeatedly that one can never, try as he will, get around to the front of the universe. Man is destined to see only its far side, to realize nature only in retreat.   24

Yet here was the thing in the midst of the bones, the wide-eyed, innocent fox inviting me to play, with the innate courtesy of its two fore-paws placed appealingly together, along with a mock shake of the head. The universe was swinging in some fantastic fashion around to present its face, and the face was so small that the universe itself was laughing.   25

It was not a time for human dignity. It was a time only for the careful observance of amenities written behind the stars. Gravely I arranged my forepaws while the puppy whimpered with ill-concealed excitement. I drew the breath of a fox's den into my nostrils. On impulse, I picked up clumsily a whiter bone and shook it in teeth that had not entirely forgotten their original purpose. Round and round we tumbled for one ecstatic moment. We were the innocent thing in the midst of the bones, born in the egg, born in the den, born in the dark cave with the stone ax close to hand, born at last in human guise to grow coldly remote in the room with the rifle rack upon the wall.*   26

But I had seen my miracle. I had seen the universe as it begins for all things. It was, in reality, a child's universe, a tiny and laughing universe. I rolled the pup on his back and ran, literally ran for the nearest ridge. The sun was half out of the sea, and the world was swinging back to normal. The adult foxes would be already trotting home.   27

A little farther on, I passed one on a ridge who knew well I had no gun, for it swung by quite close, stepping delicately with brush and head held high. Its face was watchful but averted. It did not matter. It was what I had experienced and the fox had experienced, what we had all experienced in adulthood. We passed carefully on our separate ways into the morning, eyes not meeting.†   28

But to me the mist had come, and the mere chance of two lifted sunlit ears at morning. I knew at last why the man on the bed had smiled finally before he dropped his hands. He, too, had worked around to the front of things in his death agony. The hands were playthings and had to be cast aside at last like a little cherished toy. There was a meaning and there was not a meaning, and therein lay the agony.‡   29

The meaning was all in the beginning, as though time was awry. It was a little beautiful meaning that did not stay, and the sixty-year-old man on the hospital bed had traveled briefly toward it through the dark at the end of the universe. There was something in the desperate nature of the world that had to be reversed, but he had been too weak to tell me, and the hands had dropped helplessly away.   30

After forty years I had been just his own age when the fog had come groping for my face. I think I can safely put it down that I had been allowed my miracle. It was very small, as is the way of great things. I had been permitted to correct time's arrow for a space of perhaps five minutes—and that is a boon not granted to all men. If I were to render a report upon this episode, I would say that men must find a way to run the arrow backward. Doubtless it is impossible in the physical world, but in the memory and the will man might achieve the deed if he would try.   31

* Paragraph 26: Try to place the thought of the last sentence in a sentence of your own.

† Paragraph 28: How does the incident relate to the point that the author has now made in his essay?

‡ Paragraph 29: What was the "meaning" and what was "not a meaning"?

For just a moment I had held the universe at bay by the simple expedient of sitting on my haunches before a fox den and tumbling about with a chicken bone. It is the gravest, most meaningful act I shall ever accomplish, but, as Thoreau once remarked of some peculiar errand of his own, there is no use reporting it to the Royal Society.*   32

* Paragraph 32: Why would there be "no use reporting it to the Royal Society"?

The Whole Selection

1 If this essay appears incomprehensible to you even after following the suggestion which we made in footnote question 3 on page 88, you might be helped by reading W. H. Auden's review (see page 609) of Eiseley's book from which the essay was taken.
2 How is the "hole in the hedge," which is referred to in paragraphs 4 and 5, illustrated by the experience of the author with the little fox?
3 In paragraph 8, the fog is described as if it were an animate being. How does this device effectively prepare us for the encounter with the fox?
4 How do the brief examples which the author uses in paragraph 10 contribute to the main point of this essay as it is illustrated in the encounter with the fox?

Word Study dryad, indefatigable, peruse, ephemeral, poignant, tenuous, palpate, interstice, congelation

---

ROARERS, WHISPERERS, AND MODERATORS

SAMUEL JOHNSON

The Rambler. No. 144. Saturday, August 3, 1751

————Daphnidis arcum
Fregisti et calamos: quæ tu, perverse Menalca,
Et cum vidisti puero donata, dolebas;
Et, si non aliqua nocuisses, mortuus esses.
Virg. [Ec. III 12]

The bow of Daphnis and the shafts you broke;
When the fair boy receiv'd the gift of right;
And but for mischief, you had dy'd for spite.
Dryden

It is impossible to mingle in conversation without observing the difficulty with which a new name makes its way into the world. The first appearance of excellence unites multitudes against it; unexpected opposition rises up on every side; the celebrated and the obscure join in the confederacy; subtilty furnishes arms to impudence, and invention leads on credulity.   1

The strength and unanimity of this alliance is not easily conceived. It might be expected that no man should suffer his heart to be inflamed with malice, but by injuries; that none should busy himself in contesting the pretensions of another, but when some right of his own was involved in the question; that at least hostilities commenced without cause, should quickly cease; that the armies of malignity should soon disperse, when no common interest could be found to hold them together; and that the attack upon a rising character should be left to those who had something to hope or fear from the event.   2

The hazards of those that aspire to eminence would be much diminished if they had none but acknowledged rivals to encounter. Their enemies would then be few, and what is of yet greater importance, would be known. But what caution is sufficient to ward off the blows of invisible assailants, or what force can stand against unintermitted attacks, and a continual succession of enemies? Yet such is the state of the world, that no sooner can any man emerge from the crowd, and fix the eyes of the publick upon him, than he stands as a mark to the arrows of lurking calumny, and receives, in the tumult of hostility, from distant and from nameless hands, wounds not always easy to be cured.   3

It is probable that the onset against the candidates for renown, is originally incited by those who imagine themselves in danger of suffering by their success; but when war is once declared, volunteers flock to the standard, multitudes follow the camp only for want of employment, and flying squadrons are dispersed to every part, so pleased with an opportunity of mischief that they toil without prospect of praise, and pillage without hope of[1] profit.   4

When any man has endeavoured to deserve distinction, he will be surprised to hear himself censured where he could not expect to have been named; he will find the utmost acrimony of malice among those whom he never could have offended.   5

As there are to be found in the service of envy men of every diversity of temper and degree of understanding, calumny is diffused by all arts and methods of propagation. Nothing is too gross or too refined, too cruel or too trifling to be practised; very little regard is had to the rules of honourable hostility, but every weapon is accounted lawful; and those that cannot make a thrust at life are content to keep themselves in play with petty malevolence, to teaze with feeble blows and impotent disturbance.   6

But as the industry of observation has divided the most miscellaneous and confused assemblages into proper classes, and ranged the insects of the summer, that torment us with their drones or stings, by their several tribes; the persecutors of merit, notwithstanding their numbers, may be likewise commodiously distinguished into Roarers, Whisperers, and Moderators.   7

The Roarer is an enemy rather terrible than dangerous. He has no other qualification for a champion of controversy than a hardened front and strong voice. Having seldom so much desire to confute as to silence, he depends rather upon vociferation than argument, and has very little care to adjust one part of his accusation to another, to preserve decency in his language, or probability in his narratives. He has always a store of reproachful epithets and contemptuous appellations, ready to be produced as occasion may require, which by constant use he pours out with resistless volubility. If the wealth of a trader is mentioned, he without hesitation devotes him to bankruptcy; if the beauty and elegance of a lady be commended, he wonders how the town can fall in love with rustick deformity; if a new performance of genius happens to be celebrated, he pronounces the writer a hopeless ideot, without knowledge of books or life, and without the understanding by which it must be acquired. His exaggerations are generally without effect upon those whom he compels to hear them; and though it will sometimes happen that the timorous are awed by his violence, and the credulous mistake his confidence for knowledge, yet the opinions which he endeavours to suppress soon recover their former strength, as the trees that bend to the tempest erect themselves again when its force is past.   8

The Whisperer is more dangerous. He easily gains attention by a soft address, and excites curiosity by an air of importance. As secrets are not to be made cheap by promiscuous publication, he calls a select audience about him, and gratifies their vanity with an appearance of trust by com-

[1] 1756: or.

municating his intelligence in a low voice. Of the trader he can tell that though he seems to manage an extensive commerce, and talks in high terms of the funds, yet his wealth is not equal to his reputation; he has lately suffered much by an expensive project, and had a greater share than is acknowledged in the rich ship that perished by the storm. Of the beauty he has little to say, but that they who see her in a morning do not discover all these graces which are admired in the park. Of the writer he affirms with great certainty, that though the excellence of the work be incontestable, he can claim but a small part of the reputation; that he owed most of the images and sentiments to a secret friend; and that the accuracy and equality of the stile was produced by the successive correction of the chief criticks of the age.   9

As every one is pleased with imagining that he knows something not yet commonly divulged, secret history easily gains credit; but it is for the most part believed only while it circulates in whispers, and when once it is openly told, is openly confuted.   10

The most pernicious enemy is the man of Moderation. Without interest in the question, or any motive but honest curiosity, this impartial and zealous enquirer after truth, is ready to hear either side, and always disposed to kind interpretations and favourable opinions. He has heard the trader's affairs reported with great variation, and after a diligent comparison of the evidence, concludes it probable that the splendid superstructure of business being originally built upon a narrow basis, has lately been found to totter; but between dilatory payment and bankruptcy there is a great distance; many merchants have supported themselves by expedients for a time, without any final injury to their creditors; and what is lost by one adventure may be recovered by another. He believes that a young lady pleased with admiration, and desirous to make perfect what is already excellent, may heighten her charms by artificial improvements, but surely most of her beauties must be genuine, and who can say that he is wholly what he endeavours to appear? The author he knows to be a man of diligence, who perhaps does not sparkle with the fire of *Homer,* but has the judgment to discover his own deficiencies, and to supply them by the help of others; and in his opinion modesty is a quality so amiable and rare, that it ought to find a patron wherever it appears, and may justly be preferred by the publick suffrage to petulant wit and ostentatious literature. 11

He who thus discovers failings with unwillingness, and extenuates the faults which cannot be denied, puts an end at once to doubt or vindication; his hearers repose upon his candour and veracity, and admit the charge without allowing the excuse.   12

Such are the arts by which the envious, the idle, the peevish, and the thoughtless, obstruct that worth which they cannot equal, and by artifices thus easy, sordid, and detestable, is industry defeated, beauty blasted, and genius depressed.   13

THE MAN WHO WAS PUT IN A CAGE

ROLLO MAY

> *What a piece of work is man! how noble in reason! how infinite in faculty! in form and moving how express and admirable! . . . The paragon of animals!*
> —Shakespeare, *Hamlet*

We have quite a few discrete pieces of information these days about what happens to a person when he is deprived of this or that element of freedom. We have our studies of sensory deprivation and of how a person reacts when put in different kinds of authoritarian atmosphere, and so on. But recently I have been wondering what pattern would emerge if we put these various pieces of knowledge together. In short, what would happen to a living, whole person if his total freedom—or as nearly total as we can imagine—were taken away? In the course of these reflections, a parable took form in my mind.   1

The story begins with a king who, while standing in reverie at the window of his palace one evening, happened to notice a man in the town square below. He was apparently an average man, walking home at night, who had taken the same route five nights a week for many years. The king followed this man in his imagination—pictured him arriving home, perfunctorily kissing his wife, eating his late meal, inquiring whether everything was all right with the children, reading the paper, going to bed, perhaps engaging in the sex relation with his wife or perhaps not, sleeping, and getting up and going off to work again the next day.   2

And a sudden curiosity seized the king, which for a moment banished his fatigue: "I wonder what would happen if a man were kept in a cage, like the animals at the zoo?" His curiosity was perhaps in some ways not unlike that of the first surgeons who wondered what it would be like to perform a lobotomy on the human brain.   3

So the next day the king called in a psychologist, told him of his idea, and invited him to observe the experiment. When the psychologist demurred saying, "It's an unthinkable thing to keep a man in a cage," the monarch replied that many rulers had in effect, if not literally, done so, from the time of the Romans through Genghis Khan down to Hitler and the totalitarian leaders; so why not find out scientifically what would happen? Furthermore, added the king, he had made up his mind to do it whether the psychologist took part or not; he had already gotten the Greater Social Research Foundation to give a large sum of money for the experiment, and why let that money go to waste? By this time the psychologist also was feeling within himself a great curiosity about what would happen if a man were kept in a cage.   4

And so the next day the king caused a cage to be brought from the zoo—a large cage that had been occupied by a lion when it was new, then later by a tiger; just recently it had been the home of a hyena who died the previous week. The cage was put in an inner private court in the palace grounds, and the average man whom the king had seen from the window was brought and placed therein. The psychologist, with his Rorschach and Wechsler-Bellevue tests in his brief case to administer at some appropriate moment, sat down outside the cage.   5

At first the man was simply bewildered, and he kept saying to the psychologist, "I have to catch the tram, I have to get to work, look what time it is, I'll be late for work!" But later on in the afternoon the man began soberly to realize what was up, and then he protested vehemently, "The king can't do this to me! It is unjust! It's against the law." His voice was strong, and his eyes full of anger. The psychologist liked the man for his anger, and he became vaguely aware that this was a mood he had encountered often in people he worked with in his clinic. "Yes," he realized, "this anger is the attitude of people who—like the healthy adolescents of any era—want to fight what's wrong, who protest directly against it. When people come to the clinic in this mood, it is good—they can be helped."   6

During the rest of the week the man continued his vehement protests. When the king walked by the cage, as he did every day, the man made his protests directly to the monarch.   7

But the king answered, "Look here, you are getting plenty of food, you have a good bed, and you don't have to work. We take good care of you; so why are you objecting?"   8

After some days had passed, the man's protests lessened and then ceased. He was silent in his cage, generally refusing to talk. But the psychologist could see hatred glowing in his eyes. When he did exchange a few words, they were short, definite words uttered in the strong, vibrant, but calm voice of the person who hates and knows whom he hates.   9

Whenever the king walked into the courtyard, there was a deep fire in the man's eyes. The psychologist thought, "This must be the way people act when they are first conquered." He remembered that he had also seen that expression of the eyes and heard that tone of voice in many patients at his clinic: the adolescent who had been unjustly accused at home or in school and could do nothing about it; the college student who was required by public and campus opinion to be a star on the gridiron, but was required by his professors to pass courses he could not prepare for if he were to be successful in football—and who was then expelled from college for the cheating that resulted. And the psychologist, looking at the active hatred in the man's eyes, thought, "It is still good; a person who has this fight in him can be helped."   10

Every day the king, as he walked through the courtyard, kept reminding the man in the cage that he was given food and shelter and taken good care of, so why did he not like it? And the psychologist noticed that, whereas at first the man had been entirely impervious to the king's statements, it now seemed more and more that he was pausing for a moment after the king's speech—for a second the hatred was postponed from returning to his eyes—as though he were asking himself if what the king said were possibly true.   11

And after a few weeks more, the man began to discuss with the psychologist how it was a useful thing that a man is given food and shelter; and how man had to live by his fate in any case, and the part of wisdom was to accept fate. He soon was developing an extensive theory about security and the acceptance of fate, which sounded to the psychologist very much like the philosophical theories that Rosenberg and others worked out for the fascists in Germany. He was very voluble during this period, talking at length, although the talk was mostly a monologue. The psychologist noticed that his voice was flat and hollow as he talked, like the voice of people in TV previews who make an effort to look you in the eye and try hard to sound sincere as they tell you that you should see the program they are advertising, or the announcers on the radio who are paid to persuade you that you should like highbrow music.   12

And the psychologist also noticed that now the corners of the man's mouth always turned down, as though he were in some gigantic pout. Then the psychologist suddenly remembered: this was like the middle-aged, middle-class people who came to his clinic, the respectable bourgeois people who went to church and lived morally but who were always full of resentment, as though everything they did was conceived, born, and nursed in resentment. It reminded the psychologist of Nietzsche's saying that the middle class was consumed with resentment. He then for the first time began to be seriously worried about the man in the cage, for he knew that once resentment gets a firm start and becomes well rationalized and structuralized, it may become like cancer. When the person no longer knows whom he hates, he is much harder to help.   13

During this period the Greater Social Research Foundation had a board of trustees meeting, and they decided that since they were expending a fund to keep a man supported in a cage, it would look better if representatives of the Foundation at least visited the experiment. So a group of people, consisting of two professors and a few graduate students, came in one day to look at the man in the cage. One of the professors then proceeded to lecture to the group about the relation of the autonomic nervous system and the secretions of the ductless glands to human existence in a cage. But it occurred to the other professor that the verbal communications of the victim himself might just possibly be interesting, so he asked the man how he felt about living in a cage. The man was friendly toward the professors and students and explained to them that he had chosen this way of life, that there were great values in security and in being taken care of, that they would of course see how sensible this course was, and so on.   14

"How strange!" thought the psychologist, "and how pathetic; why is it he struggles so hard to get them to approve his way of life?"   15

In the succeeding days when the king walked through the courtyard, the man fawned upon him from behind the bars in his cage and thanked him for the food and shelter. But when the king was not in the yard and the man was not aware that the psychologist was present, his expression was quite different—sullen and morose. When his food was handed to him through the bars by the keeper, the man would often drop the dishes or dump over the water and then would be embarrassed because of his stupidity and clumsiness. His conversation became increasingly one-tracked; and instead of the involved philosophical theories about the value of being taken care of, he had gotten down to simple sentences such as "It is fate," which he would say over and over again, or he would just mumble to himself, "It is." The psychologist was surprised to find that the man should now be so clumsy as to drop his food, or so stupid as to talk in those barren sentences, for he knew from his tests that the man had originally been of good average intelligence. Then it dawned upon the psychologist that this was the kind of behavior he had observed in some anthropological studies among the Negroes in the South—people who had been forced to kiss the hand that fed and enslaved them, who could no longer either hate or rebel. The man in the cage took more and more to simply sitting all day long in the sun as it came through the bars, his only movement being to shift his position from time to time from morning through the afternoon.   16

It was hard to say just when the last phase set in. But the psychologist became aware that the man's face now seemed to have no particular expression; his smile was no longer fawning, but simply empty and meaningless, like the grimace a baby makes when there is gas on its stomach. The man ate his food and exchanged a few sentences with the psychologist from time to time; but his eyes were distant and vague, and though he looked at the psychologist, it seemed that he never really *saw* him.   17

And now the man, in his desultory conversations, never used the word "I" any more. He had accepted the cage. He had no anger, no hate, no rationalizations. But he was now insane.   18

The night the psychologist realized this, he sat in his apartment trying to write a concluding report. But it was very difficult for him to summon up words, for he felt within himself a great emptiness. He kept trying to reassure himself with the words, "They say that nothing is ever lost, that matter is merely changed to energy and back again." But he could not help feeling that something *had* been lost, that something had gone out of the universe in this experiment.   19

He finally went to bed with his report unfinished. But he could not sleep; there was a gnawing within him which, in less rational and scientific ages, would have been called a conscience. Why didn't I tell the king that this is the one experiment that no man can do—or at least why didn't I shout that I would have nothing to do with the whole bloody business? Of course, the king would have dismissed me, the foundations would never have granted me any more money, and at the clinic they would have said that I was not a real scientist. But maybe one could farm in the mountains and make a living, and maybe one could paint or write something that would make future men happier and more free. . . .   20

But he realized that these musings were, at least at the moment, unrealistic, and he tried to pull himself back to reality. All he could get, however, was this feeling of emptiness within himself, and the words, "Something has been taken out of the universe, and there is left only a void."   21

Finally he dropped off to sleep. Some time later, in the small hours of the morning, he was awakened by a startling dream. A crowd of people had gathered, in the dream, in front of the cage in the courtyard, and the man in the cage—no longer inert and vacuous—was shouting through the bars of the cage in impassioned oratory. "It is not only I whose freedom is taken away!" he was crying. "When the king puts me or any man in a cage, the freedom of each of you is taken away also. The king must go!" The people began to chant. "The king must go!" and they seized and broke out the iron bars of the cage, and wielded them for weapons as they charged the palace.   22

The psychologist awoke, filled by the dream with a great feeling of hope and joy—an experience of hope and joy probably not unlike that experienced by the free men of England when they forced King John to sign the Magna Charta. But not for nothing had the psychologist had an orthodox analysis in the course of his training, and as he lay surrounded by this aura of happiness, a voice spoke within him: "Aha, you had this dream to make yourself feel better; it's just a wish fulfillment."   23

"The hell it is!" said the psychologist as he climbed out of bed. "Maybe some dreams are to be acted on."   24

Suggestions for Writing

1 Using the technique of a single example, as David Riesman does, or of a series of examples, write an essay which explains the meaning of any one of the following items:

a The state of secondary school education.
b The typical college student.
c "Never say 'no' when the world says 'yes'."

2 Using a single, extended example, explain the meaning of any one of the following in an essay of no more than 500 words:
a A true friend.
b "A stitch in time saves nine."
c "Don't cross a bridge until you come to it."
d "A bird in the hand is worth two in the bush."

3 Using either an extended example or several examples, as Loren Eiseley and Samuel Johnson do, write an essay explaining the meaning of any one of the following:
a Controlling the air we breathe.
b The population explosion.
c Television drama worth watching.
d "Our life is frittered away by detail."—H. D. Thoreau

RESEMBLANCES AND DIFFERENCES: COMPARISON AND CONTRAST

Because it is used so frequently, comparison and contrast is a method of analysis familiar to everyone. It can be as simple or as sophisticated as the material or subject it analyzes: the preschool teacher uses it to extend the knowledge of her pupils; the literary critic uses it to develop his evaluation of a poem or novel. When Miss Jones announces to her five-year-olds that they are going to the zoo, she must take into account that many of her pupils have never been there before. "Well," she may begin, "the zoo is something like . . ." In completing her explanation, she will be using the device of comparison and contrast. Or the modern literary critic may begin his review of a poem by Peter Viereck by comparing it with a poem by Robert Lowell.

The technique of comparison points out the *similarities* that exist between two (or more) objects, terms, or ideas; contrast focuses our attention on the *differences* between two (or more) objects, terms, or ideas. In "Time, Place, and Painter" (page 107), Katharine Kuh discusses two paintings which are similar in that both are portraits of a mother and child, but her main intent is to contrast the two. On the other hand, in "Real Religion—and False" (page 127), Barbara Ward compares the shocking similarities between Soviet and Western attitudes toward religion. Though comparison and contrast seem to aim at different ends, they must be considered as one single method of analysis. There can be no comparison without some contrast: completely identical objects are not comparable. And there can be no contrast without some comparison: from a logical point of view, there would be little value in contrasting a horse and a wristwatch, because they do not have anything in common—there is no sufficient comparison to make the contrast meaningful. Of course, a poet might contrast a horse and a wristwatch; but he would probably do it by means of a metaphor, which is a way of extending the limits of language, and that is another matter. Comparison and contrast as a method of analysis, in short, depends upon man's ability to see a pattern in existence, a pattern made up of likenesses and differences.

Comparison and contrast aims at making the unknown known to the reader by calling his attention to the connection that exists between them. The essays in this section indicate ways of doing this.

To contrast two paintings, Katherine Kuh first states the general differences ("they represented two totally different worlds"), and then, in her second paragraph, indicates more specific elements of difference ("time, thought, and place"); after that, she proceeds in the next four paragraphs to explain the American painting in relation to the specific elements of contrast. Only then, and in only one paragraph (since her major interest is the American painting), does she explain the Italian painting in relation to the specific elements of difference.

Raymond-Leopold Bruckberger, in "An Assignment for Intellectuals" (page 119), uses comparison and contrast in order to answer what he considers a significant question: What should be the role of the American intellectual in the world today? He compares the American intellectual and the European intellectual with respect to a common tradition. The place held by the intellectual in the United States does not differ historically from that held by the European intellectual in his society; but Bruckberger is more concerned with the contrast between the European intellectual's sense of vocation and the American intellectual's lack of such a sense.

Barbara Ward's "Real Religion—and False" is the only essay in which comparison is used more than contrast. She does, of course, begin with a vital contrast between real religion and false religion: real religion is nonmaterialistic and puts a premium upon the individual; false religion is materialistic and puts a premium upon society. But what really interests her is a searching comparison between actual Soviet and Western attitudes toward religion. She finds that both attitudes are materialistic; both involve thinking in units and not of people. This comparison is striking, because most readers tend to think of the Soviet Union and the Western world only as contrasting elements.

A further study of these essays will indicate that the nature of comparison and contrast is such that there are only two basic ways of organizing material for the presentation of it. For simple, less complex, objects, terms, or ideas, the writer may expose one object (or term, or idea) fully before turning to a full exposition of the second. Kuh does something like this: she explains the American painting in detail in four paragraphs before turning to an explanation of the European painting. It is important to note, however, that she does not proceed exclusively in that way. The method of exposing the whole of one object and then the whole of the other is not much used in its pure form. This way of organizing material assumes that the subject being discussed is simple enough in its parts to be comprehended fully and for one part to be retained when we turn to the other part being compared or contrasted. If the subject is complex, this method is likely to make excessive demands upon the reader, since it assumes that he can keep all the detailed matter in mind when turning to the other object or term—a dangerous assumption to make under ordinary circumstances. Therefore, the writer, when dealing with a complex comparison and contrast, will tend to examine both objects, terms, or ideas part by part, turning first to one and then to the other alternately in his presentation. This is the method used by van Dresser, Ward, and Bruckberger.

Finally, it is important to note again that comparison and contrast as a method of analysis is ordinarily not used alone. Peter van Dresser provides us with examples to make his contrast clearer; Barbara Ward uses definition as well as example. Once again, too, we must note, as we did with the other methods of analysis, that comparison and contrast may be the dominant intention of the writer, as it is in Mrs. Kuh's essay, but it may also be used by the writer in order to further some other dominant purpose: van Dresser and Bruckberger, for example, use it to advance their arguments.

PLACE, TIME, AND PAINTER

KATHARINE KUH

There was no reason to compare the two paintings. They represented totally different worlds, and perhaps that was precisely why I found myself doing so. True, they both were hanging in the same building and both were variations on "the Madonna with Child" theme, but kinship ended there. I encountered them separated by several rooms in one of America's star institutions, the Worcester Art Museum, rightfully celebrated for its superior collections hand-picked over the years by a succession of knowledgeable experts. And should one question whether knowledge makes a difference, a visit to this sophisticated art gallery will dispel such doubts. Also, should one question the advantages of a well-pruned smaller museum adapted to normal human intake, Worcester is proof that size and geographic location are not what make an institution parochial.*   1

---

* Paragraph 1: The thoughts of the first two sentences seem to be contradictory. Presumably, they are not; but, if so, how are they not contradictory? In the last sentence, what does "parochial" mean in this context?

Top: "Virgin and Child," by Bartolomeo Montagna (?–1523). Painting on wood. *Worcester Art Museum. Bottom:* "Mrs. Elizabeth Freake and Baby Mary," by an anonymous seventeenth-century American artist (Boston, 1670s). Oil on canvas. *Worcester Art Museum; gift of Mr. and Mrs. Albert W. Rice.*

Among this museum's holdings is a group of rare seventeenth-century American paintings climaxed by an anonymous double portrait of *Mrs. Freake and Baby Mary,* often considered the country's outstanding canvas of the period. Much less famous but far more urbane and technically accomplished is Bartolomeo Montagna's late fifteenth-century *Virgin and Child,* probably painted in Vicenza where this Italian artist spent most of his life. Viewed on one level, both Worcester pictures are interesting works of art; viewed on another, they are reflections of wholly different periods in time, thought, and place, each offering a brief résumé of the land and mores from which it came. Worth investigating, too, is why one painting is so highly prized, the other merely accepted with polite respect.*   2

Though nothing could be more egregious than confusing esthetic reactions with historical documentation, still art has always served as a valuable clue to the past. What better way to understand the elegant frivolity of eighteenth-century France than through Boucher, Watteau, and Fragonard? What better way to understand our own abrasive scene than through its ebullient Pop imitators? Yet, *Mrs. Freake and Baby Mary* is not typically native. It is all the more provocative because method and message are somewhat divergent. The subject is clearly American, the technique not necessarily so. As Louisa Dresser, the Worcester museum's curator, points out, this carefully delineated composition might well pass for a French provincial painting—one of those crisp, slightly awkward works found frequently in France's excellent smaller museums. If technical methods have been refined by mixed memories of Europe, the sitter, her child, her costume, her stalwart character are strictly early American. Indeed, most of the details in the picture probably provide accurate data on the period in which it was painted—about 1674.†   3

Where its anonymous artist came from we do not know, but most likely it was England. One thing is certain: he was never a member of the Dutch Patroon school that settled chiefly in New York State, producing a legacy of brutally frank, brilliantly strong portraits that lack the sensitivity of Mrs. Freake's image. We also do not know too much about Elizabeth Freake herself, except that she was born in Dorchester, Massachusetts, in 1642, thus making her thirty-two at the time of the portrait. Her husband John Freake, whose likeness hangs next to hers in the Worcester museum and came no doubt from the same hand though at a less inspired moment, emigrated from England around 1660 to settle in Boston as an attorney and merchant. A year after the portraits were finished, he died in a Boston Harbor explosion.‡   4

* Paragraph 2: Why is the inverted order used in the second sentence more effective than normal word order would have been?

† Paragraph 3: In the fifth sentence, what do "method" and "message" mean as clarified in the rest of the paragraph?

‡ Paragraph 4: In the second sentence why does the author use a colon instead of a semi-colon or a period?

The question immediately confronting us is why the woman's portrait
is hailed as a major—possibly *the* major—example of primitive American
art. Surely not because of the puppet-like child, the bourgeois sitter, the
affectionately recorded garments, the wealth of subtle whites. Rather, I
think, it is the quiet, the purity, the trusting record of an authentic person
that come through to us with touching impact. Whether this same painting
would be regarded so enthusiastically in any country other than its own is
doubtful, though Daniel Rich, director of the Worcester Art Museum,
reports that "interested Europeans respond to the portrait, because they
sense in it the primitive quality we admire today. Since Le Douanier
Rousseau," he adds, "Europeans as well as Americans have been interested in self-taught artists who are involved with direct, fresh discoveries."   5

But it is more than quaint primitivism that attracts us to *Mrs. Freake
and Baby Mary* (a title, by the way, I find wonderfully American). This
strong, measured, plain woman is part of a heritage we like to remember,
especially today under less serene circumstances. She seems eminently
respectable, secure, and non-Freudian. As we emerge from historical
adolescence and begin to value our past, American art daily assumes
greater importance. Yet, admiration for this particular work goes beyond
pride in home production; it is rightfully based on the appeal of a painting
that probes deeper than the usual early American portrait. The picture has
its own individuality, its own uniqueness. The unfaltering linear design—
rigid, proud, and simple—echoes similar characteristics in the young
mother, providing us with an eloquent glimpse of an early American
personality.*   6

All of which brings me back to Montagna's *Virgin and Child,* painted
two centuries earlier than Mrs. Freake. If one were to ask a casual viewer,
who knows nothing specific about the antecedents of either picture, which
he prefers, he would, I think, choose the Montagna. To appreciate this
tender religious work presupposes little previous knowledge. One need not
be told that Montagna lived in Venice at one time, that the present painting may have derived from a print by Mantegna and may have also been
influenced by Giovanni Bellini. The close relationship of Mother and Child,
the beautiful candid Virgin, the undulating gracious design are all part of
a southern European Renaissance tradition we have long understood and
accepted. But Mrs. Freake's portrait, even more Protestant than American,
is related to an austere New World where denial of sensuality was basic to
survival. In order to relish the picture fully, one must recognize the stern
realities of the land and the time it came from. Montagna's deeply Catholic
panel combines idealized symbolism with warm human emotions. This

---

* Paragraph 6: What characteristics of Mrs. Freake are echoed by "the unfaltering linear
design—rigid, proud, and simple"?

dichotomy, implicit in much Italian Renaissance art, was characteristic of an indulgent faith. Here, though religious iconography was omnipotent, there was none of the Puritan restraint that inhibited early American expression.*   7

In the long run, however, the American portrait remains inimitable, a special and unusual encounter. I recall no other seventeenth-century painting produced in the United States that in any way duplicates or, for that matter, approximates it. The Montagna Virgin is not an individualized personality but a type dependent on familiar traditions. She is part of a safely established period, not a brave preview of a new one. More articulate and more polished than Mrs. Freake, she is the heroine of a universal story. So, too, is the American mother, but her story is related to the mundane facts of life, while the Virgin, despite her human fervency, is nonetheless a supernatural being.†   8

The Montagna, of course, is not a primitive work though it is dated some 200 years earlier than the American canvas, demonstrating how geography can become as important as chronology. It is the place *and* the time, to say nothing of the artist, that make a picture tick. But it is more than place, time, and painter; it is the audience, too. What in the second half of the twentieth century is considered a masterpiece might have seemed merely an adequate historical document to viewers a hundred years ago. And what Americans consider a chef d'œuvre today might appeal to contemporary Europeans as little more than a typical regional work of minor importance. It is rare that a country's primitive beginnings turn into a world-wide inheritance. During relatively recent centuries this has happened in Italy, the Netherlands, and, to a degree, in Germany, Spain, and France.‡   9

With great works rapidly dwindling from the market, Americans are turning back on themselves with almost hysterical zeal. Prices for older and sometimes third-rate indigenous canvases are skyrocketing in unrealistic leaps. These paintings often have value only here and now, only to us in these United States. They are scarcely negotiable elsewhere. Yet, we must not forget that on occasion a blunt early American work can hold its own with more worldly examples from abroad. *Mrs. Freake and Baby Mary* is a formidable case in point. Here honesty and innate dignity compensate for technical naïveté. And, curiously, it is this very naïveté that intensifies the picture's uncompromising integrity.   10

* Paragraph 7: With what elements in design in the early American painting does "the undulating gracious design" of the Italian painting contrast?

† Paragraph 8: What is the American painting "a brave preview" of? Why does the author call it "brave"?

‡ Paragraph 9: What is the topic thought of this paragraph?

The Whole Selection

1 Except in metaphor, one cannot compare completely identical things or contrast completely unlike things (see our introduction to this section, page 105). In what ways are the two paintings alike and in what ways are they unlike?

2 Sometimes, for certain purposes such as holding the reader in suspense, or, in the case of a complex subject, avoiding confusion for the reader, a writer will not let us know quickly what he intends to do in a piece of writing. Good exposition, however, often requires that very early in an essay the writer let us know what will be the main objects of his attention. What does Mrs. Kuh do in this regard?

3 In paragraph 2, the author says that each of the two paintings reflects "the land and mores from which it came." Where in this essay does she give us details of these reflections? Where in the essay does the author develop the subject which she introduces in the last sentence of paragraph 2?

Word Study *egregious, abrasive, dichotomy*

THE MODERN RETREAT FROM FUNCTION

PETER van DRESSER

As a people, we have not ceased congratulating ourselves on our remarkable escape from the obsessive genteelness, the overriding concern with propriety, facade and pseudo-elegance which we associate with the past century. Victorian manners and customs are perennially good for a condescending chuckle, and the voluminous garments in which the ladies and gentlemen of that epoch swathed themselves still serve as a sort of subconscious, contrasting background to the tanned mobility of bathing-briefed humanity (on billboard, beach and screen) which accompanies our neo-Hellenic savor of the joys and beauties of the flesh. Surely we have by now achieved a collective *joie de vivre* sufficient to flood away the dark world of anxieties, tensions, repressions which festered in that murky climate of self-fear within which our ancestors are said to have been reared.*   1

But there is evidence that our psychic liberation is still only skin-deep, so to speak; that the current relaxation of tabus against exposed epidermis and musculature has been countered by the proliferation of a system of far more pervasive inhibitions and pruderies than our great grandparents could have imagined. Where the Victorian culture seems to have conditioned primarily against the direct recognition of, or exposure to, the raw phenomenon of sexuality, the modern American is being perhaps even more effectively conditioned against an entire complex of physico-physiological processes.†   2

THE TRIUMPH OF THE CONTAINER

Probably the most obvious indication of this conditioning and the one most frequently commented on, is the role that the motor-car has assumed in our society. With its polished exterior and padded interior, it has become a sort of sanitary carapace within which the contemporary psyche shelters itself from the rigors of the physical world. Beginning by progressively eliminating the need for walking and for managing draft animals—two effective modes of contact with the organic environment—the automobile has evolved into the "womb with a view," and on wheels; the concrete

---

* Paragraph 1: Does the tone of this paragraph suggest that "surely," as used in the last sentence, perhaps does not really mean "surely"? What words or phrases in the paragraph suggest the tone or the attitude which the author exhibits in this paragraph toward the two different ages—the Victorian and the present?

† Paragraph 2: By referring to some specific details in this and in the preceding paragraph, show how the use of the term "skin-deep" is particularly effective here.

embodiment of revulsion against a disturbing underworld of dark fears of germs and physical contact, of exertion, effort and dirt.   3

The preparation of food, in a parallel fashion, has retreated to an esoteric domain of immaculate and hermetically sealed machinery, the culmination of which is the inevitable cellophane package or tinned container. All the old lusty smells and sensations attendant upon the grinding of corn, roasting of coffee, the fermenting of yeast in bread or beer, the pressing of apples or grapes, have been banished in favor of a hushed operating room asepsis. Gourmets have long lamented the resulting blandification of foodstuffs—the average American child now cannot tolerate foods of marked flavor and character; he subsists on an emolient of homogenized peanut-butter, triply ground hamburger and emulsified chocolate milk. Country life, which used to provide an enclave sheltered from such degeneration, has now of course become as much or more invaded by these practices as the city and suburbia.   4

The submergence of all operations of a physiological or physical nature beneath a cosmeticized camouflage can be seen at work throughout our technology. The Victorian took an honest pleasure in the construction of his machinery. He embellished its members with scrollwork and gilding, but he did not hide them. To the Modern, even the play of gear trains, connecting rods and levers has become in bad taste and his mechanisms increase in salability to the extent that they can be shrouded in nubile housings. There is of course a measure of technical justification for this kind of evolution, but the drive behind it is certainly as much psychological as functional, and the fabrication, repair and maintenance problems are often vastly complicated.*   5

A perhaps inevitable result of this trend has been, of course, the withdrawal of the repairing of machinery—especially of automobiles—to the pastel-toned laboratory of smocked specialists. The grimy, grease-stained mechanic is still to be found in an occasional backwater garage, but he is on his way out, and the typical modern repair operation tends to consist in the deft installation of a packaged "factory fresh" component, rather than the painful personal reworking of broken or worn mechanisms. And as for the old-time blacksmith-machine shop, with its Piranesi-like interior, its maze of shafting and slapping leather belts, its awesome wrestlings with red-hot metal—this traditional point of contact with the elemental Hephaestic world has almost completely vanished.†   6

The Do-It-Yourself renaissance which has aroused so much comment may be cited as a counter-movement against this general professionalization and sanitization of daily life. It seems true that the submerged need for personal manipulation of creative forces has indeed stimulated this

* Paragraph 5: What is the meaning of the last sentence in this paragraph?
† Paragraph 6: In the last sentence, why is the "Hephaestic world" called "elemental"?

thriving new segment of our tertiary economy. However, an examination of Do-It-Yourselfism reveals that it too has gone through the same process of degermination which has affected our whole way of life. It is precisely in the rough elemental stage of extracting and forming raw materials that the How-to-do-it kit bypasses contact with the crude real world. One plays with plywood or ductile aluminum extrusions or ready tanned and cut leather, or pre-compounded clay and glazes—in extreme cases one even fills in color-coded areas in a prefabricated painting. But all these operations are incomplete, emasculated, predigested. They are, in fact, hardly more than extensions of the childhood manipulations of guaranteed non-toxically colored pegboards in the hygienic nursery.   7

    Indeed, in an ideally laid out suburban development, one gets an overwhelming impression of a gay toyland peopled with brightly painted lawnmowers, baby garden tractors, prefabricated pergolas and aluminum clothes dryers. The toyland picture is completed with the gleaming two-toned icecream-sundae-colored automobiles parked beneath the carports. (Their beautiful but obscene engines and members are of course concealed beneath softly-rounded and magically glittering frostings.)*   8

THE BLENDERIZED ENVIRONMENT

The psychological shock of rough textures is carefully avoided here; walls and floors are dulcet planes of featureless plastic or enamel; lawns are uninterrupted velvet. Only an occasional token fireplace chimney of ashlar masonry, or a carefully varnished panel of knotty pine is allowed to symbolize a pioneering heritage.   9

    In this careful cosmetic world there are no gnarled people, no mature or older men and women whose faces, bodies and hands have been formed and indented through direct contact with the brines, caustics and tannins of elder nature. When these people, in response to vestigial urges, penetrate the wilderness briefly on summer vacations, they do so sheltered in their hydromatically propelled perambulators, cared for and distracted by the multitude of gay gadgets such as folding stoves, shirt-pocket radios, collapsible plastic furniture; nourished through the umbilical cord of intricate transport and communications. The Grecian exposure to sun and wind is after all achieved only in carefully selected beaches, resort spots or dude ranches, guaranteed free of chiggers, abrasive gravel and black-flies. Painful effort, sweat other than that which can be quickly removed in the locker room showers, gruelling and permanently disfiguring contacts with the elements—such ingredients are discreetly missing.   10

    More even than in play, this general and tacit evasion of the crudities of our root-contacts with the planet, permeates our mode of organization of work. The rough physical tasks are still to be done; foodstuffs and

* Paragraph 8: In the last sentence, why are the engines called "obscene"?

fibers must still be brought forth from the dirt; animals killed and gutted; minerals wrested from rock veins, smelted and forged; massive objects moved, lifted, piled; trees felled and shaped; mountains of refuse disposed of. In the past all these processes, subdivided into a thousand lesser tasks, were undertaken by men—men with muscles, nerves: men who sweated. Uncounted deeds of individual valor, judgment, skill, seasoned with anxiety, effort and pride, formed the network of man's economic relationship to his globe. Men were marked physically, spiritually and mentally by the demands of their occupations—sometimes honorably, sometimes painfully.*   11

In our emerging automated world this intimacy with the physical processes of existence is not in good taste. As on a small scale we conceal the play of vital activities behind euphemic shroudings, so on the larger stage entire regions are segregated to the massive chemurgies of our industry. Broad piedmonts and prairies are devoted to the dreary but efficient monoculture of cotton, corn, wheat or tobacco; mineralized basins and littorals to the monstrous extractions and smeltings of iron, copper, coal; prodigious intrametropolitan complexes to wildernesses of interlocking manufacturers and processings. In sheer physical extent, such areas overwhelm suburbia; psychologically they are nevertheless subservient to it. The powerful and capable men who operate the great machines here are blighted with its fatally genteel pruderies. Wherever physically or economically possible, their housing developments and shopping centers caricature the dream world of chrome store fronts, picture windows and unctuously curving asphalt motorways; wives move in a hypnotic orbit of easy-pay-plan color-styled bathrooms and living room suites, of shopping expeditions to the nearest glittering super market and its attendant beautician, seeking, unconsciously, escape from the overwhelming brutality of the technology about them.†   12

In this environment, no balance of the physical, the intellectual and the esthetic may be expected to evolve. Here, especially, because of the sheer economic pressure towards ever mounting production, labors that demand participation of body and nerve are being reorganized into cerebrally guided, automatically coordinated mechanical processes.   13

THE NEED FOR ROUGHAGE

Examples could be multiplied indefinitely and have been discussed exhaustively since the days of Ruskin and William Morris, but the general

* Paragraph 11: In this and in the preceding paragraph, point out instances of parallelism. Can you see a relationship between such phrasing and comparison and contrast?

† Paragraph 12: What do you think the author would propose as a desirable alternative to "the dreary but efficient monoculture of cotton, corn, wheat or tobacco" which, in the second sentence, he deplores? In the fifth sentence, to what does "its" refer? In the sixth sentence, is the metaphoric use of "unctuously" effective?

tendency away from human-to-nature contact with our environment and towards impersonal, cerebral, specialized manipulation continues and no doubt will proceed to a much greater degree of perfection.   14

Without questioning the basic benefits of applied science—release from drudgery, power over the blind vagaries of nature—one may entertain doubts as to the particular ends towards which the present technological evolution is rushing us. Whether we think we like it or not, it is quite probable that the healthy human psyche requires a proportion of roughage in its figurative diet. We are the heirs of a million years of a generally victorious struggle against cold, hunger, difficult terrain, carnivorous cunning; our nervous and glandular balance has evolved under the stress of exertion, effort, endurance. Individuals reared in the complete absence of such stimuli are not apt to be healthy or sane. A prudish avoidance or concealment of physical challenge in the world about us is much more apt to result in a pseudo-refinement, a pseudo-spirituality with an accompanying drive towards cruelty and violence in some specialized department of civilization, than it is to result in the development of full-blooded humans capable of the exercise of all the nobler human emotions. "Overcivilized" (i.e., culturally imbalanced) societies of the past are notorious for mass exercises in cruelty—gladiatorial combats, animal baiting, gang slave labor, massacres of prisoners and the like. After the experiences of the last world war and in the face of mounting statistics of mechanical violence in our own cities and highways, can we confidently assert that such a compensation mechanism is not at work in our own society?   15

To an indeterminate but certainly very large extent, the shape and structure of our economy is being fixed by a mistaken urge to escape all demands upon, and challenges to, our somas. "Our abundant society," says Paul Goodman, "is at present simply deficient in many of the most elementary objective opportunities and worth-while goods that could make growing up possible. It is lacking in enough man's work. . . . It is lacking in the opportunity to be useful . . . it thwarts aptitudes and creates stupidity . . . it dampers animal ardour. . . ." Is it pure coincidence that at the same time the economy as a whole is being shaped towards releases of destructive energy and collective violence on an utterly unprecedented scale?   16

It does not follow that the alternative to this mode of evolution lies in a regression towards a Spartan or a primitive social pattern. What is required is the opening up of our productive arrangements to a new intensity and opportunity for personal skill, personal creative mastery or useful processes, personal contact with the basic aliment of life. This implies a re-organization of the technical and economic landscape, a retreat from over-centralization, over-organization and over-mechanization; a re-emphasis of the human scale, a closer symbiosis between the human community, the soil and the total pattern of indigenous—both living and inorganic—resources. It implies a re-direction of the enormous social energy now consumed by the Frankenstein drive towards endlessly increasing complexity, power, size and fake refinement. Such a shift, one can guess, would result in a society boasting far less applied horsepower but far more applied science, skill and artistry; less plate-glass, plastic and chrome and more lovingly-laid masonry and beautifully worked wood; fewer superhighways but more richly diversified countrysides, towns and cities; less speed and multiplication but greater fruitfulness. Above all, the insensate lust for aggrandizement and technological-mercantile conquest which characterizes our culture would diminish before the lure of self-conquest, of internal, personal and community cultivation. But without a renaissance of pride and delight in grasping and manipulating the stubborn but priceless realities of the soil, of rock, of timber; of growth, muscular effort, discomfort and even danger, the glitteringly sterile domination of unrelieved mechanism will crystallize about us into the nightmare environment fore-shadowed by a Capek, a Huxley or an Orwell.*   17

* Paragraph 17: What type of sentence structure is used in the last sentence? Is it appropriate here?

The Whole Selection

1 The author evidently regards our contemporary society as "overcivilized" or "culturally imbalanced" when compared with Victorian society. What were the specific elements of "balance" in Victorian society, as suggested by the author?
2 Does the author depend more upon comparison or upon contrast in analyzing his subject?
3 What function does the last paragraph serve in relation to the whole essay?
4 The use of metaphor enlivens van Dresser's style. Select several metaphors from his essay, and then try to determine what they have in common. This analysis will help you understand the nature of metaphor. The essence of metaphor is the use of comparison in suggesting or applying a new meaning, thus making an old word perform new tricks. You will also be able to decide what makes one metaphor more effective than another. Decide which are the most effective among your choices. Remember that metaphors exist not only in lengthy comparisons but also in single nouns, adjectives, and other words.
5 Do you think the title of the essay is precise?

Word Study *carapace, esoteric, asepsis, enclave, nubile, Hephaestic, vestigial, unctuously, euphemic*

AN ASSIGNMENT FOR INTELLECTUALS

RAYMOND LEOPOLD BRUCKBERGER

What is the role of the American intellectual in the world today? And what should it be? In attempting to answer these questions it is natural for me, a Frenchman, to draw upon the experience of European intellectuals for comparisons.

1

Historians agree that the Encyclopedists and Rousseau prepared the French Revolution and gave it orientation. From the time of the Napoleonic enslavement of Europe, it has been the intellectuals who have dared to defy one tyranny after another—from Chateaubriand even to General de Gaulle, who declared that the two pillars of the anti-Nazi Resistance were a stump of a sword and French thought.

2

The high estate of the intellectual in Europe goes back to the Middle Ages when three powers had sovereign domain: the Pope, the Emperor, and the Universities—particularly the University of Paris. This respect for the power of the "clerics"—to use Julien Benda's term—has always been strictly a European phenomenon. As the story goes, when President Roosevelt mentioned the Pope to Stalin, Stalin laughed and asked, "How many divisions has the Pope?" This was an Asian chief speaking, not a European statesman; for though the medieval forms of the tradition may have crumbled, European thought is today alive as ever and its spiritual force commands the same power and prestige.*

3

Much as I dislike the term "intellectual," there is no other to designate the social role of those who serve in the realm of ideas exactly as the military serve by arms and the ecclesiastics serve the church. The thirteenth-century Bavarian philosopher Albertus Magnus—a Dominican who was a professor at the University of Paris—defined the intellectual's role perfectly when he said: "Our mission is to tell whether an action is good or bad, not by passing sentence as do the judges, but according to the truth as do the sages; and to do this truly, whoever may be the author of the action and whatever his position, be it below or above our own."†

4

Thus, by tradition, the European intellectual has a special character —a "vocation" beyond the limits of his own profession of writing or science or teaching. He believes himself called (*vocatus*) to a more universal responsibility: to keep watch on the world and call the plays as he sees them—at whatever risk to himself. The dangers of his position are as real as poverty, exile, prison, or death; and, unlike the soldier or the priest, he has no organized body to defend him. Someone is always accusing him of interfering in matters which do not concern him; the charge is

---

* Paragraph 3: What does the term "clerics" mean here?

† Paragraph 4: To which of the three groups in paragraph 3 does the intellectual belong?

familiar, and he is not frightened by it. But the present plight of the intellectual in Europe is something different. Today society is trying to isolate and silence him: the governing classes hate him secretly and despise him for being poor; the Communists try to use him. Yet he carries on, sowing unrest—the very kind of unrest which can ultimately bring a revolution, a revolution that will in turn cast him out once again.   5

This is the responsibility, the vocation, and the danger which the intellectual lives by. In this tradition the pamphlet and the manifesto have had a very special role—and a different meaning from that which the words carry in American. In Europe, the pamphlet is a short piece of writing essentially polemic in nature, concerned with a problem of the moment. Many of the most famous have first appeared anonymously because of the danger to the authors—Pascal, Voltaire, Chateaubriand, Victor Hugo, Zola, and Bernanos have written excellent pamphlets.   6

The manifesto is something different: a declaration on a particular or universal problem which seeks to attract attention by the inherent authority of the names of its signers. The most famous was, of course, the Communist Manifesto, but I remember an epidemic of them in France just before the war. At every street corner somebody asked for your signature —for good cause and for no cause at all.   7

When a manifesto is well phrased, appears at the right moment, and when the signers command respect, its importance may be immense. You may remember the manifesto in favor of their country's action which was issued by a few eminent Italian intellectuals when Italy changed sides at the end of the war. Published throughout the world, this manifesto rendered a service to country greater than arms.   8

Is the place of the intellectual in the United States a different one? Historically, no. Certainly the great revolutionary movement whose climax was American independence was in large part led by intellectuals. As the Encyclopedists prepared and oriented the French Revolution, the American intellectuals prepared and oriented their Revolution. Of course, the eighteenth-century American intellectuals were moved by a totally different philosophy from that of the Encyclopedists, just as the American Revolution has a totally different meaning from the French.   9

In fact, the American Revolution is the only one in modern history which, rather than devouring the intellectuals who prepared it, carried them to power. Most of the signatories of the Declaration of Independence *were* intellectuals. This tradition is ingrained in America, whose greatest statesmen have been intellectuals—Jefferson and Lincoln, for example. These statesmen performed their political functions, but at the same time they felt a more universal responsibility, and they actively defined this responsibility. Thanks to them there is in America a living school of political science. In fact, it is at the moment the only one perfectly adapted to the emergencies of the contemporary world and one which can be victoriously opposed to Communism. A European who follows American politics will be struck by the constant reference in the press and from the platform to this political philosophy, to the historical events through which it was best expressed, to the great statesmen who were its best representatives.*   10

There is, however, in America today a growing class of intellectuals who are not involved in politics—at least, this is not their profession. As all intellectuals in all countries, these people talk a great deal. What do they say about themselves; how do they define their position? Speaking in generalizations, as I am doing at the moment, one is liable to be unjust and overlook individual cases. May I be pardoned or criticized if I am wrong, but it seems to me that the attitude of the American intellectual in comparison with his European counterpart is based on frustration and an inferiority complex. I am continually meeting people who tell me that the intellectual in Europe enjoys a position which, if not happier, is at least more dignified than that of the intellectual in America. They say that he is more respected and that his influence upon the affairs of his country is infinitely greater. Whose fault is this? They go on to tell me that the fault rests with the American people, who have no appreciation for things of the intellect. I wonder whether it is not also in great measure the fault of the American intellectuals themselves.†   11

Modern philosophy, which is in essence Cartesian and idealistic, separates mind from matter, and this has facilitated the isolation of the intellectual in Europe as well as in America. The intellectual is encouraged to remain in the sphere of abstractions, leaving to cynics and realists the domains of the breadth and wealth of the world. But the fault for this state of affairs lies first of all with modern philosophy and with the intellectuals who have taught it. They have no cause to complain of the ditch which they themselves have dug between themselves and reality.‡   12

On the other hand, there hovered over the nineteenth century a utopian vision of the fraternal relations among peoples and a boundless ambition for international harmony. At that time people believed themselves to be more fully a part of humanity as they became less intensely French, for example. The contrary is true. In France we have recently learned that being less and less French does not mean becoming more human but instead, up to 1945, becoming more and more German and

* Paragraph 10: Why were Jefferson and Lincoln not merely statesmen but also intellectuals?

† Paragraph 11: What contrast is made between the European and the American intellectual?

‡ Paragraph 12: What is the meaning—obviously unfavorable—of "idealistic" here? What does it generally mean?

today, more and more Russian. For better or for worse, we are all bound to our countries. In Europe as in America, this dreamy international philosophy has left the intellectual far behind in a world which spins ever more quickly. The world has not turned down the intellectual's services; it is the intellectual who has refused to understand the profound laws of reality which, after all, govern the world. And in refusing to understand, he betrays his mission. It is not enough for a philosophy to be proclaimed as such in order to achieve dignity of the spirit; it still has got to be true. If the intellectual loses his concern with truth, does he not also lose his own title to honor?   13

What have the American intellectuals done to acquire in their country the position of authority and respect which they say the intellectual enjoys in Europe? They are serious in their own professions. If they are novelists or playwrights, they write good novels and plays. Physicists and chemists do excellent work in the world's finest laboratories. The jurists define the law. And so it goes. But are they truly aware of the additional responsibility which may draw them away from their work from time to time, which may lead them to questions which require answers on a universal level—that is, the level of intelligence itself? In general, I do not think so. Recently I dared to suggest mildly that American novelists ought to feel a somewhat deeper responsibility to their country for the false picture which the world has of her. I was answered by a whole concert of indignant replies—as if I had set fire to the temple of Minerva with my own hand. Well, let me repeat the offense. It is my conviction that the American intellectuals have an immense sin of omission on their conscience, and that it has poisoned their whole lives.*   14

In short, the American intellectual often tends to say that his country has failed him, that she will not give him the honor which is his due, and that he feels like a spiritual exile. I wonder if the contrary is not true. Perhaps the American intellectual has failed his country, and perhaps he is more deeply missed than is at first apparent. When the intellectual turns his back on his country, his place remains empty—while he complains that he has no place at all.   15

This misunderstanding would indeed be comic if a nation could get along without intellectuals. Yes, the American intellectuals should stop complaining about America. It would be more in order for America to complain about them. All too often, it seems as if their country were of no interest to them. They above all are bound to their country for better or for worse. They need America, but America needs them still more; their service and their intelligent sympathy. What is happening today in the United States has immense significance, not only on a national level but

---

* Paragraph 14: What is the "immense sin of omission"?

on the universal level—precisely there where the intellectual belongs. The American intellectual is failing his duty, the duty to which he is called. For there is no one, or at any rate almost no one, to understand and explain to the world the universal significance of the current American experiment.   16

The rights of man are at stake today throughout the world. The various kinds of socialism, and particularly Marxist socialism, tend to convince men to hand over their liberty to the State in much the same frame of mind as the patient parts with his appendix: he doesn't feel any worse, and he doesn't risk a sudden appendicitis. On the contrary, the American experiment tends to prove that freedom not only remains the best possible regime, but a necessary one for the continued existence of man as a thinking animal. Man cannot live without liberty any more than a fish can live without water; liberty is his natural element and the excellence of humanity, which each man carries within him, dies with the death of liberty.*   17

Absurd and dangerous as socialism and the Russian experiment may be for mankind, allies and defenders of them have been found everywhere among intellectuals. The same is not true of freedom and the American experiment. This is a very serious situation, serious in view of the destiny of man, and so grave that one wonders whether the game is not already lost, whether the world's intellectuals have not already cast their vote against freedom, and whether soon we will have left to us only a choice between an intellectual culture without freedom and freedom without culture. If I should be faced with this choice, I should prefer freedom a thousand times even if it means a barbarian existence. Because, finally, culture cannot survive without liberty, and freedom of thought is at the base of all culture.   18

Yet I am persuaded that if the American intellectuals saw this situation clearly they would have the courage to face it, and place themselves on the side of freedom. William Faulkner spoke for them, I think, when he said on receiving the Nobel Prize: "I decline to accept the end of man." American intellectuals have not seen, until now—in the vast moral and spiritual disorder which has seized Europe—the extent to which man and his fate are bound to America and to her own tradition of liberty. And I mean America; her people, her conception of living, her own culture—I do not mean American policy or the State Department. One may have affection for America and a high appreciation of the immense budding cultural resources inherent in the American people, and have but a very sorry esteem for the State Department and its official policy. This is an important distinction to make if one does not wish to compromise the

* Paragraphs 16 and 17: What contrast does the author see between Marxism and "the American experiment"?

American tradition with official blundering. If the American intellectual were clearly aware of the reservoir of hope which his country represents for the entire world, would he not carry his country's conception of man to a waiting world? The day he takes on this responsibility and accepts it fully, not only America but the entire world will give him the place of honor he so desperately wants. Certainly, he will have to pay the price for the honor and the place, but after all, the old European continent is built on martyrdom, that is to say, on obdurate thought bathed in its own blood.*   19

Since nothing is easier than to resort to ambiguities on this subject, I shall try to be very clear. There is a chasm between giving testimony (which may bring martyrdom and which is response to a vocation) and propaganda. This kind of testimony is essentially objective and in honor of truth, which means that it is for the good of man and for his liberation from all untruth. Propaganda, on the contrary, is committed, it has something to gain, it is in the service of a party, a nation, a class, or a commercial enterprise. Honor and truth are there only by accident when they are there at all. Propaganda exploits the needs and instincts of man and enslaves bit by bit, rather than aiding to free him. The intellectuals fall into dishonor when they stoop to the level of propaganda, but it is the essence of their mission to give testimony.   20

This does not mean that they should abandon their work. American writers must continue to write novels and plays in their own style and to the best of their ability—this is their profession. But from time to time they must concern themselves directly with the present state of stress of man and with the aid which their testimony may bring—this, to me, appears to be their vocation. When Bernanos was writing his book on the Spanish Civil War, I heard him say: "I am betraying my profession [*métier*] for my vocation." He certainly was not betraying his profession, since he was writing one of his best books, but in doing so he abandoned the novel for the pamphlet, in other words, for direct testimony in behalf of man. But he realized that he was accomplishing his highest vocation as an intellectual.   21

There is evidence that the American intellectuals are very close to a similar choice. William Faulkner recently published in this magazine an article entitled "On Privacy—The American Dream: What Happened to It." The article seemed to me to be of great significance in that it broke with isolation. In it the greatest American novelist wrote a pamphlet, in the French sense of the word. I shall not discuss the substance of the article; that is Mr. Faulkner's business and he says very well what he has to say. Yet the inferiority complex of the American intellectual, which I have already mentioned, appears in it here and there.   22

* Paragraph 19: What does "the end of man" mean here?

". . . artists in America don't have to have privacy because they don't need to be artists as far as America is concerned," Faulkner says. "America doesn't need artists because they don't count in America. . . ." 23

Why, having affirmed that his privacy has been shamefully violated, does Mr. Faulkner conclude that America has no need of artists and that they don't count in or for America? In France a writer like Camus has had to put up with similar intrusions on his privacy, and even some more serious. One day a newspaperwoman took a job as a maid in his house and spent her time reading his private letters instead of cleaning house. Camus was not very happy about the matter, but that's not the point. It never occurred to him to draw the conclusion from one bad personal experience that France doesn't need artists or that they don't count in France. The truth is, of course, that if artists count in France it is not because they are better treated than they are in America but that, first of all, France counts for them. Every day, throughout the world, America is cruelly insulted; not only for her politics, which would be of little importance, but for her institutions, her people, and her way of life. The American intellectuals remain all but silent. 24

Mr. Faulkner must have felt personally annoyed or threatened, and it was his right to fight back. I do not believe that he fell short of his function as a writer for this reason, or that he became a lesser novelist. But would it be fanciful or absurd or unjust to imagine that certain intellectuals might feel themselves touched to the quick, personally insulted or personally revolted by the stupid calumnies brought against their country every day throughout the world, to the great damage, not only of their country, but of man and of Western civilization? That civilization to which America is so cruelly necessary. Is it fanciful, absurd, or unjust to imagine that these intellectuals might some day take up the defense of their insulted country clearly, without anger but without cowardice, that they might some day put their world prestige to the service of their country, not for the benefit of a propaganda machine or a political line, not for the State Department, but in a way which would be above politics and even national interest; in honor of truth and justice? Every man has a right to truth, and it should be neither veiled nor disfigured; and America, like every human society, has a right to be known as she is, and the injustices which are done her should in one way or another be repaired.* 25

Now that I have started on the subject there seems no reason why I should stop before I have said all I think. The world needs America, not so much her money or atomic bombs as the wisdom and courage of her

---

* Paragraph 25: Is sentence 4, "That civilization . . . ," grammatically acceptable? Is it properly punctuated? In answering this question, read this and the preceding sentence aloud. Observe how sound (particularly intonation) is frequently a help in determining the structure and punctuation of written English.

people, the example of her institutions, her jealous regard for the freedom
of the individual, and her social equilibrium.*   26

If a few great American intellectuals—writers, scientists, or labor
leaders—those who have won incontestable prestige internationally as the
result of their various achievements, would gather together and write a
manifesto dictated only by their conscience—over and above even their
love for their country—and by their grave concern for the destiny of man
("I decline to accept the end of man")—such a manifesto would surely
have incredible importance and would dissipate many of the misunderstandings between the American people and the other peoples of the
earth. I believe that far from harming the quality of their intellectual effort,
such testimony would honor those whose responsibility it was. For they
would have surpassed the limitations of their profession and expressed
their vocation and their concern for the salvation of man and his truth.   27

* Paragraph 26: What is America's "social equilibrium"?

The Whole Selection

1 Bruckberger's purpose is clearly and briefly set forth in his opening
   paragraph. What are his answers to the two questions raised there?
2 Is the central purpose of this essay comparison and contrast, or are
   comparison and contrast used essentially as techniques of analysis, as
   methods of developing the central purpose?
3 What comparisons or contrasts does the author draw between the
   American intellectual and his European counterpart as well as his
   American forebears?
4 In view of Bruckberger's charge, in paragraphs 11 and 22, that the
   American intellectual has an inferiority complex, what special function
   do paragraphs 2 through 10 perform?
5 This essay is expository, but, like many explanations involving ideas, it
   tends to be persuasive. Persuasion requires the author to gain the good
   will of his particular audience, which is here the American intellectual.
   Point to some details in the essay by which the author seeks this good
   will. Also note that he does not hesitate to be forthright in his adverse
   criticisms of the American intellectual, for the author knows that his
   particular audience is one not to be coddled or cajoled. Cite some of
   these adverse criticisms.

Word Study polemic, Cartesian, utopian, ambiguity, calumny

REAL RELIGION—AND FALSE

BARBARA WARD

In the middle of 1954—a year otherwise marked in Russia by attempts to conciliate the ordinary citizens—the Soviet Government announced a new drive to wipe out religious influences among its people.   1

For some time past, in fact since the death of Stalin introduced some latitude into the movement of foreign correspondents around the country, reports have reached the West of life and growth in the supposedly moribund Russian Orthodox Church. Young people marry in church, children are baptized. The countryside takes its holidays on Saints' days.   2

Not only are old churches overflowing but many that had been left derelict are now restored to use. The Soviet citizen has the right, in theory, to petition the authorities for the building of a new church in his district. Correspondents now report that such churches are being built and that the faithful are supplying money for their upkeep and for the training and livelihood of Orthodox priests. However difficult it may be to judge the scale of this religious activity, it seems certain that it is widespread, is strongly rooted and represents a genuine movement of popular desire.   3

Yet a regime which has set itself to concilate the popular mood by such measures as a cheapening of prices, the attempt to increase consumer goods, the announcing of amnesties, a release of prisoners and concessions offered even to the unlucky peasants—this regime is apparently setting its face against the face of the church's revival and resorting once more to an antireligious campaign.*   4

But the exception is not really surprising. The concessions made in other fields leave the authority and the pretensions of the Soviet bureaucracy more or less intact. To these bureaucrats the dangerous and disturbing fact about Christianity is that, at the deepest level of human experience, in the imagination and will of the individual citizen, it can set up a divided allegiance, and that division may in time prove a loophole of freedom, a small but widening rift in the absolute claims of the total state.   5

Consider the symbolism of the story of Christmas which is being told in we know not how many thousands of Russian homes. It is hardly possible to conceive a more profound contradiction of every principle upon which the authority of the Soviet administration is based. Many of the worst excesses of the regime have been committed on the plea of raising at breakneck speed the country's material standards.   6

The forced collectivization of agriculture which killed millions of

---

* Paragraph 4: Point out the use of parallel structure in the phrasing here. What is the grammatical subject of the main clause in the sentence? Name the grammatical structure of this sentence. What is the sentence's rhetorical structure? Is the latter effective here?

peasants and left agricultural standards permanently depressed was justified by the need to feed the cities quickly. Industrialization schemes in the Urals which, according to eyewitnesses, caused casualties among untrained workers equivalent to slaughter on the battlefield, were rushed through in order to put more steel and power behind the present generation of Soviet workers.   7

Today the more or less compulsory migration of thousands of young people to new industrial areas in Central Asia—not to speak of the maintenance of forced-labor camps throughout Siberia—is based upon the need to force the growth of the whole physical apparatus of the Soviet empire. The cult of bigness and immediate results, the cult of frantic material growth, the worship of machines, of technology, the utter adulation of physical power—these are the psychological drives which spur on the Soviet rulers and which they attempt to communicate to those they rule.   8

But can such a communication be completely achieved if somewhere in the mind of individual men and women is lodged another image—of the Lord of life needing no more material convenience for His coming than a stable and a truss of straw? The story of Bethlehem does not contradict in any way the aim of realizing a reasonable and decent living for ordinary families. Part of its pathos lies explicitly in the lack, at the birth of Christ, of even the simplest standards. Equally, however, the choice of so stark a material setting and of such uncompromising simplicity passes a judgment, repeated throughout the Gospels, upon the megalomania of pursuing at headlong speed, and at whatever social and human cost, an ever more elaborate material apparatus for society.*   9

Perhaps this is simply one aspect of a larger contradiction between the purposes of Soviet state power and the natural direction of Christian faith. For the Russian bureaucrat, society is the unit. Historically the clash of classes has brought it into being. Today, as "the classless society," it alone has significance, its needs alone are dominant and bureaucrats determine what those needs may be—among them, this constant aggrandizement of material power.   10

But the story of Christmas begins with an ironic reversal of such values. The whole, ponderous machinery of the state goes into action but for one purpose only—to fix the birthplace of a single child. Joseph and Mary are brought to Bethlehem by the order of Augustus Caesar. The herding of millions of Roman subjects to their birthplace occurs as part of a general census—in other words, a centralizing act of state power, counting heads and establishing categories, comparable to the recent census in Communist China.   11

* Paragraphs 7 through 9: How do these paragraphs relate to paragraph 6?

But this vast and anonymous bureaucratic measure becomes in the event the setting for the most personal of human experiences—the birth of a child. Two thousand years later no one remembers that census. The records of Caesar Augustus, measuring his imperial power, have moldered away. But Russian children today still learn of the mother and the child and the foster father alone in the stable on a winter's night. The empire has faded. The family remains.*   12

This stamp of privacy and personality, this significance placed not on the mass but on the individual soul, marks all the ceremonies and festivals of the Christian faith. The baptism which Russian parents give their children consecrates them as children of God, not of the state. The marriage they celebrate before the priest proclaims a personal fidelity not dictated by state needs or social convenience. Each act has in it the germs of independence, for it acknowledges another order of reality in which the state, however total, has no part.   13

This is the central fact in the inability of the Soviet system to tolerate a serious revival of religious faith. So long as the state's claims are total, Caesar cannot make place for God. This fundamental hostility is the more remarkable in that in Russia the Christian Church has gone as far as religious organization can in identifying itself with the purposes and policies of the regime.   14

It is not a revolutionary church, or rather it conforms to the Soviet version of revolution. It inculcates obedience. It accepts the subject's duty of submission. It plays its part in forwarding Soviet foreign policy. It is used, by the Soviets, in their propaganda abroad. Yet no subservience can finally undo the risk of divided allegiance.   15

In the Christmas festivities, as Twelfth Night approaches, the Wise Men, the Magi, the Kings from the East, come to Bethlehem and at the feet of the Child they lay their crowns and their gifts. No total government can tolerate this reversal of roles. The state must wear the crown and command the gifts and since religion is inseparable from a dual loyalty, religion itself must cease. Here, at least, there is still no place for "co-existence" in Soviet philosophy.   16

The Western World, surveying this fateful division at the heart of Communist society, may perhaps be tempted to a certain complacency. There are many who argue that, in the West, religious influences are growing and that they work harmoniously with government. In 1954 alone, such events as Dr. Billy Graham's enormously successful evangelical mission to England or the summer gathering of Christian representatives from every nation on earth at the World Council of Churches at Evanston, Ill., have

---

* Paragraphs 10 through 12: What psychological effect does the reference to the Holy Family have upon the reader?

been demonstrations of how many millions in the West spontaneously acknowledge or seek a religious view of life.   17

In the United States there have even been moves to associate the democratic state more formally with the religious impulses of the people. While church attendance has risen to a higher level than ever before, postage stamps bearing a religious message have been inaugurated with some solemnity by the President and a vigorous campaign has been made to "put God into the Constitution" and into the school children's oath of loyalty. Is there not reason here for a certain self-congratulation, a certain thankfulness that we are "not as the rest of men," especially as these Communists who persecute religion and seek to stamp out the image of God?   18

But before we give way to any sense of security and superiority, it would be as well, perhaps, to give a rather more searching look at this comparison between Soviet and Western attitudes. What disturbs the Communist rulers is not the phraseology of religion, the lip-service that may be paid to it, or the speeches and declarations made in its favor. They are apprehensive before the profound social consequences of a religion that is carried into practice and not simply acknowledged.   19

In concrete terms, they fear a decline in the hold on men's minds of successful materialism. They fear a growing sense of the importance of persons, of individual men and women and a decline in the habit of thinking in categories, either of praise—the workers, the toiling masses—or of blame—the reactionaries, the imperialists, the Fascist-beasts.   20

Above all, they fear standards of judgment and behavior which claim autonomy from state and nation and do not regard the interests of the Soviet community as the ultimate criterion of good and evil. If all these concrete consequences of religious thinking can be observed in the West, then, indeed, there can be no doubt of the strengthening of the forces which the Communists must fear and whose extension they must bitterly oppose. But is the balance sheet really so clear?   21

In fact, in each category, there is room in the West for self-examination rather than complacency. There is admittedly a less frantic pursuit of physical aggrandizement in the West, less readiness to sacrifice the substance of human life to grandiose schemes for the material glorification of society. The web of economic life is woven in the main to satisfy the needs of ordinary families and not to magnify bureaucracy or aggrandize state power.   22

Yet no one surely can be content with standards achieved by millions of those families—least of all, say, in France, where the share of national wealth allotted to the working class is lower than before the war, or in Germany where, as a wave of strikes last summer reminded us, national income has risen more quickly than the workers' share of it.   23

Moreover, once the relatively wealthy arena of the Atlantic world is left behind, the "materialism" of Western wealth begins to appear greedy and exclusive in contrast with the misery elsewhere. It is a particularly sobering thought that the Western Powers, for all their resources, have allowed the problem of the world's refugees to continue—to permit for years in many cases conditions as pitiable and forsaken as the stable of Bethlehem itself.   24

One reason for this neglect is undoubtedly the continuance, in the West as in the East, of the habit of thinking by categories. The term "refugees" ceases to represent the suffering of individual men and women. It becomes a "problem" instead. Indeed, it seems that thinking in terms of groups, not persons, has increased, not diminished, in the West for all the supposed increase in personal religion.*   25

When people succumb to generalized suspicion, when they accept chance association as proof of guilt, when they lump men together according to degrees of orthodoxy, when they make color, not human dignity, the test of citizenship, they are in fact judging men and women as groups, categories, tendencies, problems or dangers, and no longer as individuals, each unique, each responsible, each of infinite worth.†   26

In 1954, the declaration of basic human values inherent in the Supreme Court's outlawing of segregation in American schools is tarnished, among millions of Africans, by the opposite determination of the supposedly Christian Government of South Africa to pursue, under the name of *Apartheid,* policies which condemn the black citizen to permanent inferiority.   27

This tendency to think by categories is apparent in Europe as well as in Africa. After all the brave attempts to establish a new society based on the transcendence of old groups, the 1954 debates on the European Defense Community demonstrated how many Frenchmen still think of Germans not as individual men and women sharing common problems of security and livelihood but as a menacing collectivity. And their attitude is one more proof that, in the free world as in the Soviet half, the nation-state is still very largely accepted as the ultimate source of authority and value.   28

There is little to suggest that a reviving sense of religion in the West is leading to abatements of sovereignty, to a more eager search for co-operation and partnership among the nations. In some quarters, indeed, it is almost as though God were being revived as a tribal deity to safeguard and protect the interests of particular nations, a God who is "on our side," a God who can be mobilized as an auxiliary in the "fight against atheistic

* Paragraph 25: How does the conclusion here relate to the thought of paragraph 20?

† Paragraph 26: Is the use of the periodic sentence appropriate here?

communism." In the land even of Lincoln, there seems little trace of the great President's sense of his nation standing under the judgment of God, of expiating, even while it struggled against slavery, its own sins, failures and shortcomings.   29

But religion which is a mere adjunct of national purpose is a religion that even the Soviets can tolerate. What they fear is a religion that transcends frontiers and can challenge the purpose and performance of the nation-state.*   30

It is, in fact, an irony of any religious revival in the West that so long as it is thought of in purely instrumental terms—as something which helps us in the "cold war," or something which strengthens the existing social structure—it loses its power to do any of these things. But a religious revival which sent Western material plenty to relieve want in the world at large, which restored charity and trust among citizens, which taught the nations to place the building of a common human society above the pretensions of absolute sovereignty—such a religious revival would, before long, leave the pressure of communism as no more than a fading memory in the mind of man.†   31

The Soviet instinct to crush out religion is thus not ill-judged. Potentially religion is the force that can undermine their idolatry of state power and their material megalomania. The error is to believe that such a force has yet been mobilized on any serious scale in the Western World.   32

* Paragraph 30: What is the force of the first word here?

† Paragraph 31: To be sure that you understand it, try to present the thought of this paragraph in your own words.

The Whole Selection

1 What are some of the specific comparisons and contrasts made in this essay?
2 Could the first four paragraphs have been presented as one? In answering this question, note that this essay first appeared in *The New York Times*. Why do newspapers usually use short paragraphs?
3 What transitional devices does the author use to connect her paragraphs?
4 Does the author define "real religion"?
5 What special purpose does paragraph 16 have for the organization of the whole essay?

Word Study *moribund, derelict, bureaucracy, megalomania, aggrandizement, subservience, autonomy*

KENNETH B. CLARK

Man is an organism that seeks and demands explanations. He has sought to understand the mysteries of his environment. He has asked questions, and searched for answers, about his origin and the meaning of his existence. He has been profoundly concerned and anxious about his ability to survive in the face of his comparative physical weaknesses and the multiple dangers of his enviornment. Man asks these questions and seeks their answers because he is an intelligent being who is not limited to mere behavioral interactions with his environment. He is a conscious, reflective, evaluative, anxious being who is required to be as responsive to the realities of his ideational and created environments as to his physical and biological environments. The fact of human intelligence demands this. Human intelligence also provides the key to the answers to the questions it is capable of raising. Man believes that he has survived as a species and will continue to survive in spite of his skeletal weakness because he has the intelligence necessary to probe, to seek to understand and to control the environmental forces that threaten him.   1

So far, his experience supports this intellectual circularity and chauvinism.   2

The critical question of this period of human history—the answer to which, paradoxically, must also be obtained through the critical use of man's mind—is whether human intelligence as traditionally defined offers any reliable assurance of human survival. This question may seem hopelessly abstract, even trite. But nothing could be more concrete. Is pure intelligence enough to protect man from self-inflicted destruction?   3

Paradox and irony are inherent in this question:

—The choice is between a world of leisure, of productive and creative humanity, or a world destroyed through human intelligence. Man's understanding and his mastery of matter and energy justify his claims to godlike superiority; provide him with the basis for enriching and deepening human experience; and, at the same time, provide him with the instruments for ultimate destruction.   4

—Science and technology, among the constructive benefits of human intelligence, cannot, at present, be divorced from possible destruction or inhuman uses. Some have sought to resolve this dilemma by suggesting that certain scientific discoveries be destroyed or blocked before fulfillment. Yet the power of thought cannot be artificially or arbitrarily controlled without atrophy. We cannot have the benefits of the unfettered mind without freedom and risk. To control intelligence in the attempt to insure only benevolent consequences would be a Pyrrhic victory sentencing the human race to ignorance, stagnation and decadence, and probably would be impossible.   5

—Free human intelligence and its richest consequences—science, technology, art, literature, philosophy and religion—are essential to human progress and survival. But in their pure form, they are not enough. They do not in themselves reduce the capricious dangers and hazards to life. They bring with them now the novel and awesome possibility of self-inflicted annihilation.   6

Now our gods are the gods of Intelligence, Science and Technology. These gods have their powerful priests and apostles. Their true believers are uncritically abject, obsequious and worshipful in the faith that these omnipotent and omniscient gods will protect and save them and enrich their lives. But there remains the gnawing suspicion that these contemporary gods are fickle and treacherous. They promise and they taunt. They fulfill and they tantalize. They offer the extension and the deepening of life and they threaten imminent extinction. They play with man as they dare him to question their power. They know that man dares not doubt, dares not question and dares not now reject them because to do so would be to throw him back to a state of futility, helplessness, insecurity and despair even more stultifying than that faced by his most primitive ancestors. Man now emerges as the victorious prisoner of his own intelligence. He cowers in each victory. As he rockets to the moon, he plans the futility of protection from nuclear devastation on earth.   7

This paradox of human intelligence can only be resolved through the use of courageous and creative human intelligence. A reasonable starting postulate could be that the present threats to survival do not result from too much intelligence, or too much science or even from too much technology. Like his ancestors who faced crises of survival, contemporary man is also threatened by ignorance. The ignorance of modern man, however, is not that which can be cured by the exercise of pure intelligence. His critical ignorance lies in an inadequate functional sense of social morality.   8

Social morality is illusive and difficult to define. It involves not only man's intelligence but his feelings and his total being.   9

Social morality depends upon man's capacity to give and to receive love, to be kind and to be empathic. Love in its most concrete sense is a primary emotion essential to the preservation of the species. It is a positive and adaptive emotion, which involves an affinity and desire for closeness with another human being. It is essential for survival. Kindness may be viewed as the generalized expression of love, concern and sensitivity in interpersonal relations. A kind person seeks to be helpful. Empathy is the ability to feel into and to identify with the needs of another human being. An empathic person shares another's concerns, joys, anguish, despair, frustrations, hopes and aspirations as if they were his own. Empathy, unlike love, is not concrete and primary but rather requires the capacity for abstract thought. Empathy is not possible for a limited, defective, egocentric or animalistic human organism. Without empathy, social morality, social responsibility, justice, and human society itself would not be possible. Empathy involves the convergence of human intelligence, love and kindness.   10

There are those who are described and who describe themselves as tough-minded realists who contend that love, kindness and empathy are mere disguises for more powerful and primitive egocentric and animalistic impulses in man. They contend that there is no stable basis for social morality and that all morality is a thin pretensive veneer quick to disappear under stress, deprivation or adversity. This debate between the advocates of man's moral capacity and obligations and those who contend that only egocentric power imperatives are important has dominated man's struggle to define the dimensions of his humanity from the awakening of human consciousness up to the present Vietnam protests.   11

Those who argue that man is incapable of a dependable functional form of social morality have given up and written the epitaph of the human species. This is so because the chief threat to human survival is to be found in the exercise of pure, amoral human intelligence in the service of man's irrational, primitive, egocentric, animalistic impulses harnessed to his blind quest for power and status.   12

Probably the only protection for contemporary man is to discover how to use his intelligence in the service of love and kindness. The training of human intelligence must include the simultaneous development of the empathic capacity. Only in this way can intelligence be made an instrument of social morality and responsibility—and thereby increase the chances of survival.   13

The need to produce human beings with trained morally sensitive intelligence is essentially a challenge to educators and educational institutions. Traditionally, the realm of social morality was left to religion and the churches as guardians or custodians. But their failure to fulfill this responsibility and their yielding to the seductive lures of the men of wealth and pomp and power are documented by the history of the last two thousand years and have now resulted in the irrelevant "God Is Dead" theological rhetoric. The more pragmatic men of power have had no time or inclination to deal with the fundamental problems of social morality. For them simplistic Machiavellianism must remain the guiding principle of their decisions—power is morality, morality is power. This oversimplification increases the chances of nuclear devastation. We must therefore hope that educators and educational institutions have the capacity, the commitment and the time to instill moral sensitivity as an integral part of the complex pattern of functional human intelligence. Some way must be found in the training of human beings to give them the assurance to love, the security to be kind, and the integrity required for a functional empathy. 14

This task will not be any easier for our colleges and universities than it has been for our churches, for our universities are a part of a society dominated by power. They too seek the protection, safety and status that come with identification with those who have power. The avoidance of this socially and morally responsible role takes many forms —some subtle and some flagrant. Among the more subtle forms of escape are the postures and assertions of moral relativism, of academic detachment, of philosophical purity and scientific objectivity. 15

According to the proponents of moral relativism, right and wrong, good and bad, justice and injustice are relative values which are not subject to empirical, objective or consistent definition. They assert that moral values are determined by the society or culture within which the individual is socialized, and that the prevailing social norms will determine what a person believes and how he behaves toward his fellowman. Initially this view arose from the important work of the cultural anthropologists and reflected the growing liberalism and tolerance of human differences characteristic of certain aspects of twentieth-century American social science. But the fashionable oversimplification of moral relativism and its confusion with moral nihilism masked the basic fact that man is unique as a value-seeking and moral organism. Nor can the horrors of infanticide, genocide and Hitlerian Nazism be comprehended or dealt with within moral relativism's limited and naïve conceptual framework. Literalistic moral relativism must be seen as indifference, as insensitivity, and as moral and intellectual confusion. To the extent that colleges and universities promulgate this point of view without powerful countervailing probes, they provide an adequate escape from any moral commitment for themselves and they leave their students without moral guidelines essential for the responsible use of intelligence. 16

The same must be said for the postures of academic detachment and scientific objectivity when they are defined as precluding the making of moral judgments and the rejection of the responsibility to remedy that which is wrong or unjust in our society. It is argued that detachment and objectivity are required for the discovery of truth. But of what value is a soulless truth? Does not truth require meaning? And does not meaning require a context of values? Is there any meaningful or relevant truth without commitment? 17

How is it possible to study a slum objectively? What manner of human being can remain detached as he watches the dehumanization of other human beings? Why would one want to study a sick child except to make that child well?   18

Intellectual detachment and scientific objectivity can be most insidious and dangerous forms of moral irresponsibility. Indifference, equivocation and expediency avoid the risks engendered by the use of human intelligence for the attainment of social justice and human progress. When our colleges and universities become havens from value, when our teachers become defenders of such transparent escapes, they abdicate their responsibilities for moral leadership and they contribute to, if not help to create, the profound tragedy of the moral erosion and emptiness of those who have the intellectual gifts that might make human advancement and survival possible.   19

The persistent protests of a small number of our college students extensively reported in the newspapers beginning with the first sit-ins of Negro college students, followed by the Berkeley rebellion, and the Vietnam protests can be seen as symptomatic of the deep undercurrent of moral uneasiness of sensitive young people. They are demanding of their colleges and the universities some demonstration of humanity. They are demanding honesty. They are demanding evidence of concern with justice. They are demanding that colleges and universities be socially and morally relevant. They are few, and they are anguished and confused; but they are concerned—and they assume the risks of the concerned.   20

So far our colleges and universities and the men who control and run them have not yet answered these young people affirmatively. Perhaps they do not understand them. It is probably that the years of moral denial and studied blindness to flagrant problems of social injustice that were deemed essential to the efficient financing and administration of a large and complex educational institution have made it difficult and impractical to listen to pleas for dialogue and for resolution of fundamental moral issues. Our colleges and universities have a long history of default on important moral issues. They have frequently tried to make a virtue of isolation from the problems of the marketplace and from the anguished yearnings of the deprived and powerless people of our society. They have thrown in their lot with the powerful in government, business and industry. Their concern with purity of research is reconciled with relative ease as they accept larger and larger grants and subsidies from the Defense Department, from the C.I.A., and from big business for work on practical problems—problems of power. It is only when the issue is directly or indirectly one of social justice or fundamental social change that our colleges and universities raise questions concerning the propriety of institutional involvement or the role of a professor, and ask whether involvement is consistent with the pure and detached quest for truth.   21

An attempt at a somewhat balanced appraisal of the role of American universities requires one to mention some exceptions to these severe charges. Probably the chief exception would be found in the research and teaching in the medical and public health schools of our universities, which are directly tied to human need and human welfare. Their findings must be directly or indirectly relevant. They cannot be pompously trivial. But even they are more concerned with individual cure than with the prevention of the conditions of poverty and degradation that lead to disease. 22

There are many specific and relevant areas in which American colleges and universities have defaulted in providing morally sensitive intellectual leadership for our society: 23
—They have watched silently, and facilitated, the process whereby education from the primary grades on has become ruthlessly competitive and anxiety-producing—in which the possibility of empathy, concern for one's classmate and the use of superior intelligence as a social trust are precluded, as our children are required to learn by their experiences in the classroom, by the demands of their teachers and the insistence of their parents, that education is competition and that intelligence is a device to obtain superior status and economic advantage over others.   24
—Under the guise of efficiency, the demands of mass education and the pressure of limited facilities in colleges, they have facilitated the reduction of the educational process to the level of content retention required for the necessary score on the College Boards and the Graduate Record Examinations at the price of reflective and critical thought.   25
—They have permitted our elementary and secondary schools to become contaminated by and organized in terms of the educationally irrelevant factors of race and economic status.   26
—They have watched without sustained protests the erosion of the quality of education provided for minority group children and other lower-status children—erosion to the point of criminal inefficiency and dehumanization.   27
—They have watched in silence the creeping blight of our cities and the spawning of Negro ghettos, concerned only when the pathologies associated with the ghetto come too close to the walls of the university. Only then do they seek to protect themselves, sometimes through a ruthless and callous dispossessing of the unwanted lower-status people.   28
—They have abdicated any sustained, forthright moral leadership in America's attempt to resolve the anguish of its pervasive racial problem. Leadership in the civil rights struggle has come from civil rights organizations, from the federal courts, and more recently from the executive and legislative branches of the federal and some state governments; and from the Catholic, Protestant and Jewish churches and synagogues. De-

spite the commitment of some of their faculty, American colleges and universities have, as institutions, remained detached and nonrelevant to this major domestic issue of our times. Indeed colleges and universities are major bastions of a subtle and persistent form of white supremacy.   29

In summary, the major charge that must now be made against American colleges and universities is that they have not fulfilled their responsibility and obligation to develop and train human beings with a morally relevant and socially responsible intelligence. They have operated as if it were possible for a detached, amoral intelligence to be adaptive. They have not provided their students with the moral guidelines essential for the effective, creative and adaptive use of superior intelligence. They have not provided their faculties with the stimulation or protection for a socially responsible use of their own critical intelligence. And above all they have not provided the moral leadership for society—they have not alerted the public to the urgency of finding moral and democratic solutions to critical domestic and international problems.   30

Given these real and chronic deficiencies, how can one hope that American colleges and universities can become morally relevant in time to make any difference in the destiny of man? One can hope because one must. The deficiencies in our educational system are remediable. The first step in any attempt at remedying a problem is the courage to recognize it as a problem—followed by the commitment to change.   31

A realistic basis for hope is found in the fact that man has the capacity for empathy. He struggles for values. He insists and argues and demands and dies and kills in his tortuous and often pathetic quests for moral stabilities. Another basis for hope is that empathy, like intelligence, can be made more functional and effective through education. If it is trained and directed it can become meaningful for the individual and adaptive for the society. If it is untrained it becomes unpredictable, random, misdirected, or it atrophies. The acceptance of the responsibility to reinforce man's empathic capacity as an integral part of the responsibility to train intellect is now the clear challenge of relevance confronting contemporary educational institutions.   32

American higher education need not continue to subordinate itself to the goals of efficiency, expediency, power, status and success. Young people can be trained in our schools, colleges and universities to value critical and independent thought above affability; to value individuality and creativity above conformity and packaged opinions; to value evidence of concern, commitment and social sensitivity above personal acceptance and mere social success. Once they understand the stakes and the nature of the challenge, it will be possible for our colleges and universities to produce totally educated persons.   33

A truly educated person is trained to mesh his intelligence with his feelings in a disciplined whole. He cannot deny or subordinate either his brain or his heart because each is essential to the effective functioning of the other. Our colleges must provide the opportunities for students to test their courage to stand alone—to accept the risks of alienation and aloneness that come with the anguish and the torture of the search for moral commitment and disciplined, intelligent action. Colleges must be the place where human beings are prepared to bolster intelligence with compassion, courage and increasing wisdom. American colleges and universities will demonstrate that they are relevant to the crucial issues of our times, that they are morally adaptive, and therefore that they can contribute to the survival of the human race, when they fully and functionally accept as their responsibility the need to train individuals of moral intelligence who demonstrate by the totality of their lives that they understand that an injustice perpetrated upon any human being robs them of some of their humanity and demands of them personal, constructive and intelligent action for justice. Wisdom and moral sensitivity tempering human intelligence are not now ethical abstractions. They are survival imperatives. Relevant colleges and universities can and must make them real.   34

SCIENCE AND SENSIBILITY

J. BRONOWSKI

I came to England when I was twelve, and when I landed I could speak, rather badly, two words of English which I had learnt on the channel boat. I did not read English at all easily for two or three years after. The first writers in whom I was able to distinguish what my patient schoolmasters called style were, I remember, Macaulay and Joseph Conrad. I do not remember now whether at that time I was also able to distinguish between their styles. I read greedily, with excitement, with affection, with a perpetual sense of discovering a new and, I slowly realised, a great literature. But I was handicapped then, and I have been ever since, by the disorderly way in which I fell upon my masterpieces: Dickens cheek by jowl with Aphra Behn and Bernard Shaw, and elsewhere leaving tracts of neglected literature by the century. To this day I have not read the Waverley novels, and in consequence I have remained rather insensitive to historical romance, particularly if much of the conversation is in dialect.   1

I make these confessions because they seem to me to bear on many stories besides my own. The difficulties which I had are not mine alone, and they are not in any special way literary difficulties. On the contrary, what now strikes me about them is their likeness to the trouble which other people have with science. At bottom my difficulties in facing a strange literature are precisely the difficulties which all intelligent people today have in trying to make some order out of modern science.   2

We live surrounded by the apparatus of science: the Diesel engine and the experiment, the bottle of aspirins and the survey of opinion. We are hardly conscious of them; but behind them we are becoming conscious of a new importance in science. We are coming to understand that science is not a haphazard collection of manufacturing techniques carried out by a race of laboratory dwellers with acid-yellow fingers and steel-rimmed spectacles and no home life. Science, we are growing aware, is a method and a force of its own, which has its own meaning and style and its own sense of excitement. We are aware now that somewhere within the jungle of valves and formulae and shining glassware lies a content; lies, let us admit it, a new culture.   3

How are we to reach that culture, across its jargons, and translate it into a language which we know? The difficulties of the layman are my boyhood difficulties. He opens his newspaper and there stands a revelation in capitals: THE ELECTRONIC BRAIN, or SUPERSONIC FLIGHT, or *Is there life on Mars?* But capitals or italics, the revelation remains in code for him. The language is as strange to him as *The Anatomy of Melancholy* was to me at fifteen. He has only the smallest vocabulary: a smattering from other popular articles, schoolboy memories of the stinks lab, and a few names of scientists sprinkled at random across history. His history, which might have given an order to it all, is the most maddening of his uncertainties. I knew no English history, and therefore I could not make sense of literary development. How well I recall the helplessness with which I faced a list of names such as Marlowe and Coleridge and H. G. Wells. I could not make any historical order of them. It is hard to visualize my difficulty; yet just this is the difficulty which every reader meets when he sees the names of Napier, Humphry Davy and Rutherford. These three scientists were contemporaries of the three writers, and they were by no means lesser men.   4

II

A knowledge of history of course, even the history of science, will not do duty for science. But it gives us the backbone in the growth of science, so that the morning headline suddenly takes its place in the development of our world. It throws a bridge into science from whatever humanist interest we happen to stand on. And it does so because it asserts the unity not merely of history but of knowledge. The layman's key to science is its unity with the arts. He will understand science as a culture when he tries to trace it in his own culture.   5

It has been one of the most destructive modern prejudices that art and science are different and somehow incompatible interests. We have fallen into the habit of opposing the artistic to the scientific temper; we even identify them with a creative and a critical approach. In a society like ours which practises the division of labour there are of course specialized functions, as matters of convenience. As a convenience, and only as a convenience, the scientific function is different from the artistic. In the same way the function of thought differs from, and complements, the function of feeling. But the human race is not divided into thinkers and feelers, and would not long survive the division.   6

Much of this quarrel between science and soul was trumped up by the religious apologists of Queen Victoria's day, who were anxious to find science materialistic and unspiritual. The sneer that science is only critical came from others. It was made by the timid and laboured artists of the nineties in order that they might by comparison appear to be creative and intuitive. Yet this finesse could not hide their own knowledge that the best minds were already being drawn to the more adventurous practice of the new sciences: a movement which Peacock had foreseen seventy-five years before in *The Four Ages of Poetry*.   7

The arts and the sciences ever since have been in competition for the most lively young brains. This competition is itself the clearest evidence that good minds can fulfil themselves as well in one as in the other. Here in fact is one of the few psychological discoveries of our generation to which we can hold with a reasonable certainty: that the general configuration of intelligence factors which distinguish the bright from the dull is the same in one man as another, in the humanist as in the scientist. We are divided by schooling and experience; and we do differ, though we differ less, in our aptitudes; but below these, we share a deeper basis of common ability. This is why I write with confidence for laymen and scientists, because the reader who is interested in any activity which needs thought and judgment is almost certainly a person to whom science can be made to speak. It is not he who is deaf, but the specialists who have been dumb—the specialists in the arts as well as the sciences.   8

Many people persuade themselves that they cannot understand mechanical things, or that they have no head for figures. These convictions make them feel enclosed and safe, and of course save them a great deal of trouble. But the reader who has a head for anything at all is pretty sure to have a head for whatever he really wants to put his mind to. His interest, say in mathematics, has usually been killed by routine teaching, exactly as the literary interest of most scientists (and, for that matter, of most non-scientists) has been killed by the set book and the Shakespeare play. Few people would argue that those whose taste for poetry has not survived the School Certificate are fundamentally insensitive to poetry. Yet they cheerfully write off the large intellectual pleasures of science as if they belonged only to minds of a special cast. Science is not a special sense. It is as wide as the literal meaning of its name: knowledge. The notion of the specialised mind is by comparison as modern as the specialised man, "the scientist," a word which is only a hundred years old. 9

III

Therefore I have in mind as I write a reader who is less interested in the sciences than he is in science. There was in the last century a tradition of self-teaching in the Mechanics' Institutes which in its time was a just cause for pride. But the tradition is gone and its going now is not a loss, because the interest in science has widened. We are all aware of the widening. Those who hanker after a knowledge of science today are not looking for technical information. They are no longer unfortunates who would have liked to work in a laboratory too, if fate had not sent them into a mill at twelve. I take it for granted that those who take up this book are well content with what they know and do, and are not thinking of themselves vicariously as the white-coated hero of a second feature about the discovery of Compound E. And I do not assume that they must necessarily be fascinated by the marvels of the electron microscope or of radio-active iodine. I think of them as people aware that the world into which they were born is changing during their lifetime, and who have about this change the same curiosity which they have about what is new in their closer neighbourhood—in literature or the arts or local politics or the business of the tennis club.   10

Few people today are really in doubt about the scale and the lasting importance of this change. But many people push it to the back of their minds, resolutely or in embarrassment. And much of the time they fear to face it, because they are afraid to acknowledge that this movement is changing their lives, is washing away the landmarks of their familiar world, rising round their values and in the end drowning the selves which must last them their lifetime. Yet these fears are less fears of the social change which science is working than simple personal fears. They are afraid, we are all afraid of being left out. We are afraid that something is happening which we shall not be able to understand and which will shut us out from the fellowship of the brighter and younger people.   11

These fears I believe are groundless. I believe that it is easy for a man who likes conversation and to read the second leader now and again to be comfortable with the large ideas of science: as easy as it is for a scientist to have a fancy for biography. The difficulties are those of language and the personal fear of what is unfamiliar. These are merely fed by those enthusiastic scientists who write as if the layman were to be pitied, and treat him as an erring would-be scientist who ought to be converted to an interest in the nucleus. I have no such reader in mind. I think of my readers, scientists as well as laymen, as balanced people who see about them the world in movement, and who want to know enough about the forces of science outside their own neighbourhood to assess their part in that profound and total movement of history.   12

IV

Many people affect to believe that science has progressively strangled the arts, or distorted them into some unpleasant "modern" form; and therefore that the arts can be revived only by throwing over science. Often of course this is merely an elderly sentiment in favour of the art of our younger days, and the real scapegoat is not science but change. But even where the sentiment is less partial, it springs from a misunderstanding of progress in art and science. Science today is plainly more powerful than, let us say, in the time of Isaac Newton. Against this, the arts today

seldom reach the height of, say, his contemporary John Dryden. It is therefore tempting to conclude that science continually outgrows its older ideas,
while great literature remains permanent. But this is a hopeless muddle of
concepts. Newtons are no more plentiful today than Drydens; and the work
of Newton continues to stand to modern science in precisely the relation
that the prose of Dryden stands to modern prose. Dryden and Newton each
revealed a wholly new set of possibilities in their forms of knowledge. Both
are classics in this sense, that they were at once pioneers and men of
great achievement. And neither is a classic in any other sense.   13

The belief that science destroys culture is sometimes supported by
historical statements that the arts have flourished only when the sciences
have been neglected. This thesis is so directly contrary to history that I
find it difficult to begin to debate it. What is this golden age of art un-
tarnished by the breath of rude mechanics? Where did it exist? In the
East? The civilisations of Egypt, of India, and of the Arabs belie it. The
only oriental poet at all well known in England, Omar Khayyam, was a
Persian astronomer. In the West? The culture of the West begins in
Greece; and in the great age of Greece, art and science penetrate one
another more closely than in any modern age. Pythagoras lived before
Aeschylus had created Greek drama. Socrates taught when that drama was
at its greatest; and is Socrates to be claimed by art or science? And Plato,
who did not tolerate poets in his ideal state, was a scholar when Aristo-
phanes closed the eyes of Greek drama. The example of these men in
science as much as in art set the modern world afire in the Renaissance.
And the type and symbol of Renaissance man was from the beginning and
remains Leonardo da Vinci, painter, sculptor, mathematician, and engineer. No man has shown more strikingly the universality and the unity of
the intellect.   14

In England we put the golden age into the reign of Queen Elizabeth;
and that characteristically was an age of commercial and industrial as well as
of literary invention. Voyagers and adventurers like Sir Walter Ralegh were
the Leonardos of that age; and Ralegh's own circle, which turned Christopher Marlowe into a rationalist, was dominated by a mathematician and an
astronomer. For navigation is dependent on astronomy; it went hand in
hand with the new speculations about the world and the solar system; and
in turn, the voyages of the great navigators inspired the literature of Elizabethan England. The worlds of art and of science and the physical world
unfolded then together. It was not by accident that the first table of
logarithms was published within a few years of the First Folio.   15

Sixty years after the death of Elizabeth, another great age ripened
in England, the age of Restoration literature. I shall have a great deal to
say about that in this book, because one symbol of the age is the founding

of what has remained the most important scientific society in the world. The meeting which founded it opened with a lecture on astronomy, and the lecture was given by Christopher Wren the architect. The society was given its name, the Royal Society, and its motto by the most enthusiastic of its founders. He was John Evelyn the diarist. When the society wanted to encourage the use of simple and lucid prose, it appointed a committee which included a fellow of the society with a special gift for such writing. He was the poet John Dryden.   16

V

The golden ages of literature were in fact times of greatness when science and the arts went forward hand in hand. Has all this come to an end? Literary critics say Yes, it ended in England at the Industrial Revolution, somewhere between 1760 and 1800. Yet these critics date the Romantic Revival from some point between the death of Collins in 1759, which meant so much to Wordsworth, and the publication of the *Lyrical Ballads* in 1798. These two sets of dates are almost identical, and can it be reasonable to keep them in separate compartments of the mind? Is it really tenable to think of the Industrial Revolution as a kind of death? It gave our world its structure. It turned science from astronomy to what are essentially its modern interests, which hinge on the use of mechanical power. And it created in the romantic poets and the reformers what has remained our sensibility.   17

I say created our sensibility, although of course I have pointed only to the coincidence of dates: that Blake and Coleridge and Wilberforce were after all contemporaries of Arkwright and James Watt. Against this, those who hold the illusion that pre-industrial England was more sensitive and cultured, point to the misery of the manufacturing age: women in mines, children in factories, the disasters of enclosure, famine, the Napoleonic wars, and political reaction. These were very terrible evils, but they are evils far older than 1800 and the machines. The labour of women and children for endless hours in their own homes is a commonplace in Defoe's journals in 1725. Yet the Augustan optimists of his day did not see it as matter for protest. But in the factory these evils became naked and public; and the driving force for reform came from the men of the mill, from Robert Owen and the elder Peel. We today are scandalized that boys went on climbing in chimneys for nearly eighty years after the heart-rending poems which Blake wrote about them around 1790; the last of the climbing boys, Joseph Lawrence, is still alive as I write. But the boys had been climbing for a hundred years before Blake without a line of protest from Addison or Gay or Dr. Johnson. In their broad Augustan day,

Scottish miners were legally still serfs, just as the miners of Greece had always been slaves; and neither civilisation thought anything amiss. So today in China and India and other countries with few machines, life is brutal and laborious, and sensibility is unknown; I have seen it so myself, under the rusty thin surface of mechanisation in Japan, for women and animals alike. It was the engine, it was the horsepower which created consideration for the horse; and the Industrial Revolution which created our sensibility.   18

VI

Science changes our values in two ways. It injects new ideas into the familiar culture. And it subjects it to the pressure of technical change, in the way I have just been describing, until the whole basis of our culture has imperceptibly been remade. The invention of printing does not seem to bear very directly on the content of poetry. But when a poem can be read and read again, it is natural that the interest shifts from the rhythm to the meaning and the allusion. So the invention of photography has made the painter and the patron lose interest in the likeness and transfer it to some more formal pattern. Our whole sensibility has been re-created by such subtle shifts.   19

Science and the arts today are not as discordant as many people think. The difficulties which we all have as intelligent amateurs in following modern literature and music and painting are not unimportant. They are one sign of the lack of a broad and general language in our culture. The difficulties which we have in understanding the basic ideas of modern science are signs of the same lack. Science and the arts shared the same language at the Restoration. They no longer seem to do so today. But the reason is that they share the same silence: they lack the same language. And it is the business of each of us to try to remake that one universal language which alone can unite art and science, and layman and scientist, in a common understanding.   20

Suggestions for Writing

1 Explain the resemblances and differences between any of the following (choose one pair). Be sure to be specific. Use definition and example where these methods will aid the comparison and contrast.
   a The honor student and the athlete
   b The stage play and the film
   c The American car and the foreign car

    d The college teacher and the high school teacher
    e Pagan and Christian elements in an American Christmas
    f Getting ahead and getting to heaven
    g The opinions of the majority and of the minority in your school
2 Using the resources of the library and the art collection in your college, and being guided by Katharine Kuh's essay, compare and contrast cultural elements which you can observe in the background of two paintings or sculptures having a common subject.
3 Agreeing or disagreeing with the point of view expressed in Peter van Dresser's essay, compare and contrast the jack-of-all-trades and the highly specialized craftsman in terms of the personal satisfaction which you think each derives from his work.

FUNCTIONS AND PROCEDURES: PROCESS ANALYSIS

After swimming about in a pool of tears, Alice and the strange animals all needed a drying out. The Dodo suggested a Caucus Race as the best method for getting dry. When Alice asked what a Caucus Race was, the Dodo said in that solemn way of his, "Why, the best way to explain it is to do it." We have to be only a little wiser than the Dodo to know that doing something is not the same as explaining it. Had he been able to explain a Caucus Race, which is doubtful, the Dodo would have been using process analysis. When a writer uses this method of analysis, he is concerned with the steps in a process or with the order of a series of events leading to the completion of some kind of operation, structure, or experience. Process analysis is the method of expository analysis that answers these questions: "How does it work?" "How is it made?" "How is it organized or put together?" The subject may be an idea, or a natural phenomenon, or a mechanical structure, or an explanation of human activity. Using process analysis, the writer may explain something as simple as how to fry an egg or as complex as how the heart functions. He may explain things as different as the development of our modern arithmetic and the making of the H-bomb.

Mary Ellen Chase, distinguished novelist and teacher of composition, indicates the first requisite of a good process analysis in her advice to writers: "Assume that your reader is completely, nay, colossally, ignorant of the mechanism you are about to describe or explain. . . . You must pretend, if need be, that he is foreign to all our devices, that he is blind, or only that he is stupid. His particular brand of insufficiency matters little, but that he is totally insufficient in understanding your subject is absolutely necessary for you to assume."[1] Her advice is stated in such strong language because clarity is an absolute necessity in the explanation of any process. Thus, the first requisite for a successful process analysis is that the writer make no unjustified assumptions. The second requisite is a controlled simplicity of diction, the exact character depending upon the nature of the subject. The legitimate attempt to be clear should not, however, force the writer to distort his subject for the sake of false simplicity. Third, no matter how difficult the subject matter, the writer can make his entire presentation clear by making very clear to the reader each of the steps in the process. For example, in "The Empty Column" (page 173) Tobias Dantzig takes us step by step first through the history of ancient numbering systems and then through the development of modern arithmetic. Ordinarily, the writer of a

[1] From *Constructive Theme Writing*, Holt, Rinehart, and Winston, Inc., New York, 1938.

process analysis is not only interested in listing the steps in a process or the events in a sequence but is also trying to show the relationship of each step to the whole. Dantzig is careful to indicate such relationships: the reader will particularly note his extensive use of connective words and phrases, along with other devices, to signal the connection of paragraph with paragraph, and sentence with sentence. To assist the reader further, he also sets off the major divisions of his subject in numbered sections.

Dantzig's essay and Jessica Mitford's "The Story of Service" (page 157) are alike in that each follows a chronological pattern, using time order as the means of organizing the material. Each essay has a narrative design because of this method of ordering the materials; but in both cases the narrative is used only because it supports the process analysis, which happens to be best handled in a chronological fashion. Another way of ordering or arranging the material of a process analysis can be seen in Mortimer Adler's "How to Mark a Book" (page 151). The seven steps in marking a book are arranged in the order of relative importance, beginning with the simplest kind of underlining and proceeding through the more significant comments that the reader writes in the available space within the book itself. Because of the complex nature of his subject, the order of arrangement in Robert Warshow's "The Gangster as Tragic Hero" (page 168) is somewhat more complex: the elements of what goes to make up the character of the movie gangster as tragic hero are presented in a causal order.

Like the other expository methods, process analysis may stand by itself as the dominant intention of a piece of writing or may appear incidentally in a somewhat larger context. "The Empty Column," and "Throwing Back the European Offensive" are clearly analyses of a process of some kind. Both use, of course, other methods of analysis; but the dominant intention of each is clearly to explain a process. "The Story of Service" is generally concerned with a process; the whole organization of the essay is in terms of the steps in the services provided by an undertaker. But in this essay some argument is insinuated by Miss Mitford, with the intent of persuading the reader that the need for some of those services is doubtful. "How to Mark a Book" is clearly meant to persuade the reader to "write between the lines." The process explained in the essay is there to give the reader a method of doing what Adler hopes to persuade him to do. In "The Gangster as Tragic Hero," the process analysis (found in the latter half of the essay) is used as one means to achieve the author's main purpose: to convince the reader that certain aspects of modern society account for the popularity of the movie gangster as tragic hero. These various uses of process analysis should make it clear that we must be alert to distinguish between the dominant intention of a given essay and the means used to achieve that intention. To be able to make such a distinction is a mark of a good reader.

HOW TO MARK A BOOK

MORTIMER J. ADLER

You know you have to read "between the lines" to get the most out of anything. I want to persuade you to do something equally important in the course of your reading. I want to persuade you to "write between the lines." Unless you do, you are not likely to do the most efficient kind of reading.   1

I contend, quite bluntly, that marking up a book is not an act of mutilation but of love.*   2

You shouldn't mark up a book which isn't yours. Librarians (or your friends) who lend you books expect you to keep them clean, and you should. If you decide that I am right about the usefulness of marking books, you will have to buy them. Most of the world's great books are available today, in reprint editions, at less than a dollar.   3

There are two ways in which one can own a book. The first is the property right you establish by paying for it, just as you pay for clothes and furniture. But this act of purchase is only the prelude to possession. Full ownership comes only when you have made it a part of yourself, and the best way to make yourself a part of it is by writing in it. An illustration may make the point clear. You buy a beefsteak and transfer it from the butcher's ice-box to your own. But you do not own the beefsteak in

---

* Paragraph 2: Why is this sentence set off as a separate paragraph?

the most important sense until you consume it and get it into your blood-stream. I am arguing that books, too, must be absorbed in your blood-stream to do you any good.*   4

Confusion about what it means to *own* a book leads people to a false reverence for paper, binding, and type—a respect for the physical thing —the craft of the printer rather than the genius of the author. They forget that it is possible for a man to acquire the idea, to possess the beauty, which a great book contains, without staking his claim by pasting his bookplate inside the cover. Having a fine library doesn't prove that its owner has a mind enriched by books; it proves nothing more than that he, his father, or his wife, was rich enough to buy them.†   5

There are three kinds of book owners. The first has all the standard sets and best-sellers—unread, untouched. (This deluded individual owns woodpulp and ink, not books.) The second has a great many books—a few of them read through, most of them dipped into, but all of them as clean and shiny as the day they were bought. (This person would probably like to make books his own, but is restrained by a false respect for their phys-ical appearance.) The third has a few books or many—every one of them dog-eared and dilapidated, shaken and loosened by continual use, marked and scribbled in from front to back. (This man owns books.)‡   6

Is it false respect, you may ask, to preserve intact and unblemished a beautifully printed book, an elegantly bound edition? Of course not. I'd no more scribble all over the first edition of *Paradise Lost* than I'd give my baby a set of crayons and an original Rembrandt! I wouldn't mark up a painting or a statue. Its soul, so to speak, is inseparable from its body. And the beauty of a rare edition or of a richly manufactured volume is like that of a painting or a statue.   7

But the soul of a book *can* be separated from its body. A book is more like the score of a piece of music than it is like a painting. No great musician confuses a symphony with the printed sheets of music. Arturo Toscanini reveres Brahms, but Toscanini's score of the C-minor Symphony is so thoroughly marked up that no one but the maestro himself can read it. The reason why a great conductor makes notations on his musical scores—marks them up again and again each time he returns to study them—is the reason why you should mark up your books. If your respect for magnificent binding or typography gets in the way, buy yourself a cheap edition and pay your respects to the author.§   8

* Paragraph 4: Homely examples can be effective. Is the one used here appropriate?

† Paragraph 5: Why do you suppose the author used the phrase "or his wife" instead of, say, "or some other relative"?

‡ Paragraph 6: Would the paragraph be improved by the omission of the parentheses?

§ Paragraph 8: What does "pay your respects to the author" mean here?

Why is marking up a book indispensable to reading it? First, it keeps you awake. (And I don't mean merely conscious; I mean wide awake.) In the second place, reading, if it is active, is thinking, and thinking tends to express itself in words, spoken or written. The marked book is usually the thought-through book. Finally, writing helps you remember the thoughts you had, or the thoughts the author expressed. Let me develop these three points.   9

If reading is to accomplish anything more than passing time, it must be active. You can't let your eyes glide across the lines of a book and come up with an understanding of what you have read. Now an ordinary piece of light fiction, like say, *Gone with the Wind,* doesn't require the most active kind of reading. The books you read for pleasure can be read in a state of relaxation, and nothing is lost. But a great book, rich in ideas and beauty, a book that raises and tries to answer great fundamental questions, demands the most active reading of which you are capable. You don't absorb the ideas of John Dewey the way you absorb the crooning of Mr. Vallee. You have to reach for them. That you cannot do while you're asleep.*   10

If, when you've finished reading a book, the pages are filled with your notes, you know that you read actively. The most famous *active* reader of great books I know is President Hutchins, of the University of Chicago. He also has the hardest schedule of business activities of any man I know. He invariably reads with a pencil, and sometimes, when he picks up a book and pencil in the evening, he finds himself, instead of making intelligent notes, drawing what he calls "caviar factories" on the margins. When that happens, he puts the book down. He knows he's too tired to read, and he's just wasting time.   11

But, you may ask, why is writing necessary? Well, the physical act of writing, with your own hand, brings words and sentences more sharply before your mind and preserves them better in your memory. To set down your reaction to important words and sentences you have read, and the questions they have raised in your mind, is to preserve those reactions and sharpen those questions.   12

Even if you wrote on a scratch pad, and threw the paper away when you had finished writing, your grasp of the book would be surer. But you don't have to throw the paper away. The margins (top and bottom, as well as side), the end-papers, the very space between the lines, are all available. They aren't sacred. And, best of all, your marks and notes become an integral part of the book and stay there forever. You can pick up the book the following week or year, and there are all your points of agreement,

---

* Paragraph 10: What methods are used to develop the central thought here?

disagreement, doubt, and inquiry. It's like resuming an interrupted conversation with the advantage of being able to pick up where you left off.   13

And that is exactly what reading a book should be: a conversation
between you and the author. Presumably he knows more about the subject
than you do; naturally, you'll have the proper humility as you approach
him. But don't let anybody tell you that a reader is supposed to be solely
on the receiving end. Understanding is a two-way operation; learning
doesn't consist in being an empty receptacle. The learner has to question
himself and question the teacher. He even has to argue with the teacher,
once he understands what the teacher is saying. And marking a book is
literally an expression of your differences, or agreements of opinion, with
the author.   14

There are all kinds of devices for marking a book intelligently and
fruitfully. Here's the way I do it: 15

1. Underlining: Of major points, of important or forceful statements.   16

2. Vertical lines at the margin: To emphasize a statement already
underlined.   17

3. Star, asterisk, or other doo-dad at the margin: To be used sparingly, to emphasize the ten or twenty most important statements in the
book. (You may want to fold the bottom corner of each page on which you
use such marks. It won't hurt the sturdy paper on which most modern
books are printed, and you will be able to take the book off the shelf at any
time and, by opening it at the folded-corner page, refresh your recollection of the book.)   18

4. Numbers in the margin: To indicate the sequence of points the
author makes in developing a single argument.   19

5. Numbers of other pages in the margin: To indicate where else in
the book the author made points relevant to the point marked; to tie up
the ideas in a book, which, though they may be separated by many pages,
belong together.*   20

6. Circling of key words or phrases.   21

*7. Writing in the margin, or at the top or bottom of the page, for the
sake of:* Recording questions (and perhaps answers) which a passage
raised in your mind; reducing a complicated discussion to a simple statement; recording the sequence of major points right through the book. I use
the end-papers at the back of the book to make a personal index of the
author's points in the order of their appearance.   22

The front end-papers are, to me, the most important. Some people
reserve them for a fancy bookplate. I reserve them for fancy thinking. After
I have finished reading the book and making my personal index on the

---

* Paragraph 20: Justify the punctuation used here, particularly the colon and the
  semicolon.

back end-papers, I turn to the front and try to outline the book, not page by page, or point by point (I've already done that at the back), but as an integrated structure, with a basic unity and an order of parts. This outline is, to me, the measure of my understanding of the work.   23

If you're a die-hard anti-book-marker, you may object that the margins, the space between the lines, and the end-papers don't give you room enough. All right. How about using a scratch pad slightly smaller than the page-size of the book—so that the edges of the sheets won't protrude? Make your index, outlines, and even your notes on the pad, and then insert these sheets permanently inside the front and back covers of the book.   24

Or, you may say that this business of marking books is going to slow up your reading. It probably will. That's one of the reasons for doing it. Most of us have been taken in by the notion that speed of reading is a measure of our intelligence. There is no such thing as the right speed for intelligent reading. Some things should be read quickly and effortlessly, and some should be read slowly and even laboriously. The sign of intelligence in reading is the ability to read different things differently according to their worth. In the case of good books, the point is not to see how many of them you can get through, but rather how many can get through you— how many you can make your own. A few friends are better than a thousand acquaintances. If this be your aim, as it should be, you will not be impatient if it takes more time and effort to read a great book than it does a newspaper.   25

You may have one final objection to marking books. You can't lend them to your friends because nobody else can read them without being distracted by your notes. Furthermore, you won't want to lend them because a marked copy is a kind of intellectual diary, and lending it is almost like giving your mind away.   26

If your friend wishes to read your *Plutarch's Lives,* "Shakespeare," or *The Federalist Papers,* tell him gently but firmly, to buy a copy. You will lend him your car or your coat—but your books are as much a part of you as your head or your heart.   27

The Whole Selection

1 Is this essay simply the explanation of a process? Where is the explanation of the process?
2 The essay as a whole is, as the author clearly indicates at the beginning, intended to persuade the reader. What does he intend to persuade us to do? Does he?

3 Note that Mr. Adler does not make sweeping generalizations. What kinds
of books should not or need not be marked?

4 Are the relatively short paragraphs to be explained by the demands of
the printed page—three narrow columns to a page—of magazines such as
the *Saturday Review,* in which the essay first appeared? If you are already
quite competent at writing unified and coherent paragraphs, you might
ask yourself whether or not there is something rather relative and
arbitrary about the desirable length that a paragraph may have.

5 Adler here frequently uses diction, structures, and metaphors which
effect a colloquial tone. Cite some examples of such usage. Do you approve of this effect in this particular essay?

THE STORY OF SERVICE

JESSICA MITFORD

There was a time when the undertaker's tasks were clearcut and rather obvious, and when he billed his patrons accordingly. Typical late-nineteenth-century charges, in addition to the price of merchandise, are shown on bills of the period as: "Services at the house (placing corpse in the coffin) $1.25," "Preserving remains on ice, $10," "Getting Permit, $1.50." It was customary for the undertaker to add a few dollars to his bill for being "in attendance," which seems only fair and right. The cost of embalming was around $10 in 1880. An undertaker, writing in 1900, recommends these minimums for service charges: Washing and dressing, $5; embalming, $10; hearse, $8 to $10. As Habenstein and Lamers, the historians of the trade, have pointed out, "The undertaker had yet to conceive of the value of personal services offered professionally for a fee, legitimately claimed." Well, he has now so conceived with a vengeance.*   1

When weaving in the story of service as it is rendered today, spokesmen for the funeral industry tend to become so carried away by their own enthusiasm, so positively lyrical and copious in their declarations, that the outsider may have a little trouble understanding it all. There are indeed contradictions. Preferred Funeral Directors International has prepared a mimeographed talk designed to inform people about service: "The American public receive the services of employees and proprietor alike, nine and one half days of labor for every funeral handled, they receive the use of automobiles and hearses, a building including a chapel and other rooms which require building maintenance, insurance, taxes and licenses, and depreciation, as well as heat in the winter, cooling in the summer and light and water." The writer goes on to say that while the process of embalming takes only about three hours, yet, "it would be necessary for one man to work two forty-hour weeks to complete a funeral service. This is coupled with an additional forty hours service required by members of other local allied professions, including the work of the cemeteries, newspapers, and of course, the most important of all, the service of your clergyman. These some 120 hours of labor are the basic value on which the cost of funerals rests."   2

Our informant has lumped a lot of things together here. To start with "the most important of all, the service of your clergyman," the average religious funeral service lasts no more than 25 minutes. Furthermore, it is not, of course, paid for by the funeral director. The "work of the cemeteries" presumably means the opening and closing of a grave. This

* Paragraph 1: How does the phrase "historians of the trade" suggest the author's attitude toward undertakers?

now mechanized operation, which takes 15 to 20 minutes, is likewise not billed as part of the funeral director's costs. The work of "newspapers"? This is a puzzler. Presumably reference is made here to the publication of an obituary notice on the vital statistics page. It is, incidentally, surprising to learn that newspaper work is considered an "allied profession."   3

Just how insurance, taxes, licenses and depreciation are figured in as part of the 120 man-hours of service is hard to tell. The writer does mention that his operation features "65 items of service." In general, the funeral salesman is inclined to chuck in everything he does under the heading of "service." For example, in a typical list of "services" he will include items like "securing statistical data" (in other words, completing the death certificate and finding out how much insurance was left by the deceased), "the arrangements conference" (in which the sale of the funeral to the survivors is made), and the "keeping of records," by which he means his own bookkeeping work. Evidently there is some confusion here between items that properly belong in a cost-accounting system and items of *actual* service rendered in any given funeral. In all likelihood, idle time of employees is figured in and prorated as part of the "man-hours." The up-to-date funeral home operates on a 24-hour basis, and the mimeographed speech contains this heartening news:

> The funeral service profession of the United States is proud of the fact that there is not a person within the continental limits of the United States who is more than two hours away from a licensed funeral director and embalmer in case of need. That's one that even the fire fighting apparatus of our country cannot match.   4

While the hit-or-miss rhetoric of the foregoing is fairly typical of the prose style of the funeral trade as a whole, and while the statement that 120 man-hours are devoted to a single man- (or woman-) funeral may be open to question, there really is a fantastic amount of service accorded the dead body and its survivors.   5

Having decreed what sort of funeral is right, proper and nice, and having gradually appropriated to himself all the functions connected with it, the funeral director has become responsible for a multitude of tasks beyond the obvious one of "placing corpse in the coffin" recorded in our nineteenth-century funeral bill. His self-imposed duties fall into two main categories: attention to the corpse itself, and the stage-managing of the funeral.   6

The drama begins to unfold with the arrival of the corpse at the mortuary.*   7

* Paragraph 7: What function does this paragraph serve?

Alas, poor Yorick! How surprised he would be to see how his counter-part of today is whisked off to a funeral parlor and is in short order sprayed, sliced, pierced, pickled, trussed, trimmed, creamed, waxed, painted, rouged and neatly dressed—transformed from a common corpse into a Beautiful Memory Picture. This process is known in the trade as embalming and restorative art, and is so universallly employed in the United States and Canada that the funeral director does it routinely, with-out consulting corpse or kin. He regards as eccentric those few who are hardy enough to suggest that it might be dispensed with. Yet no law requires embalming, no religious doctrine commends it, nor is it dictated by considerations of health, sanitation, or even of personal daintiness. In no part of the world but in Northern America is it widely used. The pur-pose of embalming is to make the corpse presentable for viewing in a suitably costly container; and here too the funeral director routinely, with-out first consulting the family, prepares the body for public display.   8

Is all this legal? The processes to which a dead body may be sub-jected are after all to some extent circumscribed by law. In most states, for instance, the signature of next of kin must be obtained before an autopsy may be performed, before the deceased may be cremated, before the body may be turned over to a medical school for research purposes; or such provision must be made in the decedent's will. In the case of embalming, no such permission is required nor is it ever sought. A text-book, *The Principles and Practices of Embalming,* comments on this: "There is some question regarding the legality of much that is done within the preparation room." The author points out that it would be most un-usual for a responsible member of a bereaved family to instruct the mortician, in so many words, to *"embalm"* the body of a deceased relative. The very term "embalming" is so seldom used that the mortician must rely upon custom in the matter. The author concludes that unless the family specifies otherwise, the act of entrusting the body to the care of a funeral establishment carries with it an implied permission to go ahead and embalm.   9

Embalming is indeed a most extraordinary procedure, and one must wonder at the docility of Americans who each year pay hundreds of millions of dollars for its perpetuation, blissfully ignorant of what it is all about, what is done, how it is done. Not one in ten thousand has any idea of what actually takes place. Books on the subject are extremely hard to come by. They are not to be found in most libraries or bookshops.   10

In an era when huge television audiences watch surgical operations in the comfort of their living rooms, when, thanks to the animated cartoon, the geography of the digestive system has become familiar territory even to the nursery school set, in a land where the satisfaction of curiosity about almost all matters is a national pastime, the secrecy surrounding embalming can, surely, hardly be attributed to the inherent gruesomeness of the subject. Custom in this regard has within this century suffered a complete reversal. In the early days of American embalming, when it was performed in the home of the deceased, it was almost mandatory for some relative to stay by the embalmer's side and witness the procedure. Today, family members who might wish to be in attendance would certainly be dissuaded by the funeral director. All others, except apprentices, are excluded by law from the preparation room.*   11

A close look at what does actually take place may explain in large measure the undertaker's intractable reticence concerning a procedure that has become his major *raison d'être*. Is it possible he fears that public information about embalming might lead patrons to wonder if they really want this service? If the funeral men are loath to discuss the subject outside the trade, the reader may, understandably, be equally loath to go on reading at this point. For those who have the stomach for it, let us part the formaldehyde curtain. Others should skip to page [164].†   12

The body is first laid out in the undertaker's morgue—or rather, Mr. Jones is reposing in the preparation room—to be readied to bid the world farewell.   13

The preparation room in any of the better funeral establishments has the tiled and sterile look of a surgery, and indeed the embalmer-restorative artist who does his chores there is beginning to adopt the term "derma-surgeon" (appropriately corrupted by some mortician-writers as "demi-surgeon") to describe his calling. His equipment, consisting of scalpels, scissors, augurs, forceps, clamps, needles, pumps, tubes, bowls and basins, is crudely imitative of the surgeon's, as is his technique, acquired in a nine- or twelve-month post-high-school course in an embalming school. He is supplied by an advanced chemical industry with a bewildering array of fluids, sprays, pastes, oils, powders, creams, to fix or soften tissue, shrink or distend it as needed, dry it here, restore the moisture there. There are cosmetics, waxes and paints to fill and cover features, even plaster of Paris to replace entire limbs. There are ingenious aids to prop and stabilize the cadaver: a Vari-Pose Head Rest, the Edwards Arm and Hand Positioner, the Repose Block (to support the shoulders during the embalming), and the Throop Foot Positioner, which resembles an old-fashioned stocks.   14

Mr. John H. Eckels, president of the Eckels College of Mortuary Science, thus describes the first part of the embalming procedure: "In the hands of a skilled practitioner, this work may be done in a comparatively short time and without mutilating the body other than by slight incision—

* Paragraph 11: What effect does the periodic sentence achieve here?
† Paragraph 12: Where is metaphor used here?

so slight that it scarcely would cause serious inconvenience if made upon a living person. It is necessary to remove the blood, and doing this not only helps in the disinfecting, but removes the principal cause of disfigurements due to discoloration."   15

Another textbook discusses the all-important time element: "The earlier this is done, the better, for every hour that elapses between death and embalming will add to the problems and complications encountered. . . ." Just how soon should one get going on the embalming? The author tells us, "On the basis of such scanty information made available to this profession through its rudimentary and haphazard system of technical research, we must conclude that the best results are to be obtained if the subject is embalmed before life is completely extinct—that is, before cellular death has occurred. In the average case, this would mean within an hour after somatic death." For those who feel that there is something a little rudimentary, not to say haphazard, about this advice, a comforting thought is offered by another writer. Speaking of fears entertained in early days of premature burial, he points out, "One of the effects of embalming by chemical injection, however, has been to dispel fears of live burial." How true; once the blood is removed, chances of live burial are indeed remote.   16

To return to Mr. Jones, the blood is drained out through the veins and replaced by embalming fluid pumped in through the arteries. As noted in *The Principles and Practices of Embalming,* "every operator has a favorite injection and drainage point—a fact which becomes a handicap only if he fails or refuses to forsake his favorites when conditions demand it." Typical favorites are the carotid artery, femoral artery, jugular vein, subclavian vein. There are various choices of embalming fluid. If Flextone is used, it will produce a "mild, flexible rigidity. The skin retains a velvety softness, the tissues are rubbery and pliable. Ideal for women and children." It may be blended with B. and G. Products Company's Lyf-Lyk tint, which is guaranteed to reproduce "nature's own skin texture . . . the velvety appearance of living tissue." Suntone comes in three separate tints: Suntan; Special Cosmetic Tint, a pink shade "especially indicated for young female subjects"; and Regular Cosmetic Tint, moderately pink.   17

About three to six gallons of a dyed and perfumed solution of formaldehyde, glycerin, borax, phenol, alcohol and water is soon circulating through Mr. Jones, whose mouth has been sewn together with a "needle directed upward between the upper lip and gum and brought out through the left nostril," with the corners raised slightly "for a more pleasant expression." If he should be bucktoothed, his teeth are cleaned with Bon Ami and coated with colorless nail polish. His eyes, meanwhile, are closed with flesh-tinted eye caps and eye cement.   18

The next step is to have at Mr. Jones with a thing called a trocar.

This is a long, hollow needle attached to a tube. It is jabbed into the abdomen, poked around the entrails and chest cavity, the contents of which are pumped out and replaced with "cavity fluid." This done, and the hole in the abdomen sewn up, Mr. Jones's face is heavily creamed (to protect the skin from burns which may be caused by leakage of the chemicals), and he is covered with a sheet and left unmolested for a while. But not for long—there is more, much more, in store for him. He has been embalmed, but not yet restored, and the best time to start the restorative work is eight to ten hours after embalming, when the tissues have become firm and dry.   19

The object of all this attention to the corpse, it must be remembered, is to make it presentable for viewing in an attitude of healthy repose. "Our customs require the presentation of our dead in the semblance of normality . . . unmarred by the ravages of illness, disease or mutilation," says Mr. J. Sheridan Mayer in his *Restorative Art.* This is rather a large order since few people die in the full bloom of health, unravaged by illness and unmarked by some disfigurement. The funeral industry is equal to the challenge: "In some cases the gruesome appearance of a mutilated or disease-ridden subject may be quite discouraging. The task of restoration may seem impossible and shake the confidence of the embalmer. This is the time for intestinal fortitude and determination. Once the formative work is begun and affected tissues are cleaned or removed, all doubts of success vanish. It is surprising and gratifying to discover the results which may be obtained."   20

The embalmer, having allowed an appropriate interval to elapse, returns to the attack, but now he brings into play the skill and equipment of sculptor and cosmetician. Is a hand missing? Casting one in plaster of Paris is a simple matter. "For replacement purposes, only a cast of the back of the hand is necessary; this is within the ability of the average operator and is quite adequate." If a lip or two, a nose or an ear should be missing, the embalmer has at hand a variety of restorative waxes with which to model replacements. Pores and skin texture are simulated by stippling with a little brush, and over this cosmetics are laid on. Head off? Decapitation cases are rather routinely handled. Ragged edges are trimmed, and head joined to torso with a series of splints, wires and sutures. It is a good idea to have a little something at the neck—a scarf or high collar—when time for viewing comes. Swollen mouth? Cut out tissue as needed from inside the lips. If too much is removed, the surface contour can easily be restored by padding with cotton. Swollen necks and cheeks are reduced by removing tissue through vertical incisions made down each side of the neck. "When the deceased is casketed, the pillow will hide the suture incisions . . . as an extra precaution against leakage, the suture may be painted with liquid sealer."   21

The opposite condition is more likely to present itself—that of emaciation. His hypodermic syringe now loaded with massage cream, the embalmer seeks out and fills the hollowed and sunken areas by injection. In this procedure the backs of the hands and fingers and the under-chin area should not be neglected.   22

Positioning the lips is a problem that recurrently challenges the ingenuity of the embalmer. Closed too tightly, they tend to give a stern, even disapproving expression. Ideally, embalmers feel, the lips should give the impression of being ever so slightly parted, the upper lip protruding slightly for a more youthful appearance. This takes some engineering, however, as the lips tend to drift apart. Lip drift can sometimes be remedied by pushing one or two straight pins through the inner margin of the lower lip and then inserting them between the two front upper teeth. If Mr. Jones happens to have no teeth, the pins can just as easily be anchored in his Armstrong Face Former and Denture Replacer. Another method to maintain lip closure is to dislocate the lower jaw, which is then held in its new position by a wire run through holes which have been drilled through the upper and lower jaws at the midline. As the French are fond of saying, *il faut souffrir pour être belle.*[1]   23

If Mr. Jones has died of jaundice, the embalming fluid will very likely turn him green. Does this deter the embalmer? Not if he has intestinal fortitude. Masking pastes and cosmetics are heavily laid on, burial garments and casket interiors are color-correlated with particular care, and Jones is displayed beneath rose-colored lights. Friends will say, "How well he looks." Death by carbon monoxide, on the other hand, can be rather a good thing from the embalmer's viewpoint: "One advantage is the fact that this type of discoloration is an exaggerated form of a natural pink coloration." This is nice because the healthy glow is already present and needs but little attention.   24

The patching and filling completed, Mr. Jones is now shaved, washed and dressed. Cream-based cosmetic, available in pink, flesh, suntan, brunette and blond, is applied to his hands and face, his hair is shampooed and combed (and, in the case of Mrs. Jones, set), his hands manicured. For the horny-handed son of toil special care must be taken; cream should be applied to remove ingrained grime, and the nails cleaned. "If he were not in the habit of having them manicured in life, trimming and shaping is advised for better appearance—never questioned by kin."   25

Jones is now ready for casketing (this is the present participle of the verb "to casket"). In this operation his right shoulder should be depressed

---

[1] In 1963 *Mortuary Management* reports a new development: "Natural Expression Formers," an invention of Funeral Directors Research Company. "They may be used to replace one or both artificial dentures, or over natural teeth; have 'bite-indicator' lines as a closure guide . . . Natural Expression Formers also offer more control of facial expression."

slightly "to turn the body a bit to the right and soften the appearance of lying flat on the back." Positioning the hands is a matter of importance, and special rubber positioning blocks may be used. The hands should be cupped slightly for a more lifelike, relaxed appearance. Proper placement of the body requires a delicate sense of balance. It should lie as high as possible in the casket, yet not so high that the lid, when lowered, will hit the nose. On the other hand, we are cautioned, placing the body too low "creates the impression that the body is in a box."   26

Jones is next wheeled into the appointed slumber room where a few last touches may be added—his favorite pipe placed in his hand or, if he was a great reader, a book propped into position. (In the case of little Master Jones a Teddy bear may be clutched.) Here he will hold open house for a few days, visiting hours 10 a.m. to 9 p.m.   27

All now being in readiness, the funeral director calls a staff conference to make sure that each assistant knows his precise duties. Mr. Wilber Krieger writes: "This makes your staff feel that they are a part of the team, with a definite assignment that must be properly carried out if the whole plan is to succeed. You never heard of a football coach who failed to talk to his entire team before they go on the field. They have drilled on the plays they are to execute for hours and days, and yet the successful coach knows the importance of making even the bench-warming third-string substitute feel that he is important if the game is to be won." The winning of *this* game is predicated upon glass-smooth handling of the logistics. The funeral director has notified the pallbearers whose names were furnished by the family, has arranged for the presence of clergyman, organist, and soloist, has provided transportation for everybody, has organized and listed the flowers sent by friends. In *Psychology of Funeral Service* Mr. Edward A. Martin points out: "He may not always do as much as the family thinks he is doing, but it is his helpful guidance that they appreciate in knowing they are proceeding as they should. . . . The important thing is how well his services can be used to make the family believe they are giving unlimited expression to their own sentiment."   28

The religious service may be held in a church or in the chapel of the funeral home; the funeral director vastly prefers the latter arrangement, for not only is it more convenient for him but it affords him the opportunity to show off his beautiful facilities to the gathered mourners. After the clergyman has had his say, the mourners queue up to file past the casket for a last look at the deceased. The family is *never* asked whether they want an open-casket ceremony; in the absence of their instruction to the contrary, this is taken for granted. Consequently well over 90 per cent of all American funerals feature the open casket—a custom unknown in other parts of the world. Foreigners are astonished by it. An English woman living in San Francisco described her reaction in a letter to the writer:

> I myself have attended only one funeral here—that of an elderly fellow worker of mine. After the service I could not understand why everyone was walking towards the coffin (sorry, I mean casket), but thought I had better follow the crowd. It shook me rigid to get there and find the casket open and poor old Oscar lying there in his brown tweed suit, wearing a suntan makeup and just the wrong shade of lipstick. If I had not been extremely fond of the old boy, I have a horrible feeling that I might have giggled. Then and there I decided that I could never face another American funeral—even dead.   29

The casket (which has been resting throughout the service on a Classic Beauty Ultra Metal Casket Bier) is now transferred by a hydraulically operated device called Porto-Lift to a ballon-tired, Glide Easy casket carriage which will wheel it to yet another conveyance, the Cadillac Funeral Coach. This may be lavender, cream, light green—anything but black. Interiors, of course, are color-correlated, "for the man who cannot stop short of perfection."   30

At graveside, the casket is lowered into the earth. This office, once the prerogative of friends of the deceased, is now performed by a patented mechanical lowering device. A "Lifetime Green" artificial grass mat is at the ready to conceal the sere earth, and overhead, to conceal the sky, is a portable Steril Chapel Tent ("resists the intense heat and humidity of summer and the terrific storms of winter . . . available in Silver Grey, Rose or Evergreen"). Now is the time for the ritual scattering of earth over the coffin, as the solemn words "earth to earth, ashes to ashes, dust to dust" are pronounced by the officiating cleric. This can today be accomplished "with a mere flick of the wrist with the Gordon Leak-Proof Earth Dispenser. No grasping of a handful of dirt, no soiled fingers. Simple, dignified, beautiful, reverent! The modern way!" The Gordon Earth Dispenser (at $5) is of nickel-plated brass construction. It is not only "attractive to the eye and long wearing"; it is also "one of the 'tools' for building better public relations" if presented as "an appropriate non-commercial gift" to the clergyman. It is shaped something like a saltshaker.   31

Untouched by human hand, the coffin and the earth are now united. 32

It is in the function of directing the participants through this maze of gadgetry that the funeral director has assigned to himself his relatively new role of "grief therapist." He has relieved the family of every detail, he has revamped the corpse to look like a living doll, he has arranged for it to nap for a few days in a slumber room, he has put on a well-oiled performance in which the concept of *death* has played no part whatsoever

—unless it was inconsiderately mentioned by the clergyman who conducted the religious service. He has done everything in his power to make the funeral a real pleasure for everybody concerned. He and his team have given their all to score an upset victory over death.   33

Dale Carnegie has written that in the lexicon of the successful man there is no such word as "failure." So have the funeral men managed to delete the word death and all its associations from their vocabulary. They have from time to time published lists of In and Out words and phrases to be memorized and used in connection with the final return of dust to dust; then, still dissatisfied with the result, have elaborated and revised the lists. Thus a 1916 glossary substitutes "prepare body" for "handle corpse." Today, though, "body" is Out and "remains" or "Mr. Jones" is In.   34

"The use of improper terminology by anyone affiliated with a mortuary should be strictly forbidden," declares Edward A. Martin. He suggests a rather thorough overhauling of the language; his deathless words include: "service, not funeral; Mr., Mrs., Miss Blank, not corpse or body; preparation room, not morgue; casket, not coffin; funeral director or mortician, not undertaker; reposing room or slumber room, not laying-out room; display room, not showroom; baby or infant, not stillborn; deceased, not dead; autopsy or post-mortem, not post; casket coach, not hearse; shipping case, not shipping box; flower car, not flower truck; cremains or cremated remains, not ashes; clothing, dress, suit, etc., not shroud; drawing room, not parlor."   35

This rather basic list was refined in 1956 by Victor Landig in his *Basic Principles of Funeral Service.* He enjoins the reader to avoid using the word "death" as much as possible, even sometimes when such avoidance may seem impossible; for example, a death certificate should be referred to as a "vital statistics form." One should speak not of the "job" but rather of the "call." We do not "haul" a dead person, we "transfer" or "remove" him—and we do this in a "service car," not a "body car." We "open and close" his grave rather than dig and fill it, and in it we "inter" rather than bury him. This is done, not in a graveyard or cemetery but rather in a "memorial park." The deceased is beautified, not with makeup, but with "cosmetics." Anyway, he didn't die, he "expired." An important error to guard against, cautions Mr. Landig, is referring to "cost of the casket." The phrase, "amount of investment in the service" is a wiser usage here.   36

Miss Anne Hamilton Franz, writing in *Funeral Direction and Management,* adds an interesting footnote on the use of the word "ashes" to describe (in a word) ashes. She fears this usage will encourage scattering (for what is more natural than to scatter ashes?) and prefers to speak of "cremated remains" or "human remains." She does not like the word "retort" to describe the container in which cremation takes place, but prefers "cremation chamber" or "cremation vault," because this "sounds better and softens any harshness to sensitive feelings."   37

As for the Loved One, poor fellow, he wanders like a sad ghost through the funeral men's pronouncements. No provision seems to have been made for the burial of a Heartily Disliked One, although the necessity for such must arise in the course of human events.   38

The Whole Selection

1 In paragraph 6, Miss Mitford announces the "two main categories" of the service; then in the rest of the essay she explains these categories through process analysis. What order of arrangement does she employ in each of these process analyses? (See the discussion on page 150.)

2 As the editorial comment in this textbook has emphasized, most writing uses a variety of forms and methods of analysis. Like Adler in his essay, Miss Mitford employs the form of exposition, yet her intent is argumentative—she explains in order to persuade us. Also, although she uses process analysis, she employs other methods as well, including definition, example, and comparison and contrast, which you have already studied. Which of these does she use in paragraphs 11, 12, 33, and 34?

3 Although she is entirely serious in her criticism of the undertaking business, and supports her criticism with ample documentation, Miss Mitford does not adopt a deadly earnest manner. A lightly humorous manner, a gentle ridiculing, can often be highly effective in the treatment of a subject as macabre as Miss Mitford's is. One device which she uses to achieve a light touch is the use of colloquial expression, e.g., "to chuck in," "to have at," "rather a large order." What other devices does she use to achieve this effect?

4 Cite some examples of verbal irony (see Glossary) used frequently in this selection.

5 The subject treated in paragraphs 33 to 36 is more effective placed here, toward the end of the selection, than it would have been near the beginning of the selection. Why?

6 How can the very extensive use of direct quotation in this selection be justified?

Word Study copious, intractable, reticence, raison d'être, somatic, sere

THE GANGSTER AS TRAGIC HERO

ROBERT WARSHOW

America, as a social and political organization, is committed to a cheerful view of life. It could not be otherwise. The sense of tragedy is a luxury of aristocratic societies, where the fate of the individual is not conceived of as having a direct and legitimate political importance, being determined by a fixed and supra-political—that is, non-controversial—moral order or fate. Modern equalitarian societies, however, whether democratic or authoritarian in their political forms, always base themselves on the claim that they are making life happier; the avowed function of the modern state, at least in its ultimate terms, is not only to regulate social relations, but also to determine the quality and the possibilities of human life in general. Happiness thus becomes the chief political issue—in a sense, the only political issue—and for that reason it can never be treated as an issue at all. If an American or a Russian is unhappy, it implies a certain reprobation of his society, and therefore, by a logic of which we can all recognize the necessity, it becomes an obligation of citizenship to be cheerful; if the authorities find it necessary, the citizen may even be compelled to make a public display of his cheerfulness on important occasions, just as he may be conscripted into the army in time of war.*   1

Naturally, this civic responsibility rests most strongly upon the organs of mass culture. The individual citizen may still be permitted his private unhappiness so long as it does not take on political significance, the extent of this tolerance being determined by how large an area of private life the society can accommodate. But every production of mass culture is a public act and must conform with accepted notions of the public good. Nobody seriously questions the principle that it is the function of mass culture to maintain public morale, and certainly nobody in the mass audience objects to having his morale maintained.[1] At a time when the normal condition of the citizen is a state of anxiety, euphoria spreads over our culture like the broad smile of an idiot. In terms of attitudes towards life, there is very little difference between a "happy" movie like Good News, which ignores death and suffering, and a "sad" movie like A Tree Grows in Brooklyn, which uses death and suffering as incidents in the service of a higher optimism.   2

[1] In her testimony before the House Committee on Un-American Activities, Mrs. Leila Rogers said that the movie None But the Lonely Heart was un-American because it was gloomy. Like so much else that was said during the unhappy investigation of Hollywood, this statement was at once stupid and illuminating. One knew immediately what Mrs. Rogers was talking about; she had simply been insensitive enough to carry her philistinism to its conclusion.

* Paragraph 1: What are "aristocratic societies"? In an equalitarian society, how can happiness, being "the chief political issue," "never be treated as an issue at all"?

But, whatever its effectiveness as a source of consolation and a means of pressure for maintaining "positive" social attitudes, this optimism is fundamentally satisfying to no one, not even to those who would be most disoriented without its support. Even within the area of mass culture, there always exists a current of opposition, seeking to express by whatever means are available to it that sense of desperation and inevitable failure which optimism itself helps to create. Most often, this opposition is confined to rudimentary or semi-literate forms: in mob politics and journalism, for example, or in certain kinds of religious enthusiasm. When it does enter the field of art, it is likely to be disguised or attenuated: in an unspecific form of expression like jazz, in the basically harmless nihilism of the Marx Brothers, in the continually reasserted strain of hopelessness that often seems to be the real meaning of the soap opera. The gangster film is remarkable in that it fills the need for disguise (though not sufficiently to avoid arousing uneasiness) without requiring any serious distortion. From its beginnings, it has been a consistent and astonishingly complete presentation of the modern sense of tragedy.[2]*   3

In its initial character, the gangster film is simply one example of the movies' constant tendency to create fixed dramatic patterns that can be repeated indefinitely with a reasonable expectation of profit. One gangster film follows another as one musical or one Western follows another. But this rigidity is not necessarily opposed to the requirements of art. There have been very successful types of art in the past which developed such specific and detailed conventions as almost to make individual examples of the type interchangeable. This is true, for example, of Elizabethan revenge tragedy and Restoration comedy.†   4

For such a type to be successful means that its conventions have imposed themselves upon the general consciousness and become the accepted vehicles of a particular set of attitudes and a particular aesthetic effect. One goes to any individual example of the type with very definite expectations, and originality is to be welcomed only in the degree that it intensifies the expected experience without fundamentally altering it. Moreover, the relationship between the conventions which go to make up such a type and the real experience of its audience or the real facts of whatever situation it pretends to describe is of only secondary importance

---

[2] Efforts have been made from time to time to bring the gangster film into line with the prevailing optimism and social constructiveness of our culture; *Kiss of Death* is a recent example. These efforts are usually unsuccessful; the reasons for their lack of success are interesting in themselves, but I shall not be able to discuss them here.

* Paragraph 3: In sentence 1, why is "positive" placed in quotation marks? In sentence 5, does "arousing" serve as an adjective or as a verbal noun?

† Paragraph 4: What does the third sentence mean?

and does not determine its aesthetic force. It is only in an ultimate sense that the type appeals to its audience's experience of reality; much more immediately, it appeals to previous experience of the type itself: it creates its own field of reference.*   5

Thus the importance of the gangster film, and the nature and intensity of its emotional and aesthetic impact, cannot be measured in terms of the place of the gangster himself or the importance of the problem of crime in American life. Those European movie-goers who think there is a gangster on every corner in New York are certainly deceived, but defenders of the "positive" side of American culture are equally deceived if they think it relevant to point out that most Americans have never seen a gangster. What matters is that the experience of the gangster *as an experience of art* is universal to Americans. There is almost nothing we understand better or react to more readily or with quicker intelligence. The Western film, though it seems never to diminish in popularity, is for most of us no more than the folklore of the past, familiar and understandable only because it has been repeated so often. The gangster film comes much closer. In ways that we do not easily or willingly define, the gangster speaks for us, expressing that part of the American psyche which rejects the qualities and the demands of modern life, which rejects "Americanism" itself.†   6

The gangster is the man of the city, with the city's language and knowledge, with its queer and dishonest skills and its terrible daring, carrying his life in his hands like a placard, like a club. For everyone else, there is at least the theoretical possibility of another world—in that happier American culture which the gangster denies, the city does not really exist; it is only a more crowded and more brightly lit country—but for the gangster there is only the city; he must inhabit it in order to personify it: not the real city, but that dangerous and sad city of the imagination which is so much more important, which is the modern world. And the gangster —though there are real gangsters—is also, and primarily, a creature of the imagination. The real city, one might say, produces only criminals; the imaginary city produces the gangster: he is what we want to be and what we are afraid we may become.‡   7

Thrown into the crowd without background or advantages, with only those ambiguous skills which the rest of us—the real people of the real city—can only pretend to have, the gangster is required to make his way, to make his life and impose it on others. Usually, when we come upon him, he has already made his choice or the choice has already been made for him, it doesn't matter which: we are not permitted to ask whether at some point he could have chosen to be something else than what he is.   8

* Paragraph 5: What does the last sentence mean?
† Paragraph 6: In the last sentence, why is "Americanism" placed in quotation marks?
‡ Paragraph 7: What is "that happier American culture which the gangster denies"?

The gangster's activity is actually a form of rational enterprise, involving fairly definite goals and various techniques for achieving them. But this rationality is usually no more than a vague background; we know, perhaps, that the gangster sells liquor or that he operates a numbers racket; often we are not given even that much information. So his activity becomes a kind of pure criminality: he hurts people. Certainly our response to the gangster film is most consistently and most universally a response to sadism; we gain the double satisfaction of participating vicariously in the gangster's sadism and then seeing it turned against the gangster himself.   9

But on another level the quality of irrational brutality and the quality of rational enterprise become one. Since we do not see the rational and routine aspects of the gangster's behavior, the practice of brutality—the quality of unmixed criminality—becomes the totality of his career. At the same time, we are always conscious that the whole meaning of his career is a drive for success: the typical gangster film presents a steady upward progress followed by a very precipitate fall. Thus brutality itself becomes at once the means to success and the content of success—a success that is defined in its most general terms, not as accomplishment or specific gain, but simply as the unlimited possibility of aggression. (In the same way, film presentations of businessmen tend to make it appear that they achieve their success by talking on the telephone and holding conferences and that success *is* talking on the telephone and holding conferences.)   10

From this point of view, the initial contact between the film and its audience is an agreed conception of human life: that man is a being with the possibilities of success or failure. This principle, too, belongs to the city; one must emerge from the crowd or else one is nothing. On that basis the necessity of the action is established, and it progresses by inalterable paths to the point where the gangster lies dead and the principle has been modified: there is really only one possibility—failure. The final meaning of the city is anonymity and death.   11

In the opening scene of *Scarface,* we are shown a successful man; we know he is successful because he has just given a party of opulent proportions and because he is called Big Louie. Through some monstrous lack of caution, he permits himself to be alone for a few moments. We understand from this immediately that he is about to be killed. No convention of the gangster film is more strongly established than this: it is dangerous to be alone. And yet the very conditions of success make it impossible not to be alone, for success is always the establishment of an *individual* preeminence that must be imposed on others, in whom it automatically arouses hatred; the successful man is an outlaw. The gangster's whole life is an effort to assert himself as an individual, to draw himself out of the crowd, and he always dies *because* he is an individual; the final bullet thrusts him back, makes him, after all, a failure. "Mother of God," says the dying Little Caesar, "is this the end of Rico?"—speaking of him-self thus in the third person because what has been brought low is not the undifferentiated *man*, but the individual with a name, the gangster, the success; even to himself he is a creature of the imagination. (T. S. Eliot has pointed out that a number of Shakespeare's tragic heroes have this trick of looking at themselves dramatically; their true identity, the thing that is destroyed when they die, is something outside themselves—not a man, but a style of life, a kind of meaning).   12

   At bottom, the gangster is doomed because he is under the obliga-tion to succeed, not because the means he employs are unlawful. In the deeper layers of the modern consciousness, *all* means are unlawful, every attempt to succeed is an act of aggression, leaving one alone and guilty and defenseless among enemies: one is *punished* for success. This is our intolerable dilemma: that failure is a kind of death and success is evil and dangerous, is—ultimately—impossible. The effect of the gangster film is to embody this dilemma in the person of the gangster and resolve it by his death. The dilemma is resolved because it is *his* death, not ours. We are safe; for the moment, we can acquiesce in our failure, we can choose to fail.*   13

* Paragraph 13: In the last paragraph, how does the punctuation—colons, dashes, semi-colons, commas—enhance the rhetorical effectiveness of the paragraph?

The Whole Selection

1 What function do paragraphs 1 and 2 serve in the total structure of the essay?
2 Where does the process analysis begin?
3 Be sure to note Warshow's distinction between the gangster in real life and the gangster as "a creature of the imagination," "as an experience of art." In the process analysis, which one is being explained?
4 In terms of Warshow's use of the word "optimism" in paragraphs 2 and 3, how would you define it?
5 In paragraph 11, how is the last sentence, "The final meaning of the city is anonymity and death," related to the sociological implications found in the first three paragraphs of this essay? How is the thought of the last paragraph of the essay also related to these same implications?
6 Rewrite the substance of paragraph 10 in your own words.

Word Study *supra-political, reprobation, philistinism, euphoria, attenuated, nihilism, vicariously, opulent*

THE EMPTY COLUMN

TOBIAS DANTZIG

> *It is India that gave us the ingenious method of expressing all numbers by means of ten symbols, each symbol receiving a value of position as well as an absolute value; a profound and important idea which appears so simple to us now that we ignore its true merit. But its very simplicity and the great ease which it has lent to all computations put our arithmetic in the first rank of useful inventions; and we shall appreciate the grandeur of this achievement the more when we remember that it escaped the genius of Archimedes and Apollonius, two of the greatest men produced by antiquity.*   —Laplace

As I am writing these lines there rings in my ears the old refrain:

Reading, 'Riting, 'Rithmetic,
Taught to the tune of a hickory-stick!   1

In this chapter I propose to tell the story of one of three R's, the one, which, though oldest, came hardest to mankind.   2

It is not a story of brilliant achievement, heroic deeds, or noble sacrifice. It is a story of blind stumbling and chance discovery, of groping in the dark and refusing to admit the light. It is a story replete with obscurantism and prejudice, of sound judgment often eclipsed by loyalty to tradition, and of reason long held subservient to custom. In short, it is a human story.*   3

II

Written numeration is probably as old as private property. There is little doubt that it originated in man's desire to keep a record of his flocks and other goods. Notches on a stick or tree, scratches on stones and rocks, marks in clay—these are the earliest forms of this endeavor to record numbers by written symbols. Archeological researches trace such records to times immemorial, as they are found in the caves of prehistoric man in Europe, Africa and Asia. Numeration is at least as old as written language, and there is evidence that it preceded it. Perhaps, even, the recording of numbers had suggested the recording of sounds.   4

---

* Paragraph 3: Is the repeated use of parallelism in the sentences here effective?

The oldest records indicating the systematic use of written numerals are those of the ancient Sumerians and Egyptians. They are all traced back to about the same epoch, around 3500 B.C. When we examine them we are struck with the great similarity in the principles used. There is, of course, the possibility that there was communication between these peoples in spite of the distances that separated them. However, it is more likely that they developed their numerations along the lines of least resistance, i.e., that their numerations were but an outgrowth of the natural process of tallying. (See figure below.)   5

Indeed, whether it be the cuneiform numerals of the ancient Babylonians, the hieroglyphics of the Egyptian papyri, or the queer figures of the early Chinese records, we find everywhere a distinctly *cardinal* principle. Each numeral up to nine is merely a collection of strokes. The same principle is used beyond nine, units of a higher class, such as tens, hundreds, etc., being represented by special symbols.*   6

III

The English tally-stick, of obscure but probably very ancient origin, also bears this unquestionably cardinal character. A schematic picture of the tally is shown in the accompanying figure. The small notches each represent a pound sterling, the larger ones 10 pounds, 100 pounds, etc.   7

It is curious that the English tally persisted for many centuries after the introduction of modern numeration made its use ridiculously obsolete.

	1	2	3	4	5	9	10	12	23	60	100	1000	10,000
Sumerian 3400 B.C.	𒁹	𒈫	𒐈	𒐉	𒐊	𒐘	𒌋	𒌋𒈫	𒎙𒈫	𒐏	𒐕	𒐕	𒐏
Hieroglyphics 3400 B.C.	𓏤	𓏥	𓏦	𓏦𓏦	𓏦𓏦𓏤	𓏭	𓎆	𓎆𓏥	𓎇𓏦	𓎊	𓍢	𓆼	𓂭
Greek	α′	β′	γ′	δ′	ε′	θ′	ι′	ι′β′	κ′γ′	ξ′	ρ′	,α	,ι

Ancient numerations.

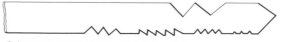

Schematic drawing of English tally-stick.

* Paragraph 6: What does *"cardinal"* mean here?

In fact it was responsible for an important episode in the history of Parliament. Charles Dickens described this episode with inimitable sarcasm in an address on Administrative Reform, which he delivered a few years after the incident occurred.

> Ages ago a savage mode of keeping accounts on notched sticks was introduced into the Court of Exchequer and the accounts were kept much as Robinson Crusoe kept his calendar on the desert island. A multitude of accountants, bookkeepers, and actuaries were born and died. . . . Still official routine inclined to those notched sticks as if they were pillars of the Constitution, and still the Exchequer accounts continued to be kept on certain splints of elm-wood called *tallies*. In the reign of George III an inquiry was made by some revolutionary spirit whether, pens, ink and paper, slates and pencils being in existence, this obstinate adherence to an obsolete custom ought to be continued, and whether a change ought not be effected. All the red tape in the country grew redder at the bare mention of this bold and original conception, and it took until 1826 to get these sticks abolished. In 1834 it was found that there was a considerable accumulation of them; and the question then arose, what was to be done with such worn-out, worm-eaten, rotten old bits of wood? The sticks were housed in Westminster, and it would naturally occur to any intelligent person that nothing could be easier than to allow them to be carried away for firewood by the miserable people who lived in that neighborhood. However, they never had been useful, and official routine required that they should never be, and so the order went out that they were to be privately and confidentially burned. It came to pass that they were burned in a stove in the House of Lords. The stove, over-gorged with these preposterous sticks, set fire to the panelling; the panelling set fire to the House of Commons; the two houses were reduced to ashes; architects were called in to build others; and we are now in the second million of the cost thereof.   8

As opposed to this purely cardinal character of the earliest records there is the ordinal numeration, in which the numbers are represented by the letters of an alphabet in their spoken succession.   9

The earliest evidence of this principle is that of the Phoenician numeration. It probably arose from the urge for compactness brought about by the complexities of a growing commerce. The Phoenician origin of both the Hebrew and the Greek numeration is unquestionable: the Phoenician system was adopted boldly, together with the alphabet, and even the sounds of the letters were retained.   10

On the other hand, the Roman numeration, which has survived to this day, shows a marked return to the earlier cardinal methods. Yet Greek influence is shown in the literal symbols adopted for certain units, such as X for ten, C for hundred, M for thousand. But the substitution of letters for the more picturesque symbols of the Chaldeans or the Egyptians does not constitute a departure from principle.   11

V

The evolution of the numerations of antiquity found its final expression in the ordinal system of the Greeks and the cardinal system of Rome. Which of the two was superior? The question would have significance if the only object of a numeration were a compact recording of quantity. But this is not the main issue. A far more important question is: how well is the system adapted to arithmetical operations, and what ease does it lend to calculations?   12

In this respect there is hardly any choice between the two methods: neither was capable of creating an arithmetic which could be used by a man of average intelligence. This is why, from the beginning of history until the advent of our modern *positional* numeration, so little progress was made in the art of reckoning.*   13

Not that there were no attempts to devise rules for operating on these numerals. How difficult these rules were can be gleaned from the great awe in which all reckoning was held in these days. A man skilled in the art was regarded as endowed with almost supernatural powers. This may explain why arithmetic from time immemorial was so assiduously cultivated by the priesthood. We shall have occasion later to dwell at greater length on this relation of early mathematics to religious rites and mysteries. Not only was this true of the ancient Orient, where science was built around religion, but even the enlightened Greeks never completely freed themselves from this mysticism of number and form.   14

And to a certain extent this awe persists to this day. The average man identifies mathematical ability with quickness in figures. "So you are a mathematician? Why, then you have no trouble with your income-tax return!" What mathematician has not at least once in his career been so addressed? There is, perhaps, unconscious irony in these words, for are not most professional mathematicians spared all trouble incident to excessive income?† 15

VI

There is a story of a German merchant of the fifteenth century, which I have not succeeded in authenticating, but it is so characteristic of the

* Paragraphs 12 and 13: Why were the Greek and Roman systems of numeration hindrances in arithmetic for a man of average intelligence?

† Paragraph 15: What unconscious irony may be found in the words in quotation marks?

situation then existing that I cannot resist the temptation of telling it. It appears that the merchant had a son whom he desired to give an advanced commercial education. He appealed to a prominent professor of a university for advice as to where he should send his son. The reply was that if the mathematical curriculum of the young man was to be confined to adding and subtracting, he perhaps could obtain the instruction in a German university; but the art of multiplying and dividing, he continued, had been greatly developed in Italy, which in his opinion was the only country where such advanced instruction could be obtained.   16

As a matter of fact, multiplication and division as practiced in those days had little in common with the modern operations bearing the same names. Multiplication, for instance, was a succession of *duplations,* which was the name given to the doubling of a number. In the same way division was reduced to *mediation,* i.e., "having" a number. A clearer insight into the status of reckoning in the Middle Ages can be obtained from an example. Using modern notations:

Today	Thirteenth century
46	$46 \times 2 = 92$
13	$46 \times 4 = 92 \times 2 = 184$
138	$46 \times 8 = 184 \times 2 = 368$
46	$368 + 184 + 46 = 598$
598		17

We begin to understand why humanity so obstinately clung to such devices as the abacus or even the tally. Computations which a child can now perform required then the services of a specialist, and what is now only a matter of a few minutes meant in the twelfth century days of elaborate work.   18

The greatly increased facility with which the average man today manipulates number has been often taken as proof of the growth of the human intellect. The truth of the matter is that the difficulties then experienced were inherent in the numeration in use, a numeration not susceptible to simple, clear-cut rules. The discovery of the modern positional numeration did away with these obstacles and made arithmetic accessible even to the dullest mind.*   19

* Paragraph 19: What is "modern positional numeration"?

VII

The growing complexities of life, industry and commerce, of landed property and slave-holding, of taxation and military organization—all called for calculations more or less intricate, but beyond the scope of the finger technique. The rigid, unwieldy numeration was incapable of meeting the demand. How did man, in the five thousand years of his civilized existence which preceded modern numeration, counter these difficulties?   20

The answer is that from the very outset he had to resort to mechanical devices which vary in form with place and age but are all the same in principle. The scheme can be typified by the curious method of counting an army which has been found in Madagascar. The soldiers are made to file through a narrow passage, and one pebble is dropped for each. When 10 pebbles are counted, a pebble is cast into another pile representing tens, and the counting continues. When 10 pepples are amassed in the second pile, a pebble is cast into a third pile representing hundreds, and so on until all the soldiers have been accounted for.   21

From this there is but one step to the *counting board* or *abacus* which in one form or another has been found in practically every country where a counting technique exists. The abacus in its general form consists of a flat board divided into a series of parallel columns, each column representing a distinct decimal class, such as units, tens, hundreds, etc. The board is provided with a set of counters which are used to indicate the number of units in each class. For instance, to represent 574 on the abacus, 4 counters are put on the last column, 7 counters on the next to the last and 5 on the third to the last column. (See figure opposite.)   22

The many counting boards known differ merely in the construction of the columns and in the type of counters used. The Greek and Roman types had loose counters, while the Chinese Suan-Pan of today has perforated balls sliding on slender bamboo rods. The Russian Szczety, like the Chinese variety, consists of a wooden frame on which are mounted a series of wire rods with sliding buttons for counters. Finally, it is more than probable that the ancient Hindu *dust board* was also an abacus in principle, the part of the counters here being played by erasable marks written on sand.   23

The origin of the word abacus is not certain. Some trace it to the Semitic *abac*, dust; others believe that it came from the Greek *abax*, slab. The instrument was widely used in Greece, and we find references to it in Herodotus and Polybius. The latter, commenting on the court of Philip II of Macedonia in his *Historia* makes this suggestive statement: 24

> Like counters on the abacus which at the pleasure of the calculator may at one moment be worth a talent and the next moment a chalcus, so are the courtiers at their King's nod at one moment at the height of prosperity and at the next objects of human pity.

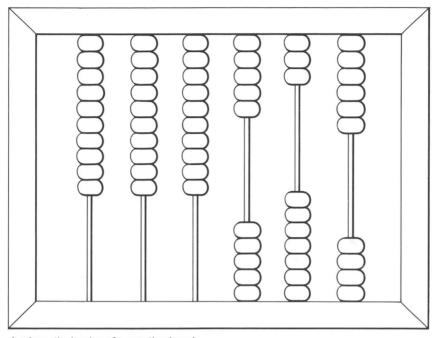

A schematic drawing of a counting board.

To this day the counting board is in daily use in the rural districts of Russia and throughout China, where it persists in open competition with modern calculating devices. But in Western Europe and America the abacus survived as a mere curiosity which few people have seen except in pictures. Few realize how extensively the abacus was used in their own countries only a few hundred years ago, where after a fashion it managed to meet the difficulties which were beyond the power of a clumsy numeration.

25

VIII

One who reflects upon the history of reckoning up to the invention of the principle of position is struck by the paucity of achievement. This long period of nearly five thousand years saw the fall and rise of many a civilization, each leaving behind it a heritage of literature, art, philosophy and religion. But what was the net achievement in the field of reckoning, the earliest art practiced by man? An inflexible numeration so crude as to make progress well-nigh impossible, and a calculating device so limited in scope that even elementary calculations called for the services of an expert. And what is more, man used these devices for thousands of years without making a single worth-while improvement in the instrument, without contributing a single important idea to the system!   26

This criticism may sound severe; after all it is not fair to judge the achievements of a remote age by the standards of our own time of accelerated progress and feverish activity. Yet, even when compared with the slow growth of ideas during the Dark Ages, the history of reckoning presents a peculiar picture of desolate stagnation.   27

When viewed in this light, the achievement of the unknown Hindu who some time in the first centuries of our era discovered the *principle of position* assumes the proportions of a world-event. Not only did this principle constitute a radical departure in method, but we know now that without it no progress in arithmetic was possible. And yet the principle is so simple that today the dullest school boy has no difficulty in grasping it. In a measure, it is suggested by the very structure of our number language. Indeed, it would appear that the first attempt to translate the action of the counting board into the language of numerals ought to have resulted in the discovery of the principle of position.   28

Particularly puzzling to us is the fact that the great mathematicians of classical Greece did not stumble on it. Is it that the Greeks had such a marked contempt for applied science, leaving even the instruction of their children to the slaves? But if so, how is it that the nation which gave us geometry and carried this science so far, did not create even a rudimentary algebra? Is it not equally strange that algebra, that cornerstone of modern mathematics, also originated in India and at about the same time when positional numeration did?   29

IX

A close examination of the anatomy of our modern numeration may shed light on these questions. The principle of position consists in giving the numeral a value which depends not only on the member of the natural sequence it represents, but also on the position it occupies with respect to the other symbols of the group. Thus, the same digit 2 has different meanings in the three numbers 342, 725, 269: in the first case it stands for two; in the second for twenty, in the third for two hundred. As a matter of fact 342 is just an abbreviation for three hundred plus four tens plus two units.   30

But that is precisely the scheme of the counting board, where 342 is represented by

And, as I said before, it would seem that it is sufficient to translate this scheme into the language of numerals to obtain substantially what we have today.   31

True! But there is one difficulty. Any attempt to make a permanent record of a counting-board operation would meet the obstacle that such an entry as $\equiv$ $=$ may represent any one of several numbers: 32, 302, 320, 3002, and 3020 among others. In order to avoid this ambiguity it is essential to have some method of representing the gaps, i.e., what is needed is a *symbol for an empty column.*   32

We see therefore that no progress was possible until a symbol was invented for an *empty* class, a symbol for *nothing*, our modern *zero*. The concrete mind of the ancient Greeks could not conceive the void as a number, let alone endow the void with a symbol.   33

And neither did the unknown Hindu see in zero the symbol of nothing. The Indian term for zero was *sunya*, which meant *empty* or *blank*, but had no connotation of "void" or "nothing." And so, from all appearances, the discovery of zero was an accident brought about by an attempt to make an unambiguous permanent record of a counting-board operation.*   34

X

How the Indian *sunya* became the zero of today constitutes one of the most interesting chapters in the history of culture. When the Arabs of the tenth century adopted the Indian numeration, they translated the Indian *sunya* by their own, *sifr*, which meant empty in Arabic. When the Indo-Arabic numeration was first introduced into Italy, *sifr* was latinized into *zephirum*. This happened at the beginning of the thirteenth century, and in the course of the next hundred years the word underwent a series of changes which culminated in the Italian *zero*.   35

About the same time Jordanus Nemerarius was introducing the Arabic system into Germany. He kept the Arabic word, changing it slightly to *cifra*. That for some time in the learned circles of Europe the word *cifra* and its derivatives denoted zero is shown by the fact that the great Gauss, the last of the mathematicians of the nineteenth century who wrote in Latin, still used *cifra* in this sense. In the English language the word *cifra* has become *cipher* and has retained its original meaning of zero.   36

The attitude of the common people toward this new numeration is reflected in the fact that soon after its introduction into Europe, the word *cifra* was used as a secret sign; but this connotation was altogether lost

* Paragraphs 30 through 34: These five paragraphs might have been presented as one, not unusually long, paragraph. Why is the five-paragraph arrangement more effective here?

in the succeeding centuries. The verb *decipher* remains as a monument of these early days.   37

The next stage in this development saw the new art of reckoning spread more widely. It is significant that the essential part played by zero in this new system did not escape the notice of the masses. Indeed, they identified the whole system with its most striking feature, the *cifra*, and this explains how this word in its different forms, *ziffer, chiffre,* etc., came to receive the meaning of numeral, which it has in Europe today.   38

This double meaning, the popular *cifra* standing for numeral and the *cifra* of the learned signifying zero, caused considerable confusion. In vain did scholars attempt to revive the original meaning of the word: the popular meaning had taken deep root. The learned had to yield to popular usage, and the matter was eventually settled by adopting the Italian zero in the sense in which it is used today.   39

The same interest attaches to the word *algorithm*. As the term is used today, it applies to any mathematical procedure consisting of an indefinite number of steps, each step applying to the result of the one preceding it. But between the tenth and fifteenth centuries *algorithm* was synonymous with positional numeration. We now know that the word is merely a corruption of Al Kworesmi, the name of the Arabian mathematician of the ninth century whose book (in Latin translation) was the first work on this subject to reach Western Europe.   40

XI

Today, when positional numeration has become a part of our daily life, it seems that the superiority of this method, the compactness of its notation, the ease and elegance it introduced in calculations, should have assured the rapid and sweeping acceptance of it. In reality, the transition, far from being immediate, extended over long centuries. The struggle between the *Abacists,* who defended the old traditions, and the *Algorists,* who advocated the reform, lasted from the eleventh to the fifteenth century and went through all the usual stages of obscurantism and reaction. In some places, Arabic numerals were banned from official documents; in others, the art was prohibited altogether. And, as usual, *prohibition* did not succeed in abolishing, but merely served to spread *bootlegging,* ample evidence of which is found in the thirteenth century archives of Italy, where, it appears, merchants were using the Arabic numerals as a sort of secret code.   41

Yet, for a while reaction succeeded in arresting the progress and in hampering the development of the new system. Indeed, little of essential value or of lasting influence was contributed to the art of reckoning in these transition centuries. Only the outward appearance of the numerals went through a series of changes; not, however, from any desire for improvement, but because the manuals of these days were hand-written. In fact, the numerals did not assume a stable form until the introduction of printing. It can be added parenthetically that so great was the stabilizing influence of printing that the numerals of today have essentially the same appearance as those of the fifteenth century.   42

XII

As to the final victory of the Algorists, no definite date can be set. We do know that at the beginning of the sixteenth century the supremacy of the new numeration was incontestable. Since then progress was unhampered, so that in the course of the next hundred years all the rules of operations, both on integers and on common and decimal fractions, reached practically the same scope and form in which they are taught today in our schools.   43

Another century, and the Abacists and all they stood for were so completely forgotten that various peoples of Europe began each to regard the positional numeration as its own national achievement. So, for instance, early in the nineteenth century we find that Arabic numerals were called in Germany *Deutsche* with a view to differentiating them from the *Roman,* which were recognized as of foreign origin.   44

As to the abacus itself, no traces of it are found in Western Europe during the eighteenth century. Its reappearance early in the nineteenth century occurred under very curious circumstances. The mathematician Poncelet, a general under Napoleon, was captured in the Russian campaign and spent many years in Russia as a prisoner of war. Upon returning to France he brought, among other curios, a Russian abacus. For many years to come, this importation of Poncelet's was regarded as a great curiosity of "barbaric" origin. Such examples of national amnesia abound in the history of culture. How many educated people even today know that only four hundred years ago finger counting was the average man's only means of calculating, while the counting board was accessible only to the professional calculators of the time?   45

XIII

Conceived in all probability as the symbol for an empty column on a counting board, the Indian *sunya* was destined to become the turning-point in a development without which the progress of modern science, industry, or commerce is inconceivable. And the influence of this great discovery was by no means confined to arithmetic. By paving the way to a generalized number concept, it played just as fundamental a rôle in practically

every branch of mathematics. In the history of culture the discovery of
zero will always stand out as one of the greatest single achievements of
the human race.   46

A great discovery! Yes. But, like so many other early discoveries,
which have profoundly affected the life of the race,—not the reward of
painstaking research, but a gift from blind chance.   47

The Whole Selection

1 What does the title of the essay mean?
2 As the opening paragraphs announce, the dominant intention of this
essay is narrative—that is, the telling of a story, in this case a factual
story. The author, however, employs a variety of methods of analysis in
his narrative, including process analysis. Process analysis occurs extensively in section IX to XII (paragraphs 30-45) in this essay. What
order of arrangement is used in section IX, and what order in sections
X to XII?
3 In what other sections or paragraphs does the author use process
analysis?
4 Where are other methods of analysis—definition, example, comparison
and contrast, which you have already studied in this textbook—used in
this essay?
5 To achieve coherence within a paragraph a writer may employ a variety
of devices: connective words or phrases; word order within sentences;
various sentence structures (as, for example, a complex sentence which
may indicate what is main and what is subordinate in thought); coherent sequence of the sentences in the paragraph; parallel and balanced
structure; repetition. Cite examples of the use of such devices in paragraphs 3 to 12.
6 State the controlling or central purpose of each of the thirteen main
sections of this essay, using one brief sentence for each, and then
determine if these main divisions represent a logical outline or arrangement.

Word Study *replete, obscurantism, paucity, amnesia*

CAMPING OUT

ERNEST HEMINGWAY

Thousands of people will go into the bush this summer to cut the high cost of living. A man who gets his two weeks' salary while he is on vacation should be able to put those two weeks in fishing and camping and be able to save one week's salary clear. He ought to be able to sleep comfortably every night, to eat well every day and to return to the city rested and in good condition. 1

But if he goes into the woods with a frying pan, an ignorance of black flies and mosquitoes, and a great and abiding lack of knowledge about cookery the chances are that his return will be very different. He will come back with enough mosquito bites to make the back of his neck look like a relief map of the Caucasus. His digestion will be wrecked after a valiant battle to assimilate half-cooked or charred grub. And he won't have had a decent night's sleep while he has been gone. 2

He will solemnly raise his right hand and inform you that he has joined the grand army of never-agains. The call of the wild may be all right, but it's a dog's life. He's heard the call of the tame with both ears. Waiter, bring him an order of milk toast. 3

In the first place he overlooked the insects. Black flies, no-see-ums, deer flies, gnats and mosquitoes were instituted by the devil to force people to live in cities where he could get at them better. If it weren't for them everybody would live in the bush and he would be out of work. It was a rather successful invention. 4

But there are lots of dopes that will counteract the pests. The simplest perhaps is oil of citronella. Two bits' worth of this purchased at any pharmacist's will be enough to last for two weeks in the worst fly and mosquito-ridden country. 5

Rub a little on the back of your neck, your forehead and your wrists before you start fishing, and the blacks and skeeters will shun you. The odor of citronella is not offensive to people. It smells like gun oil. But the bugs do hate it. 6

Oil of pennyroyal and eucalyptol are also much hated by mosquitoes, and with citronella they form the basis for many proprietary preparations. But it is cheaper and better to buy the straight citronella. Put a little on the mosquito netting that covers the front of your pup tent or canoe tent at night, and you won't be bothered. 7

To be really rested and get any benefit out of a vacation a man must get a good night's sleep every night. The first requisite for this is to have plenty of cover. It is twice as cold as you expect it will be in the bush four nights out of five, and a good plan is to take just double the bedding that you think you will need. An old quilt that you can wrap up in is as warm as two blankets.   8

Nearly all outdoor writers rhapsodize over the browse bed. It is all right for the man who knows how to make one and has plenty of time. But in a succession of one-night camps on a canoe trip all you need is level ground for your tent floor and you will sleep all right if you have plenty of covers under you. Take twice as much cover as you think that you will need, and then put two-thirds of it under you. You will sleep warm and get your rest.   9

When it is clear weather you don't need to pitch your tent if you are only stopping for the night. Drive four stakes at the head of your made-up bed and drape your mosquito bar over that, then you can sleep like a log and laugh at the mosquitoes.   10

Outside of insects and bum sleeping the rock that wrecks most camping trips is cooking. The average tyro's idea of cooking is to fry everything and fry it good and plenty. Now, a frying pan is a most necessary thing to any trip, but you also need the old stew kettle and the folding reflector baker.   11

A pan of fried trout can't be bettered and they don't cost any more than ever. But there is a good and bad way of frying them.   12

The beginner puts his trout and his bacon in and over a brightly burning fire the bacon curls up and dries into a dry tasteless cinder and the trout is burned outside while it is still raw inside. He eats them and it is all right if he is only out for the day and going home to a good meal at night. But if he is going to face more trout and bacon the next morning and other equally well-cooked dishes for the remainder of two weeks he is on the pathway to nervous dyspepsia.   13

The proper way is to cook over coals. Have several cans of Crisco or Cotosuet or one of the vegetable shortenings along that are as good as lard and excellent for all kinds of shortening. Put the bacon in and when it is about half cooked lay the trout in the hot grease, dipping them in corn meal first. Then put the bacon on top of the trout and it will baste them as it slowly cooks.   14

The coffee can be boiling at the same time and in a smaller skillet pancakes being made that are satisfying the other campers while they are waiting for the trout.   15

With the prepared pancake flours you take a cupful of pancake flour and add a cup of water. Mix the water and flour and as soon as the lumps are out it is ready for cooking. Have the skillet hot and keep it well greased. Drop the batter in and as soon as it is done on one side loosen it in the skillet and flip it over. Apple butter, syrup or cinnamon and sugar go well with the cakes.   16

While the crowd have taken the edge from their appetites with flap-jacks the trout have been cooked and they and the bacon are ready to serve. The trout are crisp outside and firm and pink inside and the bacon is well done—but not too done. If there is anything better than that combination the writer has yet to taste it in a lifetime devoted largely and studiously to eating.   17

The stew kettle will cook you dried apricots when they have resumed their predried plumpness after a night of soaking, it will serve to concoct a mulligan in, and it will cook macaroni. When you are not using it, it should be boiling water for the dishes.   18

In the baker, mere man comes into his own, for he can make a pie that to his bush appetite will have it all over the product that mother used to make, like a tent. Men have always believed that there was something mysterious and difficult about making a pie. Here is a great secret. There is nothing to it. We've been kidded for years. Any man of average office intelligence can make at least as good a pie as his wife.   19

All there is to a pie is a cup and a half of flour, one-half teaspoonful of salt, one-half cup of lard and cold water. That will make pie crust that will bring tears of joy into your camping partner's eyes.   20

Mix the salt with the flour, work the lard into the flour, make it up into a good workmanlike dough with cold water. Spread some flour on the back of a box or something flat, and pat the dough around a while. Then roll it out with whatever kind of round bottle you prefer. Put a little more lard on the surface of the sheet of dough and then slosh a little flour on and roll it up and then roll it out again with the bottle.   21

Cut out a piece of the rolled out dough big enough to line a pie tin. I like the kind with holes in the bottom. Then put in your dried apples that have soaked all night and been sweetened, or your apricots, or your blueberries, and then take another sheet of the dough and drape it gracefully over the top, soldering it down at the edges with your fingers. Cut a couple of slits in the top dough sheet and prick it a few times with a fork in an artistic manner.   22

Put it in the baker with a good slow fire for forty-five minutes and then take it out and if your pals are Frenchmen they will kiss you. The penalty for knowing how to cook is that the others will make you do all the cooking.   23

It is all right to talk about roughing it in the woods. But the real woodsman is the man who can be really comfortable in the bush.   24

ROBERT BENCHLEY

This is probably the hardest time of year for those of us who didn't go to Europe last summer. It was bad enough when the others were packing and outlining their trips for you. It was pretty bad when the postcards from Lausanne and Venice began coming in. But now, in the fall, when the travelers are returning with their Marco Polo travelogs, now is when we must be brave and give a cheer for the early frost. 1

There are several ways to combat this menace of returning travelers. The one that I have found most effective is based on the old football theory that a strong offense is the best defense. I rush them right off their feet, before they can get started. 2

In carrying out this system, it is well to remember that very few travelers know anything more about the places they have visited than the names of one hotel, two points of interest, and perhaps one street. You can bluff them into insensibility by making up a name and asking them if they saw that when they were in Florence. My whole strategy is based on my ability to make up names. You can do it, too, with practice. 3

Thus, let us say that I am confronted by Mrs. Reetaly who has just returned from a frantic tour of Spain, southern France, and the Ritz Hotel, Paris. You are inextricably cornered with her at a tea, or beer night, or something. Following is a transcript of the conversation. (Note the gathering power of my offense.) 4

Mrs. R.: Well, we have just returned from Europe, and everything seems so strange here. I simply can't get used to our money. 5

Mr. B.: I never see enough of it to get used to it myself. (*Just a pleasantry*) 6

Mrs. R.: When we were in Madrid, I just gave up trying to figure out the Spanish money. You see, they have *pesetas* and———— 7

Mr. B.: A very easy way to remember Spanish money is to count ten *segradas* to one *mesa,* ten *mesas* to one *rintilla* and twenty *rintillas* to one *peseta.* 8

Mrs. R.: Oh, you have been to Spain? Did you go to Toledo? 9

Mr. B.: Well, of course, Toledo is just the beginning. You have pushed on to Mastilejo, of course? 10

Mrs. R.: Why——er——no. We were in quite a hurry to get to Granada and———— 11

Mr. B.: You didn't see Mastilejo? That's too bad. Mastilejo is Toledo multiplied by a hundred. Such mountains! Such coloring! Leaving Mastilejo, one ascends by easy stages to the ridge behind the town from which

188

is obtained an incomparable view of the entire Bobadilla Valley. It was
here that, in 1476, the Moors——   12

Mrs. R.: The Moorish relics in Granada——   13

Mr. B.: The Moorish relics in Granada are like something you buy
from Sears-Roebuck compared to the remains in Tuna. You saw Tuna, of
course?   14

Mrs. R.: Well, no (*lying her head off*), we were going there, but Harry
thought that it would just be repeating what——   15

Mr. B.: The biggest mistake of your life, Mrs. Reetaly, the biggest
mistake of your life! Unless you have seen Tuna, you haven't seen Spain.   16

Mrs. R.: But Carcassonne——   17

Mr. B.: Ah, Carcassonne! Now you're talking! Did you ever see anything to beat that old diamond mill in the *Vielle Ville?* Would they let you
go through it when you were there?   18

Mrs. R.: Why, I don't think that we saw any old diamond mill. We
saw an old——   19

Mr. B.: I know what you're going to say! You saw the old wheat sifter.
Isn't that fascinating? Did you talk with the old courier there?   20

Mrs. R.: Why, I don't remember——   21

Mr. B.: And the hole in the wall where Louis the Neurotic escaped
from the Saracens?   22

Mrs. R.: Yes, wasn't that——? (*Very weak*)   23

Mr. B.: And the stream where they found the sword and buckler of
the Man with the Iron Abdomen?   24

Mrs. R. (*edging away*): Yes, indeed.   25

Mr. B.: And old Vastelles? You visited Vastelles, surely? . . . Mrs.
Reetaly, come back here, please! I just love talking over these dear places
with someone who has just been there. . . . May I call on you some day
soon and we'll just have a feast of reminiscence? . . . Thank you. How
about tomorrow?   26

And from that day to this, I am never bothered by Mrs. Reetaly's
European trip, and you needn't be, either, if you will only study the above
plan carefully.   27

The other method is based on just the opposite theory—that of no
offense, or defense, at all. It is known as "dumb submission," and should
be tried only by very phlegmatic people who can deaden their sensibilities
so that they don't even hear the first ten minutes of the traveler's ha-
rangue. The idea is to let them proceed at will for a time and then give un-
mistakable evidence of not having heard a word they have said. Let us say
that Mr. Thwomly has accosted me on the train.   28

Mr. T.: It certainly seems funny to be riding in trains like this again.
We have been all summer in France, you know, and those French trains

are all divided up into compartments. You get into a compartment—
compartimon, they call them—and there you are with three or five other
people, all cooped up together. On the way from Paris to Marseilles we
had a funny experience. I was sitting next to a Frenchman who was getting
off at Lyons—Lyons is about half way between Paris and Marseilles—and
he was dozing when we got in. So I——   29

Mr. B.: Did you get to France at all when you were away?   30

Mr. T.: This was in *France* that I'm telling you about. On the way
from Paris to Marseilles. We got into a railway carriage——   31

Mr. B.: The railway carriages there aren't like ours here, are they?
I've seen pictures of them, and they seem to be more like compartments
of some sort.   32

Mr. T. (*a little discouraged*): That was a French railway carriage I
was just describing to you. I sat next to a man——   33

Mr. B.: A Frenchman?   34

Mr. T.: Sure, a Frenchman. That's the *point*.   35

Mr. B.: Oh, I see.   36

Mr. T.: Well, the Frenchman was asleep, and when we got in I stumbled over his feet. So he woke up and said something in French, which I
couldn't understand, and I excused myself in English, which *he* couldn't
understand, but I saw by his ticket that he was going only as far as
Lyons——   37

Mr. B.: You were across the border into France, then?   38

Mr. T.: (*giving the whole thing up as a bad job*): And what did *you*
do this summer?   39

Whichever way you pick to defend yourself against the assults of
people who want to tell you about Europe, don't forget that it was I who
told you how. I'm going to Europe myself next year, and if you try to pull
either of these systems on *me* when I get back, I will recognize them at
once, and it will just go all the harder with you. But, of course, *I* will
have something to tell that will be worth hearing.   40

Suggestions for Writing

1 Write an essay explaining something which seems to be a relatively
   simple and ordinary process, but of which many people have missed the
   essential techniques. Keep Mortimer Adler's essay in mind.
   a How to study successfully
   b How to win at tennis (any sport)
   c Borrowing money from a friend
   d The art of polishing the apple

2 Write an essay explaining a complex process which you know but which your reader may not know. Take special pains to make your language clear and simple: you will have to be especially careful to use language with which your reader is familiar, or you will have to define those terms essential to your explanation which the reader may not know.

a What television is

b Explaining the "hi" in hi-fi

c Developing your own photographs

d The operation of radar

3 Write an essay on any one of the following topics, taking special care to make the steps in the process clear to the reader.

a Following a bill through Congress

b Making the most of a small (large) yard

c Planning a trip to Europe (South America, anywhere)

d Giving a party, or how not to give a party

4 In the same way Warshow analyzed the gangster as tragic hero, write an essay explaining what goes to make up the character of the Western film hero as a type, or the character of the politician, the campus radical, or the nonstudent.

THE PARTS AND THE WHOLE: CLASSIFICATION AND DIVISION

Although classification and division is one of the more sophisticated methods of analysis, it is used at some time or another by everyone. A favorite indoor sport of Americans has come to be applying labels to the rest of the population. We speak glibly in these years of the twentieth century of the "organization man," the "man in the gray flannel suit," the suburbanite, the exurbanite, the hawk, the dove. What we are really doing is classifying certain people, putting them into a category suggested by the characteristics that they appear to possess. An economist might classify Americans, according to their economic standing, as low-income group, middle-income group, and high-income group. In each case, certain characteristics have been classified, assigned to a category. In the first essay in this section, Aldous Huxley calls classification "the first and indispensable condition of systematic thought."

In many essays, however, we discover a contrasting tendency, the expression of division or partition—that is, taking a whole and separating it into its parts. A historian, for instance, might divide the history of America into four periods—the era of discovery, colonial times, the age of national consciousness, and modern times. Aristotle divided the concept of government into three parts—rule by a king, rule by an aristocracy, and rule by the citizens at large. In both cases, the subject has been divided into distinct parts. Some rhetoricians regard division as so crucial that they treat it as a separate rhetorical category. What was said previously, however, about comparison and contrast (page 105) is just as true of classification and division. Even though a given essay might emphasize one more than the other, the two must be considered together as one method of analysis because the use of one implies, at least, the presence of the other. The two aspects of this method of analysis are intimately joined—so intimately that the rules for an adequate division are inversely the rules for a legitimate classification.

When we classify a subject, we are concerned with it in its relationship to the whole of which it is a part. When we divide a subject, we are concerned with it in its relationship to the parts which make up the whole. Or, to put it another way, a subject is classifiable when it is regarded as a part of a whole, and a subject is divisible when it is regarded as a whole. In classification we relate the individual subject to a class larger than itself; in division we relate the subject to parts smaller than itself. Classification is, therefore, an upward movement, while division is a downward movement. It is obvious that classification and division as a method of analysis is closely related to definition (see pages 41–44). Classification explains or establishes the genus; division explains or establishes the species.

Aldous Huxley's "Who Are You?" (page 196) and Aaron Copland's "What to Listen for in Music" (page 220) are illustrations of the methods of classification and division. Huxley's essay is a classification of the varieties of the human physique on the basis of certain physical characteristics. Because of the relationship of the physiological and the psychological, this first classification leads to a second classification—temperaments by type: viscerotonia, somatotonia, and cerebrotonia. A careful reading of the essay will show that each class was arrived at only after an extensive investigation of characteristic likenesses which could be grouped together into a class or category. Whereas Huxley's essay uses an upward movement, Copland's uses a downward movement. After telling the reader that we all listen to music on three distinct planes, Copland says, "The whole listening process may become clearer if we break it up into its component parts." And so he divides the listening process into the sensuous plane, the expressive plane, and the sheerly musical plane. When we divide or partition, we take something apart that is regarded as a whole and not as a part. The process of listening to music is here regarded by Copland as a whole with distinct parts.

Any given subject may be either classified or divided, depending upon how it is regarded, as part of a class or as a whole having parts. The government of the United States, for example, can be divided into the legislative, executive, and judicial branches. Or it can be classified as a republic to distinguish it from other classes of government, such as monarchies or dictatorships.

An essay that uses classification and division as a method of analysis must observe the criteria for the method. First, a clear basis for the classification or division at any stage of the operation must be established. We cannot, for instance, divide an egg on the basis of the chemical elements it contains and then cite size as one of the parts. Surely size is a "part" of the egg, but it is not a part for the writer who is interested in analyzing its chemical elements. In "What Every Writer Must Learn" (page 211), once having made his major divisions on the basis of what can be learned by the creative writer, John Ciardi does not introduce as one of his major divisions something so illogically related to his parts as, for example, advice to a young writer.

The second criterion for classification and division demands that the writer follow the principle of his classification or division through consistently and logically until it is as complete as it needs to be. The extent to which a writer exhausts his analysis depends upon the purpose of his writing. The scientist or the philosopher

writing a formal exposition must be as exhaustive as the possibilities
will allow. Aldous Huxley's explanation of this point is worth quoting.
"For the purposes of pure and applied science, the best classification
is comprehensive, covering as many of the indefinitely numerous
facts as it is possible for thought to cover without becoming
confused, and yet it is simple enough to be readily understood and
used without being so simple as to be untrue to the essentially
complex nature of reality."

Sheldon's classification, which Huxley explains, is complete,
exhaustive. This system, in terms of which the continuous variations
of the human physique can adequately be described, is based upon the
discrimination of three factors, present to a varying degree in every
individual. For rhetorical purposes, however, all classifications or
divisions need not be this complete, so long as the writer makes it
quite clear to the reader that he does not intend to exhaust the
subject completely. Ulf Hannerz, for example, makes it quite clear, in
"The Rhetoric of Soul" (page 226), that he will deal with only "a
few characteristics of what is 'soul'." Ciardi tells the reader that he
intends to present only the main elements of what he believes every
writer must learn, and he exhausts his division only as regards
this intent.

Any classification or division will be made on the basis of some
special interest in the subject being analyzed. A book, for instance,
might be divided into its chapters by a reviewer, classified on the
basis of its weight by the post office, divided on the basis of the
major points it makes about its subject by a student, or classified
as a kind of contribution to the scholarship of the field with which it
deals by a scholar. In all examples of classification and division some
special interest on the part of the writer will determine the kind of
category he works up to or the partition he works down to.

ALDOUS HUXLEY

The most striking fact about human beings is that, in many respects, they are very unlike one another. Their bodies vary enormously in size and shape. Their modes of thought and speech and feeling are startlingly different. Startlingly different, too, are their reactions to even such basic things as food, sex, money, and power. Between the most highly gifted and those of least ability, and between persons endowed with one particular kind of talent or temperament and persons endowed with another kind, the gulfs are so wide as to be bridgeable only by the most enlightened charity.   1

These are facts which from time immemorial have been recognized, described in plays and stories, commented on in proverbs, aphorisms, and poems. And yet, in spite of their obviousness and their enormous practical importance, these facts are still, to a very great extent, outside the pale of systematic thought.*   2

The first and indispensable condition of systematic thought is classification. For the purposes of pure and applied science, the best classification is comprehensive, covering as many of the indefinitely numerous facts as it is possible for thought to cover without becoming confused, and yet is simple enough to be readily understood and used without being so simple as to be untrue to the essentially complex nature of reality. The categories under which it classifies things and events are easily recognizable, lend themselves to being expressed in quantitative terms, and can be shown experimentally to be meaningful for our specifically human purposes.   3

Up to the present, all the systems in terms of which men have attempted to think about human differences have been unsatisfactory. Some, for example, have conspicuously failed to cover more than a part of the relevant facts. This is especially true of psychology and sociology as commonly taught and practised at the present time. How many of even the best of our psychologists talk, write, think, and act as though the human body, with its innate constitution and its acquired habits, were something that, in an analysis of mental states, could safely be ignored! And even when they do admit, rather reluctantly, that the mind always trails its carcass behind it, they have little or nothing to tell us about the ways in which mental and physical characteristics are related.†   4

---

* Paragraphs 1 and 2: What is the function of the first two paragraphs?

† Paragraph 4: How does the example cited show that all systems of thinking about human differences have been unsatisfactory?

Sociologists deal with abstractions even more phantasmally bodiless. For example, they will carry out laborious researches into the problems of marriage. But when we read the results, we are flabbergasted to find that the one factor never taken into account by the researchers is who the men and women under investigation actually *are*. We are told every detail about their social and economic background; nothing at all about their inherited psycho-physical constitution.*   5

There are other classificatory systems which claim to be comprehensive, but in which the indispensable process of simplification has been carried so far that they are no longer true to the facts. The interpretation of all human activity in terms of economics is a case in point. Another type of oversimplification is to be found in such theories as those of Helvétius in the eighteenth century and of certain Behaviorists in the twentieth—theories which profess to account for everything that men do or are in terms of environment, education, or conditioned reflexes. At the other extreme of oversimplification we find some of the more rabid Eugenists, who attribute all the observable differences between human beings to hereditary factors, and refuse to admit that environmental influences may also play a part.†   6

It may be remarked in passing that most of the hypotheses and classification systems we use in our everyday thinking are grossly oversimplified and therefore grossly untrue to a reality which is intrinsically complex. Popular theories about such things as morals, politics, economics, and religion are generally of the either-or, A-causes-B variety. But in any real-life situation there are almost always more than two valid and workable alternatives and invaribly more than one determining cause. That is why the utterances of speech-making politicians can never, in the very nature of things, be true. In half an hour's yelling from a platform it is intellectually impossible for even the most scrupulous man to tell the delicately complex truth about any of the major issues of political or economic life.   7

We come now to the classification systems which attempt to cover the whole ground, but which have proved scientifically unsatisfactory because (though founded, as they often are, upon profound insights into the nature of human reality) they have made use of categories which could not be expressed in quantitative terms. Thus, for several thousands of years, the Hindus have been classifying human beings within the framework of four main psycho-physico-social categories. Because the caste system in India has become petrified into a rigidity that is untrue to the facts of life and therefore often unjust, the whole idea of caste is repellent

---

* Paragraph 5: In the third sentence, what does the last "are" mean?

† Paragraph 6: What are the three types of oversimplification which Huxley cites here?

to Western minds. And yet that special branch of applied psychology which deals with vocational guidance is concerned precisely with assigning individuals to their proper place in the natural caste system. The work of the specialists in "human engineering" has made it quite clear that individuals belong congenitally to one kind of caste, and that they hurt themselves and their society if, by some mistake, they get enrolled in another caste. Some time in the next century or two the empirical findings of the vocational guidance experts will be linked up with a satisfactory method of analyzing the total psycho-physical organism. When that happens, society will be in a position to reorganize itself on the basis of a rejuvenated and thoroughly beneficent, because thoroughly realistic, caste system.   8

In the West, for more than two thousand years, men were content with a classification system devised by the Greek physician, Hippocrates. His theory was that one's innate psycho-physical constitution was determined by the relative predominance within one's body of one or other of the four "humors"—blood, phlegm, black bile, and yellow bile. (We still describe temperaments as "sanguine" or "phlegmatic"; we still talk of "choler" and "melancholia.") Humoral pathology persisted into the nineteenth century. Diseases were attributed to a derangement of the normal balance of the individual's humors, and treatment was directed to restoring the equilibrium. This relating of disease to inherited constitution was essentially realistic, and one of the things that modern medicine most urgently needs is a new and sounder version of the Hippocratic hypothesis —a classification of human differences in terms of which the physician may interpret the merely mechanical findings of his diagnostic instruments.   9

Finally we come to those classification systems which are unsatisfactory because the categories they make use of, although susceptible of being expressed in quantitative terms, have not, in practice, turned out to be particularly meaningful. Thus the anthropometrists have measured innumerable skulls, determined the coloring of innumerable heads of hair and pairs of eyes, but have told us very little of genuinely scientific or practical value about human beings. Why? Because, as a matter of empirical fact, these records and measurements could not be related in any significant way to human behavior.   10

And, not content with telling us very little by means of a colossal volume of statistics, the anthropometrists proceeded to confuse the whole issue by trying to think about human differences in terms of fixed racial types—the Nordic, the Alpine, the Mediterranean, and so forth. But the most obvious fact about all the existing groups of human beings, at any rate in Europe and America, is that each one of them exhibits a large number of individual variations. In certain areas, it is true, a single closely related set of such variations may be more common than in other areas. It is upon this fact that the whole theory of racial types has been built up —a system of classification which has proved extremely unfruitful as an instrument of pure and applied science, and, in the hands of the Nazi ideologists, extremely fruitful as an instrument of discrimination and persecution.   11

II

So much, then, for the classification systems which have proved to be unsatisfactory. Does there exist a more adequate system? This is a question which it is now possible, I think, to answer with a decided yes. A classification system more adequate to the facts and more potentially fruitful than any other devised hitherto has been formulated by Dr. W. H. Sheldon in two recently published volumes, *The Varieties of Human Physique* and *The Varieties of Temperament*.   12

Sheldon's classification system is the fruit of nearly fifteen years of research, during which he and his collaborators have made, measured, and arranged in order many thousands of standardized photographs of the male body, taken from in front, from behind, and in profile. A careful study of these photographs revealed that the most basic (first order) classification system in terms of which the continuous variations of human physique could adequately be described was based upon the discrimination of three factors, present to a varying degree in every individual. To these three factors Sheldon has given the names of *endomorphy, mesomorphy,* and *ectomorphy.*   13

Endomorphy is the factor which, when predominant, expresses itself in a tendency for anabolism to predominate over catabolism, which often results in soft and comfortable roundness of physique. At school the extreme endomorph is called Slob or Fatty. By middle life he or she may be so enormously heavy as to be practically incapable of walking. The endomorphic physique is dominated by its digestive tract. Autopsies show that the endomorphic gut is often more than twice as long and weighs more than twice as much as the intestine of a person in whom there is an extreme predominance of the ectomorphic constituent.   14

Predominant mesomorphy expresses itself in a physique that is hard and muscular. The body is built around strong heavy bones and is dominated by its extraordinarily powerful muscles. In youth, the extreme mesomorph tends to look older than his years, and his skin, instead of being soft, smooth, and unwrinkled, like that of the endomorph, is coarse and leathery, tans easily, and sets in deep folds and creases at a comparatively early age. It is from the ranks of extreme mesomorphs that successful boxers, football players, military leaders, and the central figures of the more heroic comic strips are drawn.   15

The extreme ectomorph is neither comfortably round nor compactly hard. His is a linear physique with slender bones, stringy unemphatic muscles, a short and thin-walled gut. The ectomorph is a lightweight, has little muscular strength, needs to eat at frequent intervals, is often quick and highly sensitive. The ratio of skin surface to body mass is higher than in endomorphs or mesomorphs, and he is thus more vulnerable to outside influences, because more extensively in contact with them. His body is built, not around the endomorph's massively efficient intestine, not around the mesomorph's big bones and muscles, but around a relatively predominant and unprotected nervous system.   16

Endomorphy, mesomorphy, and ectomorphy occur, as constituting components, in every human individual. In most persons the three components are combined fairly evenly, or at least harmoniously. Extreme and unbalanced predominance of any one factor is relatively uncommon.   17

For example, less than ten boys out of every hundred are sufficiently mesomorphic to engage with even moderate success in the more strenuous forms of athletics, requiring great strength and physical endurance. Hence the almost criminal folly of encouraging all boys, whatever their hereditary make-up, to develop athletic ambitions. By doing this, educators condemn large numbers of their pupils to an unnecessary disappointment and frustration, plant the seed of neurosis among the unsuccessful, and foster a conspicuous bumptiousness and self-conceit in the extreme mesomorph. A rational policy with regard to athletics would be to tell all boys the simple truth, which is that very few of them can expect to excel in the more violent sports, that such excellence depends primarily on a particular inheritance of size and shape, and that persons of other shapes and sizes not suited to athletic proficiency have as good a right to realize their own *natural* capacities as the extreme mesomorph and can contribute at least as much to society.   18

In order to calculate the relative amounts of each component in the total individual mixture, Sheldon divides the body into five regions and proceeds to make a number of measurements in each zone. The records of these measurements are then subjected to certain mathematical procedures, which yield a three-digit formula. This formula expresses the amount of endomorphy, mesomorphy, and ectomorphy present within the organism, as measured on a seven-point scale of values. Thus the formula 7–1–1 indicates that the individual under consideration exhibits endomorphy in its highest possible degree, combined with the lowest degree of mesomorphy and ectomorphy. In practice, he would probably be extremely fat, gluttonous and comfort-loving, without drive or energy, almost sexless, and pathetically dependent on other people. How different from the well-balanced 4–4–4, the formidably powerful and aggressive 3–7–1, the thin, nervous, "introverted" 1–2–7!   19

The relationships between the components are such that only a certain number of the mathematically possible combinations can occur in nature. Thus it is obviously impossible for a human being to be a 7–1–7, or a 7–7–7, or a 1–7–7; for nobody can be simultaneously extremely round and soft and extremely hard and compact or extremely narrow, small-gutted, and stringy-muscled. Sheldon and his collaborators have found that, in terms of their seven-point scale of values for three components, seventy-six varieties of human physique can be clearly recognized. If a value scale of more than seven points were used, the number would of course be correspondingly greater. But they have found empirically that the seven-point scale provides an instrument of analysis sufficiently precise for most practical purposes.   20

The three-digit formula given by an analysis of the basic components tells some of the story, but not all. It needs to be supplemented by additional information in respect to three secondary components present in all individuals—the factor of *dysplasia* or disharmony; the factor of *gynandromorphy*, or the possession of characteristics typical of the opposite sex; and the factor of *texture*, whether fine or coarse, aesthetically pleasing or the reverse.   21

Dysplasia occurs when one region or feature of the body is more or less markedly in disharmony with the rest of the physique. We are all familiar, for example, with the big, barrel-chested man whose legs or arms taper off to an absurdly slender inefficiency. And who has not had to listen to the despairing complaints of the ladies to whom ironic nature has given an elegantly ectomorphic torso, with hips and thighs of the most amply endomorphic scale? Such disharmonies are significant and must be observed and measured, for they provide many clues to the explorers of human personality.   22

All persons exhibit characteristics of the opposite sex, some to a very slight degree, others more or less conspicuously. Again, the variations are significant. And the same is true of the factor of texture. Of two individuals having the same fundamental pattern one may be markedly fine-textured, the other markedly coarse-textured. The difference is one which cannot be neglected. That is why the basic formula is always supplemented by other descriptive qualifications expressing the amount of dysplasia, gynandromorphy, and fineness of texture observed in the individual under analysis. 23

III

So much for the varieties of physique and the methods by which they can be classified and measured. Inevitably two questions now propound themselves. First, is it possible for an individual to modify his basic physical pattern? Is there any system of dieting, hormone therapy, or exercise by means of which, say, a 1–1–7 can be transformed into a 7–1–1 or a 3–4–3? The answer would seem to be no. An individual's basic formula cannot be modified. True, an endomorph may be undernourished to the point of looking like a thing of skin and bones. But this particular thing of skin and bones will be measurably quite unlike the thing of skin and bones which is an undernourished, or even tolerably well nourished, ectomorph. Our fundamental physical pattern is something given and unalterable, something we can make the best of but can never hope to change.   24

The second question which naturally occurs to us is this: how closely is our fundamental psychological pattern related to our physical pattern? That such a relationship exists is a subject upon which every dramatist and story-teller, every observant student of men and women, has always been agreed. No writer in his senses would dream of associating the character of Pickwick with the body of Scrooge. And when the comic strip artist wants to portray an athletic hero, he gives him the physique of Flash Gordon, not of Rosie's Beau. Further, men have always clearly recognized that individuals of one psycho-physical type tend to misunderstand and even dislike individuals whose basic psycho-physical pattern is different from their own. Here are the words which Shakespeare puts into the mouth of Julius Caesar:

> Let me have men about me that are fat;
> Sleek-headed men and such as sleep o' nights:
> Yond Cassius has a lean and hungry look;
> He thinks too much: such men are dangerous.

Translated into Sheldon's terminology, this means that the mesomorph is one kind of animal, the ectomorph another; and that their mutual incomprehension very often leads to suspicion and downright antipathy.*   25

In a general way all this has been perfectly well known for the past several thousand years. But it has been known only in an intuitive, empirical way. No organized scientific thinking about the subject has been possible hitherto, because (in spite of some valuable work done in Europe and America) nobody had worked out a satisfactory classification system for describing temperamental differences.   26

---

* Paragraph 25: What balanced structures can you cite in this paragraph? Would balanced structure have improved the fifth sentence?

Modern chemistry classifies matter in terms of a system of ninety-two first-order elements. In earlier times, men tried to do their thinking about matter in terms of only four elements—earth, air, fire, and water. But earth, air, and water are not first-order elements, but elaborate combinations of such elements; while fire is not an element at all, but something that happens to all kinds of matter under certain conditions of temperature. In terms of so inadequate a classification system it was impossible for scientific thought to go very far.   27

The problem of psychological analysis is identical in principle with that of the analysis of matter. The psychologist's business is to discover first-order elements, in terms of which the facts of human difference may be classified and measured. The failure of psychology—and it has conspicuously failed to become the fruitful Science of Man which ideally it should be—is due to the fact that it has done its analysis of human differences in terms of entities that were not first-order elements, but combinations of elements. Sheldon's great contribution to psychology consists in this: that he has isolated a number of genuine first-order elements of the basic psychological pattern which we call temperament, and has demonstrated their close correlation with the individual's basic physical pattern.* 28

What follows is a summing up—necessarily rather crude and over-simplified—of the conclusions to which his research has led.†   29

Endomorphy, mesomorphy, and ectomorphy are correlated very closely with specific patterns of temperament—endomorphy with the temperamental pattern to which Sheldon gives the name of *viscerotonia,* mesomorphy with *somatotonia,* and ectomorphy with *cerebrotonia.* Close and prolonged observation of many subjects, combined with an adaptation of the technique known as factor-analysis, resulted in the isolation of sixty descriptive or determinative traits—twenty for each of the main, first-order components of temperament. From these sixty, I select a smaller number of the more striking and easily recognizable traits.   30

Conspicuous among the elements of the viscerotonic pattern of temperament are relaxation in posture and movement, slow reaction, profound sleep, love of physical comfort, and love of food. With this love of food for its own sake goes a great love of eating in company, an almost religious feeling for the social meal as a kind of sacrament. Another conspicuous viscerotonic trait is love of polite ceremony, with which goes a love of company, together with indiscriminate amiability and marked dependence on, and desire for, the affection and approval of other people. The viscerotonic does not inhibit his emotions, but tends to give expression to them as they arise, so that nobody is ever in doubt as to what he feels.   31

* Paragraph 28: Why has psychology failed?
† Paragraph 29: Describe the function of this paragraph.

Somatotonia, the temperament associated with the hard and power-ful mesomorphic physique, is a patterning of very different elements. The somatotonic individual stands and moves in an assertive way, loves phys-ical adventure, enjoys risk and loves to take a chance. He feels a strong need for physical exercise, which he hugely enjoys and often makes a fetish of, just as the viscerotonic enjoys and makes a fetish of eating. When in trouble, he seeks relief in physical action, whereas the viscero-tonic turns in the same circumstances to people and the cerebrotonic retires, like a wounded animal, into solitude. The somatotonic is essentially energetic and quick to action. Procrastination is unknown to him; for he is neither excessively relaxed and comfort-loving, like the viscerotonic, nor inhibited and 'sicklied o'er with the pale cast of thought,' like the cere-brotonic. The social manner of the somatotonic is uninhibited and direct. The voice is normally unrestrained, and he coughs, laughs, snores and, when passion breaks through his veneer of civilization, speaks loudly. He is physically courageous in combat and enjoys every kind of competitive activity.   32

From a sociological point of view, the most significant of the somato-tonic traits is the lust for power. The individual who is high in somatotonia loves to dominate, and since he is (when somatotonia is extreme) con-genitally insensitive to other people's feelings, since he lacks the indis-criminate amiability and tolerance of viscerotonia and is devoid of cere-brotonic squeamishness, he can easily become a ruthless bully and tyrant. The somatotonic individual is always an extrovert in the sense that his attention is firmly fixed upon external reality, to such an extent that he is necessarily unaware of what is going on in the deeper levels of his own mind.   33

It should be noted that somatotonic extroversion is quite different from the extroversion of the viscerotonic; for while the latter is continually spilling the emotional beans and turning for support and affection to his fellows, the former tends to be insensitive to other people, feels little need to confide his emotions, and pursues his trampling course through ex-ternal reality with an effortless callousness. For him the period of youth is the flower of life; he hates to grow old and often makes desperate efforts, even in advanced middle age, to live as actively as he did at twenty. The viscerotonic, on the other hand, is orientated toward childhood —his own and that of his offspring. He is the great family man. The cerebrotonic, on the other hand, looks forward, even in youth, to the tranquillity and the wisdom which, he hopes or imagines, are associated with old age.   34

With cerebrotonia we pass from the world of Flash Gordon to that of Hamlet. The cerebrotonic is the over-alert, over-sensitive introvert, who is more concerned with the inner universe of his own thoughts and feelings and imagination than with the external world to which, in their different ways, the viscerotonic and the somatotonic pay their primary attention and allegiance. In posture and movements, the cerebrotonic person is tense and restrained. His reactions may be unduly rapid and his physiological responses uncomfortably intense. It is the cerebrotonic who suffers from nervous indigestion, who gets stage fright and feels nauseated with mere shyness, who suffers from the various skin eruptions often associated with emotional disturbances.   35

Extreme cerebrotonics have none of the viscerotonic love of company; on the contrary, they have a passion for privacy, hate to make themselves conspicuous, and have none of the exhibitionistic tendencies displayed both by somatotonics and viscerotonics. In company they tend to be shy and unpredictably moody. When they are with strangers they fidget, their glances are shifting, sometimes furtive; their facial expression is apt to change frequently and rapidly. (For all these reasons no extreme cerebrotonic has ever been a good actor or actress.) Their normal manner is inhibited and restrained and when it comes to the expression of feelings they are outwardly so inhibited that viscerotonics suspect them of being heartless. (On their side, cerebrotonics tend to feel a strong repugnance for the viscerotonic's emotional gush and florid ceremoniousness.)   36

With self-conscious general restraint goes a marked restraint of voice and of all noise in general. To be compelled to raise the voice, as when speaking to the deaf, is, for the cerebrotonic, sheer torture. And it is also torture for him to have to endure noise made by other people. One of the best recipes for an unhappy marriage is to combine a high degree of noise-hating cerebrotonia with a high degree of loud-speaking, loud-laughing, loud-snoring and, in general, noise-making somatotonia. Cerebrotonics are extremely sensitive to pain, sleep poorly, and suffer from chronic fatigue; nevertheless they often live to a ripe old age—provided always that they do not permit themselves to be forced by the pressure of somatotonic public opinion into taking too much violent exercise. They do not easily form habits and are extremely bad at adapting themselves to an active routine, such as military life. They tend to look younger than their age and preserve a kind of youthful intensity of appearance far into middle life. Alcohol, which increases the relaxed amiability of viscerotonics and heightens the aggressiveness of the somatotonic, merely depresses the cerebrotonic and makes him feel thoroughly ill.   37

To determine the degree of viscerotonia, somatotonia, and cerebrotonia present in any given individual, Sheldon makes use of specially designed interviews, supplemented by a medical history and, where possible, by observation over a considerable period. The sixty traits are then assessed on a seven-point scale, in which one represents the minimum manifestation and seven the most extreme.   38

How do these temperamental assessments compare with the corresponding physical assessments of endomorphy, mesomorphy, and ectomorphy? The answer is that there is a high positive correlation. In some persons the correlation is complete, and the three-digit formula for temperament is identical with the three-digit formula for physique. More frequently, however, there is a slight deviation, as when a *four* in physical endomorphy is correlated with a *three* or a *five* in temperamental viscerotonia. Where there is a deviation, it is seldom of more than one point in any of the three components. Occasionally, however, the discrepancy between physique and temperament may be as much as two points; when this happens, the individual is under very considerable strain and has much difficulty in adapting himself to life. Deviations of more than two points do not seem to occur in the normal population, but are not uncommon among the insane.   39

The discrepancies between physique and temperament are probably due, in the main, to what the French philosopher, Jules de Gaultier, has called "bovarism." Mme. Bovary, the heroine of Flaubert's novel, was a young woman who consistently tried to be what in fact she was not. To a greater or less degree we are all bovarists, engaged from earliest childhood in the process of building up what the psychologists call a *persona*, to suit the tastes of the society surrounding us. The sort of *persona* we try to build up depends very largely upon our environment, physical and mental. Thus, in pioneering days, every Westerner tried to bovarize himself into the likeness of an Indian fighter. This was necessary, partly because people had to be tough, wary, and extroverted if they were to survive under frontier conditions, partly because local public opinion condemned and despised the introverted, the tender-minded, the aesthetes, and the abstract thinkers. Sheldon's researches show exactly how far bovarism can go without risk of compromising the individual's sanity; and the highly significant fact is that the borderline between normal and abnormal is reached pretty quickly. Hence the enormous psychological dangers inherent in such dogmatic and intolerant philosophies of life as Puritanism or Militarism—philosophies which exert an unrelenting pressure on those subjected to their influence, forcing a majority to try to change their fundamental psycho-physical constitution, to become something other than what they basically are.*   40

Here a word of warning is necessary. Knowledge of an individual's constitutional make-up is not the same as complete knowledge of his character. Persons with the same temperamental formula may behave in very different ways and exhibit very different characters. Temperamentally similar individuals can make dissimilar uses of their constitutional endow-

---

* Paragraph 40: Define "bovarism" in your own words.

ments. It all depends on circumstances, upbringing, and the exercise of free will. Of three men with the same high degree of somatotonia one may become a suavely efficient executive, another a professional soldier of the explosive, blood-and-guts variety, and the third a ruthless gangster. But each in his own way will be aggressive and power-loving, daring and energetic, extroverted and insensitive to other people's feelings. And no amount of training, no effort of the will, will serve to transform them into relaxed and indiscriminately amiable viscerotonics, or into inhibited, hyperattentional, and introverted cerebrotonics.

41

IV

We are now in a position to consider a few of the things that constitutional analysis and appraisal can do for us. First and most important, it makes it possible for us to know who we and other people really are— of what psychological and bodily elements we and they are composed. Having determined the statics of physique and the closely related dynamics of temperament, we can begin to think in a genuinely intelligent and fruitful way about the environment and the individual's reaction to it. Moreover, to understand is to forgive; and when we realize that the people who are different from us did not get that way out of wickedness or perversity, when we understand that many of the profoundest of such differences are constitutional and that constitution cannot be changed, only made the best of, we may perhaps learn to be more tolerant, more intelligently charitable than we are at present.

42

Passing from the general to the particular, we find that constitutional appraisal has many important practical applications. In medicine, for example, the constitutional approach will undoubtedly prove helpful both in diagnosis and prognosis, in cure and prevention. To some extent, it is true, all physicians make use of the constitutional approach, and have been doing so for twenty-five centuries at least; but considering the importance of the subject, very little systematic research has been undertaken along these lines.

43

Education can never in the nature of things be one hundred per cent efficient. Teaching is an art and, in every field, bad artists vastly outnumber good ones. Great educators are almost as rare as great painters and composers. The best we can hope to do is to improve the system within which teachers of average ability do their work. In this improvement of the system, constitutional analysis is likely to prove extremely helpful. Ideally, there should be several educational systems, one adapted to each of the main varieties of human beings. Of the progressive education which in recent years has largely ousted from our schools the formal, suppressive type of training that was at one time universal, Dr. Sheldon makes the following significant remark. "This vigorous progressive education is actually as suppressive as was Christian education at its darkest. It suppresses the third instead of the second component. It is as suppressive to a young cerebrotonic to press him to join in the dance or in the swim, and to make noise and mix and socialize, as it is suppressive to a young somatotonic to make him sit still."   44

In the fields of history, sociology, and religion, the concepts of constitutional analysis may turn out to be extremely fruitful. From the constitutional point of view, civilization may be defined as a complex of devices for restraining extreme somatotonics from destroying society by their reckless aggressiveness. Of the great world religions one, Confucianism, has been pre-eminently viscerotonic; it has sought to tame somatotonia by inculcating ceremonious good manners, general amiability, and the cult of the family. Most of the other world religions—Buddhism, the higher forms of Hinduism, and, until recent years, Christianity—have been predominantly cerebrotonic. (The figure of Christ in traditional Christian art is almost always that of a man with a high degree of ectomorphy and therefore of cerebrotonia.) These cerebrotonic religions have tried to keep somatotonics in order by teaching them the virtues of self-restraint, humility, and sensitiveness. At the same time they tried to sublimate somatotonic aggressiveness, or to direct it into channels thought to be desirable, such as crusades and wars of religion. On their side, the somatotonics have often succeeded in modifying the cerebrotonic philosophies and institutions of the prevailing religion. For example, no cerebrotonic or viscerotonic would ever have thought of talking about the Church Militant.   45

V

In recent years there has been, in Sheldon's phrase, a great Somatotonic Revolution, directed against the dominance of cerebrotonic values as embodied in traditional Christianity. Thus, for traditional Christianity, it was axiomatic that the life of contemplation was superior to the life of action. Today the overwhelming majority even of Christians accept without question the primacy of action.   46

For traditional Christianity the important thing was the development of the right state of mind about the environment. Today, the important thing is not the state of the mind, but the state of the environment. We believe that men and women will be happy when they are surrounded with the right kind of gadgets. Our forefathers believed that they would be happy if they achieved what one of the greatest of Christian saints called "a holy indifference" to their material surroundings. The change is from a cerebrotonic point of view to the point of view of a somatotonic extrovert.   47

The Somatotonic Revolution has been greatly accelerated by technological advances. These have served to turn men's attention outward, and have encouraged the belief in a material apocalypse, a progress toward a mechanized New Jerusalem. Such beliefs have been carefully fostered by the writers of advertising copy—the most influential of all authors because they are the only ones whose works are read every day by every member of the population. In a world peopled by cerebrontonics, living an inward-turning life in a state of holy, or even unholy, indifference to their material surroundings, mass production would be doomed. That is why advertisers consistently support the Somatotonic Revolution.   48

It is hardly necessary to add that total war is another potent factor in creating and sustaining the Somatotonic Revolution. Nazi education, which was specifically education for war, aimed at encouraging the manifestations of somatotonia in those most richly endowed with it, and making the rest of the population feel ashamed of its tendencies towards relaxed amiability or restrained and inward-looking sensitivity. During the war the enemies of Nazism have had to borrow from the Nazi educational philosophy. All over the world millions of young men and even young women are now being educated to be tough, and to admire toughness beyond every other moral quality. Never has somatotonia been so widely or so systematically encouraged as at the present time. Indeed, most societies in the past systematically discouraged somatotonia, because they did not wish to be destroyed by the unrestrained aggressiveness of their most active minority. What will be the result of the present worldwide reversal of what hitherto has been an almost universal social policy? Time alone will show.*   49

* Paragraph 49: What has been the "almost universal social policy"?

The Whole Selection

1 In paragraph 3, Huxley has analyzed, in a summary way, the characteristics of the "best classification" for purposes of pure and applied science. Is his analysis of this subject a division or a classification?

2 In the development of the thought, what relation do paragraphs 4–11 bear to paragraph 3?

3 Is the analysis in paragraphs 12–16 rhetorically a classification or a division (partition) of the subject being analyzed?

4 In paragraphs 13–16, does the classification of the body meet the requirements for good classification which Huxley has explained in paragraphs 3–11?

5 Although the material in this essay is technical, Huxley has succeeded in making it comprehensible to the intelligent lay reader. To do so, he uses a variety of methods of analysis, most of which you have met in earlier sections of this book. In paragraph 14, to develop his definition of endomorphy, what methods does he use? Does he use the same methods in paragraphs 15–16 and 21–23? Which does he use in paragraphs 25–28?

6 Is the analysis of various individuals in paragraphs 30–37 a contradiction of the view expressed on oversimplification in paragraph 6? After you answer this question, refer to paragraphs 17, 29, and 41 for qualifications which you may have missed.

WHAT EVERY WRITER MUST LEARN

JOHN CIARDI

The teaching of writing has become practically a profession by now. There is hardly a college in the land that does not offer at least one course in "creative writing" (whatever that is) by some "teacher of writing" (whoever he is). There are, moreover, at least fifty annual writers' conferences now functioning among us with something like fifty degrees of competence. And there seems to be no way of counting the number of literary counsellors, good and bad, who are prepared to promise that they can teach a writer what he needs to know.   1

I am myself a "teacher of writing," but though it be taken as a confession of fraud I must insist, in the face of all this "teaching" apparatus, that writing cannot in fact be taught. What a writer must have above all else is inventiveness. Dedication, commitment, passion—whatever one chooses to call the writer's human motivation—must be there, to be sure. But to require human motivation is only to assume that the writer is a human being—certainly not a very hard assumption to make. Art, however, is not humanity but the *expression of* humanity, and for enduring expression the one gift above all is inventiveness.   2

But where, in what curriculum ever, has there been, or can there be, a course in inventiveness—which is to say, in creativity? The truly creative—whether in art, in science, or in philosophy—is always, and precisely, that which cannot be taught. And yet, though it seem paradoxical, creativity cannot spring from the untaught. Creativity is the imaginatively gifted recombination of known elements into something new.   3

And so, it may be seen, there is no real paradox. The elements of an invention or of a creation can be taught, but the creativity must be self-discovered and self-disciplined. A good teacher—whether in a college classroom, a Parisian café, or a Greek marketplace—can marvelously assist the learning. But in writing, as in all creativity, it is the gift that must learn itself.*   4

The good teacher will be able to itemize a tremendous amount of essential lore. He can tell a would-be novelist that if an incidental character is given a name that character had best reappear in the later action, and that if he is not going to reappear he should be identified simply as "the Supply Sergeant," "the big blonde," "the man in the red waistcoat," or whatever. He can point out that good dialogue avoids "he averred," "he bellowed," "he boomed," "he interpolated," and that it is wise to write simply "he said," indicating any important direction for the tone of voice

---

* Paragraph 4: What is a "paradox"? Why is there no real paradox here?

in a separate sentence. He can demonstrate that in all fiction the action must be perceived by someone, and he can defend in theory and support by endless instances that in effective fiction one does not allow more than one means of perception within a single scene. He can point out to would-be poets that traditional rhyme and traditional metrics are not indispensable, but that once a pattern has been established the writer must respect it. And he can then point out that within the pattern established at the start of the student's poem certain lines are metrically deficient and certain rhymes forced.*   5

He may "teach" (or preach) any number of such particulars. And if he is a good man for the job he will never forget that these particulars are simply rules of thumb, any one of which may be violated by a master, but none of which may be safely ignored by a writer who has not yet learned they exist.   6

Belaboring such particulars is useful service to the would-be writer who under a competent teacher may save himself years of floundering trial-and-error. Writers are forever being produced by literary groups of one sort or another, and one of the most important things a writer acquires in the give-and-take of a good literary group is a headful of precisely such particulars. The most important thing a teacher of writing can do is to create a literary group in which he teaches minimums while the most talented of his students learn maximums—very largely from fighting with one another (rarely, if ever, from mutual admiration).†   7

But if writing requires a starting talent that a man either has or has not and which he cannot learn, and if the teachable elements are not enough to make a writer of him, what is it he must learn? What are the measures by which his gift comes to know itself?‡   8

The answers to that question must be given separately, and if they are so given they must be put down one after the other with some sort of natural implication that the order in which they are given is keyed to their importance. Such mechanical necessity (and it is one of the most constant seductions of the classroom) must not be allowed to obscure the far greater likelihood that the answers all exist at the same time in the behavior of a good writer, and that all are equally important. That, too, is part of what must be learned. As is the fact that no one set of generalizations will ever suffice. But one must begin somewhere. I offer the following six points as the most meaningful and the most central I have been able to locate.§   9

* Paragraph 5: What is the topic sentence of this paragraph?
† Paragraph 7: In the second sentence, precisely to what particulars is Ciardi referring?
‡ Paragraph 8: This is one of the most important paragraphs so far. Why? What is its function?
§ Paragraph 9: How does the function of this paragraph differ from that of the one immediately preceding it?

1   SOMETHING TO WRITE ABOUT

"You have to give them something to write about," Robert Frost once said in discussing his classroom principles. His own poems are full of stunning examples of the central truth that good writers deal in information, and that even the lofty (if they are lofty) acreages of poetry are sown to fact. Consider the opening lines of "Mending Wall":

> Something there is that doesn't love a wall,
> That sends the frozen-groundswell under it,
> And spills the upper boulders in the sun;
> And makes gaps even two can pass abreast.
> The work of hunters is another thing:
> I have come after them and made repair
> Where they have left not one stone on a stone,
> But they would have the rabbit out of hiding,
> To please the yelping dogs. The gaps I mean,
> No one has seen them made or heard them made,
> But at spring mending-time we find them there . . .

I intend no elaborate critique of this passage. I want simply to make the point that it contains as much specific information about stone walls as one could hope to find in a Department of Agriculture pamphlet.*   10

Frost states his passion for the *things* of the world both in example and in precept. "The fact is the sweetest dream the labor knows," he writes in "The Mowing." One has only to compare that line with R. P. T. Coffin's "Nothing so crude as fact could enter here" to understand an important part of the difference between a poet and something less than a poet.   11

Even so mystical a poet as Gerard Manley Hopkins (I misuse the word "mystical" in order to save three paragraphs, but let me at least file an apology) is gorgeously given to the fact of the thing. Consider: "And blue bleak embers, ah my dear,/Fall, gall themselves, and gash gold-vermilion" (*i.e.,* "Coal embers in a grate, their outside surfaces burned out and blue-bleak, sift down, fall through the grate, strike the surface below or the side of the grate, and are gashed open to reveal the gold-vermilion fire still glowing at their core").   12

The writer of fiction deals his facts in a different way, but it will not do to say that he is more bound to fact than is the poet: he simply is not required to keep his facts under poetic compression; keep hard to them he still must. Consider Melville's passion for the details of whaling; or DeFoe's for the details of criminality, of ransoming an English merchant captured by a French ship, or of Robinson Crusoe's carpentry. The passion for fact was powerful enough in these masters to lure them into shattering

---

* Paragraph 10: What is the purpose of quoting the opening lines of "Mending Wall"?

the pace of their own best fiction, and to do so time and time again. And who is to say that a man reading for more than amusement, a man passionate to touch the writer's mind in his writing, has any real objection to having the pace so shattered? All those self-blooming, lovingly-managed, chunky, touchable facts!   13

For a writer is a man who must know something better than anyone else does, be it so little as his own goldfish or so much as himself. True, he is not required to know any one specific thing. Not at least until he begins to write about it. But once he has chosen to write about X then he is responsible for knowing everything the writing needs to know about X. I know of no writer of any consequence whatever who did not treasure the world enough to gather to himself a strange and wonderful headful and soulful of facts about its going and coming.   14

2   AN OUTSIDE EYE

Nothing is more difficult than for the writer to ride his passion while still managing to observe it critically. The memoirs of good writers of every sort are studded with long thoughts on this essential duplicity, this sense of esthetic detachment, of a second attention lurking in the mind at the very moment they have felt the need to be most indivisibly absorbed in what they are doing.   15

The writer absolutely must learn to develop that eye outside himself, for the last action every writer must perform for his writing is to become its reader. It is not easy to approach one's own output as if he were coming on it fresh. Yet unless the writer turns that trick any communication that happens will either be by accident or by such genius as transcends the possibility of discussion.   16

For the writer's relation to his writing is a developing relation. The writing starts as a conceptual buzz. Approaching the writing thus with the buzz loud in the head, one may easily believe that anything he sets down is actually full of that starting-buzz. But one must remember that the buzz is there before the writing, and that should some accident interfere with the actual writing the buzz would still be there. A writer in a really heightened state could jot down telephone numbers and actually believe that he has set down a piece of writing that accurately conveys his original inpulse.   17

The reader, however, is a very different situation. He comes to the writing committed to no prior emotion. There is no starting buzz in his head, except by irrelevant accident. It is the writer's job to make that reader buzz. Not, to be sure, to make every reader buzz—the world is full of the practically unbuzzable—but to make the competent reader buzz. Simply to say "I buzz" is not enough. To make the reader experience the original buzz with nothing but the writing to create the buzz within him —that is the function of every sort of literature, the communication of experience in experienceable terms. The disciplines of any art form are among other things ways of estimating the amount of buzz the form is transmitting.*   18

3   FLUENCY

As noted, one does not hope to reach all readers, but only the competent. In one way the qualifications of a good reader are the same as those of a competent writer. Both must achieve fluency. By fluency I mean the ability to receive more than one impression at the same time. To create or to experience art one must be both technically and emotionally fluent.   19

A pun is a simple example of the necessity for technical fluency. The two or more faces of a pun must be received at the same instant or all is lost. The news comes over the radio that the Communist leader of Pisa has been chastised by Moscow for making overtures to the left-center parties for a united front, and the happy punster says, "Aha, a Lenin tower of a-Pisa-ment!" then settles back in his moment of personal splendor. This golden instant from my autobiography—but what good is even glory if it has to be explained? "I don't get it," says the guest who will never be invited again, and the evening is ruined.   20

The pun, of course, is only the simplest example of the need for technical fluency. Unless the writer and the reader have in common the necessary language of simultaneity in its millions of shadings, the best will die en route.   21

The need for emotional fluency is analogous. Good writing constantly requires the writer to perceive and the reader to receive different sets of feelings at the same instant. Both the writer and the reader must be equal to the emotion of the subject dealt with. Shakespeare can put a world into *Hamlet,* but where is that world when a five-year-old child or an emotionally five-year-old adult attempts to read or to see the play? Whatever he may see, it is certainly not Shakespeare. A reader who is emotionally immature or who is too psychically rigid (the same thing really) to enter into the simultaneity of the human experiences commonly portrayed in literature, is simply not capable of any sort of writing with the possible exception of the technical report, the statistical summary, or that semi-literate combination, the Ph.D. thesis.†   22

* Paragraphs 17 and 18: Precisely what does Ciardi mean by the phrase "conceptual buzz"? Do you think that this combination of an ordinarily formal word and a colloquial one is effective? How does the "buzz" idea hold these two paragraphs together?

† Paragraph 22: Analyze the structure of the concluding sentence. Is the punctuation correct?

4 A SENSE OF THE PAST

No painter can produce a good canvas without a broad knowledge of what has been painted before him, no architect can plan a meaningful building except as he has pondered the architecture of the past, and no writer can produce good writing without a sure sense of what has been accomplished in the past within his form.*   23

There are legions of poets today who are trying belatedly to be Wordsworth, and legions of fictioneers who are trying to be Louisa May Alcott. I imply no attack here on either Wordsworth or Alcott. I simply make the point that it is too late to be either of them again. Both of them, moreover, did a better job of being themselves than any of their imitators can aspire to. As the Kitty-cat bird in Theodore Roethke's poem said: "Whoever you are, be sure it's you."   24

Nor does one learn the past of his form only to adhere to it. Such an adherence, if overdedicated, would be a death in itself. I mean, rather, that it is impossible to venture meaningful innovation unless one knows what he is *innovating-from.* With no exception I am able to think of, the best innovators in our literature have been those who best knew their past tradition.   25

I am saying simply that a writer must learn to read. He must read widely and thoughtfully, and he must learn to read not as an amateur spectator but as an engaged professional. Just as the football coach sees more of the play than do the coeds, so the writer must learn to see more of what is happening under the surface of the illusion than does the reader who simply yields to the illusion. William Dean Howells, then editor of *The Atlantic,* paid what he intended as a supreme compliment to one of Mark Twain's books when he reported that he had begun the book and for the first time in many years had found himself reading as a reader rather than as an editor. A happy indulgence and a gracious compliment, but once the writer has allowed himself that much it becomes his duty to reread the book with his glasses on—not only to enter into the illusion of the writing, but to identify the devices (*i.e.,* the inventions) by which the illusion was created and made to work upon him. And here, too, he must experience his essential duplicity, for the best reading is exactly that reading in which the passion of the illusion and the awareness of its technical management arrive at the same time.   26

5 A SENSE OF THE AGE

The true writer, that is to say the writer who is something more than a competent technician, has a yet more difficult thing to learn. He must not

---

* Paragraph 23: This paragraph is made up of only one sentence. Rhetorically, what kind of sentence is it?

only know his human and artistic past; he must learn to read the mood of his world under its own names for itself. He must become an instrument, tuned by devices he can never wholly understand, to the reception of a sense of his age, its mood, its climate of ideas, its human position, and its potential of action. And he must not let himself be deceived into thinking that the world answers to the names it gives itself. Hitler's agencies once gave a great deal of attention to what they called "Strength-through-Joy." It was the product of this Strength-through-Joy that Lord Beaverbrook called at the time "the stalwart young Nazis of Germany." The names were "strength," "joy," and "stalwarts." Yet any man today can see that those who answered to these shining names contained within themselves possibilities for action that must answer to much darker names. Any man can see it—now. I think it is very much to the point that all of the best writers sensed it then, and that the better the German writers were the earlier they left Germany. Good writing must be of its times and must contain within itself—God knows how but the writer must learn for himself—a sense of what Hippolyte Taine called "the moral temperature of the times," what the Germans call der Zeitgeist, and what English and American writers have come to call "the climate."*   27

6   ART IS ARTIFICE

And along with all else, as an essential part of his duplicity, his commitment, his fluency, and his sense of past and present, the writer must learn beyond any flicker of doubt within himself that art is not life itself but a made representation of life. He must learn that it is no defense of a piece of fiction, for example, to argue "but that's the way it happened." The fact that it happened that way in the world of the Daily News does not make it happen to the reader within the world of the writing.   28

The writer's subject is reality but his medium is illusion. Only by illusory means can the sense of reality be transmitted in an art form. That complex of pigment-on-canvas is not four maidens dancing, but it is the managed illusion whereby Botticelli transmits his real vision of the four seasons. Those words on paper are not Emma Bovary but they are the elements of the illusion whereby we experience her as a living creation. The writer, like every artist, deals in what I have come to call the AS-IF. AS-IF is the mode of all poetry and of all imaginative writing. IS is the mode of what passes for reality and of all information-prose. Is IS more real than AS-IF? One must ask: "More real for what purposes?" I have no argument with, for example, the research chemists. I mean rather to hold them in considerable admiration. But though many of them think of themselves as the IS-iest men in the world, which of them has ever deter-

---

* Paragraph 27: What is the advantage of using three different terms or expressions to identify what good writing must contain within itself?

mined a piece of truth except by setting up and pursuing a starting hypothesis (let me leave accident out of consideration)? And what is a starting hypothesis but an AS-IF? "Let us act AS-IF this hypothesis were true," says the researcher, "and then see how it checks out." At the end of ten, or a hundred, or ten thousand starting AS-IF's lurks the nailed-down IS of valence, or quanta, or transmutation of elements. Maybe. And then only until the next revolution in IS outdates the researcher's results.*   29

At the far end of all the AS-IF's a man, and particularly a writer, can summon from himself lurks that final IS (maybe) that will be a truth for him. But not all of the truth will be told at one time. Part of the truth, I think the most truth, a writer must learn is that writing is not a decorative act, but a specific, disciplined, and infinitely viable means of knowledge. Poetry and fiction, like all the arts, are a way of perceiving and of understanding the world. Good writing is as positive a search for truth as is any part of science, and it deals with kinds of truth that must forever be beyond science. The writer must learn, necessarily of himself and within himself, that his subject is the nature of reality, that good writing always increases the amount of human knowledge available, and that the one key to that knowledge of reality is AS-IF. His breadth and depth as a human being are measured by the number of AS-IF's he has managed to experience; his stature as a writer, by the number he has managed to bring to life in his work.   30

For no man in any one lifetime can hope to learn by physical experience (IS) all that he must know and all that he must have experienced in order to be an adequate human being. No writer can hope to engage physically enough worlds of IS to make his imagination and his humanity pertinent. Only by his vicarious assumptions of AS-IF can the writer learn his real human dimension, and only as he dedicates his writing to the creation of a meaningful and experienceable new AS-IF can he hope to write well—to write as no school can teach him to write, but as he must learn for himself if he cares enough, and if he has gift enough.†   31

---

* Paragraph 29: How do we know from the first sentence that a certain method of paragraph development will be used in this paragraph? Relate "AS-IF" and "IS" to the idea stated in the first sentence of the paragraph. Distinguish between "AS-IF" and "IS" in your own words.

† Paragraph 31: This paragraph summarizes part 6 of the division of the technique of creative writing. Why is there no final paragraph summarizing all six parts of the division?

The Whole Selection

1 At what point do the introductory paragraphs end and the division of the subject begin? Discuss the function of these introductory paragraphs in the light of the meaning of the whole essay.

2 Notice the formality of the statement of the parts of the division. Is this an aid or a hindrance to the reader? To the writer? Is this method applicable to all topics or to all kinds of writing?

3 Point out Ciardi's use of definition throughout the essay as an aid to his division. Then show how he uses example for this purpose.

Word Study *vicarious, viable, transmutation, hypothesis, psyche, conceptual*

WHAT TO LISTEN FOR IN MUSIC

AARON COPLAND

We all listen to music according to our separate capacities. But, for the sake of analysis, the whole listening process may become clearer if we break it up into its component parts, so to speak. In a certain sense we all listen to music on three separate planes. For lack of a better terminology, one might name these: (1) the sensuous plane, (2) the expressive plane, (3) the sheerly musical plane. The only advantage to be gained from mechanically splitting up the listening process into these hypothetical planes is the clearer view to be had of the way in which we listen.*   1

The simplest way of listening to music is to listen for the sheer pleasure of the musical sound itself. That is the sensuous plane. It is the plane on which we hear music without thinking, without considering it in any way. One turns on the radio while doing something else and absent-mindedly bathes in the sound. A kind of brainless but attractive state of mind is engendered by the mere sound appeal of the music.   2

You may be sitting in a room reading this book. Imagine one note struck on the piano. Immediately that one note is enough to change the atmosphere of the room—proving that the sound element in music is a powerful and mysterious agent, which it would be foolish to deride or belittle.   3

The surprising thing is that many people who consider themselves qualified music lovers abuse the plane in listening. They go to concerts in order to lose themselves. They use music as a consolation or an escape. They enter an ideal world where one doesn't have to think of the realities of everyday life. Of course they aren't thinking about the music either. Music allows them to leave it, and they go off to a place to dream, dreaming because of and apropos of the music yet never quite listening to it.   4

Yes, the sound appeal of music is a potent and primitive force, but you must not allow it to usurp a disproportionate share of your interest. The sensuous plane is an important one in music, a very important one, but it does not constitute the whole story.†   5

There is no need to digress further on the sensuous plane. Its appeal to every normal human being is self-evident. There is, however, such a thing as becoming more sensitive to the different kinds of sound stuff as used by various composers. For all composers do not use that sound stuff in the same way. Don't get the idea that the value of music is commensurate with its sensuous appeal or that the loveliest sounding music is

---

* Paragraph 1: Copland states clearly his three major parts. What has he divided?

† Paragraphs 2 through 5: What means does Copland use in these paragraphs to make clear his definition of the sensuous plane of listening?

made by the greatest composer. If that were so, Ravel would be a greater creator than Beethoven. The point is that the sound element varies with each composer, that his usage of sound forms an integral part of his style and must be taken into account when listening. The reader can see, therefore, that a more conscious approach is valuable even on this primary plane of music listening.*   6

The second plane on which music exists is what I have called the expressive one. Here, immediately, we tread on controversial ground. Composers have a way of shying away from any discussion of music's expressive side. Did not Stravinsky himself proclaim that his music was an "object," a "thing," with a life of its own, and with no other meaning than its own purely musical existence? This intransigent attitude of Stravinsky's may be due to the fact that so many people have tried to read different meanings into so many pieces. Heaven knows it is difficult enough to say precisely what it is that a piece of music means, to say it definitely, to say it finally so that everyone is satisfied with your explanation. But that should not lead one to the other extreme of denying to music the right to be "expressive."†   7

My own belief is that all music has an expressive power, some more and some less, but that all music has a certain meaning behind the notes and that that meaning behind the notes constitutes, after all, what the piece is saying, what the piece is about. This whole problem can be stated quite simply by asking, "Is there a meaning to music?" My answer to that would be, "Yes." And "Can you state in so many words what the meaning is?" My answer to that would be, "No." Therein lies the difficulty. 8

Simple-minded souls will never be satisfied with the answer to the second of these questions. They always want music to have a meaning, and the more concrete it is the better they like it. The more the music reminds them of a train, a storm, a funeral, or any other familiar conception the more expressive it appears to be to them. This popular idea of music's meaning—stimulated and abetted by the usual run of musical commentator—should be discouraged wherever and whenever it is met. One timid lady once confessed to me that she suspected something seriously lacking in her appreciation of music because of her inability to connect it with anything definite. That is getting the whole thing backward, of course.   9

Still, the question remains, How close should the intelligent music lover wish to come to pinning a definite meaning to any particular work? No closer than a general concept, I should say. Music expresses, at different moments, serenity or exuberance, regret or triumph, fury or delight. It

* Paragraph 6: What is the function of this paragraph?

† Paragraph 7: Does the rest of this paragraph demonstrate Copland's statement (in sentence 2) that we are treading on controversial ground?

expresses each of these moods, and many others, in a numberless variety of subtle shadings and differences. It may even express a state of meaning for which there exists no adequate word in any language. In that case, musicians often like to say that it has only a purely musical meaning. They sometimes go farther and say that *all* music has only purely musical meaning. What they really mean is that no appropriate word can be found to express the music's meaning and that, even if it could they do not feel the need of finding it.   10

But whatever the professional musician may hold, most musical novices still search for specific words with which to pin down their musical reactions. That is why they always find Tschaikovsky easier to "understand" than Beethoven. In the first place, it is easier to pin a meaning-word on a Tschaikovsky piece than on a Beethoven one. Much easier. Moreover, with the Russian composer, every time you come back to a piece of his it almost always says the same thing to you, whereas with Beethoven it is often quite difficult to put your finger right on what he is saying. And any musician will tell you that that is why Beethoven is the greater composer. Because music which always says the same thing to you will necessarily soon become dull music, but music whose meaning is slightly different with each hearing has a greater chance of remaining alive.   11

Listen, if you can, to the forty-eight fugue themes of Bach's *Well-Tempered Clavichord*. Listen to each theme, one after another. You will soon realize that each theme mirrors a different world of feeling. You will also soon realize that the more beautiful a theme seems to you the harder it is to find any word that will describe it to your complete satisfaction. Yes, you will certainly know whether it is a gay theme or a sad one. You will be able, in other words, in your own mind, to draw a frame of emotional feeling around your theme. Now study the sad one a little closer. Try to pin down the exact quality of its sadness. Is it pessimistically sad or resignedly sad; is it fatefully sad or smilingly sad?   12

Let us suppose that you are fortunate and can describe to your own satisfaction in so many words the exact meaning of your chosen theme. There is still no guarantee that anyone else will be satisfied. Nor need they be. The important thing is that each one feel for himself the specific expressive quality of a theme or, similarly, an entire piece of music. And if it is a great work of art, don't expect it to mean exactly the same thing to you each time you return to it.   13

Themes or pieces need not express only one emotion, of course. Take such a theme as the first main one of the *Ninth Symphony*, for example. It is clearly made up of different elements. It does not say only one thing. Yet anyone hearing it immediately gets a feeling of strength, a feeling of power. It isn't a power that comes simply because the theme is played loudly. It is a power inherent in the theme itself. The extraordinary strength and vigor of the theme results in the listener's receiving an impression that a forceful statement has been made. But one should never try to boil it down to "the fateful hammer of life," etc. That is where the trouble begins. The musician, in his exasperation, says it means nothing but the notes themselves, whereas the nonprofessional is only too anxious to hang on to any explanation that gives him the illusion of getting closer to the music's meaning.*   14

Now, perhaps, the reader will know better what I mean when I say that music does have an expressive meaning but that we cannot say in so many words what that meaning is.†   15

The third plane on which music exists is the sheerly musical plane. Besides the pleasurable sound of music and the expressive feeling that it gives off, music does exist in terms of the notes themselves and of their manipulation. Most listeners are not sufficiently conscious of this third plane. . . .   16

Professional musicians, on the other hand, are, if anything, too conscious of the mere notes themselves. They often fall into the error of becoming so engrossed with their arpeggios and staccatos that they forget the deeper aspects of the music they are performing. But from the layman's standpoint, it is not so much a matter of getting over bad habits on the sheerly musical plane as of increasing one's awareness of what is going on, in so far as the notes are concerned.   17

When the man in the street listens to the "notes themselves" with any degree of concentration, he is most likely to make some mention of the melody. Either he hears a pretty melody or he does not, and he generally lets it go at that. Rhythm is likely to gain his attention next, particularly if it seems exciting. But harmony and tone color are generally taken for granted, if they are thought of consciously at all. As for music's having a definite form of some kind, that idea seems never to have occurred to him.   18

It is very important for all of us to become more alive to music on its sheerly musical plane. After all, an actual musical material is being used. The intelligent listener must be prepared to increase his awareness of the musical material and what happens to it. He must hear the melodies, the rhythms, the harmonies, the tone colors in a more conscious fashion. But above all he must, in order to follow the line of the composer's thought, know something of the principles of musical form. Listening to all of these elements is listening on the sheerly musical plane.   19

---

* Paragraph 14: What is his purpose in coming back to the "musician" and the "non professional"?

† Paragraph 15: What is the function of this paragraph? How does it differ from the function of paragraph 6?

Let me repeat that I have split up mechanically the three separate planes on which we listen merely for the sake of greater clarity. Actually, we never listen on one or the other of these planes. What we do is to correlate them—listening in all three ways at the same time. It takes no mental effort, for we do it instinctively.*   20

Perhaps an analogy with what happens to us when we visit the theater will make this instinctive correlation clearer. In the theater, you are aware of the actors and actresses, costumes and sets, sounds and movements. All these give one the sense that the theater is a pleasant place to be in. They constitute the sensuous plane in our theatrical reactions.   21

The expressive plane in the theater would be derived from the feeling that you get from what is happening on the stage. You are moved to pity, excitement, or gaiety. It is this general feeling, generated aside from the particular words being spoken, a certain emotional something which exists on the stage, that is analogous to the expressive quality in music.   22

The plot and plot development is equivalent to our sheerly musical plane. The playwright creates and develops a character in just the same way that a composer creates and develops a theme. According to the degree of your awareness of the way in which the artist in either field handles his material will you become a more intelligent listener.   23

It is easy enough to see that the theatergoer never is conscious of any of these elements separately. He is aware of them all at the same time. The same is true of music listening. We simultaneously and without thinking listen on all three planes.†   24

In a sense, the ideal listener is both inside and outside the music at the same moment, judging it and enjoying it, wishing it would go one way and watching it go another—almost like the composer at the moment he composes it; because in order to write his music, the composer must also be inside and outside his music, carried away by it and yet coldly critical of it. A subjective and objective attitude is implied in both creating and listening to music.   25

What the reader should strive for, then, is a more *active* kind of listening. Whether you listen to Mozart or Duke Ellington, you can deepen your understanding of music only by being a more conscious and aware listener—not someone who is just listening, but someone who is listening *for* something.   26

---

* Paragraph 20: What is the function of this paragraph? Could it be omitted?

† Paragraphs 21 through 24: Why is the analogy of the theatergoer introduced? Is it effective?

The Whole Selection

1 Copland has divided the listening of music into three parts. He devotes four paragraphs to the first part, nine paragraphs to the second part, and four paragraphs to the third part. Can you discover reasons for this proportion? Why isn't more time spent on the third part, since "most listeners are not sufficiently conscious" of it?

2 Select any one of the examples or references that Copland uses and examine it to see if it fulfills its function as an illustration.

3 Usually in any good division in formal writing the parts exhaust the whole. Is that true here?

4 How do we know from the essay itself that Copland is writing for the general reader and not for the professional musician?

THE RHETORIC OF SOUL: IDENTIFICATION IN NEGRO SOCIETY

ULF HANNERZ

The last few years have witnessed the emergence of a concept of "soul" as signifying what is "essentially Negro" in the black ghettos of the large cities of the Northern United States. In this paper, I will attempt to place this concept of "soul" in its social and cultural matrix, in particular with respect to tendencies of social change as experienced by ghetto inhabitants. In doing so, I will emphasise what I believe to be the dominant purpose of a "soul" vocabulary among its users. There will be clear points of convergence between my view of "soul" and that stated by Charles Keil in his book *Urban Blues*.[1] However, I believe that Keil's personal evaluation of some of the features of black ghetto culture tends to obscure the issue in some ways, and I also feel that a clearer picture of the essential social-structural and social-psychological features may be achieved.

This paper is based on field work in a lower-class Negro neighbourhood in Washington, D.C. The field site seems to be in many ways typical of Negro slums in Northern American cities. It is situated at the edge of a large, ethnically homogeneous area. Its inhabitants share the common characteristics of America's lower-class urban Negroes: poverty, a high rate of unemployment, a considerable amount of crime, including juvenile delinquency, and widely varying family role-structures according to which it is relatively common that the adult woman dominates the family while the male is either absent or only temporarily attached—even when he is a permanent member of the household his participation in household affairs may be quite limited. (It should be noted that this is not said to be true of all households—it is only pointed out that unstable family relationships and female dominance are much more common among lower-class Negroes than among the American people in general.) Of the adults at the field site —a block-long street lined by two- or three-story row houses—a minority was born in Washington, D.C. The majority are immigrants from the South. particularly from Virginia, North Carolina, and South Carolina. Apart from conducting field work in this area by means of participant observation in the traditional sense, I have paid attention to those impersonal media which have a significant part in ghetto life; these are particularly important in the context of this study. I refer here to media which are specifically intended for a lower-class Negro audience: radio (three stations in Washington, D.C. are clearly aimed at Negroes), the recording industry, and stage shows featuring Negro rock-and-roll artists and comedians. (The term "rhythm and blues" used by whites to denote Negro rock-and-roll is

1

[1] Charles Keil, *Urban Blues* (Chicago, University of Chicago Press, 1966).

now only infrequently used by the Negroes themselves.) These media have played a prominent part in promoting the vocabulary of "soul." (It may be added, on the other hand, that both the local Negro press such as the Washington *Afro-American,* and the national Negro publications, for example the monthly *Ebony,* are largely middle-class oriented and thus of limited value in the understanding of life in the ghetto where few read them.)*   2

II

What, then, is "soul"? As the concept has come to be used in urban ghettos over the last number of years, it stands for what is "the essence of Negroness" and, it should be added, this "Negroness" refers to the kind of Negro with which the urban slum dweller is most familiar—people like himself. The question whether a middle-class, white-collar suburban Negro also has "soul" is often met with consternation. In fact, "soul" seems to be a folk conception of the lower-class urban Negro's own "national character." Modes of action, personal attributes, and certain artifacts are given the "soul" label. Typically, in conversations, one hears statements such as, "Man, he got a lot of soul." This appreciative opinion may be given concerning anybody in the ghetto, but more often by younger adults or adolescents about others of their own categories. In particular, speaking in terms of "soul" is common among younger men. This sex differentiation of the use of "soul" conceptions, I will suggest below, may be quite important in the understanding of the basis of the use of the "soul" concept.†   3

The choice of the term "soul" for this "Negroness" is in itself noteworthy. First of all, it shows the influence of religion on lower-class Negroes, even those who are not themselves active church members—expressions of religious derivation, such as "God, have mercy!" are frequent in everyday speech among lower-class Negroes of all age and sex categories, and in all contexts. A very great number of people, of course, have been regular church-goers at some point or other, at least at the time when they attended Sunday school, and many are actively involved in church activities, perhaps in one of the large Baptist churches but at least as often in small spiritualist storefront churches. Although the people who use the "soul" vocabulary in which we are interested here are seldom themselves regular church-goers, they have certainly been fully (although

---

* Paragraph 2: Why is the last sentence placed in parentheses? What purpose do the first two paragraphs serve?

† Paragraph 3: In the second sentence, by whom would the "question" be "met with consternation"?

sometimes indirectly) exposed to the religious idiom; including such phrases as "a soul-stirring revival meeting."   4

Furthermore, the choice of a term which in church usage has a connotation of "the essentially human" to refer to "the essentially Negro," as the new concept of "soul" does, certainly has strong implications of ethnocentrism. If "soul" is Negro, the non-Negro is "non-soul," and, it appears, somewhat less human. Although I have never heard such a point of view spelled out, it would seem to me that it is implicitly accepted as part of an incipient "soul" ideology. It is very clear that what is "soul" is not only different from what is not "soul" (particularly what is mainstream middle-class American); it is also superior. "Soul" is an appraisive as well as designative concept.[2] If one asks a young man what a "soul brother" is, the answer is usually something like "someone who's hip, someone who knows what he's doing." It may be added here that although both "soul brother" and "soul sister" are used for "soul" personified, the former is more common. Like "soul," "soul brother" and "soul sister" are terms used particularly by younger males.*   5

Let us now note a few fields that are particularly "soul." One area is that of music (where the concept may have originated—see the article on the "soul" movement among jazz musicians by Szwed),[3] particularly the field of progressive jazz and rock-and-roll. This has been seized upon by those actively engaged in these fields. James Brown, a leading rock-and-roll singer, is often referred to as "Soul Brother Number One"; two of the largest record stores in Washington, D.C., with practically only Negro customers, are the "Soul Shack" and the "Soul City." Recently a new magazine named "Soul" appeared; its main outlet seems to be these de facto segregated record stores. It contains stories on rock-and-roll artists, disc jockeys, and the like. Excellence in musical expression is indeed a part of the lower-class Negro self-conception, and white rock-and-roll is often viewed with scorn as a poor imitation of the Negro genius. Resentment is frequently aimed at the Beatles who stand as typical of white intrusion into a Negro field. (Occasionally, a Beatle melody has become a hit in the Negro ghetto as well, but only when performed in a local version by a Negro group, such as the recordings of "Day Tripper" by the Vontastics. In such a case, there is little or no mention of its Beatles origin.)†   6

The commercial side of Negro entertainment is, of course, directly tied to "soul" music. With counterparts in other large Negro ghettos in the United States, the Howard Theater in Washington stages shows of tour-

[2] Charles Morris, Signification and Significance (Cambridge, Mass., The M.I.T. Press, 1964).
[3] John F. Szwed, "Musical Style and Racial Conflict," Phylon (vol. 27, 1966), pp. 358–66.

* Paragraph 5: What does the fifth sentence mean?

† Paragraph 6: What does "de facto segregated" mean?

ing rock-and-roll groups and individual performers—each show usually runs a week, with four or five performances every day. Larger shows also make one-night only appearances at the Washington Coliseum. Occasionally, a comedian also takes part; Moms Mabley, Pigmeat Markham, or Red Foxx are among those who draw large Negro audiences but few whites.   7

The "emcees" of these shows are often celebrities in their own right—some, such as "King" Coleman and "Georgeous George" tour regularly with the shows, others are local disc jockeys from the Negro radio stations. In Washington, such disc jockeys as "The Nighthawk" (Bob Terry), and "Soulfinger" (Fred Correy), make highly appreciated appearances at the Howard. The leading local black station is WOL "Soul Radio": it is clear that the commercial establishments with a vested interest in a separate Negro audience have seized upon the "soul" vocabulary, using it to further their own interests as well as supporting its use among the audience. Thus there is also for instance a WWRL "soul brother radio" in New York. However, one should not view the "soul" vocabulary solely as a commercial creation. It existed before it was commercialized, and the fact that it seems so profitable for commercial establishments to fly the banner of "soul" also indicates that whatever part these establishments have had in promoting it, it has fallen into fertile ground.*   8

A second area of widespread "soul" symbolism is that of food. The dishes that are now "soul food" were once—and still are to some extent —referred to simply as "Southern cooking"; but in the Northern ghettos they increasingly come to stand for race rather than region. In the centre of the Washington area, for instance, there is a "Little Harlem Restaurant" advertising "soul food." There are a number of such foods; some of those which are most frequently mentioned as "soul foods" are chitterlings (a part of the intestine of the pig), hog maw (pig tripe), black-eyed peas, collard greens, corn bread, and grits (a kind of porridge). Typically, they were the poor man's food in the rural South—in the urban North, they may still be so to some extent, but in the face of the diversity of the urban environment, they also come to stand as signs of ethnicity. (Thus in some Northern cities there are "soul food" restaurants catering to curious whites, much in the same way as any exotic cuisine.) One may note that references to "soul food" occur frequently in "soul music"; two of the hits of the winter 1966–7 were "Grits and Cornbread" by the Soul Runners and the Joe Cuba Sextet's "Bang! Bang!" with the refrain "corn bread, hog maw and chitterling." Sometimes, the names of "soul foods" may themselves be used as more or less synonymous with "soul"—Negro entertainers on stage, talking of their experiences while journeying between ghetto shows around the country, sometimes refer to it as "the chitterling

---

* Paragraphs 7 and 8: Why does the author present the many details that appear in these two paragraphs?

circuit," and this figure of speech usually draws much favorable audience reaction.   9

What, then, is "soul music" and "soul food"? It may be wise to be cautious here, since there is little intellectualizing and analyzing on the part of the ghetto's inhabitants on this subject. I believe that this comparative absence of defining activity may itself be significant, and I will return to this possibility below. Here, I will only point to a few basic characteristics of what is "soul" which I feel make it particularly "essentially Negro"—referring again, of course, to urban lower-class Negroes rather than to any other category of people.*   10

There is, of course, the Southern origin. The "Down Country" connotations are particularly attached to "soul food"; however, although Negro music has changed more and the contemporary commercial rock-and-roll is an urban phenomenon, it is certainly seen as the latest stage of an unfolding musical heritage. Thus the things that are "soul," while taking on new significance in the urban environment, provide some common historical tradition for ghetto inhabitants. One might also speculate on the possibility that the early and from then on constant and intimate exposure to these foods and to this music—for radios and record players seem to belong to practically every poor ghetto home—may make them appear particularly basic to a "Negro way of life."†   11

When it comes to "soul" music, there are a couple of themes in style and content which I would suggest are pervasive in ghetto life and which probably make them appear very close to the everyday experience of ghetto inhabitants.   12

One of these is the lack of control over the social environment. There is a very frequent attitude among "soul brothers"—that is, the ghetto's younger males—that one's environment is somewhat like a jungle where tough, smart people may survive and where a lot happens to make it worth while and enjoyable just to "watch the scene" if one does not have too high hopes of controlling it. Many of the reactions in listening to "progressive jazz" seem to connect to this view; "Oooh, man, there just ain't nothing you can do about it but sit there and feel it goin' all the way into you." Without being able to do much about proving it, I feel that exposure to experiences—desirable or undesirable—in which one can only passively perceive events without influencing them is an esential fact of ghetto life, for better or for worse; thus it is "soul."   13

Related to this is the experience of unstable personal relationships, in particular between the sexes. It is a well-known fact that among lower-

---

* Paragraph 10: What purpose does this paragraph serve?

† Paragraph 11: In this paragraph, the author explains why "soul food" and "soul music" are "particularly basic" to the culture which he is describing. What function do paragraphs 6 through 9, which deal with these same topics, serve?

class urban Negroes there are many "broken" families (households without a husband and father), many temporary common-law unions, and in general relatively little consensus on sex roles. Thus, it is not much of an exaggeration to speak of a constant "battle of the sexes," and the achievement of success with the opposite sex is a focal concern in lower-class Negro life. From this area come most of the lyrics of contemporary rock-and-roll music. It may be objected that this is true of white rock-and-roll as well; to this it may be answered that this is very much to the point. For white rock-and-roll is predominantly adolescent music, thus reaching people with similar problems of unstable personal relationships. In the case of lower-class urban Negroes, such relationships are characteristic of a much wider age-range, and music on this theme also reaches this wider range. Some titles of recent rock-and-roll hits may show this theme: "I'm losing you" (Temptations), "Are you lonely" (Freddie Scott), "Yours until tomorrow" (Dee Dee Warwick), "Keep me hangin' on" (Supremes). "Soul" stands for a bitter-sweet experience; this often arises from contacts with the other sex, although there are certainly also other sources. This bitter-sweetness, of course, was typical already of the blues.   14

Turning to style, a common element in everyday social interaction as well as among storefront church preachers, Negro comedians, and rock-and-roll singers is an alternation between aggressive, somewhat boasting behaviour, and plaintive behaviour from an implicit under-dog position.   15

This may not be the place to give a more detailed account of this style of behaviour. However, as I said, it occurs in many situations and may itself be related to the unstable personal relationships . . . mentioned above. In any case, it seems that this style is seen as having "soul"; without describing its occurrences in a variety of contexts.*   16

As I noted above, I have hesitated to try to analyze and define "soul," because what seems to be important in the emergence of the present "soul" concept is the fact that there is felt to be *something* which is "soul" rather than *what* that something is. There is, of course, some logic to this; if "soul" is what is "essentially Negro," it should not be necessary for "soul brothers" to spend too much time analyzing it. Asking about "soul" one often receives answers such as "you know, we don't talk much about it, but we've all been through it, so we know what it is anyway." Probably, this is to some extent true. What the lack of pronounced definition points to, in that case, is that "soul" vocabulary is predominantly for in-group consumption. It is a symbol of solidarity among the people of the ghetto, but not in more than a weak and implicit sense of solidarity *against* anybody else. "Soul" is turned inward; and so everybody who is touched

---

* Paragraph 16: How may the "style" referred to here "be related to the unstable relationships" discussed in paragraph 14?

by it is supposed to know what it means. So far there has been little interference with the "soul" vocabulary by outsiders, at least in any way
noticeable to the ghetto dwellers. There have been none of the fierce arguments about its meaning which have developed around "black power," a
concept which did not really evolve in the ghetto but is largely the creation
of white mass media. "Black power" is controversial, and so white people
insist on a definition. (And many black people, also depending on white
media for news, tend to accept the interpretations of these media.) "Soul"
is not equally threatening, and so ghetto dwellers can keep its mystique to
themselves.   17

     We may note in this context that the few interpreters of "soul" to
the outside world are, in fact, outsiders; a kind of cultural brokers who
give interested members of the larger society the "inside stuff" on the
ghetto. But serving as such brokers, they hardly affect the uses of "soul"
within the ghetto community. LeRoi Jones, the author, a convert to ghetto
life who like so many converts seems to have become more militantly
partisan than the more authentic ghetto inhabitants, has moved from a
position where he rather impartially noted the ethnocentric bias of "soul"[4]
to one where he preaches for the complete destruction of the present
American society,[5] an activist programme which I am sure is far out of
step with the immediate concerns of the average "soul brother." Bennett,
an editor of the middle-class *Ebony* magazine, is not particularly interested in "the folk myth of soul" but explains what he feels that "soul"
really is.[6] I am not convinced that his conception is entirely correct; it is
certainly not expressed in the idiom of the ghetto. Keil, an ethnomusicol-
ogist, probably comes closer to the folk conception than anyone else, by
giving what amounts to a catalogue of those ghetto values and experiences
which its inhabitants recognize as their own.[7] In doing so, of course, one
does not get a short and comprehensive definition of "soul" that is acceptable to all and in every situation—one merely lists the fields in which
a vocabulary of "soul" is particularly likely to be expressed. This, of
course, is what has been done in a partial and parsimonious way above.   18

     Here we end the exposition of the "soul" concept. Summing up what
has been said so far, the vocabulary of "soul," which is a relatively recent
phenomenon, is used among younger Negro ghetto dwellers, and particularly young men, to designate in a highly approving manner the experiences and characteristics which are "essentially Negro." As such it is not
an activist vocabulary for use in inter-group relations but a vocabulary
which is employed within the group, although it is clear that by discussing

---

[4] LeRoi Jones, *Blues People* (New York, William Morrow & Co., 1963), p. 219.

[5] LeRoi Jones, *Home: Social Essays* (New York, William Morrow & Co., 1966).

[6] Lerone Bennett, Jr., *The Negro Mood* (New York, Ballantine Books, 1965), p. 89.

[7] Charles Keil, op. cit., pp. 164 et seq.

what is "typically Negro" one makes an implicit reference to the non-Negro society. We turn now to an interpretation of the emergence of such a vocabulary in this group at this point of Negro history.   19

III

For a long time, the social boundaries which have constituted barriers to educational, economic and other achievement by Negro Americans have been highly impermeable. Although lower-class Negroes have to a considerable degree accepted the values of mainstream American culture in those areas, the very obviousness of the impermeability of social boundaries has probably prevented a more complete commitment to the achievement of those goals which have been out of reach. Instead, there has been an adjustment to the lower-class situation in which goals and values more appropriate to the ascribed social position of the group have been added to, and to some extent substituted for, the mainstream norms. Whether these lower-class concerns, experiences, and values are direct responses to the situation or historically based patterns for which the lower-class niche provides space is not really important here. What is important is that the style of life of the lower class, in this case the Negro lower class, is different from that of the upper classes, and that the impermeability of group boundaries and the unequal distribution of resources between groups have long kept the behavioural characteristics of the groups relatively stable and distinct from one another, although to a great extent, one of the groups—the lower-class Negroes—would have preferred the style of life of the other group—the middle-class whites—had it been available to them. As it has been, they have only been able to do the best with what they have had. In a way, then, they have had two cultures, the mainstream culture with which they are relatively familiar, which has in many ways appeared superior and preferable, and which has been closed to them, and the ghetto culture which is a second choice and based on the circumstances of the ascribed social position. (I will not dwell here on the typical features of the two cultures and the relationship between them; articles by Miller[8] and Rodman[9] are enlightening discussions of these topics.)   20
    This, of course, sounds to some extent like the position of what has often been called "the marginal man." Such a position may cause psychological problems. However, when the position is very clearly defined and where the same situation is shared by many, the situation is perhaps

---

[8] Walter B. Miller, "Lower Class Culture as a Generating Milieu of Gang Delinquency," *Journal of Social Issues* (vol. 14, 1958), pp. 5–19.

[9] Hyman Rodman, "The Lower-Class Value Stretch," *Social Forces* (vol. 42, 1963), pp. 205–15.

reasonably acceptable—there is a perfectly understandable reason for one's failure to reach one's goal. Nobody of one's own kind is allowed to reach that goal, and the basis of the condition is a social rule rather than a personal failure. There are indications that marginality is more severely felt if the barrier is not absolute but boundary permeability is possible although uncertain. According to Kerckhoff and McCormick,

> . . . an absolute barrier between the two groups is less conducive to personality problems than "grudging, uncertain and unpredictable acceptance." The impact of the rejection on an individual's personality organization will depend to some extent upon the usual treatment accorded members of his group by the dominant group. If his group as a whole faces a rather permeable barrier and he meets with more serious rejection, the effect on him is likely to be more severe than the same treatment received by a more thoroughly rejected group (one facing an impermeable barrier).[10]

My thesis here is that recent changes in race relations in the United States have indeed made the social barriers to achievement at least seem less impermeable than before to the ghetto population. One often hears people in the ghetto expressing opinions such as, "Yeh, there are so many programs, job-training and things, going on, man, so if you got anything on the ball you can make it." On the other hand, there are also assertions about the impossibility of getting anywhere which contradict the first opinion. Obviously, the clear-cut exclusion from mainstream American culture is gradually being replaced by ambivalence about one's actual chances. This ambivalence, of course, seems to represent an accurate estimate of the situation; the lower-class Negro continues to be disadvantaged, although probably his chances of moving up and out are somewhat better than earlier—people do indeed trickle out of the ghetto.*   21

It is in this situation that the ethnocentric vocabulary of "soul" has emerged, and I want to suggest that it is a response to the uncertainty of the ghetto dweller's situation. This uncertainty is particularly strong for the younger male, the "soul brother." While women have always been able to live closer to mainstream culture norms, as homemakers and possibly with a type of job keeping them in touch with the middle-class world, men have had less chance to become competent in mainstream culture as well as to practice it. Older men tend to feel that current social changes come too late for them but put higher expectations on the following generation. Thus the present generation of young men in the Negro ghettos of the United States are placed in a new situation to which it is making new

---

[10]Alan C. Kerckhoff and Thomas C. McCormick, "Marginal Status and Marginal Personality," *Social Forces* (vol. 34, 1955), p. 51.

---

* Paragraph 21: Try to clarify for yourself the "ambivalence" referred to in the last two sentences by briefly defining it in your own words.

responses, and much of the unrest in the ghettos today is perhaps the result of these emerging pressures.   22

I will suggest here that this new situation must be taken into account if we are to understand the basis of the emergence of the "soul" vocabulary. The increasing ambivalence in conceptions of one's opportunities in the changing social structure may be accompanied by doubts about one's own worth. Earlier, the lack of congruence between mainstream culture norms and the lower-class Negro's achievements could easily be explained by referring to the social barriers. Under-achievement with respect to mainstream norms was an ascribed characteristic of lower-class Negroes. However, when as at present the suspicion arises, which may very well be mistaken, that under-achievement is not ascribed but due to one's own failure, self-doubt may be the result. Such doubt can be reduced in different ways. Some, of course, are able to live up to mainstream norms of achievement, thereby reducing the strain on themselves (but at the same time increasing that on others). Higher self-esteem can also be arrived at by affirming that the boundaries are still impermeable. A third possibility is to set new standards for achievement, proclaiming one's own achievements to be the ideals. It is not necessary, of course, that the same way of reducing self-doubt is always applied. In the case of "soul," the method is that of idealizing one's own achievements, proclaiming one's own way of life to be superior. Yet the same "soul brother" may argue at other times that they are what they are because they are not allowed to become anything else.   23

In any case, "soul" is by native public definition "superior," and the motive of the "soul" vocabulary, I believe, is above all to reduce self-doubt by persuading "soul brothers" that they are successful. Being a "soul brother" is belonging to a select group instead of to a residual category of people who have not succeeded. Thus, the "soul" vocabulary is a device of rhetoric. By talking about people who have "soul," about "soul music" and about "soul food," the "soul brother" attempts to establish himself in an expert and connoisseur role; by talking to others of his group in these terms, he identifies with them and confers the same role on them. Using "soul" rhetoric is a way of convincing others of one's own worth and of their worth; it also serves to persuade the speaker himself. As Burke expresses it,

> A man can be his own audience, insofar as he, even in his secret thoughts, cultivates certain ideas or images for the effect he hopes they may have upon him; he is here what Mead would call "an 'I' addressing its 'me' "; and in this respect he is being rhetorical quite as though he were using pleasant imagery to influence an outside audience rather than one within.[11]   24

[11]Kenneth Burke, A Grammar of Motives and a Rhetoric of Motives (Cleveland, Meridian Books, 1962), p. 562.

The "soul" vocabulary has thus emerged from the social basis of a number of individuals, in effective interaction with one another, with similar problems of adjustment to a new situation. The use of "soul" rhetoric is a way of meeting their needs as long as it occurs in situations where they can mutually support each other. Here is, of course, a clue to the confinement of the rhetoric to in-group situations. If "soul" talk were directed toward outsiders, they might not accept the claims for its excellence—it is not their "folk myth." Viewing "soul" as such a device of rhetoric, it is also easier to understand why it is advantageous for its purposes not to have made it the topic of too much intellectualizing. As Geertz makes clear in his paper on "Ideology as a Cultural System,"[12] by analyzing and defining activity, one achieves maximum intellectual clarity at the expense of emotional commitment. It is doubtful that "soul" rhetoric would thrive on too much intellectual clarity; rather, by expressing "soul" ideals in a circumspect manner in terms of emotionally charged symbols such as "soul food" and "soul music," one can avoid the rather sordid realities underlying these emotions. As I pointed out above, the shared lower-class Negro experiences which seem to be the bases of "soul" are hardly in themselves such as to bring out a surge of ethnic pride. That is a psychological reason for keeping the "soul" concept diffuse. There is also, I believe, a sociological basis for the diffuseness. The more exactly a "soul brother" would define "soul," the fewer others would probably agree upon the "essential Negroness" of his definition; and, as we have seen, a basic idea of the rhetoric of "soul" is to cast others into roles which satisfy them and at the same time support one's own position. If people are cast into a role of "soul brother" and then find that there has been a definition established for that role which they cannot accept, the result may be overt disagreement and denial of solidarity rather than mutual deference. As it is, "soul" can be an umbrella concept for a rather wide variety of definitions of one's situation, and the "soul brothers" who are most in need of the ethnocentric core conception can occasionally get at least fleeting allegiance to "soul" from others with whom in reality they share relatively little, for instance individuals who are clearly upwardly mobile. On one occasion I listened to a long conversation about "soul music" in a rather heterogeneous group of young Negro men who all agreed on the "soulfulness" of the singers whose records they were playing, and afterwards I asked one of the men who is clearly upwardly mobile of his conception of "soul." He answered that "soul" is earthy, "there is nothing specifically Negro about it." Yet the very individuals with whom he had just agreed on matters of "soul" had earlier given me the opposite answer—only Negroes have "soul." Thus by avoid-

[12]Clifford Geertz, "Ideology as a Cultural System," in David E. Apter (ed.), *Ideology and Discontent* (New York, The Free Press, 1964).

ing definitions, they had found together an area of agreement and satisfaction in "soul" by merely assuming that there was a shared basis of opinion.*   25

IV

Summing up what has been said, "soul" is a relatively recent concept used in the urban Negro ghetto, in particular by young men, to express what is "essential Negroness" and to convey appreciation for it. The point of view which has been expressed here is that the need for such a concept has arisen at this point because of increasingly ambivalent conceptions of the opportunity structure. While earlier, lack of achievement according to American mainstream ideals could easily be explained in terms of impermeable social barriers, the impression is gaining ground in the ghetto that there are now ways out of the situation. The young men who come under particularly great strain if such a belief is accepted must either achieve some success (which many of them are obviously still unable to do, for various reasons), explain that achievement is impossible (which is probably not as true as it has been), or explain that achievement according to mainstream ideals is not necessarily achievement according to their ideals. The emergence of "soul," it has been stated here, goes some way toward meeting the need of stating alternative ideals and also provides solidarity among those with such a need. In implying or stating explicitly that ghetto culture has a superiority of its own, the users of the "soul" vocabulary seem to take a step beyond devices of established usage which are terms of solidarity but lack or at least have less clear cultural references—for example the use of "brother" as a term of either reference or address for another Negro. That is, it is more in the cultural than in the social dimension that "soul" is an innovation rather than just one more term of a kind. Of course, the two are closely connected. It is advantageous to maintain a diffuse conception of "soul," for if an intellectually clear definition were established, "soul" would probably be both less convincing and less uniting.   26

The view of "soul" taken here is one of a piecemeal rhetoric attempt to establish a satisfactory self-conception. For the great majority of "soul brothers" I am sure this is the major basis of "soul." It may be added that for instance LeRoi Jones[13] and Charles Keil[14] tend to give the impres-

---

[13]LeRoi Jones, *Home: Social Essays.*
[14]Charles Keil, op. cit.

---

* Paragraphs 24 and 25: What does the author mean by referring to the "soul" vocabulary as "a device of rhetoric"?

sion of a more social-activist conception of "soul," although Keil tends to make it a prophecy rather than an interpretation. At least at present, I think that there is little basis for connecting the majority of "soul brothers" with militant black nationalism—there is hardly a "soul movement." "Soul" became publicly associated with black militancy as the term "soul brother" made its way to international prominence during recent ghetto uprisings—Negro businessmen posted "soul brother" signs in their windows, it was noted by mass media all over the world. However, it is worth noting that this was an internal appeal to the ghetto moral community by black shopkeepers, not a sign of defiance of the outside world by the participants. It may be said that the outsiders merely caught a glimpse of an internal ghetto dialogue. Yet organized black nationalism may be able to recruit followers by using some kind of transformed "soul" vocabulary, and I think there are obviously attempts on its side to make more of "soul" than it is now. Certainly, there is seldom any hostility to black militants among the wider groups of self-defined "soul brothers," although the vocabulary of "soul" has not been extensively employed for political purposes. If it is so used, however, it could possibly increase the ghetto dwellers' identification with political nationalism. Thus, if at present it is not possible to speak of more than a "rhetoric of soul," it may be that in the future we will find a "soul movement." If that happens, of course, "soul" may become a more controversial concept, as "black power" is now.   27

The Whole Selection

1 Although his basic intent is to define "soul," the author of this essay makes considerable use of classification and division. In paragraphs 4 and 5 he gives us two classifications which are bases for the initial use of the term "soul" by blacks. Then, in paragraphs 6 through 9, he moves to another element, that of the "areas" in which "soul" is evident. Does he exhaust the possibilities under which the areas might be classified?

2 In the fourth sentence in section IV of his essay (page 237), Hannerz sums up the three classifications which he has made of the alternatives that are open to the young men of the black ghetto. Where, in the body of his essay, has he developed the three classifications?

3 Cite the author's use of other methods of development, such as example and comparison and contrast.

4 Observe how the author avoids absolute generalizations. For example, he says, "The field site *seems* to be typical . . ." (sentence 2, paragraph

2) and "This sex differentiation . . . *may* be quite important" (last sentence, paragraph 3). What effect does this achieve?

5 In paragraph 19, Hannerz summarizes what he has said up to that point in his essay, and in paragraph 26 he summarizes the body of the whole essay. Is it always necessary for a writer to provide summaries? Why does Hannerz do so?

A RHETORICAL ANALYSIS OF THE GETTYSBURG ADDRESS

HAROLD ZYSKIND

The analysis of the Gettysburg Address presented below is intended to exemplify one way of treating literary texts in undergraduate, preferably junior college, discussions. The treatment or method, roughly speaking, is generic: the meaning, structure, and purpose of the text are sought on the hypothesis that the Address is an instance of a literary genre; and the general nature of the Address is sought on the hypothesis that its parts converge to create a unity of meaning or effect. In application to any particular text, the hypotheses need not be wholly true: they are employed to suggest a mode of analysis, not aesthetic criteria. Since such an approach seeks to recover meaning in context, it is applicable to readings in almost any field of knowledge. And, since the concern is, in equal measure, with the literary construction and the genre of a work, the approach is peculiarly relevant to the humanities.[1]

---

*Address Delivered at the Dedication
of the Cemetery at Gettysburg*[2]

Four score and seven years ago our fathers brought forth on this continent, a new nation, conceived in Liberty, and dedicated to the proposition that all men are created equal.

[2.] Now we are engaged in a great Civil War, testing whether that nation, or any nation so conceived and so dedicated, can long endure. [3.] We are met on a great battlefield of that war. [4.] We have come to dedicate a portion of that field, as a final resting place for those who here gave their lives that that nation might live. [5.] It is altogether fitting and proper that we should do this.

[6.] But, in a larger sense, we cannot dedicate—we cannot consecrate—we cannot hallow—this ground. [7.] The brave men, living and dead, who struggled here, have consecrated it far above our poor power to add or detract. [8.] The world will little note, nor long remember what we say here, but it can never forget what they did here. [9.] It is for us the living, rather, to be dedicated here to the unfinished work which they who fought here have thus far so nobly advanced. [10.] It is rather for us to be here dedicated to the great task remaining before us—that from these honored dead we take increased devotion to that cause for which they gave the last full measure of devotion—that we here highly resolve that these dead shall not have died in vain—that this nation, under God, shall have a new birth of freedom—and that government of the people, by the people, for the people, shall not perish from the earth.

Abraham Lincoln

November 19, 1863

---

[1] For the role of analysis in a humanities program see Richard McKeon, "The Nature and Searching of the Humanities," *Journal of General Education*, III, No. 4 (July, 1949), 290–303.

[2] Text taken from the "final manuscript" copy appearing in William E. Barton, *Lincoln at Gettysburg* (Indianapolis: Bobbs-Merrill Co., 1930), plate facing p. 208.

I

A generic analysis obviously depends on a particular definition of the genre in question (in this case, rhetoric) and on the principles supporting it. I do not believe it relevant to argue the principle here, however, since the defense assumed for the definition of rhetoric employed in this article is pedagogic, not philosophic. If the grounds of greatness of the Gettysburg Address were the primary consideration, perhaps a preliminary discussion of principle would be in order. But a final judgment as to its greatness is not involved necessarily in a generic analysis. The primary questions are: Does the Address belong to the genre as defined (however arbitrarily defined)? Are the meaning and purpose of the Address—is its uniqueness—in any way illuminated by an analysis of it as belonging to that genre? The latter question is predominant; only for its sake is the former one asked. In general terms, the familiar notion is used here of a rhetorical work as one designed primarily to create a certain effect on, or to persuade, a particular audience, by whatever means. The merit of the definition, for immediate purposes, is simply that it suggests specific questions to ask about the Gettysburg Address—for example, it immediately suggests an inquiry to discover the traits of the audience envisaged in the statements of Lincoln's speech. Thus, although originating in part from a more or less specific notion as to what rhetoric is (the details of this notion are at least implicit throughout the article), the analysis proceeds— and may be tested for fruitfulness—by reference to the Address itself.   1

This approach lends itself well to creative participation by students in class discussion. Since no great body of auxiliary or background facts is essential for an intelligent analysis within the framework of the approach, discussion need not consist of attempts by students to anticipate what is in the mind of an instructor better informed than they. In addition, of course, the approach allows for the formulation of questions whose answers require thought about the text rather than recitation from it. The discussion will go better, I believe, if the students are aware generally of the nature of the approach. Otherwise, the instructor's questions may appear to reflect his ingenuity, but they are not likely to suggest the particular and sharply limited purpose of the inquiry.   2

One way of helping students become clearer about a generic or analytic inquiry is to differentiate it from two other approaches closely related to it. The first kinsman is the biographer. His interests will coincide with the analyst's frequently enough so that the latter must be alert against being diverted by the kinds of biographical questions which do not concern him except incidentally. Does the Address reveal how Lincoln truly felt about the conscripted soldiers and the substitutes? Was Lincoln sincere in all that he said, or was he pretending for the occasion? These may be significant questions for politics or that kind of history called "biography." But, at best, they would be tangential to the analyst's chief emphasis. Whether an orator made a statement because he truly believed it or because he felt it expedient to pretend that he believed it, the statement remains the same. Once delivered, the speech exists. The analyst's primary interest is to discover its meaning and power, as it stands, since he views the Address in the particular compass of his approach as an artistic creation designed for some end. The biographer, on the other hand, sees the speech ultimately as a clue, a piece of evidence which may yield valuable information about the facts of Lincoln's life.   3

Another approach akin to the analyst's but different in emphasis is that of the geneticist, who works hand in hand with the biographer, but in rather a reverse direction. The biographer seeks to understand the forces and facts of Lincoln's life by studying the speech as evidence, while the geneticist seeks to understand the speech by studying the facts or forces in Lincoln's life as evidence. Quite properly for his interests, the geneticist discovers the historical or psychological causes which motivated Lincoln to write the Address.   4

One unkind and narrow geneticist explanation of Lincoln's purpose in writing the Gettysburg Address that might be presented to students as an example could run roughly as follows: In November, 1863, the month in which the speech was delivered, Lincoln was concerned about the coming presidential campaign of 1864. For his campaign to be successful, he knew he needed the support of Pennsylvania's governor, Andrew H. Curtin. At the time, however, this support was in doubt. And so, since Curtin was the chief sponsor of the national cemetery at Gettysburg and had been widely advertised as such, Lincoln therefore decided to lay aside his pressing duties at Washington and to accept the invitation to speak at the dedication ceremony, as a way of pleasing and indorsing Curtin publicly. So evident was Lincoln's purpose that he rode up to Gettysburg the day before the ceremony in the hope of seeing the governor at some of the preliminary social affairs, although Secretary of War Stanton had arranged for him to leave Washington the following day in ample time for the actual dedication. Finally, the intention of pleasing Curtin is made clear in the speech itself, for in the fifth sentence Lincoln makes a point of declaring that the ceremony—Curtin's ceremony—is altogether fitting and proper. 5

Whether or not this explanation were accepted, if one began to search Lincoln's letters and records in order to confirm or disprove it, he would be turning away from the chief focus of the generic analysis. The latter does seek to determine the purpose or intention of the speech. But by that is meant the aim which the words and ideas of the Address seem designed to achieve. What I am saying may be made clearer, I think, by glancing again at the fifth sentence. What one geneticist might find significant in this sentence already has been seen. If his kind of explanation of it were accepted as adequate for the analyst, the latter would be distracted from observing, for example, that the fifth sentence marks the last stage of a steady process of inward narrowing or contraction in the Address. Let us trace this process.   6

The first sentence opens broadly on the concepts of the continent, the nation, liberty, and equality. Then in the second sentence Lincoln narrows attention to the Civil War; then the circle contracts to the battlefield of that war; next, attention is pinpointed on that part of the battlefield which is being dedicated; and, finally, in the fifth sentence the narrowing movement from continent-nation to war to battlefield to cemetery plots ends in the statement that the dedication of this cemetery is altogether fitting and proper. The termination of the inward movement here, accompanied appropriately as it is by the matter-of-fact diction of this fifth sentence, prepares in tone and thought for the subsequent statement of the inadequacy of the ceremony. More important, since it raises the question of the fittingness of the ceremony, it creates a need, and opens the way, for the expansion and rising emphasis which begin in the sixth sentence with the words "but in a *larger* sense," and which continue until the final plea that this nation and democratic government may not perish from the earth. In this final statement Lincoln has reascended to concepts similar to those with which he began: that is, this continent, the nation, liberty, and equality of the opening are paralleled in the closing statement —though not in the same order—by the earth, this nation, freedom, and government of the people. The movement is like the shape of an hourglass, a steady contraction from broad considerations, followed by progressive expansion back to those considerations. The fifth sentence functions in diction and tone and thought as the narrow passageway connecting the two periods of the movement. There will be more to say of the fifth sentence later, but the point here is that this kind of observation about it is immediately relevant to the analyst's interest, and he should not be diverted from it by an exclusive concern with the relation between Lincoln and the governor of Pennsylvania.   7

I have distinguished between the approaches with perhaps excessive rigidity. Just as the sound geneticist will relate Lincoln's habits of thought and composition to the structure of the Address, so the generic analyst cannot read the Address in a vacuum of indifference to its genesis in Lincoln's mind and environment. But the emphasis in the two approaches is nonetheless distinct. The geneticist sees the speech primarily as a historical event which is to be interpreted by discovering its external causes and consequences; the analyst sees the Address primarily as a construction which may be interpreted by discovering its intrinsic causes—its aim, its structure, its assumptions about the audience, its parts and their interrelations.   8

II

With such an interest, the analysis[3] may begin in a preliminary and tentative fashion by considering the literary form or genre of the Address, since the initial conception of the form will suggest a more specific direction that questions may take. The fact that the speech is oratory and was delivered on a ceremonial occasion does not classify it automatically as rhetoric. Orton H. Carmichael says the Address will last through time—because, in his words, "Truth only is eternal."[4] He here obviously is treating the speech as political philosophy. And it is true that Lincoln speaks strongly of fundamental principles of government. One might assert, even, that the Address is history, since it lays down in the second sentence a thesis as to the historical significance of the Civil War. No law requires that the Address lie meekly in any rigorous category or that it not have value for us—like Herodotus' work—as philosophy, history, and rhetoric. But there are reasons which suggest a rhetorical analysis as primary: The Gettysburg Address assumes—it does not seek to demonstrate—the truth of the political propositions that it lays down. The listeners are presumed in advance to believe that democratic government is desirable. The same applies to the broader historical statements. No substantiation is offered. Lincoln simply asserts what the significance of the Civil War is. He apparently relies for substantiation on the audience's existing convictions rather than on the kind of evidence and interpretations observed in most histories. Lincoln's method in this regard is characteristic of rhetoric. If the aim is to create an effect on a particular audience, the relevant question for the rhetorician is not whether a proposition necessary to the argument really is true but whether the listeners believe it to be true. Consequently, what would have to be demonstrated in some fashion for the historian or scientist often is offered in rhetoric as an assumed premise, just as Lincoln's broad historical and philosophic statements are offered here. In addition, the Address has an obvious emotional pitch and makes frequent references to the audience, thus further suggesting its essentially persuasive character. Although the Address has not been shown by any means to be exclusively rhetorical, it seems clear that an inquiry into it as rhetoric should yield some insight into its meaning and aim. First, then, to the question of its rhetorical effect or aim.   9

The ceremonial occasion, as Lincoln expressly describes it in the speech, suggests that he sought to bestow honor on the dead of Gettys-

---

[3] Among the works consulted in the preparation of this analysis was a lecture by Andrew Meyer, professor of English, Hood College. I wish here to express thanks for insights obtained from his paper.

[4] *Lincoln's Gettysburg Address* (New York: Abingdon Press, 1917), p. 113.

burg and all those who had fought that the Union might live. This aim is supported especially by the emphasis that Lincoln gives to the inadequacy of the ceremony in contrast to the larger and more genuine dedication of the ground achieved by the soldiers who fought there. The speech thus would be epideictic rhetoric; that is, its aim would be to exhibit the deeds or memory of the fallen soldiers in such solemn and stirring manner as to excite the audience's immediate, present praise of them. Another possibility is that Lincoln's aim is deliberative; that is, that his concern is to persuade the audience to take some specified course of action represented as desirable for its future consequences. This is supported chiefly by the two final sentences, each of which begins with an injunction to the audience to devote themselves to actions on behalf of the Union's survival.   10

Is either of these two aims dominant over the other? Is the Address primarily epideictic or primarily deliberative, or some combination of the two? These are the questions to be posed at this point. But the analyst's ultimate aim is not to bury the Address in some neat verbal category. His primary purpose is not to label it deliberate or epideictic. Rather he tries to place it in one or both of these categories because such an attempt requires him to examine the Address itself in a somewhat systematic manner. For example, since a temporal distinction is involved in the categories being considered—present honor and future action—one must look for the temporal emphases in the structure of the Address. This search leads to awareness of a quite evident pattern: first, Lincoln tells what happened eighty-seven years before; then, in the second sentence, attention turns to what is happening now; and, finally, the Address closes with reference to what must happen in the future. On this basis Part I of the speech would consist of the first sentence. Part II would move from the second into the eighth sentence, since the shift to the present is made explicit when the Civil War is introduced, and this emphasis on the present tense —in connection with the war, the battlefield, and the dedication ceremony —continues into the transitional eighth sentence. There the phrase "the world will little note" foreshadows the shift to the future which becomes dominant in the ninth and tenth sentences, as in such phrases as "that these dead shall not have died in vain" or that this nation "shall not perish from the earth."   11

This division by itself, however, does not help appreciably in deciding whether the Address aims at present praise or future action, for all stages of the temporal stream are represented, and not always in connection with honor or action. The division needs to be explored further before it becomes meaningful, for Lincoln obviously is not concerned with the nature of time itself but with what takes place in the temporal stream. What or who moves along it? The most apparent and constant element is the audience itself—or, rather, the speaker and audience combined, who constitute the general "we" of the Address. This "we" appears in some form at least once in every statement in the speech. Sometimes it changes to the possessive "our" or the accusative "us," but the plural pronoun in the first person still is there. A glance down the speech reveals: "our fathers"; "we are engaged"; "we are met"; "we have come"; "that we should do this," "we cannot dedicate"; "our poor power"; and so on in each sentence through "that we here highly resolve."   12

Thus, whatever it is whose temporal sequence Lincoln is following, he explicitly underlines his and the listeners' roles at each stage of the sequence. From the standpoint solely of what this role of the audience is, a climactic rise is apparent from stage to stage. In Part I the phrase "our fathers" incidentally implies the audience's role as inheritors of the nation founded eighty-seven years before; the listeners here are passive beneficiaries, inactive heirs. Part II represents them as engaged in a Civil War generally, but their particular role in it at the present moment is to dedicate the cemetery: the point of the dedication is what is said. The listeners are here, therefore, mere talkers or utterers of words. Part III begins in the ninth sentence to urge them to more positive action in the future, to carry on the unfinished work, so that they now become, potentially, doers of deeds. Thus as the speech moves in temporal climax from past to present to future, the role ascribed to the audience moves climactically from that of receivers to speakers to doers. It may be noticed, incidentally, how complete these divisions are: just as past, present, and future cover the whole of a temporal stream, so also passivity, speech, and action cover all kinds of external service which the listeners or any men could render to a cause.   13

At any rate, when the two patterns of time and the listeners' role are linked, the emphasis in the final section falls on the audience's future action; and the inquiry has shown that the solemn call to action emerges in this final section not as an appendage or afterthought but rather as the systematic culmination and climax (in time and kind of service) to the two preceding sections. The implication therefore is that the epideictic elements of the speech must be subordinate to and must help achieve its deliberative aim.   14

To test this implication, one may examine the way in which the epideictic elements do figure in the pattern already observed. These elements are "our fathers" and the soldiers, since they are the only persons in the Address for whom there is any strong note of praise. Notice that the praise given is for the high degree of worthy action or doing which Lincoln ascribes to them. In Part I, when one barely thinks of the passive role implied for the audience, the fathers are engaged in the mighty task of bringing forth a nation. In Part II, the deeds of the soldiers—"what they did here"—are expressly contrasted with "what we say here."   15

Hence the pattern of the analysis must be expanded to include doers at every stage of the Address. In the first, it is our fathers who are the doers; in the second, it is the soldiers; in the third, as evident from the earlier analysis, it is the audience potentially. The connection is clear and explicit. Because in Parts I and II the deeds of the fathers and soldiers are represented to some extent epideictically as praiseworthy in contrast to the mere talk of the audience, therefore in Part III Lincoln urges the audience to act as the soldiers have acted in preserving what was achieved through action by the fathers. The dominance of the deliberative aim is therefore clear.[5]   16

What it might have meant for Lincoln to have made the epideictic aim dominant instead may be indicated vividly by drawing on the speech delivered on the same occasion by Edward Everett. As chief orator of that day at Gettsyburg, he spoke magnificently for some two hours. Here are the concluding sentences of his speech:

> "The whole earth," said Pericles, as he stood over the remains of his fellow-citizens, who had fallen in the first year of the Peloponnesian War, "the whole earth is the sepulchre of illustrious men." All time, he might have added, is the millennium of their glory. Surely I would do no injustice to the other noble achievements of the war, which have reflected such honor on both arms of the service, and have entitled the armies and the navy of the United States, their officers and men, to the warmest thanks and the richest rewards which a grateful people can pay. But they, I am sure, will join us in saying, as we bid farewell to the dust of these martyr-heroes, that wheresoever throughout the civilized world the accounts of this great warfare are read, and down to the latest periods of recorded time, in the glorious annals of our common country there will be no brighter page than that which relates The Battles of Gettysburg.[6]

Mr. Everett's eloquent concern at this point with nobility, honor, and glory has an epideictic emphasis which ought to illuminate, by contrast, the quite different end of the Gettysburg Address.   17

[5] A simple diagram of analysis up to this point would be as follows:

Part	Sentences	Time	Audience Role	Models
I	1	Past	Passivity	Action (fathers)
II	2–8	Present	Speech	Action (soldiers)
III	8/9–10	Future	Action	

[6] *Address of the Hon. Edward Everett, at the Consecration of the National Cemetery at Gettysburg, 19th November, 1863, with the Dedicatory Speech of President Lincoln.* . . . (Boston: Little, Brown & Co., 1864), p. 82.

III

While the interpretation up to this point presumably is justified, there is a rather striking omission from it. No mention has been made of a usual characteristic by which a speech is recognized as deliberative. Milton's *Areopagitica*, or virtually any contemporary political speech, exemplifies this trait well. Milton wants the licensing act repealed. Consequently, he tells Parliament that the passage of the act produces bad ends and that the repeal of the act will be the means for restoring truth and virtue. As in most deliberative oratory, the argument turns on the issue of means and ends, since the aim is to stimulate a course of action by showing the desirable effect which it will have.   18

If the Gettysburg Address is deliberative, what about its argument? This question may be explored by looking at the Address for a moment solely from the standpoint of its concern with means and ends. In the opening sentence what is important about our fathers is the end which they achieved—the founding of the nation. Then the Civil War is identified by the fact that it also has as its end the survival of that nation. The battlefield and the cemetery plot are next presented implicitly in terms of the same end, since, as Lincoln develops the narrowing process observed earlier, the Civil War's arena includes the battlefield, which, in turn, includes the plot of ground being dedicated. The connection thus established between the cemetery and the welfare of the nation is reaffirmed when Lincoln expressly describes the cemetery as the resting place for those who gave their lives that that nation might live. Accordingly, the fifth sentence may declare the ceremonial dedication altogether fitting and proper, because—and here I shall go back up the ladder from the fifth to the first sentence—the cemetery contains the dead who fought on the battlefield of the war whose end is the survival of the nation that our fathers founded. Thus these opening sentences comprise more than the narrowing movement noticed earlier; they form a unit in which the career of the Union is established and held to steadfastly by Lincoln as the one end or standard by which to understand or judge our fathers, the war, the soldiers, the cemetery, and the ceremony.   19

Next, one may notice how, after Stage I of the argument—i.e., the unit formed by the first five sentences—has been completed, Lincoln begins in the sixth sentence to shift his emphasis from the end of action to a consideration of the most noble and effective means. In Stage I there is no mention of the bravery of the soldiers, that is, of the way they fought, but only of the end for which they fought. Now in Stage II (sentences six, seven, eight) their bravery becomes important because it characterizes the means which they employed toward the end. Similarly, it is in this second stage that Lincoln considers the audience's poor power to add or detract, that is, the ineffectiveness of the ceremony as a means. Ostensibly, Lincoln here in Stage II of the argument is modifying and expanding his former judgment of the ceremony. It is incapable of truly dedicating the ground, because the soldier's deeds have done this more genuinely and because their deeds—not the words of the ceremony—will be memorable to the world. This contrast between words and deeds is an opposition between two kinds of means for serving the same end.   20

In the light, now, of the first five sentences as comprising Stage I and the next three sentences as comprising Stage II, of what is loosely called the "argument," we may summarize the grounds on which two apparently opposed judgments of the dedication ceremony are offered. Stage I judges it by the end toward which it is directed and therefore finds the ceremony, like the soldier's deeds, to be altogether fitting and proper. Stage II, however, judges the ceremony by the means employed and therefore finds it, unlike the soldier's brave deeds, to be altogether inadequate and transitory.   21

Thus not only has Lincoln passed judgment on the ceremony, but, in doing so, he has employed broad and basic criteria for action in any crucial period of the democratic Union's career. Even should the audience forget the particular judgment of the ceremony, Lincoln has impressed on them the principles by which they should live and act in the future—they know the right end and the most effective means. With such criteria for future action established, the way is open for the third and final stage of the argument, which begins with the ninth sentence and needs only to press the listeners with deep emotion to act according to these principles. 22

Lincoln does not once mar the beauty of his words or the fluency of his thought by speaking expressly of means and ends. But when in Stage III he encourages the listeners rather to be doers, like the soldiers, so that the nation may live, he is urging them to carry on the means which had been established as preferable in Stage II of the argument, for the end which had been premised as desirable in Stage I.[7]   23

IV

The inquiry thus far has yielded some conception of what Lincoln's speech seeks to persuade its listeners to do. It is necessary, next, to try to identify these listeners. Until one knows whom the Address seeks to

---

[7] A simple diagram of the argument of the speech would be as follows:

Stage	Sentences	Judgment	Criterion
I	1–5	Ceremony fitting	End
II	6–8	Ceremony inadequate	Means
III	9–10	Therefore, act for the Union (means) (end)	

arouse to action, the conception of its aim as deliberative rhetoric remains somewhat empty. Of course, there was the physical audience seated before Lincoln at the ceremony. But some of them may have been distracted at the moment of the speech—especially since the speech is so short—by a neighbor's sneezing fit. Indeed, the evidence is not at all clear as to whether Lincoln produced much of an effect of any kind on the persons seated before him. Perhaps he had in mind the newspaper readers who would see the Address on the morning after the ceremony. Or, again, to the extent that modern readers or listeners are affected by the speech, perhaps they constitute the true audience. Such questions will have to be left chiefly to the biographer or the geneticist, who are more concerned with discovering just whom Lincoln had in mind and precisely what historical consequences the Address has had on the oratory and emotions of America. In view of the practical difficulties alone, an analysis on the undergraduate level could hardly attempt to define the audience by such research. But there is a limited kind of inquiry appropriate here which is germane to the analyst's interests. He can try to discover, from the Address, roughly the kind of persons to whom it is likely to appeal.   24

For example, it is quite apparent that an atheist is not a member of the envisaged audience, so far as the phrase "under God," which appears in the tenth sentence, is concerned. If we are right about Lincoln's purpose, then the phrase "under God"—like any other phrase in the Address—ought to help lead the listener toward being an active doer in the service of the nation. That fact that the nation is said to be under God will have no such effect on an atheist, and in that respect—though perhaps in no other—he will be excluded from the envisaged audience. If this line of reasoning is pursued in a more general and practicable manner, we should say that the true or envisaged audience will comprise those who have some kind of positive and favorable feelings about the Founding Fathers, this continent, liberty, equality, bravery in battle, and so on. From such a beginning one could go on to build up a more detailed picture of the sort of person to whom the speech is appealing.   25

Notice how broad and inclusive this audience is. Nowhere does Lincoln touch on particular issues which might tend to cut off some partisan group from his reach. Nor does he make any nice distinctions about the definition of liberty or democratic government. Whatever theoretic or even practical differences about methods may separate believers in political democracy, Lincoln chooses the terms[8] dear to all of them and appeals

---

[8] The orientation of this analysis may perhaps best be indicated at this point, since Lincoln's use of undefined generalities is considered here only for its persuasive qualities, whereas often such a device is praised or blamed as the declaration of true ideals or the misleading exploitation of glittering generalities, depending on whether one supports or opposes the particular rhetorician under consideration.

to the basic convictions which they have in common. Whatever disadvantages in specificity of appeal this method may entail, the audience is envisaged with a breadth that will attract nearly all persons who bring to the speech a feeling that they have a genuine attachment to American democracy.   26

It is not enough, however, to designate the listeners whom Lincoln is trying to reach, for Lincoln is doing more than appealing *to* them. He is *using* them as part of his means of persuasion. The audience constitutes material for the skillful rhetorician as surely as words do. With perhaps a single symbol, the skillful rhetorician awakens emotions and convictions already possessed by his listeners, though perhaps vaguely or dormantly; and he then channels these emotions toward the end that he has in mind. Among the already existent feelings which Lincoln awakens and stimulates are admiration for the Founding Fathers, respect for liberty, emulation of bravery, love and veneration of God. But, having aroused this diversity of emotions and convictions, what does Lincoln do with them? By what means does he turn them to his purpose? To answer this in part, one may notice the systematic way in which Lincoln implicitly defines all the diverse objects which have emotional significance for the audience. All such objects take on meaning, for the instant of the Address, only insofar as they relate to the concept of the free nation. Our fathers, whatever else they may have done in fact, have meaning in the Address only as the founders of the nation. Bravery is here a virtue only insofar as it prompts brave deeds in the service of the nation. Liberty is defined only as a characteristic of the nation. And God, whatever other significance he may have in our lives, is represented in the Address only as the Being who stands over the nation. One could proceed thus with all the major emotional terms in the speech. The point here is that, since all these terms have meaning in the Address only as they relate to the nation, then all the emotions associated with the terms tend to be transferred to the nation. Thus all the diverse feelings and sympathies which Lincoln awakens are channeled so as to crystallize into an instant of intense devotion to the free Union in peril.   27

The cumulative channeling of this feeling is not interrupted by any aspect of the Address, not even by an attempt on Lincoln's part to tell how deeply moved he himself is as President. In other speeches he does not hesitate to use the pronoun "I" and thereby to represent his own character, motives, and position in a favorable light. He could have done the same in the Gettysburg Address. But he represents himself only as an indistinguishable member among those gathered to honor the dead. In representing himself in such a way, Lincoln adds emotionally to the idea that the only touchstone of importance is one's relation to the nation's survival. At the moment he is engaged, like the audience, in honoring the dead with words; therefore, he and the audience are one.   28

The resultant sense of unity is sustained by the Address as a whole. Lincoln, the audience, the soldiers, the Founding Fathers, even God—all are united in the Address in their concern with the same end. Though a war is in progress, nowhere does Lincoln introduce a single note of division; he forgoes all the advantages he could have gained from emotional condemnations of the unpopular Copperheads of the North or the hated slave barons of the South. Nowhere does he mention enemies, and it is obvious that "our fathers" were from Virginia as well as from New York. Whatever Lincoln may forfeit in partisan emotional appeal by this method he gains back in a sense of emotional unity.   29

V

A final stage in the inquiry still is necessary before it may be considered adequate. We have some notion now of Lincoln's aim and of the ideas and emotional associations that he employs to achieve this aim. But, unless the ideas and emotions are presented stirringly and appropriately, the speech will lack effectiveness. I shall not inquire thoroughly here into this topic of style or tone, for it is what is so often emphasized in "rhetorical" analysis. One may observe the biblical tone of such a word as "consecrate" and of such a phrase as "Four score and seven years ago"; this diction imparts a solemnity appropriate both to the dedication ceremony and to the larger dedication which Lincoln urges upon his audience. Or one may contrast the matter-of-fact form of the sentence—"We are met on a great battlefield of that war"—to the parallelism in the sixth sentence: ". . . we cannot dedicate—we cannot consecrate—we cannot hallow—this ground." And the symphonic progression represented by that contrast may be traced as it builds up further from that sixth sentence to the more extended climactic parallels, the solemn rhythms, and the periodic form of the final appeal in the tenth sentence.   30

But I prefer here to emphasize the basic metaphor that Lincoln employs for the nation, since the emotional tone is derived in such large measure from it; that is, from the figure of the nation as a single being moving through an organic life-cycle. The ideas of the speech, and the diction as well, emphasize the vicissitudes of this metaphoric cycle. Our fathers *brought forth* the nation. It was *conceived* in liberty. The war tests whether it can *endure*. The soldiers fought that it might *live*. And we must see that it has a new *birth* of freedom and *not perish* from the earth. No figure could have been more appropriate to an occasion commemorating the dead. Its appropriateness—and the religious tone set by solemn discussion of generation and death—are sustained by the characterization of the audience as the living in contrast to the dead of the battlefield, who gave their lives that the nation might live.   31

VI

On the day following Lincoln's delivery of the Address, he received a note from Edward Everett, who said: "I should be glad if I could flatter myself that I came as near to the central idea of the occasion in two hours as you did in two minutes.[9] What Everett had in mind, perhaps, was the central point seen re-emerging successively in the various rhetorical aspects of the Address as analyzed here—that is, that the dedication ceremony and all the ideas and actions appropriate to it take on in Lincoln's address a solemn significance precisely because they are exhibited to us so skillfully and so exclusively from the perspective of their bearing on the Union in peril. As an argument, the Address establishes service to the nation as the end of action and positive deeds as the proper means. In the process of the argument a wide range of the envisaged audience's sympathies and convictions are channeled and brought to focus on the nation and the necessity for its survival. And, in style, the occasion is made the basis of a metaphor which transforms appropriate thoughts about the soldiers' deaths into a consideration of the nation's life. 32

In stirring his audience thus to action on behalf of the Union, Lincoln's subordination of what may be called the "logical" element to the emotional and intuitive has been evident. The argument itself sets up its criteria of means and ends in its first two stages, so that the final stage of even so brief a speech has nothing to establish—it has only to drive home emotionally the implications of these principles for the listeners' choice of future action. The emotional process is stimulated further by the sense of unity created in the audience and by the skillful evoking of a wide range of their traditional feelings. And, finally, the kind of simplicity and solemnity created by the metaphor of birth and death, by the religious diction and the climactic progressions, lends a quality of timelessness to Lincoln's statements. 33

Thus the deliberative aim of the Address, as it may be reformulated now in the light of the entire analysis, is not to persuade the listeners of the truth of the idea that the Union must be reborn. In a logical sense the truth of the general idea that future action is needed is largely taken for granted. The aim rather is to take this accepted general idea and sink it deeply into the feelings of the audience, fix it as an emotional experience so powerful that each listener will, at any crucial time, do what he can specifically for the future of the nation to which he is here dedicated. 34

[9] Barton, *op. cit.*, p. 105.

INAUGURAL ADDRESS

JOHN F. KENNEDY

We observe today not a victory of party but a celebration of freedom, symbolizing an end as well as a beginning, signifying renewal as well as change. For I have sworn before you and Almighty God the same solemn oath our forebears prescribed nearly a century and three-quarters ago.　1

The world is very different now. For man holds in his mortal hands the power to abolish all forms of human poverty and all forms of human life. And yet the same revolutionary belief for which our forebears fought is still at issue around the globe, the belief that the rights of man come not from the generosity of the state but from the hand of God.　2

We dare not forget today that we are the heirs of that first revolution. Let the word go forth from this time and place, to friend and foe alike, that the torch has been passed to a new generation of Americans, born in this century, tempered by war, disciplined by a hard and bitter peace, proud of our ancient heritage, and unwilling to witness or permit the slow undoing of those human rights to which this nation has always been committed, and to which we are committed today at home and around the world.　3

Let every nation know, whether it wishes us well or ill, that we shall pay any price, bear any burden, meet any hardship, support any friend, oppose any foe to assure the survival and the success of liberty.　4

This much we pledge—and more.　5

To those old allies whose cultural and spiritual origins we share, we pledge the loyalty of faithful friends. United, there is little we cannot do in a host of co-operative ventures. Divided, there is little we can do, for we dare not meet a powerful challenge at odds and split asunder.　6

To those new states whom we welcome to the ranks of the free, we pledge our word that one form of colonial control shall not have passed away merely to be replaced by a far more iron tyranny. We shall not always expect to find them supporting our view. But we shall always hope to find them strongly supporting their own freedom, and to remember that, in the past, those who foolishly sought power by riding the back of the tiger ended up inside.　7

To those peoples in the huts and villages of half the globe struggling to break the bonds of mass misery, we pledge our best efforts to help them help themselves, for whatever period is required, not because the Communists may be doing it, not because we seek their votes, but because it is right. If a free society cannot help the many who are poor, it cannot save the few who are rich.　8

To our sister republics south of our border, we offer a special pledge: to convert our good words into good deeds, in a new alliance for progress, to assist free men and free governments in casting off the chains of poverty. But this peaceful revolution of hope cannot become the prey of hostile powers. Let all our neighbors know that we shall join with them to oppose aggression or subversion anywhere in the Americas. And let every other power know that this hemisphere intends to remain the master of its own house.   9

To that world assembly of sovereign states, the United Nations, our last best hope in an age where the instruments of war have far outpaced the instruments of peace, we renew our pledge of support: to prevent it from becoming merely a forum for invective, to strengthen its shield of the new and the weak, and to enlarge the area in which its writ may run. 10

Finally, to those nations who would make themselves our adversary, we offer not a pledge but a request: that both sides begin anew the quest for peace, before the dark powers of destruction unleashed by science engulf all humanity in planned or accidental self-destruction.   11

We dare not tempt them with weakness. For only when our arms are sufficient beyond doubt can we be certain beyond doubt that they will never be employed.   12

But neither can two great and powerful groups of nations take comfort from our present course—both sides overburdened by the cost of modern weapons, both rightly alarmed by the steady spread of the deadly atom, yet both racing to alter that uncertain balance of terror that stays the hand of mankind's final war.   13

So let us begin anew, remembering on both sides that civility is not a sign of weakness, and sincerity is always subject to proof. Let us never negotiate out of fear, but let us never fear to negotiate.   14

Let both sides explore what problems unite us instead of belaboring those problems which divide us.   15

Let both sides, for the first time, formulate serious and precise proposals for the inspection and control of arms, and bring the absolute power to destroy other nations under the absolute control of all nations. 16

Let both sides seek to invoke the wonders of science instead of its terrors. Together let us explore the stars, conquer the deserts, eradicate disease, tap the ocean depths and encourage the arts and commerce.   17

Let both sides unite to heed in all corners of the earth the command of Isaiah to "undo the heavy burdens . . . [and] let the oppressed go free."   18

And if a beachhead of co-operation may push back the jungle of suspicion, let both sides join in creating a new endeavor, not a new balance of power, but a new world of law, where the strong are just and the weak secure and the peace preserved.   19

All this will not be finished in the first one hundred days. Nor will it be finished in the first one thousand days, nor in the life of this Administration, nor even perhaps in our lifetime on this planet. But let us begin. 20

In your hands, my fellow citizens, more than mine, will rest the final success or failure of our course. Since this country was founded, each generation of Americans has been summoned to give testimony to its national loyalty. The graves of young Americans who answered the call to service surround the globe. 21

Now the trumpet summons us again—not as a call to bear arms, though arms we need; not as a call to battle, though embattled we are; but a call to bear the burden of a long twilight struggle, year in and year out, "rejoicing in hope, patient in tribulation," a struggle against the common enemies of man: tyranny, poverty, disease and war itself. 22

Can we forge against these enemies a grand and global alliance, North and South, East and West, that can assure a more fruitful life for all mankind? Will you join in that historic effort? 23

In the long history of the world, only a few generations have been granted the role of defending freedom in its hour of maximum danger. I do not shrink from this responsibility; I welcome it. I do not believe that any of us would exchange places with any other people or any other generation. The energy, the faith, the devotion which we bring to this endeavor will light our country and all who serve it, and the glow from that fire can truly light the world. 24

And so, my fellow Americans, ask not what your country can do for you; ask what you can do for your country. 25

My fellow citizens of the world, ask not what America will do for you, but what together we can do for the freedom of man. 26

Finally, whether you are citizens of America or citizens of the world, ask of us here the same high standards of strength and sacrifice which we ask of you. With a good conscience our only sure reward, with history the final judge of our deeds, let us go forth to lead the land we love, asking His blessing and His help, but knowing that here on earth God's work must truly be our own. 27

Suggestions for Writing

Listed below are a number of topics which lend themselves to development by the method of classification and division. Be sure to make the principle used in classifying or dividing clear in the essay you write.

1 Types of students I like (or dislike)
2 Types of men (women) to avoid for a date

3 The types of music which appeal to me
4 Painting as a fine art
5 Automobile buyers
6 Weekend guests
7 Snobs I have known
8 The voters in my community
9 "Sportsmen (golfers, baseball fans) are in a class by themselves"
10 The contributions of science to our happiness
11 Schools of painting
12 Bourgeois elements in American life

WHY, WHENCE, WHAT ENDS AND RESULTS: CAUSE AND EFFECT

That cause and effect is a frequently used and important method of analysis can be demonstrated if we think of the countless problems in the course of our education that have been phrased in terms of cause and effect. What were the causes of Lincoln's election in 1861? What are the effects of poor housing on adolescents? What caused Italy's entrance into World War II? What were the effects of Pearl Harbor on the American people? It should be noted at once that the strictly logical implications of cause and effect can be extremely complex. Trying to discover the complete cause in the past of an existing situation may become so involved as to be unmanageable. And trying to predict the final effects in the future of any given cause seems almost hopeless, since a cause can send out effects with the consequences as far-reaching as those of a transmitter sending out sound waves. Writers do, however, face up to the challenge. They adapt the principles of causal analysis to the rhetorical purposes it can be made to serve, using them freely rather than with scientific precision. The essays in this section demonstrate that cause and effect as a method of analysis can be understood from a rhetorical point of view and can be fruitfully used by a writer.

"Cause" can be defined most simply as "that by which an effect is produced." Some causes are *immediate*: that is, they can be discovered in time, close to the effect produced. Some causes are *remote*. For example, we read in the newspaper about a teen-ager dead as a result of an automobile crash: the crash is an immediate cause of his death. But if he had been in a hurry to get someplace, someone will surely say at his funeral, "If he hadn't been in such a hurry, he'd be alive today"—his haste is suggested as a cause for his death, and, if it is, it is still an immediate cause, but a less immediate one. If he was a poor driver, the neighbors will attribute his death to this fact; this cause is relatively still less immediate. An indignant reformer may, as a result of this death, blame the state for giving a driver's license to anyone under twenty-one; the cause now is becoming more remote. It often happens that complicated and involved effects have very important remote causes which cannot be ignored. In "The Federalist, No. X" (page 276) James Madison says that the "latent" (remote) cause of faction is in the very nature of man himself. This is a remote cause that cannot be ignored, for self-love dominates man's fallible reason and causes faction. This latent cause, he continues, is brought into action in the circumstances of civil society by more immediate causes, such as a zeal for different opinions concerning religion and government or an attachment to different leaders. "But," he emphasizes, "the most common and durable source of factions has been the various and unequal distribution of property." Madison, therefore, deals with both remote and immediate causes. The tendency of most writers is to deal with the immediate causes only. Often it is almost impossible to ferret out in the vast forest of the past the proper remote cause as carefully as Madison has been able to do it.

"Causes of the Restless Spirit of the Americans" (page 283), by Alexis de Tocqueville, is another example of the use of causal analysis. What are the causes, he asks, of the restless spirit of the Americans in the midst of their abundance? He describes Americans as brooding—despite their prosperity—over advantages which they do not possess. His causal analysis in an attempt to answer the central question is clearly set forth. The Americans' taste for physical gratification leads to an inordinate concern for their worldly welfare and a pathetic consciousness of the passage of time. The flexibility and mobility of American society, caused by the lack of laws and customs which would keep people confined to a certain status, makes no social condition permanent. And, finally, he asserts that where equality of conditions leads every citizen to have lofty hopes and desires, it is apparent that all citizens will be less able to realize them. The exact use of causal analysis in this essay makes it an excellent model for study.

Although it happens that one essay will emphasize cause and another effect, cause and effect must be regarded as a single method. One is impossible without the other: de Tocqueville, for example, describes the effects as well as the causes of restlessness amidst abundance; Madison describes both the causes and effect of faction. In "The Revolt of the Diminished Man (page 287), Archibald MacLeish describes some of the effects of student unrest; then he considers what some people regard as the causes of the unrest—for example, urban disorder, racial prejudice, the war in Vietnam—and admits that these are immediate causes, but finally argues that these immediate causes are really the effects of a more remote cause. In general, trying to separate cause and effect completely would be like trying to separate the two sides of a coin— even if this could be done, the result would have little value.

Since even rhetorical causal analysis can be quite complex, it is important to discuss certain fallacies to be avoided. When using cause and effect as a method of analysis, the writer must be careful to distinguish between a true cause and the conditions necessary for the successful operation of the cause. In order to crash at all, the teen-ager of our first example had to be in an automobile. The automobile in order to run had to have gasoline, oil, and the requisite number of parts. All of these, and many others, make up the *condition* for the crash to take place. The condition is a combination of the factors in a situation which will allow the effect of the cause to appear; it is not a cause. We cannot say that the automobile or the gasoline or the oil caused the crash.

Because we often think of cause and effect within a time sequence, there is one more fallacy that should be discussed. Not everything that precedes an effect is for that reason its cause. Hence, in the development of causal analysis, the connection between the given effect and the cause for it should be clearly shown. Blurred and confused thinking results from the assumption that if Y follows X, then X is the cause of Y (*post hoc, ergo propter hoc*). Suppose the teen-ager of our example had stopped for a Coke at a drive-in before crashing; it would be unwise to conclude that stopping at a drive-in for a Coke causes automobile crashes.

Cause and effect is supported by and used with the other methods of expository analysis and the other forms of discourse. In Madison's essay it is used along with contrast when Madison deals with a republic and a pure democracy. Although George Carter's essay "The American Civilization Puzzle" (page 262) is basically cause and effect, Carter uses a long process analysis in order to explain *how* civilization arose in America. MacLeish, in his essay, compares and contrasts the attitudes of his own college generation toward education with the attitude of the present college generation before he begins to clarify what he considers the remote cause of student unrest. No matter how cause and effect is used rhetorically, as dominant or auxiliary, it will be an effective method of analysis only if it is used as systematically and carefully as the writer's specific purpose permits.

THE AMERICAN CIVILIZATION PUZZLE

GEORGE F. CARTER

Why, people ask, do professors like me study the things we do? Of course, they tell me, Indians are interesting—but are they important? Even if we do manage to find out when and how they developed their civilizations, is the knowledge really worth our working so hard to acquire it?   1

To such questions I give an emphatic Yes.   2

We need to know a good deal about the origin of civilization in general. We must know *how* civilization arose. And to answer the "how" we must know when and where. Did civilization arise just once, or several times? What part, if any, did climate and soil and landform and race play in its growth or growths? To give it a modern application: if we get careless with our super-bombs and wipe out civilization, what is the likelihood of a new civilization springing up? How soon? What kind? And where?   3

Behind these questions lies a further set of questions. Is man largely controlled or directed or influenced by his physical environment, or is he relatively independent of it? And another: Is man predominantly inventive or retentive? There have been whole schools of thought, and still are, that take one side or another on these questions. And we still know little, with any certainty, about how civilization arose, spread, and grows.*   4

The growth of the American Indian civilizations has come to be of crucial importance to the whole problem. For some, it is an example of the inventiveness of man. For others it is an example of the overwhelming force of the physical environment in the molding of man. For still others, it is an example of how uninventive man really is, of how extremely retentive he is, and of the complete dominance of the *spread* of ideas—or "diffusion"—over the *invention* of ideas.   5

Great battles—really fierce battles—have raged over such things. The current battleground, the current testing-ground, is America.   6

And, in these battles, I find myself in the thick of things.   7

In the area from southern Mexico to northern Chile, civilization apparently began rather suddenly, possibly about 1000 B.C. and probably not earlier than 2000 or 3000 B.C.   8

The peopling of America had been accomplished very much earlier, most probably by small bands of rather primitive people who wandered across from northeastern Asia into Alaska and then wandered slowly southward into the open, unpopulated continents that spread before them. They did not "discover" America. They simply drifted in. They did not "migrate" through the Americas. They simply multiplied and each generation moved a few miles. In such a manner it would take only a few thousand years for

* Paragraph 4: What is the significance of the question asked in sentence 3 in this paragraph?

such people to reach all parts of North and South America. We know they had plenty of time: by the most advanced methods of measuring past time, we now know that man was here more than thirty-eight thousand years ago. If my current research is right, he was here far earlier than that.   9

Our present problem, however, is not with this original peopling, but with what happened once these people had settled down. They entered with simple cultures, lacking domestic animals except the dog, lacking the bow and arrow, lacking any knowledge of pottery-making. When we Europeans discovered them many thousands of years later, the Indian peoples in Middle America were practicing agriculture, making pottery, raising some domesticated animals, practicing metallurgy, using practically all the known techniques of weaving, living in organized city states and even empires, and having great capitals that would rival Rome or Athens or Thebes or Babylon.*   10

Just how did all of this come about? Did they do all of it by themselves, with no help? Or did ideas dribble across the great watery moats of the seas? Or, perhaps, did whole floods of ideas reach them from overseas?   11

On the answers, scholars violently disagree. This is the Diffusion controversy, and for more than one hundred years it has rustled the ivy on academic halls. Some professors, "Diffusionists," think the evidence indicates that man crossed the oceans carrying ideas with him. Others, "Independent Inventionists," fiercely defend the doctrine that nothing of the sort ever happened. They believe that, lacking strong evidence that such transmission of knowledge took place, it is more likely that groups of men all over the world, faced with similar problems, reached similar solutions— even though these groups never had contact with one another.†   12

Gradually, the Independent Inventionists have had to retreat. Gradually, diffusion has been demonstrated over wider and wider areas, through greater and greater time depths, and for more and more things. In the Old World, agriculture, metallurgy, architecture, and the alphabets tended to arise in one center or another and spread to the others. Each area took the basic ideas and wove them into its own particular way of life, giving them a special local flavor. But fundamentally, most of the basic ideas used in this great area of civilization's early growth had their origins in one center or the other. It has been clear for some time now that the growth of civilization in the Old World was a closely interrelated phenomenon.   13

The New World was the Independent Inventionist's last great stronghold. Here, he could point out, the American Indians developed *in isolation* from the culture growths of the Old World. And in this isolation they had developed nearly everything that the Old World had. They had invented agriculture, but none of the plants were like the domestic plants of the

* Paragraph 10: Cite examples of balanced or parallel phrasing in this paragraph.
† Paragraph 12: Does this paragraph suggest the slant that the rest of the essay will take on the questions raised?

Old World. They had domesticated a few animals: ducks, turkeys, camels (llamas), guinea pigs. And while these might seem uncomfortably close to ducks, chickens, camels, and rabbits of the Old World, the Indians never domesticated any cowlike animal such as the buffalo. They never used any animal for draft purposes, never milked an animal, never made animal domestication an important part of their lives. So, said the Independent Inventionist (with obvious relief), the seeming similarities are not really significant, after all.   14

The Old World—New World similarities kept piling up, however. In Middle America (a convenient term to designate the area from southern Mexico to northern Chile) the Indian people built pyramids somewhat as some of the people in the Old World did. But the pyramids were built primarily as commanding locations for temples, rather than for the burial of kings as in Egypt. The Independent Inventionists tended to overlook the presence of just such pyramids in Southeast Asia, with temples on *their* truncated tops. Some of the Diffusionists were equally guilty, and played right into the Independent Inventionists' hands, by insisting that nearly all ideas came from Egypt, where of course the pyramids were royal tombs.   15

The list of men who have entered the debate over the separateness of the Americas from Asia and Eurafrica, and the mountains of evidence and nonsense that have been presented, could be fitted into a doctoral dissertation only with difficulty. Almost from the beginning there were rumblings of Asiatic contacts with America. The Spaniards learned from the Incas of Peru that they had legends of people coming from across the Pacific to trade. And the Incas insisted that they had sent out a great fleet of balsa-log rafts that were gone for two years and finally returned with stories of lands across the sea. This strange tale was believed by the Spaniards, and there followed a series of intrigues over who should head the expedition that would discover another source of wealth like Mexico or Peru. In the political maneuvering, the wrong man ended up in the job. He followed the wrong directions, and the Spaniards found themselves in the impoverished, Negro-populated islands of the southwest Pacific. The Incas' tale was discredited.   16

The sequel has been written in this decade of the twentieth century. The intrepid Thor Heyerdahl has demonstrated that the Incas could have done just what they said they did; that balsa rafts *can* be sailed across the Pacific. And Heyerdahl has since learned enough about such rafts that, should he wish to, he could now sail on to Asia and then turn around and sail back. By studies in the Galapagos Islands he has shown that the Incas used these islands, six hundred miles offshore, as a base for their fishing fleet—no mean bit of navigation for people using rafts. But it was long denied that the Indians possessed such ability.   17

The evidence was difficult to throttle. It was pointed out that the game of parchesi, which we got from India, was practically the national pastime in Mexico when the Spanish reached there. There was no mistaking the game. All the rules, and the shape of the board on which it was played, were as we know the game today. In addition, it had special meanings that were duplicated in India.   18

In America, the Indians blew on pipes of Pan. The pipes blew the identical notes, in the same scale, on both sides of the Pacific. As if this were not enough, in Peru they were played in pairs. Two people stood facing each other, connected by a string that led from one set of pipes to the other. One set of pipes was called Mama and the other Father. The same thing was done in Southeast Asia.   19

Surely this is stretching coincidence extremely far. Is it really reasonable that the same scale, the same notes, and the identical customs would all be reinvented? There is nothing in the climate or in the soil or in man himself that compels such detailed parallels.   20

Mathematical and recording systems showed similar strange parallels. In Peru, records of taxes, populations, and histories were kept by tying knots in strings. The system for numbers was a decimal one. A knot tied in one string stood for one, in the next string for ten, in the next for one hundred, and so on.   21

This is a remarkable invention. It involves the idea that the value of a number is established by its position, and this includes the idea of a decimal place and a zero. It leads directly into negative numbers. All of these concepts we of the Western World received from India.   22

But when one begins tracing the distribution of such systems as the Peruvian knots in strings, one finds them in the islands of the Pacific and, anciently, in China, Tibet, and India. The Chinese say that they recorded their history by tying knots in strings, before writing was invented.   23

Thus we have one of the most difficult of mathematical ideas, associated with a particular way of recording it, with a continuous distribution from the probable source, India, to the exact part of America that has a whole host of other parallels to the Southeast Asian center.   24

The material is formidable in extent. A partial list of further parallels appears below.

COINCIDENCE?

Here is a sampling of ideas, inventions, and legends suggesting varied contacts between America and the Old World:

Place Numeral Systems, India to China; Peru and Mexico.
Knot-in-String Records, Peru, Polynesia, China (before script).
The Zodiac, Asia and Mexico.

Mathematical
The Zero, Used in India, Peru, and Mexico.

Technological
The Loom, In Peru, with all its Old-World parts.

Cloth, In Peru, all known Old-World weaves.

The Wheel, On toys, only in America.

Alcoholic Beverages, Close parallels in Polynesia and Peru.

Metals, Elaborate smelting, casting, and alloying techniques duplicated in Old World and Middle America.

Seamanship, Centerboards used for sailing in Peru and China.

Obsidian Mirrors, Polynesia and Peru.

Racial

Vivid Portraits in stone, clay, and paint, showing Indian, Mongolian, and bearded European types.

Legends giving emphatic, clear-cut descriptions of blond, bearded, learned visitors.

Chinese Palm Prints among the Maya.

Artistic

Jade emphasized in Mexico, Peru, and China.

Trefoil Arch, Maya and India.

Sacred Tree Design, Maya and India.

Tiger Thrones, Maya and Southeast Asia.

Lotus Staff, lotus stone, lotus panels: detailed similarities between Maya and India.

Serpent Columns, balustrades: Mexico and Southeast Asia.

The Diving God, Mexico and Bali.

Copper Bells, Made by same technique and with same designs in Mexico and Indochina.

Featherwork Cloaks, Peru and Polynesia.

Legendary

Peruvian Tales of an expedition across the Pacific.

Chinese Document, possibly describing a Buddhist missionary effort in America about 500 A.D.

Polynesian Legends of voyages to and from America.

Explicit Stories of tall, bearded men who came and taught the Indians.

Serpent Deities in Asia and Middle America.

Corn Mother Myth (and others) common to Southeast Asia and Middle America.

Agricultural

Sweet Potato, Surely carried across seas, probably from America.

Coconut, Most probably carried to America.

Bottle Gourd, Probably carried to America.

Cotton, Most probably carried to America.

Pineapple, Probably carried from America.

Terracing of mountainsides.

Specialized Irrigation techniques.

A Long List of possible (unconfirmed) plant transfers.

Musical

Panpipe, Identical scale, notes, and ceremonial use in Middle America and Southeast Asia.

Nose Flute.

Gourd Whistle.

Conch-shell Trumpet with similar names in both America and Polynesia. (One Polynesian shell trumpet found in Peru.)

Hollowed Log with slit: Used both for music and for signaling in Africa, Middle America, and Polynesia.

One would think from all this that it would quickly be agreed that ideas were indeed carried in some quantity directly from Asia to America. But such has not been the case. Instead, it has been claimed that such transoceanic voyages were impossible, especially for such landlubbers as Chinese or Hindus. The Polynesians were discounted as people with only wooden dugouts totally incapable of such voyages. The Incas were pictured as comical fellows possessed of the world's clumsiest shipping—rafts that could not stay afloat more than a week or so before they had to be pulled out and dried in order to maintain their buoyancy.   25

The Inca raft, built of great logs of balsa, is now revealed as an excellent ocean-going vessel, capable of voyaging across the Pacific and back, of sailing before the wind or, by ingenious use of centerboards, of sailing into the wind, and of tacking and performing all the maneuvers of the square-rigged vessels of the days of sail. The Polynesian dugouts were often one hundred feet long, more than twice the length of Columbus's smallest ship and fully capable of making great sea voyages. The Hindus and the Chinese had large ocean-going ships when written history began in that area, and we have no evidence of how long they had them before that.   26

Still, we could *prove* nothing one way or the other. I could argue that the pipes of Pan and parchesi and the system of recording things decimally by tying knots in strings are most unlikely to be independently reinvented. But the opposition could well reply that this was only my opinion. In *their* opinion there was nothing unusual about such independent invention on two sides of the vast ocean. And so there it would rest—unless there were other ways to determine which opinion was more likely right. Fortunately, there is other evidence—and evidence of such nature that opinion plays no part in it.   27

Man invents pottery, mathematics, pyramids, and metallurgy. And, in a very real sense, man invents agriculture.   28

But he does not invent plants.*   29

Plants are natural creations. Man may modify them, and he most certainly did so in developing wild plants into the useful ones of today. But plants have definite homelands. We know for certain that oranges came from Southeast Asia, that wheat came from the Near East, and that olives came from the Mediterranean. We also know that all pumpkins and squashes, tomatoes, potatoes, and chocolate, came from America. No one, not even the Independent Inventionists, has ever claimed that men independently created identical or even similar plants in different parts of the world. Here, then, were markers that offered an opportunity to test the separateness of the two worlds.   30

This knowledge could not be used immediately. We did not know

* Paragraphs 28 and 29: What particular effect do these short paragraphs achieve?

until rather recently just where our domestic plants came from. One of the pioneers in gathering that information was Alphonse De Candolle, who wrote his great work in 1884. At that time there was still uncertainty about such ultra-American crops as squashes and pumpkins, and their American origin was finally established as late as 1931.   31

About the turn of the century, O. F. Cook became interested in the coconut. He found that practically all the palms of the coconut family were American. He thought it strange indeed that only the domesticated member of this family should be non-American and concluded that it would be more natural for the domestic coconut to come *from* America.   32

Cook then went on to investigate a number of other plants. He found that there was considerable evidence that coconuts were not the only foreigners on the pre-Columbian American shores. Further, he found that a few American plants had strayed overseas, also. Of these, two seemed to have carried their names with them. One was the sweet potato; the other was the hibiscus. The names were the same both in parts of Middle America and in Polynesia, the island world of the mid-Pacific. On this and other evidence, Cook built the idea that agriculture had originated in America and spread across the Pacific Ocean to Southeast Asia. He was an early Diffusionist, and a pretty extreme one at that.   33

His ideas were attacked very sharply. Should they stand, whole schools of thought about the independent growth of civilizations, the psychic unity of mankind, the nature of the growth of culture, the nature of man, the influence of the physical environment on man, and many other beloved theories would have to be discarded. This was a grave threat to academic peace of mind. It was all the more serious because it was backed by an expert in a science.   34

The way out of this type of difficulty is to get another expert in the same science to counteract the first. (This is a well-known maneuver in more professions than the academic one, by the way.) The Independent Inventionists soon found a champion in the late E. D. Merrill, of Harvard. Merrill assured them that Cook was a very poor expert, indeed. The evidence of pre-Columbian coconuts was not valid. Besides, coconuts could float, so that even if they had been in America in pre-Columbian times it would not mean that men had carried them across the Pacific. The seeds of some hibiscus varieties can also float and stay alive. And as for the sweet potato—well, that was just a case of poor historical research. Merrill was a devastating critic, and he demonstrated to the utter satisfaction of the Independent Inventionists, and to the considerable discomfiture of the Diffusionists, that Cook could be ignored. The botanical evidence was destined to be let alone for a few decades.   35

Meanwhile another champion of diffusion, a most interesting man, entered the battle. G. Elliot Smith was a physician and surgeon. He worked for many years in Egypt and, among other things, became interested in the Egyptian mummies. This is a fascinating subject, and particularly intriguing to a surgeon. In the preparation of the body for embalming, certain parts had to be removed. This was a professional problem, and Dr. Smith took a keen professional interest in the problem of the removal of the viscera and the brain, the closing of the openings so created, the problem of retaining the fingernails during the pickling process. It was enough to make an inquiring doctor wish that he could have been right there to discuss stitches and incisions, and to inquire into just why some of the operations were performed in such deucedly awkward and stylized ways. Dr. Smith was interested enough to read all that he could get his hands on concerning the funerary arts, processes, and rituals of the Egyptians.   36

Dr. Smith was also a great traveler. He visited the Trobriand Islanders, in the island world north of Australia. Here, to his astonishment, he found people practicing practically the identical embalming techniques: the incisions in the same awkward places, the same sort of stitches, and even some of the same rituals. His interest was aroused, and he began to trace other spreads of ideas from Egypt. Soon he was tracing everything imaginable to Egypt. Eventually, he was tracing things even farther, for he had begun to look at Inca mummies. Here again he found the same improbable surgical procedures. (I hesitate to discuss the details of the preparation of a body for mummification, for it is a grisly subject to those not used to dealing rather offhandedly with cadavers. The resemblances are specific and detailed, however, and entail such singular solutions of the problem as to leave little doubt of their singular origin, if I may be allowed an apt pun.)*   37

G. Elliot Smith marshaled vast amounts of evidence. However, he destroyed his case by insisting that *everything* came from Egypt. (It seems only fair to record that his critics have been equally extreme in discarding his evidence because of flaws in his presentation of it. This technique is known in best scientific parlance as throwing the baby out with the bathwater. It is probably the major contributor to the high infant mortality in the world of ideas, especially of those ideas that run counter to the notions held by powerful and vocal critics.)   38

Plant evidence was in disrepute due to the efforts of E. D. Merrill, who had overly brilliantly picked the flaws in Cook's arguments. Cook had opened the door to attack on himself by some uncritical work, and by his enthusiasm's leading him to think that the origin of agriculture, *the* origin of agriculture, was in America. Smith had made the same mistakes. He became too enthused with his Egyptian origins. The battle went to the critics. The Independent Inventionists ruled in peace. All the textbooks and

* Paragraph 37: What is the pun in the last sentence?

all the lectures assured the rising generation that there had been no contact between America and Asia. The Pacific was a vast and impregnable moat.   39

But this was an uneasy peace. For facts are a bit like the fires of a volcano. They may lie dormant, but actually they are smoldering away, awaiting only the touch of an investigator's hand to spring into life, capable of destroying the most elaborate of philosophical structures.*   40

In the world of knowledge there is utterly no way of knowing where a given piece of research will lead. The work that was to reopen the Diffusionist controversy began with an attempt by a group of botanists to untangle the relationships of the cottons of the world. Hutchinson, Silow, and Stevens teamed up on this job, using the modern techniques of genetics. They soon found that they could divide the cottons of the world into three groups: the wild and domestic cottons of the Old World, the wild cottons of the New World, and the domestic cottons of the New World. The New World domestic cottons particularly interested them. When they studied cells under high-powered microscopes they found that they contained twice as many hereditary units (chromosomes) as did the other cottons. Further, they could tell that there were two sets of chromosomes there, one the Old World type and the other the New World type. The most probable explanation they could find was that man had brought a domestic cotton from the Old World into the New, and that the two cottons had crossed, combined the full sets of chromosomes from both plants, and created this new plant.   41

They then did a very interesting thing. They examined the New World domestic cotton and carefully catalogued all its characteristics. Next they searched the cottons of the world to see just what two cottons, if combined, would give them these characteristics. They found the answer in an Asiatic domestic cotton and in a Peruvian wild cotton. They then succeeded in crossing these two plants and producing a near-duplicate of the American domesticated cotton.   42

We cannot get much nearer to proof than this. Thus the whole question of voyages to America was again wide open. Cotton seeds are not particularly tough. Plant men do not believe that they can float around the ocean and remain alive. To have got to America they must have been carried by someone. (Just how cotton got to America *and* the Old World in the first place is quite another problem of an utterly different time, and I will not try to deal with it here.)   43

It was at this point that I entered the controversy. Having been "properly" educated in the field of anthropology, I knew that once the

---

* Paragraphs 38 through 40: Do you think that the metaphors used in these paragraphs are effective?

American Indians entered America, they had been sealed off and had developed entirely on their own. They were of stupendous interest as the living examples of how inevitable the growth and development of cultures and civilization really were. They were the final answer to the Diffusionist. "Why just look, even the minute details are alike! Weaving, casting of metals, the shape of helmets, feathered robes for royalty. Name it and you can have it. There was almost nothing in the Old World that had not been independently reinvented in the New World. This certainly proves independent invention, doesn't it?"* 44

Ah, yes. But *did* it prove it? Or did it prove just the opposite? Those mischievous geneticists were threatening to lift the lid of Pandora's box. If someone had brought cotton to the New World, how could we be sure that other things, such as zeros, Panpipes, metallurgy, and parchesi hadn't been brought in, also? Obviously this required looking into. 45

Since I had just finished a doctoral thesis in which I had used plants as tracers for determining the spread of peoples and ideas within America, it was quite natural for me to turn to the plant evidence to see just what there was to this controversy. To begin with, I knew the classical position. There were, in pre-Columbian times, no domestic plants from the Old World in the Americas, and conversely there were no American plants in the Old World. To be specific, the Indians had no wheat or rice, and the peoples of the Old World had no corn, American beans, or squash. 46

Work began with a review of the cotton situation. Stevens sent me a manuscript discussing the cultural implications of what he and his colleagues had done. It was a disturbing document for a man thoroughly indoctrinated with the idea of the separateness of the Old and New Worlds. I took it to a Johns Hopkins geneticist to have it read from a geneticist's point of view. (In retrospect I must secretly have been hoping that there was a gross error in the work. Otherwise there was an awful lot of reading and thinking ahead of me.) The reply was that the genetics was sound, the conclusions from the data reasonable, and the probability quite good that Hutchinson, Silow, and Stevens had drawn the right conclusion. This left me no alternative but to dive into the problem and see what more evidence there was. The results were shocking. 47

Cotton was not the only plant involved. The sweet potato had been investigated by a professor hostile to the idea of voyages to and from America. But he had shown that the sweet potato had been in the Pacific area before any possible European spread. Further, there was positive proof in the form of a letter written by one of Cortes's lieutenants that coconuts were in America when Cortes landed there. Still further, tests on

---

* Paragraph 44: In the second sentence, why does Carter put the word "properly" in quotation marks?

the ability of coconuts to survive a long period of drifting in the ocean currents had raised considerable doubts that the coconut could get across the Pacific in that way. And when I applied my knowledge of ocean currents and wind directions, it seemed to me that these chances vanished. Further, there were other plants. The bottle gourd was present in America in the earliest levels, and very ancient in the Old World. (I was later to prove by experiments in the Chesapeake Bay that these gourds *could* have floated to America.) But there were American weeds in the islands of the Pacific that certainly could not have blown or drifted there. There *were* American plants that had got out of America and there *were* Asiatic plants that had got into America. Someone *had* crossed the Pacific both ways. Pandora's box was open. The moat was crossed. The Independent Inventionists' vessel had sprung a leak.   48

This was not a leak that could be readily repaired by referring to the similarity of men's minds and claiming that the zero concept, wheels, pyramids, and games of chance are so natural to man that they prove nothing when they reappear in similar forms in distant parts of the world. Man does not invent plants. To quote O. F. Cook, "The same plant does not originate twice, and varieties dependent everywhere for their very existence on human care must also have been distributed by human agency." And again: "For the present purposes it suffices to remember that the actual introduction of plants by human agency discounts in advance all objections on the ground of distances and difficulties of communication, and justifies the fullest use of biological or other data in tracing the origin and dissemination of agricultural civilization in the tropics of both hemispheres." The plant evidence was an iceberg that in one rending crash ripped the bottom out of the isolation of pre-Columbian America.   49

The sequels to the plant story are of interest. The list of plants possibly carried is quite extensive, and almost nothing is now safe from question. It is suspected that Indian corn was known in Africa and in Southeast Asia before Columbus. (The reason that the Europeans first called Indian corn "Turkish wheat" is again being examined, and the old answers no longer satisfy.) Questions are being asked about the time of appearance of the American peanut in Asia, and of the Old World bananas in the Americas. The chicken from Southeast Asia is strongly suspected of being in America in pre-Columbian times, and no one claims that it could either fly or swim the Pacific.   50

The plant evidence is unshakable, and it is now admitted, at least in part, by its bitterest foes. They tend to retreat firing such Parthian shots as "unimportant in number," "probably a few unimportant accidental landings," "not important to the story of the growth and development of the American Indian civilizations." But I like the simile of Pandora's box. The lid has been lifted and all sorts of ideas have escaped to buzz about our heads.   51

Quite independently a further line of attack has been reopened. This is the investigation of art resemblances on the two sides of the Pacific. This work has been done by Professor Robert Heine-Geldern of Austria and Dr. Gordon Ekholm of the American Museum of Natural History in New York.   52

Comparison of the art and architecture of Southeast Asia with that of some parts of the Americas led to the discovery of some remarkable parallels. Not only were there truncated pyramids in Cambodia with temples on top of them, just as there were in Yucatan and in Peru, but they were sometimes almost identical down to small architectural details. The dragons on Chou-dynasty bronze vases were duplicated in minute detail in Mayan Indian art. And these details were multiplied. Criticism immediately centered on the fact that the similarities were picked more or less at random over a considerable range of time and space. This has since been met with a vengeance. Heine-Geldern's latest work names the individual Asiatic city states and points out their art influence in specific times and places in the Americas.   53

Such thoughts are met with some skepticism. If the people of Southeast Asia actually did such things, why do we have no records of all this? How could such a discovery ever be lost? My reply is to point out that the Norse discovered America about 1000 A.D. and maintained colonies in Greenland until about 1400 A.D. This is in the full light of modern European history. Yet most people are surprised to hear of this, and the effective discovery of America was left to Columbus. Further there is at least one Chinese document that probably refers to a Chinese voyage to America and return.*   54

There are all sorts of strange bits of other evidence. The palm prints of the Maya are specifically like those of the Chinese. The Polynesian legends tell of reaching America, and the American Indian told the Spaniards that people from the Pacific came to them for trading purposes. Then there are the plants, the mathematics, the games, the arts and architecture, and all the other clues.   55

In capsule form, what we have learned, or are in the process of learning, is this: all the Old World civilizations were interconnected and drew on each other for ideas and inspiration. We do not know just where and how this civilization began. It seems to have started in that area we call the Near East. It is not too difficult to make a case for the single origin

---

* Paragraph 54: How does Carter's "reply" answer the question "How could such a discovery ever be lost?"

of civilization there. The New World civilizations seem to be to some
as-yet-unknown degree dependent on the Old World growth of civilization.* 56

Peering into the future, guessing at things to come, I would estimate
that the American Indians had made some very modest advances toward
agriculture and the beginnings of settled village life. The peoples of the
Old World, sometime after 3000 B.C. and before 500 B.C., discovered the
New World. They maintained contact over a long period of time. During
this time they colonized parts of America, introduced arts, crafts, science,
and governmental forms, and carried some domestic plants back and
forth. It was this impact that set off the civilizations of Middle America. 57

We cannot say that civilization would never have been achieved by
the American Indians had they been left alone. Neither do we know that
they ever would have. The natives of Australia, Africa, America north of
Mexico, and south and east of Peru and Bolivia certainly never did.   58

The interesting by-product of all this is that we are faced with the
possibility that civilization has but one beginning. One could seriously argue
for this view. We do not know that any particular people or any particular
geography gave rise to it. Nor would we know how to start the process
over again should the present civilization be extinguished. It appears to
me from such studies as these that the civilization that we carry today is a
unique growth.†   59

If this is true, then man is certainly to be viewed as basically non-
inventive. He proves, rather, to be a splendid copyist, infinitely more able
to borrow an idea than to invent a new one. To answer one of our earlier
questions: man is retentive and not particularly inventive. Civilization,
once the germ is implanted, can flourish in desert or jungle, on mountain
plateau or lowland plain. It is not the physical environment that is all-
important; it is the cultural environment.   60

These are important things to know, and it is the pursuit of this
type of knowledge that underlies the professional passion for study of such
seemingly exotic things as the long-dead civilizations of the American
Indians.   61

* Paragraph 56: What causes and effects that have been set forth by Carter up to this
point in his essay might support the statement that he makes in the fourth sentence of
this paragraph?

† Paragraph 59: In the last sentence of this paragraph, what does "unique" growth mean?

The Whole Selection

1 Where does Carter's introduction end? Is the extent of his introduction
  justified?
2 Where in the beginning of his essay does Carter specify that he is

writing for the general literate public rather than for fellow professional anthropologists? What elements in the substance of the essay and what aspects of the form of the essay illustrate the direction of the essay to a nonprofessional audience?

3 In which of the paragraphs in the first part of the essay does Carter state the central purpose of the essay?

4 Is Carter trying to discover causes or effects? In the essay as a whole, do you think that the author has properly related the causes to the effects?

5 What causal relationships do you see between the conclusions that Carter presents to us and the questions that he raises in paragraph 3?

6 By the end of the essay, what answers has Carter given to the questions that he raises in paragraph 4?

7 Although this essay exemplifies the use of cause and effect, it contains as well the exposition of a process. What is the process that is explained in this essay?

Word Study *parlance, dormant, geneticist*

THE FEDERALIST, NO. X

JAMES MADISON

To the People of the State of New York

Among the numerous advantages promised by a well-constructed Union, none deserves to be more accurately developed than its tendency to break and control the violence of faction. The friend of popular governments never finds himself so much alarmed for their character and fate as when he contemplates their propensity to this dangerous vice. He will not fail, therefore, to set a due value on any plan which, without violating the principles to which he is attached, provides a proper cure for it. The instability, injustice, and confusion introduced into the public councils, have, in truth, been the mortal diseases under which popular governments have everywhere perished; as they continue to be the favourite and fruitful topics from which the adversaries to liberty derive their most specious declamations. The valuable improvements made by the American constitutions on the popular models, both ancient and modern, cannot certainly be too much admired; but it would be an unwarrantable partiality, to contend that they have as effectually obviated the danger on this side, as was wished and expected. Complaints are everywhere heard from our most considerate and virtuous citizens, equally the friends of public and private faith, and of public and personal liberty, that our governments are too unstable, that the public good is disregarded in the conflicts of rival parties, and that measures are too often decided, not according to the rules of justice and the rights of the minor party, but by the superior force of an interested and overbearing majority. However anxiously we may wish that these complaints had no foundation, the evidence of known facts will not permit us to deny that they are in some degree true. It will be found, indeed, on a candid review of our situation, that some of the distresses under which we labour have been erroneously charged on the operation of our governments; but it will be found, at the same time, that other causes will not alone account for many of our heaviest misfortunes; and, particularly, for that prevailing and increasing distrust of public engagements, and alarm for private rights, which are echoed from one end of the continent to the other. These must be chiefly, if not wholly, effects of the unsteadiness and injustice with which a factious spirit has tainted our public administrations.*   1

By a faction, I understand a number of citizens, whether amounting to a majority or minority of the whole, who are united and actuated by some common impulse of passion, or of interest, adverse to the rights of

---

* Paragraph 1: In sentence 6, what does "interested" mean?

other citizens, or to the permanent and aggregate interests of the community.   2

There are two methods of curing the mischiefs of faction: the one, by removing its causes; the other, by controlling its effects.   3

There are again two methods of removing the causes of faction: the one, by destroying the liberty which is essential to its existence; the other, by giving to every citizen the same opinions, the same passions, and the same interests.   4

It could never be more truly said than of the first remedy, that it was worse than the disease. Liberty is to faction what air is to fire, an element without which it instantly expires. But it could not be less folly to abolish liberty, which is essential to political life, because it nourishes faction, than it would be to wish the annihilation of air, which is essential to animal life, because it imparts to fire its destructive agency.*   5

The second expedient is as impracticable as the first would be unwise. As long as the reason of man continues fallible, and he is at liberty to exercise it, different opinions will be formed. As long as the connection subsists between his reason and his self-love, his opinions and his passions will have a reciprocal influence on each other; and the former will be objects to which the latter will attach themselves. The diversity in the faculties of men, from which the rights of property originate, is not less an insuperable obstacle to a uniformity of interests. The protection of these faculties is the first object of government. From the protection of different and unequal faculties of acquiring property, the possession of different degrees and kinds of property immediately results; and from the influence of these on the sentiments and views of the respective proprietors, ensues a division of the society into different interests and parties.   6

The latent causes of faction are thus sown in the nature of man; and we see them everywhere brought into different degrees of activity, according to the different circumstances of civil society. A zeal for different opinions concerning religion, concerning government, and many other points, as well of speculation as of practice; an attachment to different leaders ambitiously contending for pre-eminence and power; or to persons of other descriptions whose fortunes have been interesting to the human passions, have, in turn, divided mankind into parties, inflamed them with mutual animosity, and rendered them much more disposed to vex and oppress each other than to cooperate for their common good. So strong is this propensity of mankind to fall into mutual animosities, that where no substantial occasion presents itself, the most frivolous and fanciful distinctions have been sufficient to kindle their unfriendly passions and excite their most violent conflicts. But the most common and durable

* Paragraph 5: Is the comparison appropriate?

source of factions has been the various and unequal distribution of property. Those who hold and those who are without property have ever formed distinct interests in society. Those who are creditors, and those who are debtors, fall under a like discrimination. A landed interest, a manufacturing interest, a mercantile interest, a moneyed interest, with many lesser interests, grow up of necessity in civilised nations, and divide them into different classes, actuated by different sentiments and views. The regulation of these various and interfering interests forms the principal task of modern legislation, and involves the spirit of party and faction in the necessary and ordinary operations of the government.   7

No man is allowed to be a judge in his own cause, because his interest would certainly bias his judgment, and, not improbably, corrupt his integrity. With equal, nay, with greater reason, a body of men are unfit to be both judges and parties at the same time; yet what are many of the most important acts of legislation, but so many judicial determinations, not indeed concerning the rights of single persons, but concerning the rights of large bodies of citizens? And what are the different classes of legislators but advocates and parties to the causes which they determine? Is a law proposed concerning private debts? It is a question to which the creditors are parties on one side and the debtors on the other. Justice ought to hold the balance between them. Yet the parties are, and must be, themselves the judges; and the most numerous party, or, in other words, the most powerful faction must be expected to prevail. Shall domestic manufacturers be encouraged, and in what degree, by restrictions on foreign manufactures? are questions which would be differently decided by the landed and the manufacturing classes, and probably by neither with a sole regard to justice and the public good. The apportionment of taxes on the various descriptions of property is an act which seems to require the most exact impartiality; yet there is, perhaps, no legislative act in which greater opportunity and temptation are given to a predominant party to trample on the rules of justice. Every shilling with which they overburden the inferior number is a shilling saved to their own pockets.*   8

It is in vain to say that enlightened statesmen will be able to adjust these clashing interests, and render them all subservient to the public good. Enlightened statesmen will not always be at the helm. Nor, in many cases, can such an adjustment be made at all without taking into view indirect and remote considerations, which will rarely prevail over the immediate interest which one party may find in disregarding the rights of another or the good of the whole.†   9

The inference to which we are brought is that the *causes of faction*

---

* Paragraph 8: Comment on the punctuation of the second sentence.

† Paragraph 9: What does the last sentence mean?

cannot be removed, and that relief is only to be sought in the means of controlling its *effects*.*   10

If a faction consists of less than a majority, relief is supplied by the republican principle, which enables the majority to defeat its sinister views by regular vote. It may clog the administration, it may convulse the society; but it will be unable to execute and mask its violence under the forms of the Constitution. When a majority is included in a faction, the form of popular government, on the other hand, enables it to sacrifice to its ruling passion or interest both the public good and the rights of other citizens. To secure the public good and private rights against the danger of such a faction, and at the same time to preserve the spirit and the form of popular government, is then the great object to which our inquiries are directed. Let me add that it is the great desideratum by which this form of government can be rescued from the opprobrium under which it has so long laboured, and be recommended to the esteem and adoption of mankind.†   11

By what means is this object obtainable? Evidently by one of two only: Either the existence of the same passion or interest in a majority at the same time must be prevented, or the majority, having such coexistent passion or interest, must be rendered, by their number and local situation, unable to concert and carry into effect schemes of oppression. If the impulse and the opportunity be suffered to coincide, we well know that neither moral nor religious motives can be relied on as an adequate control. They are not found to be such on the injustice and violence of individuals, and lose their efficacy in proportion to the number combined together, that is, in proportion as their efficacy becomes needful.   12

From this view of the subject it may be concluded that a pure democracy, by which I mean a society consisting of a small number of citizens, who assemble and administer the government in person, can admit of no cure for the mischiefs of faction. A common passion or interest will, in almost every case, be felt by a majority of the whole; a communication and concert result from the form of government itself; and there is nothing to check the inducements to sacrifice the weaker party or an obnoxious individual. Hence it is that such democracies have ever been spectacles of turbulence and contention; have ever been found incompatible with personal security or the rights of property; and have in general been as short in their lives as they have been violent in their deaths. Theoretic politicians, who have patronised this species of government, have erroneously supposed that by reducing mankind to a perfect equality in

---

* Paragraph 10: What function does this paragraph serve in the structure of the essay at this point?

† Paragraph 11: In sentence 1, what is the antecedent of "its"? What is the main object to which, Madison says, his inquiry is directed? Is he concerned more with the minority faction or the majority faction?

their political rights, they would, at the same time, be perfectly equalised and assimilated in their possessions, their opinions, and their passions.* 13

A republic, by which I mean a government in which the scheme of representation takes place, opens a different prospect, and promises the cure for which we are seeking. Let us examine the points in which it varies from pure democracy, and we shall comprehend both the nature of the cure and the efficacy which it must derive from the Union. 14

The two great points of difference between a democracy and a republic are: first, the delegation of the government, in the latter, to a small number of citizens elected by the rest; secondly, the greater number of citizens, and greater sphere of country, over which the latter may be extended. 15

The effect of the first difference is, on the one hand, to refine and enlarge the public views, by passing them through the medium of a chosen body of citizens, whose wisdom may best discern the true interest of their country, and whose patriotism and love of justice will be least likely to sacrifice it to temporary or partial considerations. Under such a regulation, it may well happen that the public voice, pronounced by the representatives of the people, will be more consonant to the public good than if pronounced by the people themselves, convened for the purpose. On the other hand, the effect may be inverted. Men of factious tempers, of local prejudices, or of sinister designs, may, by intrigue, by corruption, or by other means, first obtain the suffrages, and then betray the interests, of the people. The question resulting is, whether small or extensive republics are more favourable to the election of proper guardians of the public weal; and it is clearly decided in favour of the latter by two obvious considerations: 16

In the first place, it is to be remarked that, however small the republic may be, the representatives must be raised to a certain number, in order to guard against the cabals of a few; and that, however large it may be, they must be limited to a certain number, in order to guard against the confusion of a multitude. Hence, the number of representatives in the two cases not being in proportion to that of the two constituents, and being proportionally greater in the small republic, it follows that, if the proportion of fit characters be not less in the large than in the small republic, the former will present a greater option, and consequently a greater probability of a fit choice.† 17

In the next place, as each representative will be chosen by a greater number of citizens in the large than in the small republic, it will be more difficult for unworthy candidates to practise with success the vicious arts

---

* Paragraph 13: What kinds of democracies "have ever been spectacles of turbulence"?

† Paragraph 17: In this paragraph, is Madison contradicting what he said in paragraph 12?

by which elections are too often carried; and the suffrages of the people, being more free, will be more likely to centre in men who possess the most attractive merit and the most diffusive and established character.   18

It must be confessed that in this, as in most other cases, there is a mean, on both sides of which inconveniences will be found to lie. By enlarging too much the number of electors, you render the representative too little acquainted with all their local circumstances and lesser interests; as by reducing it too much, you render him unduly attached to these, and too little fit to comprehend and pursue great and national objects. The federal Constitution forms a happy combination in this respect; the great and aggregate interests being referred to the national, the local and particular to the State legislatures.   19

The other point of difference is, the greater number of citizens and extent of territory which may be brought within the compass of republican than of democratic government; and it is this circumstance principally which renders factious combinations less to be dreaded in the former than in the latter. The smaller the society, the fewer probably will be the distinct parties and interests composing it; the fewer the distinct parties and interests, the more frequently will a majority be found of the same party; and the smaller the number of individuals composing a majority, and the smaller the compass within which they are placed, the more easily will they concert and execute their plans of oppression. Extend the sphere, and you take in a greater variety of parties and interests; you make it less probable that a majority of the whole will have a common motive to invade the rights of other citizens; or if such a common motive exists, it will be more difficult for all who feel it to discover their own strength, and to act in unison with each other. Besides other impediments, it may be remarked that, where there is a consciousness of unjust or dishonourable purposes, communication is always checked by distrust in proportion to the number whose concurrence is necessary.   20

Hence, it clearly appears, that the same advantage which a republic has over a democracy, in controlling the effects of faction, is enjoyed by a large over a small republic,—is enjoyed by the Union over the States composing it. Does the advantage consist in the substitution of representatives whose enlightened views and virtuous sentiments render them superior to local prejudices and to schemes of injustice? It will not be denied that the representation of the Union will be most likely to possess these requisite endowments. Does it consist in the greater security afforded by a greater variety of parties, against the event of any one party being able to out-number and oppress the rest? In an equal degree does the increased variety of parties comprised within the Union increase this security? Does it, in fine, consist in the greater obstacles opposed to the concert and accomplishment of the secret wishes of an unjust and interested majority? Here, again, the extent of the Union gives it the most palpable advantage.*   21

The influence of factious leaders may kindle a flame within their particular States, but will be unable to spread a general conflagration through the other States. A religious sect may degenerate into a political faction in a part of the Confederacy; but the variety of sects dispersed over the entire face of it must secure the national councils against any danger from that source. A rage for paper money, for an abolition of debts, for an equal division of property, or for any other improper or wicked project, will be less apt to pervade the whole body of the Union than a particular member of it; in the same proportion as such a malady is more likely to taint a particular county or district, than an entire State.   22

In the extent and proper structure of the Union, therefore, we behold a republican remedy for the diseases most incident to republican government. And according to the degree of pleasure and pride we feel in being republicans, ought to be our zeal in cherishing the spirit and supporting the character of Federalists.   23

* Paragraph 21: Is the argument in this paragraph convincing?

The Whole Selection

1 Note that Madison uses classification in paragraphs 3 and 4 and then immediately thereafter uses cause and effect. What other methods of development are used in this selection?

2 Why does Madison believe it impracticable to remove the second of the two causes of "faction"?

3 Where does Madison consider the relation of the rights of property to the individual's talents or abilities? Would Madison favor the equal distribution of wealth in a nation?

4 In the beginning of paragraph 7, Madison says, "The latent causes of faction are thus sown in the nature of man." What are these causes?

5 In paragraph 10, Madison suggests that "the causes of faction cannot be removed." What evidence has he given for this view?

6 In paragraphs 13 through 21, Madison outlines what he believes are certain differing effects resulting from a democracy on the one hand and a republic on the other. Briefly outline these effects under each of the causes. Are the causes here immediate or remote?

7 Which of the two means noted by Madison in paragraph 12 does he regard as feasible for controlling the effects of faction?

Word Study *propensity, specious, declamation, obviate, aggregate, fallible, insuperable, latent, animosity, desideratum, opprobrium, palpable*

CAUSES OF THE RESTLESS SPIRIT OF THE AMERICANS

ALEXIS de TOCQUEVILLE

In certain remote corners of the Old World you may still sometimes stumble upon a small district which seems to have been forgotten amid the general tumult, and to have remained stationary while everything around it was in motion. The inhabitants are for the most part extremely ignorant and poor; they take no part in the business of the country, and they are frequently oppressed by the government; yet their countenances are generally placid, and their spirits light. In America I saw the freest and most enlightened men placed in the happiest circumstances that the world affords: it seemed to me as if a cloud habitually hung upon their brow, and I thought them serious and almost sad even in their pleasures. The chief reason of this contrast is that the former do not think of the ills they endure—the latter are forever brooding over advantages they do not possess. It is strange to see with what feverish ardour the Americans pursue their own welfare; and to watch the vague dread that constantly torments them lest they should not have chosen the shortest path which may lead to it. A native of the United States clings to this world's goods as if he were certain never to die; and he is so hasty in grasping at all within his reach that one would suppose he was constantly afraid of not living long enough to enjoy them. He clutches everything, he holds nothing fast, but soon loosens his grasp to pursue fresh gratifications.   1

In the United States a man builds a house to spend his latter years in it, and he sells it before the roof is on: he plants a garden, and lets it just as the trees are coming into bearing: he brings a field into tillage, and leaves other men to gather the crops: he embraces a profession, and gives it up: he settles in a place, which he soon afterward leaves, to carry his changeable longings elsewhere. If his private affairs leave him any leisure, he instantly plunges into the vortex of politics; and if at the end of a year of unremitting labour he finds he has a few days' vacation, his eager curiosity whirls him over the vast extent of the United States, and he will travel fifteen hundred miles in a few days to shake off his happiness. Death at length overtakes him, but it is before he is weary of his bootless chase of that complete felicity which is forever on the wing.*   2

At first sight there is something surprising in this strange unrest of so many happy men, restless in the midst of abundance. The spectacle itself is, however, as old as the world; the novelty is to see a whole people furnish an exemplification of it. Their taste for physical gratifications must

---

* Paragraph 2: How is the thought of this paragraph related to that of the preceding one? How does the use of parallelism in the first sentence contribute to the sense which the author wishes to communicate to the reader?

be regarded as the original source of that secret inquietude that the actions of the Americans betray, and of that inconstancy of which they afford fresh examples every day. He who has set his heart exclusively upon the pursuit of worldly welfare is always in a hurry, for he has but a limited time at his disposal to reach it, to grasp it, and to enjoy it. The recollection of the brevity of life is a constant spur to him. Besides the good things which he possesses, he every instant fancies a thousand others which death will prevent him from trying if he does not try them soon. This thought fills him with anxiety, fear, and regret, and keeps his mind in ceaseless trepidation, which leads him perpetually to change his plans and his abode. If in addition to the taste for physical well-being a social condition be superadded, in which the laws and customs make no condition permanent, here is a great additional stimulant to this restlessness of temper. Men will then be seen continually to change their track, for fear of missing the shortest cut to happiness. It may readily be conceived that if men, passionately bent upon physical gratifications, desire eagerly, they are also easily discouraged: as their ultimate object is to enjoy, the means to reach that object must be prompt and easy, or the trouble of acquiring the gratification would be greater than the gratification itself. Their prevailing frame of mind, then, is at once ardent and relaxed, violent and enervated. Death is often less dreaded than perseverance in continuous efforts to one end.*   3

The equality of conditions leads by a still straighter road to several of the effects which I have here described. When all the privileges of birth and fortune are abolished, when all professions are accessible to all, and a man's own energies may place him at the top of any one of them, an easy and unbounded career seems open to his ambition, and he will readily persuade himself that he is born to no vulgar destinies. But this is an erroneous notion, which is corrected by daily experience. The same equality which allows every citizen to conceive these lofty hopes renders all the citizens less able to realize them: it circumscribes their powers on every side, while it gives freer scope to their desires. Not only are they themselves powerless, but they are met at every step by immense obstacles, which they did not at first perceive. They have swept away the privileges of some of their fellow-creatures which stood in their way, but they have opened the door to universal competition: the barrier has changed its shape rather than its position. When men are nearly alike, and all follow the same track, it is very difficult for any one individual to walk quick and cleave a way through the dense throng which surrounds and presses him. This constant strife between the propensities springing from the equality

---

* Paragraph 3: In the eighth sentence, what does "the laws . . . make no condition permanent" mean? Does the author mean that our laws are inadequate? What is the cause of the fact that the American "frame of mind" is "at once ardent and relaxed, violent and enervated" (in the second to last sentence of the paragraph)?

of conditions and the means it supplies to satisfy them harasses and
wearies the mind.*   4

It is possible to conceive men arrived at a degree of freedom which
should content them; they would then enjoy their independence without
anxiety and without impatience. But men will never establish any equality
with which they can be contented. Whatever efforts a people may make,
they will never succeed in reducing all the conditions of society to a perfect level; and even if they unhappily attained that absolute and complete
depression, the inequality of minds would still remain, which, coming
directly from the hand of God, will forever escape the laws of man. However democratic, then, the social state and the political constitution of a
people may be, it is certain that every member of the community will
always find out several points about him that command his own position;
and we may foresee that his looks will be doggedly fixed in that direction.
When inequality of conditions is the common law of society, the most
marked inequalities do not strike the eye: when everything is nearly on the
same level, the slightest are marked enough to hurt it. Hence the desire of
equality always becomes more insatiable in proportion as equality is more
complete.†   5

Among democratic nations men easily attain a certain equality of
conditions: they can never attain the equality they desire. It perpetually
retires from before them, yet without hiding itself from their sight, and in
retiring draws them on. At every moment they think they are about to
grasp it; it escapes at every moment from their hold. They are near enough
to see its charms, but too far off to enjoy them; and before they have
fully tasted its delights they die. To these causes must be attributed that
strange melancholy that oftentimes will haunt the inhabitants of democratic countries in the midst of their abundance, and that disgust at life
that sometimes seizes upon them in the midst of calm and easy circumstances. Complaints are made in France that the number of suicides
increases; in America suicide is rare, but insanity is said to be more common than anywhere else. These are all different symptoms of the same disease. The Americans do not put an end to their lives, however disquieted
they may be, because their religion forbids it; and among them materialism may be said hardly to exist, notwithstanding the general passion for
physical gratification. The will resists—reason frequently gives way.‡   6

---

* Paragraph 4: What are the "propensities" and what are "the means" referred to in the
last sentence of this paragraph?

† Paragraph 5: In the fourth sentence, the statement that "every member . . . will always
find out several points about him that command his own position" is obviously a
metaphor (drawn from the military). What does it mean? Be sure to observe that in the
statement "about" means "around" (not "concerning"). What is the grammatical
structure of this sentence?

‡ Paragraph 6: In the last sentence, what does "the will resists" mean? What does the
will resist? Turn this into a literal statement, in your own words.

In democratic ages enjoyments are more intense than in the ages of aristocracy, and especially the number of those who partake in them is larger: but, on the other hand, it must be admitted that man's hopes and his desires are oftener blasted, the soul is more stricken and perturbed, and care itself more keen.   7

The Whole Selection

1 Although de Tocqueville's main, general interest is in ascribing causes, cause and effect are—as we noted in our introduction to this section— inseparable. Indeed, the relationships between the two may not always be easily perceived by a reader. In paragraphs 3 and 4 of this essay, which elements or details represent causes and which represent effects?

2 In his first paragraph, de Tocqueville compares and contrasts two different groups of people. Do you find his comparison valid? What other methods of analysis, besides cause and effect and comparison and contrast, does de Tocqueville use?

3 The author makes considerable use of colons in the first sentence in paragraph 2. Why is their use here, and also in sentences 4 and 6 in paragraph 4, rhetorically more effective than the use of semicolons or periods would have been?

THE REVOLT OF THE DIMINISHED MAN

ARCHIBALD MacLEISH

Robert Frost had the universe, not the university, in mind when he wrote his laconic couplet about the secret in the middle, but the image fits the academic world in crisis as well as the mysteries of space.

1

> We dance around in a ring and suppose
> But the secret sits in the middle and knows.

2

Indeed, we do. Faculty committees, state legislatures, alumni associations, police departments, and all the rest of us whirl in a circle with our favorite suppositions—which increasingly tend to roll up into one supposition: that the crisis in the university is really only a student crisis, or, more precisely, a crisis precipitated by a small minority of students, which would go away if the students would stop doing whatever it is they are doing or whatever they plan to do next.*

3

Which, needless to say, is not a wholly irrational supposition. Those who have seen a purposeful task force of Harvard students take over University Hall, carry out reluctant deans, break into files, shout down professors are within their logical rights when they conclude that the occupying students were the cause of the crisis thus created. But the supposition remains a supposition notwithstanding for it does not follow—did not follow at Harvard certainly—that the crisis is a student crisis in the critical sense that it can be ended merely by suppressing the students involved. When the students involved were suppressed at Harvard, the crisis (as at other universities) was not reduced but enlarged. Which suggests, if it suggests anything, that the actual crisis is larger than its particular incidents or their perpetrators.

4

And there are other familiar facts which look in the same direction; as, for example, the fact that it is only when the general opinion of an entire student generation supports, or at least condones, minority disruptions that they can hope to succeed. The notion that the activist tail wags the huge, indifferent student dog is an illusion. Had a minority of the kind involved at Harvard attempted to bring the University to that famous "grinding halt" in the Forties or the Fifties it would have had its trouble for its pains no matter how forceful the police. It succeeded in the Sixties for one reason and for one reason only—because the climate of student opinion as a whole had changed in the Sixties; because there has been a

---

* Paragraph 3: What does the first sentence—"Indeed, we do"—mean?

change in the underlying beliefs, the accepted ideas, of an entire academic
generation, or the greater part of it.*   5

To look for the cause of crisis, therefore, is to examine, not the
demands of the much discussed minorities but something larger—the
changes in belief of the generation to which they belong. And there at
once a paradox appears. The most striking of these changes far from
disturbing the academic world should and does encourage it. There are, of
course, romantics in the new generation who talk of destroying the university as a symbol of a defunct civilization, but the great mass of their
contemporaries, however little they sometimes seem to understand the
nature of the university—the vulnerability, fragility even, of that free and
open community of minds which a university is—are nevertheless profoundly concerned with the university's well-being and, specifically, its relation to the world and to themselves.†   6

This is a new thing under the academic sun—and, in itself, a hopeful thing. Down to the decade now closing, demands by any considerable
number of American undergraduates for changes in the substance or manner or method or purpose of their instruction were rare indeed. In my day
at Yale, back before the First World War, no one concerned himself less
with matters of curriculum and teaching and the like than a college undergraduate. We were not, as undergraduates, indifferent to our education,
but it never occurred to any of us to think of the curriculum of Yale College
as a matter within our concern, or the policies of the university as decisions about which we—we of all creatures living—were entitled to an
opinion. Some of my college classmates protested compulsory chapel
(largely because of its interference with breakfast), but no one to my
knowledge ever protested, even in a letter to the News, the pedantic
teaching of Shakespeare, from which the college then suffered, or the non-
teaching of Karl Marx, who was then on the point of changing the history
of the world.   7

And the same thing was true of the relation between the university
and the world outside. We in the class of 1915 spent our senior year in a
Yale totally surrounded by the First World War, but we were "inside" and
all the rest were "outside," and it was not for us to put the two together—
not even for those of us who were to go from New Haven to die on the
Marne or in the Argonne under extremely unpleasant circumstances in the
most murderous, hypocritical, unnecessary, and generally nasty of all
recorded wars, the present one included. Our deaths, as we came to know,
would be our own but not their reasons. When I myself was asked by a
corporal in my battery what we were there for—"there" being the second

* Paragraph 5: What are the "familiar facts" which MacLeish refers to in the first sentence?
† Paragraph 6: What is the "paradox" MacLeish suggests?

battle of the Marne—I quoted President Wilson: "to make the world safe
for democracy." It was not my war. President Wilson was running it.   8

And the generation which fought the next war twenty years later
saw things in much the same way. They too were in a sense observers—
observers, in their case, of their own heroism. When the war came they
fought it with magnificent courage: no citizen army in history ever fought
better than theirs after that brutal North African initiation. But until the
war came, while it was still in the agonizing process of becoming, it was
somebody else's war—President Roosevelt's, as the Chicago *Tribune* kept
insinuating, or Winston Churchill's. "America First" was, in part, a campus
movement but the terrible question posed by Adolf Hitler—a question of
life or death for thousands of young Americans and very possibly for the
Republic itself—was little argued by the undergraduates of 1941. The
political aspects of fascism they left to their elders at home and the moral
agony to their contemporaries in the French Resistance. They themselves
merely fought the war and won it—fought it with a kind of gallant indifference, an almost ironic gallantry, which was, and still remains, the hallmark
of that incredible generation and its improbable triumph.*   9

It is in this perspective and against this background that the attitudes of the undergraduates of the Sixties must be seen. Here, suddenly
and almost without warning, is a generation of undergraduates that re-
verses everything that has gone before, rejects the traditional undergraduate isolation, refuses the conventional segregation of the university from
the troubled world, and not only accepts for itself but demands for itself
a measure of responsibility for both—for university *and* world, for life as
well as for education.†   10

And the question, if we wish to understand this famous crisis of ours,
is: Why? Why has this transformation of ideas—metamorphosis more
precisely—taken place? Why does the generation of the Sixties make itself
morally responsible for the war in Vietnam, while the generation of 1917
stood on the Marne quoting Woodrow Wilson and the generation of 1941
smashed the invincible Nazi armor from Normandy to the Rhine without
a quotation from anybody? Why, for the first time in the remembered history of this Republic, do its college and university students assert a responsibility for their own education, demand a part in the process? Are we
really to believe with some of our legislators that the whole thing is the
result of a mysterious, country-wide conspiracy among the hairier of the
young directed perhaps by a sinister professor somewhere? Or is it open
to us to consider that the crisis in the university may actually be what we

* Paragraph 9: In the last sentence, why does MacLeish call the "triumph" "improbable"?

† Paragraph 10: What function do the three preceding paragraphs serve with relation to
this paragraph?

call it: a crisis *in* the university—a crisis in education itself precipitated
by a revolution in ideas, a revolution in the ideas of a new generation of
mankind?   11

There are those who believe we must find the answer to that question where we find the question: in the decade in which we live. Franklin
Ford, dean of the Faculty of Arts and Sciences at Harvard and one of the
ablest and most admired of university administrators, attributes this
changed mentality in great part to "the particular malaise of the Sixties."
Undertaking to explain to his colleagues his view of what we have come to
call "student unrest," Dean Ford defined it in terms of concentric circles,
the most important of which would include students who had been profoundly hurt by the anguish of these recent years: "The thought-benumb-
ing blows of successive assassinations, the equally tragic though more
comprehensible crisis of the cities, the growing bitterness of the poor amid
the self-congratulations of affluence, the even greater bitterness of black
Americans, rich or poor . . . all these torments of our day have hit
thoughtful young people with peculiar force. . . . Youth is a time of extreme
vulnerability to grief and frustration, as well as a time of impatient, generous sympathy." And to all this, Dean Ford continues, must be added the
war in Vietnam, which he sees as poisoning and exacerbating everything
else, contributing "what can only be described as (a sense) of horror."   12

Most of us—perhaps I should qualify that by saying most of those
with whom I talk—would agree. We would agree, that is to say, that the
war in Vietnam has poisoned the American mind. We would agree that
the affluent society—more precisely the affluent half-society—has turned
out to be a sick society, for the affluent half as well as for the other. We
would agree that the cancer of the cities, the animal hatred of the races,
the bursting pustule of violence has hurt us all and particularly those of
us who are young and they in particular *because* they are young, because,
being young, they are generous, because, being young and generous, they
are vulnerable. We would agree to all this, and we would agree in consequence that there is a relationship between the malaise in the universities and Dean Ford's "particular malaise of the Sixties."*   13

But would we agree, reflecting on those considerations and this conclusion, that it is the tragic events of the decade which, alone, are the
root cause—the effective cause—of the unrest of which Dean Ford is
speaking? If the bitterness, the brutality, the suffering of the last few years
were the effective cause, would the *university* be the principal target of
resentment? If Vietnam were the heart of the trouble, would the university
curriculum be attacked—the methods of teaching, the teachers them-

---

* Paragraph 13: What purpose is served by the repetition of "We would agree . . ." at the
  beginning of most of the sentences in this paragraph?

selves? Would the reaction not have expressed itself, as indeed it once did, at the Pentagon?   14

What is resented, clearly, is not only the present state of the Republic, the present state of the world, but some relation or lack of relation between the state of the Republic, the state of the world, and the process of education—the process of education at its most meaningful point—the process of education in the university.   15

But what relation or lack of relation? A direct, a one-to-one, relationship? Is the university blamed *because* the war is being fought, *because* the ghettos exist, *because* the affluent society is the vulgar, dull, unbeautiful society we see in our more ostentatious cities? Is the demand of the young a demand that the university should alter its instruction and its practices so as to put an end to this ugliness, these evils—reshape this society?   16

There are some undergraduates, certainly, who take this position. There are some who would like to bring the weight and influence of the university to bear directly on the solution of economic and social problems through the management of the university's real estate and endowments. There are others who would direct its instruction toward specific evils by establishing courses in African affairs and urban studies. Both attitudes are familiar: they are standard demands of student political organizations. They are also reasonable—reasonable at least in purpose if not always in form. But do they go to the heart of the matter? Is this direct relationship of specific instruction to specific need—of specific land-use program to specific land-use evil—the relation undergraduates have in mind when they complain, as they do, over and over, that their courses are not "relevant," that their education does not "respond to their needs," "preach to their condition"? Is it only "applicability," only immediate pertinence, the generation of the young demands of us? Is the deep, almost undefinable restlessness of the student generation—the dark unhappiness of which Senator Muskie spoke in that unforgettable speech at Chicago—an unhappiness which Centers of Urban Studies, however necessary, can cure?   17

I do not think so and neither, if you will forgive me for saying it, do you. The distress, the very real and generous suffering and distress of an entire generation of young men and young women is related certainly to the miseries of the Sixties, but it is not founded in them and it will not disappear when they vanish—when, if ever, the war ends and the hot summers find cool shade and the assassinations cease. The "relevance" these students speak of is not relevance to the *Huntley-Brinkley Report*. It is relevance to their own lives, to the living of their lives, to themselves as men and women living. And their resentment, their very real resentment and distress, rises not only from the tragedies and mischances of the last ten years but from a human situation, a total human situation involving human life as human life, which has been three generations in the making, and which this new generation now revolts against—rejects.   18

At the time of the Sorbonne riots a year ago a French politician spoke in terms of apocalypse: We had come to a point in time like the fall of Rome when civilizations collapse because belief is dead. What was actually happening in Paris and elsewhere was, of course, the precise opposite. Belief, passionate belief, had come alive for the first time in the century and with it rage and violence. The long diminishment, the progressive diminution, of value put upon man, upon the idea of man, in modern society had met the revulsion of a generation of the young who condemned it in all its aspects, left as well as right, Communist as well as capitalist, the indifference of the Marxist bureaucracies as well as the bureaucratic industrial indifference of the West.*   19

This diminishment of the idea of man has been a long time in progress. I will not claim for my generation that we witnessed its beginning, I will assert only that we were the first to record it where alone it could be recorded. The arts with us became aware of a flatness in human life, a loss of depth as though a dimension had somehow dropped from the world— as though our human shadows had deserted us. The great metaphor of the journey of mankind—Ulysses among the mysteries and monsters— reduced itself in our youth to that other Ulysses among the privies and the pubs of Dublin, Ireland. Cleopatra on her flowery barge floated through a Saturday night in the Bloomsbury Twenties. Even death itself was lessened: the multitudes of Dante's damned crossed T. S. Eliot's London Bridge, commuters in the morning fog. Nothing was left remarkable beneath the visiting moon.   20

And in the next generation—the generation, as we are now beginning to see, of Joyce's secretary and disciple, Samuel Beckett—the testimony of the arts went on. The banality of the age turned to impotence and numbness and paralysis, a total anesthesia of the soul. Leopold Bloom no longer maundered through the musty Dublin streets. He was incapable even of maundering, incapable of motion. He sat to his neck in sand, like a head of rotting celery in an autumn garden, and waited, or did not even wait— just sat there. While as for Cleopatra—Cleopatra was an old man's youthful memory played back upon a worn-out tape.   21

The arts are honest witnesses in these matters. Pound was right enough, for all the well-known plethora of language, when he wrote in praise of Joyce's *Ulysses* that "it is a summary of pre-war Europe, the blackness and mess and muddle of a 'civilization'," and that "Bloom very

---

* Paragraph 19: In MacLeish's opinion, what is the "passionate belief" that has come alive?

much *is* the mess." The arts, moreover, are honest witnesses in such matters not only when they achieve works of art as with Joyce and Eliot and frequently with Beckett. They testify even when they fail. The unpoem, the nonpainting of our era, the play that does not play, all bear their penny's worth of witness. The naked, half-embarrassed boy displaying his pudenda on an off Off-Broadway stage is not an actor nor is his shivering gesture a dramatic act, but still he testifies. He is the last, sad, lost reincarnation of L. Bloom, the resurrection of the head of celery. Odysseus on his lonely raft in the god-infested sea has come to this.   22

What was imagined in Greece, reimagined in the Renaissance, carried to a passion of pride in Europe of the Enlightenment and to a passion of hope in the Republic of the New World—John Adams's hope as well as Jefferson's and Whitman's; Lincoln's that he called "the last, best hope" —all this grimaces in pitiful derision of itself in that nude, sad, shivering figure. And we see it or we hear about it and protest. But protest *what?* The nakedness! The morals of the playwright! Undoubtedly the playwright needs correction in his morals and above all in the practice of his art, but in his *vision?* His *perception?* Is he the first to see this? On the contrary, his most obvious failure as playwright is precisely the fact that he is merely one of thousands in a thronging, long contemporary line—a follower of fashion. He testifies as hundreds of his betters have been testifying now for years—for generations—near a century.   23

Why have they so testified? They cannot tell you. The artist's business is to see and to show, not answer why: to see as no one else can see, and to show as nothing else can show, but not to explain. He knows no more of explanation than another. And yet *we* canot help but wonder why —why the belief in man has foundered; why it has foundered *now*— precisely *now*—now at the moment of our greatest intellectual triumphs, our never equaled technological mastery, our electronic miracles. Why was man a wonder to the Greeks—to Sophocles of all the Greeks—when he could do little more than work a ship to windward, ride a horse, and plow the earth, while now that he knows the whole of modern science he is a wonder to no one—certainly not to Sophocles' successors and least of all, in any case, to himself?   24

There is no easy answer, though thoughtful men are beginning to suggest that an answer may be found and that, when it is, it may very well relate precisely to this vast new knowledge. George W. Morgan states the position in his *The Human Predicament*. "The sheer weight of accumulated but uncontrolled knowledge and information, of print, views, discoveries, and interpretations, of methods and techniques, inflicts a paralyzing sense of impotence. The mind is overwhelmed by a constant fear of its ignorance. . . . The individual man, feeling unable to gain a valid perspective of the world and of himself, is forced to regard both as consisting of innumerable isolated parts to be relinquished, for knowledge and control, to a legion of experts." All this, says Mr. Morgan, diminishes human understanding in the very process of augmenting human knowledge. It also, I should wish to add, diminishes something else. It diminishes man. For man, as the whole of science as well as the whole of poetry, will demonstrate, is not what he thinks he knows, but what he thinks he *can* know, can become.*   25

But however much or little we comprehend of the cause of our paradoxical diminishment in our own eyes at the moment of our greatest technological triumphs, we cannot help but understand a little of its consequences and particularly its relation to the crisis in the university. Without the belief in man, the university is a contradiction in terms. The business of the university is education at its highest possible level, and the business of education at its highest possible level is the relation of men to their lives. But how is the university to concern itself with the relation of men to their lives, to the living of their lives, to the world in which their lives are lived, without the bold assumption, the brave, improbable hypothesis, that these lives matter, that these men count—that Odysseus on his battered, drifing raft still stands for a reality we take for real?   26

And how can a generation of the young, born into the world of the diminished man and in revolt against it—in revolt against its indifference to humanity in its cities and in its wars and in the weapons of its wars— how can a generation of the young help but demand some teaching from the universities which will interpret all this horror and make cause against it?   27

Centuries ago in a world of gods and mysteries and monsters when man's creativity, his immense creative powers, had been, as Berdyaev put it, "paralyzed by the Middle Ages"—when men had been diminished in their own eyes by the demeaning dogma of the Fall—centuries ago the university conceived an intellectual and spiritual position which released mankind into a new beginning, a rebirth, a Renaissance. What is demanded of us now in a new age of gods and mysteries and monsters, not without dogmas and superstitions of its own, is a second humanism that will free us from our new paralysis of soul as the earlier humanism freed us from that other. If it was human significance which was destroyed by the Middle Ages, it is human significance which we ourselves are now destroying. We are witnessing, as the British critic F. R. Leavis phrases it, the elimination of that "day-by-day creativity of human response which manifests itself in the significances and values without which there is no reality—nothing but emptiness that has to be filled with drink, sex, eating, background music, and . . . the papers and the telly."   28

* Paragraph 25: What is the meaning of the last sentence in this paragraph?

Mr. Leavis, not the most optimistic of dons on any occasion, believes that something might be done to revive "the creative human response that maintains cultural continuity" and that gives human life a meaning. I, with fewer qualifications to speak, would go much further. I would say that a conscious and determined effort to conceive a new humanism which would do for our darkness what that earlier humanism did for the darkness of the Middle Ages is not only a present dream but a present possibility, and that it is a present possibility not despite the generation of the young—the generation of the Sixties—but because of it.   29

That generation is not perhaps as sophisticated politically as it—or its activist spokesmen—would have us think. Its moral superiority to earlier generations may not, in every instance, be as great as it apparently believes. But one virtue it does possess to a degree not equaled by any generation in this century: It believes in man.   30

It is an angry generation, yes, but its resentment is not the disgust of the generation for which Beckett speaks. Its resentment is not a resentment *of* our human life but a resentment *on behalf* of human life; not an indignation that we exist on the Earth but that we *permit* ourselves to exist in a selfishness and wretchedness and squalor which we have the means to abolish. Resentment of this kind is founded, can only be founded, on belief in man. And belief in man—a return to a belief in man—is the reality on which a new age can be built.   31

Thus far, that new belief has been used by the young largely as a weapon—as a justification of an indictment of earlier generations for their exploitation and debasement of human life and earth. When it is allowed to become itself—when the belief in man becomes an affirmative effort to re-create the life of man—the crisis in the university may well become the triumph of the university.   32

For it is only the university in this technological age which can save us from ourselves. And the university, as we now know, can only function effectively when it functions as a common labor of all its generations dedicated to the highest purpose of them all.   33

The Whole Selection

1 What paragraphs serve as introduction to the body of the essay?
2 In the last sentence of paragraph 5, MacLeish sets forth the general area in which he feels the cause for student unrest resides. Where in the essay does he first state what he regards as the specific cause? Why does he delay his statement of the specific cause until he is well on in his essay?

3 In paragraphs 12 through 14, the author presents Dean Ford's answers about the causes of student unrest and then indicates that he is not satisfied with the causes offered by Ford. Does the cause which Mac-Leish ultimately presents in his essay differ materially from the causes presented by Ford?

4 How is the author's view, expressed in paragraphs 20 through 23, that the literary arts for almost a century bore honest witness to the "banality," "impotence," and "numbness" of the preceding two or three generations, related to his central thesis or purpose?

LETTER FROM BIRMINGHAM JAIL

MARTIN LUTHER KING, JR.

April 16, 1963

My dear Fellow Clergymen,

While confined here in the Birmingham City Jail, I came across your recent statement calling our present activities "unwise and untimely." Seldom, if ever, do I pause to answer criticism of my work and ideas. If I sought to answer all of the criticisms that cross my desk, my secretaries would be engaged in little else in the course of the day and I would have no time for constructive work. But since I feel that you are men of genuine good will and your criticisms are sincerely set forth, I would like to answer your statement in what I hope will be patient and reasonable terms.

1

I think I should give the reason for my being in Birmingham, since you have been influenced by the argument of "outsiders coming in." I have the honor of serving as president of the Southern Christian Leadership Conference, an organization operating in every Southern state with headquarters in Atlanta, Georgia. We have some eighty-five affiliate organizations all across the South—one being the Alabama Christian Movement for Human Rights. Whenever necessary and possible we share staff, educational, and financial resources with our affiliates. Several months ago our local affiliate here in Birmingham invited us to be on call to engage in a nonviolent direct action program if such were deemed necessary. We readily consented and when the hour came we lived up to our promises. So I am here, along with several members of my staff, because we were invited here. I am here because I have basic organizational ties here. Beyond this, I am in Birmingham because injustice is here. Just as the eighth century prophets left their little villages and carried their "thus saith the Lord" far beyond the boundaries of their home town, and just as the Apostle Paul left his little village of Tarsus and carried the gospel of Jesus Christ to practically every hamlet and city of the Graeco-Roman world, I too am compelled to carry the gospel of freedom beyond my particular home town. Like Paul, I must constantly respond to the Macedonian call for aid.

2

Moreover, I am cognizant of the interrelatedness of all communities and states. I cannot sit idly by in Atlanta and not be concerned about what happens in Birmingham. Injustice anywhere is a threat to justice everywhere. We are caught in an inescapable network of mutuality tied in a single garment of destiny. Whatever affects one directly affects all indirectly. Never again can we afford to live with the narrow, provincial "outside agitator" idea. Anyone who lives inside the United States can never be considered an outsider anywhere in this country.

3

You deplore the demonstrations that are presently taking place in Birmingham. But I am sorry that your statement did not express a similar concern for the conditions that brought the demonstrations into being. I am sure that each of you would want to go beyond the superficial social analyst who looks merely at effects, and does not grapple with underlying causes. I would not hesitate to say that it is unfortunate that so-called demonstrations are taking place in Birmingham at this time, but I would say in more emphatic terms that it is even more unfortunate that the white power structure of this city left the Negro community with no other alternative.   4

In any nonviolent campaign there are four basic steps: (1) collection of the facts to determine whether injustices are alive; (2) negotiation; (3) self-purification; and (4) direct action. We have gone through all of these steps in Birmingham. There can be no gainsaying of the fact that racial injustice engulfs this community. Birmingham is probably the most thoroughly segregated city in the United States. Its ugly record of police brutality is known in every section of this country. Its unjust treatment of Negroes in the courts is a notorious reality. There have been more unsolved bombings of Negro homes and churches in Birmingham than any city in this nation. These are the hard, brutal, and unbelievable facts. On the basis of these conditions Negro leaders sought to negotiate with the city fathers. But the political leaders consistently refused to engage in good faith negotiation.   5

Then came the opportunity last September to talk with some of the leaders of the economic community. In these negotiating sessions certain promises were made by the merchants—such as the promise to remove the humiliating racial signs from the stores. On the basis of these promises Rev. Shuttlesworth and the leaders of the Alabama Christian Movement for Human Rights agreed to call a moratorium on any type of demonstrations. As the weeks and months unfolded we realized that we were the victims of a broken promise. The signs remained. As in so many experiences of the past we were confronted with blasted hopes, and the dark shadow of a deep disappointment settled upon us. So we had no alternative except that of preparing for direct action, whereby we would present our very bodies as a means of laying our case before the conscience of the local and national community. We were not unmindful of the difficulties involved. So we decided to go through a process of self-purification. We started having workshops on nonviolence and repeatedly asked ourselves the questions, "Are you able to accept blows without retaliating?" "Are you able to endure the ordeals of jail?"   6

We decided to set our direct action program around the Easter season, realizing that with the exception of Christmas, this was the largest shopping period of the year. Knowing that a strong economic withdrawal program would be the by-product of direct action, we felt that this was the best time to bring pressure on the merchants for the needed changes. Then it occurred to us that the March election was ahead, and so we speedily decided to postpone action until after election day. When we discovered that Mr. Connor was in the run-off, we decided again to postpone action so that the demonstrations could not be used to cloud the issues. At this time we agreed to begin our nonviolent witness the day after the run-off.   7

This reveals that we did not move irresponsibly into direct action. We too wanted to see Mr. Connor defeated; so we went through postponement after postponement to aid in this community need. After this we felt that direct action could be delayed no longer.   8

You may well ask, "Why direct action? Why sit-ins, marches, etc.? Isn't negotiation a better path?" You are exactly right in your call for negotiation. Indeed, this is the purpose of direct action. Nonviolent direct action seeks to create such a crisis and establish such creative tension that a community that has constantly refused to negotiate is forced to confront the issue. It seeks so to dramatize the issue that it can no longer be ignored. I just referred to the creation of tension as a part of the work of the nonviolent resister. This may sound rather shocking. But I must confess that I am not afraid of the word tension. I have earnestly worked and preached against violent tension, but there is a type of constructive nonviolent tension that is necessary for growth. Just as Socrates felt that it was necessary to create a tension in the mind so that individuals could rise from the bondage of myths and half-truths to the unfettered realm of creative analysis and objective appraisal, we must see the need of having nonviolent gadflies to create the kind of tension in society that will help men rise from the dark depths of prejudice and racism to the majestic heights of understanding and brotherhood. So the purpose of the direct action is to create a situation so crisis-packed that it will inevitably open the door to negotiation. We, therefore, concur with you in your call for negotiation. Too long has our beloved Southland been bogged down in the tragic attempt to live in monologue rather than dialogue.   9

One of the basic points in your statement is that our acts are untimely. Some have asked, "Why didn't you give the new administration time to act?" The only answer that I can give to this inquiry is that the new administration must be prodded about as much as the outgoing one before it acts. We will be sadly mistaken if we feel that the election of Mr. Boutwell will bring the millennium to Birmingham. While Mr. Boutwell is much more articulate and gentle than Mr. Connor, they are both segregationists dedicated to the task of maintaining the status quo. The hope I see in Mr. Boutwell is that he will be reasonable enough to see the futility of massive resistance to desegregation. But he will not see this without pressure from the devotees of civil rights. My friends, I must say to you that we have not made a single gain in civil rights without determined legal and non-violent pressure. History is the long and tragic story of the fact that privileged groups seldom give up their privileges voluntarily. Individuals may see the moral light and voluntarily give up their unjust posture; but as Reinhold Niebuhr has reminded us, groups are more immoral than individuals.   10

We know through painful experience that freedom is never volun-tarily given by the oppressor; it must be demanded by the oppressed. Frankly I have never yet engaged in a direct action movement that was "well timed," according to the timetable of those who have not suffered unduly from the disease of segregation. For years now I have heard the word "Wait!" It rings in the ear of every Negro with a piercing familiarity. This "wait" has almost always meant "never." It has been a tranquilizing thalidomide, relieving the emotional stress for a moment, only to give birth to an ill-formed infant of frustration. We must come to see with the dis-tinguished jurist of yesterday that "justice too long delayed is justice denied." We have waited for more than three hundred and forty years for our constitutional and God-given rights. The nations of Asia and Africa are moving with jet-like speed toward the goal of political independence, and we still creep at horse and buggy pace toward the gaining of a cup of coffee at a lunch counter.   11

I guess it is easy for those who have never felt the stinging darts of segregation to say wait. But when you have seen vicious mobs lynch your mothers and fathers at will and drown your sisters and brothers at whim; when you have seen hate filled policemen curse, kick, brutalize, and even kill your black brothers and sisters with impunity; when you see the vast majority of your twenty million Negro brothers smothering in an air-tight cage of poverty in the midst of an affluent society; when you sud-denly find your tongue twisted and your speech stammering as you seek to explain to your six-year-old daughter why she can't go to the public amusement park that has just been advertised on television, and see tears welling up in her little eyes when she is told that Funtown is closed to colored children, and see the depressing clouds of inferiority begin to form in her little mental sky, and see her begin to distort her little per-sonality by unconsciously developing a bitterness toward white people; when you have to concoct an answer for a five-year-old son asking in agonizing pathos: "Daddy, why do white people treat colored people so mean?"; when you take a cross country drive and find it necessary to sleep night after night in the uncomfortable corners of your automobile because no motel will accept you; when you are humiliated day in and day out by nagging signs reading "white" men and "colored"; when your first name becomes "nigger" and your middle name becomes "boy" (however old you are) and your last name becomes "John," and when your wife and mother are never given the respected title "Mrs."; when you are harried by day and haunted by night by the fact that you are a Negro, living constantly at tip-toe stance never quite knowing what to expect next, and plagued with inner fears and outer resentments; when you are forever fighting a degenerating sense of "nobodiness";—then you will understand why we find it difficult to wait. There comes a time when the cup of endurance runs over, and men are no longer willing to be plunged into an abyss of injustice where they experience the bleakness of corroding despair. I hope, sirs, you can understand our legitimate and unavoidable impatience. 12

You express a great deal of anxiety over our willingness to break laws. This is certainly a legitimate concern. Since we so diligently urge people to obey the Supreme Court's decision of 1954 outlawing segregation in the public schools, it is rather strange and paradoxical to find us consciously breaking laws. One may well ask, "How can you advocate breaking some laws and obeying others?" The answer is found in the fact that there are two types of laws. There are *just* laws and there are *unjust* laws. I would be the first to advocate obeying just laws. One has not only a legal but moral responsibility to obey just laws. Conversely, one has a moral responsibility to disobey unjust laws. I would agree with Saint Augustine that "An unjust law is no law at all." 13

Now what is the difference between the two? How does one determine when a law is just or unjust? A just law is a man-made code that squares with the moral law or the law of God. An unjust law is a code that is out of harmony with the moral law. To put it in the terms of Saint Thomas Aquinas, an unjust law is a human law that is not rooted in eternal and natural law. Any law that uplifts human personality is just. Any law that degrades human personality is unjust. All segregation statutes are unjust because segregation distorts the soul and damages the personality. It gives the segregator a false sense of superiority and the segregated a false sense of inferiority. To use the words of Martin Buber, the great Jewish philosopher, segregation substitutes an "I-it" relationship for the "I-thou" relationship, and ends up relegating persons to the status of things. So segregation is not only politically, economically, and sociologically unsound, but it is morally wrong and sinful. Paul Tillich has said that sin is separation. Isn't segregation an existential expression of man's tragic separation, an expression of his awful estrangement, his terrible sinfulness? So I can urge men to obey the 1954 decision of the Supreme Court because it is morally right, and I can urge them to disobey segregation ordinances because they are morally wrong. 14

Let us turn to a more concrete example of just and unjust laws. An unjust law is a code that a majority inflicts on a minority that is not binding on itself. This is *difference* made legal. On the other hand a just law is a code that a majority compels a minority to follow that it is willing to follow itself. This is *sameness* made legal.   15

Let me give another explanation. An unjust law is a code inflicted upon a minority which that minority had no part in enacting or creating because they did not have the unhampered right to vote. Who can say the legislature of Alabama which set up the segregation laws was democratically elected? Throughout the state of Alabama all types of conniving methods are used to prevent Negroes from becoming registered voters and there are some counties without a single Negro registered to vote despite the fact that the Negro constitutes a majority of the population. Can any law set up in such a state be considered democratically structured?   16

These are just a few examples of unjust and just laws. There are some instances when a law is just on its face but unjust in its application. For instance, I was arrested Friday on a charge of parading without a permit. Now there is nothing wrong with an ordinance which requires a permit for a parade, but when the ordinance is used to preserve segregation and to deny citizens the First Amendment privilege of peaceful assembly and peaceful protest, then it becomes unjust.   17

I hope you can see the distinction I am trying to point out. In no sense do I advocate evading or defying the law as the rabid segregationist would do. This would lead to anarchy. One who breaks an unjust law must do it *openly, lovingly* (not hatefully as the white mothers did in New Orleans when they were seen on television screaming "nigger, nigger, nigger") and with a willingness to accept the penalty. I submit that an individual who breaks a law that conscience tells him is unjust, and willingly accepts the penalty by staying in jail to arouse the conscience of the community over its injustice, is in reality expressing the very highest respect for law.   18

Of course there is nothing new about this kind of civil disobedience. It was seen sublimely in the refusal of Shadrach, Meshach, and Abednego to obey the laws of Nebuchadnezzar because a higher moral law was involved. It was practiced superbly by the early Christians who were willing to face hungry lions and the excruciating pain of chopping blocks, before submitting to certain unjust laws of the Roman Empire. To a degree academic freedom is a reality today because Socrates practiced civil disobedience.   19

We can never forget that everything Hitler did in Germany was "legal" and everything the Hungarian freedom fighters did in Hungary was "illegal." It was "illegal" to aid and comfort a Jew in Hitler's Germany. But I am sure that, if I had lived in Germany during that time, I would have aided and comforted my Jewish brothers even though it was illegal.

If I lived in a communist country today where certain principles dear to the Christian faith are suppressed, I believe I would openly advocate disobeying these antireligious laws.   20

I must make two honest confessions to you, my Christian and Jewish brothers. First I must confess that over the last few years I have been gravely disappointed with the white moderate. I have almost reached the regrettable conclusion that the Negroes' great stumbling block in the stride toward freedom is not the White Citizens' "Counciler" or the Ku Klux Klanner, but the white moderate who is more devoted to "order" than to justice; who prefers a negative peace which is the absence of tension to a positive peace which is the presence of justice; who constantly says "I agree with you in the goal you seek, but I can't agree with your methods of direct action"; who paternalistically feels that he can set the time-table for another man's freedom; who lives by the myth of time and who constantly advises the Negro to wait until a "more convenient season." Shallow understanding from people of good will is more frustrating than absolute misunderstanding from people of ill will. Luke-warm acceptance is much more bewildering than outright rejection.   21

I had hoped that the white moderate would understand that law and order exist for the purpose of establishing justice, and that when they fail to do this they become the dangerously structured dams that block the flow of social progress. I had hoped that the white moderate would understand that the present tension in the South is merely a necessary phase of the transition from an obnoxious negative peace, where the Negro passively accepted his unjust plight, to a substance-filled positive peace, where all men will respect the dignity and worth of human personality. Actually, we who engage in nonviolent direct action are not the creators of tension. We merely bring to the surface the hidden tension that is already alive. We bring it out in the open where it can be seen and dealt with. Like a boil that can never be cured as long as it is covered up but must be opened with all its pus-flowing ugliness to the natural medicines of air and light, injustice must likewise be exposed, with all of the tension its exposing creates, to the light of human conscience and the air of national opinion before it can be cured.   22

In your statement you asserted that our actions, even though peaceful, must be condemned because they precipitate violence. But can this assertion be logically made? Isn't this like condemning the robbed man because his possession of money precipitated the evil act of robbery? Isn't this like condemning Socrates because his unswerving commitment to truth and his philosophical delvings precipitated the misguided popular mind to make him drink the hemlock? Isn't this like condemning Jesus because His unique God consciousness and never-ceasing devotion to His will precipitated the evil act of crucifixion? We must come to see, as federal courts have consistently affirmed, that it is immoral to urge an individual to withdraw his efforts to gain his basic constitutional rights because the quest precipitates violence. Society must protect the robbed and punish the robber.   23

I had also hoped that the white moderate would reject the myth of time. I received a letter this morning from a white brother in Texas which said: "All Christians know that the colored people will receive equal rights eventually, but is it possible that you are in too great of a religious hurry? It has taken Christianity almost 2000 years to accomplish what it has. The teachings of Christ take time to come to earth." All that is said here grows out of a tragic misconception of time. It is the strangely irrational notion that there is something in the very flow of time that will inevitably cure all ills. Actually time is neutral. It can be used either destructively or constructively. I am coming to feel that the people of ill will have used time much more effectively than the people of good will. We will have to repent in this generation not merely for the vitriolic words and actions of the bad people, but for the appalling silence of the good people. We must come to see that human progress never rolls in on wheels of inevitability. It comes through the tireless efforts and persistent work of men willing to be co-workers with God, and without this hard work time itself becomes an ally of the forces of social stagnation.   24

We must use time creatively, and forever realize that the time is always ripe to do right. Now is the time to make real the promise of democracy, and transform our pending national elegy into a creative psalm of brotherhood. Now is the time to lift our national policy from the quick-sand of racial injustice to the solid rock of human dignity.   25

You spoke of our activity in Birmingham as extreme. At first I was rather disappointed that fellow clergymen would see my nonviolent efforts as those of the extremist. I started thinking about the fact that I stand in the middle of two opposing forces in the Negro community. One is a force of complacency made up of Negroes who, as a result of long years of oppression, have been so completely drained of self-respect and a sense of "somebodiness" that they have adjusted to segregation, and of a few Negroes in the middle class who, because of a degree of academic and economic security, and because at points they profit by segregation, have unconsciously become insensitive to the problems of the masses. The other force is one of bitterness and hatred and comes perilously close to advocating violence. It is expressed in the various black nationalist groups that are springing up over the nation, the largest and best known being Elijah Muhammad's Muslim movement. This movement is nourished by the contemporary frustration over the continued existence of racial discrimination. It is made up of people who have lost faith in America, who have absolutely repudiated Christianity, and who have concluded that the white man is an incurable "devil." I have tried to stand between these two forces saying that we need not follow the "do-nothingism" of the complacent or the hatred and despair of the black nationalist. There is the more excellent way of love and nonviolent protest. I'm grateful to God that, through the Negro church, the dimension of nonviolence entered our struggle. If this philosophy had not emerged I am convinced that by now many streets of the South would be flowing with floods of blood. And I am further convinced that if our white brothers dismiss us as "rabble rousers" and "outside agitators"—those of us who are working through the channels of nonviolent direct action—and refuse to support our nonviolent efforts, millions of Negroes, out of frustration and despair, will seek solace and security in black nationalist ideologies, a development that will lead inevitably to a frightening racial nightmare.   26

Oppressed people cannot remain oppressed forever. The urge for freedom will eventually come. This is what has happened to the American Negro. Something within has reminded him of his birthright of freedom; something without has reminded him that he can gain it. Consciously and unconsciously, he has been swept in by what the Germans call the *Zeitgeist,* and with his black brothers of Africa, and his brown and yellow brothers of Asia, South America, and the Caribbean, he is moving with a sense of cosmic urgency toward the promised land of racial justice. Recognizing this vital urge that has engulfed the Negro community, one should readily understand public demonstrations. The Negro has many pent-up resentments and latent frustrations. He has to get them out. So let him march sometime; let him have his prayer pilgrimages to the city hall; understand why he must have sit-ins and freedom rides. If his repressed emotions do not come out in these nonviolent ways, they will come out in ominous expressions of violence. This is not a threat; it is a fact of history. So I have not said to my people, "Get rid of your discontent." But I have tried to say that this normal and healthy discontent can be channeled through the creative outlet of nonviolent direct action. Now this approach is being dismissed as extremist. I must admit that I was initially disappointed in being so categorized.   27

But as I continued to think about the matter I gradually gained a bit of satisfaction from being considered an extremist. Was not Jesus an extremist in love? "Love your enemies, bless them that curse you, pray for them that despitefully use you." Was not Amos an extremist for justice— "Let justice roll down like waters and righteousness like a mighty stream." Was not Paul an extremist for the gospel of Jesus Christ—"I bear in my body the marks of the Lord Jesus." Was not Martin Luther an extremist— "Here I stand; I can do none other so help me God." Was not John Bunyan an extremist—"I will stay in jail to the end of my days before I make a butchery of my conscience." Was not Abraham Lincoln an extremist—"This nation cannot survive half slave and half free." Was not Thomas Jefferson an extremist—"We hold these truths to be self evident that all men are created equal." So the question is not whether we will be extremist but what kind of extremist will we be. Will we be extremists for hate or will we be extremists for love? Will we be extremists for the preservation of injustice—or will we be extremists for the cause of justice? In that dramatic scene on Calvary's hill three men were crucified. We must never forget that all three were crucified for the same crime—the crime of extremism. Two were extremists for immorality, and thus fell below their environment. The other, Jesus Christ, was an extremist for love, truth, and goodness, and thereby rose above His environment. So, after all, maybe the South, the nation, and the world are in dire need of creative extremists. 28

I had hoped that the white moderate would see this. Maybe I was too optimistic. Maybe I expected too much. I guess I should have realized that few members of a race that has oppressed another race can understand or appreciate the deep groans and passionate yearnings of those that have been oppressed, and still fewer have the vision to see that injustice must be rooted out by strong, persistent, and determined action. I am thankful, however, that some of our white brothers have grasped the meaning of this social revolution and committed themselves to it. They are still all too small in quantity, but they are big in quality. Some like Ralph McGill, Lillian Smith, Harry Golden, and James Dabbs have written about our struggle in eloquent, prophetic, and understanding terms. Others have marched with us down nameless streets of the South. They have languished in filthy, roach-infested jails, suffering the abuse and brutality of angry policemen who see them as "dirty nigger lovers." They, unlike so many of their moderate brothers and sisters, have recognized the urgency of the moment and sensed the need for powerful "action" antidotes to combat the disease of segregation. 29

Let me rush on to mention my other disappointment. I have been so greatly disappointed with the white Church and its leadership. Of course there are some notable exceptions. I am not unmindful of the fact that each of you has taken some significant stands on this issue. I commend you, Rev. Stallings, for your Christian stand on this past Sunday, in welcoming Negroes to your worship service on a non-segregated basis. I commend the Catholic leaders of this state for integrating Springhill College several years ago. 30

But despite these notable exceptions I must honestly reiterate that I have been disappointed with the Church. I do not say that as one of those negative critics who can always find something wrong with the Church. I say it as a minister of the gospel, who loves the Church; who was nurtured in its bosom; who has been sustained by its spiritual blessings and who will remain true to it as long as the cord of life shall lengthen. 31

I had the strange feeling when I was suddenly catapulted into the leadership of the bus protest in Montgomery several years ago that we would have the support of the white Church. I felt that the white ministers, priests, and rabbis of the South would be some of our strongest allies. Instead, some have been outright opponents, refusing to understand the freedom movement and misrepresenting its leaders; all too many others have been more cautious than courageous and have remained silent behind the anesthetizing security of stained glass windows.   32

In spite of my shattered dreams of the past, I came to Birmingham with the hope that the white religious leadership of this community would see the justice of our cause and, with deep moral concern, serve as the channel through which our just grievances could get to the power structure. I had hoped that each of you would understand. But again I have been disappointed.   33

I have heard numerous religious leaders of the South call upon their worshippers to comply with a desegregation decision because it is the law, but I have longed to hear white ministers say follow this decree because integration is morally right and the Negro is your brother. In the midst of blatant injustices inflicted upon the Negro, I have watched white churches stand on the sideline and merely mouth pious irrelevancies and sanctimonious trivialities. In the midst of a mighty struggle to rid our nation of racial and economic injustice, I have heard so many ministers say, "Those are social issues with which the Gospel has no real concern," and I have watched so many churches commit themselves to a completely other-worldly religion which made a strange distinction between body and soul, the sacred and the secular.   34

So here we are moving toward the exit of the twentieth century with a religious community largely adjusted to the status quo, standing as a tail light behind other community agencies rather than a headlight leading men to higher levels of justice.   35

I have travelled the length and breadth of Alabama, Mississippi, and all the other Southern states. On sweltering summer days and crisp autumn mornings I have looked at her beautiful churches with their spires pointing heavenward. I have beheld the impressive outlay of her massive religious education buildings. Over and over again I have found myself asking: "Who worships here? Who is their God? Where were their voices when the lips of Governor Barnett dripped with words of interposition and nullification? Where were they when Governor Wallace gave the clarion call for defiance and hatred? Where were their voices of support when tired, bruised, and weary Negro men and women decided to rise from the dark dungeons of complacency to the bright hills of creative protest?"   36

Yes, these questions are still in my mind. In deep disappointment, I have wept over the laxity of the Church. But be assured that my tears have been tears of love. There can be no deep disappointment where there is not deep love. Yes, I love the Church; I love her sacred walls. How could I do otherwise? I am in the rather unique position of being the son, the grandson, and the great grandson of preachers. Yes, I see the Church as the body of Christ. But, oh! How we have blemished and scarred that body through social neglect and fear of being nonconformist.   37

There was a time when the Church was very powerful. It was during that period when the early Christians rejoiced when they were deemed worthy to suffer for what they believed. In those days the Church was not merely a thermometer that recorded the ideas and principles of popular opinion; it was a thermostat that transformed the mores of society. Wherever the early Christians entered a town the power structure got disturbed and immediately sought to convict them for being "disturbers of the peace" and "outside agitators." But they went on with the conviction that they were a "colony of heaven" and had to obey God rather than man. They were small in number but big in commitment. They were too God-intoxicated to be "astronomically intimidated." They brought an end to such ancient evils as infanticide and gladiatorial contest.   38

Things are different now. The contemporary Church is so often a weak, ineffectual voice with an uncertain sound. It is so often the arch-supporter of the status quo. Far from being disturbed by the presence of the Church, the power structure of the average community is consoled by the Church's silent and often vocal sanction of things as they are.   39

But the judgment of God is upon the Church as never before. If the Church of today does not recapture the sacrificial spirit of the early Church, it will lose its authentic ring, forfeit the loyalty of millions, and be dismissed as an irrelevant social club with no meaning for the twentieth century. I am meeting young people every day whose disappointment with the Church has risen to outright disgust.   40

Maybe again I have been too optimistic. Is organized religion too inextricably bound to the status quo to save our nation and the world? Maybe I must turn my faith to the inner spiritual Church, the church within the Church, as the true *ecclesia* and the hope of the world. But again I am thankful to God that some noble souls from the ranks of organized religion have broken loose from the paralyzing chains of conformity and joined us as active partners in the struggle for freedom. They have left their secure congregations and walked the streets of Albany, Georgia, with us. They have gone through the highways of the South on torturous rides for freedom. Yes, they have gone to jail with us. Some have been kicked out of their churches and lost the support of their bishops and fellow ministers. But they have gone with the faith that right defeated is stronger than evil triumphant. These men have been the leaven in the lump of the race. Their witness has been the spiritual salt that has preserved the true meaning of the Gospel in these troubled times. They have carved a tunnel of hope through the dark mountain of disappointment.   41

I hope the Church as a whole will meet the challenge of this decisive hour. But even if the Church does not come to the aid of justice, I have no despair about the future. I have no fear about the outcome of our struggle in Birmingham, even if our motives are presently misunderstood. We will reach the goal of freedom in Birmingham and all over the nation, because the goal of America is freedom. Abused and scorned though we may be, our destiny is tied up with the destiny of America. Before the pilgrims landed at Plymouth, we were here. Before the pen of Jefferson etched across the pages of history the majestic words of the Declaration of Independence, we were here. For more than two centuries our fore-parents labored in this country without wages; they made cotton "king"; and they built the homes of their masters in the midst of brutal injustice and shameful humiliation—and yet out of a bottomless vitality they continued to thrive and develop. If the inexpressible cruelties of slavery could not stop us, the opposition we now face will surely fail. We will win our freedom because the sacred heritage of our nation and the eternal will of God are embodied in our echoing demands.   42

I must close now. But before closing I am impelled to mention one other point in your statement that troubled me profoundly. You warmly commended the Birmingham police force for keeping "order" and "preventing violence." I don't believe you would have so warmly commended the police force if you had seen its angry violent dogs literally biting six unarmed, nonviolent Negroes. I don't believe you would so quickly commend the policemen if you would observe their ugly and inhuman treatment of Negroes here in the city jail; if you would watch them push and curse old Negro women and young Negro girls; if you would see them slap and kick old Negro men and young Negro boys; if you will observe them, as they did on two occasions, refuse to give us food because we wanted to sing our grace together. I'm sorry that I can't join you in your praise for the police department.   43

It is true that they have been rather disciplined in their public handling of the demonstrators. In this sense they have been rather publicly "nonviolent." But for what purpose? To preserve the evil system of segregation. Over the last few years I have consistently preached that non-violence demands that the means we use must be as pure as the ends we seek. So I have tried to make it clear that it is wrong to use immoral means to attain moral ends. But now I must affirm that it is just as wrong, or even more so, to use moral means to preserve immoral ends. Maybe Mr. Connor and his policemen have been rather publicly nonviolent, as Chief Prichett was in Albany, Georgia, but they have used the moral means of nonviolence to maintain the immoral end of flagrant racial injustice. T. S.

Eliot has said that there is no greater treason than to do the right deed for the wrong reason.   44

I wish you had commended the Negro sit-inners and demonstrators of Birmingham for their sublime courage, their willingness to suffer, and their amazing discipline in the midst of the most inhuman provocation. One day the South will recognize its real heroes. They will be the James Merediths, courageously and with a majestic sense of purpose, facing jeering and hostile mobs and the agonizing loneliness that characterizes the life of the pioneer. They will be old, oppressed, battered Negro women, symbolized in a seventy-two year old woman of Montgomery, Alabama, who rose up with a sense of dignity and with her people decided not to ride the segregated buses, and responded to one who inquired about her tiredness with ungrammatical profundity: "My feets is tired, but my soul is rested." They will be young high school and college students, young ministers of the gospel and a host of the elders, courageously and nonviolently sitting in at lunch counters and willingly going to jail for conscience sake. One day the South will know that when these disinherited children of God sat down at lunch counters they were in reality standing up for the best in the American dream and the most sacred values in our Judeo-Christian heritage, and thus carrying our whole nation back to great wells of democracy which were dug deep by the founding fathers in the formulation of the Constitution and the Declaration of Independence.   45

Never before have I written a letter this long (or should I say a book?). I'm afraid that it is much too long to take your precious time. I can assure you that it would have been much shorter if I had been writing from a comfortable desk, but what else is there to do when you are alone for days in the dull monotony of a narrow jail cell other than write long letters, think strange thoughts, and pray long prayers?   46

If I have said anything in this letter that is an overstatement of the truth and is indicative of an unreasonable impatience, I beg you to forgive me. If I have said anything in this letter that is an understatement of the truth and is indicative of my having a patience that makes me patient with anything less than brotherhood, I beg God to forgive me.   47

I hope this letter finds you strong in the faith. I also hope that circumstances will soon make it possible for me to meet each of you, not as an integrationist or a civil rights leader, but as a fellow clergyman and a Christian brother. Let us all hope that the dark clouds of racial prejudice will soon pass away and the deep fog of misunderstanding will be lifted from our fear-drenched communities and in some not too distant tomorrow the radiant stars of love and brotherhood will shine over our great nation with all of their scintillating beauty.   48

Yours for the cause of Peace and Brotherhood
Martin Luther King, Jr.

AMERICAN CENTURY

LEOPOLD TYRMAND

Voices are to be heard sounding a despondent note concerning America's disappointing historical performance and consequent decline. America-haters, both outside and inside the country, outdo one another in making gloomy predictions and preaching America's inevitable failure. One of them, a distinguished Briton, has said, not without *Schadenfreude,* "This is not going to be the American century. Very few people are enamored of the American way of life." The gentleman is perfectly right in expressing doubt about the future. This need not be said to be *going* to be an American century, because it already *is* one, and has been almost from its beginning. It became American not through cohorts and legions, not through anything that rules the waves, not through the exporting of a homemade revolution but through its glorious share in the two most important wars of liberation that mankind has experienced, and its unheard-of position, in both, as the principal winner who did not annex one single inch of the soil of its defeated foes. Neither tanks and cannon and a constant readiness to use them nor an unlimited, never-before-seen economic magnitude is what denotes an American century, but, rather, an unprecedented civilizational influence upon the rest of humanity. Hence the gentleman's grave error. To check how wrong he is, he has but to look around his native England and recognize how thoroughly Americanized it has grown during the last twenty-five years—how many American words have become indispensable to his native language, how many people from London, Glasgow, and Dublin have opted for the American way of life. The objection that they make this choice merely because America is richer and pays better wages has no validity, for if one country is more affluent than another and provides better rewards to those who work for it, this testifies to a superiority that, if it was not achieved by conquest, must have stemmed from the skills and the quality of its people and from its institutions. However, re-sourcefulness and industriousness cannot explain the evident fact that there exist few places on this planet where little boys do not play cowboys and bigger boys do not sing rock and roll, where the word "Hollywood" has never been pronounced or "Star Dust" hummed or the New York skyline seen either on the screen or in illustrations. No one forces human-ity to watch American movies, listen to American music, dance American dances, read American books, and wear American clothes. Nevertheless, all over the world these products of American civilization are best-selling items. If the gentleman were only aware of the piety with which some Europeans today listen to a ragtime tune totally forgotten in America, of how well acquainted they are with American history, of the fanatical curiosity with which they leaf through old American illustrated magazines, he would probably understand what the phrase "American century" means. In the Communist empire, as a matter of fact, people are persecuted for their craving for Americanism, and the persecution only intensifies the craving, endows everything American with greater magic, and gives names like Max Factor, Coca-Cola, and William Faulkner more content than the names of Lenin, Socialism, and Sholokhov. Charlie Chaplin's California and Gary Cooper's Wild West have become the world's most romantic landscapes for several generations on five continents, and countless millions have melted in tears at the end of "West Side Story," although no one sheds tears anymore on reaching the end of "Romeo and Juliet." As M. de Talleyrand once said, "I do not say it is good, I do not say it is bad, I say it is the way it is."   1

For me, the idea of an American century has a deeper meaning. We are now witnessing a strange exodus from Communist-dominated Eastern Europe. People are fleeing, inconspicuously but in very large numbers, from martyred Czechoslovakia; from Poland, held in a neo-Nazi grip; from lethargic Hungary. Many of them might do better on several continents that are ready to provide them with material opportunities infinitely superior to the daily hardship of American competition. Nevertheless, the most coveted prize in life's lottery is free entry into the United States. One can find among the arrivals from Eastern Europe political rascals who have devoted the past twenty-five years to besmirching America and its institutions, to lying about this country, to slandering it according to the most insolent and obscurantist Communist gospel. Yet it is here that they seek refuge. This act of providing enemies with shelter shines through the moral darkness enveloping our epoch and does more than anything else to bestow on it the title "American."   2

Suggestions for Writing

1 Answering the question "Why?"—and thus using the technique of cause and effect—write an essay explaining why you accept (or do not accept) one of the following generalizations:
   a The business of education is to improve the moral condition of mankind.
   b "The artist's business is to see and to show, not answer why."— Archibald MacLeish
   c "An unjust law is no law at all."—St. Augustine, as quoted by Martin Luther King, Jr.
   d "Old friends are best."—John Selden

    e "Be slow in choosing a friend, slower in changing."—Benjamin Franklin

    f The life of man on earth is one long tragedy.

2 Using the method of cause and effect, develop any one of the following topics in an extended essay:

    a The causes (or effects) of racial prejudice

    b The effects of the ethnic patterns in my home state

    c "The risks involved in a democratic society are to be preferred to the security or stability provided in a monarchical or totalitarian one."

    d Why men seek power (money, fame)

    e Why clowns are funny

    f Why I prefer to live in a small town (large city)

    g The results of studying too much (too little) science

SYNTHESIS: A COMBINATION OF THE METHODS

It must be recognized that the methods of analysis that have been studied separately are most often used in combination with one another. Although it is both important and necessary to isolate an individual method of analysis so that it can be closely observed and clearly understood, it is also important to observe how the methods of analysis are combined by a careful writer in a given essay. This kind of synthesis is essential for a thorough understanding of the essentials of prose composition. Even though the major intention of each preceding section has been to concentrate on a single method, the introductions to these sections and the questions in the text have also emphasized the way one method of analysis may be used in combination with others. This section provides a special opportunity for the study and observation of a variety of methods of analysis in combination. It will also help us to review our understanding of the use of the individual methods already studied. And it should underscore the crucial fact, so often referred to, that any good writing is, in a sense, the sum of all its parts.

In "The Romantic Generation" (page 316) Peter F. Drucker explains why students of today, unlike those of the 1950s, are inner-directed rather than outer-directed—are interested "in personal (if not spiritual) values, rather than . . . social utility or community mores." After an introduction in which he uses personal narrative, in paragraphs 4 through 9 he shows how much of the literature read by the students of today illustrates their inner-directions; the use of such illustration also clarifies Drucker's definition of "inner-direction." In paragraph 6, he classifies some of the characteristics of the literature. In paragraphs 28 and 30 he briefly employs process analysis (how some modern organizations function). The footnote questions which we have provided for this essay will direct your attention to Drucker's use of the other methods of analysis, such as comparison and contrast and cause and effect.

In "The Indispensable Opposition" (page 325), Walter Lippmann explains why the opposition, in a political sense, is indispensable for the continuing success of a real democracy. Since he is dealing with such controversial terms as "liberty of opinion" and "freedom of speech," we can expect him, as a careful writer, to use definition frequently to establish the meaning of such terms for the reader. His very first paragraph, for example, defines "political freedom." It is not surprising that in paragraphs 3, 4, 9, 13, 17, and 19 he repeats and extends the definition of this term, so essential for our adequate understanding of the essay. And it is logical that he should make a significant effort in the first nine paragraphs to point out the deficiencies in the commonly accepted notion, "a naively self-righteous view" as he calls it, that political freedom is a matter of toleration. In order to make what he considers the correct definition of "political freedom" more graphic, he quite naturally introduces an example, "the natural means of producing conviction." The story of the patient and the physician is an illustration of an extended example, used in much the same way as the example in David Riesman's "Tootle: A Modern Cautionary Tale." Lippmann's application of the creative principle of freedom of speech to the system of public speech in a totalitarian state is a well-worked-out instance of process analysis. It explains *how* the essential process of give and take of opinion works in a nondemocratic state.

These two essays very obviously demonstrate what has been true of the essays covered to this point: a "pure" use of any one of the methods of analysis will rarely be found. The study of the methods of analysis singly and then in combination should be an effective means for learning the character of each within actual writing situations.

THE ROMANTIC GENERATION

PETER F. DRUCKER

"I am Mother O'Rourke," the voice on the telephone said. "I am Dean of Students at a large Catholic women's college. Mother President and all our faculty very much hope that you will accept our invitation to talk to our girls on social issues and their importance. Ten years ago our students were deeply interested in labor relations, international relations, and in other major social and political problems. Now they care only for matters of conscience and personal behavior, such as civil rights, a 'personal philosophy of life,' or the size of their own future family and how to raise it. That's wonderful, of course, and we are all for it. But economic and political questions still exist and are far from solved. The girls surely ought to know something about them and not just concern themselves all the time with their little selves and their own conscience."   1

A dean trying to con a prospective speaker (especially if there is no fee) has no more truth in him than a Texas wildcatter raising sucker money. Yet Mother O'Rourke's call pulled together for me a lot of observations that have made me question the accepted picture of an important group of today's young adults—the men and women between twenty and twenty-five who are in college or graduate school. This picture, it seems to me, does not fit at all the influential, though not very large, group which sets the intellectual fashions on campuses from San Diego State to the Harvard Yard.   2

"Everybody knows" for instance that these educated young adults have discarded the Protestant Ethic of their forefathers. And ever since David Riesman's brilliant book *The Lonely Crowd* in 1950, it has been almost an axiom that the young American is increasingly outer-directed. But when I hung up, after extricating myself from Mother O'Rourke's invitation, it suddenly dawned on me that many of the young Americans now in college and graduate school are searching for an ethic based on personal (if not spiritual) values, rather than on social utility or community mores—what one might call an Ecumenical Ethic. The old ideologies and slogans leave these young adults cold—as does President Johnson's Great Society. But there is a passionate groping for personal commitment to a philosophy of life. Above all, a new inner-directedness is all the rage in this group.*   3

The clearest symptom of this is, perhaps, the books that are the fashion on campus. Undergraduates and graduate students alike read a great deal of what one of them—a teaching assistant in history—aptly calls "Instant Zen." They read Erich Fromm. They devour those two apparently incompatible but actually complementary pamphleteers: (1) Paul Goodman (*Growing Up Absurd, Utopian Essays*), a latter-day Thoreau opposed to society and all its work whose Walden Pond is the graduate psychology department; and (2) Ayn Rand (*Fountainhead, Atlas Shrugged,* and a new book, just out, *The Virtue of Selfishness*), a Nietzsche of the NAM, preaching the organization superman. And they read Sartre. (Despite their professed interest in Existentialism, they tend to consign Camus to the limbo of "required reading"; his very compassion, generosity and concern for his fellowman make him suspect as a "classic.")   4

Ever since adolescence was invented two hundred years ago, in Goethe's *Young Werther* (incidentally the first international bestseller), it has always had a literature it claimed for its very own. Salinger's *Catcher in the Rye*—another *Young Werther*, though one living in an affluent society which can afford salvation by psychoanalysis, instead of by suicide

* Paragraph 3: In the first sentence, why does the author place "Everybody knows" in quotation marks? Why might "an ethic based on personal (if not spiritual) values" be called "an Ecumenical Ethic"?

as in Goethe's book—was the "in" book of the young adults ten years ago. Our grandmothers hid in their bosoms tear-stained albums of Swinburne's slightly rancid sensuality. Generations of levelheaded, no-nonsense New England girls have got drunk on the low-calorie carbonated syrup of Kahili Gibran's The Prophet. Generations of equally levelheaded European boys, diligently preparing to be German engineers or French customs inspectors, have swooned over Stendhal's passionately passionless male Lolitas. When my own generation reached young adulthood around 1930, T. S. Eliot's The Waste Land and the early Donne were our Bibles; we missed the H. L. Mencken and Nietzsche fashions by only a few years.*   5

The specific authors and books of the campus fashion thus vary greatly from one generation to the other—and not only in their literary merits. But the whole genre has common characteristics. It is naïvely sentimental, for instance, or saturated with the bittersweet sadness the Germans call Weltschmerz (and which only the very healthy, vigorous, and hopeful—that is the young—can afford). They tend to wallow in self-pity (in which department The Sorrows of Young Werther still holds the unchallenged world record). The idols of every campus generation have always been against everything and for nothing. The twenty-year-olds, after all, while mature in body and mind, are still exempted from responsibility—are indeed being encouraged in the pleasant delusion that Daddy will take care of everything, whether they smash an automobile fender or an institution.†   6

This literature always reflects the mood of its generation. It is the young adult's own, precisely because it says what he feels but is unable to express himself. These books do not talk to their reader; they talk for him. Even though ephemeral—and, often enough, trash—the books faithfully mirror how the campus generation of the moment sees itself, or at the least how it wants to see itself.   7

The books of this kind in fashion today are contemptuous of, if not hostile to, society and its demands, values, and rewards. They proclaim that truth can be found only in one's own inner experience, and that the demands of one's own personal conscience are a trustworthy guide to behavior and action. Sartre is "in"—as Camus is not—because only the cocoon of his own words and thoughts exists for him.   8

The "moderate" among these authors today is clearly Erich Fromm, the neo-Freudian psychoanalyst. He plays in today's campus culture the role that Reinhold Niebuhr played thirty years ago. Niebuhr even then

---

* Paragraphs 4 and 5: What method of analysis is used in these two paragraphs?

† Paragraph 6: What is "the whole genre" referred to in the second sentence? In giving some "common characteristics" of the genre, what method of analysis is the author using?

warned against forgetting the person and his spiritual needs. But he was the idol of the young because in those days he preached the "social gospel" of public responsibility and liberal reform. Fromm today, by contrast, warns against forgetting community and society; but he is accepted because his main stress is on the person and his relationship to himself. Niebuhr asked, What society do you, as a moral man, want? Fromm asks, What kind of person do you want to be? Like the other writers who speak for the young adults—from "Instant Zen" to Paul Goodman and Ayn Rand—Fromm is self-centered.   9

There are a good many other symptoms of the new "inner-directedness." The vogue of the word "sincerity" is one. To the older generation this is an embarrassing word; we remember the appeasers and quislings of thirty years ago saying, "At least Hitler is *sincere.*" But to today's young adult "sincerity" is again a valid, if not the ultimate, test of behavior, especially in public life. I listened a year ago to some graduate students, bright and well-informed, discussing an all-night teach-in at Columbia University. They were not a bit interested in logic or in the arguments, let alone in the factual assertions of the various speakers. All they wanted to know was, "Do you think he was sincere?"   10

A related phenomenon is the current interest in the "mind drugs" such as LSD. Whatever else they do, the hallucinations they produce are entirely self-centered inner experiences of one's own consciousness, with no outside world, no other person, no relationships in them.   11

On a mountain hike last summer—a few weeks after Mother O'Rourke's telephone call—a psychologist friend began to talk about the "management problems" of a Midwestern mental-health center which trains postgraduate students in sizable numbers to become psychiatrists, psychologists, and social workers.   12

"To what do you attribute these management problems," I interrupted. "Your growth?"   13

"We have grown of course very rapidly—fourfold since 1950," he answered. "But this is a minor factor. Our big problem is the radical shift in student attitude. The men who came to us ten or fifteen years ago wanted to be scientists. They were research-oriented. They got upset when they found out that in psychology or psychiatry empirical data and scientific theory are not enough. We had to hammer home day after day that the practitioner always deals with a unique human being, his emotions, aspirations, experiences, values—and that the practitioner himself is a human being too.   14

"The men we get today are scientifically much better trained as a rule. But they tend to be frustrated clergymen who only come to us because there is no ecumenical, nondenominational seminary around. We have to tell them every day that fulfilling oneself, compassion, and love for one's neighbor aren't enough—indeed, will do damage unless supported by empirical facts and buttressed by sound theory. The men we got ten or fifteen years ago were out to find the facts; the men we get today are out to find themselves."*   15

What explains such a shift from the outer-directed student of the 1950s to the inner-directed student of today?   16

One cause is certainly the disenchantment of this particular group of young people with the traditional social issues. However important they may be, such issues are not very exciting in the 1960s. It is hard for anybody to get up much emotional steam about the pension demands of the newspaper unions. And who is the "wicked imperialist" in the conflict between India and Pakistan? Indeed, most social problems have ceased to be "issues" and have become "fields of study." Where they used to call for passion leading to commitment and action, they now call for hard, plodding work leading to a Ph.D. thesis. And very few Ph.D. theses have ever fired the imagination and engrossed the emotions even of the men who wrote them, let alone of a generation of young people.   17

A second factor is that there are so many more graduate students in pursuit of a higher degree. The emergence and rapid growth of a distinct graduate-student community fosters emphasis on "inner experience," on "sincerity," and on the search for a "personal philosophy." Many graduate students have an outsized guilt feeling and therefore need an inner-directed ethic to justify themselves to themselves.   18

In part, they need a rationalization for their economic status. Most graduate students, while far from rich, live well above the poverty line. Their income, however, comes from fellowships or grants rather than from wages. If there is a wage earner in the family it is the wife rather than the husband. As consumers they are part of the affluent society. But as producers they are outside of it. Some graduate students are so self-conscious about this that they seriously advocate the payment of regular wages for going to graduate school. But many more search for an ethic which would base economic reward on what work means to a man and contributes to his self-development, rather than on its social utility and its value to others.†   19

Above all, however, the graduate student needs such an inner-directed ethic to rationalize his own motives. To be sure, love of scholarship is the main motivation for some, others are attracted by the rewards which our economy offers the man with advanced specialized training. But a good many graduate students know perfectly well that they decided to stay in school in large part because grants and fellowships made it

---

* Paragraphs 12 through 15: What purpose do these paragraphs serve with relation to paragraphs 10 and 11?

† Paragraph 19: How is the view expressed in the last sentence of this paragraph related to what the author has said up to this point?

easy. Often they secretly suspect that they use graduate school as a pleasant way to postpone growing up, with its many commitments and decisions. Others are in graduate school for the sake of the draft exemption—and they cannot help knowing it. When they talk about their reasons for staying on in school—and they talk about them on and on and on—they therefore tend to stress "self-fulfillment," "sincerity," "basic values," and "personal philosophy of life."   20

Though going on to graduate school is fast becoming the correct thing to do in the better colleges, the graduate-school community is quite small—maybe half a million people at any one time, counting the students, their wives, and children. This group however has influence out of all proportion to its size. It is highly concentrated in a very few large universities—such as the University of California at Berkeley, Harvard, MIT, Cal Tech, New York University, Chicago, and Stanford. As a result it tends to dominate the prestige schools, which are of course the pace-setters and fashion makers for the entire academic world, faculty as well as students. Indeed, for the first time—in the Berkeley riots and in a good many of the teach-ins—graduates rather than undergraduate students took the lead.   21

The great catalyst of the new mood has of course been the civil-rights campaign. It gave the campus generation the Cause it had been waiting for: a cause of conscience. The young people are much closer in their views on civil rights to the abolitionists of a century ago than they are to yesterday's liberals. The oppression of the Negro is to them a sin rather than a wrong. "We Shall Overcome" has the ring of a gospel hymn rather than that of a *New Republic* editorial. This explains in large part the tremendous impact the civil-rights movement has had on the mood, vision, and world-view of the campus generation. In addition, civil rights has offered scope for individual initiative and effectiveness, something our society otherwise does not readily grant to men or women in their early twenties. These are the students, white and colored, who have gone South to teach in the Freedom Schools. There are the white college girls up North who in considerable numbers venture into the meanest Negro ghettos of the big cities to tutor or counsel, often entirely on their own.* 22

Yet developments in this country alone cannot explain the shift in mood. It is by no means an American phenomenon. It is indeed going on in all industrially developed countries, regardless of race or political and economic systems. In both Western and Eastern Europe those apostles of inner-directedness, the American Beat poets such as Allen Ginsberg, are extraordinarily popular. The Idol of Russia's university students is Yevgeni Yevtushenko—a poet of the individual conscience, before which society is all but irrelevant. And the one mass movement in any industrial

* Paragraph 22: In the second sentence, why is "Cause" capitalized?

country today that has attracted large numbers of the college generation is the Japanese Soka Gakkai—half religious fundamentalism preaching the absolute primacy of inner experiences, half political fanaticism with "sincerity" its only slogan.   23

Fashions—especially adolescent fashions—do not as a rule outlast their generation. There is just a slim chance, however, that the mood of this campus generation will prove to be one of the rare exceptions: a first premonition of a change in the consciousness and vision of modern man.   24

The present disinterest on campus in social problems may possibly —just barely possibly—be a first hint that the conventional social issues are increasingly becoming red herrings. Terms such as "management and labor," the "concentration of economic power," or "big government" all assume that there are a few big organizations in a society which is otherwise relatively power-free. But actually in our society all social tasks tend to ball together into large and complex organizations of tremendous power.   25

The institution that has grown the most in this century is not in the economic or political sphere at all. It is the university. There is actually more concentration of brainpower in the twenty largest universities than there ever was a concentration of economic power in the heyday of the Morgans and the Rockefellers, before the passage of the antitrust laws. The hospital has also become big and complex—and so has the Catholic Diocese in the modern metropolis, the American Medical Association, the armed forces, the civil service, and so on. The fact of big, complex organization, rather than this or that embodiment of it, is now the matter of central significance. To single out any one institution as *the* organization is to make impossible an understanding of the issue, let alone a solution. 26

This, I think, is beginning to be felt. Or is it pure coincidence that we recently had two totally unconnected revolts against organizational power structures which were never before seen as problem areas: the Berkeley student riot and the attack on the Roman bureaucracy of the Catholic Church at the Vatican Council, especially in its first two sessions before Pope John's death?*   27

The big complex modern organization does indeed present a number of strange problems. In the first place, there is plenty of evidence that we do not yet really know how to make it work or how to control it. It tends to be overadministered but undermanaged, tends to mistake procedures and "proper channels" for direction and energy. The student riots at Berkeley were greatly aggravated by management malfunctioning and

---

* Paragraph 27: Does the author believe that the two revolts he cites here occurred as the result of "pure coincidence"?

by a ludicrous failure of communications within a very small top-management group sitting in adjoining offices. Yet Clark Kerr, the university's president, is one of the most accomplished professional managers in the country. Similarly, management malfunctioning and communications failure seem to have greatly aggravated the grievances of the Catholic bishops against the Roman Curia.   28

Even more important, of course, is the new set of problems which confronts a society of big organizations—their relationship to each other and to the common good; their effective control by government; the effective control of government by the public and its representatives; and the power, authority, and responsibility of these institutional monsters.   29

Despite everything Paul Goodman—one of the heroes of the campus —has been saying in his all-out attacks on the very idea of organization, we will not do away with it. On the contrary we clearly need more large organizations—for the task of running the modern metropolis, for instance, and for a good many new jobs in the international community such as the policing and traffic control of outer space. But despite everything Miss Ayn Rand—another hero of the campus—has been saying, the problems of the big organization will not disappear if only we give free rein to the superman executive. McNamaras and Hammarskjölds (not to mention the executive-suite Genghis Khans of Miss Rand's *Atlas Shrugged*) are in very short supply.*   30

The problems of the big organization demand new political theory and new social policy. At the moment, indeed, both politics and society require greater skill and greater responsibility precisely because no generally accepted and understood theory is available to statesmen and politicians. The example of Sartre and of some of the more extreme splinter groups of the student leftists show clearly, I submit, how fast in such a situation inner-directedness degenerates into irresponsibility. Yet one can also understand why the young might conclude that the major tasks in society are jobs for the professional, the political philosopher, and the social innovator, for which amateurs, such as they are, need not apply.   31

But a society of big organizations also raises in new and acute form the question of the person. What is his relationship to these new leviathans which are at one and the same time his servants and his master, his opportunity and his restraint, his tool and his environment? How can the individual maintain his integrity and privacy in such a society? Is individual freedom necessarily limited to whatever small air space will be left between the towering organizational skyscrapers? In such a society of big organizations, the need becomes more urgent for new answers to the old questions: "Who am I?" "What am I?" "What should I be?" These

---

* Paragraph 30: What method of analysis is used in this paragraph?

are questions the West has tended to consider either as solved or as unimportant, for the last few hundred years, while it put its main emphasis on the nature of matter rather than on the nature of man. But now these questions, the young may rightly feel, cannot be ignored. They are their own direct, personal concerns.   32

The present mood of the present campus generation is not without serious dangers. It is being exploited by some dubious people—on the Right and the Left—for political purposes of their own; but this, while undoubtedly a threat, may not be the major danger. For the present mood encourages irresponsibility. And the emphasis on "sincerity" might only too easily degenerate into adulation of that professional specialist in sincerity, the demagogue, or of the synthetic TV personality. Is it pure accident that California, the state most strongly influenced by the young adults and their fashions, is also the one state where TV or movie success seems increasingly to be accepted as adequate preparation for the job of Governor or U.S. Senator?   33

The present campus mood is above all drearily futile. Most of the rebels against big organization will end up—and very soon—as well-paid and fairly successful members of big organizations, whether big university, big government, or big business. They will then predictably impose their own emotional need for security and conformity on their organization, despite all their fine contempt for the Organization Man. The odds are astronomical against Instant Zen's fathering anything but another bull session.   34

Yet in its return to "inner-directedness," today's college crowd may, just may, play-act in their school years their homework as tomorrow's adults. The bull session may, for once, be awareness rather than echo. For once, today's young-adult fashions may foretell the concerns, and prefigure the intellectual landscape, of tomorrow.   35

The Whole Selection

1 How does paragraph 1 serve effectively as an introduction to the whole essay?

2 In paragraphs 17 through 22, the author makes considerable use of cause and effect. In which of these paragraphs is attention given dominantly to causes, and in which to effects? What other methods of analysis are used in these paragraphs?

3 In paragraph 22, the author says, "The oppression of the Negro is to them [the students of today] a sin rather than a wrong." Explain what this means in the light of the differences which the author sees between the students of today and those of the preceding generation.

4 What is the significance of the title of this essay?

THE INDISPENSABLE OPPOSITION

WALTER LIPPMANN

Were they pressed hard enough, most men would probably confess that political freedom—that is to say, the right to speak freely and to act in opposition—is a noble ideal rather than a practical necessity. As the case for freedom is generally put to-day, the argument lends itself to this feeling. It is made to appear that, whereas each man claims his freedom as a matter of right, the freedom he accords to other men is a matter of toleration. Thus, the defense of freedom of opinion tends to rest not on its substantial, beneficial, and indispensable consequences, but on a somewhat eccentric, a rather vaguely benevolent, attachment to an abstraction.* 1

It is all very well to say with Voltaire, "I wholly disapprove of what you say, but will defend to the death your right to say it," but as a matter of fact most men will not defend to the death the rights of other men: if they disapprove sufficiently what other men say, they will somehow suppress those men if they can.† 2

So, if this is the best that can be said for liberty of opinion, that a man must tolerate his opponents because everyone has a "right" to say what he pleases, then we shall find that liberty of opinion is a luxury, safe only in pleasant times when men can be tolerant because they are not deeply and vitally concerned.‡ 3

Yet actually, as a matter of historic fact, there is a much stronger foundation for the great constitutional right of freedom of speech, and as a matter of practical human experience there is a much more compelling reason for cultivating the habits of free men. We take, it seems to me, a naïvely self-righteous view when we argue as if the right of our opponents to speak were something that we protect because we are magnanimous, noble, and unselfish. The compelling reason why, if liberty of opinion did not exist, we should have to invent it, why it will eventually have to be restored in all civilized countries where it is now suppressed, is that we must protect the right of our opponents to speak because we must hear what they have to say.§ 4

We miss the whole point when we imagine that we tolerate the freedom of our political opponents as we tolerate a howling baby next door, as

---

* Paragraph 1: How is "political freedom" defined? Is the definition explained? How? Why are the terms "right" and "toleration" distinguished from each other?

† Paragraph 2: Is the quotation from Voltaire relevant to the initial definition of "political freedom"?

‡ Paragraph 3: What makes "liberty of opinion" a "luxury"? Is "liberty of opinion" the same as "political freedom"?

§ Paragraph 4: How does the first sentence indicate that a contrast will now be made with what went before? Does the author disagree with the initial definition of "political freedom," or does he disagree with the interpretation of it?

we put up with the blasts from our neighbor's radio because we are too peaceable to heave a brick through the window. If this were all there is to freedom of opinion, that we are too good-natured or too timid to do anything about our opponents and our critics except to let them talk, it would be difficult to say whether we are tolerant because we are magnanimous or because we are lazy, because we have strong principles or because we lack serious convictions, whether we have the hospitality of an inquiring mind or the indifference of an empty mind. And so, if we truly wish to understand why freedom is necessary in a civilized society, we must begin by realizing that, because freedom of discussion improves our own opinions, the liberties of other men are our own vital necessity.*   5

We are much closer to the essence of the matter, not when we quote Voltaire, but when we go to the doctor and pay him to ask us the most embarrassing questions and to prescribe the most disagreeable diet. When we pay the doctor to exercise complete freedom of speech about the cause and cure of our stomachache, we do not look upon ourselves as tolerant and magnanimous, and worthy to be admired by ourselves. We have enough common sense to know that if we threaten to put the doctor in jail because we do not like the diagnosis and the prescription it will be unpleasant for the doctor, to be sure, but equally unpleasant for our own stomachache. That is why even the most ferocious dictator would rather be treated by a doctor who was free to think and speak the truth than by his own Minister of Propaganda. For there is a point, the point at which things really matter, where the freedom of others is no longer a question of their right but of our own need.†   6

The point at which we recognize this need is much higher in some men than in others. The totalitarian rulers think they do not need the freedom of an opposition: they exile, imprison, or shoot their opponents. We have concluded on the basis of practical experience, which goes back to Magna Carta and beyond, that we need the opposition. We pay the opposition salaries out of the public treasury.‡   7

In so far as the usual apology for freedom of speech ignores this experience, it becomes abstract and eccentric rather than concrete and human. The emphasis is generally put on the right to speak, as if all that mattered were that the doctor should be free to go out into the park and explain to the vacant air why I have a stomachache. Surely that is a miserable caricature of the great civic right which men have bled and died for. What really matters is that the doctor should tell *me* what ails me, that I should listen to him; that if I do not like what he says I should be free

---

* Paragraph 5: Point out one use of example. Tolerant people are divided on the basis of the cause of their tolerance; list these divisions.

† Paragraph 6: How does using an example get to the essence of the matter better than quoting Voltaire? Point out one instance of definition.

‡ Paragraph 7: What transitional word links paragraphs 6 and 7? How is contrast used?

to call in another doctor; and that then the first doctor should have to listen to the second doctor; and that out of all the speaking and listening, the give-and-take of opinions, the truth should be arrived at.   8

This is the creative principle of freedom of speech, not that it is a system for the tolerating of error, but that it is a system for finding the truth. It may not produce the truth, or the whole truth all the time, or often, or in some cases ever. But if the truth can be found, there is no other system which will normally and habitually find so much truth. Until we have thoroughly understood this principle, we shall not know why we must value our liberty, or how we can protect and develop it.*   9

II

Let us apply this principle to the system of public speech in a totalitarian state. We may, without any serious falsification, picture a condition of affairs in which the mass of the people are being addressed through one broadcasting system by one man and his chosen subordinates. The orators speak. The audience listens but cannot and dare not speak back. It is a system of one-way communication; the opinions of the rulers are broadcast outwardly to the mass of the people. But nothing comes back to the rulers from the people except the cheers; nothing returns in the way of knowledge of forgotten facts, hidden feelings, neglected truths, and practical suggestions.†   10

But even a dictator cannot govern by his own one-way inspiration alone. In practice, therefore, the totalitarian rulers get back the reports of the secret police and of their party henchmen down among the crowd. If these reports are competent, the rulers may manage to remain in touch with public sentiment. Yet that is not enough to know what the audience feels. The rulers have also to make great decisions that have enormous consequences, and here their system provides virtually no help from the give-and-take of opinion in the nation. So they must either rely on their own intuition, which cannot be permanently and continually inspired, or, if they are intelligent despots, encourage their trusted advisers and their technicians to speak and debate freely in their presence.   11

On the walls of the houses of Italian peasants one may see inscribed in large letters the legend, "Mussolini is always right." But if that legend is taken seriously by Italian ambassadors, by the Italian General Staff, and

---

* Paragraph 9. What is summarized here? What pivotal sentence defines freedom of speech? How is freedom of speech related to "political freedom"? Why does a summary paragraph appear relatively early in the essay?

† Paragraph 10: What method of analysis is chiefly used in this paragraph? How do we know this from the first sentence? What transitional phrase connects paragraphs 9 and 10?

by the Ministry of Finance, then all one can say is heaven help Mussolini, heaven help Italy, and the new Emperor of Ethiopia.   12

For at some point, even in a totalitarian state, it is indispensable that there should exist the freedom of opinion which causes opposing opinions to be debated. As time goes on, that is less and less easy under a despotism; critical discussion disappears as the internal opposition is liquidated in favor of men who think and feel alike. That is why the early successes of despots, of Napoleon I and of Nepoleon III, have usually been followed by an irreparable mistake. For in listening only to his yes men— the others being in exile or in concentration camps, or terrified—the despot shuts himself off from the truth that no man can dispense with.   13

We know all this well enough when we contemplate the dictatorships. But when we try to picture our own system, by way of contrast, what picture do we have in our minds? It is, is it not, that anyone may stand up on his own soapbox and say anything he pleases, like the individuals in Kipling's poem who sit each in his separate star and draw the Thing as they see it for the God of Things as they are. Kipling, perhaps, could do this, since he was a poet. But the ordinary mortal isolated on his separate star will have an hallucination, and a citizenry declaiming from separate soapboxes will poison the air with hot and nonsensical confusion.   14

If the democratic alternative to the totalitarian one-way broadcasts is a row of separate soapboxes, then I submit that the alternative is unworkable, is unreasonable, and is humanly unattractive. It is above all a false alternative. It is not true that liberty has developed among civilized men when anyone is free to set up a soapbox, is free to hire a hall where he may expound his opinions to those who are willing to listen. On the contrary, freedom of speech is established to achieve its essential purpose only when different opinions are expounded in the same hall to the same audience.   15

For, while the right to talk may be the beginning of freedom, the necessity of listening is what makes the right important. Even in Russia and Germany a man may still stand in an open field and speak his mind. What matters is not the utterance of opinions. What matters is the confrontation of opinions in debate. No man can care profoundly that every fool should say what he likes. Nothing has been accomplished if the wisest man proclaims his wisdom in the middle of the Sahara Desert. This is the shadow. We have the substance of liberty when the fool is compelled to listen to the wise man and learn; when the wise man is compelled to take account of the fool, and to instruct him; when the wise man can increase his wisdom by hearing the judgment of his peers.*   16

* Paragraphs 14 through 16: What method of analysis is used chiefly in these paragraphs? Why is it appropriate here? What examples reinforce the dominant method?

That is why civilized men must cherish liberty—as a means of promoting the discovery of truth. So we must not fix our whole attention on the right of anyone to hire his own hall, to rent his own broadcasting station, to distribute his own pamphlets. These rights are incidental; and though they must be preserved, they can be preserved only by regarding them as incidental, as auxiliary to the substance of liberty that must be cherished and cultivated.   17

Freedom of speech is best conceived, therefore, by having in mind the picture of a place like the American Congress, an assembly where opposing views are represented, where ideas are not merely uttered but debated, or the British Parliament, where men who are free to speak are also compelled to answer. We may picture the true condition of freedom as existing in a place like a court of law, where witnesses testify and are cross-examined, where the lawyer argues against the opposing lawyer before the same judge and in the presence of one jury. We may picture freedom as existing in a forum where the speaker must respond to questions; in a gathering of scientists where the data, the hypothesis, and the conclusion are submitted to men competent to judge them; in a reputable newspaper which not only will publish the opinions of those who disagree but will reëxamine its own opinion in the light of what they say.*   18

Thus the essence of freedom of opinion is not in mere toleration as such, but in the debate which toleration provides: it is not in the venting of opinion, but in the confrontation of opinion. That this is the practical substance can readily be understood when we remember how differently we feel and act about the censorship and regulation of opinion purveyed by different media of communication. We find then that, in so far as the medium makes difficult the confrontation of opinion in debate, we are driven towards censorship and regulation.†   19

There is, for example, the whispering campaign, the circulation of anonymous rumors by men who cannot be compelled to prove what they say. They put the utmost strain on our tolerance, and there are few who do not rejoice when the anonymous slanderer is caught, exposed, and punished. At a higher level there is the moving picture, a most powerful medium for conveying ideas, but a medium which does not permit debate. A moving picture cannot be answered effectively by another moving picture; in all free countries there is some censorship of the movies, and there would be more if the producers did not recognize their limitations by avoiding political controversy. There is then the radio. Here debate is difficult: it is not easy to make sure that the speaker is being answered

---

* Paragraph 18: Account for the difference in the examples used here from the long example introduced in paragraph 6.

† Paragraph 19: Why does the author define his major topic again? Compare this definition with the ones given in paragraphs 1, 3, 4, 9, 13, and 17.

in the presence of the same audience. Inevitably, there is some regulation
of the radio.   20

When we reach the newspaper press, the opportunity for debate is so
considerable that discontent cannot grow to the point where under normal
conditions there is any disposition to regulate the press. But when newspapers abuse their power by injuring people who have no means of reply-
ing, a disposition to regulate the press appears. When we arrive at Congress we find that, because the membership of the House is so large, full
debate is impracticable. So there are restrictive rules. On the other hand,
in the Senate, where the conditions of full debate exist, there is almost
absolute freedom of speech.   21

This shows us that the preservation and development of freedom of
opinion are not only a matter of adhering to abstract legal rights, but
also, and very urgently, a matter of organizing and arranging sufficient
debate. Once we have a firm hold on the central principle, there are many
practical conclusions to be drawn. We then realize that the defense of
freedom of opinion consists primarily in perfecting the opportunity for an
adequate give-and-take of opinion; it consists also in regulating the freedom
of those revolutionists who cannot or will not permit or maintain debate
when it does not suit their purposes.*   22

We must insist that free oratory is only the beginning of free speech;
it is not the end, but a means to an end. The end is to find the truth.
The practical justification of civil liberty is not that self-expression is one
of the rights of man. It is that the examination of opinion is one of the
necessities of man. For experience tells us that it is only when freedom of
opinion becomes the compulsion to debate that the seed which our fathers
planted has produced its fruit. When that is understood, freedom will be
cherished not because it is a vent for our opinions but because it is the
surest method of correcting them.   23

The unexamined life, said Socrates, is unfit to be lived by man. This
is the virtue of liberty, and the ground on which we may best justify our
belief in it, that it tolerates error in order to serve the truth. When men
are brought face to face with their opponents, forced to listen and learn
and mend their ideas, they cease to be children and savages and begin to
live like civilized men. Then only is freedom a reality, when men may
voice their opinions because they must examine their opinions.   24

III

The only reason for dwelling on all this is that if we are to preserve
democracy we must understand its principles. And the principle which

---

* Paragraphs 20 through 22: What purpose, considering the meaning of the essay, do the
examples herein serve? What specific sentence helps the reader to answer this question?
Where is cause and effect used briefly?

distinguishes it from all other forms of government is that in a democracy the opposition not only is tolerated as constitutional but must be maintained because it is in fact indispensable.*   25

The democratic system cannot be operated without effective opposition. For, in making the great experiment of governing people by consent rather than by coercion, it is not sufficient that the party in power should have a majority. It is just as necessary that the party in power should never outrage the minority. That means that it must listen to the minority and be moved by the criticisms of the minority. That means that its measures must take account of the minority's objections, and that in administering measures it must remember that the minority may become the majority.   26

The opposition is indispensable. A good statesman, like any other sensible human being, always learns more from his opponents than from his fervent supporters. For his supporters will push him to disaster unless his opponents show him where the dangers are. So if he is wise he will often pray to be delivered from his friends, because they will ruin him. But, though it hurts, he ought also to pray never to be left without opponents; for they keep him on the path of reason and good sense.†   27

The national unity of a free people depends upon a sufficiently even balance of political power to make it impracticable for the administration to be arbitrary and for the opposition to be revolutionary and irreconcilable. Where that balance no longer exists, democracy perishes. For unless all the citizens of a state are forced by circumstances to compromise, unless they feel that they can affect policy but that no one can wholly dominate it, unless by habit and necessity they have to give and take, freedom cannot be maintained.   28

The Whole Selection

1 Why does the author begin his essay by discussing an interpretation of political freedom with which he disagrees?
2 Repetition is a useful and familiar rhetorical device for securing unity, coherence, and emphasis. Point out places in this essay where it is used to achieve each of these principles of good composition.
3 "Abstract" and "concrete" are two words used by the author in the writing of the essay that have some relevance to his method of presentation. Where in the essay is he "abstract," and where is he "concrete,"

* Paragraph 25: Into what classification does "democracy" fit? How is it divided from the other members of its class? Could the meaning of "democracy," as divided from the other members of its class, become a new classification that could be further divided?

† Paragraph 27: What is the topic sentence of this paragraph? What purpose does the example serve?

in his analysis of the subject? Discuss the aptness of his being one or the other in the particular instances discovered.

4 In what ways does freedom of speech make censorship and regulation necessary?

5 The author uses many examples. Are they all of the same kind? Citing two or three particular instances, show how each is successful or not successful in accomplishing its purpose.

THE IMAGE OF CULTURE

RICHARD M. WEAVER

No one can deny that there is widespread discussion of the decline of Western culture, however much opinions of the realities involved may differ. This has been present in philosophical works for more than half a century; the shock of the First World War brought it into more popular organs of discussion, and today one may encounter it, though usually in frivolous forms, in the columns of daily newspapers. That the idea has not merely persisted but has seeped increasingly into the modern consciousness is itself a cultural and social fact of great importance which cannot be overlooked among the signs of the times.　　　　1

Attempts to dismiss the idea often take the easy route of attributing it to temperamental pessimism or some other condition of the critic. It is alleged that those who say our culture is decaying are those who regularly take an apprehensive view of the future, or they are those who have lost their nerve amid the complexities of an age of transition, or they are those who suffer from nostalgia. The presence of such persons, it is argued, is not peculiar to this age, and hence their warnings are not to be taken as a serious sign that our way of life is deteriorating. The properly constituted man adopts the red-blooded attitude toward things; he goes along with changes because he realizes that change and progress are the law of life and that, although some valued institutions may be disappearing, they will more than be made up for by new ones that are in the process of creation. The upholders of this view retort, in brief, that the world instead of growing worse is growing better and that it is really one's civic duty to believe this and to proclaim it.　　　　2

Thus two largely antithetical views are regularly placed before the public. It is well to see that both of these views are capable of support. One can argue that our culture is in serious decline, and one can argue that it is flourishing and improving. But both arguments cannot be equally valid. Whenever large-scale tendencies are being examined, facts taken from a superficial level and facts taken from a profound one may conflict or point in opposite directions. Like two air masses, one moving at ground level and one moving at a high altitude, they can for awhile pursue opposite courses. If one reads from the top level of phenomena, one may get many signs of assurance which will be contradicted by a look lower down. The real issue in this controversy, then, is one of depth of implication. Yet there can be no implication at all unless one is willing to contemplate an order of human values. The nature and proper end of man are central to any discussion, not only of whether a certain culture is weakening, but also of whether such a culture is worth preserving. It is when we look at the depth of implication that we see the real difference between the parties to this argument.   3

Those who contend that things are going well enough or are improving are found to be nonserious, in the sense of refusing to look at serious things. They glean their data from the novel, or flashy, or transitory sort of development, which often does indicate a sort of vitality, but shows at the same time a lack of direction and a purposelessness. Their data are likely to be the kind that can be quantified in the style of the social scientists or at least of the publicist—so many more people owning record players, so many more books circulating from public libraries, and the like. They ignore the deep sources of tendency which can very easily render nugatory any gains of the above kind. In short, their fact-finding is superficial and simplistic, and their claims are made sometimes in a strident tone which is itself a demerit to their case.   4

Moreover, it is certain that some if not many of the defenders of this optimistic position have a vested interest in "progress," or the present trend of things. A continuation of this trend means for them reputation and money, and they fall in with it as supporters who expect to be rewarded. There are many disintegrative processes which are immediately profitable to those engaged in promoting them, and it is human weakness to covet even such ill-gotten rewards. Therefore it is not hypercritical to look closely at the situation of those who argue for the excellence of modernism to see whether they stand to profit in practical ways from these developments. Not only advertising and journalism but considerable areas of education now invite this kind of scrutiny.   5

When we turn to the other view, we find that it is made up predominantly of persons who are concerned with the nature of man and the problem of value. They are people with definite ideas of right and wrong, possessing the faculty of taste and consciences which can be offended. Furthermore, they usually will be historically informed with the result that to them novelty is not always originality nor a fresh departure toward a new horizon. If they are conservative, it is because they have learned the truth of the maxim, "The good is hard," and they know how tempting it is to try to circumvent this. It is my observation that these people suffer a great deal, and their suffering is sometimes used to condemn them, as if failure to achieve complacency were an indictable thing. But it is only those who are capable of discrimination and of feelings *against* things who can be the custodians of culture. Accordingly, I am satisfied that T. S. Eliot made a true appraisal of our times in asserting that "our own period is one of decline; that the standards of culture are lower than they were fifty years ago; and that the evidences of this decline are visible in every department of human activity." [1]   6

[1] T. S. Eliot, *Notes Toward the Definition of Culture* (New York, 1949), 17.

Another way of understanding this conflict of opinion is to recognize that the "optimists" have the current rhetoric on their side even while the "pessimists" have the proof. The modern world has a terrific momentum in the direction in which it is going, and many of the words of our everyday vocabulary are terms implicit with approval of modern tendencies. To describe these tendencies in the language that is used most widely is to endorse them, whereas to oppose them is to bring in words that connote half-forgotten beliefs and carry disturbing resonances. Thus the signs and probabilities are with the optimists, and their task of expression is an easy one, since they have so many ready-made terms at hand. They have the rhetorician's advantage of a language in circulation and a set of "prejudices" in the mind of the majority. It is the object of this writing to bring a rhetoric along with a proof to show that the present course of our culture is not occasion for complacency but for criticism and for possible reconstruction. This requires meeting a rhetoric derived from circumstances with one based more on definition and causal analysis.   7

I anticipate the further objection that all ages are ages of anxiety just because all ages are in some respect ages of transition. Since transition is a passage to the unknown, a degree of apprehensiveness over what is tentative, unformed, and uncertain is natural. There is some truth in this generalization, yet it would be as absurd to say that every period in the history of a culture is equally healthy and fruitful as to say that every period in the life of an individual is equally happy. It would in fact be intellectual and moral skepticism to deny that some periods are distinct as crises, and the troubled consciousness of modern man gives ample ground for believing that ours is such a period.   8

The need then is great for a revisionist view of what is known as modernism. The mindless approval of everything modern—indeed, of each dissolution of an old pattern—as something better than what preceded it, or acceptance of the Spenglerian thesis of inevitable decay, massive and intellectually serious as this is, does not constitute a true dilemma for the man who wishes to orient himself with reference to the culture of our time. There is the answer of some third alternative, involving basic principles and leading through free will and effort to some creative results. The imagination of the time cannot, at least, leave this possibility unexamined. 9

One more thing needs to be said about the relation of a critic to his culture. There is an opinion, by no means easy to refute, that culture is like a brotherhood: either you are of it or you are not. If you are of it, you can do something about it to the extent of carrying it on by living according to its prescriptions. If you are not of it, there is nothing you can do about it, except perhaps describe it from a distance while missing the real *Innigkeit*. On this assumption there is no such thing as aiding a culture from the outside or of aiding it consciously in any way. If you belong to it, you live in and by it; if you are outside it, you find the gulf impassable, except to certain superficial contacts. "Culture is culturing," and when a culture has lost its will to live, outside ministrations are of no use.   10

But in a further view, there is more than one way of being outside a culture. One can be outside it simply in the sense of having been born outside its pale and of having received no nurture through it. People in this position constitute the kind of "foreigners" the Greeks called *barbaroi*—"those speaking a different language." Certainly not to speak the language of a culture, in the figurative sense, is to suffer effective disbarment. These persons are alien, even when they belong to another culture of high development. The man of a different culture has different intellectual and moral bearings, and except in the case of gifted individuals having long periods to assimilate, there is no crossing over, nor any real desire for it. The men of another culture are outsiders, and one expects no more from them than from a friendly stranger, although there is sometimes critical value in an outside view.   11

There is another type of outsider, however, who may entertain hope of doing something about a culture that is weakening. He is a member of the culture who has to some degree estranged himself from it through study and reflection. He is like the *savant* in society; though in it, he is not wholly of it; he has acquired knowledge and developed habits of thought which enable him to see it in perspective and to gauge it. He has not lost the intuitive understanding which belongs to him as a member, but he has added something to that. A temporary alienation from his culture may be followed by an intense preoccupation with it, but on a more reflective level than that of the typical member. He has become sufficiently aware of what is outside it to see it as a system or an entity. This person may be a kind of doctor of culture; in one way he is crippled by his objectivity, but in another way he is helped to what he must have, a point of view and a consciousness of freedom of movement.   12

It has been observed, to cite a kind of parallel, that nearly all of the leaders of strong nationalistic movements in the present age were men who had some type of "outside" experience in their rearing or their education. They were men who knew their nations from the inside, but who had also seen them from a vantage point elsewhere. Thus it was with Parnell and Ireland, with Sun Yat-sen and China, with Hitler and Germany, with Gandhi and India. Even Franco is a "Gallego"—not a Spaniard in the true sense. These men had all at one time been far enough removed from their future nations to see what these were, and what they saw engendered in them an urge to define the reality and the consciousness of that nationhood. Although they were "doctors" of nationalism rather than "doctors" of culture, their case shows enough analogy to provide guiding points here. The man who is simply a carrier of his culture may not be armed in the same way to do something about it when it flags. His role may be too much that of simply acting; he can keep in stride, but he cannot coach. For diagnostic and remedial work we may have to turn to those who have in a way mutilated themselves by withdrawal, by a special kind of mental discipline, and by the kind of fixation upon a task which even impedes free cultural participation.[2] We may therefore regard it as no anomaly, but rather as an understandable event, if a person not conspicuously cultured himself should discern what is impairing the health of a culture. Thus it is not the person who has contributed most to a culture who will necessarily have the most useful things to say when the culture shows signs of dissolution.   13

But what can this person, who is not a paragon of the culture, but who finds himself profoundly stirred by its uneasy situation, actually contribute? From his mixed position he probably can recognize the hostile or disruptive forces. Like the doctor again, he cannot make the object of his attention live, but he can combat those things which would keep it from living. He can point out: this is a disease, this is a poison, this is a bad diet. If the inimical conditions are removed and if there is a true vitality, the sufferer should recover. There are, of course, limits of the analogy of a human culture to an organism, yet culture is a creation in the world, and it must obey certain fundamental conditions of existence.   14

A radical perspective on the subject may even start with the question of whether culture as such is something we ought to cherish and defend. It would be uncritical to assume that the answer has always been affirmative. Now and in the past culture in the sense meant here has had to meet open and covert hostility. Certain religions have been largely hostile to it; moralists have condemned it as a frivolity or an indulgence; men of business have been impatient with its demands and its "extravagance"; statesmen of a certain type have opposed it as producing "effeminacy." At present there is a fairly widespread feeling that culture "costs too much" in the sense of gratifying certain educated appetites at considerable expense

---

[2] An example of this is often seen in the relation of the academic person to the culture in which he lives. He may be and often is learned in it, but he is not exactly of it. I have felt more than once that this fact is proved by the peculiar explicitness of the speech of college professors. They are usually at great pains to draw out the meaning of their phrases and to verbalize all the connections of thought. Some of this may result from the habit of simplifying things for youthful learners, but this is not the whole account of it. In the speech of a culture maintained by a traditional society, there will occur many elisions and ellipses of meaning. It is not necessary to state them, because anyone can supply the omissions; it is rather the awkwardness of pedantry to put them into words. But the man who is outside the tradition, or who is self-consciously halfway between the tradition and something else, goes about it in a different way: its beliefs, values, and institutions are "objects" to him, and he refers to them with something of the objective completeness of the technical description. This is why professors "sound so funny" when they talk of something that is an everyday subject to the ordinary man. The ordinary man wonders why the professor, instead of using lumbering phrases to designate the obvious, cannot assume more. It may also explain why professors as a class are suspected of dissidence. Their speech does not sound like the speech of a person who is perfectly solid with his tradition, which is oftentimes the case.

while the masses are deprived. If the friends of culture were to allow the matter to be put to a popular vote, they might still win, but I do not think that the size of the majority would be reassuring. The public of today does not understand clearly either the nature or the role of culture, and general literacy has not helped the situation.   15

The claim of culture as such to exist is best explained through its genesis. Man is a special creature in the respect that he has to live with two selves. One of these is his existential part, his simple animal being, which breathes and moves and nourishes itself. This is man without quali- fication or adornment, an organism living in an environment. In this ex- istence he is a very predictable animal—or would be except that the second self can have effects upon his somatic appearance and behavior. 16

The second self is an image which he somehow evolves from his spirit. It is made up of wishes and hopes, of things transfigured, of imaginations and value ascriptions. It is a picture to which the subjective part of our being necessarily gives a great deal, and hence the danger of trying to read it literally from external facts. A culture expresses itself very extensively through artistic creation, and, as Suzanne Langer has pointed out in her *Problems of Art,* we cannot infer artistic vision from a symptom. That is to say, a mere noting of details without insight and some construc- tive use of the imagination will not produce an understanding of a culture. 17

It appears that even the most primitive people have this urge to depict themselves in some fashion. Without the picturization, man feels an unendurable nakedness in the face of his environment and before the questions of life. From such poverty he rescues himself through projec- tions that include the natural environment and whatever is suggested by his spirit regarding the mystery that broods over creation. Look beneath the surface of the most brilliant cultures of history, and you find a hunger and a wonderment, reaching even to a kind of melancholia. Nietzsche has shown how this impelled the Greeks to create their splendid world of illu- sion in myth and art. Impulses of like kind can be found beneath the efflorescence of Elizabethan England. The more man is impressed with the tragic nature of his lot, the more he dramatizes his relation with the world. A strain of artist in the race causes it to reach out in proportion as its awareness deepens and to throw up great protective creations.   18

This great yearning of man to be *something* in the imaginative sense, that is, to be something more than he is in the simple existential way or in the reductionist formula of materialism, is both universal and proper to him. The latter may be asserted because he is the only creature who asks the question why he is here and who feels thwarted in his self-realization until some kind of answer is produced. This urge to be representative of something higher is an active ingredient of his specific humanity; it has created everything from the necklace of animal teeth with which the primitive adorns his body to the elaborate constructions which the men of high cultures have made to interpret the meaning of life and their mission in it. This is the point at which he departs from the purely utilitarian course and makes of himself a being with significance. It is a refutation of all simplistic histories and psychologies, but it is one of the most verifiable facts about man.   19

No one has been able to define exactly how a culture integrates and homologizes the ideas and actions of many men over a long period of time any more than how the consciousness gives a thematic continuity to the life of an individual. As far as one can tell, the collective consciousness of the group creates a mode of looking at the world or arrives at some imaginative visual bearing. It "sees" the world metaphorically according to some felt need of the group, and this entails an ordering which denotes dissatisfaction with "things as they are." Of course, cultures do respond to differences in what nature has provided, such as the sea, or a kind of terrain, or a hot or cold climate, these having the power to initiate imaginative reactions. But man meets the given part way, and then proceeds with something of his own. So cultures reflect different regions and varying kinds of historical endowment. But the decisive thing is the work of the spirit, which always operates positively by transfiguring and excluding. It is of the essence of culture to feel its own imperative and to believe in the uniqueness of its worth. In doing so, it has to reject others which are "objectively" just as good, yet for it irrelevant. Syncretistic cultures like syncretistic religions have always proved relatively powerless to create and to influence; there is no weight of authentic history behind them. The very concept of eclectic religion and eclectic culture derives from an inappropriate analogy which suggests that a plurality can be greater than one. Culture derives its very desire to continue from its unitariness. Perhaps some deep force which explains our liking for figures of repetition is here involved; we feel confirmed through seeing things repeated in the same way, and departures from the form are viewed as laxity or ignorance.   20

Evidently this is the reason that every culture in the course of its formation sets up directions from which the members are constrained not to depart. Penalties for violation may be no more than cultural, although sometimes they have been moral and legal. The truth is that if the culture is to assume form and to bring the satisfactions for which cultures are created, it is not culturally feasible for everyone to do everything "any way he wants to." There is at the heart of every culture a center of authority from which there proceed subtle and pervasive pressures upon us to conform and to repel the unlike as disruptive. So culture too is faced with the metaphysical problem of freedom and organization, which rules out the possibility of uncircumscribed liberty. Like all forces which shape and direct, it must insist on a pattern of inclusion and exclusion. This is a

necessity of integral being and a fundamental fact to deal with in any plan
for its protection.   21

At this center there lies a "tyrannizing image," which draws everything toward itself. This image is the ideal of its excellence. The forms that
it can take and the particular manifestations that it can find are various. In
some instances it has been a religious ritual; in others a sacred scripture;
in others a literature which everyone is expected to know; codes of conduct
(and even of warfare) may be the highest embodied form. But examine
them as we will, we find this inward facing toward some high representation. This is the sacred well of the culture from which inspiring waters like
magnetic lines of force flow out and hold the various activities in a subservience of acknowledgment. Not to feel this magnetic pull toward identification and assimilation is to be outside the culture.   22

Such centripetalism is the essence of culture's power to cohere and
to endure. There is a center which commands all things, and this center is
open to imaginative but not logical discovery. It is a focus of value, a law
of relationships, an inspiriting vision. By its very nature it sets up rankings
and orders; to be near it is to be higher; to be far from it in the sense of
not feeling its attraction is to be lower. Culture is thus by nature aristocratic, for it is a means of discriminating between what counts for much
and what counts for little; this no doubt explains the necessity man feels
to create it. It is his protest against the uniformity and dead level of simple
succession. He *will* establish a center of value and see to it that the group
is oriented toward it. This is his rejection of any merely naturalistic ordering of his life, his declaration of independence from mere environment.
Discrimination, selection, and preference with regard to the tyrannizing
image are its constitutives.   23

For this reason it is the very nature of culture to be exclusive. Without the power to reject that which does not understand or acknowledge its
center of force, it would disintegrate. We might say that a culture continues by attracting and attracts by continuing. In this way it maintains
its identity. There can be no such thing as a "democratic" culture in the
sense of one open to everybody at all times on equal terms. To *know* the
right thing, without mediating thoughts as to what and when, is to be
native born to the culture. An individual absorbs his native culture as he
acquires his native tongue, with the most subtle shades of intonation;
again, like the idioms of a language, the ways of a culture are rooted too
deep in immemorial bias and feeling to be analyzed. If a culture appears
arbitrary in the preferences it makes and the lines it draws, this is because
it is a willed creation.   24

The truth most important for us to recognize in our present crisis is
this principle of integration, and exclusiveness. There is for all things, as
Aristotle pointed out, an entelechy, a binding, type-determining factor,

which gives to a thing its specific form and property of coherence. The
fact that a culture is a spiritual and imaginative creation does not mean
that it is any less bound by this pervading law. Just as the skin of a sound
fruit protects it from dispersion or evaporation, so the form of a culture
keeps it from ceasing to exist through a miscellaneous commingling. Form
is intellectual and negative; it sets boundaries which affirm in the very
process of denying. The form of a culture is its style, which it asserts
against the world of meaningless "democratic" existence. In a highly developed culture this sense of style permeates everything; it is in dress and
manners, in art and institutions, in architecture and cookery. It imparts
tone to the whole of society by keeping before its members a standard of
the right and not right. But this form depends upon the centripetal image
of an ideal of perfection and goodness and upon confidence in ruling out
what is unlike or fortuitous.   25

The task of the conservative in our time is to defend this concentration and to expose as erroneous attempts to break down the discrimina-
tions of a culture. For once the inward-looking vision and the impulse to
resist the alien are lost, disruption must ensue. What was a whole ceases
to feel its reason for being a whole, and the different parts may suffer a
random distortion—random just because there is no longer a unifying idea
to prescribe fitness and size. Parts then get out of line and begin to
usurp the places and roles belonging to other parts. This is the chaos that
the true friend of culture beholds with deepest apprehension, not only
because it deprives him of so much but because in the masses it can
induce monstrous outbursts of irrationality. All men, and not merely the
sensitive and the gifted, need the integrating service of this vision,
although not all realize that they need it. Lancelot Law Whyte in his *Next
Development in Man* has vividly expressed the power of this urge:

> Man abhors the absence of integration. He demands integration, and
> will create religions, achieve heroic self-sacrifice, pursue mad ambitions,
> or follow the ecstasy of danger rather than live without. If society
> refuses him this satisfaction in constructive form, he will seize a
> destructive principle to which he can devote himself and will take
> revenge on the society which thought his only demand was pleasure.
> Vice, in this sense, shows the integrating power of virtue, of which it
> is merely the negative form. The mass-man readily rejected the utili-
> tarian philosophy which had created him and accepted in its place the
> new mass religion of national suicide.[3]

The final sentence, written with reference to the fascist movements of
Europe, reminds us that if no reasonable cultural unification is offered, an
unreasonable one may be invented and carried to frightful lengths.   26

[3] Lancelot Law Whyte, *The Next Development in Man* (New York, 1948), 188.

The greatest perversion of culture in our time is a misconception of the role of democracy. As the preceding definition makes clear, a culture integrates a people qualitatively. Under the widely current misconception, it is supposed that democracy can integrate them as quantitative units— that is, as units without relation to the value structure of the ideal. The most pressing duty of the believer in culture today is to define democracy and keep it within its place, in doing which he not only will preserve it as a viable form but also will protect those other areas of activity which are essential to supply a different kind of need.   27

Democracy is not a pattern for all existence any more than a form of economic activity is a substitute for the whole of living. Truly considered, democracy is nothing more than an ideal of equity among men in their political relationships. Its roots are in the truth that every individual has an inviolable personality, a private experience, and an authentic voice. Every individual is a reporter of what affects him, and he offers motions, as it were, concerning the general political welfare. To make this possible, a democratic state decrees a certain limited equality among its citizens. Even so, this equality is more theoretical than actual. But theories of this kind may have their practical usefulness as well as their noble objects. Thus in a parliamentary assembly we might give each speaker ten minutes to express his views, although we know that one man can say more in ten minutes than another can in an hour. Still, the equality serves the larger purpose. And so with democracy in its consulting of opinions and its counting of votes.   28

But democracy has to do with citizenship, and as Ortega has pointed out in one of his trenchant essays, our citizenship is the most insipid of our qualities. It concerns the things we have to get done in order to be in position to do things higher in the scale. It is account-keeping or household management, an essentially low order of practical activity. It is better to do this well than poorly, and it should be done with equity to the individuals involved. But it is senseless to say that dutiful household management is the highest commission of man and that whatever proves instrumental in this must be our principle of ordering all social and cultural life. In our present confusion over the role of culture, this is what is being done with the limited concept "democracy."   29

When democracy is taken from its proper place and is allowed to fill the entire horizon, it produces an envious hatred not only of all distinction but even of all difference. The ensuing distortion conceals its very purpose, which is to keep natural inequalities from obtruding in the one area where equality has intelligible function. The reason we consent to treat men as equals in this area of activity is that we know they are not equals in other areas. The fanatical democrat insists upon making them equal in all departments, regardless of the type of activity and vocation. It is of course the essence of fanaticism to seize upon some fragment of truth or value and to regard it as the exclusive object of man's striving. So democracy, a valuable but limited political concept, has been elevated by some into a creed as comprehensive as a religion or a philosophy, already at the cost of widespread subversion.   30

Ortega has wisely pointed out that this is not the spirit of true democracy, but of plebeianism. It exalts the very things that democracy was hopefully inaugurated to combat in the ranks of the people.

> The initial result is the wounding of the very sentiment which gave rise to democracy: for the concept of democracy springs from the desire to save the plebs from their low condition. But the doctrinaire democrat, who has converted a technique, democracy, into an end, soon finds himself sympathizing with the plebs precisely because of their plebeianism—their customs, manners, and intellectual tone. An example of this is the socialist creed (for we are dealing here with a creed, a secular religion) which has for one article of faith the dogma that only a proletarian head is fit for true science and reformed morality.[4]   31

Today we are being asked to accept "democratic living." The eulogistic tone with which this phrase is pronounced invites the question of whether this could be the "tyrannizing image" of some new culture. The answer is "no," if by democracy one means simple communism. Now there are in fact some places where a large measure of equality is in effect among the members without prejudice to the cultural life which they support. Such is true of the communities of some religious orders, where, for example, no outward discrimination is made between those who carry on the work of teaching and those who look after maintenance. It is true also of some educational institutions where the students do a large part of the work; no real distinction is made between those who hold "white collar" jobs and those who labor in the cow barns. Anyone who has visited such a community knows that the social atmosphere there is most agreeable and relaxing. But when one studies the impulse that sustains them, one realizes that the democracy is made possible by a consecration to and a hierarchy of purpose. In the religious communities it is of course the service of the religion; in the schools it is the furtherance of education. Nobody pretends that in these areas all are equal. There is selection according to ability, vocation, and dedication. This structure of purpose and calling is really the insurer of the democracy that exists; equality is maintained where it is useful because there is an overriding aim to be served. If this overriding aim were conceivably withdrawn, it is easy to picture even such communities breaking up into competitive pressure groups among "unequals." It is the authority of the mission which they carry on that keeps

[4] José Ortega y Gasset, "Morbid Democracy," *Modern Age* (Summer, 1957), 54.

inequalities of service in a manageable and pleasing order. Thus the cohesiveness of such communities lies in the idea that informs and possesses them.   32

What I have here spoken of as true of small associations bears analogy with peoples and nations: a culture is a means of uniting society by making provision for differences. Differences do not create resentment unless the seed of resentment has been otherwise planted. A just man finds satisfaction in the knowledge that society has various roles for various kinds of people and that they in the performance of these roles create a kind of symphony of labor, play, and social life. There arises in fact a distinct pleasure from knowing that society is structured, diversified, balanced, and complex. Blind levelers do not realize that people can enjoy seeing things above them as well as on a plane with them. Societies with differentiation afford pleasure to the moral imagination as an aesthetic design affords rest to the eye. The propaganda of egalitarianism encourages belief that any society embodying distinctions must necessarily be torn with envy and hatred. But theory does not show and empirical observation does not discover that societies having a proper internal differentiation are unhappy. On the contrary, they may be reposeful and content. Of a number of examples which could be used to support this, I choose one described by Goethe in *Poetry and Truth.* Commenting on the Germany in which he had grown up, this great poet and philosopher of life—"Europe's wisest head"—had this to say:

> The tranquillized condition of Germany, of which my native town had formed a part for more than a century, had remained intact in spite of many wars and convulsions. The existence of the most varied social grades, including as they did the highest as well as the lowest, the Emperor as well as the Jew, instead of separating the various members, seemed rather to unite them; and this condition of things was conducive to a feeling of contentment.[5]

Goethe, whose insight told him the true nature of the French Revolution while many of the romantics and rationalists were still befooled, was not deceived by the effect of classes.   33

> In Germany it had hardly occurred to anyone yet to look with envy on this vast privileged class, or to grudge its obviously worldly advantages. The middle classes had quietly devoted themselves to commerce and the sciences, and by these pursuits, as well as by the practice of the mechanical arts, had raised themselves to a position of importance which fully compensated their political inferiority; the free or partially free cities encouraged their activities, so that members of these classes were able to lead lives of peace and comfort. The man who increased

[5] Goethe, *Poetry and Truth From My Life* (2 vols.; London, 1913), II, 240.

his wealth or enhanced his intellectual influence, especially in matters of law or state, could always be sure of both respect and authority. In the Supreme Court of the Empire and elsewhere, the bench of nobles was faced by one of learned lawyers; the freer, less restricted outlook of the one worked in friendly harmony with the other, and not a trace of rivalry could be detected between them in everyday life. The noble felt secure in his exclusive and time-hallowed privileges, and the burgher felt it beneath his dignity to pretend to their possession by adding a prefix to his name.[6]

This was the Germany of poets, musicians, and philosophers. The classes thrived on a mutual dependence, and the principle of distinction, far from being felt as invidious, was the cement that held the whole together. One senses the kind of satisfaction that was felt in seeing different kinds of people to the right and left of one and, since it is in the nature of things, above and below. Not to be overlooked is the fact that a "lowest" class often finds satisfaction in knowing itself "superior" to other classes in certain respects—in hardihood, in industry, or in religiousness.   34

A society which is cohesive in this way, through classes which have developed naturally out of civic and cultural vocation, is in point of fact stronger than one which is undifferentiated. The latter tends to be inflexible and brittle; it does not have the internal give and take of the former. The inner organizations of a structural society act as struts and braces and enable it to withstand a blow which would shatter the other. The whole is sustained by its parts, which afford, as it were, a protection in depth. Nations composed of such societies have proved themselves very tough in international encounters. English society, despite a high degree of classness, has displayed intense patriotism and great power of endurance in crises. The society of the American South, which is formed somewhat upon the English model, has stood up under strong attacks and pressures from the outside through its sense of being organized. All the evidence shows that differentiation which is not fragmentation is a source of strength. But such differentiation is possible only if there is a center toward which the parts look for their meaning and validation. One of the functions of cultural activity is to objectify this center so that it will exist as an ever-present reminder of one's place and one's vocation. A high degree of cultural orientation is, accordingly, a symptom of a healthy society.   35

In brief, culture is an exclusive, which is to say, self-defining creation, which satisfies needs arising from man's feeling and imagination. Every culture has a kind of ontological basis in social life, and this social life does not express itself in equality, but in a common participation from different levels and through different vocations.   36

[6] *Ibid.*, II, 241.

Because of these facts and because of the political contentiousness of our time the question has actually been raised as to whether culture is "reactionary." The question itself reveals a confusion of categories which should never have been permitted. But we know from the words and deeds of Communists and their sympathizers that they make much of this subject and that they are prone to condemn artistic or cultural expression which deviates from their harsh political line. Now it is true, if one takes a very narrow and false view of progress, that much which the world has valued as culture could be condemned as "reactionary." For one thing, the very concept of culture runs counter to blind progressivism, by which I mean that state of mind which cannot measure anything except by number and linear extension. Since culture operates in the realm of quality and offers not greater magnitudes but more refined and intense sentiments, it is an engagement of the spirit lying beyond the thinking of those who have allowed their minds to be dominated by material categories. Speed and mass, virtually the slogans of contemporary Western civilization, are the antitheses of culture. The pointless series of "new developments" and expansions which the modern barbarian delights in look poor and hollow when placed beside authentic creations of the spirit. Since the two impulses move in opposite directions, the one does recede from the other. The barbarian, were he capable of a critical vocabulary, might brand what frustrates his kind of pleasure as "reaction." The possession of culture by historical elites gives some edge to this as a political weapon, but the charge of course mistakes the true gift brought by this creation of the spirit.   37

Under another aspect culture can be viewed as "reactionary" because it involves much ceremonial waste, which cannot be explained to those whose vision of life is merely economic and sensate.   38

This brings up the supremely important matter of style. All culture incorporates the idea of style, which is an homage to an intangible but felt need of the spirit. We hear references to "the modern style" in buildings and other creations where man customarily expresses his desire to impose order and design, yet this seems really to be a negation of style, relieved a little perhaps by imaginative attempts to suggest mass.   39

True style displays itself in elaboration, rhythm, and distance, which demand activity of the imagination and play of the spirit. Elaboration means going beyond what is useful to produce what is engaging to contemplation. Rhythm is a marking of beginnings and endings. In place of a meaningless continuum, rhythm provides intelligibility and the sense that the material has been handled in a subjective interest. It is human to dislike mere lapse. When one sees things in rhythmical configuration, he feels that they have been brought into the realm of the spirit. Rhythm is thus a way of breaking up nihilistic monotony and of proclaiming that there is a world of value. Distance is what preserves us from the vulgarity of immediacy. Extension and proportion in space, as in architecture, and extension in time, as in manners and deportment, help to give gratifying form to these creations. All style has in it an element of ritual, which signifies steps which cannot be passed over.   40

Today these factors of style, which are of the essence of culture, are regarded as if they were mere persiflage. Elaboration is suspected of spending too much on nonutilitarian needs, and the limited ends of engineering efficiency take precedence. Rhythm suffers because one cannot wait for the period to come around. In regard to distance, it is felt that there *should* be nothing between man and what he wants; distance is a kind of prohibition; and the new man sees no sanction in arrangements that stand in the way of immediate gratification. He has not been taught the subtlety to perceive that what one gains by immediate seizure one pays for by more serious losses. Impatience with space and time seems to be driving the modern to an increasing surrender of all ideas of order. Everywhere there is reversion to the plain and the casual, and style itself takes on an obsolescent look, as if it belonged to some era destined never again to appear.   41

It may be thought negligent that in this exposition I have made no reference to the now extensive studies of various cultures by anthropologists. The reason is that anthropological relativism is the chief quandary to be avoided in the kind of search that is undertaken here. The method of the anthropologists is descriptive, as everyone who has looked at their type of study knows. Essentially geographers and cataloguers of cultures, they are interested in a wide collection of particulars, so that their object could be summed up as *polymathein* rather than *polynoein:* to know much rather than to understand much. I may do some of them less than justice by this charge, yet it is by and large true. What I am certain of is that their practice constitutes a distraction for the one whose interest is in the value of culture and especially of his own culture.   42

For him the main object is to seize the formal *Innigkeit* of cultural expression and then to decide in what way his own is being menaced or vitiated. Thereafter he is in position to be both doctor and preacher, and indeed it is hard to conceive of a man's being thus interested in culture without feeling moved to proceed against its enemies.   43

I have pointed to the fact that a culture comes into being under the influence of a "tyrannizing" image or vision. I use the word "tyrannizing" hoping that it will be excused its sinister connotations and understood as meaning unifying and compelling. A culture then is a complex of values polarized by an image or idea. It cannot be perfectly tolerant or even tolerant to any large extent, because it lives by homogeneity. It therefore has to exclude on grounds which are cultural and not "rational" what does not comport with its driving impulse.   44

A grave danger arises when this principle is challenged by rationalistic thinkers, as is happening today. In speaking of a culture's power to influence and to bind I have more than once used the word "integrate," since a culture is something unitary gathered about the dominating idea. But "integration" and "segregation" are two sides of the same operation. A culture integrates by segregating its forms of activity and its members from those not belonging. The right to self-segregate then is an indispensable ground of its being. Enough has been said to show that our culture today is faced with very serious threats in the form of rationalistic drives to prohibit in the name of equality cultural segregation. The effect of this would be to break up the natural cultural cohesion and to try to replace it with artificial, politically dictated integration. Such "integration" would of course be a failure, because where deep inner impulse is lacking, cohesiveness for any length of time is impossible. This crisis has been brought to our attention most spectacularly in the attempt to "integrate" culturally distinct elements by court action. It is, however, only the most publicized of the moves; others are taking place in areas not in the spotlight, but all originate in ignorance, if not in a suicidal determination to write an end to the heritage of Western culture.   45

CIVIL DISOBEDIENCE (1849)

HENRY DAVID THOREAU

I heartily accept the motto,—"That government is best which governs least;" and I should like to see it acted up to more rapidly and systematically. Carried out, it finally amounts to this, which also I believe,—"That government is best which governs not at all;" and when men are prepared for it, that will be the kind of government which they will have. Government is at best but an expedient; but most governments are usually, and all governments are sometimes, inexpedient. The objections which have been brought against a standing army, and they are many and weighty, and deserve to prevail, may also at last be brought against a standing government. The standing army is only an arm of the standing government. The government itself, which is only the mode which the people have chosen to execute their will, is equally liable to be abused and perverted before the people can act through it. Witness the present Mexican war, the work of comparatively a few individuals using the standing government as their tool; for, in the outset, the people would not have consented to this measure.   1

This American government,—what is it but a tradition, though a recent one, endeavoring to transmit itself unimpaired to posterity, but each instant losing some of its integrity? It has not the vitality and force of a single living man; for a single man can bend it to his will. It is a sort of wooden gun to the people themselves. But it is not the less necessary for this; for the people must have some complicated machinery or other, and hear its din, to satisfy that idea of government which they have. Governments show thus how successfully men can be imposed on, even impose on themselves, for their own advantage. It is excellent, we must all allow. Yet this government never of itself furthered any enterprise, but by the alacrity with which it got out of its way. *It* does not keep the country free. *It* does not settle the West. *It* does not educate. The character inherent in the American people has done all that has been accomplished; and it would have done somewhat more, if the government had not sometimes got in its way. For government is an expedient by which men would fain succeed in letting one another alone; and, as has been said, when it is most expedient, the governed are most let alone by it. Trade and commerce, if they were not made of India-rubber, would never manage to bounce over the obstacles which legislators are continually putting in their way; and, if one were to judge these men wholly by the effects of their actions and not partly by their intentions, they would deserve to be classed and punished with those mischievous persons who put obstructions on the railroads.   2

But, to speak practically and as a citizen, unlike those who call themselves no-government men, I ask for, not at once no government, but *at
once a better government.* Let every man make known what kind of government would command his respect, and that will be one step toward
obtaining it.   3

After all, the practical reason why, when the power is once in the
hands of the people, a majority are permitted, and for a long period continue, to rule is not because they are most likely to be in the right, nor
because this seems fairest to the minority, but because they are physically
the strongest. But a government in which the majority rule in all cases
cannot be based on justice, even as far as men understand it. Can there
not be a government in which majorities do not virtually decide right and
wrong, but conscience?—in which majorities decide only those questions
to which the rule of expediency is applicable? Must the citizen ever for a
moment, or in the least degree, resign his conscience to the legislator?
Why has every man a conscience, then? I think that we should be men
first, and subjects afterward. It is not desirable to cultivate a respect for
the law, so much as for the right. The only obligation which I have a right
to assume is to do at any time what I think right. It is truly enough said,
that a corporation has no conscience; but a corporation of conscientious
men is a corporation *with* a conscience. Law never made men a whit more
just; and, by means of their respect for it, even the well-disposed are
daily made the agents of injustice. A common and natural result of an
undue respect for law is, that you may see a file of soldiers, colonel,
captain, corporal, privates, powder-monkeys, and all, marching in admirable order over hill and dale to the wars, against their wills, ay, against
their common sense and consciences, which makes it very steep marching
indeed, and produces a palpitation of the heart. They have no doubt that
it is a damnable business in which they are concerned; they are all peace-
ably inclined. Now, what are they? Men at all? or small movable forts and
magazines, at the service of some unscrupulous man in power? Visit the
Navy-Yard, and behold a marine, such a man as an American government
can make, or such as it can make a man with its black arts,—a mere
shadow and reminiscence of humanity, a man laid out alive and standing,
and already, as one may say, buried under arms with funeral accompani-
ments, though it may be,—

> Not a drum was heard, not a funeral note,
>   As his corse to the rampart we hurried;
> Not a soldier discharged his farewell shot
>   O'er the grave where our hero we buried.   4

The mass of men serve the state thus, not as men mainly, but as
machines, with their bodies. They are the standing army, and the militia,
jailors, constables, posse comitatus, etc. In most cases there is no free

exercise whatever of the judgment or of the moral sense; but they put themselves on a level with wood and earth and stones; and wooden men can perhaps be manufactured that will serve the purpose as well. Such command no more respect than men of straw or a lump of dirt. They have the same sort of worth only as horses and dogs. Yet such as these even are commonly esteemed good citizens. Others—as most legislators, politicians, lawyers, ministers, and office-holders—serve the state chiefly with their heads; and, as they rarely make any moral distinctions, they are as likely to serve the Devil, without *intending* it, as God. A very few, as heroes, patriots, martyrs, reformers in the great sense, and *men,* serve the state with their consciences also, and so necessarily resist it for the most part; and they are commonly treated as enemies by it. A wise man will only be useful as a man, and will not submit to be "clay," and "stop a hole to keep the wind away," but leave that office to his dust at least:—

> *I am too high-born to be propertied,*
> *To be a secondary at control,*
> *Or useful serving-man and instrument*
> *To any sovereign state throughout the world.*   5

He who gives himself entirely to his fellow-men appears to them useless and selfish; but he who gives himself partially to them is pronounced a benefactor and philanthropist.   6

How does it become a man to behave toward this American government to-day? I answer, that he cannot without disgrace be associated with it. I cannot for an instant recognize that political organization as *my* government which is the *slave's* government also.   7

All men recognize the right of revolution; that is, the right to refuse allegiance to, and to resist, the government, when its tyranny or its inefficiency are great and unendurable. But almost all say that such is not the case now. But such was the case, they think, in the Revolution of '75. If one were to tell me that this was a bad government because it taxed certain foreign commodities brought to its ports, it is most probable that I should not make an ado about it, for I can do without them. All machines have their friction; and possibly this does enough good to counterbalance the evil. At any rate, it is a great evil to make a stir about it. But when the friction comes to have its machine, and oppression and robbery are organized, I say, let us not have such a machine any longer. In other words, when a sixth of the population of a nation which has undertaken to be the refuge of liberty are slaves, and a whole country is unjustly overrun and conquered by a foreign army, and subjected to military law, I think that it is not too soon for honest men to rebel and revolutionize. What makes this duty the more urgent is the fact that the country so overrun is not our own, but ours is the invading army.   8

Paley, a common authority with many on moral questions, in his chapter on the "Duty of Submission to Civil Government," resolves all civil obligation into expediency; and he proceeds to say, "That so long as the interest of the whole society requires it, that is, so long as the established government cannot be resisted or changed without public inconveniency, it is the will of God that the established government be obeyed, and no longer. . . . This principle being admitted, the justice of every particular case of resistance is reduced to a computation of the quantity of the danger and grievance on the one side, and of the probability and expense of redressing it on the other." Of this, he says, every man shall judge for himself. But Paley appears never to have contemplated those cases to which the rule of expediency does not apply, in which a people, as well as an individual, must do justice, cost what it may. If I have unjustly wrested a plank from a drowning man, I must restore it to him though I drown myself. This, according to Paley, would be inconvenient. But he that would save his life, in such a case, shall lose it. This people must cease to hold slaves, and to make war on Mexico, though it cost them their existence as a people.   9

In their practice, nations agree with Paley; but does any one think that Massachusetts does exactly what is right at the present crisis?

> A drab of state, a cloth-o'-silver slut,
>   To have her train borne up, and her soul trail in the dirt.

Practically speaking, the opponents to a reform in Massachusetts are not a hundred thousand politicians at the South, but a hundred thousand merchants and farmers here, who are more interested in commerce and agriculture than they are in humanity, and are not prepared to do justice to the slave and to Mexico, *cost what it may*. I quarrel not with far-off foes, but with those who, near at home, coöperate with, and do the bidding of, those far away, and without whom the latter would be harmless. We are accustomed to say, that the mass of men are unprepared; but improvement is slow because the few are not materially wiser or better than the many. It is not so important that many should be as good as you, as that there be some absolute goodness somewhere; for that will leaven the whole lump. There are thousands who are *in opinion* opposed to slavery and to the war, who yet in effect do nothing to put an end to them; who, esteeming themselves children of Washington and Franklin, sit down with their hands in their pockets, and say that they know not what to do, and do nothing; who even postpone the question of freedom to the question of free-trade, and quietly read the prices-current along with the latest advices from Mexico, after dinner, and, it may be, fall asleep over them both. What is the price-current of an honest man and patriot to-day? They hesitate, and they regret, and sometimes they petition; but they do nothing in earnest and with effect. They will wait, well disposed, for others to remedy the evil, that they may no longer have it to regret. At most, they give only a cheap vote, and a feeble countenance and Godspeed, to the right, as it goes by them. There are nine hundred and ninety-nine patrons of virtue to one virtuous man. But it is easier to deal with the real possessor of a thing than with the temporary guardian of it.   10

All voting is a sort of gaming, like checkers or backgammon, with a slight moral tinge to it, a playing with right and wrong, with moral questions; and betting naturally accompanies it. The character of the voters is not staked. I cast my vote, perchance, as I think right; but I am not vitally concerned that that right should prevail. I am willing to leave it to the majority. Its obligation, therefore, never exceeds that of expediency. Even voting *for the right* is *doing* nothing for it. It is only expressing to men feebly your desire that it should prevail. A wise man will not leave the right to the mercy of chance, nor wish it to prevail through the power of the majority. There is but little virtue in the action of masses of men. When the majority shall at length vote for the abolition of slavery, it will be because they are indifferent to slavery, or because there is but little slavery left to be abolished by their vote. *They* will then be the only slaves. Only *his* vote can hasten the abolition of slavery who asserts his own freedom by his vote.   11

I hear of a convention to be held at Baltimore, or elsewhere, for the selection of a candidate for the Presidency, made up chiefly of editors, and men who are politicians by profession; but I think, what is it to any independent, intelligent, and respectable man what decision they may come to? Shall we not have the advantage of his wisdom and honesty, nevertheless? Can we not count upon some independent votes? Are there not many individuals in the country who do not attend conventions? But no: I find that the respectable man, so called, has immediately drifted from his position, and despairs of his country, when his country has more reason to despair of him. He forthwith adopts one of the candidates thus selected as the only *available* one, thus proving that he is himself *available* for any purposes of the demagogue. His vote is of no more worth than that of any unprincipled foreigner or hireling native, who may have been bought. O for a man who is a *man,* and, as my neighbor says, has a bone in his back which you cannot pass your hand through! Our statistics are at fault: the population has been returned too large. How many *men* are there to a square thousand miles in this country? Hardly one. Does not America offer any inducement for men to settle here? The American has dwindled into an Odd Fellow,—one who may be known by the development of his organ of gregariousness, and a manifest lack of intellect and cheerful self-reliance; whose first and chief concern, on coming into the world, is to see that the

Almshouses are in good repair; and, before yet he has lawfully donned the virile garb, to collect a fund for the support of the widows and orphans that may be; who, in short, ventures to live only by the aid of the Mutual Insurance company, which has promised to bury him decently.   12

It is not a man's duty, as a matter of course, to devote himself to the eradication of any, even the most enormous wrong; he may still properly have other concerns to engage him; but it is his duty, at least, to wash his hands of it, and, if he gives it no thought longer, not to give it practically his support. If I devote myself to other pursuits and contemplations, I must first see, at least, that I do not pursue them sitting upon another man's shoulders. I must get off him first, that he may pursue his contemplations too. See what gross inconsistency is tolerated. I have heard some of my townsmen say, "I should like to have them order me out to help put down an insurrection of the slaves, or to march to Mexico;—see if I would go;" and yet these very men have each, directly by their allegiance, and so indirectly, at least, by their money, furnished a substitute. The soldier is applauded who refuses to serve in an unjust war by those who do not refuse to sustain the unjust government which makes the war; it is applauded by those whose own act and authority he disregards and sets at naught; as if the state were penitent to that degree that it hired one to scourge it while it sinned, but not to that degree that it left off sinning for a moment. Thus, under the name of Order and Civil Government, we are all made at last to pay homage to and support our own meanness. After the first blush of sin comes its indifference; and from immoral it becomes, as it were, *un*moral, and not quite unnecessary to that life which we have made.   13

The broadest and most prevalent error requires the most disinterested virtue to sustain it. The slight reproach to which the virtue of patriotism is commonly liable, the noble are most likely to incur. Those who, while they disapprove of the character and measures of a government, yield to it their allegiance and support are undoubtedly its most conscientious supporters, and so frequently the most serious obstacles to reform. Some are petitioning the state to dissolve the Union, to disregard the requisitions of the President. Why do they not dissolve it themselves,—the union between themselves and the state,—and refuse to pay their quota into its treasury? Do not they stand in the same relation to the state that the state does to the Union? And have not the same reasons prevented the state from resisting the Union which have prevented them from resisting the state?   14

How can a man be satisfied to entertain an opinion merely, and enjoy *it*? Is there any enjoyment in it, if his opinion is that he is aggrieved? If you are cheated out of a single dollar by your neighbor, you do not rest satisfied with knowing that you are cheated, or with saying that you are cheated, or even with petitioning him to pay you your due; but you take effectual steps at once to obtain the full amount, and see that you are never cheated again. Action from principle, the perception and the performance of right, changes things and relations; it is essentially revolutionary, and does not consist wholly with anything which was. It not only divides states and churches, it divides families; ay, it divides the *individual,* separating the diabolical in him from the divine.   15

Unjust laws exist: shall we be content to obey them, or shall we endeavor to amend them, and obey them until we have succeeded, or shall we transgress them at once? Men generally, under such a government as this, think that they ought to wait until they have persuaded the majority to alter them. They think that, if they should resist, the remedy would be worse than the evil. But it is the fault of the government itself that the remedy *is* worse than the evil. *It* makes it worse. Why is it not more apt to anticipate and provide for reform? Why does it not cherish its wise minority? Why does it cry and resist before it is hurt? Why does it not encourage its citizens to be on the alert to point out its faults, and *do* better than *it* would have them? Why does it always crucify Christ, and excommunicate Copernicus and Luther, and pronounce Washington and Franklin rebels?   16

One would think, that a deliberate and practical denial of its authority was the only offense never contemplated by government; else, why has it not assigned its definite, its suitable and proportionate penalty? If a man who has no property refuses but once to earn nine shillings for the state, he is put in prison for a period unlimited by any law that I know, and determined only by the discretion of those who placed him there; but if he should steal ninety times nine shillings from the state, he is soon permitted to go at large again.   17

If the injustice is part of the necessary friction of the machine of government, let it go, let it go: perchance it will wear smooth,—certainly the machine will wear out. If the injustice has a spring, or a pulley, or a rope, or a crank, exclusively for itself, then perhaps you may consider whether the remedy will not be worse than the evil; but if it is of such a nature that it requires you to be the agent of injustice to another, then, I say, break the law. Let your life be a counter friction to stop the machine. What I have to do is to see, at any rate, that I do not lend myself to the wrong which I condemn.   18

As for adopting the ways which the state has provided for remedying the evil, I know not of such ways. They take too much time, and a man's life will be gone. I have other affairs to attend to. I came into this world, not chiefly to make this a good place to live in, but to live in it, be it good or bad. A man has not everything to do, but something; and because he cannot do *everything,* it is not necessary that he should do *something* wrong. It is not my business to be petitioning the Governor or the Legislature any more than it is theirs to petition me; and if they should not hear my petition, what should I do then? But in this case the state has provided no way: its very Constitution is the evil. This may seem to be harsh and stubborn and unconciliatory; but it is to treat with the utmost kindness and consideration the only spirit that can appreciate or deserves it. So is all change for the better, like birth and death, which convulse the body. 19

I do not hesitate to say, that those who call themselves Abolitionists should at once effectually withdraw their support, both in person and property, from the government of Massachusetts and not wait till they constitute a majority of one, before they suffer the right to prevail through them. I think that it is enough if they have God on their side, without waiting for that other one. Moreover, any man more right than his neighbors constitutes a majority of one already. 20

I meet this American government, or its representative, the state government, directly, and face to face, once a year—no more—in the person of its tax-gatherer; this is the only mode in which a man situated as I am necessarily meets it; and it then says distinctly, Recognize me; and the simplest, most effectual, and, in the present posture of affairs, the indispensablest mode of treating with it on this head, of expressing your little satisfaction with and love for it, is to deny it then. My civil neighbor, the tax-gatherer, is the very man I have to deal with,—for it is, after all, with men and not with parchment that I quarrel,—and he has voluntarily chosen to be an agent of the government. How shall he ever know well what he is and does as an officer of the government, or as a man, until he is obliged to consider whether he shall treat me, his neighbor, for whom he has respect, as a neighbor and well-disposed man, or as a maniac and disturber of the peace, and see if he can get over this obstruction to his neighborliness without a ruder and more impetuous thought or speech corresponding with his action. I know this well, that if one thousand, if one hundred, if ten men whom I could name,—if ten *honest* men only,—if *one* HONEST man, in this State of Massachusetts, *ceasing to hold slaves,* were actually to withdraw from this copartnership, and be locked up in the county jail therefor, it would be the abolition of slavery in America. For it matters not how small the beginning may seem to be: what is once well done is done forever. But we love better to talk about it: that we say is our mission. Reform keeps many scores of newspapers in its service, but not one man. If my esteemed neighbor, the State's ambassador, who will devote his days to the settlement of the question of human rights in the Council Chamber, instead of being threatened with the prisons of Carolina, were to sit down the prisoner of Massachusetts, that State which is so anxious to foist the sin of slavery upon her sister,—though at present she can discover only an act of inhospitality to be the ground of a quarrel with her,—the Legislature would not wholly waive the subject the following winter.   21

Under a government which imprisons any unjustly, the true place for a just man is also a prison. The proper place to-day, the only place which Massachusetts has provided for her freer and less desponding spirits, is in her prisons, to be put out and locked out of the State by her own act, as they have already put themselves out by their principles. It is there that the fugitive slave, and the Mexican prisoner on parole, and the Indian come to plead the wrongs of his race should find them; on that separate, but more free and honorable ground, where the State places those who are not *with* her, but *against* her,—the only house in a slave State in which a free man can abide with honor. If any think that their influence would be lost there, and their voices no longer afflict the ear of the State, that they would not be as an enemy within its walls, they do not know by how much truth is stronger than error, nor how much more eloquently and effectively he can combat injustice who has experienced a little in his own person. Cast your whole vote, not a strip of paper merely, but your whole influence. A minority is powerless while it conforms to the majority; it is not even a minority then; but it is irresistible when it clogs by its whole weight. If the alternative is to keep all just men in prison, or give up war and slavery, the State will not hesitate which to choose. If a thousand men were not to pay their tax-bills this year, that would not be a violent and bloody measure, as it would be to pay them, and enable the State to commit violence and shed innocent blood. This is, in fact, the definition of a peaceable revolution, if any such is possible. If the tax-gatherer, or any other public officer, asks me, as one has done, "But what shall I do?" my answer is, "If you really wish to do anything, resign your office." When the subject has refused allegiance, and the officer has resigned his office, then the revolution is accomplished. But even suppose blood should flow. Is there not a sort of blood shed when the conscience is wounded? Through this wound a man's real manhood and immortality flow out, and he bleeds to an everlasting death. I see this blood flowing now.   22

I have contemplated the imprisonment of the offender, rather than the seizure of his goods,—though both will serve the same purpose,—because they who assert the purest right, and consequently are most dangerous to a corrupt State, commonly have not spent much time in accumulating property. To such the State renders comparatively small service, and a slight tax is wont to appear exorbitant, particularly if they are obliged to earn it by special labor with their hands. If there were one who lived wholly without the use of money, the State itself would hesitate to demand it of him. But the rich man—not to make any invidious comparison—is always sold to the institution which makes him rich. Absolutely speaking, the more money, the less virtue; for money comes between a man and his objects, and obtains them for him; and it was certainly no great virtue to obtain it. It puts to rest many questions which he would otherwise be taxed to answer; while the only new question which it puts is the hard but superfluous one, how to spend it. Thus his moral ground is taken from under his feet. The opportunities of living are diminished in proportion as what are called the "means" are increased. The best thing a man can do for his culture when he is rich is to endeavor to carry out those schemes which he entertained when he was poor. Christ answered the Herodians according to their condition. "Show me the tribute-money," said he;—and one took a penny out of his pocket;—if you use the money which has the image of Cæsar on it and which he has made current and valuable, that is, *if you are men of the State,* and gladly enjoy the advantages of Cæsar's government, then pay him back some of his own when he demands it. "Render therefore to Cæsar that which is Cæsar's, and to God those things which are God's,"—leaving them no wiser than before as to which was which; for they did not wish to know.   23

When I converse with the freest of my neighbors, I perceive that, whatever they may say about the magnitude and seriousness of the question, and their regard for the public tranquillity, the long and the short of the matter is, that they cannot spare the protection of the existing government, and they dread the consequences to their property and families of disobedience to it. For my own part, I should not like to think that I ever rely on the protection of the State. But, if I deny the authority of the State when it presents its tax-bill, it will soon take and waste all my property, and so harass me and my children without end. This is hard. This makes it impossible for a man to live honestly, and at the same time comfortably, in outward respects. It will not be worth the while to accumulate property; that would be sure to go again. You must hire or squat somewhere, and raise but a small crop, and eat that soon. You must live within yourself, and depend upon yourself always tucked up and ready for a start, and not have many affairs. A man may grow rich in Turkey even, if he will be in all respects a good subject of the Turkish government. Confucius said: "If a state is governed by the principles of reason, poverty and misery are subjects of shame; if a state is not governed by the principles of reason, riches and honors are the subjects of shame." No: until I want the protection of Massachusetts to be extended to me in some distant Southern port, where my liberty is endangered, or until I am bent solely on building up an estate at home by peaceful enterprise, I can afford to refuse allegiance to Massachusetts, and her right to my property and life. It costs me less in every sense to incur the penalty of disobedience to the State than it would to obey. I should feel as if I were worth less in that case.   24

Some years ago, the State met me in behalf of the Church, and commanded me to pay a certain sum toward the support of a clergyman whose preaching my father attended, but never I myself. "Pay," it said, "or be locked up in the jail." I declined to pay. But, unfortunately, another man saw fit to pay it. I did not see why the schoolmaster should be taxed to support the priest, and not the priest the schoolmaster; for I was not the State's schoolmaster, but I supported myself by voluntary subscription. I did not see why the lyceum should not present its tax-bill, and have the State to back its demand, as well as the Church. However, at the request of the selectmen, I condescended to make some such statement as this in writing:—"Know all men by these presents, that I, Henry Thoreau, do not wish to be regarded as a member of any incorporated society which I have not joined." This I gave to the town clerk; and he has it. The State, having thus learned that I did not wish to be regarded as a member of that church, has never made a like demand on me since; though it said that it must adhere to its original presumption that time. If I had known how to name them, I should then have signed off in detail from all the societies which I never signed on to; but I did not know where to find a complete list.   25

I have paid no poll-tax for six years. I was put into a jail once on this account, for one night; and, as I stood considering the walls of solid stone, two or three feet thick, the door of wood and iron, a foot thick, and the iron grating which strained the light, I could not help being struck with the foolishness of that institution which treated me as if I were mere flesh and blood and bones to be locked up. I wondered that it should have concluded at length that this was the best use it could put me to, and had never thought to avail itself of my services in some way. I saw that, if there was a wall of stone between me and my townsmen, there was a still more difficult one to climb or break through before they could get to be as free as I was. I did not for a moment feel confined, and the walls seemed a great waste of stone and mortar. I felt as if I alone of all my townsmen had paid my tax. They plainly did not know how to treat me, but behaved like persons who are underbred. In every threat and in every compliment there was a blunder; for they thought that my chief desire was to stand the other side of that stone wall. I could not but smile to see how industriously they locked the door on my meditations, which followed them out again without let or hindrance, and *they* were really all that was dangerous. As they could not reach me, they had resolved to punish my body; just as boys, if they cannot come at some person against whom they have a spite, will abuse his dog. I saw that the State was half-witted, that it was timid as a lone woman with her silver spoons, and that it did not know its friends from its foes, and I lost all my remaining respect for it, and pitied it.   26

Thus the State never intentionally confronts a man's sense, intellectual or moral, but only his body, his senses. It is not armed with superior wit or honesty, but with superior physical strength. I was not born to be forced. I will breathe after my own fashion. Let us see who is the strongest. What force has a multitude? They only can force me who obey a higher law than I. They force me to become like themselves. I do not hear of *men* being *forced* to live this way or that by masses of men. What sort of life were that to live? When I meet a government which says to me, "Your money or your life," why should I be in haste to give it my money? It may be in a great strait, and not know what to do: I cannot help that. It must help itself; do as I do. It is not worth the while to snivel about it. I am not responsible for the successful working of the machinery of society. I am not the son of the engineer. I perceive that, when an acorn and a chestnut fall side by side, the one does not remain inert to make way for the other, but both obey their own laws, and spring and grow and flourish as best they can, till one, perchance, overshadows and destroys the other. If a plant cannot live according to its nature, it dies; and so a man.   27

The night in prison was novel and interesting enough. The prisoners in their shirt-sleeves were enjoying a chat and the evening air in the doorway, when I entered. But the jailer said, "Come, boys, it is time to lock up;" and so they dispersed, and I heard the sound of their steps returning into the hollow apartments. My roommate was introduced to me by the jailer as "a first-rate fellow and a clever man." When the door was locked, he showed me where to hang my hat, and how he managed matters there. The rooms were whitewashed once a month; and this one, at least, was the whitest, most simply furnished, and probably the neatest apartment in the town. He naturally wanted to know where I came from, and what brought me there; and, when I had told him, I asked him in my turn how he came there, presuming him to be an honest man, of course; and, as the world goes, I believe he was. "Why," said he, "they accuse me of burning a barn; but I never did it." As near as I could discover, he had probably gone to bed in a barn when drunk, and smoked his pipe there; and so a barn was burnt. He had the reputation of being a clever man, had been there some three months waiting for his trial to come on, and would have to wait as much longer; but he was quite domesticated and contented, since he got his board for nothing, and thought that he was well treated.   28

He occupied one window, and I the other; and I saw that if one stayed there long, his principal business would be to look out the window. I had soon read all the tracts that were left there, and examined where former prisoners had broken out, and where a grate had been sawed off, and heard the history of the various occupants of that room; for I found that even here there was a history and a gossip which never circulated beyond the walls of the jail. Probably this is the only house in the town where verses are composed, which are afterward printed in a circular form, but not published. I was shown quite a long list of verses which were composed by some young men who had been detected in an attempt to escape, who avenged themselves by singing them.   29

I pumped my fellow-prisoner as dry as I could, for fear I should never see him again; but at length he showed me which was my bed, and left me to blow out the lamp.   30

It was like traveling into a far country, such as I had never expected to behold, to lie there for one night. It seemed to me that I never had heard the town-clock strike before, nor the evening sounds of the village; for we slept with the windows open, which were inside the grating. It was to see my native village in the light of the Middle Ages, and our Concord was turned into a Rhine stream, and visions of knights and castles passed before me. They were the voices of old burghers that I heard in the streets. I was an involuntary spectator and auditor of whatever was done and said in the kitchen of the adjacent village-inn,—a wholly new and rare experience to me. It was a closer view of my native town. I was fairly inside of it. I never had seen its institutions before. This is one of its peculiar institutions; for it is a shire town. I began to comprehend what its inhabitants were about.   31

In the morning, our breakfasts were put through the hole in the door, in small oblong-square tin pans, made to fit, and holding a pint of chocolate, with brown bread, and an iron spoon. When they called for the vessels again, I was green enough to return what bread I had left; but my comrade seized it, and said that I should lay that up for lunch or dinner. Soon after he was let out to work at haying in a neighboring field, whither he went every day, and would not be back till noon; so he bade me good-day, saying that he doubted if he should see me again.   32

When I came out of prison,—for some one interfered, and paid that tax,—I did not perceive that great changes had taken place on the common, such as he observed who went in a youth and emerged a tottering and gray-headed man; and yet a change had to my eyes come over the scene,—the town, and State, and country,—greater than any that mere time could effect. I saw yet more distinctly the State in which I lived. I saw to what extent the people among whom I lived could be trusted as good neighbors and friends; that their friendship was for summer weather only; that they did not greatly propose to do right; that they were a distinct race from me by their prejudices and superstitions, as the Chinamen and Malays are; that in their sacrifices to humanity they ran no risks, not even to their property; that after all they were not so noble but they treated the thief as he had treated them, and hoped, by a certain outward observance and a few prayers, and by walking in a particular straight though useless path from time to time, to save their souls. This may be to judge my neighbors harshly; for I believe that many of them are not aware that they have such an institution as the jail in their village.   33

It was formerly the custom in our village, when a poor debtor came out of jail, for his acquaintances to salute him, looking through their fingers, which were crossed to represent the grating of a jail window, "How do ye do?" My neighbors did not thus salute me, but first looked at me, and then at one another, as if I had returned from a long journey. I was put into jail as I was going to the shoemaker's to get a shoe which was mended. When I was let out the next morning, I proceeded to finish my errand, and, having put on my mended shoe, joined a huckleberry party, who were impatient to put themselves under my conduct; and in half an hour,—for the horse was soon tackled,—was in the midst of a huckleberry field, on one of our highest hills, two miles off, and then the State was nowhere to be seen.   34

This is the whole history of "My Prisons."   35

I have never declined paying the highway tax, because I am as desirous of being a good neighbor as I am of being a bad subject; and as for supporting schools, I am doing my part to educate my fellow-countrymen now. It is for no particular item in the tax-bill that I refuse to pay it. I simply wish to refuse allegiance to the State, to withdraw and stand aloof from it effectually. I do not care to trace the course of my dollar, if I could, till it buys a man or a musket to shoot with,—the dollar is innocent, —but I am concerned to trace the effects of my allegiance. In fact, I quietly declare war with the State, after my fashion, though I will still make what use and get what advantage of her I can, as is usual in such cases.   36

If others pay the tax which is demanded of me, from a sympathy with the State, they do but what they have already done in their own case, or rather they abet injustice to a greater extent than the State requires. If they pay the tax from a mistaken interest in the individual taxed to save his property, or prevent his going to jail, it is because they have not considered wisely how far they let their private feelings interfere with the public good.   37

This, then, is my position at present. But one cannot be too much on his guard in such a case, lest his action be biased by obstinacy or an undue regard for the opinions of men. Let him see that he does only what belongs to himself and to the hour.   38

I think sometimes, Why, this people mean well, they are only ignorant; they would do better if they knew how: why give your neighbors this pain to treat you as they are not inclined to? But I think again, This is no reason why I should do as they do, or permit others to suffer much greater pain of a different kind. Again, I sometimes say to myself, When many millions of men, without heat, without ill will, without personal feeling of any kind, demand of you a few shillings only, without the possibility, such is their constitution, of retracting or altering their present demand, and without the possibility, on your side, of appeal to any other millions, why expose yourself to this overwhelming brute force? You do not resist cold and hunger, the winds and the waves, thus obstinately; you quietly submit to a thousand similar necessities. You do not put your head into the fire. But just in proportion as I regard this as not wholly a brute force, but partly a human force, and consider that I have relations to those millions as to so many millions of men, and not of mere brute or inanimate things, I see that appeal is possible, first and instantaneously, from them to the Maker of them, and, secondly, from them to themselves. But if I put my head deliberately into the fire, there is no appeal to fire or to the Maker of fire, and I have only myself to blame. If I could convince myself that I have any right to be satisfied with men as they are, and to treat them accordingly, and not according, in some respects, to my requisitions and expectations of what they and I ought to be, then, like a good Mussulman and fatalist, I should endeavor to be satisfied with things as they are, and say it is the will of God. And, above all, there is this difference between resisting this and a purely brute or natural force, that I can resist this with some effect; but I cannot expect, like Orpheus, to change the nature 39 of the rocks and trees and beasts.

I do not wish to quarrel with any man or nation. I do not wish to split hairs, to make fine distinctions, or set myself up as better than my neighbors. I seek rather, I may say, even an excuse for conforming to the laws of the land. I am but too ready to conform to them. Indeed, I have reason to suspect myself on this head; and each year, as the tax-gatherer comes round, I find myself disposed to review the acts and position of the general and State governments, and the spirit of the people, to discover a pretext for conformity.

> We must affect our country as our parents,
> And if at any time we alienate
> Our love or industry from doing it honor,
> We must respect effects and teach the soul
> Matter of conscience and religion,
> And not desire of rule or benefit.

I believe that the State will soon be able to take all my work of this sort out of my hands, and then I shall be no better a patriot than my fellow-countrymen. Seen from a lower point of view, the Constitution, with all its faults, is very good; the law and the courts are very respectable; even this State and this American government are, in many respects, very admirable, and rare things, to be thankful for, such as a great many have described them; but seen from a point of view a little higher, they are what I have

described them; seen from a higher still, and the highest, who shall say
what they are, or that they are worth looking at or thinking of at all?   40
        However, the government does not concern me much, and I shall
bestow the fewest possible thoughts on it. It is not many moments that I
live under a government, even in this world. If a man is thought-free,
fancy-free, imagination-free, that which *is not* never for a long time appearing *to be* to him, unwise rulers or reformers cannot fatally interrupt him.   41
        I know that most men think differently from myself; but those whose
lives are by profession devoted to the study of these or kindred subjects
content me as little as any. Statesmen and legislators, standing so completely within the institution, never distinctly and nakedly behold it. They
speak of moving society, but have no resting-place without it. They may be
men of a certain experience and discrimination, and have no doubt invented ingenious and even useful systems, for which we sincerely thank
them; but all their wit and usefulness lie within certain not very wide
limits. They are wont to forget that the world is not governed by policy and
expediency. Webster never goes behind government, and so cannot speak
with authority about it. His words are wisdom to those legislators who contemplate no essential reform in the existing government; but for thinkers,
and those who legislate for all time, he never once glances at the subject.
I know of those whose serene and wise speculations on this theme would
soon reveal the limits of his mind's range and hospitality. Yet, compared
with the cheap professions of most reformers, and the still cheaper
wisdom and eloquence of politicians in general, his are almost the only
sensible and valuable words, and we thank Heaven for him. Comparatively,
he is always strong, original, and, above all, practical. Still, his quality is
not wisdom, but prudence. The lawyer's truth is not Truth, but consistency
or a consistent expediency. Truth is always in harmony with herself, and is
not concerned chiefly to reveal the justice that may consist with wrong-
doing. He well deserves to be called, as he has been called, the Defender
of the Constitution. There are really no blows to be given by him but defensive ones. He is not a leader, but a follower. His leaders are the men
of '87. "I have never made an effort," he says, "and never propose to
make an effort; I have never countenanced an effort, and never mean to
countenance an effort, to disturb the arrangement as originally made, by
which the various States came into the Union." Still thinking of the
sanction which the Constitution gives to slavery, he says, "Because
it was a part of the original compact,—let it stand." Notwithstanding
his special acuteness and ability, he is unable to take a fact out of its
merely political relations, and behold it as it lies absolutely to be disposed
of by the intellect,—what, for instance, it behooves a man to do here in
America to-day with regard to slavery,—but ventures, or is driven to make
some such desperate answer as the following, while professing to speak

absolutely, and as a private man,—from which what new and singular code of social duties might be inferred? "The manner," says he, "in which the governments of those States where slavery exists are to regulate it is for their own consideration, under their responsibility to their constituents, to the general laws of propriety, humanity, and justice, and to God. Associations formed elsewhere, springing from a feeling of humanity, or other cause, have nothing whatever to do with it. They have never received any encouragement from me, and they never will."   42

They who know of no purer sources of truth, who have traced up its stream no higher, stand, and wisely stand, by the Bible and the Constitution, and drink at it there with reverence and humility; but they who behold where it comes trickling into this lake or that pool, gird up their loins once more, and continue their pilgrimage toward its fountain-head.   43

No man with a genius for legislation has appeared in America. They are rare in the history of the world. There are orators, politicians, and eloquent men, by the thousand; but the speaker has not yet opened his mouth to speak who is capable of settling the much-vexed questions of the day. We love eloquence for its own sake, and not for any truth which it may utter, or any heroism it may inspire. Our legislators have not yet learned the comparative value of free-trade and of freedom, of union, and of rectitude, to a nation. They have no genius or talent for comparatively humble questions of taxation and finance, commerce and manufactures and agriculture. If we were left solely to the wordy wit of legislators in Congress for our guidance, uncorrected by the seasonable experience and the effectual complaints of the people, America would not long retain her rank among the nations. For eighteen hundred years, though perchance I have no right to say it, the New Testament has been written; yet where is the legislator who has wisdom and practical talent enough to avail himself of the light which it sheds on the science of legislation?   44

The authority of government, even such as I am willing to submit to, —for I will cheerfully obey those who know and can do better than I, and in many things even those who neither know nor can do so well,—is still an impure one: to be strictly just, it must have the sanction and consent of the governed. It can have no pure right over my person and property but what I concede to it. The progress from an absolute to a limited monarchy, from a limited monarchy to a democracy, is a progress toward a true respect for the individual. Even the Chinese philosopher was wise enough to regard the individual as the basis of the empire. Is a democracy, such as we know it, the last improvement possible in government? Is it not possible to take a step further towards recognizing and organizing the rights of man? There will never be a really free and enlightened State until the State comes to recognize the individual as a higher and independent power, from which all its own power and authority are derived, and treats him accordingly. I please myself with imagining a State at last which can afford to be just to all men, and to treat the individual with respect as a neighbor; which even would not think it inconsistent with its own repose if a few were to live aloof from it, not meddling with it, nor embraced by it, who fulfilled all the duties of neighbors and fellowmen. A State which bore this kind of fruit, and suffered it to drop off as fast as it ripened, would prepare the way for a still more perfect and glorious State, which also I have imagined, but not yet anywhere seen.   45

Suggestions for Writing

Develop any one of the following topics in an extended expository essay; of the methods of analysis that you have studied, use the ones that seem appropriate to your development of the topic.

1 "The value of an idea has nothing whatever to do with the sincerity of the man who expresses it."—Oscar Wilde
2 "A society of big organizations . . . raises in new and acute form the question of the person. . . . How can the individual maintain his integrity and privacy?"—Peter F. Drucker
3 It is in the nature of men that some shall always be leaders and some followers.
4 "The wise only possess ideas; the greater part of mankind are possessed by them."—S. T. Coleridge
5 The greatness of the United States lies in its diversity—its pluralism—in religions and in racial and national groups.

3

ARGUMENT

Where there is much desire to learn, there of necessity will be much arguing, much writing, many opinions; for opinion in good men is knowledge in the making. John Milton

rgument is the form of discourse that aims at convincing the reader of the truth of a proposition. Milton's words, quoted above, should remind us that argument is one of the most commonly used of the forms of discourse. Since argument is an essential medium in our political and social life, it is well for us to remember Walter Lippmann's insistence (page 325) that the presentation of opposing points of view is essential for democratic decision. As Thomas Jefferson has pointed out, uniformity of opinion in many matters is no more desirable than uniformity of face and stature. The energizing of truth through argument leads man from darkness into light. The ancient Greeks, in their early development of a democracy, knew the great value of argument and prized the method highly. A large part of the great tradition of ancient oratory is argumentative in character. One of the greatest figures, Aristotle, defined all of rhetoric as we might define argument today: the use in any given situation of the available means of persuasion.

Our present society especially needs to take argument seriously and to use it wisely. John Courtney Murray has warned us that "nothing is more damaging to democracy than lack of rationality in public argument." The powerful mass media of communication—the press, radio, television—use the techniques of argumentation frequently and sometimes loosely. We must understand the use of these techniques in order to protect our own clarity of decision. As future leaders and members of a democratic society, we must be able to use these techniques in speech and writing.

When we want an audience *to be convinced* of what we have to say, we present an *argument*. When we want it to be moved to some kind of *action* as a result of what we say, we *persuade* it. Although this distinction is both practical and accepted, we should remember that argument, like the other forms of discourse, is a complex of many things considered together. We will seldom discover a purely rational argument, even in the Declaration of Independence (page 384); nor do we generally find a serious piece of writing that is *all* persuasion. Aristotle, for instance, considered argument a single thing: making others see our point, acting on the truth of our assertions physically or cerebrally, in deed or in idea. To achieve this purpose, we may present a logical and rational approach, convincing the reader because of the force and power of our reasoning, as Joseph Wood Krutch does in "Is Our Common Man Too Common?" (page 373). We may engage the emotions of our reader psychologically and try to persuade him as do Daniel Boorstin in "The New Barbarians" (page 417) and Seymour Krim in "Literature Makes Plenty Happen" (page 412). Or, since good men do not deceive other men knowingly, we may be convinced or persuaded by the character of the man who is advancing the point, as is the case with Thomas Jefferson in "A Natural Aristocracy" (page 459) and Jonathan Swift in "A Modest Proposal" (page 464).

In every argumentative essay we will find a mixture of these things: (1) the power of reasoning, (2) an emotional appeal, (3) an ethical appeal. In recent speculation about the theory of argument, this third principle has almost been abandoned. In the practical order, good men still convince us, but their goodness is seldom formally cited as a reason for our belief. Admittedly it is difficult to analyze formally the goodness of the proposer of a judgment—much more difficult than analyzing the grounds for the argument proposed by him, which is something quite different. We shall, therefore, be concerned with argument from two points of view: (1) the logic of argument, which convinces the reader because of its power of reasoning, and (2) the psychology of argument, which persuades the reader because of its power of emotion.

The study of exposition has been an excellent preparation for analyzing any argument, since the two forms of discourse have much in common, using many of the same techniques. The two forms of discourse differ fundamentally because each has a separate primary intention. If the aim is primarily to explain or inform, the result is exposition. If the aim is to influence the reader to accept a certain proposition, to give assent to one of various possibilities, the result is argument. The argumentative writer assumes that the possibility of conflict exists, that there is more than one position possible. He believes his to be the correct position. Obviously Phyllis McGinley knows that one can like suburban living or dislike it; she attempts to persuade us to accept her position as the preferable one.

We can identify an essay whose primary intention is argumentative by certain characteristics. Somewhere, expressed or implied, we will discover a *proposition,* a judgment that can be accepted or denied. George P. Elliot presents a proposition of fact in his essay. In the essay by Jonathan Swift, which advocates a change of belief or a course of action, we have a proposition of policy. Any single proposition brings to mind points for it and against it. When any one of these points becomes essential to the acceptance of the proposition, we call it an "issue." Propositions, thus, depend upon issues. These issues are discovered (never invented) by analyzing the proposition. Some of the issues may be "audience admissable," or agreed upon by both sides of the controversy. Both Elliot and Krim agree that literature has significance. This is an "admitted issue," requiring no proof. The "crucial issues" are those about which disagreement exists. The writer must prove that these are valid in themselves and that they support his proposition. He does this by the use of evidence.

The writer has an opportunity to use two kinds of evidence. He may find authorities whose judgments substantiate his point of view. (A "judgment" is an opinion presumably based upon the right operation of reason.) Or the writer may offer facts that can be verified by the general experience of mankind or attested to by a witness. (A "fact" is something that has been, has happened, or is.) Once the "evidence of opinion" and the "evidence of fact" have been collected, they must be reasoned about. "Reasoning" may be defined as the process by which the mind moves from certain known or given evidence to a conclusion that is not known or not given.

The writer may begin with a multitude of particular details and reach a generalization, as does Daniel P. Moynihan. This is *induction*. He may prove his point by beginning with a generally accepted truth and then, by using a syllogism, showing how the truth applies to his specific point, as did the writers of the Declaration of Independence. This is *deduction*. The difference between induction and deduction has been stated with unerring lucidity in a famous essay by Thomas Huxley:

> Suppose you go into a fruiterer's shop, wanting an apple—you take one up, and, on biting, you find it is sour; you look at it, and see that it is hard, and green. You take up another one and that too is hard, green, and sour. The shop man offers you a third; but, before biting it, you examine it, and find that it is hard and green, and you immediately say that you will not have it, as it must be sour, like those that you have already tried.
>
> Nothing can be more simple than that, you think; but if you will take the trouble to analyse and trace out into its logical elements what has been done by the mind, you will be greatly surprised. In the first place, you have performed the operation of induction. You found, that, in two experiences, hardness and greenness in apples went together with sourness. It was so in the first case, and it was confirmed by the second. True, it is a very small basis, but still it is enough to make an induction from; you generalize the facts, and you expect to find sourness in apples where you get hardness and greenness. You found upon that a general law, that all hard and green apples are sour; and that, so far as it goes, is a perfect induction. Well, having got your natural law in this way, when you are offered another apple which you find is hard and green, you say, "All hard and green apples are sour; this apple is hard and green, therefore this apple is sour." That train of reasoning is what logicians call a syllogism, and has all its various parts and terms—its major premise, its minor premise, and its conclusion. And, by the help of further reasoning, which, if drawn out, would have to be exhibited in two or three other syllogisms, you arrive at your final determination. "I will not have that apple." So that, you see, you have, in the first place, established a law by induction, and upon that you have founded a deduction, and reasoned out the special conclusion of the particular case.

The writer, on the other hand, may argue in favor of his point by com paring the subject, object, or idea under discussion with other subjects, objects, or ideas and by inferring that certain known resemblances imply other probable resemblances. Such comparison, called "reasoning by

analogy," is basically an employment of simile—more or less extended—
or of metaphor. The first, analogy by simile (sometimes called "literal"
analogy), clearly states the comparison: "A general will make a good president because the qualities needed by him are the same as those needed by
a good president." The second, analogy by metaphor, implies the comparison: "Without baking powder, a cake would not rise: advertising is the
necessary leavening agent in the development of the competitive enterprise
system." Strictly, analogy is not a valid source for logical reasoning; it
has very little probative force. Its value is in its persuasive effects: a fertile
source of illustration, it can hold the reader's interest and engage his
emotions. Obviously, the effective use of analogy in argument requires that
the writer emphasize similarities that are of fundamental and not of trivial
significance for his argument.

The skillful argumentative writer does all the things described
above, but he also does more than this—to the clarity of his reasoning he
adds a passionate appeal for acceptance, using the techniques of the psychology of argument. He knows the truth of what La Rochefoucauld said
in 1665: "The simplest man with passion will be more persuasive than
the most eloquent without." Aristotle made the pioneer attempt to discover
what men responded to emotionally. Modern psychologists are helping
modern rhetoricians to determine with some precision the importance of
the emotions in making judgments. The persuasive writer is a pragmatist,
using, within the limits of morality and truth, those persuasive devices
which work. We are still certain that the major emotional appeals (to our
sense of survival, to family, to sex, to virtue) have validity. What we
know of man through tradition in a classical sense has not much changed.
Pericles aroused the Greeks not much differently, in essence, than did
Lincoln his Illinois audiences. And Winston Churchill differs little, in this
respect, from Lincoln. Needless to say, the psychology of argument has
been much abused in our own time. There is seldom any justification for
the use of the psychology of argument by itself. We should always assume
that the reader wishes to be convinced by the power of reasoning as well
as moved by the power of emotion. As readers, we should expect this
combination from writers. On the other hand, the argumentative writer
gives up one of his chief means for persuasion if he does not make his
appeal vivid by colorful language, aptly chosen metaphor, and the many
techniques of style at his disposal.

Most of the essays presented here are informal arguments, since informality characterizes most argumentative writing. Do not expect the
essays to have the precision of a legal brief; nevertheless, good informal
arguments contain an adequate representation of the techniques of formal
argument in order to be convincing and moving.

IS OUR COMMON MAN TOO COMMON?

JOSEPH WOOD KRUTCH

The Age of the Common Man is not merely a phrase; it is also a fact. Already we are definitely entered upon it, and in all probability it is destined to continue for a long time to come, intensifying its characteristics as it develops in some of the directions which it has already begun to take. 1

Most people welcome the fact, but we have only begun to assess it or even to ask ourselves what choices are still open to us once the grand decision has been made, as by now it has. How common does the common man need to be? Does his dominance necessarily mean that the uncommon man will cease to be tolerated or that the world will become less suited to his needs, less favorable to the development of his talents, than it now is? Will excellence be looked upon as in itself unworthy or "undemocratic"? Can we have an Age of the Common Man without making it an Age of the Common Denominator? Do any dangers lie ahead?* 2

One way to approach these questions is, of course, to ask what has happened already, what changes in attitudes have demonstrably taken place, how the culture of the first era of the Age of the Common Man differs from that which preceded it. What, in other words, is the culture of present-day America like, and are there aspects of it, directly traceable to the emphasis on the common man and his tastes, which are not wholly reassuring? And if there are, then to what extent are the defects corrigible, to what extent are they necessary consequences of the premises we have already accepted?† 3

Unfortunately, but not surprisingly, there is no general agreement concerning the real nature of the situation at the present moment, though it does seem clear enough that most Americans judge both the present and the future a good deal more favorably than many observers from the Old World do. 4

Thus, in his recent book *The Big Change*, Frederick Lewis Allen summed up very cogently the case for contemporary American culture. Hundreds of thousands read the selections of the book clubs; hundreds of thousands more attend concerts of serious music; millions listen to debates, symphonies, and operas on the radio. Never before in the history of the world has so large a proportion of any population been so interested in and so alert to intellectual and artistic activities. Ours is the most cultured nation which ever existed. 5

* Paragraph 2: Are all the questions here related to a single topic?
† Paragraph 3: What premises have we already accepted?

Compare this with any one of the typical fulminations which proceed at regular intervals from European commentators and the result is both astonishing and disturbing. In Europe the prevalent opinion seems to be that this same civilization of ours constitutes a serious threat to the very existence of anything which can properly be called a culture.   6

We are told, in the first place, that for every American who does read the Book of the Month and attend a symphony concert there are a dozen who live in a vulgar dream-world induced by a perpetual diet of soap operas, comic books, torch songs, and "B" movies. Moreover, the material prosperity and political power of this majority of sick barbarians enable them to become, as no cultural proletariat ever was before, a threat to every civilized minority. They rule the roost, and they are becoming less and less tolerant of anyone or anything superior to them.   7

In the second place—and perhaps even more importantly—the culture of even the minority is described as largely an imitation. It consumes but does not produce art. The best of the books it reads and the music it listens to is imported. Its members are really only parasites feeding upon European culture, and their sterility will in time kill it completely. Even their power to "appreciate" is essentially shallow—the result of superficial education, propaganda, advertisement, and a general pro-cultural hoop-la, all of which produce something very different indeed from that deep, personal, demanding passion for Truth and Beauty which has always been the dynamic force in the production of any genuine culture.*   8

Now it is easy enough to dismiss this European view as merely the product of ignorance, prejudice, and envy. But it is dangerous to do so. To look candidly at the two pictures is to perceive something recognizable in both of them. Nobody really knows what the American phenomenon means or what it portends. And the reason is that it is actually something genuinely new. Whether you call it the Dawn of the First Democratic Culture or call it the Triumph of Mediocrity, the fact remains that there is no obvious parallel in human history. Mr. Allen and those who agree with him are obviously right as far as they go. But the unique phenomenon which they describe can stand further analysis.†   9

A college education for everybody and two cars in every garage are ideals not wholly unrelated. An even closer analogy can be drawn with the earlier, more modest ideal of universal literacy. America was the first country to teach nearly everybody to read. Whether we are quite aware of it or not, we are now embarked upon the pursuit of what is really an extension of the same ideal, namely, a minimum cultural literacy for all. There

---

* Paragraphs 5 through 8: What method of analysis is being used to develop Krutch's approach through these paragraphs?

† Paragraph 9: Why have the two pictures been introduced?

is a vast difference between being barely able to spell out a newspaper and being able to read in the full sense of what the term implies. There is a similar and probably no greater difference between, say, being able to get something out of the movie *The Great Caruso* or the latest volume dispatched to the members of a book club by editors who have trained themselves to understand the limitations of their average subscriber, and a genuine grasp of either music or literature. The term "literacy" covers a large area whether we are using it in its limited sense or extending it to include what I have called "cultural literacy." A few generations ago we pointed with pride to the fact that most Americans "could read"; we now point with pride to the fact that an astonishing proportion of them "read serious books" or "listen to serious music," and in both cases we take satisfaction in a mass capacity which exists only if we define it in minimum terms. In neither case does the phenomenon mean quite as much as those who celebrate it most enthusiastically sometimes seem to assume.*   10

But, what, one may ask, is either disturbing or surprising about that? The minimum remains something more than any people as a whole ever before achieved. Is it likely that fewer people will read well just because a larger number can read a little? Is not, indeed, the opposite likely to be true? Is anything but good likely to come from the establishment of a broad base of even a minimum cultural literacy?   11

Any hesitation in answering "no" to the last question might seem at first sight to spring inevitably from nothing except arrogance, snobbishness, and a desire to preserve the privileges of an aristocracy. Yet a good many Europeans and an occasional American do seem inclined to take the negative position. The wide spread of our minimum culture does seem to them to constitute some sort of threat.   12

At least one fact or alleged fact they can cite as possible evidence on their side of the argument. So far, the number of recognized masterpieces produced by native-born Americans does seem disappointingly small when compared with the number of literate citizens we have produced. Is that because American art is inadequately recognized, or because we just haven't had time to mature? Or is it, perhaps, somehow connected—as some would say it is—with mass culture itself? Is the Good always the friend of the Best or is it sometimes and somehow the enemy? Is Excellence more likely to lose out to Mediocrity than it is to mere Ignorance or Nullity?†   13

The line being taken in Europe today has a good deal in common with that of the American intellectual of the Twenties. To some extent in-

* Paragraph 10: What is an analogy? What is the purpose of using any one of them? Why is it important to define the terms "literacy" and "cultural literacy"? What are his definitions? State the assumption referred to in the final sentence.

† Paragraph 13: How is repetition used effectively here?

deed it may have been learned from our post-World War I intellectuals; the disdainful European conception of American society is a good deal like Mencken's Boobocracy. At the present moment, however, the current of opinion at home is running in the opposite direction, and it is no longer unusual for the confessed intellectual to defend the culture which his predecessor of a generation ago despised and rejected. But complacency has its dangers too, and it may be worth while to examine a little further what can be said in support of the European's thesis.   14

This, he hears us say, is the Age of the Common Man. But we as well as he are not quite certain what we mean by that. In so far as we mean only the age of universal opportunity, what was once called simply "the career open to talents," nothing but good could seem to come of it. But many people do, sometimes without being entirely aware of it, mean something more. When we make ourselves the champion of any particular group we almost inevitably begin to idealize that group. From defending the common man we pass on to exalting him, and we find ourselves beginning to imply, not merely that he is as good as anybody else, but that he is actually better. Instead of demanding only that the common man be given an opportunity to become as uncommon as possible, we make his commonness a virtue, and even in the case of candidates for high office, we sometimes praise them for being nearly indistinguishable from the average man in the street. Secretly, no doubt, we hope that they are somehow superior, but we feel at the same time that a kind of decency requires them to conceal the fact as completely as possible.   15

The logical extreme of this opinion would be the conviction that any deviation in either direction from the statistical average is unadmirable; even, to take a concrete example, that the ideal man or woman could best be represented, not by an artist's dream, but by a composite photograph of the entire population. And though few would explicitly acknowledge their acceptance of this extreme position, there is a very strong tendency to emphasize quantitative rather than qualitative standards in estimating achievement. We are, for instance, more inclined to boast how many Americans go to college than to ask how much the average college education amounts to; how many people read books rather than how good the books are; how many listen to the radio rather than how good what they hear from it really is.   16

Argue, as I myself have argued, that more can be learned from almost any subject from ten minutes with printed page than from half an hour with even one of the better educational programs and you will be met with the reply: "Perhaps. But so many more people will listen to the radio." In a democracy quantity is important. But when the stress upon it becomes too nearly exclusive, then democracy itself threatens to lose its promise of moving on to higher levels. Thus the Good really can become

the enemy of the Best if one insists upon exclusively quantitative standards.*   17

Certainly one of the striking—some would say one of the inevitable
—characteristics of our society is its penchant for making widely and
easily accessible either substitutes for, or inferior versions of, a vast number of good things, like the vile substitute for bread available at any
grocer's. That bread can be come by without effort, and it may be true that
fewer people are in want of bread of some kind than ever were in want of it
in any society before. But that does not change the fact that it is a very
inferior product.   18

Another and related tendency of this same society is its encouragement of passivity. A generation ago moralists viewed with alarm the popularity of "spectator sports": the fact that people gathered in stadia to
watch others play games for them. But we have gone far beyond that and
today the baseball fan who takes the trouble to make a journey to the Polo
Grounds instead of watching the game on his TV set has almost earned
the right to call himself an athlete. One wonders, sometimes, if the popularity of "discussion" programs does not mean very much the same thing;
if most people have not now decided to let others hold remote conversations for them—as well as play remote games—even though the conversations are often no better than those they could hold for themselves.†   19

As John Stuart Mill—certainly no anti-democrat—wrote a century
ago:

> Capacity for the noble feeling is in most natures a very tender plant. . . .
> Men lose their high aspirations as they lose their intellectual tastes,
> because they have not time or opportunity for indulging them; and they
> addict themselves to inferior pleasures, not because they deliberately
> prefer them, but because they are either the only ones to which they
> have access, or the only ones which they are any longer capable of
> enjoying.   20

In the history books of the future this age of ours may come to be
known as the Age of Statistics. In the biological and physical as well as the
sociological sciences, statistics have become, as they never were before,
the most important tool of investigation. But as every philosophical scientist knows, the conclusions drawn by a science depend to a considerable
extent upon the tools used. And it is in the nature of statistics not only
that they deal with quantity but that they emphasize the significance of
averages and medians. What usually exists or usually happens establishes

---

* Paragraph 17: Why does Krutch recall a personal argument but not prove it? What form
of the syllogism concludes the paragraph?

† Paragraphs 18 and 19: What two characteristics of our society are delineated here? Can
they be classified as effects, causes, or conditions?

The Law, and The Law is soon thought of as identical with the Truth. In all the arts, nevertheless, it is the exceptional and the unpredictable which really count. It is the excellent, not the average, which is really important. And there is, therefore, one aspect of the cultural condition of a civilization to which statistical study is curiously inappropriate.   21

No one, it may be said, needs to accept the inferior substitute or hold himself down to the average level. But simple and complete as that answer may seem to be, there are facts and forces which do tend to encourage an almost unconscious acceptance of mediocrity. One, of course, is that the inferior substitute—whether it be baker's bread or the movie show playing at the neighborhood house—is so readily accessible and so forced upon one's attention by all the arts of advertising as well as by the very way in which our lives have been organized. Another and more serious one is the tendency of the mass media to force out of the field every enterprise which is not based upon mass appeal. Whatever the reason may be, it is a generally recognized fact that it is becoming increasingly difficult, economically, to publish a book which is not a best seller or produce a play which is not a smash hit. More and more, therefore, artistic enterprise must be abandoned to the movies and to television where the mass audience is sufficient to defray the staggering cost.*   22

Besides these economic reasons why the new media tend to concern themselves only with mass appeals, there is the additional technical reason why the two newest of such media tend to confine themselves to it. Since TV and radio channels are limited in number, all the arguments in favor of democracy as it is sometimes defined justify the existing fact that these channels should be used to communicate what the greatest number of people seem to want. That is the argument of the great broadcasting chains, and on the premise assumed it is a valid one.   23

The only mechanical instrument of communication which can make a reasonable case for the claim that it has actually served to increase the popularity of the thing communicated on its highest level of excellence is the phonograph, and it is significant that the phonograph is the only such device for communication which—especially since the invention of tape recording and LP—has found it economically feasible to cater to relatively small minorities. The fact that it does not cost much to produce a record may well have an incalculably great effect upon American musical taste.†   24

* Paragraph 22: What are the causes for "an almost unconscious acceptance of mediocrity"?

† Paragraphs 22 through 24: Why is so much more space devoted to the second of "the facts and forces"? Are both induction and deduction used to prove this second point? Trace the reasoning process used from "the unconscious acceptance of mediocrity" through the end of paragraph 24. Paragraph 24: How is the exception to the point accounted for?

What the question comes down to in the simplest possible terms is one of those which we asked at the very beginning of this discussion: Can we have an Age of the Common Man without having also an Age of the Common Denominator? That question has not been answered, probably cannot be convincingly answered, at the present moment. But it is a fateful question and the one with which this discussion is concerned.   25

One must not, of course, idealize the past to the extent of assuming that the best works were always, inevitably, and immediately the most popular. Two years ago James D. Hart's thorough and amusing *The Popular Book* (Oxford University Press) demonstrated conclusively that since colonial times there have always been absurd best sellers. The year that Hawthorne earned $144.09 royalty in six months was the year his own publisher paid Susan Warner $4,500 for the same period and another publisher sold 70,000 copies of one of Fanny Fern's several works.*   26

Neither, I think, should it be supposed that any society ever has been or ever will be so organized as to favor exclusively the highest artistic excellence. As a system, aristocratic patronage is absurdly capricious; capitalistic democracy tends to favor vulgarity; Socialism would probably favor official mediocrity. The question here is not whether contemporary America provides ideal conditions for cultural developments on the highest level, but whether it renders such development unusually difficult instead of making it, as the optimists insist, almost inevitable.†   27

Of the unfavorable influences which I have mentioned, it seems to me that the most serious is the tendency to confuse the Common Denominator with a standard of excellence. The mechanical and economic facts which tend to give the purveyors of mediocrity a monopoly—highly developed in the case of radio and TV, probably growing in the publishing business—may possibly be changed by new developments, as they have already been changed in the case of the phonograph. But to confuse The Best with the most widely and the most generally acceptable is to reveal a spiritual confusion which is subtle and insidious as well as fundamental. It could easily nullify any solution of the mechanical and economic problems created by the age of mass production.   28

How real and how general does this confusion seem actually to be?   29

More than one sociologist has recently pointed out that as technology integrates larger and larger populations into tighter and tighter groups the members of these groups tend inevitably to work, live, and recreate themselves in the same way and in accordance with the standardized patterns which the facilities provided for these various activities lay down. For ill as well as for good, "community living" becomes more

---

* Paragraph 26: What is the purpose of the example? Does it accomplish this purpose as a mere illustration or as factual proof?

† Paragraph 27: Why is the central question of the essay stated again?

and more nearly inevitable and individual temperament or taste finds less
and less opportunity to express itself.   30

   One result of this is that the natural tendency of the adolescent to
practice a desperate conformity is prolonged into adult life and the grown
man continues to want what his neighbors have, to do what his neighbors
do, to enjoy what his neighbors enjoy. This is one of the things which the
European may have in mind when he calls us a nation of adolescents, and
commercial interests take advantage of our adolescent characteristics by
stressing, through all sorts of publicity, the fact that this is the kind of
cigarette most people smoke, the kind of breakfast food most people eat,
and the torch singer or crooner most people like. The best-selling book
is not only the one easiest to buy, but it is also the one we must read
unless we are willing to be made to seem somehow inferior. What is most
popular must be best. As a broadcast official recently said, to call the most
popular radio programs vulgar is to call the American people vulgar. And
that, he seemed to imply, was not merely nonsense but pretty close to
treason. The voice of the people is the voice of God. God loves the common man. If the common man loves Bob Hope then God must love Bob
Hope also. In musical taste as in everything else the common man is
divine.*   31

   It is this logic which, unfortunately, the purveyors to the mass audience are very prone to follow. Undoubtedly, it leads them to the line of
least resistance at the same time that it provides them with a smug excuse
for both inanity and vulgarity. They are, they say, servants of the public
and have no right to doubt that the people know not only what they want
but what is good for them. The age of the common man has no place for
any holier-than-thou attitude. It believes in government "by" as well as
"for" the people. Totalitarianism is what you get when you accept the
"for" but not the "by," and the attitude of, for example, the British
Broadcasting Company, with its notorious Third Program, merely demonstrates that England has not yet learned what democracy really means.†   32

   No doubt the questions involved are too complicated to be discussed
here. A few years ago, Charles A. Siepmann in his *Radio, Television, and
Society* fully and impartially reported on both the policies and the arguments as they affect the media with which he was dealing. But at least one
conclusion seems obvious. If there is any such thing as responsibility on
the part of those most powerful and best informed towards those whose
appetites they feed, then no provider of movies or records or television pro-

---

* Paragraph 31: Trace the reasoning process of the broadcast official. In Krutch's example
  of the logic of the controllers of the mass media demonstrating God's approval of Bob
  Hope, two syllogisms are suggested. State both of them in their complete forms. What
  is wrong with each of them?

† Paragraph 32: Where is irony used here as a rhetorical device?

grams can escape the minimal duty of giving his public the best rather than the worst it will stand for. Mr. Mencken once declared that no one had ever gone bankrupt by underestimating the taste of the American public, but there is an increasing tendency to believe that, by dint of long trying, certain commercial exploiters of the mass media have succeeded only too well in underestimating it considerably. 33

What is obviously called for is a public opinion less ready than it now is to excuse the failure to meet even minimal responsibilities; but that public opinion is not likely to arise unless those responsible for public thinking play their own parts, and there is a tendency for them to yield rather than protest. Unfortunately, the fanatical exaltation of the common denominator has been taken up not only by the common man himself and by those who hope to profit by his exploitation but also and increasingly by those who are supposed to be educators and intellectual leaders. Instead of asking "What would a good education consist of?" many professors of education are asking "What do most college students want?"; instead of asking "What books are wisest and best and most beautiful?" they conduct polls to determine which the largest number of students have read with least pain. Examination papers are marked, not in accordance with any fixed standard, but in accordance with a usual level of achievement; the amount of work required is fixed by the amount the average student does; even the words with which the average student is not familiar are edited out of the books he is given to read. How, granted such methods, is it other than inevitable both that the average will seldom be exceeded and that the average itself will gradually drop? 34

As David Reisman and his collaborators pointed out two years ago in their brilliant analysis called *The Lonely Crowd* (Yale University Press), the ideal now persistently held before the American citizen from the moment he enters kindergarten to the time when he is buried under the auspices of a recognized funeral parlor is a kind of conformity more or less disguised under the term "adjustment." "Normality" has almost completely replaced "Excellence" as an ideal. It has also rendered all but obsolescent such terms as "Righteousness," "Integrity," and "Truth." The question is no longer how a boy ought to behave but how most boys do behave; not how honest a man ought to be but how honest men usually are. Even the Robber Baron, who represented an evil manifestation of the determination to excel, gives away to the moneymaker who wants only to be rich according to the accepted standards of his group. Or, as Mr. Reisman sums it up, the American who used to be conspicuously "inner-directed" is now conspicuously "outer-directed."* 35

---

* Paragraph 35: What is the purpose of citing Reisman's book? Can you determine the validity of Reisman as an authority? How does Krutch try to make him acceptable to the reader? What word (words) used by Krutch is (are) the equivalent of "outer-directed"?

According to the anthropologists, many primitive societies are based almost exclusively upon the idea of conformity and generate what are, in the anthropologist's meaning of the term, remarkable cultures. It may, of course, be argued that America and the whole world which follows in America's wake is evolving in the direction of this kind of culture. But if by "culture" we mean something more narrowly defined, if we mean a culture which is continuous with that of the Western world since the Renaissance, then it is my contention that it cannot flourish where the stress is as nearly exclusively as it threatens to become upon "adjustment," "normality," or any of the other concepts which, in the end, come down to mean that the Common Denominator is identical with the Ideal. Especially, it cannot flourish under those conditions if the result which they tend to produce is intensified by the fact that ingenious methods of mass production and mass propaganda help impose upon all the tyranny of the average.   36

Salvation, if salvation is possible, may be made so by technological developments like those in the phonograph industry which tend to break monopoly and permit the individual to assert his preferences and his tastes. But the possible will not become the actual if in the meantime the desire for excellence has been lost and those who should be leaders have willingly become followers instead. If the Age of the Common Man is not to become the Age of the Common Denominator rather than what it was originally intended to be—namely an age in which every man had the opportunity to become as superior as he could—then the cultural as well as the political rights of minorities must somehow be acknowledged. There is not really anything undemocratic about either the desire for, or the recognition of, excellence. To prove that ours is the most cultured nation which ever existed will constitute only a barren victory if we must, to prove our point, use nothing but quantitative standards and reconcile ourselves to the common denominator as a measure of excellence.   37

One might sum up the situation in a series of propositions. (1) The Age of the Common Man has begun. (2) Despite all the gains that it may legitimately claim, they are threatened by those confusions which arise when the common denominator is consciously or unconsciously allowed to function as a standard of excellence. (3) The dominance of mass media almost exclusively under the control of those who are little concerned with anything except immediate financial gain does tend to debase taste. (4) Ultimate responsibility for the future rests with the thinkers and the educators whose most important social task at the moment is to define democratic culture in some fashion which will both reserve a place for uncommon excellence and, even in connection with the largest masses, emphasize the highest rather than the lowest common denominator.   38

The Whole Selection

1 Can you determine the character of the audience at which this essay was directed from the essay itself and from the place where it first appeared? Can you conclude that there is a relationship between the author's attitude toward his material and his attitude toward his audience?

2 It is very important to your comprehension of the essay to understand how Krutch proves that the "Best" tends to become what is most widely and generally acceptable in the Age of the Common Man. How does he arrive at this conclusion? Trace his reasoning process.

3 Point out passages in which Krutch appears to be most persuasive to the reader. Try to determine what techniques of persuasion he is using.

4 In the final paragraph Krutch lists four propositions. These four points, divided and subdivided, will give the reader the structure of the essay. Using this structure, outline in detail the development of the essay.

    I   The Age of the Common Man has begun.

    II   Despite all the gains . . .

    III   The dominance of mass media . . .

    IV   Ultimate responsibility of the future . . .

Remember that this is not a paragraph outline; you may have to skip around throughout the essay to get the proper divisions under each point. This kind of development is proper to informal argument.

5 In paragraph 38, how has Krutch proved any one of the "propositions" listed? After studying the four propositions listed here, phrase the single proposition that gives us the dominant intention of the essay. What is the rhetorical effect of this kind of summary paragraph in an essay of this character?

Word Study   *assess, corrigible, cogently, fulminations, sterility, complacency, divergence, penchant, passivity, capricious, insidious, nullify, purveyors, inanity, minimal*

THE DECLARATION OF INDEPENDENCE

[The composition of the Declaration of Independence is substantially that of Thomas Jefferson, but it was altered and amended by the Congress. The parts struck out by Congress are here printed in italics and enclosed in brackets, and those inserted by it are placed in the margin or in a concurrent column.]

When, in the course of human events, it becomes necessary for one people to dissolve the political bands which have connected them with another, and to assume among the powers of the earth the separate and equal station to which the laws of nature and of nature's God entitle them, a decent respect to the opinions of mankind requires that they should declare the causes which impel them to the separation.*

1

We hold these truths to be self-evident: that all men are created equal; that they are endowed by their creator with [inherent and] inalienable rights; that among these are life, liberty, and the pursuit of happiness: that to secure these rights, governments are instituted among men, deriving their just powers from the consent of the governed; that whenever any form of government becomes destructive of these ends, it is the right of the people to alter or to abolish it, and to institute new government, laying its foundation on such principles, and organizing its powers in such form, as to them shall seem most likely to effect their safety and happiness. Prudence, indeed, will dictate that governments long established should not be changed for light and transient causes; and accordingly all experience hath shown that mankind are more disposed to suffer while evils are sufferable, than to right themselves by abolishing the forms to which they are accustomed. But when a long train of abuses and usurpations, [begun at a distinguished period and] pursuing invariably the same object, evinces a design to reduce them under absolute despotism, it is their right, it is their duty to throw off such government, and to provide new guards for their future security. Such has been the patient sufferance of these colonies; and such is now the necessity which constrains them to [expunge] their former systems of government. The history of the

certain

alter

* Paragraph 1: What is the specific purpose of this paragraph?

present king of Great Britain is a history of [*unremitting*]   repeated
injuries and usurpations, [*among which appears no soli-*
tary fact to contradict the uniform tenor of the rest, but
all have] in direct object the establishment of an absolute   all having
tyranny over these states. To prove this, let facts be submitted to a candid world [*for the truth of which we pledge*
a faith yet unsullied by falsehood.]*   2

He has refused his assent to laws the most whole-
some and necessary for the public good.   3

He has forbidden his governors to pass laws of immediate and pressing importance, unless suspended in
their operation till his assent should be obtained; and,
when so suspended, he has utterly neglected to attend
them.   4

He has refused to pass other laws for the accommodation of large districts of people, unless those people
would relinquish the right of representation in the legislature, a right inestimable to them, and formidable to
tyrants only.   5

He has called together legislative bodies at places
unusual, uncomfortable, and distant from the depository
of their public records, for the sole purpose of fatiguing
them into compliance with his measures.   6

He has dissolved representative houses repeatedly
[*and continually*] for opposing with manly firmness his
invasions on the rights of the people.   7

He has refused for a long time after such dissolu-
tions to cause others to be elected, whereby the legislative
powers, incapable of annihilation, have returned to the
people at large for their exercise, the state remaining, in
the meantime, exposed to all the dangers of invasion
from without and convulsions within.   8

He has endeavored to prevent the population of
these states; for that purpose obstructing the laws for
naturalization of foreigners, refusing to pass others to
encourage their migrations hither, and raising the conditions of new appropriations of lands.   9

---

* Paragraphs 1 and 2: What indication has the reader that this is a very serious undertaking? Can you characterize the tone of the essay or the authors' attitude toward their
subject and toward their audience?

* Paragraph 2: Enumerate the number of "self-evident" truths listed. What is a "self-
evident" truth? Can you cite other "self-evident" truths? How does the use of "facts" in
the final sentence compare with the definition of "fact" given in your dictionary? What
are the conditions (as opposed to the causes) of rebellion?

He has [*suffered*] the administration of justice   obstructed
[*totally to cease in some of these states*] refusing his   by
assent to laws for establishing judiciary powers.   10

He has made [*our*] judges dependent on his will
alone for the tenure of their offices, and the amount and
payment of their salaries.   11

He has erected a multitude of new offices, [*by a
self-assumed power*] and sent hither swarms of new
officers to harass our people and eat out their substance.   12

He has kept among us in times of peace standing
armies [*and ships of war*] without the consent of our legislatures.   13

He has affected to render the military independent
of, and superior to, the civil power.   14

He has combined with others to subject us to a
jurisdiction foreign to our constitutions and unacknowledged by our laws, giving his assent to their acts of pretended legislation for quartering large bodies of armed
troops among us; for protecting them by a mock trial from
punishment for any murders which they should commit
on the inhabitants of these states; for cutting off our
trade with all parts of the world; for imposing taxes on
us without our consent; for depriving us [   ] of the   in many cases
benefits of trial by jury; for transporting us beyond seas
to be tried for pretended offences; for abolishing the free
system of English laws in a neighboring province, establishing therein an arbitrary government, and enlarging its
boundaries, so as to render it at once an example and fit
instrument for introducing the same absolute rule into
these [*states*]; for taking away our charters, abolishing   colonies
our most valuable laws, and altering fundamentally the
forms of our governments; for suspending our own legislatures, and declaring themselves invested with power to
legislate for us in all cases whatsoever.   15

He has abdicated government here [*withdrawing his*   by declaring us
governors, and declaring us out of his allegiance and pro-   out of his pro-
tection].   tection, and
                                                                        waging war   16
He has plundered our seas, ravaged our coasts,   against us.
burnt our towns, and destroyed the lives of our people.   17

He is at this time transporting large armies of
foreign mercenaries to complete the works of death, desolation, and tyranny already begun with circumstances of

cruelty and perfidy [   ] unworthy the head of a civilized nation.

He has constrained our fellow citizens taken captive on the high seas to bear arms against their country, to become the executioners of their friends and brethren, or to fall themselves by their hands.

He has [   ] endeavored to bring on the inhabitants of our frontiers, the merciless Indian savages, whose known rule of warfare is an undistinguished destruction of all ages, sexes, and conditions [of existence]*

[He has incited treasonable insurrections of our fellow citizens, with the allurements of forfeiture and confiscation of our property. He has waged cruel war against human nature itself, violating its most sacred rights of life and liberty in the persons of a distant people who never offended him, captivating and carrying them into slavery in another hemisphere, or to incur miserable death in their transportation thither. This piratical warfare, the opprobrium of INFIDEL powers, is the warfare of the CHRISTIAN king of Great Britain. Determined to keep open a market where MEN should be bought and sold, he has prostituted his negative for suppressing every legislative attempt to prohibit or to restrain this execrable commerce. And that this assemblage of horrors might want no fact of distinguished die, he is now exciting those very people to rise in arms among us, and to purchase that liberty of which he has deprived them, by murdering the people on whom he also obtruded them: thus paying off former crimes committed against the LIBERTIES of one people, with crimes which he urges them to commit against the LIVES of another.]

In every stage of these oppressions we have petitioned for redress in the most humble terms: our repeated petitions have been answered only by repeated injuries.†

A prince whose character is thus marked by every act which may define a tyrant is unfit to be the ruler of a [   ] people [who mean to be free. Future ages will scarcely believe that the hardiness of one man adven-

Sidenote: scarcely paralleled in the most barbarous ages, and totally **18**

19

Sidenote: excited domestic insurrection among us, and has **20**

21

22

Sidenote: free

---

* Paragraphs 3 through 20: What rhetorical principle is illustrated by the structure of these paragraphs?

† Paragraph 22: What is the function of this paragraph?

tured, within the short compass of twelve years only, to lay a foundation so broad and so undisguised for tyranny over a people fostered and fixed in principles of freedom].   23

Nor have we been wanting in attentions to our British brethren. We have warned them from time to time of attempts by their legislature to extend [a] jurisdiction over [*these our states*]. We have reminded them of the circumstances of our emigration and settlement here, [*no one of which could warrant so strange a pretension: that these were effected at the expense of our own blood and treasure, unassisted by the wealth or the strength of Great Britain: that in constituting indeed our several forms of government, we had adopted one common king, thereby laying a foundation for perpetual league and amity with them: but that submission to their parliament was no part of our constitution, nor ever in idea, if history may be credited: and,*] we [   ] appealed to their native justice and magnanimity [*as well as to*] the ties of our common kindred to disavow these usurpations which [*were likely to*] interrupt our connection and correspondence. They too have been deaf to the voice of justice and of consanguinity. [*and when occasions have been given them, by the regular course of their laws, of removing from their councils the disturbers of our harmony, they have, by their free election, re-established them in power. At this very time too, they are permitting their chief magistrate to send over not only soldiers of our common blood but Scotch and foreign mercenaries to invade and destroy us. These facts have given the last stab to agonizing affection, and manly spirit bids us to renounce forever these unfeeling brethren. We must endeavor to forget our former love for them, and hold them as we hold the rest of mankind, enemies in war, in peace friends. We might have been a free and a great people together; but a communication of grandeur and of freedom, it seems, is below their dignity. Be it so, since they will have it. The road to happiness and to glory is open to us, too. We will tread it apart from them, and*] acquiesce in the necessity which denounces our [*eternal*] separation [   ]!

Marginal notes:

an unwarrantable/us

have
and we have conjured them by
would inevitably

We must therefore
and hold them as we hold the rest of mankind, enemies in war, in peace friends.   24

We, therefore, the representatives of the United States of America in General Congress assembled, do in the name, and by the authority of the good people of these [*states reject and renounce all allegiance and subjection to the kings of Great Britain and all others who may hereafter claim by, through, or under them; we utterly dissolve all political connection which may heretofore have subsisted between us and the people or parliament of Great Britain; and finally we do assert and declare these colonies to be free and independent states,*] and that as free and independent states, they have full power to levy war, conclude peace, contract alliances, establish commerce, and to do all other acts and things which independent states may of right do.

And for the support of this declaration, we mutually pledge to each other our lives, our fortunes, and our sacred honor.

We, therefore, the representatives of the United States of America in General Congress assembled, appealing to the supreme judge of the world for the rectitude of our intentions, do in the name, and by the authority of the good people of these colonies, solemnly publish and declare, that these united colonies are, and of right ought to be free and independent states; that they are absolved from all allegiance to the British crown, and that all political connection between them and the state of Great Britain is, and ought to be, totally dissolved; and that as free and independent states, they have full power to levy war, conclude peace, contract alliances, establish commerce, and to do all other acts and things which independent states may of right do.   25

And for the support of this declaration, with a firm reliance on the protection of divine providence, we mutually pledge to each other our lives, our fortunes, and our sacred honor.   26

The Whole Selection

1 The principal form of evidence used to prove the proposition in this essay is reasoning by deduction, which takes the form of a syllogism. In a simplified manner, construct the syllogism that supports the line of reasoning:
Major Premise:
Minor Premise:
Conclusion:
2 Both types of reasoning, induction and deduction, are often used in the

same essay to support the proposition. In what way is induction used in this essay?

3 It is obvious from the second paragraph and from the final paragraph that this document is a call to action. The reader is required not only to give his assent to the proposition but also to do something about it or, at least, to concur with something that is being done. As a result, the persuasive elements in the document should be apparent to the reader. Using the following categories, find evidence from the Declaration to demonstrate its persuasive effect:

a Choice of words (diction)

b Selection of details

4 We know that it is important to define the terms used in argumentation. We know, as well, that the definition of some terms may be assumed under certain conditions: if the terms are familiar to the audience or to mankind in general and if they have already been defined acceptably by the opposition. How are the following terms defined?

a Government

b Laws of nature

c Unalienable rights

d Tyrant

5 From the following points of view, study the additions and subtractions that the Continental Congress made:

a Has the meaning of the document been altered in any way? Jefferson tells us in his autobiography that "the sentiments of men are known not only by what they receive, but what they reject also."

b Has the line of reasoning been strengthened or weakened?

c Are the persuasive elements emphasized, altered, or diminished?

d Some pieces of writing must be considered in relation to the era in which they were written for complete understanding. Would the circumstances of the time explain any of the alterations or amendments?

SUBURBIA: OF THEE I SING

PHYLLIS McGINLEY

Twenty miles east of New York City as the New Haven Railroad flies
sits a village I shall call Spruce Manor. The Boston Post Road, there,
for the length of two blocks, becomes Main Street, and on one side of
that thundering thoroughfare are the grocery stores and the drug stores
and the Village Spa where teen-agers gather of an afternoon to drink their
cokes and speak their curious confidences. There one finds the shoe re-
pairers and the dry cleaners and the second-hand stores which sell "an-
tiques" and the stationery stores which dispense comic books to ten-year-
olds and greeting cards and lending library masterpieces to their mothers.
On the opposite side stand the bank, the fire house, the public library. The
rest of this town of perhaps four or five thousand people lies to the south
and is bounded largely by Long Island Sound, curving protectively on
three borders. The movie theater (dedicated to the showing of second-
run, single-feature pictures) and the grade schools lie north, beyond the
Post Road, and that is a source of worry to Spruce Manorites. They are
always a little uneasy about the children, crossing, perhaps, before the
lights are safely green. However, two excellent policemen—Mr. Crowley
and Mr. Lang—station themselves at the intersections four times a day,
and so far there have been no accidents.   1

    Spruce Manor in the spring and summer and fall is a pretty town,
full of gardens and old elms. (There are few spruces, but the village Council is considering planting a few on the station plaza, out of sheer patriotism.) In the winter, the houses reveal themselves as comfortable, well-
kept, architecturally insignificant. Then one can see the town for what it is
and has been since it left off being farm and woodland some sixty years
ago—the epitome of Suburbia, not the country and certainly not the city.
It is a commuter's town, the living center of a web which unrolls each
morning as the men swing aboard the locals, and contracts again in the
evening when they return. By day, with even the children pent in schools,
it is a village of women. They trundle mobile baskets at the A&P, they sit
under driers at the hairdressers, they sweep their porches and set out
bulbs and stitch up slip covers. Only on weekends does it become heterogeneous and lively, the parking places difficult to find.*   2

    Spruce Manor has no country club of its own, though devoted golfers
have their choice of two or three not far away. It does have a small yacht
club and a beach which can be used by anyone who rents or owns a

---

* Paragraph 2: What method of analysis is applied to Spruce Manor in order to clarify
the community's definition for the reader? What metaphor reinforces the descriptive
definition of paragraph 1?

house here. The village supports a little park with playground equipment and a counselor, where children, unattended by parents, can spend summer days if they have no more pressing engagements.   3

It is a town not wholly without traditions. Residents will point out the two-hundred-year-old manor house, now a minor museum; and in the autumn they line the streets on a scheduled evening to watch the Volunteer Firemen parade. That is a fine occasion, with so many heads of households marching in their red blouses and white gloves, some with flaming helmets, some swinging lanterns, most of them genially out of step. There is a bigger parade on Memorial Day with more marchers than watchers and with the Catholic priest, the rabbi, and the Protestant ministers each delivering a short prayer when the paraders gather near the War Memorial. On the whole, however, outside of contributing generously to the Community Chest, Manorites are not addicted to municipal get-togethers.   4

No one is very poor here and not many families rich enough to be awesome. In fact, there is not much to distinguish Spruce Manor from any other of a thousand suburbs outside of New York City or San Francisco or Detroit or Chicago or even Stockholm, for that matter. Except for one thing. For some reason, Spruce Manor has become a sort of symbol to writers and reporters familiar only with its name or trivial aspects. It has become a symbol of all that is middle-class in the worst sense, of settled-downness or rootlessness, according to what the writer is trying to prove; of smug and prosperous mediocrity—or even, in more lurid novels, of lechery at the country club and Sunday morning hangovers.   5

To condemn Suburbia has long been a literary cliché, anyhow. I have yet to read a book in which the suburban life was pictured as the good life or the commuter as a sympathetic figure. He is nearly as much a stock character as the old stage Irishman: the man who "spends his life riding to and from his wife," the eternal Babbitt who knows all about Buicks and nothing about Picasso, whose sanctuary is the club locker room, whose ideas spring ready-made from the illiberal newspapers. His wife plays politics at the P.T.A. and keeps up with the Joneses. Or—if the scene is more gilded and less respectable—the commuter is the high-powered advertising executive with a station wagon and an eye for the ladies, his wife a restless baggage given to too many cocktails in the afternoon.   6

These clichés I challenge. I have lived in the country, I have lived in the city. I have lived in an average Middle Western small town. But for the best eleven years of my life I have lived in Suburbia and I like it.*   7

"Compromise!" cried our friends when we came here from an expensive, inconvenient, moderately fashionable tenement in Manhattan. It was the period in our lives when everyone was moving somewhere. Farther uptown, farther downtown, across town to Sutton Place, to a

* Paragraph 7: What is the function of this paragraph?

half-dozen rural acres in Connecticut or New Jersey or even Vermont. But no one in our rather rarefied little group was thinking of moving to the suburbs except us. They were aghast that we could find anything appealing in the thought of a middle-class house on a middle-class street in a middle-class village full of middle-class people. That we were tired of town and hoped for children, that we couldn't afford both a city apartment and a farm, they put down as feeble excuses. To this day they cannot understand us. You see, they read the books. They even write them.   8

Compromise? Of course we compromise. But compromise, if not the spice of life, is its solidity. It is what makes nations great and marriages happy and Spruce Manor the pleasant place it is. As for its being middle-class, what is wrong with acknowledging one's roots? And how free we are! Free of the city's noise, of its ubiquitous doormen, of the soot on the windowsill and the radio in the next apartment. We have released ourselves from the seasonal hegira to the mountains or the seashore. We have only one address, one house to keep supplied with paring knives and blankets. We are free from the snows that block the countryman's roads in winter and his electricity which always goes off in a thunderstorm. I do not insist that we are typical. There is nothing really typical about any of our friends and neighbors here, and therein lies my point. The true suburbanite needs to conform less than anyone else; much less than the gentleman farmer with his remodeled salt-box or than the determined cliff dweller with his necessity for living at the right address. In Spruce Manor all addresses are right. And since we are fairly numerous here, we need not fall back on the people nearest us for total companionship. There is not here, as in a small city away from truly urban centers, some particular family whose codes must be ours. And we could not keep up with the Joneses even if we wanted to, for we know many Joneses and they are all quite different people leading the most various lives.*   9

The Albert Joneses spend their weekends sailing, the Bertram Joneses cultivate their delphinium, the Clarence Joneses—Clarence being a handy man with a cello—are enthusiastic about amateur chamber music. The David Joneses dote on bridge, but neither of the Ernest Joneses understands it, and they prefer staying home of an evening so that Ernest Jones can carve his witty caricatures out of pieces of old fruit wood. We admire each other's gardens, applaud each other's sailing records; we are too busy to compete. So long as our clapboards are painted and our hedges decently trimmed, we have fulfilled our community obligations. We can live as anonymously as in a city or we can call half the village by their first names.   10

* Paragraphs 8 and 9: Why is "compromise" introduced in paragraph 8 but not developed until paragraph 9? How is it defined? How may her friends have defined it? Is there any relationship between her definition of "compromise" and the idea of freedom? What is the connection between her "point" and paragraph 7? Point out an example of the use of contrast.

On our half-acre or three-quarters, we can raise enough tomatoes for our salads and assassinate enough beetles to satisfy the gardening urge. Or we can buy our vegetables at the store and put the whole place to lawn without feeling that we are neglecting our property. We can have privacy and shade and the changing of the seasons and also the Joneses next door from whom to borrow a cup of sugar or a stepladder. Despite the novelists, the shadow of the country club rests lightly on us. Half of us wouldn't be found dead with a golf stick in our hands, and loathe Saturday dances. Few of us expect to be deliriously wealthy or world-famous or divorced. What we do expect is to pay off the mortgage and send our healthy children to good colleges.   11

For when I refer to life here, I think, of course, of living with children. Spruce Manor without children would be a paradox. The summer waters are full of them, gamboling like dolphins. The lanes are alive with them, the yards overflow with them, they possess the tennis courts and the skating pond and the vacant lots. Their roller skates wear down the asphalt, and their bicycles make necessary the twenty-five-mile speed limit. They converse interminably on the telephones and make rich the dentist and the pediatrician. Who claims that a child and a half is the American middle-class average? A nice medium Spruce Manor family runs to four or five, and we count proudly, but not with amazement, the many solid households running to six, seven, eight, nine, even up to twelve. Our houses here are big and not new, most of them, and there is a temptation to fill them up, let the décor fall where it may.*   12

Besides, Spruce Manor seems designed by providence and town planning for the happiness of children. Better designed than the city; better, I say defiantly, than the country. Country mothers must be constantly arranging and contriving for their children's leisure time. There is no neighbor child next door for playmate, no school within walking distance. The ponds are dangerous to young swimmers, the woods full of poison ivy, the romantic dirt roads unsuitable for bicycles. An extra acre or two gives a fine sense of possession to an adult; it does not compensate children for the give-and-take of our village, where there is always a contemporary to help swing the skipping rope or put on the catcher's mitt. Where in the country is the Friday evening dancing class or the Saturday morning movie (approved by the P.T.A.)? It is the greatest fallacy of all time that children love the country as a year-around plan. Children would take a dusty corner of Washington Square or a city sidewalk, even, in preference to the lonely sermons in stones and books in running brooks which their contemporaries cannot share.   13

As for the horrors of bringing up progeny in the city, for all its

* Paragraph 12: List the verbs that are used metaphorically.

museums and other cultural advantages (so perfectly within reach of sub-urban families if they feel strongly about it), they were summed up for me one day last winter. The harried mother of one, speaking to me on the telephone just after Christmas, sighed and said, "It's been a really wonder-ful time for me, as vacations go. Barbara has had an engagement with a child in our apartment house every afternoon this week. I have had to take her almost nowhere." Barbara is eleven. For six of those eleven years, I realized, her mother must have dreaded Christmas vacation, not to men-tion spring, as a time when Barbara had to be entertained. I thought thankfully of my own daughters whom I had scarcely seen since school closed, out with their skis and their sleds and their friends, sliding down the roped-off hill half a block away, coming in hungrily for lunch and disappearing again, hearty, amused, and safe—at least as safe as any sled-borne child can be.*   14

Spruce Manor is not Eden, of course. Our taxes are higher than we like, and there is always that eight-eleven in the morning to be caught, and we sometimes resent the necessity of rushing from a theater to a train on a weekday evening. But the taxes pay for our really excellent schools and for our garbage collections (so that the pails of orange peels need not stand in the halls overnight as ours did in the city) and for our water supply which does not give out every dry summer as it frequently does in the country. As for the theaters—they are twenty miles away and we don't get to them more than twice a month. But neither, I think, do many of our friends in town. The eight-eleven is rather a pleasant train, too, say the husbands; it gets them to work in thirty-four minutes and they read the papers restfully on the way.†   15

"But the suburban mind!" cry our die-hard friends in Manhattan and Connecticut. "The suburban conversation! The monotony!" They imply that they and I must scintillate or we perish. Let me anatomize Spruce Manor, for them and for the others who envision Suburbia as a congrega-tion of mindless housewives and amoral go-getters.‡   16

From my window, now, on a June morning, I have a view. It contains neither solitary hills nor dramatic skyscrapers. But I can see my roses in bloom, and my foxglove, and an arch of trees over the lane. I think com-fortably of my friends whose houses line this and other streets rather like it. Not one of them is, so far as I know, doing any of the things that subur-ban ladies are popularly supposed to be doing. One of them, I happen to

---

* Paragraphs 12 through 14: What is the new topic developed in these paragraphs? How is it related to the proposition? What is the thesis statement of these three paragraphs as a unit? By what methods of analysis is it developed?

† Paragraph 15: What advantage does the author gain by bringing up the disadvantages of Spruce Manor?

‡ Paragraph 16: State in your own words what the "die-hard friends in Manhattan and Connecticut" mean by "the suburban mind."

know, has gone bowling for her health and figure, but she has already tidied up her house and arranged to be home before the boys return from school. Some, undoubtedly, are ferociously busy in the garden. One lady is on her way to Ellis Island, bearing comfort and gifts to a Polish boy—a seventeen-year-old stowaway who did slave labor in Germany and was liberated by a cousin of hers during the war—who is being held for attempting to attain the land of which her cousin told him. The boy has been on the Island for three months. Twice a week she takes this tedious journey, meanwhile besieging courts and immigration authorities on his behalf. This lady has a large house, a part-time maid, and five children.   17

My friend around the corner is finishing her third novel. She writes daily from nine-thirty until two. After that her son comes back from school and she plunges into maternity; at six, she combs her pretty hair, refreshes her lipstick, and is charming to her doctor husband. The village dancing school is run by another neighbor, as it has been for twenty years. She has sent a number of ballerinas on to the theatrical world as well as having shepherded for many a successful season the white-gloved little boys and full-skirted little girls through their first social tasks.   18

Some of the ladies are no doubt painting their kitchens or a nursery; one of them is painting the portrait, on assignment, of a very distinguished personage. Some of them are nurses' aides and Red Cross workers and supporters of good causes. But all find time to be friends with their families and to meet the 5:32 five nights a week. They read something besides the newest historical novel, Braque is not unidentifiable to most of them, and their conversation is for the most part as agreeable as the tables they set. The tireless bridge players, the gossips, the women bored by their husbands live perhaps in our suburb, too. Let them. Our orbits need not cross.   19

And what of the husbands, industriously selling bonds or practicing law or editing magazines or looking through microscopes or managing offices in the city? Do they spend their evenings and their weekends in the gaudy bars of Fifty-second Street? Or are they the perennial householders, their lives a dreary round of taking down screens and mending drains? Well, screens they have always with them, and a man who is good around the house can spend happy hours with the plumbing even on a South Sea island. Some of them cut their own lawns and some of them try to break par and some of them sail their little boats all summer with their families for crew. Some of them are village trustees for nothing a year and some listen to symphonies and some think Milton Berle ought to be President. There is a scientist who plays wonderful bebop, and an insurance salesman who has bought a big old house nearby and with his own hands is gradually tearing it apart and reshaping it nearer to his heart's desire. Some of them are passionate hedge-clippers and some read Plutarch for fun. But I do not know many—though there may be such—who either kiss their neighbor's wives behind doors or whose idea of sprightly talk is to tell you the plot of an old movie.*   20

It is June, now, as I have said. This afternoon my daughters will come home from school with a crowd of their peers at their heels. They will eat up the cookies and drink up the ginger ale and go down for a swim at the beach if the water is warm enough, that beach which is only three blocks away and open to all Spruce Manor. They will go unattended by me, since they have been swimming since they were four, and besides there are lifeguards and no big waves. (Even our piece of ocean is a compromise.) Presently it will be time for us to climb into our very old Studebaker—we are not car-proud in Spruce Manor—and meet the 5:32. That evening expedition is not vitally necessary, for a bus runs straight down our principal avenue from the station to the shore, and it meets all trains. But it is an event we enjoy. There is something delightfully ritualistic about the moment when the train pulls in and the men swing off, with the less sophisticated children running squealing to meet them. The women move over from the driver's seat, surrender the keys, and receive an absent-minded kiss. It is the sort of picture that wakes John Marquand screaming from his sleep. But, deluded people that we are, we do not realize how mediocre it all seems. We will eat our undistinguished meal, probably without even a cocktail to enliven it. We will drink our coffee at the table, not carry it into the living room; if a husband changes for dinner here it is into old and spotty trousers and more comfortable shoes. The children will then go through the regular childhood routine—complain about their homework, grumble about going to bed, and finally accomplish both ordeals. Perhaps later the Gerard Joneses will drop in. We will talk a great deal of unimportant chatter and compare notes on food prices; we will also discuss the headlines and disagree. (Some of us in the Manor are Republicans, some are Democrats, a few lean plainly leftward. There are probably anti-Semites and anti-Catholics and even anti-Americans. Most of us are merely anti-antis.) We will all have one highball, and the Joneses will leave early. Tomorrow and tomorrow and tomorrow the pattern will be repeated. This is Suburbia.   21

But I think that some day people will look back on our little interval here, on our Spruce Manor way of life, as we now look back on the

* Paragraphs 17 through 20: The author is reasoning inductively to answer an unfair generalization with a valid generalization of her own. What is her exact phrasing (in paragraph 16) of the unfair generalization? Considering her purpose in this informal argument, does she provide a fair number of instances to achieve probability for her own generalization? Are the instances sufficiently typical or representative? Do they point to the same conclusion? How does she explain away negative instances? Is her explanation satisfactory?

Currier and Ives kind of living, with nostalgia and respect. In a world of
terrible extremes, it will stand out as the safe, important medium.   22
    Suburbia, of thee I sing!*   23

* Paragraph 23: This is an illustration of her ability to adapt well-known phrases or
stereotyped expressions to her own purposes by altering the words or adding to them.
Find at least three other illustrations of this technique.

The Whole Selection

1 Although this is an informal argument characterized by a light tone, the
  author is nonetheless serious in making her point. She does this by
  using the structure of a formal argument, disguised perhaps by her
  easy, casual, and colorful style. Point out where in the essay each of the
  following parts of a formal argument can be found:
  a Definition of terms
  b History of the question (understood as the reason why the topic is
    taken up by the writer)
  c Statement of the proposition
  d Statement of the issues
    i Those which rise from her refutation of her opponent
    ii Those introduced by the author as positive reasons for accepting
       the proposition
2 An introduction to any essay usually presents an exposition of the
  writer's subject and purpose, creates through the strategies of style
  some interest in the reader, and gives the reader some basis for accepting the author as someone with an acceptable point of view. Considering
  paragraphs 1 through 7 as the introduction to the essay, evaluate the
  success of Phyllis McGinley's beginning.
3 Various methods of refutation are used by the author. Since her essay is
  largely an answer to an attitude expressed by various writers by means
  of literary clichés, we will not expect the techniques of refutation to be
  obviously constructed. For each of the following, however, find an
  appropriate illustration in the essay:
  a Denial of the validity of the argument advanced by her opponents and
    offer of proof for her counterargument
  b Turning her opponents' argument to her own advantage
  c Attacking her opponents' competence, concerning this proposition
  d Distinction in the use of terms to point up a different meaning that
    will support her view of the proposition
4 Selecting specific illustrations, show whether or not her use of example
  is effective in holding the interest of the reader and effective in proving
  her issues.

SUBURBIA RECONSIDERED: DIVERSITY AND THE CREATIVE LIFE

DOROTHY LEE

Is the suburb a "paradise regained?" Yes, certainly one image of paradise: the paradise of harp players agreeably getting along with one another; a paradise of lights without shadows, of virtue rather than of vibrant good; a paradise where people do the right, the acceptable, perhaps even what they ought to do. But it is not a paradise which is the "blooming, buzzing confusion" of the senses.   1

At one time I had thought of the suburb as a good place to bring up my children. There was the country for my children to know, to see, to feel, to incorporate

> . . . the gay
> great happening illimitably earth.

There would be available to them the kind of music I liked, the kind of people I liked, the kind of experience I liked. I did not take my children to a suburb, but I did take them to a homogeneous community in the country, to the edge of the Vassar College campus, near the woods and hills, the brooks, the ponds, the fields, where they could be with deer, and rabbits, and woodchucks, and all the wild growing things. After some years, at tremendous personal expense, and against my children's resistance, I fled from this paradise. I fled, not from the country, but from the filtered experience which I had been providing for my children. We went to where the children could be tempted to join street corner society, where they could see brute poverty, and vice and exultation, and the bewilderment of the rejected immigrant; where they could be exposed to bad English and despicable music. I took them where they could meet taste that had not been labeled good or bad, so that they could make their own decisions about it; where their associates had not been implicitly preselected and pre-labeled as desirable.   2

After a period of disorientation and anguish, my children were all glad of the move. We mourned the loss of the country; we had to get it in the summer alone. But, of course, this loss is not relevant to a discussion of suburbs, because if we had been living in a true suburb the country would have been lost to us in time in any case.   3

In many respects the culture of the suburbs is only an intensification of the official American culture—the culture implicit in the curricula of the schools of education, expressed in the structure and the teaching of our public school system; the culture underlying all policy-making, and even the appeal we make in our advertising and in the mass-oriented movies produced in Hollywood. It is this culture which the urbanite takes to the suburbs with him and finds there in his children's school. But here the suburb with its relative homogeneity approximates a closed system and intensifies certain aspects of culture.*   4

I would like to consider suburban culture from the following point of view: to what extent does suburban life make it possible for the individual to grow, to maintain inner consistency, to exercise autonomy? What is the range of experience, the variety of society which it offers for the transaction of the self? I should like to discuss the prerequisites for personal growth and strength as offered on the one hand by the city and on the other hand by the suburb.†   5

I shall take up first the subject of the strength of the self. To what extent is the individual enabled and incited to excel, not in a comparative sense, but rather in the sense of exercising all the muscles of his person, intellectual, emotional, physical, with joy and pride? Does suburban living help the individual find and give expression to his own peculiar pattern to the minutest detail, and beyond that, to transcend his potential?‡   6

To my mind, one essential for the strengthening of the self is the presence of diversity. The self needs variety of experience directly for its own growth for richer transaction. Diversity is also needed indirectly so that an individual can exercise his powers of perception and discrimination in the area of making a choice, so that in making his own choice he can be an agent in creating his own experience. In fact, I believe that the exercise of one's agency is one way to excellence, and I use "exercise" here in the sense that I exercise my muscles. In the suburbs, diversity is largely absent as compared with the city. David Riesman speaks of this lack of diversity in the paper which he entitles "Suburban Sadness." And I agree with him that this is sad. Sometimes the homogeneity happens without deliberate intent, though people are naturally guided by their own likes. In the case of the establishment of Crestwood Heights, it seems to have been done with deliberation. The authors who in *Crestwood Heights: A Study of the Culture of Suburban Life* describe this pseudonymous community write that the establishment of the suburb was for the purpose of creating "a smaller area in which they and *others like* them" (the italics are added) could agree on a policy.§   7

Now there is a second aspect in which diversity can contribute to, in fact is necessary for, the strength of the self, and that is through

* Paragraphs 1 through 4: What function do these paragraphs serve?

† Paragraph 5: Restate the central idea of this thesis paragraph.

‡ Paragraph 6: Where has "strength of self" been defined previously? Why is it defined again?

§ Paragraph 7: Is the use of authority effective?

making conflict possible. Conflict may be bad when it is overwhelming; but it can evoke an answering strength, and through the exertion of this strength, can mean the growth of the self through experience, an experience which demands the output of all that is available to the self. A lawyer was speaking to me recently about his early years in this country. He arrived from Greece as a boy of eleven and went to live in an industrial city as an immigrant, as a poor boy, as the nephew of a man who owned a pool hall and who employed the little boy as an assistant. He said to me that when finally he managed to go to Princeton, he had deplored this experience of his as poverty stricken. But now, after years of living, thinking, and experience, he sees these early years of conflict as the years which had made it possible for him to grow from strength to strength. This is the kind of experience which a city does provide usually and which is generally not available to the child growing up in the suburb.*   8

In fact official American culture in general tends more and more to view conflict as bad and to eliminate it. Two years ago I was teaching a seminar in which vigorous discussion of freedom was taking place when suddenly a student asked that we agree on a definition of freedom, that we abandon our differences so that we could all be able to state the same thing. Diversity was happily present in this seminar. The members had come from all over the world. But this diversity, the contrapuntal discussion which created the theme in its rich variety of ramifications, threatened the American student's value of "getting along."†   9

Somehow in the official American culture, harmony, the symphonic unification of diversity, has been reinterpreted to mean monotony. In the name of agreement difference is being eliminated—certainly not fostered —giving place to sameness and to agreement as a desired good. There is a trend toward eliminating difference in taste, in values, in standards, in education, in ways of living. And this trend, I believe is at its strongest in the suburb, because here there is a feedback from the relatively homogeneous situation. But in eliminating diversity we deprive ourselves of the opportunity to strengthen ourselves in our own stand, and, in fact, to create our own position. We have little opportunity to learn to respect difference, or knowing the difference, to despise it or reject it according to our own act of decision.‡   10

The city at least does offer more diversity. Cities, of course, vary in idiosyncrasy and in the degree of differentiation which they offer. Yet, it is in the city that we meet the extremes, the immigrant as well as the old American, the laborer and the president of the corporation. Here is where

---

* Paragraph 8: Is it clear by now what is meant by "diversity"?

† Paragraph 9: Does the example prove the generalization in sentence 1?

‡ Paragraph 10: How are "harmony" and "monotony" defined?

we encounter the thrill of the refugee who for the first time lays eyes on the Statue of Liberty or sets foot on American soil. It is here that we meet the hardship, the sordidness, as well as the gracious living of the established. Here to some extent existence is not quite filtered for the growing individual. This is not to say that a girl in the city would end up by having a different assortment of friends than she would have had in the suburb. The point I want to make is that in the city she would have arrived possibly at the same kind of friends after having lived through the experience of choice, through perhaps the anguish of rejection and the doubts revolving around selection, and thus would have grown as a person, would have strengthened her own idiosyncratic pattern. In a sense, she would have created her own experience, and she would have been an agent in her own existence.   11

Yet, whatever the actuality, the ideal of official American culture is that of overcoming differentiation. Agreement is "good," because it is the sign of "getting along." To "get along" is one of the goals of living offered to the growing child in the school, whether in the city or in the suburb. When I analyzed manuals for the teachers of Family Life Education and of Home Economics, I found the emphasis on "getting along" strong in a variety of the situations discussed. These manuals represented suggestions for teachers across the country. In one lesson on Family Relationships, the term "get along" was found to occur seven times. Under the heading of Personality, in the chapters which were actually concerned with teaching the student how to be pleasing to others, "getting along" was also given a high ranking. Getting along means agreement; and as a matter of fact when it was used in connection with one's family relations, it spelled the elimination of diversity, the by-passing of conflict rather than living through conflict or facing the situation of conflict.*   12

Thus agreement is good in itself. It is also good because it is the elimination of conflict. Conversely, conflict must be eliminated in the name of agreement. However, there is another sanction which supports the elimination of conflict. This is the sanction against competition.   13

The aim of the schools is to teach cooperation; cooperation is seen as good and competition as the enemy of cooperation. Yet competition has been decried without enough reflection and understanding. There is one competition that is seen as leading to a standard of success. There is, however, the other competition, the competition that demands a good and strong antagonist, a respected antagonist so as to make exertion of the self possible. Take a chess player. He needs a strong chess player if he is to play well at all. Or take a tennis player. Not only does he need an

---

* Paragraph 12: If "getting along" is the goal of both suburban and city schools, what point is there in preferring city to suburban living?

antagonist, he also needs a strong one, possibly one stronger than himself, a player who calls forth skill and the strength which cannot emerge without this strong competition. In fact, in my experience, a tennis player prefers to play against a competitor who will defeat him rather than against one who, being weak, will not call for an answering strength and will be defeated as a matter of course.   14

Now the suburbs are often criticized for the competitive life they offer. But in my opinion it is the other kind of competition, the rivalry within approximate sameness, within a similarity of standards, which rages in the suburbs. The contrapuntal competition which calls forth the hidden forces of the self and helps create a new whole, this is thrown away along with the undesired diversity. Agreement engenders at least a surface placidity. And it often is achieved by means of a Procrustean bed, and—to mix my metaphors—establishes the comfortable, rigid ceiling of the golden mean.*   15

In fact, the exertion itself has ceased to be a value; both exertion and the agency of the self. Writers now deplore the fact that things "happen to us" instead of "our doing them." To my mind, they have reason to do so. I have heard of a suburb in New York where the parents became aware of this and decided they would find some way to get their children to do things for themselves. One of the obvious ways was to have the children walk to school instead of being driven by their parents. But when the parents tried to put this into practice, they found it was impossible. The passivity, the non-exertion, had been built into the suburb. There were no sidewalks anywhere except in the one or two blocks of the shopping district.†   16

I have been speaking of diversity as necessary to the growth of the self in affording situations of choice, in offering an agentival role, and, through providing conflict, in encouraging the exertion which is a dimension of commitment and engagement. In addition to this, diversity in the sense of the "blooming, buzzing confusion" is, I believe, the prime requisite of creativity. The individual must create from the source. He must see the peas roll for himself, to use Fromm's illustration, not depend on someone else's experience. It is imperative that he create his own experience, perceiving his own pattern in the chaos. This, I believe to be true of all creative work. Even in the area of law, according to Charles P. Curtis, the language of law is vague (and I should say deplorably bewildering) so as to give an opportunity to each lawyer to recreate the law for himself in terms of the specific situation. It is certainly true of poetry where "naming an

---

* Paragraph 15: After reading paragraph 15, are you satisfied that the writer has used paragraphs 12, 13, and 14 as part of a valid argument?

† Paragraph 16: Does the fact that there are no sidewalks prove or even illustrate the "passivity . . . built into the suburb?"

object suppresses three-quarters of the enjoyment of a person about it
. . ."; and where "an author knows he will give the reader more only by
getting him to do more, to take a larger share in the creation." The unfinished evokes because everything is not organized and on the surface.*   17

Now—if I may continue to generalize—all this is lacking in the
suburbs; or, rather, what is offered is just the opposite. The suburbs do
name the object for their denizens. Experience is offered, organized, pre-
labeled, preselected, prefabricated. Stephen Birmingham in his "Commuter's Lament" dreams of going back to New York and "wasting" time
doing things like taking a ride on the Staten Island Ferry. He wonders "is
it still a nickel" and rushes to say, "don't tell me, I want to find out for
myself." This freedom to find out for himself he associates with the city,
not with the suburbs. This is the tune that Robert Paul Smith sings in his
book *Where Did You Go? Out* . . . when he compares his own growing up
in New York with the life of his children in a New York suburb. He says,
"My kid went to play soccer the other day. The way you play soccer now
is this: You bring home from school a mimeographed schedule for the
Saturday morning Soccer League. . . . There are always exactly eleven men
on each team, the ball is regulation size, the games are played on a regulation-sized field with regulation-sized soccer balls, and there is a regulation-sized adult referee." In contrast, he describes his own life. "When I
was a kid, the way we got to play baseball was this: We . . . grabbed a
beat-up fielder's glove, went out on the block and met a friend who had
an old first baseman's mitt, a ball, went down the block a little and hol-
lered at the kid who had the bat. . . . We went to the vacant lot and played
a game resembling major league baseball, only in that it was played with a
bat and bases. It was fun. . . . You see it was our game. I think my kid
was playing someone else's game."†   18

Of course the father in his own childhood was wasting a lot of time
trying to find the bat and ball, rounding up the kids, getting to the vacant
lot. In the suburb, there is efficiency, at least in Birmingham's and Smith's
description of suburban life. There is no waste of time; and indeed, at least
for the commuting fathers, there is no time to waste. When two or three
or more hours of commuting are added to the regular day's work, the remaining very few hours of the waking day have to be utilized in an organized and efficient way. Birmingham, in his "Lament," writes of this aspect
of suburban life. He says that you can tell the suburbanite by the fact that
he drives around in New York. The New Yorker likes to walk because he

---

* Paragraph 17: What is the function of sentence 1? If "the unfinished evokes because
everything is not organized," wouldn't the suburb without sidewalks and all that represents encourage more creativity than the organized and structured city?

† Paragraph 18: Put the generalization of sentence 1 in your own words. It is particularly
important to understand the reference for "all this."

likes to look around, to smell the smells, to discover what is going on. But then his day is longer; there is more time in it. Perhaps this is why he has not moved to the suburbs. It is not clear here which is the chicken and which is the egg; but I would agree that this stress on efficiency, organization, this battle against wasting time, though a part of official American culture, is perhaps intensified in suburban living. Certainly when I spent three and a half hours on the road commuting, my very few "free" hours had to be rigidly goal-oriented. There was no time to waste on exploration which had not been already mapped and diagrammed and robbed of all creativity.   19

I must repeat here that this is only an intensification. Throughout our society today there is an emphasis on the streamlined, the efficient. We give our students bibliographies, not so that they may explore, but so that they may save time, so that they may take the shortest route between two points and never have a chance to take a wrong turning and wander around the countryside. In this way they need not "waste" their time looking through poor articles and discovering the inadequacy for themselves, or even in forming their own standards by which to judge a book (and, of course, reading fewer "good" books). We give them a map, not a compass, and quite often we substitute the map for the territory. Now that they have the map, now that they know what other people thought of this book, or of the Renaissance, why should they have to discover for themselves?   20

A teacher in one of the leading colleges told me how at one time she asked a class in literature to read a book about which they had never heard, and report on it. More than half the class came to her and asked her whether it was a "good book"; because, without knowing this, they did not know how to read it, how to relate to it, what to think of it.   21

This is the picture I found in the manuals for the teaching of Home Economics which I analyzed in 1954. According to these, the students were to be guided to use even their leisure time with the utmost efficiency. For example, it was suggested that they drive out in the country for a purpose, such as "in order to see the sunset." They were urged to read a book "that had been recommended." They were urged to investigate the radio programs first and then to turn on only the program which had been branded as good. No wandering about, no vagary of the spirit, no sudden exultant discovery of something which had not been approved by a superior beforehand. Here the self is not clearly recognized. It has no validity. Someone outside makes the decisions, clears away the underbrush, smoothes the road, and allows the self to move on only as a zombie, protected against its own mistakes, deprived of its own experience.*   22

---

* Paragraphs 20 through 22: Do these paragraphs advance the author's argument? Is the "emphasis" described characteristic of both city and suburb?

This treatment of the self as not significant is seen also, for example, when parents prepare a room for an "eight-year-old boy"; not for John, not for *this* boy. The authors of *Crestwood Heights* speak among other things of the rumpus room and the children's room, "meticulously fitted to what decorators and the furniture trade consider the taste of a child." That is, the child does not create his own room out of the ragged, dreadful bits and treasures that go into the making of his own personal history, the things which eventually produce a room that could be an expression only of his own self and no one else's self.   23

The Crestwood Heights house in general is described as lacking idiosyncracy. The authors write that it is "reminiscent of a series of department store windows, charmingly arranged, harmoniously matched in color." This statement reminded me of a generalization which a French informant in the Columbia Research Project for Contemporary Cultures said about the French living room, in which one found "the habits, the reminders, the family pictures, the family furniture," a room that grew with the family. This would be a living room uniquely expressing the history, the idiosyncracy of this particular family.   24

I would say then that for a suburbanite more so than for a city dweller experience comes filtered and preordered. The range of experience has been preselected and highly narrowed. The goal of efficiency is more than elsewhere realized here. And, in the suburb, no less than in the city, the individual is viewed and dealt with as a representative of a category rather than as a person in his own right.*   25

If we are to speak in the language of the existentialist, I would say that all this spells alienation to me. The individual is set on a track which leads and moves him away from encounter with the heterogeneous data of experience. He is provided with a life which does not evoke the exertion of the self, a life which does not call forth commitment. Since experience comes to a large degree prefabricated, the individual is not incited to engage himself in the process of living, to take on his responsibility of choice, and his role as agent. This I believe to be more true of the suburbs than of the city. If suburban life is "paradise regained," it is, to my mind, the wrong kind of paradise.   26

* Paragraph 25: Have these assertions, a summary, been proved to your satisfaction?

The Whole Selection

1 The author says that she believes it "to be more true of the suburb than of the city" that "the individual is not incited to engage himself in the process of living, to take on his responsibility of choice, and

his role as agent." Has her informal argument proved this to your satisfaction?

2 Has the author used authority effectively? Cite the authorities used. Were you persuaded by her use of them?

3 Could you make a list of the prerequisites (see paragraph 5) for personal growth and strength as offered, first, by the city and, second, by the suburb? If you can, does the "city" list appear to be a stronger argument for personal growth and strength?

4 Is there some problem in the author's admission that "I did not take my children to a suburb, but I did take them to a homogeneous community in the country. . . ."?

5 Contrast Lee's essay with that of McGinley in the following terms:
   a Definition of terms
   b Statement of proposition
   c Statement of issues
   d Use of examples

"POETRY MAKES NOTHING HAPPEN"

GEORGE P. ELLIOTT

Auden said it a generation ago in his elegy for Yeats, and Auden is one to listen to. He is our wisdom poet; more than any other, he has taken it upon himself to state memorably what this age believes to be true. That is, he says what he believes to be true, and the age remembers. "Poetry makes nothing happen."* 1

Here I am taking these four words as a saying rather than as part of a poem. So viewed, "poetry" means what it used to mean centuries ago and what is indicated these days by "creative literature." Paraphrased, the saying reads: To the extent that a piece of writing is art, it makes nothing happen.† 2

Whereupon out march squads of objections, to which one can only respond: "Yes, of course, poetry makes something happen." It causes books to be printed and lots of young people to strive to put some words together that way too. It consoles the bereaved and softens lovers (so does mood music). If you chop your logic fine enough, you can say that poetry makes a lot of things happen—except it doesn't, not really, not the way the expression "makes something happen" is normally used.‡ 3

Death of a Salesman caused some middle-aged salesmen to walk out of the theater while the play was being performed, so I have heard; but I've never heard of a salesman who quit selling or began selling differently because of seeing that play. Poetry has no influence whatever on the stock market's whizzes and frizzes. (I have this on the authority of a friend who is both a stockbroker and a poet, and an editor of a literary review to boot.)§ 4

Scientists find in short stories no inspirations leading to fresh discoveries, powerful formulations. (A psychologist can use a poem as evidence, raw material, but that has no more to do with its literary qualities, its essence, than a merchandiser's peddling it as a commodity or a linguist's quarrying it for phonemes.) 5

A few years ago the British were encroaching on Iceland's fishing waters. The Thing of Iceland met in prolonged emergency session. The 12-mile limit? Diplomatic relations? War? Suddenly a Communist legislator

---

* Paragraph 1: Of what value are the first three sentences in encouraging the reader to take the proposition seriously?

† Paragraph 2: Why does Elliott paraphrase the W. H. Auden quotation?

‡ Paragraph 3: What is the value of taking up an objection early in the argument?

§ Paragraph 4: Is this paragraph meant to be proof?

requested a recess of a few minutes, during which he read a poem he had just written for and about the occasion. The Thing applauded the poet, then returned to its deliberation undisturbed. So much for politics and poetry.*   6

But, you say, what about *Uncle Tom's Cabin?* Didn't it help cause the Civil War? Myself, I doubt it. I doubt that if the story had never been written and published the course of our history would have been altered in the least. The ideas and attitudes the novel promulgates were essential to bringing about the Civil War when and as it occurred, but *Uncle Tom's Cabin* was only one of many agents promulgating these ideas and attitudes. Similarly, I find it hard to believe that that monstrous child-murdering couple in England a year or two ago needed Sade's novels to butcher their victims. They used the novels, to be sure, but their purpose would have been served quite as well by a meatcutter's handbook. The decision to act, like the action itself, was theirs, not Sade's.   7

Any self-respecting Ministry of Propaganda would fire a copywriter who made as little happen in a month as Melville, Mark Twain, Henry James and Faulkner made happen in all their fiction. "Put a tiger in your tank" has made more happen than *The Divine Comedy.*†   8

Oracles whose prophecies visibly affected men's actions spoke in doggerel. One of the recurrent themes of great prophetic poetry is the prophet's complaint that his people do not heed his verses.   9

Which is all very discouraging to a passionate poet burning, as a young Negro poet of my acquaintance burns, with the pain of injustice. Must he leave the good fight to lawyers, journalists, preachers, rabble-rousers? Yes, as a poet he must. He must be true to what he knows and feels, but he must not expect the expression of those feelings, though he were a very Blake, to alter the social conditions which made him feel that way. He may be pretty sure that any poem of his that made something happen would be doggerel.

> *Rap Brown does more than Baldwin can
> To trigger the rage of the black man.*   10

A great thing about sayings is that they often come in contradictory pairs. Shelley said in another age, "Poets are the unacknowledged legislators of the world," and I think he was as right as Auden, though a lot more hyperbolic.‡   11

---

* Paragraph 6: What is the incident meant to illustrate?

† Paragraph 8: What is the purpose of contrasting a popular advertising slogan for gasoline with one of the greatest poems ever written?

‡ Paragraph 11: Why is this paragraph a vital transitional paragraph?

I believe that poetry—"creative literature"—has pervasive and profound effects on mankind. But these effects cannot be demonstrated. In *The Republic* Plato was imagining a society totally dominated by the idea of justice. That appallingly unfree society approved poetry whose immediate effects could be demonstrated useful to the state, uplifting martial verses, for example; but it banned every other kind, that is, nearly all true poetry. Plato knew how powerful the effects of literature can be, softening, private, indefinable, not directly transferrable into actions, of dubious use to the state. He ought to have known; he was a splendid poet himself.   12

The Marquis de Sade is a danger to society, but not because anyone who reads his novels must necessarily be forever corrupted. His danger is, I believe, that he modifies the souls of some who read his stories, disposes them to hate society as such, encourages them to exalt cruelty, muddies their minds till they doubt that there is such a thing as love or the good. But this cannot be proved to the satisfaction of those who believe that only that is true which can be proved, demonstrated statistically.   13

Legislators—the acknowledged kind—in nearly all the countries of the Western world prohibit Sade's novels. They are for sale, in English, in the United States now. Is this because we are so pragmatic we do not credit the power of a thing for which cause and effect cannot be demonstrated in a seemingly scientific fashion? Or is it, as I sometimes fear, because by and large we doubt that literature has any real power at all except to amuse, divert? That at least is what I conclude from the frequent argument that books should not be censored because no book ever hurt anybody. It follows as the night the day that, if no book ever hurt anybody, no book ever did anybody any good either. Art for kick's sake. Why not take LSD? It's quicker.*   14

Well, what does poetry do beyond amusing, entertaining? I believe that, if it is good and if it is read well, it modifies what its reader feels, wants, thinks is good. Whether he acts on these modified feelings is his business, not the poet's. Which is why "poetry makes nothing happen." Dante intended his poem to be morally efficacious. To accomplish this end, he offered the reader a clear vision of moral order. What the reader does with this vision is for him to choose. Most readers, it seems, choose to look at it as an object of esthetic admiration only, with some historical curiosity thrown in. (Either that or else the Revolution is dead and gone: an excellent new translation of *The Comedy*, fully annotated, is available in the U.S.S.R.)†   15

---

* Paragraphs 13 and 14: How can Elliott have quoted Auden with approval, "Poetry makes nothing happen"?

† Paragraph 15: What is meant to be proved by the fact that Dante's poem is available in the U.S.S.R.?

Poetry makes an invisible community of those who feel its power. But at any given time they are not many. They do not band together, so that the community they make never becomes an army, a lobby, a church. Poetry reaches something immortal in them, whether glancingly or strangely suffusing their hiddenmost recesses. But it does not have a discernible effect on their prayers, their purchases, how they vote, whom they are willing to kill if ordered. Tax-collectors leave it alone. "It survives in the valley of its saying," as Auden said in that same poem. "A way of happening; a mouth." Of the world, unworldly.   16

LITERATURE MAKES PLENTY HAPPEN

SEYMOUR KRIM

George P. Elliott's defense of literature as a gentleman's art ("Poetry Makes Nothing Happen," Speaking of Books, January 28) is just about the most deadening invitation to become a writer today that I can imagine. Mr. Elliott, his eye trained on the museum of the past and the most pedestalled busts of the present (Yeats, Auden, Faulkner) seems to have no notion of the crisis that literature is facing in 1968: whether it can compete with newer and, for today's public, groovier art-forms in the mere excitement of being alive. For him to dote on the very questionable fact that, in his paraphrase of W. H. Auden, "literature makes nothing happen" —so questionable that I think it's untrue in spite of Mr. Auden's slick generalization—is almost throwing in the white rag for writing when everything from acid-rock to new cinema to the revolutionary street theater is trying harder than at any time in recent memory to bust wide-open our preconceptions about the possibilities of reality.   1

Why not admit that much current U.S. "creative writing" is fighting a sickly fight against its hungry young competitors because self-elected custodians like Mr. Elliott and Headmaster Auden want to stick it under glass, or in the freezer, in the over-civilized conceit that it is too good for action out in the riot-torn cities. Whoever heard of a great literature written with the express purpose of being kept from smiting its audience, or teaching it humility before it was sent winging? You'd almost think from Mr. Elliott's timid guardianship that writing actually belonged to writers (ha!) and not to the deepest needs of a generation, especially a totally shook-up one like the short fuses, you and I included, who smolder on the modern streets. How can Elliott speak so blandly and genially about the final ineffectiveness of serious writing when more besieged people than you can count write primarily in order to survive—surely an effectiveness second to none.*   2

And if the writer writes to survive there must be readers who also depend on communication from this swaying parachute, who desperately hold to the life-line of sentences. As the noises of unreality, hard sell, coy buy and official computerthink sneer in our ears, perhaps the entire balance of our country and the new values we need to redeem ourselves as a once-decent people hinge on great and vengeful words that are also art. Let Mr. Elliott not deceive himself that literature was ever made, in any time, without the intention of changing something: the writer himself, the

---

* Paragraphs 1 and 2: Comment on the diction Krim uses to characterize Elliott's position.

outer world around him, the disorganized materials of existence that had to be shaped in pain to make sense and even a glimmer of justice out of the mortal mess.   3

Examine the word "change" any way you like and it still represents the alteration of a process. What I am saying is that there are many important kinds of change or "making something happen" that writing can produce even if until now it has not revolutionized society. But who has the authority to say that writing is essentially a superior kind of word-game that may result in, to use Elliott's words, "esthetic admiration" (sounds like "interior decoration") when the people who play it are in each generation—or were before Elliott, Auden and Co. cooled them—the most serious spirits of their time? Believe me, literature up through the bloodbath of history had other little purposes beyond "amusing, entertaining," as Mr. Elliott puts it, and the first of these was to protest against the world and the conditions of life so fiercely that a hole was forever burnt into the conscience of mankind. Think about the Bible and go back or forward from that point in time and you can not evade the fear and trembling that literature has not only changed men, it has created them.*   4

Mr. Elliott says that "these effects [of literature] cannot be demonstrated," but he is wrong. The effect of his article could be demonstrated to have driven a young would-be writer, who might otherwise have attended a session of a prose workshop that I umpire for the Poetry Project on the Lower East Side, into the movie or theater workshops instead. Young literary talent today wants action, rough body contact with society, and if Mr. Elliott says it is an illusion to find it in prose you can bet your inflated dollar that should he be taken seriously a new generation will happily leave the field to his pipe-smoking literary club—why should they want it?†   5

That is a clue to your effectiveness in a practical sense, Mr. Elliott. It all seems to depend on *how* you take your role as writer, as to whether and to what degree and to what end you will cause change. Let me hazard a guess—namely, that your own removed view of the power of literature will help remove from its ranks those kids who want a more immediate form of expression. And it will draw closer to literature those "literary" types who agree with your conception of the pragmatic futility of writing. That's "making something happen," isn't it? And then along comes a writer like myself who may attract into writing those activists who agree with me that "creative literature" should be equivalent to an implosion/explosion and can blast a doorway that didn't exist before into the inner and

---

* Paragraph 4: Comment on the device, growing more popular in contemporary prose, "What I am saying is . . ."

† Paragraph 5: What is the effect of coupling "esthetic admiration" and "interior decoration"? Compare this paragraph with paragraph 14 in Elliott's essay.

outer future. And others, who may resent today's writing being represented by high-explosive freaks like myself, may well prefer a safer area
of activity than their conception of what the new writing style is.*   6

So it seems that both of us can provoke change at an elementary
level—affect the kind of literary climate that will exist—and this is only a
prelude to a broader change in values depending on which of us prevails.
In other words, I think that whether one believes writing can "make something happen" or not is entirely up to the writer himself and what he
imposes on his reader. It is the lone individual who turns on literature's
flame and banks it in this direction or that, not an Elliott-type program that
presumes to speak for others—there can be no program, no certainty, no
scientific poll of effectiveness, because we are dealing with faith, which is
spiritual and probably the essence of literature. It must be in faith only
that I believe the will to action can be created in men through written
language, and Elliott does not. And on the basis of these two attitudes
we act as writers and virtually predict our own effectiveness or lack of it.   7

In my view Mr. Elliott's inability to believe even in the desirability of
literature's influence on events shows the narrowness of imagination that
has made serious writing in this country recently take a back seat to the
new journalism, film, multimedia theater, truth-comedy (Lord Buckley,
Bruce, Sahl), and pop song-poetry (Dylan, Baez, Leonard Cohen). These
communications to a present-tense public have nothing to do with "an
object of esthetic admiration" as a goal; that is the talk of tired, over-
sophisticated men; like all fresh art today, the intention of these long-
suppressed bursts is to stab their audience into transcendental awareness.
They are made for the moment of their performance, like a metaphor of
modern living. History (assuming there will be one) will judge whether
these performances are to be singled out as lasting art, but at least their
practitioners do not get confused as to what should come first: existential
communication from I to Thou with the fate of We possibly hanging in the
balance.   8

Maybe it will take this invasion of the performing arts into ground
that literature always accepted as its own—that it was the most serious
conceivable comment on an age—to wake up elite contemporary writing to
the gloomy self-knowledge that it has been hiding out entranced in the
classical ruins. Can there be any question that over the last 10 years
"fine" literature in our country has abdicated hitting power to the new
nonliterary forms that have not been weighed down by the curse of too

---

* Paragraphs 5 and 6: What are these two paragraphs meant to prove? Paragraph 6:
Comment on the device of direct address in sentence 1.

much wisdom ("Auden . . . is our wisdom poet," says Mr. Elliott with genocidal pride) and are proud to be alive?*   9

    To be alive, as I understand it, is to fight for change; a person or an art-form can't live significantly without using energy differently than it has been used before. And the time one lives in determines by its needs what is done with this life-force. It is no accident, for example, that a number of writers, myself included, have in the last decade stripped down to bearing personal witness to their experience rather than "fictionalizing" it in order to force public acceptance of the subjective mind in motion. Show me what's in your head, I ask of a writer, and if it is closer to the vital grain than mine I will gladly yield up my reality to yours and selfishly incorporate your head in mine—because I want to be where the most brilliant action is.† 10

    But Mr. Elliott gives me no action that I can use; because of his philosophy he "makes nothing happen" to me; he'll leave that to Bob Dylan or the Beatles and then write a piece telling me what third-rate or adolescent poets they are. What he refuses to understand is that his "mature" comments are beside the point if they aren't replaced with something better than what the new generation of wordmen are already doing—energizing, enlarging, deepening my sense of being, increasing my awe before the possible, making me more aware of what I and the world are not but could be (and if not in this lifetime then in those I can conceive of). This is the real change: because once my imagination is stretched by a convincing new literary experience I can never be totally the same and the artists who have done this to me change the sliding scale of truth that motivates my actions—even to writing this answer.‡   11

    "To the extent that a piece of writing is art, it makes nothing happen": a beautiful epitaph for that stone under which George P. Elliott would lovingly bury the power of The Word!   12

---

* Paragraph 9: With respect to the psychology of argument, what is the remark in parentheses meant to do?

† Paragraph 10: Can a reader tell from this paragraph what Krim assumes the fundamental purpose of literature to be?

‡ Paragraph 11: If the first half of sentence 1 were true, would Krim have written this essay? Compare this paragraph with paragraph 16 of Elliott's essay.

The Two Selections

1 Study the quotation from Elliott in Krim's final paragraph with great care. Is the qualification, "To the extent that a piece of writing is art . . . ," much more significant than Krim takes into account?

2 After looking at the two essays carefully, can you determine if Elliott

and Krim are using "literature" ("poetry") in the same way? Is there sufficient common ground for a real debate to have taken place?

3 After looking at Elliott's essay again, determine whether or not Krim states Elliott's position correctly. Summarize in your own words briefly Krim's essential objection to Elliott.

4 List some of the assumptions in both essays which the authors think of as "audience acceptable."

5 List some of the ways in which both writers attempt to win the confidence of the reader.

THE NEW BARBARIANS

DANIEL J. BOORSTIN

For centuries, men here have been discovering new ways in which the happiness and prosperity of each individual revolves around that of the community. Now suddenly we are witnessing the explosive rebellion of small groups, who reject the American past, deny their relation to the community, and in a spiritual Ptolemaism insist that the U.S.A. must revolve around each of them. This atavism, this New Barbarism, cannot last, if the nation is to survive.* 1

Because the New Barbarians seek the kudos of old labels—"Nonviolence," "Pacifism," "Leftism," "Radicalism," etc.—we too readily assume that they really are just another expression of "good old American individualism," of "healthy dissent," of the red-blooded rambunctious spirit which has kept this country alive and kicking. 2

Nothing could be further from the truth. We are now seeing something new under the American sun. And we will be in still deeper trouble if we do not recognize what has really happened. The New Barbarism is not simply another expression of American vitality. It is not simply another expression of the utopianism of youth. On the contrary. What it expresses, in tornado-potence, is a new view of America and of the world. It expresses a new notion of how the world should be grasped.† 3

The Depression Decade beginning in 1929 saw in the United States a host of radicalisms, perhaps more numerous and more influential than at any earlier period of our history. Many of these were left-wing movements, which included large numbers of our academics, intellectuals, and men of public conscience, who became members or fellow travelers of groups dominated by Marxist ideas. They favored a reconstruction of American life on a base of socialism or communism. They had a great deal to do with promoting a new and wider American labor movement, with helping F.D.R. popularize the need for a welfare state, and with persuading Americans to join the war to stop Hitler. Although they fenced in American social scientists by new orthodoxies, they did have a generally tonic effect on American society. However misguided were many of the policies they advocated, these radicals did awaken and sensitize the American conscience. They confronted Americans with some facts of life which had been swept under the rug. 4

---

* Paragraph 1: What is meant by "spiritual Ptolemaism"?

† Paragraph 1 through 3: How has comparison and contrast been used to help the author express his proposition?

That was radicalism. And those of us who were part of it can attest to some of its features. It was radicalism in the familiar and traditional sense of the word. The word "radical" does, of course, come from the Latin "radix," meaning "root," and a radical, then, is a person trying to go to the root of matters.*   5

Of course those radicals never were quite respectable. Their message was that things were not what they seemed, and that inevitably makes respectable people uncomfortable. But we would be mistaken if we assumed, as many do nowadays, that a radical is anybody who makes lots of other people uncomfortable.   6

What makes a radical radical is not *that* he discomfits others but *how* he does it. A drunk is not a radical, neither is a psychotic, though both can make us quite uncomfortable. Nor does mere rudeness or violence make a person a radical, though a rude or violent man can make everybody around him quite miserable. Nor is a man who is unjustly treated and resents it necessarily a radical. Caryl Chessman may not have been guilty as charged—yet that did not make him a radical.†   7

The most vocal and most violent disrupters of American society today are not radicals at all, but a new species of barbarian. In the ancient world, "barbarian" was a synonym for foreigner, and meant an alien who came from some far-off savage land. He himself was "barbarous," wild, and uncivilized. He was a menace not because he wanted to reform or reshape the society he invaded but because he did not understand or value that society, and he aimed to destroy it.   8

The New Barbarians in America today come not from without, but from within. While they are not numerous anywhere—comprising perhaps less than two percent of our two hundred million Americans—they pose a special threat precisely because they are diffuse, wild, and disorganized. They have no one or two headquarters to be surveyed, no one or two philosophies to be combated. But they are no less rude, wild, and uncivilized than if they had come from the land of the Visigoths or the Vandals. The fact that they come from within—and are somehow a product of—our society makes them peculiarly terrifying, but it does not make them any the less barbarians.   9

We must not be deceived by our own hypersensitive liberal consciences, nor by the familiar, respected labels under which the New Barbarians like to travel. If American civilization is to survive, if we are to resist and defeat the New Barbarism, we must see it for what it is. Most

---

* Paragraphs 4 and 5: What is the value of the short review of the history of the question?

† Paragraphs 5 through 7: In formal terms, what are the genus and species in Boorstin's definition? What is the advantage of pointing out what the radical is *not*?

important, we must see that in America the New Barbarism is something
really new.*   10

A first step in this direction is to cease to confuse the New Barbarians with the members of other, intellectually respectable groups which
can and must claim tolerance in a free society. The New Barbarians are
not radicals. This will be obvious if we recall the characteristics of the
radicalisms that in one form or another have discomfited and awakened
generations of Americans.†   11

Radicalism in the United States has had several distinctive and interrelated characteristics: 12

1. Radicalism Is a Search for Meaning. The search for meaning is
the search for significance, for what else something connotes. The socialist, for example, denies that the capitalist system of production and distribution makes sense; he wants to reorganize it to produce a new meaning
in the institutions of property and in the economy of the whole society. The
religious pacifist, if he is a Christian, seeks the meaning of society in the
Christian vision of peace and the brotherhood of man. When the true
radical criticizes society he demands that the society justify itself according to some new measure of meaning.‡   13

2. Radicalism Has a Specific Content. The radical is distinguished
from the man who simply has a bad digestion by the fact that the radical's
belief has some solid subject matter, while the other man is merely
dyspeptic. A stomachache or sheer anger or irritability cannot be the substance of radicalism. Thus, while a man can be ill-natured or irritable in
general, he cannot be a radical in general. Every radicalism is a way of
asserting *what* are the roots. Radicalism, therefore, involves affirmation. It
is distinguished from conservatism precisely in that the conservative can be
loose and vague about his affirmation. The conservative is in fact always
tempted to let his affirmation become mere complacency. But the true
radical cannot refuse to affirm, and to be specific, although of course he
may be utopian. The radical must affirm that *this* is more fundamental than
that. One great service of the radical, then, is that by his experimental
definitions he puts the conservative on the defensive and makes him discover, decide, and define what is really worth preserving. The radical does
this by the specificity (sometimes also by the rashness) of his affirmation
—of the dictatorship of the proletariat, of the Kingdom of God on earth, or
of whatever else.   14

* Paragraphs 8 through 10: What is the author's preliminary descriptive definition of the
"New Barbarians"? Compare these paragraphs with paragraphs 1 through 3.

† Paragraph 11: Do you see now the importance of the author's use of comparison and
contrast in paragraphs 1 through 3?

‡ Paragraph 13: Why are the socialist and religious pacifist "true radicals"?

3. Radicalism Is an Affirmation of Community. It affirms that we all share the same root problems, that we are all in the same boat, though the radical may see the boat very differently than do others. For example, if he is a pacifist radical he insists that the whole society bears the blame for even a single man killed in war; if he is an anarchist radical he insists that the whole society bears the blame for the injustice of property and the violence of government. Radicalism, then, involves a commitment to the interdependence of men, and to the sharing of their concerns, which the radical feels with an especially urgent, personal intensity.*   15

These are only general characteristics. Of course, there are border-line cases. We might be uncertain whether Henry George's Single Taxers or Tom Watson's Populists were real radicals. But a full-fledged radicalism, of the kind which can serve and has served as a tonic to the whole society, does have at least the three characteristics I have mentioned. There have been many such radicalisms in American History—from the Antinomians of Massachusetts Bay, through the Quakers of Pennsylvania, the Aboli-tionists and the Mormons down to the Jehovah's Witnesses and the Com-munists in our own day. But the most prominent, the most vocal, the most threatening, and the most characteristic disruptive movements in the United States within the last few years do not belong in this tradition. Whatever they or their uncritical observers may say to the contrary, they are not radicalisms. They do not exhibit the characteristics I have listed. 16

It is characteristic of the Student Power and the Black Power "move-ments" that in them the quest for meaning has been displaced by the quest for power. Among students, the Bull Session tends to be displaced by the Strategy Session. The "discussions" of activist students are not explorations of the great questions that have troubled civilized men as they come to manhood, since the days of the Old Testament and of Ancient Greece. They are not concerned with whether there is a God, with what is the true nature of art, or of civilization, or of morals. The Student Power Barbarians and the Black Power Barbarians pose not questions but answers. Or, as one of their recent slogans says: "Happiness Is Student Power." Their answer to everything is uncharmingly simple: Power. And to the more difficult questions their answer is: More Power.†   17

These New Barbarians offer no content, no ideology, hardly even a jargon. While dissident students thirty-five years ago spoke an esoteric Marxist lingo, and debated "dialectical materialism," "the transformation of quantity into quality," etc., etc., the dissident students and Black

---

* Paragraph 15: Compare the substance of this paragraph with the "spiritual Ptolemaism" of paragraph 1.

† Paragraph 17: Contrast this paragraph with paragraph 13.

Powerites today scream four-letter obscenities and expletives. While the radicals explored an intricate ideology in the heavy volumes of Marx, the cumbersome paragraphs of Lenin, and the elaborate reinterpretations of Stalin and Trotsky, today's power-seekers are more than satisfied by the hate slogans of Mao Tse-tung, Che Guevara, or Malcolm X. They find nothing so enchanting as the sound of their own voices, and their bibliography consists mainly of the products of their own mimeographing. They seem to think they can be radicals without portfolio. If they call themselves "anarchists" they have not bothered to read their Thoreau or Proudhon, Bakunin or Tolstoy. If they call themselves "leftists" they have not bothered to read Marx or Engels, Lenin or Trotsky. If they call themselves Black Power Nationalists, they mistake the rattle of ancient chains for the sound of facts and ideas.   18

Having nothing to say, the New Barbarians cannot interest others by *what* they say. Therefore they must try to shock by *how* they say it. Traditionally, radicals have addressed their society with a question mark, but the new frustrates' favorite punctuation is the exclamation point! Having no new facts or ideas to offer, they strain at novelty with their latrine words. The Black Powerites, whose whole program is their own power, must wrap up their emptiness in vulgarisms and expletives. For racism is the perfect example of a dogma without content.   19

The appeal to violence and "direct action" as if they were ends rather than means is eloquent testimony of the New Barbarians' lack of subject matter. An act of violence may express hate or anger, but it communicates nothing precise or substantial. Throwing a rock, like hurling an epithet, proclaims that the thrower has given up trying to say anything.*   20

These Student Powerites and Black Powerites are not *egalitarians* seeking a just community; they are *egolitarians,* preening the egoism of the isolationist self. Students seek power for "students," Negroes seek power for "blacks"—and let the community take the hindmost! Unlike the radicalisms which affirm community and are preoccupied or obsessed by its problems, the Student Power and Black Power movements deny any substantial community—even among their own "members." A novel feature of S.N.C.C. and S.D.S., too little noted, is the fact that they are, strictly speaking, "nonmembership" organizations. Members do not carry cards, membership lists are said not to exist. A person does not "join" as a result of long and solemn deliberation, he is not trained and tested (as was the case in the Thirties with candidates for membership in the Communist Party). Instead the New Barbarian simply affiliates, and stays with the group as long as it pleases him. "I'm with you today, baby, but who

* Paragraphs 18 through 20: Contrast these paragraphs with paragraph 14.

knows where I'll be tomorrow?" A desperate infant-instantism reveals the uncertainty and vagrancy of these affiliations. The leader better act this afternoon, for maybe they won't be with him tomorrow morning!*   21

All these unradical characteristics of the New Barbarians express a spiritual cataclysm. This is what I mean by the Ptolemaic Revolution: a movement from the community-centered to the self-centered. While radicals see themselves and everything else revolving around the community and its idealized needs, each of these new frustrates tries to make the world revolve around himself. The depth and significance of this shift in focus have remained unnoticed. It has been the harder to grasp because it is in the nature of the New Barbarism that it should lack philosophers. Being closer to a dyspepsia than to an ideology, the New Barbarism has tried to generalize its stomachaches but has been unable to cast them into a philosophy. It is much easier, therefore, to describe the direction in which the chaotic groups comprising the New Barbarism are moving than to fix the precise position where they stand.†   22

The New Barbarism, in a word, is the social expression of a movement from Experience to Sensation. Experience, the dictionary tells us, means *actual observation of or practical acquaintance with facts or events; knowledge resulting from this.* A person's experience is what he has lived through. Generally speaking, experience is (a) cumulative, and (b) communicable. People add up their experiences to become wiser and more knowledgeable. We can learn from our own experience and, most important, we can learn from other people's experiences. Our publicly shared experience is history. Experience is distinguished, then, by the very fact that it can be shared. When we have an experience, we enter into the continuum of a society. But the dramatic shift now is away from Experience and toward Sensation.   23

Sensation is personal, private, confined, and incommunicable. Our sensations (hearing, seeing, touching, tasting, and smelling) are what we *receive.* Or, as the dictionary says, sensation is *consciousness of perceiving or seeming to perceive some state or affection of one's body or its parts or senses of one's mind or its emotions; the contents of such consciousness.* If an experience were totally incommunicable, if I could not describe it to anyone else, If I could not share it, it would not really be an experience. It would simply be a sensation, a message which came to me and to me alone. Sensations, from their very nature, then, are intimate and ineffable. Experience takes us out of ourselves, sensation affirms and emphasizes the self.

---

* Paragraph 21: Contrast this paragraph with paragraph 15. Define "a desperate infant-instantism" in your own words.

† Paragraph 22: Why does the author reach the conclusion stated in the final sentence?

What history is to the person in quest of experience, a "happening" is to the person in quest of sensation. For a "happening" is something totally discrete. It adds to our sensations without increasing our experience.   24

Experience and Sensation, then, express attitudes to the world as opposite as the poles. The experience-oriented young person suffers Weltschmerz—the discovery of the pain and suffering that are his portion of the world. The sensation-oriented suffers an "identity crisis": he is concerned mostly about defining the boundaries of that bundle of private messages which is himself. The experience-oriented seeks, and finds, continuity, and emphasizes what is shared and what is communicable. The sensation-oriented seeks the instantaneous, the egocentric, the inexpressible. The accumulation of experience produces the expert. Its cumulative product is expertise—competence, the ability to handle situations by knowing what is tried and familiar about them. And the name for accumulated experience is knowledge.   25

While sensations can be more or less intense, they are not cumulative. A set of simultaneous, intense and melodramatic sensations is not instructive, but it is shocking: we say it is sensational. Experience is additive, it can be organized, classified, and rearranged; sensation is miscellaneous, random, and incapable of being generalized.*   26

Everywhere in the United States nowadays—and not only among the New Barbarians—we see a desperate quest for sensation and a growing tendency to value sensation more than experience. We note this in what people seek, in what they find, in what they make, and in what they like to watch. We note a tendency in painting to produce works which do not appeal to a common, sharable fund of experience, but which, instead, set off each viewer on his own private path of sensation. In the theatre and in movies which lack a clear and intelligible story line, the spectators are offered sensations from which each is expected to make his own private inward adventure.   27

An example of the current quest for the indescribable, the ineffable, the transcendent—aiming to maximize sensation rather than experience— is the current vogue for LSD and for other so-called "consciousness-expanding" drugs. Precisely speaking, they aim to expand not experience but consciousness. They aim somehow to increase the intensity and widen the range of the vivid, idiosyncratic self.   28

The special appeal of an LSD "trip" is that it leads to the ineffable: what one person gets is as different as possible from what is obtained by another. And it is all quite individual and quite unpredictable. "Instead

---

* Paragraphs 23 through 26: Why is it essential for the reader to understand Boorstin's distinction between "experience" and "sensation" in order to follow his argument?

of a communion," one psychologist explains, "it [the LSD state] is a withdrawal into oneself. The *religio* (binding together) is not visible here." This
is how Richard Alpert, the archbishop of LSD, explains the sensations
under the drug: 29

" 'Nowhere' is Sidney's prediction of where the psychochemical
(r)evolution is taking the 'young people' who are exploring inner space. I
prefer to read that word as NowHere, and fervently hope he is right—that
LSD is bringing man back 'to his senses'. . . . Do not be confused! The
issue is not LSD. . . . Your control and access to your own brain is at
stake."   30

LSD sensations, Alpert insists, are "eyewitness reports of what is,
essentially, a private experience." "It was," in the words of a girl who had
just been on an LSD trip, "like a shower on the inside."*   31

The search for sensation is a search for some way of reminding
oneself that one is alive—but without becoming entangled with others or
with a community. "I have never felt so intense, alive, such a sense of
well-being. . . . I have chosen to be outside of society after having been
very much inside. . . . My plans are unstructured in regards to anything
but the immediate future. I believe in freedom, and must take the jump, I
must take the chance of action." This is not the report of an LSD trip, but
the explanation by a young white student of his sensations on joining
S.N.C.C. The vocabulary of the Student Power movement reveals the same
desperate quest for sensation. "Direct Action" is the name for spasmodic
acts of self-affirmation. It is a way of making the senses scream. It matters
not whether the "Direct Action" has a purpose, much less whether it can
attain any purpose, since it gives satisfaction enough by intensifying the
Direct Actor's sense of being alive and separate from others. "Direct
Action" is to politics what the Frug or the Jerk is to the dance. It identifies
and explodes the self without attaching the self to groups or to individuals
outside. And now the "New Left" has become the LSD of the intellectuals. 32

The man who is pathologically experience-oriented will be timid,
haunted by respectability. His motto is apt to be that posted over the desk
of an English civil servant: "Never do anything for the first time!" On the
other hand, the man pathologically obsessed by Sensation makes his
motto: "Do everything only for the first time!"†   33

All about us, and especially in the Student Power and Black Power
movements of recent years, we see the pathology of the sensation-oriented.
Contrary to popular belief, and to the legends which they would like to
spread about themselves, they are not troubled by any excessive concern

* Paragraphs 28 through 31: Why is LSD an example of sensation as opposed to
experience?

† Paragraph 33: What is the purpose of this paragraph?

for others. Their feelings cannot accurately be described as a concern, and it is surely not for others. Their ailment might best be called *apathy*. For apathy is a feeling apart from others and, as the dictionary reminds us, *an indolence of mind*. The Direct Actionists, as President W. Allen Wallis of the University of Rochester has explained, "are the students who are truly apathetic." They do not care enough about the problems of their society to burn the midnight oil over them. Impatient to sate their egoes with the sensations of "Direct Action," they are too indolent intellectually to do the hard work of exploring the problems to which they pretend a concern. Theirs is the egoism, the personal chauvinism of the isolationist self. Their "Direct Action" slogan means nothing but "Myself, Right or Wrong!"

These people I would call the *Apathetes*. Just as the Aesthetes of 34 some decades ago believed in "Art for Art's Sake," so the Apathetes believe in "Me for My Own Sake." They try to make a virtue of their indolence of mind (by calling it "Direct Action") and they exult in their feeling-apartness (by calling it "Power"). Thus these Apathetes are at the opposite pole from the radicals of the past.

They abandon the quest for meaning, for fear it might entangle their 35 thoughts and feelings with those of others, and they plunge into "Direct Action" for fear that second thoughts might deny them this satisfaction to their ego. Theirs is a mindless, obsessive quest for power. But they give up the very idea of man's need for quest. Instead they seek explosive affirmations of the self.*

They deny the existence of subject matter, by denying the need for 36 experience. How natural, then, that Youth should lord it over Age! For in youth, they say, the senses are most sensitive and most attuned. The accumulated experience of books or of teachers becomes absurdly irrelevant. There is no Knowledge, but only Sensation, and Power is its Handmaiden!

They deny the existence of time, since Sensation is instantaneous 37 and not cumulative. They herald the age of Instant Everything! Since time can do nothing but accumulate experience and dull the senses, experience is said to be nothing but the debris which stifles our sensations! There must be no frustration. Every program must be instantaneous, every demand must be an ultimatum.

This movement from Experience to Sensation accelerates every day. 38 Each little victory for Student Power or Black Power—or any other kind of Power—is a victory for the New Barbarism. Appropriately, the New Barbarism makes its first sallies and has its greatest initial success, against the universities, which are the repositories of Experience, and in the cause of Racism, which—whether it is Black or whether it is Aryan—is the emptiness to end all emptinesses.
39

The Whole Selection

1 What is the proposition of Boorstin's argument? Is it a proposition of fact or of policy?
2 Evaluate paragraphs 35 through 39 from the point of view of the psychology of argument.
3 Explain in one paragraph of your own writing precisely what you understand Boorstin to mean by the "New Barbarism."
4 Boorstin explains the generalizations which open paragraphs 13, 14, and 15. Suppose he had not explained them. Substitute "Democracy" for "Radicalism" in the opening sentence in each paragraph. Does this tell us something of the care with which one should use generalizations?

REBELS IN SEARCH OF A CAUSE

RENE DUBOS

This book should have been written in anger. I should be expressing in the strongest possible terms my anguish at seeing so many human and natural values spoiled or destroyed in affluent societies, as well as my indignation at the failure of the scientific community to organize a systematic effort against the desecration of life and nature. Environmental ugliness and the rape of nature can be forgiven when they result from poverty, but not when they occur in the midst of plenty and indeed are produced by wealth. The neglect of human problems by the scientific establishment might be justified if it were due to lack of resources or of methods of approach, but cannot be forgiven in a society which can always find enough money to deal with the issues that concern selfish interests. 1

Unfortunately, writing in anger requires talents I do not possess. This is my excuse for presenting instead a mild discussion of our collective guilt.* 2

We claim that human relationships and communion with nature are the ultimate sources of happiness and beauty. Yet we do not hesitate to spoil our surroundings and human associations for the sake of efficiency in acquiring power and wealth. Our collective sense of guilt comes from a general awareness that our praise of human and natural values is hypocrisy as long as we practice social indifference and convert our land into a gigantic dump.† 3

Phrases like "one world" and the "brotherhood of man" occur endlessly in conversations and official discourses at the very time that political wars and race riots are raging all over the world. Politicians and real-estate operators advocate programs for the beautification of cities and highways, while allowing the exciting grandeur of the American wilderness to degenerate into an immense ugliness. Brush is overgrowing mountain slopes that were once covered with majestic forests; industrial sewers are causing sterility in streams that used to team with game fish; air pollutants generate opaque and irritating smogs that dull even the most brilliant and dramatic skies. The price of power, symbolized by superhighways and giant factories, is a desecration of nature and of human life. 4

Aggressive behavior for money or for prestige, the destruction of scenic beauty and historic landmarks, the waste of natural resources, the threats to health created by thoughtless technology—all these character-

---

* Paragraphs 1 and 2: Of what value as an introduction is the author's personal comment on his style?
† Paragraph 3: Can you think of other things which might be the "ultimate" sources of happiness and beauty?

istics of our society contribute to the dehumanization of life. Society cannot be reformed by creating more wealth and power. Instead economic and technologic considerations must be made subservient to the needs, attributes, and aspirations that have been woven into the fabric of man's nature during his evolutionary and historical development.*   5

The most hopeful sign for the future is the attempt by the rebellious young to reject our social values. Their protests indicate that mankind is becoming disturbed by increasing dehumanization and so may act in time to reverse the trend. Despite so many intellectual and ethical setbacks, despite so much evidence that human values are being spoiled or cheapened, despite the massive destruction of beauty and of natural resources, as long as there are rebels in our midst, there is reason to hope that our societies can be saved.   6

The social role of the rebel is symbolized by Honoré Daumier's picture L'Emeute (The Uprising) in the Phillips Memorial Gallery in Washington, D.C. The painting represents a revolutionary outbreak in nineteenth-century Paris. A handsome young man, with outstretched arms and clenched fists, is leading a crowd which appears hypnotized by his charismatic determination. His expression is intense, yet his dreamer's eyes are not focused on any particular object, person, or goal. He contemplates a distant future so indistinct that he probably could not describe the precise cause for which he and his followers are risking their lives.   7

Daumier's painting does not portray a particular type of rebel, or a particular cause for rebellion. Its theme is rebellious man ready to confront evil and to undertake dangerous tasks even if the goal is unclear and the rewards uncertain. The rebel is the standard-bearer of the visionaries who gradually increase man's ethical stature; because there is always evil around us, he represents one of the eternal dimensions of mankind.   8

The nineteenth-century rebels symbolized in Daumier's painting fought for political liberty and social equality. Today's rebels also try to identify themselves with political and social issues, such as world peace, equality of opportunities for all, or simply freedom of speech for college students. There comes to mind the caption of a popular cartoon, "Pick your own picket," which conveys with sad irony that civilized nations still have a wide range of social wrongs.   9

Rebellion, however, should reach beyond conventional political and social issues. Even if perfect social justice and complete freedom from want were to prevail in a world at peace, rebels would still be needed wherever the world is out of joint, which now means everywhere. Rebellion

---

* Paragraph 5: Is the last sentence a conclusion of all that has gone before (paragraphs 1 through 5), or is it an "audience acceptable" assumption?

permeates all aspects of human life. It originates from the subconscious will of mankind not to surrender to destructive forces. But rebelling is not the same as defining a cause that would improve the quality of human life, or formulating a constructive program of action. Marching in a parade is easier than blazing a trail through a forest or creating a new Jerusalem. Daumier's hero looks like many rebels in our midst. He is fighting against evil rather than for a well-defined cause. Like most of us, he is a rebel without a program.*

10

Our society is highly expert in controlling the external world and even the human mind, but our relationships with other human beings and the rest of creation are constantly diminishing in significance. This society has more comfort, safety, and power than any before it, but the quality of life is cheapened by the physical and emotional junk heap we have created. We know that life is being damaged by the present social conditions, but we participate nevertheless in a system that spoils both the earth and human relationships. Most contemporary rebels, like the rest of us, are unwilling to give up the personal advantages so readily derived from the conditions we all know to be objectionable. Nevertheless, rebels play a useful social role; at least they voice our collective concern and make us aware of our collective guilt. But the acknowledgment of guilt is not enough.

11

Rumblings against the present state of things remain amorphous and ineffective largely because existing trends, customs, and policies cannot be changed merely by negative acts. Positive beliefs are required. Alternatives will not emerge through piecemeal evolution; their development demands an intellectual and emotional revolution. We cannot transform the world until we eliminate from our collective mind the concept that man's goals are the conquest of nature and the subjection of the human mind. Such a change in attitude will not be easy. The search for the mastery of nature and for unlimited growth generates a highly stimulating, almost intoxicating atmosphere, whereas the very hint of approaching stabilization creates apathy. For this reason, we can change our ways only if we adopt a new social ethic—almost a new social religion. Whatever form this religion takes, it will have to be based on harmony with nature as well as man, instead of the drive for mastery.†

12

We have already accepted in principle, even though we rarely put into practice, the concept of human brotherhood. We must now take to

---

* Paragraphs 7 through 10: Comment on the effectiveness of the example. Compare this portrait of the rebel without a cause with the portrait Boorstin sketched of the New Barbarians. Paragraph 10. Comment on the logic of sentence 2.

† Paragraph 12: Compare the first two sentences of this paragraph with the last two sentences of paragraph 10.

heart the biblical teaching, "The Lord God took the man and put him into the Garden of Eden to dress it and to tend it" (Genesis 2:15). This means not only that the earth has been given to us for our enjoyment, but also that it has been entrusted to our care. Technicized societies thus far have exploited the earth; we must reverse this trend and learn to take care of it with love.   13

On the occasion of the annual meeting of the American Association for the Advancement of Science in 1966, the American historian Lynn White, Jr., pleaded for a new attitude toward man's nature and destiny. He saw as the only hope for the world's salvation the profoundly religious sense that the thirteenth-century Franciscans had for the spiritual and physical interdependence of all parts of nature. Scientists, and especially ecologists, he urged, should take as their patron Saint Francis of Assisi (1182–1226). But was not Francis one of the rebellious youths of his time—before the Church recognized that he was serving God by reidentifying man with nature? Francis, like Buddha, spent his early years in ease and luxury but rejected bourgeois comforts in search of more fundamental values. The contemporaries of both probably regarded them as beatniks.* 14

The name Saint Francis and the word ecology are identified with an attitude toward science, technology, and life very different from that which identified man's future with his ability to dominate the cosmos. The creation of an environment in which scientific technology renders man completely independent of natural forces calls to mind a dismal future in which man will be served by robots and thereby himself become a robot. The humanness of life depends above all on the quality of man's relationships to the rest of creation—to the winds and the stars, to the flowers and the beasts, to smiling and weeping humanity.†   15

Shortly before his death in 1963, the English novelist and essayist Aldous Huxley lamented on several occasions the fact that literature and the arts have not derived any worthwhile inspiration from modern science and technology. He thought the reason for this failure was that writers and artists are unaware of modern scientific and technological developments. This may be part of the explanation but only a very small part. Like most other human beings, writers and artists are primarily concerned with perceptions, emotions, and values which the scientific enterprise must deliberately ignore. Yet scientists should not be satisfied with studying the biological machine whose body and mind can be altered and controlled by drugs and mechanical gadgets. They should become more vitally concerned about the nature and purpose of man. Only thus can they learn to speak to man not in a specialist's jargon but in a truly human language. 16

---

* Paragraph 14: Is the use of authority effective?

† Paragraphs 14 and 15: For what purpose is St. Francis referred to?

The Whole Selection

1 Some of the devices used in the psychology of argument are these: getting the confidence of the reader, appealing to emotions, using irony, and using a selection of words in context to bring out connotations that are moving. Find illustrations of some of these devices in this essay.

2 An assumption is generally defined as the act of taking for granted or supposing. Some assumptions are "audience acceptable"; others are not. Writers may use an assumption because they feel that proof is not needed or because proof cannot be given. But assumptions may also be used carelessly—when they are not "audience acceptable" and when proof is needed and can be found. From this essay, list what assumptions you can discover and indicate whether each is justifiable or not.

3 Compare the tone of Dubos (attitude toward the reader and attitude toward the subject) with that of Boorstin.

4 Do Dubos and Boorstin agree or disagree concerning the values of rebels without a cause?

NIRVANA NOW

DANIEL P. MOYNIHAN

One of the defining qualities of the period of current history that began, roughly, with the assassination of President Kennedy has been the emergence of widespread, radical protest on the part of American youth. As it happens, this development has been congruent, and in some measure associated, with even wider protest against the current course of American foreign policy, but there is a distinction between those who differ with decisions made by the existing system, and those who reject the system itself. There is at this moment a high level of both kinds of protest, but the latter is the more singular, and almost certainly the more significant.   1

Following a period when college youth in particular were repeatedly accused of quiescent conformism, this development has taken the World War II generation rather by surprise. More than one college president given to deploring "the silent generation" appears in retrospect not half so bold, and considerably less prescient than he would have had his charges suppose. Never to trust anyone under thirty has become almost a first principle of prudence for academic administrators, and not a bad rule for politicians. It is yet to be seen, however, what if anything we shall learn from this surprising and unexpected development.   2

Of necessity, we tend to interpret present events in terms of past experience, there being, despite the efforts of the American Academy of Arts and Sciences, as yet but little future experience to guide us. I would, however, argue that we have so far been looking to misleading analogues. We have been seeing in the flamboyance of the hippies, the bitterness of the alienated college youth, the outrageousness of the New Left, little more than mutants of the old bohemianism, the never-ending conflict of generations, and perhaps the persistence of neo-Marxist radicalism. We may be wrong. Just possibly, something more important is abroad. We may be witnessing the first heresies of liberalism.   3

In its familiar setting heresy refers to religious views contrary to the established dogma of a church. It will seem odd to use it to describe such assertively nonreligious phenomena as the Students for a Democratic Society. Some also will object that inasmuch as the doctrines of liberalism are derived from experience, rather than right reason, there can be no final liberal view about anything, and therefore no finally heretical dissent from such views. I suggest, however, that the phenomenon of protest we observe today is more psychological than doctrinal in origin, and that to the youth of this time secular liberalism presents itself as every bit as much a system of "established and commonly received doctrine" as did Christianity, for example, when it was the legally prescribed belief of the Holy Roman Empire, or the Massachusetts Bay Colony. To be sure, the doctrines of liberalism can be elusive. It is a conviction, Learned Hand might say, that is not too sure of itself—save on the point that it is vastly to be preferred to any creed that is. Liberals are not without tracts—hardly—but tend more to look to institutions as repositories of their beliefs, liberalism being in every sense as much a *way* of doing things, as it is a set of propositions as to what is to be done. It is not without its schisms and assuredly not without its confusions. But in all its essentials of an optimistic belief in progress, in toleration, in equality, in the rule of law, and in the possibility of attaining a high and sustained measure of human happiness here on earth, liberalism is the nigh universally accepted creed of the ruling elites of the Western world. Religious faith persists, even grows. But it does so as a private matter: supernatural beliefs have almost no influence on the course of events. Secular liberalism is triumphant. Not surprisingly, then, given especially the great value liberalism places on skepticism and inquiry, liberalism itself is beginning to be questioned. 4

It is notorious, of course, that among the most eminent of the literary men of this century the liberal values of the larger society have been viewed with a detachment ranging from indifference to detestation. But these were men born in the nineteenth century, and raised in a world that still had, or thought it had, some options with respect to forsaking the traditionalist, hierarchical, Christian past and embracing the new creed. To these writers it had been a mistake to do so; they withheld their own assent. Thus it may have been incongruous, even perhaps unpatriotic, for a St. Louis boy such as Mr. Eliot to show such enthusiasm for the Church of England and the Royal Family, but it was not absurd. American youth today have no such option. The liberal present is the only world they know, and if it is not to their liking, as for many it is not, their only alternative is to consider how it might evolve into something new, there being no possibility of reverting to something old. What follows is very like a spiritual crisis, and in the manner of individuals and communities that have confronted such in the past, some lapse into indifference and quietism, others escape into varied forms of stabilized hysteria, while still others turn to confront doctrine itself, and in a mood of intensely felt revelation reject the very foundations of orthodoxy. 5

What indeed is most striking about the current surge of protest is the degree to which it reenacts in matters of style and structure the great heresies that have assailed the religious establishments of other ages. "The sun shone," Samuel Beckett writes in the opening passage of *Murphy*, "having no alternative, on the nothing new."

The forms of youthful protest at this time are many, and not all, of course, visible. But there are three clusters of behavior that are sufficiently coherent as to suggest a central tendency in each, and to offer the possibility of analogies with earlier phenomena. 6

The most familiar-seeming, and for that reason possibly the most deceptive of the new tendencies, is that of the New Left itself. It is familiar because it has taken a familiar form: the organization of a group defined by political objectives. Yet in truth something profoundly new may be present here, for the object of the New Left is not to capture the system but to transform it. The older radicalisms were inextricably involved with things-as-they-are, and, owing especially to Marx's view of economic determinism, they largely deprived the radical challenge to liberal capitalism of any *moral* basis: the system had a destiny that was working itself out regardless of any intentions, good or evil, on the part of mortals so innocent of the laws of economics as to suppose they, rather than things, were in the saddle. The Old Left was so utterly "materialistic" and "realistic" as to use those very terms to describe one of its defining dogmas. As Richard Blumenthal, of the Harvard Class of 1967, recently observed in the *Nation,* it is precisely this "crass materialism" that the Students for a Democratic Society reject. It is precisely the "dehumanizing" of modern society that they resent. Society's "main and transcending" concern, Tom Hayden writes, "must be the unfolding and refinement of the moral, aesthetic and logical capacities of men in a manner that creates genuine independence." However that is to be achieved, Blumenthal adds, it is not likely to be by way of "a house in the country and a two-car garage." The movement is purposely "anti-ideological, even anti-intellectual." It is precisely that rational commitment to logic and consistency—of the kind that can lead from game theory at the RAND Corporation to the use of napalm in Vietnam—that these young persons abhor.   7

Of late they have set about building things called "independent power bases" among the poor (a concept one fears may have been borrowed from the Strategic Air Command), but the striking fact about the famous Port Huron Statement adopted by S.D.S. in 1962 is that it barely, and then only indirectly, touches on problems such as poverty. It is addressed exclusively to middle-class intellectuals and college students: the "people of this generation, bred in at least modest comfort, housed now in universities, looking uncomfortably to the world we inherit." The world about them was so content with material affluence as to suppose it had attained stability, where in truth there was only stagnation. The theme of the Port Huron Statement is that men must *live,* not simply exist. "Some would have us believe that Americans feel contentment amidst prosperity —but might it not better be called a glaze above deeply felt anxieties about their role in the new world?" Man, they declared, had acquired a role of consumer rather than creator. His capacity for love, for creativity, for meaningful relations with others was being lost amidst the machinery of government. S.D.S. proclaimed a social system in which men would not only share one another's fate, but participate, each one, in shaping that destiny: "We believe in generosity of a kind that imprints one's unique

individual qualities in the relation to other men, and to all human activity."
For such a goal the Gross National Product is indeed a crude indicator of
success.   8

Who are these outrageous young people? I suggest to you they
are Christians arrived on the scene of Second Century Rome. The quality
of life of that time remains difficult to assess, not least because triumphant Christianity did so much to put an end to it. James Anthony Froude,
however, in his great Victorian essay "Origen and Celsus," gives us a
glimpse of that world in his reconstruction of the mind of the Epicurean
Celsus, a contemporary of Marcus Aurelius, who composed a tract concerning the illogicalities and misstatements of fact in Christian doctrine of
such apparent force that Origen himself undertook to refute him. The
second century was not unlike the twentieth, and, leaving aside the somewhat gratuitous assumptions of Europeans that they are the Greeks of this
age, let there be no doubt that we are the Romans. It was a world, Froude
writes, in which "Moral good and moral evil were played with as fancies in
the lecture rooms; but they were fancies merely, with no bearing on life.
The one practical belief was that pleasure was pleasant. The very memory
disappeared that there was any evil except bodily pain. . . ." It was a
tolerant world that knew too much about itself to expect words and deeds
invariably to conform. "Into the midst of this strange scene of imposture,
profligacy, enthusiasm and craving for light," Froude continues, "Christianity emerged out of Palestine with its message of lofty humility."   9

Who were these Christians? They were first of all outrageous. They
were "bad citizens, refusing public employment and avoiding service in the
army; and while . . . they claimed toleration for their own creed, they had
no toleration for others; every god but their own they openly called a
devil. . . ." They had no temples, no altars, no images, and boasted just
that. "Fathers and tutors, they say, are mad or blind, unable to understand
or do any good thing, given over to vain imaginations. The weavers and
cobblers only are wise, they only have the secret of life, they only can show
the way to peace and happiness." Of learning they had little and cared
less. Nor had they any great interest in respectable people who observed
the rules of society and tried to keep it running; they cared only for the
outcast and miserable. To be a sinner, they seemed to say, was the one
sure way to be saved. They were altogether of a seditious and revolutionary
character.   10

Such people were a bafflement to Celsus. If he spoke bitterly about
them, he observed, it was because he was bitter. One can imagine him
thinking, if not quite putting to paper: "Do they not see how precarious
is the balance of things; how readily it might all be brought down?" He was
every bit an admirable, reasonable man. "He considered," Froude writes,
"that human affairs could be best ordered by attention and obedience to

the teaching of observed facts, and that superstition, however accredited by honorable objects or apparent good effects, could only be mischievous in the long run. Sorcerers, charlatans, enthusiasts were rising thick on all sides, pretending a mission from the invisible world. Of such men and such messages Celsus and his friends were inexorable antagonists." His is the tone of the sensitive, and in ways holy, Inquisitor speaking before the trial of the Maid in Shaw's *Saint Joan:* "If you have seen what I have seen of heresy, you would not think it a light thing even in the most apparently harmless and even lovable and pious origins. Heresy begins with people who are to all appearances better than their neighbors. A gentle and pious girl, or a young man who has obeyed the command of our Lord by giving all his riches to the poor, and putting on the garb of poverty, the life of austerity, and the rule of humility and charity, may be the founder of a heresy that will wreck both Church and Empire if not ruthlessly stamped out in time." The Christians, Celsus declared, were welcome to stay and become part of the commonwealth, but if that was to be their choice, they must live by its rules. Otherwise be gone. Nothing was required that a reasonable man need find objectionable: to salute the sun, or to sing a hymn to Athene did no harm to anyone. Whatever private views one might have on the subject were one's own affair. But society had a right to allegiance.   11

Point by point Celsus took on Christianity. Point by point he won the intellectual argument, and lost the moral and spiritual one. For he was thinking about the world, and Christians were thinking about the soul. "Most persons," Froude notes, "would now admit that Celsus spoke with wise diffidence when he hesitated at the assumption that the universe and all that it contained was created solely for the sake of man. Origen is perfectly certain that God had no other object. Sun, moon, and stars, and earth and everything living upon it were subordinated to man. In man alone, or in reference to man, the creation had its purpose and meaning." God commanded that the world provide that which is needed by man: as he is weak there must be compassion; as he is sinful there must be the forgiveness of sins; and above all, as he is Godlike, his life must be seen as sacred. If that condition has never been achieved, neither has the Western world ever been the same since first embracing the belief that it should be. Can there be any mistaking that the New Left speaks to the rational, tolerant, reasonable society of the present with the same irrationality, intolerance and unreasonableness, but possibly also the same truth with which the absurd Christians spoke to Imperial Rome? Even Froude, professed and militant Christian, was not less a product of Imperial Britain, and in his grasp of Celsus' arguments, a certain affinity shows through. One recalls the curious moral judgments on display in his own essay, "The English in Ireland in the Eighteenth Century."

Among reasonable beings right is forever tending to make might. Inferiority of numbers is compensated by superior cohesiveness, intelligence, and daring. The better sort of men submit willingly to be governed by those who are nobler and wiser than themselves; organization creates superiority of force; and the ignorant and the selfish may be and are justly compelled for their own advantage to obey a rule which rescues them from their natural weakness. . . . And the right of a people to self-government consists and can consist in nothing but their power to defend themselves. No other definition is possible. . . . When resistance has been tried and failed—when the inequality has been proved beyond dispute by long and painful experience—the wisdom, and ultimately the duty, of the weaker party is to accept the benefits which are offered in exchange for submission.

In truth, is there not a touch of this in the liberal doctrines of the American Empire, with its panoply of technical assistance, constitutional conventions, mutual assistance treaties and development loans, accompanied as it seems to be by the untroubled, or at least willing, use of astonishing degrees of violence to help others perceive the value of going along?   12

The young people of the New Left know what they want; a larger, more diffuse group can best be described as knowing what they do not want, which is what they have. These are so-called alienated students of the present generation. The psychiatrist Seymour L. Halleck recently described them as "existing in a state of chronic identity crisis. . . . [their] constant cries of 'Who am I, I don't know what I believe, I have no self' are accompanied by anxiety which while subdued is nevertheless pervasive and relentless." Affluence means nothing and the increase in personal freedom that comes with growing up is as much as anything a threat to which the individual responds with "a peculiar kind of apathy and withdrawal. . . . Having failed to develop an internalized value system which allows him to determine his direction in life, he is paralyzed when the external world removes its guidelines and restraints." Such persons, Dr. Halleck reports, will occasionally involve themselves in campus protest movements and sustain the interest for a short while, but not long, which is perhaps just as well as "When he does become involved with the activist groups he can be characterized as the most angry and irrational member of that group." Sex and drugs are outlets, but joyless ones. They have everything, but nothing works.   13

Have we not seen this person through history, turning away from a religion that was failing him, rejecting its laws and opting instead for standards of conduct derived wholly from internal personal resources? The object of a liberal secular society being to induce human happiness, it more or less follows that those who reject it will choose to be unhappy and evoke their spirituality in despair more than ecstasy, but *mutatis mutandis*, are we not witnessing the emergence of secular antinomianism?   14

Not a precise, but an interesting parallel is to be seen in Sabbatianism, the mystical Jewish heresy that sprang up in the Holy Land in the seventeenth century and spread through large sections of Sephardic and then Ashkenazic Jewry. Gershom G. Scholem described this heresy in the Hilda Stich Stroock Lectures delivered in New York in 1938. Judaism faced a series of crises at this time: persecution, apostasy and, for some reason, a sudden impatience with the Lord: how long were the Jews to wander in exile? Scholem writes: "Doctrines arose which had one thing in common: That they tried to bridge the gap between the inner experience and the external reality which had ceased to function as its symbol." Sabbatai Zevi, a Cabalistic ascetic, and almost certainly a manic depressive, proclaimed himself the Messiah in Gaza in 1665, and eventually won a great following even though—and seemingly because—he went on to become an apostate! A singular quality of the man was that under the influence of his manic enthusiasms he would commit acts counter to religious law. Harmless enough at first, this practice developed among his radical followers into full-fledged antinomianism. "The Torah," the radical Sabbatians were fond of declaring, "is the seed-corn of Salvation, and just as the seed-corn must rot in the earth in order to sprout and bear fruit, the Torah must be subverted in order to appear in its true Messianic glory." This developed in time into a doctrine of the holiness of sin when committed by an elect who are fundamentally different from the crowd. It was of course a profound affront to Rabbinical Judaism, and in its extreme forms acquired a sinister cast indeed, but Scholem writes, "The religious . . . and moral nihilism of the radicals is after all only the confused and mistaken expression of their urge towards a fundamental regeneration of Jewish life, which under the historic conditions of those times could not find a normal expression." The heresy plagued Jewry for a century or more, and seems to have some influence in the rise of the openly antireligious doctrines of the French Revolution. Nathan M. Pusey has voiced his own serious doubts about "the idea that the way to advance civilization is to start over," but one cannot deny the attraction of just this view for persons who find themselves inexplicably not getting from society exactly those satisfactions society most confidently promises them.   15

Of course, far the most visible of the new protestants are those who do not protest at all, who simply smile, wave daffodils, cover the walls of their *quartiers* with graffiti suggesting we "Legalize Living," and wear their own variety of campaign buttons the quintessential of which demands with purest obstinacy, "Nirvana Now." These are the hippies. Lilies of the field. Bearded and sandaled, they live on air, and love and, alas, drugs. They seek not to change our society, but simply to have nothing to do with it. They are in quest of experiences wholly mystical and internal on the one hand, and tribal on the other. The modern American style of the effective individual functioning in a coherent but competitive society is not for them. Hunter S. Thompson in *The New York Times Sunday Magazine* recently reported an interview with such a young woman living in the Haight-Ashbury section of San Francisco: "I love the whole world," she said, "I am the divine mother, part of Buddha, part of God, part of everything." How did she live? "From meal to meal. I have no money, no possessions, money is beautiful only when it's flowing; when it piles up it's a hang-up. We take care of each other." Did she use drugs? Yes: "When I find myself becoming confused I drop out and take a dose of acid. It's a shortcut to reality; it throws you right into it." Did she pray? "Oh yes, I pray in the morning sun. It nourishes me with its energy so I can spread love and beauty and nourish others. I never pray *for* anything; I don't need anything. Whatever turns me on is a sacrament: LSD, sex, my bells, my colors . . . that is the holy communion, you dig?"   16

Perhaps not. Yet those assertions would have seemed perfectly clear and altogether admirable to a member of the Brethren of the Free Spirit (or the Spiritual Libertines), a mystical Christian heresy that permeated vast areas of medieval Europe, notably the teeming cities of Flanders and the lowlands, from the twelfth century onward almost to our time. Perhaps because its adepts lived in communities within larger polities, and never took over regions for themselves, and also, being clearly heretical, tended at most times to be more or less underground, little attention has been given the Brethren. But they appear to have significantly influenced the political, if not the religious, development of Europe.   17

In their mystical craving for an immediate experience of God, their antinomianism, and emphasis on ecstasy, the Brethren of the Free Spirit were not unlike the Jewish Sabbatians, or for that matter the early Christians. Indeed a certain correspondence obtains among all these movements. When they took matters to an extreme of public display, the Brethren, like those before and after them, both fascinated and horrified the orthodox. "The core of the heresy," Norman Cohn writes in *The Pursuit of the Millenium*, ". . . lay in the adept's attitude towards himself: he believed that he had attained a perfection so absolute that he was incapable of sin." Sexual promiscuity became a matter of principle, and marriage was denounced as an impure state. Eroticism and ecstasy were valued beyond all things as symbols of having achieved what was in truth a state of self-deification. In an age when wealth suddenly appeared in Europe, these heretics characteristically preached a communism of property, and chose to be utterly penniless: In Cohn's words, an elite of amoral supermen.   18

As with Celsus, we are forced to learn most about the views of the Brethren from denunciations by their enemies. Documents from Cromwell's England, a time when the Brethren, known as Ranters, were flourishing, leave no doubt, again in Cohn's words, that the " 'Free Spirit' really was exactly what it was said to be: a system of self-exaltation often amounting to self-deification; a pursuit of total emancipation which in practice could result in anti-nomianism and particularly in anarchic erot-icism; often also a revolutionary social doctrine which denounced the institution of private property; and aimed at its abolition." The Quakers at first saw them as kindred spirits—and the two were often lumped together by others—but efforts at rapprochement were unavailing. The saintly George Fox came upon a group of them as fellow prisoners at Charing Cross. He proposed, we cannot doubt, that they meditate together on the love of God. They called instead for beer and tobacco. A comedy of 1651 by Samuel Sheppard describes the "Character of the roaring Ranters of these Times" in terms that are familiar to say the least:

> . . . our women are all in common.
> We drink quite drunk together, share our Oaths,
> If one man's cloak be rent, all their Cloaths.

A chorus goes:

> Come away, make no delay, of mirth we are no scanters,
> Dance and sing all in a Ring, for we are Jovial Ranters

And the verses fearfully so:

> All lie down, as in a swown,
> To have a pleasing vision.
> And then rise with bared thighs,
> Who'd fear such sweet incision?

> About, about, ye Joviall rout,
> Dance antick like Hob-goblins;
> Drink and roar, and swear and whore,
> But yet no brawls or squoblings.   19

It is said the youth of Haight-Ashbury are not much addicted to scholarship, and they may be pardoned for giving to their service corps the name of "Diggers," after the primitivist community established near Cobham in Surrey in 1649–50. (Such folk have an instinct for agreeable settings.) But they are nonetheless mistaken. Hippies are Ranters.   20

Supposing all this to be so, does it matter? I believe it does. In the first place these persons matter: they number some of the fine spirits of the age. A liberal must regret the loss of belief in another as much as a decent churchman would. In the second place, these youths are trying to tell us something. It was Chesterton, surely, who described heresy as truth gone astray.   21

Seen in large terms, it is clear that these protests have been generated by at least three problems facing our society, each one of which can be said to arise from tendencies that are distinctively those of secular liberalism.   22

The first tendency is that our optimism, belief in progress, and the possibility of achieving human happiness on earth, combined with our considerable achievement in this respect at home, have led us to an increasingly dangerous and costly effort to extend our system abroad. We are in the grip of what Reinhold Niebuhr has called "The Myth of Democratic Universality," the idea that democracy is a "universal option for all nations." The irony, of course, is that it is just because our own history has been so unique that we are led to suppose that the system that has emerged from it can be made worldwide. It is an effort doomed to fail.   23

No civilization has ever succeeded in doing anything of the kind, and surely none whose qualities are as historically conditioned as ours should even try. But it is not just that we shall fail: something more serious is involved. In his inaugural lecture at the London School of Economics and Political Science, Michael Oakeshott, succeeding Harold Laski, made a remark of some significance here. ". . . To try to do something which is inherently impossible," he said, "is always a corrupting enterprise." That, in a word, is what I believe has happened to us overseas. As our efforts repeatedly fall short of their pronounced goals, we begin covering up, taking shortcuts, and in desperation end up doing things we would never conceivably start out to do. Princes of the Church, modest sons of small-town grocers, begin proclaiming holy wars in Asia, while the man in the street acquires an appallingly troubled vision of those who protest. In the words of a Columbia student, describing the mood of a crowd watching a peace march: "War is virility; love of peace is bohemianism and quite probably a sexual perversion."   24

Liberals have simply got to restrain their enthusiasm for civilizing others. It is their greatest weakness and ultimate arrogance. Bertrand Russell suggests that the great Albigensian heresy, with its quest for personal holiness and cult of poverty, was due at least in part to "disappointment of the failure of the crusades." Very likely it will be the success rather than the failure of *our* crusades that will most repel youth. Nathan Glazer has suggested that this generation is already marked by the belief that its government is capable of performing abhorrent deeds.   25

Not the least reason the American commitment to the diffusion of liberal democracy abroad has become a corrupting enterprise is that those values are not yet genuinely secure at home. This is an ugly fact we somehow never finally confront. At just those moments when we seem about to do so, something, somehow, comes along to distract us. Yet there persists in American opinion a powerful component that is illiberal, irrational, intolerant, anti-intellectual, and capable if unleashed of doing the most grievous damage to the fabric of our own society. A century of universal education has not destroyed this tendency, it has only made it more articulate. And it can drive the liberal elite to astonishing distortions. During this past year we have had to begin admitting that during the height of the cold war the United States government began secretly using intelligence funds to support organizations of liberal and even left-leaning students and intellectuals. This was done out of a sincere and almost certainly sound conviction that the activities of these groups would aid in the struggle against totalitarianism. Observe the irony: the liberals running American foreign policy were forced to resort, in effect, to corrupt practices—totalitarian practices if you will—in order to advance liberal causes —*because the popularly elected Congress would never dream of doing so.* The man most commonly blamed, of course, is a decent enough Irish Democrat from Brooklyn: his voting record is impeccably progressive, but neither he nor his constituents share the elite enthusiasm for intellectuals. In the explanations of it all a note even of poignancy enters: can you imagine, writes one former member of the intelligence establishment, trying to get the F.B.I. to grant security clearances to the Boston Symphony Orchestra? The problem goes beyond an affinity for Culture. We have not been able to get rid of racism, or to secure an equal place for Negroes in our society. (An effort in which liberals themselves have not been unfailingly helpful: Woodrow Wilson restored segregation to federal employment policies.) And we begin to perceive that Negroes are not immune to some of the less attractive qualities of their persecutors. We have not been able to get rid of poverty, and begin to perceive that some of our more treasured liberal reforms may have had unanticipated consequences that may even make it more difficult to do so. (Thus, having destroyed the power of the working class political party organization in our cities, we now pour millions of dollars of federal funds into projects designed to overcome the psychic effects of "powerlessness" among the poor.) And we have not rid ourselves of a brutal streak of violence. If the Administration has escalated the conflict in Vietnam, remember that the largest body of opinion in the United States would bomb the yellow bastards into the stone age, and a solid quarter specifically favors using the atom bomb. Cohn reports that the Ranters really began to flourish after the execution of Charles I.   26

A third problem that has contributed to the rise of youthful protest is, I would suggest, that as the life of the educated elite in America becomes more rational, more dogged of inquiry and fearless of result, the wellsprings of emotion *do* dry up, and in particular the primal sense of community begins to fade. As much for the successful as for the failed, society becomes, in Durkheim's phrase, "a dust of individuals." But to the rational liberal, the tribal attachments of blood and soil appear somehow unseemly and primitive. They repress or conceal them, much as others might a particularly lurid sexual interest. It is for this reason, I would suggest, that the nation has had such difficulties accepting the persistence of ethnicity and group cohesion as a fact both of domestic and of world politics.   27

Thus it is possible not only to sympathize with the new protest, but to see much that is valid in it. At the same time we are required to note that which is dangerous. The protest movement is likely to grow rather than otherwise, for the educated middle class from which it draws its strength is growing, and will soon be the dominant American social group. Moreover, the forms of protest are likely to have a striking impact for the very reason that their object is not to redirect the system, but to disrupt it, and this is never a difficult thing to do. It is entirely possible that this disruption could bring to power the forces of the right, and this is indeed an avowed strategy. *Nach Hitler uns.* As the traditional radical Tom Kahn wrote recently in *Partisan Review,* it would be silly to blame the 1966 liberal defeat in California on the New Left and the advocates of Black Power, but "it is enough to say that what they could do, they did." In some forms the rejection of existing society is merely confused, and essentially sophomoric. This winter at Harvard, for example, a document was distributed by a left group that brought to light the fact that in certain regions of Alaska community affairs are under the control of "local politicians, a control that in practice has often been responsive to local interests." At another level, it is anything but. This year, also at Harvard, when a member of the Cabinet came as an invited guest, but under arrangements that did not suit them, the students of the New Left took possession of his person. Such tactics in the early days of Fascist Italy appalled civilization. They are not less objectionable on the Harvard campus. Kahn has described the New Left as "panic disguised as moral superiority" and others have noted how that panic subtly induces a fascination with violence —the most grievous of all possible liberal heresies.   28

To see history as an earnest evolution from the peat bogs to John Stuart Mill, or to the 1964 Democratic platform, is a simplicity that will not much commend itself to anyone any longer. Having read Mill and having helped draft that platform, I am for one aware of greater shortcomings than, say, the former's need to read Wordsworth at the onset of middle age. But neither would I reject the theme of J. H. Plumb's new series, *The History of Human Society,* "that the condition of man now is superior to what it was." Things are better, and where they are best is in the liberal industrial democracies of the North Atlantic world. I hold these regimes to be the best accommodation to the human condition yet devised, and will demand to know of those who reject it, just what they have in mind as a replacement. By and large the central religious and philosophical traditions of the West have led us to where we are now. Some of the heresies against that tradition have helped, and some indeed have been incorporated into it. But just as many have evidenced ugly and dangerous tendencies, of which a terrible certainty about things is surely the foremost.   29

The ancient Gnostics were a charming people, and there is much to be learned from their contact between the hidden, benevolent God, and the Old Testament, law-giving one. But as Scholem writes, "The term *Jewish God, or God of Israel,* is abusive and meant to be so. The Gnostics regarded the confusion between the two Gods, the higher, loving one, and the lower who is merely just, as a misfortune for religion. It is metaphysical antisemitism in its profoundest and most effective form which has found expression in these ideas and continues to do so." The Brethren of the Free Spirit are nothing if not a lovable folk, but Cohn notes, "They were in fact gnostics intent upon their own individual salvation; but the gnosis at which they arrived was a quasi-mystical anarchism—an affirmation of freedom so reckless and unqualified that it amounted to a total denial of every kind of restraint and limitation." They were in fact the "remote precursors" of Bakunin and of Nietzsche: "Nietzsche's Superman, in however vulgarized a form, certainly obsessed the imagination of many of the 'armed bohemians' who made the National-Socialist revolution; and many a Communist intellectual, whether he knows it or not, owes more to Bakunin than to Marx."   30

To protect dissent, no matter how noxious, is one thing. To be indifferent to its growth is another. Men who would undo the system may speak: but they must be answered. The less than soul stirring belief of the liberal in due process, in restraint, in the rule of law is something more than a bourgeois *apparat*: it involves, I argue, the most profound perception of the nature of human society that has yet been achieved, and, precisely in its acknowledgement of the frailty of man and the persistence of sin and failure, it is in the deepest harmony with the central tradition of Judeo-Christian theology. It is not a belief to be frittered away in deference to a mystique of youth.   31

What we must do first of all is listen. Young people are trying to tell us something. They are probably right in much of what they say, however wrong their prescriptions for righting matters. Then we must respond. American liberalism needs to bring its commitments in balance with its resources—overseas and at home. Some years ago Robert Warshaw noted that "So much of 'official' American culture has been cheaply optimistic that we are likely almost by reflex to take pessimism as a measure of seriousness." It is just this unthinking encouragement of bloated expectation that leads young persons to compare forecast with outcome and to conclude that hypocrisy and duplicity are at work. What is asked of us is honesty: and what that requires is a great deal more rigor in matching our performance to our standards. It is now the only way to maintain the credibility of those standards.

If we do this we shall find, of course, that there is altogether too much that is shoddy and derivative, and in a final sense dishonest, about American life. I suspect we will also find that the awareness of this fact is more diffused within the American electorate than it will have suited the mildly dissenting liberal *cognoscenti* to imagine. It is one thing to read in Richard Rovere's "Letter from Washington" in the *New Yorker* that "This city is awash with lies and deceptions . . ." It is another to learn, as Rovere with his unmatched toughness of mind would insist, that two-thirds of the American people believe the assassination of President Kennedy to have been part of a broader conspiracy. The Catholic philosopher Michael Novak, commenting in *Commonweal* on the growing rejection of the American system by the New Left, has suggested:

> Perhaps the rumors that wealthy businessmen hired former CIA agents to assassinate Kennedy are the mythical expression of a growing perception of reality: a majority of Americans, and certainly a very wealthy and politically powerful minority, do not wish to see a further social or political revolution in America.

These are signs of danger, as much as are the rioting cities and turbulent campuses. The foundations of popular confidence in the American system are proving to be nothing like so solid and enduring as the confident liberal establishment has supposed. The ability to respond to signs of danger is the essential condition of the ability to survive. It is not too much to declare that our ability is now being tested: it is always being tested. If we respond well to these signs of danger—and if we find a meaningful role in helping to transform the system for those who now attack it—we are likely to evolve a society of considerable nobility. But the first requirement is to acknowledge that what we have so far made of our opportunity is very much less than we should have. 32

The story is told of the building of the great Catholic Shrine of the Immaculate Conception in Washington: generations of truck drivers, coal miners, and cleaning women contributed their pittances to the coffers of the American hierarchy which slowly amassed the fortune required to construct this most fabulous edifice. It was a building that had everything. Nothing was spared of precious metal and lustrous stone. Nothing was spared by way of design: elements of every architectural tradition in the world were skillfully incorporated in the soaring facade and billowing dome. At last it was finished, and there followed a triumphant week of procession and ceremony, chorus and sermon. Then silence fell. The next morning a child was praying in the crypt when a vision of Our Lady appeared. Smiling that most beatific of all smiles, she looked down and said, "Build a beautiful church on this site." 33

The Whole Selection

1 After consulting a dictionary, determine as carefully as you can how Moynihan is using "antinomianism" and "gnostic."

2 What is Moynihan's definition of "liberalism"? Of what importance is it that liberalism be characterized as "secular"? What are its essential characteristics? What are its weaknesses? Why are the weaknesses a significant element in the proposition the author is developing?

3 State Moynihan's central proposition in a few sentences.

4 Why is the analogy between contemporary protest movements and certain historical religious heresies introduced? Do you think the analogy valid? In the extended reference to "Origen and Celsus," could one suggest that second-century Christians were distinguished by a profound and meaningful belief, as the modern protesters are not (see Boorstin's essay)?

5 At any point in the essay, does the author provide the reader with a brief history of the question?

6 What are the three clusters of behavior mentioned in paragraph 6? What is the central tendency in each?

7 What are the three problems (beginning with paragraph 22) facing our society which are "distinctly those of secular liberalism"?

8 Is there any way in which the three "problems" are related to the "three clusters of behavior"?

9 Comment on the distinction being made in the first two sentences of paragraph 31: "To protect dissent, no matter how noxious, is one thing. To be indifferent to its growth is another."

10 Is the title of the essay in any way a part of the argument?

11 What is the point of the story concluding the essay?

12 Compare Moynihan's essay with the essays by Boorstin, Dubos, Kirk, and Schlesinger.

THE MARKET v. THE BUREAUCRAT

MILTON FRIEDMAN

There is today a widespread tendency to take it for granted that growth of population, advancing technology, expanding output of goods and services, increasing complexity of our industrial structure—the whole set of developments we label economic growth—necessarily repress individuality and enforce conformity. In the words of the brochure describing a recent symposium, "many thoughtful persons view these [scientific and technological] advances as creating new forms of bondage and as grave threats to the integrity of the individual." 1

I believe that this view is, to say the least, a great oversimplification. True, new forms of bondage are being created, and there are grave threats to the integrity of the individual. But the history of mankind—from primitive times to the present—is mostly a record of bondage, of tyranny of man over man. We do not need any sophisticated analysis to explain why freedom is threatened. Tyranny is the natural state of mankind. The remarkable thing about our era is the freedom we enjoy, not the threats to that freedom. And these threats themselves are not an inevitable consequence of the growing complexity of our society. They are a result of the social policies we have chosen to adopt. They are a result of a lack of understanding, not of harsh inevitability. 2

The causal relation between growth and freedom is almost the opposite of that which is commonly assumed: freedom produces growth and prosperity, and growth and prosperity in turn provide greater scope for freedom—though imperfect man may fail to grasp this potentiality and may instead use his material wealth to exploit his fellow man, in which case he will also destroy his prosperity. 3

Whether we look at the Golden Age of ancient Greece, or at the early centuries of the Roman era, or at the Renaissance, we see that widening individual freedom and quickening of economic growth went hand in hand —and that when freedom was destroyed, economic decline was not far behind. To come closer to our own times, the breaking down of feudal relations, the loosening of control over economic activity by the state, the widening of the scope assigned to individual initiative produced the great scientific and technological advances of the seventeenth and eighteenth centuries. It is no accident that the industrial revolution which followed had its home in Britain, where the ties of bondage were loosest, or that it had its greatest flowering after Britain adopted laissez faire as a national policy, or that the leadership moved to the United States at a time when we too had limited intervention by the government into economic affairs. 4

These developments illustrate that great insight which Adam Smith expounded so effectively. The free market enables millions of men to co-operate with one another in complex tasks without compulsion and without centralized control. The invisible hand of the free market, whereby men who intend only to serve their own interests are led to serve the public interest, is a far more sensitive and effective source of both growth and freedom than the dead hand of the bureaucrat, however well intentioned he may be. 5

Growth and development do of course produce new problems of reconciling the freedom of one man with the freedom of others—problems of congestion, pollution, and so on. And many of these can best be met by coordinated action through governmental channels. But growth and development also reduce the problems of preserving freedom in other areas. For example, growth of population and improvements in transportation and communication have greatly widened the scope for effective competition and so have reduced the need for governmental concern with monopolistic behavior—though unfortunately, as most notably in transportation itself, we have often reacted by protecting entrenched monopoly from competition rather than taking full advantage of the new scope for competition.   6

Whatever may be the net balance of the effects of growth, the most obvious threats to the integrity of the individual have a very different source: in area after area of our national life, we have adopted policies that unnecessarily threaten the integrity of the individual. In each of these, there are alternative policies that would both promote our objective better and strengthen individual freedom. The areas in which this is true are varied, and they refer to many different aspects of our lives. Yet there runs through them a common element: the substitution of bureaucratic organization and control for market arrangements, the rejection of Adam Smith's great insight.   7

I shall illustrate this generalization by discussing three specific areas: radio and television, schooling, and public welfare. I have chosen three different areas out of the many available to show under how varied a guise the same basic issue arises.   8

RADIO AND TELEVISION

Here are marvelous technological achievements that we are failing to ex-ploit effectively. We have a "wasteland" of highly repetitive, standardized programs directed at the great masses—which by itself is all to the good —but with all too little in the way of imaginative, exploratory, or simply high quality programs directed at minorities. The medium promotes dead-ening uniformity rather than variety, diversity, and individuality. The pref-erences of a minority, however strong they may be, must give way to the preferences of the mass audience, however weak.   9

Equally important, a medium that could promote vigorous and lively discussion of public issues seldom ventures into controversial areas. Truly free speech is held in check by the fear of losing a license and is replaced by "fair" speech. The occasional slightly venturesome documentary or exposé is trumpeted far and wide as a sign of the independence of the station or network. The magnificent coverage of many news events—from the Olympics to the moon landing by American astronauts—shows the potential of the medium, so far largely unexploited.   10

This indictment is widely accepted. What has been the response? A string of privately supported educational television stations and, because these seemed inadequate, the enactment of a new Public Broadcasting Act under which the Federal Government will subsidize the production and distribution of programs. Talk about carrying coals to Newcastle. As we shall see, the problem is that there is now too much control by the Federal Government—through the Federal Communications Commission— over radio and televsion. To cure this, we establish another federal body to be a monopoly supplier of programs. To quote my colleague, Ronald Coase, who dubbed the measure "a wholly objectionable poverty program for the well-to-do," "the Public Broadcasting Act of 1967 is unnecessary, inefficient, inequitable and subject to dangerous political influences."   11

I suggest that the key to the present defect is the federal licensing of broadcasters. This gives the Federal Communications Commission the power of life and death over a station. If a person wants to start a newspaper, and has the capital, he needs merely buy a printing press, rent a location, publish his paper, and see if he can get the public to buy it. Once he is in business, his readers and advertisers are the only ones he must satisfy. But if he wants to set up a radio or television station, he also must convince the FCC that he is a person of good moral character and that there is a "need" for additional facilities. This may not be easy to do —ask those who have tried to get a license for Austin, Texas. And once the FCC grants him a license, he must satisfy it that he is presenting a "balanced" and "fair" program.   12

If newspapers were subject to the same controls, the New York Times would have to change its motto to "All the news that the FCC believes fit to print," and neither the New York Times nor the Chicago Tribune, as presently constituted, could conceivably get a clean bill of health. Fortunately, newspapers developed in an earlier era and have so far escaped control. Had they first developed in, say, the 1920s or 1930s, there would almost surely be today a Federal Publications Commission—as indeed was recommended in the famous Hutchins Report on the press.   13

One specific measure taken by the FCC has perhaps done more than any other single thing to stifle diversity and enshrine mediocrity. That is its refusal to authorize subscription or pay television. The FCC has ruled that we may not spend our money to see programs we wish to see. We must accept the programs that are provided as a by-product of advertising. We cannot, even if we wish to, pay to suppress the advertising, except by contributing to and watching an educational television station.   14

To understand how this measure has such a far-reaching effect in enshrining mediocrity in television and radio, let us consider what the effect would be of applying the same rule in a comparable area to which it is not now applied. Suppose it were legislated that reading matter could not be sold but must be given away, that all newspapers must be like the "throwaways" now often given out, that all magazines must be available without charge, financed only by the revenue from the advertising they contain or by a subsidy from a church, foundation, or other organization, and similarly that any books published must be financed in the same way and distributed without charge to readers. It takes no great act of the imagination to see the results: those books and magazines that appeal to relatively small groups with specialized tastes would disappear. Few if any advertisers would deem it worthwhile to pay for the publication of avant-garde poetry in order to be able to insert pages extolling the virtue of Gleem or Dream or Steem. Far better to put those pages in a Western that millions would pick up and read avidly. The book publishing industry would become like television—a wasteland of Westerns, mysteries, and popular romances, with an occasional serious work appealing to a limited audience sponsored by a firm trying to improve its public image, or just with unusual tastes.   15

Your immediate reaction will be to regard this as a fantastic horror story and to dismiss it out of hand. But let me urge you not to let yourself be a victim of the tyranny of the status quo. The distribution of reading matter is almost strictly comparable to the distribution of television programs. I have not seen any argument in favor of forbidding pay television that does not apply with roughly equal force to forbidding pay publishing. And conversely—no argument in favor of pay publishing that does not apply with roughly equal force to permitting pay television. The two strike us as "of course" different only because they happen to have developed differently.   16

Why has the FCC prohibited pay television these past many years, except for a few so-called "pilot" projects? Because the networks are firmly established as the dominant distributors of national advertising, and they believe, rightly or wrongly, that they would fare less well than they do now if a new way of distributing programs were permitted. The networks exert enormous influence over the FCC—and it is inevitable that they should, just as it is inevitable that the railroads will exert enormous influence over the ICC, the banks over the Federal Reserve, and the producers of automobiles over the federal agency to promote automobile safety. If the FCC had not stood in the way, pay television would now be a major factor, and the range, quality, and variety of television programs would now be far closer to that of book publishing.   17

How can we take advantage of the potentialities of television and radio and eliminate the present standardizing hand of the state? By abolishing the FCC and having a truly free radio and television to parallel a free press. But I will be told, that is absurd. There are only a limited number of television channels; someone must assign them. It is regrettable that we should have to have federal control over radio and television, but that simply reflects the technological characteristics of the industry. Nothing of the sort. There are only a limited number of pieces of land on which a newspaper plant can stand. Why does that not require assignment of land? Because there is private property in land and the allocation of land can be performed by purchase and sale.   18

Precisely the same solution is available for radio and television. Let the FCC auction off to the highest bidders the right to specified channels now embodied in licenses (for example, the right to broadcast on a specified frequency from a specified location at specified times at a specified maximum power). That was what the Federal Government did a century and more ago with its land. The FCC could then be abolished. The private owners could trade these rights back and forth and rearrange them in various ways to make them more valuable. There would be problems of interference—of one man trespassing on another's frequency—but they would be handled as trespassing on land now is, through the regular courts.   19

I cannot here elaborate this proposal and consider all its implications in full detail, even if I had the competence to do so. Let me only state that this is not a crackbrained, off-the-cuff suggestion. It is a proposal that has been extensively studied, in particular by R. H. Coase. All the serious objections raised have been examined. There is little doubt that it is a perfectly feasible way to handle the allocation and use of radio and television channels without special government control, little doubt that it would produce a far more efficient use of the radio spectrum, in many different ways, than prevails today. And there is little doubt that it would convert what is today a homogenizing influence into a major force widening the avenues for the expression of individuality.   20

SCHOOLING

For reasons of space, I shall restrict myself to higher schooling—or as it is euphemistically called, higher education. (Personally, I prefer the more descriptive term because not all schooling is education nor all education schooling.) I may, however, note that lower schooling offers an equally striking example of my main theme.   21

The trend is clear. Government expenditure on higher schooling has been growing rapidly. A steadily increasing fraction of students is enrolled in governmentally run institutions. There are more complaints about the impersonality of the mega-universities, the neglect of the individual student, the standardization and routinization of the educational process. And the private schools, like Reed, that provide a welcome contrast and that have been the leaders in fostering quality education, find it more and more difficult to compete for students and funds with the governmental institutions. They are themselves becoming increasingly dependent on tax monies for support.   22

These developments raise two separate issues: First, how much of a governmental subsidy, if any, there should be for higher schooling; second, how any subsidy should be distributed.   23

Strictly speaking, only the second of these issues is relevant for my theme—how we have been unnecessarily curbing individuality by the social policies we have been following. But I cannot forbear from a few comments on the first issue, because I feel so strongly about it.[1]   24

The present use of tax monies to subsidize higher schooling seems to me one of the great suppressed scandals of our day. Compare the young men and women who receive this subsidy by attending state-supported institutions with their contemporaries who do not go to college at all. The youngsters in college come from higher income families than those who are not in college—but both sets of families pay taxes. More important, the youngsters in college will on the average have higher incomes for the rest of their lives than the youngsters who do not go to college. We have imposed a major tax on the poor to subsidize the not-so-poor. We in the middle- and upper-income classes have in this area—as I am afraid we have in many others—conned the poor into supporting us in a style that we take to be no more than our just deserts.   25

It is eminently desirable that every young man and woman, regardless of the wealth or religion or color or social standing of his or her family, have the opportunity to get whatever schooling he or she can qualify for, *provided that he or she is willing to pay for it, either currently or out of the subsequent higher income that the schooling will make possible.* There is, that is, a strong case for assuring the availability of loans or their equivalent, by governmental means, if necessary. There is no case that I can see for providing subsidies.   26

Having relieved myself of these obiter dicta, let me turn to the second question: How should any subsidy be distributed? Currently, we

---

[1] These comments refer only to schooling, not to government expenditures for support of research, which raise a different set of issues.

distribute the subsidy primarily by having the government run institutions of higher learning and by charging tuition to students that is far below the costs incurred on their behalf. This is both inequitable and inefficient. Moreover, it is this practice, much more than the subsidization of higher schooling, that promotes conformity and threatens individuality.   27

Under current arrangements, the state of Oregon says to its young men and women, "If you meet certain academic standards, we shall automatically grant you a scholarship worth something like fifteen hundred or two thousand dollars a year regardless of 'need'—provided that you are smart enough to go to the University of Oregon or Oregon State. If you are so perverse as to want to go to Reed, let alone to Stanford or Harvard or Yale or the University of Chicago, not a penny for you." Surely, it would be more equitable to proceed instead along the lines of the G.I. educational benefits for veterans. Let whatever money the state of Oregon wants to spend on higher schooling be divided into the appropriate number of scholarships, each of, say, $2000 per year, tenable for four years. Let there be a competitive exam—or some other method of selection—and let these scholarships be awarded to individuals to be used to attend any approved institution of their choice that will in turn accept them. If Oregon wants to continue to run the University of Oregon, let that institution charge tuition sufficient to cover its costs, and compete on even terms with other institutions. If it is more attractive to students than other institutions, the University will flourish; if not, it will decline.   28

Today, there is no reason for faculties and administrators of the existing state institutions to pay any attention to their students, except as this will indirectly affect the legislature which votes them funds. The thing for them to do, as they well know, is to engage in activities that will appeal to the legislature while paying to students the minimum attention that will keep them from being too obstreperous. This is the valid element in the drive for student power.   29

The arrangement I suggest gives the student a wider range of choice and enables him to exert more influence on the kind of schooling he is offered. It eliminates the present unfair competition between state-run and other institutions.   30

It gives the faculties and administrations of state-run institutions an incentive to serve their students. It would open up the opportunity for new institutions to enter the field and seek to attract customers. The strengthening of competition would promote improvements in quality and foster diversity and experimentation. Because the money would go to individuals, not institutions, it would be clear who are the recipients of the subsidy and bring into the open this question of who should be subsidized. Also, it would give the individual greater freedom of choice, greater opportunity to express his own values and to develop his own capacities as effectively as possible.   31

All of these are advantages of the scholarship plan. But they are also, to speak cynically, the major political obstacles to its enactment. As usual in such matters, the people who would benefit from the change do not know that they would; the vested interests that have developed under the present arrangement will recognize the threat to them at once.   32

PUBLIC WELFARE

The methods by which we subsidize the poor have the same defects as those by which we subsidize the rich: they involve giving too much power to bureaucrats to determine who gets the subsidy and in what form, too little power to the people who are being subsidized, and too little incentive to them to reduce the subsidy they receive.   33

The defects of our present welfare program are by now widely recognized. In the midst of great prosperity, the welfare rolls mount. Once on the rolls, many people find it difficult to get off. We have been creating a permanent class of welfare recipients, who devote their energies to wheedling a bit more welfare for themselves or bringing pressure to bear to improve welfare payments rather than to raising their own incomes to a level at which they can be off welfare. We have an army of welfare workers administering the system. They find themselves bogged down in paper work, engaged in being policemen and spies, with little time left to perform their proper function—helping the unfortunate people who are under their charge. The whole process is degrading for the welfare recipient and demeaning for the welfare workers.   34

What is wrong? At bottom, I conjecture, the belief that the state through administrative machinery can deal with persons needing assistance in the way one person spending his own money can deal with another person. If, out of charitable inclinations, a man takes an interest in someone suffering misfortune, it is entirely understandable that he may want to make a detailed investigation of that person's circumstances, to assure himself that the misfortune is real, that he will want to explore the items needed and provide help for those he thinks most urgent, and then try to guide the person he is assisting to use the help most effectively. But translate this into a large-scale governmental program, and it ends up as the kind of administrative nightmare we now have. The welfare workers are not distributing their own money, so there must be controls over them. The criteria of need must be standardized. The forms of help must be specified. The dispersers of funds must be supervised. In the process, the human element is squeezed out and replaced by frustration and mutual distrust.   35

This system clearly is a "grave threat to the integrity of the individual" receiving welfare. Before a welfare recipient may move from one apartment to another, he must get the approval of a civil servant; equally, before he may buy second-hand furniture, have the gas turned on, or make any one of a thousand other deviations from an approved budget. Needless to say, the welfare recipients have become skilled in finding ways around the regulations, but nonetheless, the whole atmosphere is one in which they are treated like irresponsible wards of the state, like children, not like responsible citizens. Clearly, if the taxpayer does subsidize them, he has in some sense the moral right to impose such requirements. But is it wise to do so?   36

Most important of all, carrying over the notion of meeting the other person's "needs" has had the unfortunate effect of largely eliminating any incentive for the welfare recipient to help himself. If a welfare recipient earns an extra $100, that is interpreted as meaning that he or she can meet an additional $100 of "needs," and therefore that welfare aid can be reduced by $100. In consequence, the recipient has no incentive to earn money unless he can earn enough completely to replace welfare. This is the main reason why there tends to develop a permanent class of welfare recipients.   37

As in each of the two prior examples, the way to improve the situation is to put greater reliance on impersonal market arrangements and less on bureaucratic administration. For welfare, the device that recommends itself is the negative income tax, under which all persons with incomes below the level now taxable would be entitled to receive a fraction of their unused exemptions and deductions. This method would give assistance to the poor in the form of money, which they could spend as they wish, on the basis of the impersonal criteria of the size of their income and the number of persons in their family, and in such a way as to give them an incentive to raise their income from other sources.   38

This is not the place for a detailed exposition of the way a negative income tax would work or of its advantages and disadvantages. It is sufficient for the present purpose to note that it has been studied carefully and that there is every reason to believe that it would be a feasible substitute for the present direct relief and aid to dependent children programs; that it would, over a period, simultaneously give more assistance to the truly needy and cost the taxpayers less.   39

The crucial point for our present purpose is that a negative income tax would permit the elimination of the bulk of our present welfare bureaucracy, would end the division of our population into two classes, would give those receiving assistance greater freedom and independence to shape their own life and greater opportunity to take advantage of their own abilities and capacities. In addition, whereas our present programs have essentially destroyed private philanthropy, the negative income tax, by assuming the basic load of income maintenance, would reduce the hardship cases, which no general program can eliminate, to a level that private charity could handle. We have been stifling private philanthropic agencies, converting them to agents or contractors of the state, by our conception of government welfare. The negative income tax would give them a new function to perform. The diversity, flexibility, and efficiency of free enterprise has a role to play in philanthropy no less than in other areas.   40

CONCLUSION

In recent decades, there has been a steady tendency to enlarge the role of the government, either to undertake new tasks or to take over tasks formerly entrusted to private and voluntary action. By now the process has gone very far indeed, even in a country like the United States which prides itself on being the country of free enterprise. Today, probably over one-third of all the income of the people in this country is channeled through the government—being extracted by taxes and loans, and spent for governmental programs. And this grossly understates the influence of the government. The wages many an employer may pay, the prices many an industry may charge, the businesses we may enter, the countries to which we may travel, and many other aspects of our daily lives are subject to governmental control.   41

This expansion of the role of the government has been sold to the American people on the ground that it would enhance both their material well-being and their personal freedom. And further expansion is now being sold to them on the same ground. The promises have been and remain glowing. Yet, when we look at performance and not promise, the story is very different. We have adopted reform after reform, program after program, without achieving the promised objectives. Consider those programs which have one after the other been proclaimed as great progressive achievements: the National Recovery Administration, the Agricultural Adjustment Act and its successors; the Securities and Exchange Commission; public housing; the Wagner Labor Act; social security; relief and aid to dependent children; urban renewal; federal aid to education—which of them has achieved the objectives that aroused such high hopes in their disinterested supporters? The problems each was touted as solving are with us yet, often in exaggerated form. Or pass from the dramatic federal level to the local level. What are the major governmental responsibilities at the local level? Schooling and police protection. What are major areas of social concern? Inadequate schooling and crime on the streets.   42

It is a fascinating question of political science to explain this sequence of events. What is it that explains what activities are taken over by government and when? Why is it that so many measures work in accordance with the original intentions of the disinterested for a year or two, but then soon become devices whereby special interests enrich themselves? Why is it, that is, that well-intentioned liberals have so often turned out to be front men for special interests they would never knowingly have supported? Why is it that, in a democracy supposedly run by a majority, there are so many measures pandering to special interests?   43

These questions take us far afield from the more limited object of this paper: to show by example that the lack of success of many government programs and the threats they raise to freedom and individuality is a necessary consequence of neither the objectives sought nor the increasing complexity of our society. Television and radio, higher schooling, and welfare arrangements are very different areas in which we have very different objectives. Yet there is a common strand running through all three. In all, we have tried to substitute central direction and bureaucratic control for voluntary arrangements. In all, we could achieve our objectives far better by using arrangements that give a greater scope to the market, that rely on "participatory democracy" rather than on bureaucratic democracy.   44

If we are to meet the recurrent threats to freedom that are bound to arise, it is important that the informed public become more sophisticated than it is now about government programs. It must come to understand that the business community has no monopoly on misleading advertising, that promises must be distinguished from performance. We must try to repress the tendency to say, "Let's pass a law," whenever a problem arises and recognize that the indirect route through voluntary action may be surer and safer than the direct route through government action. And when we do turn to government action, we shall do best if, so far as possible, we try to restrict government action either to setting up arrangements under which private action can be effective (as in radio or television), or to giving money in an open and aboveboard way to specific individuals under specified conditions rather than to providing the relevant good or service by a government organization.   45

The Whole Selection

1 Although the content of Friedman's essay appears very complex, its structure is simple enough:
   A. He begins with an assumption to be questioned.
   B. He provides a major basis for his view of the matter and an answer to the assumption of the first paragraph.
   C. His principal thesis is stated.
   D. He provides a brief history of the question.
   E. The central thesis is repeated.

F. He introduces a significant qualification of his central thesis.

G. He indicates specifically from where the threat to freedom comes.

H. He illustrates this generalization in three areas:
   1. Radio and television
   2. Schooling
   3. Public welfare

I. He provides us with a restatement and summary.

Amplify the details of this brief outline in order to get a sense of the major thrust of his argument.

2 Adam Smith can be regarded as the principal authority quoted by Friedman. Find out what you can about him. On the basis of information which you can discover, apply to him the tests for an authority:

a Does he have the intellectual ability to make a judgment in this area?

b Has he been a success (or has he been recognized) in his field?

c Does his authority have an apt relationship to the time (or era) to which it is being applied?

d Does he have sufficient experience in the field, if experience is necessary?

e Does his reasoning process, if revealed by the quoted matter, stand the test of scrutiny?

f Is there any reason to suspect a bias that would be harmful to his opinion?

Apply these same tests to Milton Friedman or any of the other authors in this section on argument.

3 How specifically does each case (radio and television, schooling, public welfare) prove Friedman's thesis? What common strand, from the author's viewpoint, runs through all three, making them adequate case histories?

4 How are "market arrangements" and "growth and freedom" connected?

5 In what way exactly does government bureaucracy act as a threat to individuality and enforced conformity?

6 Certain terms, essential to Friedman's argument, are defined directly or indirectly in the essay. What are Friedman's definitions of the following?

Market

Freedom

Growth

Bureaucracy

Participatory democracy

Free enterprise

A NATURAL ARISTOCRACY

THOMAS JEFFERSON

I agree with you that there is a natural aristocracy among men. The grounds of this are virtue and talents. Formerly, bodily powers gave place among the aristoi. But since the invention of gunpowder has armed the weak as well as the strong with missile death, bodily strength, like beauty, good humor, politeness and other accomplishments, has become but an auxiliary ground for distinction. There is also an artificial aristocracy, founded on wealth and birth without either virtue or talents; for with these it would belong to the first class. The natural aristocracy I consider as the most precious gift of nature, for the instruction, the trusts, and government of society. And indeed, it would have been inconsistent in creation to have formed man for the social state, and not to have provided virtue and wisdom enough to manage the concerns of the society. May we not even say, that that form of government is the best, which provides the most effectually for a pure selection of these natural *aristoi* into the offices of government? The artificial aristocracy is a mischievous ingredient in government, and provision should be made to prevent its ascendency. On the question, what is the best provision, you and I differ; but we differ as rational friends, using the free exercise of our own reason, and mutually indulging its errors. You think it best to put the *pseudo-aristoi* into a separate chamber of legislation, where they may be hindered from doing mischief by their co-ordinate branches, and where, also, they may be a protection to wealth against the agrarian and plundering enterprises of the majority of the people. I think that to give them power in order to prevent them from doing mischief, is arming them for it, and increasing instead of remedying the evil. For if the co-ordinate branches can arrest their action, so may they that of the co-ordinates. Mischief may be done negatively as well as positively. Of this, a cabal in the Senate of the United States has furnished many proofs. Nor do I believe them necessary to protect the wealthy; because enough of these will find their way into every branch of the legislature, to protect themselves. From fifteen to twenty legislatures of our own, in action for thirty years past, have proved that no fears of an equalization of property are to be apprehended from them. I think the best remedy is exactly that provided by all our constitutions, to leave to the citizens the free election and separation of the *aristoi* from the *pseudo-aristoi*, of the wheat from the chaff. In general they will elect the really good and wise. In some instances, wealth may corrupt, and birth blind them; but not in sufficient degree to endanger the society. [1]

It is probable that our difference of opinion may, in some measure, be produced by a difference of character in those among whom we live.

From what I have seen of Massachusetts and Connecticut myself, and still more from what I have heard, and the character given of the former by yourself, who know them so much better, there seems to be in those two States a traditionary reverence for certain families, which has rendered the offices of the government nearly hereditary in those families. I presume that from an early period of your history, members of those families happening to possess virtue and talents, have honestly exercised them for the good of the people, and by their services have endeared their names to them. In coupling Connecticut with you, I mean it politically only, not morally. For having made the Bible the common law of their land, they seem to have modeled their morality on the story of Jacob and Laban. But although this hereditary succession to office with you, may, in some degree, be founded in real family merit, yet in a much higher degree, it has proceeded from your strict alliance of Church and State. These families are canonised in the eyes of the people on common principles, "you tickle me, and I will tickle you." In Virginia we have nothing of this. Our clergy, before the Revolution, having been secured against rivalship by fixed salaries, did not give themselves the trouble of acquiring influence over the people. Of wealth, there were great accumulations in particular families, handed down from generation to generation under the English law of entails. But the only object of ambition for the wealthy was a seat in the King's Council. All their court then was paid to the crown and its creatures; and they Philipised in all collisions between the King and the people. Hence they were unpopular; and that unpopularity continues attached to their names. A Randolph, a Carter, or a Burwell must have great personal superiority over a common competitor to be elected by the people even at this day. At the first session of our legislature after the Declaration of Independence, we passed a law abolishing entails. And this was followed by one abolishing the privilege of primogeniture, and dividing the lands of intestates equally among all their children, or other representatives. These laws, drawn by myself, laid the ax to the foot of pseudo-aristocracy. And had another which I prepared been adopted by the legislature, our work would have been complete. It was a bill for the more general diffusion of learning. This proposed to divide every country into wards of five or six miles square, like your townships; to establish in each ward a free school for reading, writing, and common arithmetic; to provide for the annual selection of the best subjects from these schools, who might receive, at the public expense, a higher degree of education at a district school; and from these district schools to select a certain number of the most promising subjects, to be completed at an University, where all the useful sciences should be taught. Worth and genius would thus have been sought out from every condition of life, and completely prepared by education for defeating the competition of wealth and birth for public trusts. My proposition had, for a further object, to impart to these wards those portions of self-government for which they are best qualified, by confiding to them the care of their poor, their roads, police, elections, the nomination of jurors, administration of justice in small cases, elementary exercises of militia; in short, to have made them little republics, with a warden at the head of each, for all those concerns which, being under their eye, they would better manage than the larger republics of the county or State. A general call of ward meetings by their wardens on the same day through the State, would at any time produce the genuine sense of the people on any required point, and would enable the State to act in mass, as your people have so often done, and with so much effect by their town meeting. The law for religious freedom, which made a part of this system, having put down the aristocracy of the clergy, and restored to the citizen the freedom of the mind, and those of entails and descents nurturing an equality of conditions among them, this on education would have raised the mass of the people to the high ground of moral respectability necessary to their own safety, and to orderly government; and would have completed the great object of qualifying them to select the veritable *aristoi,* for the trusts of government, to the exclusion of the pseudalists; and the same Theognis who has furnished the epigraphs of your two letters, assures us that "Not yet, Kurmus, have good men destroyed a state."   2

Although this law has not yet been acted on but in a small and inefficient degree, it is still considered as before the legislature, with other bills of the revised code, not yet taken up, and I have great hope that some patriotic spirit will, at a favorable moment, call it up, and make it the keystone of the arch of our government.   3

With respect to aristocracy, we should further consider, that before the establishment of the American States, nothing was known to history but the man of the old world, crowded within limits either small or overcharged, and steeped in the vices which that situation generates. A government adapted to such men would be one thing; but a very different one, that for the man of these States. Here every one may have land to labor for himself, if he chooses; or, preferring the exercise of any other industry, may exact for it such compensation as not only to afford a comfortable subsistence, but wherewith to provide for a cessation from labor in old age. Every one, by his property, or by his satisfactory situation, is interested in the support of law and order. And such men may safely and advantageously reserve to themselves a wholesome control over their public affairs, and a degree of freedom, which, in the hands of the *Canaille* of the cities of Europe, would be instantly perverted to the demolition and destruction of everything public and private. The history of the last twenty-five years of France, and of the last forty years in America, nay of its last two hundred years, proves the truth of both parts of this observation.　　　　4

But even in Europe a change has sensibly taken place in the mind of man. Science had liberated the ideas of those who read and reflect, and the American example had kindled feelings of right in the people. An insurrection has consequently begun, of science, talents, and courage, against rank and birth, which have fallen into contempt. It has failed in its first effort, because the mobs of the cities, the instrument used for its accomplishment, debased by ignorance, poverty, and vice, could not be restrained to rational action. But the world will recover from the panic of this first catastrophe. Science is progressive, and talents and enterprise on the alert. Resort may be had to the people of the country, a more governable power from their principles and subordination; and rank, and birth, and tinsel-aristocracy will finally shrink into insignificance, even there. This, however, we have no right to meddle with. It suffices for us, if the moral and physical condition of our own citizens qualifies them to select the able and good for the direction of their government, with a recurrence of elections at such short periods as will enable them to displace an unfaithful servant, before the mischief he meditates may be irremediable.　　　　5

The Whole Selection

1　In the letters of 1813 Jefferson and John Adams, former political rivals, occupied themselves with a theoretical debate of what had been for them a practical issue in politics—the nature and character of an aristocracy in a democratic state. Jefferson's points will be clearer to you if you study the following excerpts from Adams' letters to Jefferson.

> *Adams to Jefferson: July 9, 1813*
> Your *aristoi* are the most difficult animals to manage of anything in the whole theory and practice of government. They will not suffer themselves to be governed. They not only exert all their own subtlety, industry, and courage, but they employ the commonalty to knock to pieces every plan and model that the most honest architects in legislation can invent to keep them within bounds. . . . Who are these *aristoi*? Who shall judge? Who shall select these choice spirits from the rest of the congregation? Themselves? We must find out and determine who "themselves" are. . . . Nobility in men is worth as much as it is in horses, asses, or rams. Yet birth and wealth prevailed over virtue and talents in all ages. The many will acknowledge no other *aristoi*.

> *Adams to Jefferson: August 1813*
> Has science, or morals, or philosophy, or criticism, or Christianity advanced, or improved, or enlightened mankind upon this subject, and

shown them that the idea of the "well-born" is a prejudice, a phantom, a point-no-point, a Cape Flyaway, a dream? I say it is the ordinance of God Almighty, in the constitution of human nature, and wrought into the fabric of the universe. Philosophers and politicians may nibble and quibble, but they never will get rid of it. . . . It is a part of the natural history of man, and politicians and philosophers may as well project to make the animal live without bones or blood, as society can pretend to establish a free government without attention to it.

Adams to Jefferson: September 2, 1813
The five pillars of aristocracy are beauty, wealth, birth, genius, and virtue. Any one of [the first three] can, at any time, overbear any one of the two last. . . .

Any debate must have some common ground on which the participants can agree. As suggested by these excerpts as well as by Jefferson's reply, what is the common ground on which these two debaters meet? Precisely where do they part company—that is, what is the essential issue about which they disagree?
2 From Jefferson's point of view, what is the essential purpose of a natural aristocracy?
3 Distinguish the *aristoi* from the *pseudo-aristoi* as Jefferson does.
4 In what ways do the eminent families of Massachusetts differ from those of Virginia? Of what importance is this to Jefferson's argument?
5 Jefferson appeals to history (especially to the history of America and France from about 1775 to 1813) to prove a point that is crucial to his argument—that the American is different from the European. What is the difference and how did it come about?

A MODEST PROPOSAL FOR PREVENTING THE CHILDREN OF POOR PEOPLE IN IRELAND FROM BEING A BURDEN TO THEIR PARENTS OR COUNTRY, AND FOR MAKING THEM BENEFICIAL TO THE PUBLIC (1729)

JONATHAN SWIFT

It is a melancholy object to those who walk through this great town or travel in the country, when they see the street, the roads, and cabin doors, crowded with beggars of the female sex, followed by three, four, or six children, all in rags, and importuning every passenger for an alms. These mothers, instead of being able to work for their honest livelihood, are forced to employ all their time in strolling to beg sustenance for their help-less infants, who, as they grow up, either turn thieves for want of work, or leave their dear native country, to fight for the Pretender in Spain, or sell themselves to the Barbadoes.   1

I think it is agreed by all parties that this prodigious number of children in the arms, or on the backs, or at the heels of their mothers, and frequently of their fathers, is in the present deplorable state of the king-dom a very great additional grievance; and therefore whoever could find out a fair, cheap, and easy method of making these children sound and useful members of the common-wealth, would deserve so well of the public as to have his statue up for a preserver of the nation.   2

But my intention is very far from being confined to provide only for the children of professed beggars; it is of much greater extent, and shall take in the whole number of infants at a certain age, who are born of parents in effect as little able to support them, as those who demand our charity in the streets.   3

As to my own part, having turned my thoughts, for many years, upon this important subject, and maturely weighed the several schemes of other projectors, I have always found them grossly mistaken in their computa-tion. It is true, a child just dropt from its dam, may be supported by her milk for a solar year with little other nourishment, at most not above the value of two shillings, which the mother may certainly get, or the value in scraps, by her lawful occupation of begging; and it is exactly at one year old that I propose to provide for them in such a manner, as, instead of being a charge upon their parents, or the parish, or wanting food and raiment for the rest of their lives, they shall, on the contrary, contribute to the feeding and partly to the clothing of many thousands.   4

There is likewise another great advantage in my scheme, that it will prevent those voluntary abortions, and that horrid practice of women murdering their bastard children, alas! too frequent among us—sacrificing the poor innocent babes, I doubt, more to avoid the expense than the shame—which would move tears and pity in the most savage and inhuman

5

The number of souls in this kingdom being usually reckoned one million and a half, of these I calculate there may be about two hundred thousand couples whose wives are breeders; from which number I subtract thirty thousand couples, who are able to maintain their own children, although I apprehend there cannot be so many, under the present distresses of the kingdom; but this being granted, there will remain an hundred and seventy thousand breeders. I again subtract fifty thousand, for those women who miscarry, or whose children die by accident or disease within the year. There only remain an hundred and twenty thousand children of poor parents annually born: The question therefore is, How this number shall be reared, and provided for: which, as I have already said, under the present situation of affairs, is utterly impossible by all the methods hitherto proposed; for we can neither employ them in handicraft or agriculture; we neither build houses, (I mean in the country) nor cultivate land: They can very seldom pick up a livelihood by stealing till they arrive at six years old, except where they are of towardly parts, although, I confess, they learn the rudiments much earlier; during which time they can however be properly looked upon only as probationers; as I have been informed by a principal gentleman in the county of Cavan, who protested to me, that he never knew above one or two instances under the age of six, even in a part of the kingdom so renowned for the quickest proficiency in that art.   6

I am assured by our merchants, that a boy or a girl before twelve years old, is no saleable commodity, and even when they come to this age, they will not yield above three pounds, or three pounds and a half crown at most, on the exchange; which cannot turn to account either to the parents or kingdom, the charge of nutriment and rags having been at least four times that value.   7

I shall now therefore humbly propose my own thoughts, which I hope will not be liable to the least objection.   8

I have been assured by a very knowing American of my acquaintance in London, that a young healthy child well nursed is at a year old a most delicious nourishing and wholesome food, whether stewed, roasted, baked, or boiled; and I make no doubt that it will equally serve in a fricassee, or a ragout.   9

I do therefore humbly offer it to publick consideration, that of the hundred and twenty thousand children, already computed, twenty thousand may be reserved for breed, whereof only one fourth part to be males; which is more than we allow to sheep, black cattle, or swine; and my reason is that these children are seldom the fruits of marriage, a circumstance not much regarded by our savages; therefore one male will be sufficient to serve four females. That the remaining hundred thousand may, at a year old, be offered in the sale to the persons of quality and fortune through the kingdom; always advising the mother to let them suck plentifully in the last month, so as to render them plump and fat for a good table. A child will make two dishes at an entertainment for friends; and when the family dines alone, the fore or hind quarter will make a reasonable dish, and seasoned with a little pepper or salt will be very good boiled on the fourth day, especially in winter.   10

I have reckoned upon a medium that a child just born will weigh 12 pounds, and in a solar year, if tolerably nursed, increaseth to 28 pounds. I grant this food will be somewhat dear, and therefore very proper for landlords, who, as they have already devoured most of the parents, seem to have the best title to the children.   11

Infant's flesh will be in season throughout the year, but more plentiful in March, and a little before and after; for we are told by a grave author, and eminent French physician, that fish being a prolific diet, there are more children born in Roman Catholic countries about nine months after Lent than at any other season; therefore, reckoning a year after Lent, the markets will be more glutted than usual, because the number of popish infants is at least three to one in this kingdom: and therefore, it will have one other collateral advantage, by lessening the number of papists among us.   12

I have already computed the charge of nursing a beggar's child (in which list I reckon all cottagers, laborers, and four-fifths of the farmers) to be about two shillings per annum, rags included; and I believe no gentleman would repine to give ten shillings for the carcass of a good fat child, which, as I have said, will make four dishes of excellent nutritive meat, when he hath only some particular friend or his own family to dine with him. Thus the squire will learn to be a good landlord, and grow popular among his tenants; the mother will have eight shillings net profit, and be fit for work till she produces another child.   13

Those who are more thrifty (as I must confess the times require) may flay the carcass, the skin of which artificially dressed will make admirable gloves for ladies, and summer boots for fine gentlemen.   14

As to our city of Dublin, shambles may be appointed for this purpose in the most convenient parts of it, and butchers we may be assured will not be wanting; although I rather recommend buying the children alive and dressing them hot from the knife, as we do roasting pigs.   15

A very worthy person, a true lover of his country, and whose virtues I highly esteem, was lately pleased in discoursing on this matter to offer a refinement upon my scheme. He said that many gentlemen of this kingdom, having of late destroyed their deer, he conceived that the want of venison might be well supplied by the bodies of young lads and maidens, not exceeding fourteen years of age nor under twelve; so great a number of both sexes in every country being now ready to starve for want of work and service; and these to be disposed of by their parents if alive, or otherwise by their nearest relations. But with due deference to so excellent a friend, and so deserving a patriot, I cannot be altogether in his sentiments; for as to the males, my American acquaintance assured me from frequent experience, that their flesh was generally tough and lean, like that of our schoolboys, by continual exercise, and their taste disagreeable, and to fatten them would not answer the charge. Then as to the females, it would, I think with humble submission, be a loss to the publick, because they soon would become breeders themselves: And besides it is not improbable that some scrupulous people might be apt to censure such a practice (although indeed very unjustly) as a little bordering upon cruelty, which, I confess, hath always been with me the strongest objection against any project, how well soever intended.   16

But in order to justify my friend, he confessed, that this expedient was put into his head by the famous Psalmanazar, a native of the island Formosa, who came from thence to London, about twenty years ago, and in conversation told my friend, that in his country when any young person happened to be put to death, the executioner sold the carcass to persons of quality, as prime dainty, and that, in his time, the body of a plump girl of fifteen, who was crucified for an attempt to poison the Emperor, was sold to his Imperial Majesty's prime minister of state, and other great mandarins of the court, in joints from the gibbet, at four hundred crowns. Neither indeed can I deny, that if the same use were made of several plump young girls in this town, who, without one single groat to their fortunes, cannot stir abroad without a chair, and appear at a play-house and assemblies in foreign fineries which they never will pay for, the kingdom would not be the worse.   17

Some persons of a desponding spirit are in great concern about that vast number of poor people, who are aged, diseased, or maimed, and I have been desired to employ my thoughts what course may be taken, to ease the nation of so grievous an encumbrance. But I am not in the least pain upon that matter, because it is very well known, that they are every day dying, and rotting, by cold, and famine, and filth, and vermin, as fast as can be reasonably expected. And as to the younger labourers, they are now in almost as hopeful a condition. They cannot get work, and consequently pine away for want of nourishment, to a degree, that if at any time they are accidentally hired to common labour, they have not enough strength to perform it, and thus the country and themselves are happily delivered from the evils to come.   18

I have too long digressed, and therefore shall return to my subject. I think the advantages by the proposal which I have made are obvious and many, as well as of the highest importance.   19

For *first*, as I have already observed, it would greatly lessen the number of papists, with whom we are yearly over-run, being the principal breeders of the nation, as well as our most dangerous enemies, and who stay at home on purpose with a design to deliver the kingdom to the Pretender, hoping to take their advantage by the absence of so many good Protestants, who have chosen rather to leave their country, than stay at home, and pay tithes against their conscience to an Episcopal curate.   20

Secondly, the poorer tenants will have something valuable of their own, which by law may be made liable to distress and help to pay their landlord's rent, their corn and cattle being already seized, and money a thing unknown.   21

Thirdly, whereas the maintenance of an hundred thousand children, from two years old and upward, cannot be computed at less than ten shillings apiece per annum, the nation's stock will be thereby increased fifty thousand pounds per annum, besides the profit of a new dish introduced to the tables of all gentlemen of fortune in the kingdom who have any refinement in taste. And the money will circulate among our selves, the goods being entirely of our own growth and manufacture.   22

Fourthly, the constant breeders, beside the gain of eight shillings sterling per annum by the sale of their children will be rid of the charge of maintaining them after the first year.   23

Fifthly, this food would likewise bring great custom to taverns, where the vintners will certainly be so prudent as to procure the best receipts for dressing it to perfection, and consequently have their houses frequented by all the fine gentlemen who justly value themselves upon their knowledge in good eating; and a skillful cook, who understands how to oblige his guests, will contrive to make it as expensive as they please.   24

Sixthly, this would be a great inducement to marriage, which all wise nations have either encouraged by rewards or enforced by laws and penalties. It would increase the care and the tenderness of mothers toward their children, when they were sure of a settlement for life to the poor babes, provided in some sort by the public, to their annual profit instead of expense. We should soon see an honest emulation among the married women, which of them could bring the fattest child to the market. Men would become as fond of their wives during the time of their pregnancy as they are now of their mares in foal, their cows in calf, their sows when they are ready to farrow; nor offer to beat or kick them (as is too frequent a practice) for fear of a miscarriage.   25

Many other advantages might be enumerated. For instance, the addition of some thousand carcasses in our exportation of barreled beef, the propagation of swine's flesh, and improvement in the art of making good bacon, so much wanted among us by the great destruction of pigs, too frequent at our table; which are no way comparable in taste or magnificence to a well-grown, fat, yearling child, which roasted whole will make a considerable figure at a lord mayor's feast or any other public entertainment. But this and many others I omit, being studious of brevity.   26

Supposing that one thousand families in this city would be constant customers for infants' flesh, besides others who might have it at merry-meetings, particularly at weddings and christenings, I compute that Dublin would take off annually about twenty thousand carcasses; and the rest of the kingdom (where probably they will be sold somewhat cheaper) the remaining eighty thousand.   27

I can think of no one objection that will possibly be raised against this proposal, unless it should be urged that the number of people will be thereby much lessened in the kingdom. This I freely own, and 'twas indeed one principal design in offering it to the world. I desire the reader will observe that I calculate my remedy for this one individual kingdom of Ireland, and for no other that ever was, is, or, I think, ever can be upon earth. Therefore let no man talk to me of other expedients: of taxing our absentees at five shillings a pound: of using neither clothes, nor household furniture, except what is of our own growth and manufacture: of utterly rejecting the materials and instruments that promote foreign luxury: of curing the expensiveness of pride, vanity, idleness, and gaming in our women: of introducing a vein of parsimony, prudence and temperance: of learning to love our country, where in we differ even from Laplanders, and the inhabitants of Topinamboo: of quitting our animosities, and factions, nor act any longer like the Jews, who were murdering one another at the very moment their city was taken: of being a little cautious not to sell our country and consciences for nothing: of teaching landlords to have at least one degree of mercy towards their tenants. Lastly, of putting a spirit of honesty, industry, and skill into our shop-keepers, who, if a resolution could now be taken to buy only our native goods, would immediately unite to cheat and exact upon us in the price, the measure, and the goodness, nor could ever yet be brought to make one fair proposal of just dealing, though often and earnestly invited to it.   28

Therefore I repeat, let no man talk to me of these and the like expedients, till he hath at least some glimpse of hope, that there will ever be some hearty and sincere attempt to put them in practice.   29

But as to my self, having been wearied out for many years with offering vain, idle, visionary thoughts, and at length utterly despairing of success, I fortunately fell upon this proposal, which as it is wholly new, so it hath something solid and real, of no expense and little trouble, full in our own power, and whereby we can incur no danger in disobliging England. For this kind of commodity will not bear exportation, the flesh being of too tender a consistence, to admit a long continuance in salt, although perhaps I could name a country, which would be glad to eat up our whole nation without it.   30

After all, I am not so violently bent upon my own opinion, as to reject any offer, proposed by wise men, which shall be found equally innocent, cheap, easy, and effectual. But before something of that kind shall be advanced in contradiction to my scheme, and offering a better, I desire the author or authors, will be pleased maturely to consider two points. *First,* as things now stand, how they will be able to find food and raiment for a hundred thousand useless mouths and backs. And *Secondly,* there being a round million of creatures in human figure throughout this kingdom, whose whole subsistence put into a common stock would leave them in debt two millions of pounds sterling, adding those who are beggars by profession, to the bulk of farmers, cottagers and labourers, with their wives and children, who are beggars in effect; I desire those politicians, who dislike my overture, and may perhaps be so bold to attempt an answer, that they will first ask the parents of these mortals, whether they would not at this day think it a great happiness to have been sold for food at a year old, in the manner I prescribe, and thereby have avoided such a perpetual scene of misfortunes as they have since gone through, by the oppression of landlords, the impossibility of paying rent without money or trade, the want of common sustenance, with neither house nor clothes to cover them from the inclemencies of the weather, and the most inevitable prospect of entailing the like or greater miseries upon their breed for ever. 31

I profess, in the sincerity of my heart, that I have not the least personal interest in endeavoring to promote this necessary work, having no other motive than the public good of my country, by advancing our trade, providing for infants, relieving the poor, and giving some pleasure to the rich. I have no children by which I can propose to get a single penny; the youngest being nine years old, and my wife past child-bearing. 32

Suggestions for Writing

1 The informal argument so evident in Phyllis McGinley's essay appears often in our leading periodicals. Trying to capture her brightness of style, write an informal argument on one of the following topics:
   a A defense of the small town (large city)
   b Television: pro or con
   c "Americans are too money-minded."

2 When a writer asks the serious kind of question, as Joseph Wood Krutch does in his essay, the tone of the piece of writing will probably be serious and the author will be quite direct in his argumentative prose. Keeping Krutch's essay in mind, write an argumentative essay dealing with one of the challenging topics below. You need not, of course, agree with the statement of the topic.
   a "Let others praise the past; I am glad that I was born in these times."—Ovid
   b A defense of the common man

    c "The tendency of democracies is, in all things, to mediocrity."—
    James Fenimore Cooper

    d "In large states public education will always be mediocre, for the
    same reason that in large kitchens the cooking is usually bad."—
    Nietzsche

3 Examine the following quotation from William Pinkney and then write
an essay defending or attacking his view:

    "The self-evident truths announced in the Declaration of Independ-
    ence are not truths at all, if taken literally; and the practical conclu-
    sions contained in the same passage of the Declaration prove that
    they were never designed to be so received."

4 Using argumentation, develop the thesis expressed in one of the following quotations:

    a "Where the press is free and every man able to read, all is safe."—
    Thomas Jefferson

    b "The first thing will be to establish a censorship of fiction. Let the
    censor accept any tale which is good, and reject any which is bad."—
    Plato

5 Using the resources of the library, discover what you can concerning the
full correspondence of the two eminent statesmen, Jefferson and John
Adams, about education and democracy. After reading what you have
been able to discover, write an essay indicating why you think either
Jefferson or Adams was right.

6 Miscellaneous topics:

    a "Is advertising a plot?" (Give a personal opinion containing fresh
    evidence.)

    b Film versus stage

    c Billboards and the highways

    d "There is a demand today for men who can make wrong appear to be
    right."—Terence

    e "Mass education is the keystone of democracy."

    f Censorship: public or private?

ANYTHING SIGNIFICANTLY LOOKED AT IS SIGNIFICANT_____

DESCRIPTION

My task which I am trying to achieve is, by the power of the written word to make you feel—it is, before all, to make you see. That—and no more, and it is everything.   Joseph Conrad

Everyone is familiar with the human tendency to describe, to re-create for another the fiber, the "feel," the warp and woof, the very texture of what we have ourselves experienced in things. The "things" in this case refer to the phenomena of the world—the people we see and know, the places we visit, the world of nature we live in. Description is the form of discourse that deals primarily with the appearance of the world as we experience it through our senses. When we describe something, we want someone else to appreciate our own sense experience. As we have noted earlier in our discussion of exposition (page 40), "describe" and "description" are sometimes used with reference to what we would call "exposition," as, for example, the explanation of some structure, or condition, or process, or technique. For example, a want ad "describes" a car for sale: "1962 Oldsmobile 98 Starfire convertible; red and white two-tone with whitewalls and hydramatic transmission." This is basically an exposition, an explanation of the structure of the object, and not a description in our sense of the word. A true description of an automobile would create through the use of suggestion an immediate sense of the beauty, power, and richness of the object. It would appeal to our imagination by communicating a sense of the real, the vital character of the object.

Description is seldom used by itself; and it is rarely the primary, dominant intention in a piece of writing. Most often it is in a subordinate position, helping out one of the other forms of discourse. Exposition uses description especially when it aims at being concrete, when it presents the details of information vividly, as in Loren Eiseley's "The Innocent Fox" (Page 88) or in Robert Warshaw's enumeration of the characteristics of the gangster (page 168). Argument uses description also, especially when it is most persuasive, relying heavily on rich connotations, as Phyllis McGinley does in her description of Suburbia (page 391) or as Joseph Wood Krutch does in describing the common man (page 373). It is probably in narrative writing that description is employed most extensively. Notice, for instance, how Bernal Diaz del Castillo (page 506) and William H. Prescott (page 509) use description to make the details of their scenes vivid to the reader. Storytellers want the reader to realize—to see the reality of—the scene or the person. It is not an accident that four of the six descriptions reprinted here are taken from novels.

Description may be used in a short sentence or two to catch the reader's attention, or it may appear in extended paragraphs. No matter how long or short it may be, a piece of descriptive writing should be specific, vivid, and lively. The writer attempts to choose words that are colorful, imaginative, and alive. Look first at the following passage:

The *Narcissus* rounded the South Foreland, passed through the Downs, and, in tow, entered the river. She wound after the tug through the channels. As she passed them, the light-vessels seemed to sail with speed in the rush of the tide, and the next moment were left behind. The big buoys slipped past her sides and tugged at their chains. The reach narrowed; and the land was close to her on each side. She went steadily up the river.

Compare it, clear as it is, with the following passage—the way it was originally written by Joseph Conrad in "The Landing of the *Narcissus*":

The *Narcissus, heeling over to off-shore gusts*, rounded the South Foreland, passed through the Downs, and, in tow, entered the river. Shorn of the glory of her white wings, she wound *obediently* after the tug through the *maze of invisible* channels. As she passed them the *red-painted* light-vessels, *swung at their moorings*, seemed *for an instant* to sail with *great speed* in the rush of the tide, and next moment were *hopelessly* left behind. The big buoys *on the tails of banks* slipped past her sides *very low*, and, *dropping in her wake*, tugged at their chains *like fierce watchdogs*. The reach narrowed; *from both sides the land approached the ship*. She went steadily up the river.

Looking at the words and phrases printed in italics, we come to understand that sensuous, vividly presented details create an artistic illusion of reality.

Another means for vivid description is the use of figurative language— that is, "metaphor" in its widest meaning: the technique of comparison. Although it may be perverted to serve as merely ornament or decoration, figurative language is an essential part of our linguistic experience: it is necessary for the specific interpretation of experience. In "The Landing of the *Narcissus*" Conrad tells us that the ship skimmed "under white wings . . . like a great tired bird speeding to its nest." This image is his interpretation of the movement of the ship; it is not just a "pretty" picture. In "Genesis" Hervey Allen tells us that "a necklace of great lakes glittered across the breast of the continent," and this suggests the specific reality of the thing pictured. Notice in both of these selections how the verbs are often metaphorical: the place beneath the trees was "aisled," the shadow "brooded" in the forest, the boat "skimmed," the channel "glittered." We find figurative language in all expression, but it is especially prominent in descriptive writing.

What is the controlling purpose in expository writing or the proposition in argumentative writing we can call the dominant impression in descriptive writing. The writer tries to communicate to the reader a dominant attitude or feeling about or toward the thing described. To do so, he must select only those details which are significant. Notice how Conrad makes the *Narcissus* the center of attention by his selection of details: the clouds race with her, the coast steps out of space to welcome her, the land approaches the ship, a bridge breaks in two before her. Notice how these details emphasize the pride and loftiness of the ship. In descriptive writing, leaving out the wrong details is as important as including the right details. Notice in the essays by Allen, Elizabeth Bowen, and James Agee how much is *left out* of the description. It might be said with some truth that the success of this kind of writing depends as much upon what is left out as upon what is put in.

Another means of achieving unity is the careful manipulation of point of view, physically or emotionally. The writer may give us the illusion of being fixed in space, seeing the object from a stationary point of view, from just one angle. Or he may provide a moving point of view, changing his position in space to see the scene from many angles. Again, the writer may communicate the dominant impression by a specific emotional point of view, maintaining a single, dominant mood or attitude toward the thing described. William Maxwell and Hervey Allen clearly want us to have a certain emotional response to their more or less panoramic descriptions. We cannot read the character sketch by Katherine Anne Porter without acquiring a distinct attitude toward the person described. The writer's own attitude toward his subject matter creates a tone to which the reader responds. The physical point of view has to do with the spatial relationship of the describer to the thing described; the emotional point of view has to do with the mood, atmosphere, impression, or feeling of the thing described.

Any person or thing lends itself to the kind of description we have been discussing. Most of the essays chosen for this section describe simple experiences. The writer need not seek the exotic in his selection of subject matter; he need only see a subject freshly—for the first time, as it were. As the poet and writer John Ciardi has said, "Anything significantly looked at is significant."

PORTRAIT: OLD SOUTH

KATHERINE ANNE PORTER

I am the grandchild of a lost War, and I have blood-knowledge of what life can be in a defeated country on the bare bones of privation. The older people in my family used to tell such amusing little stories about it. One time, several years after the War ended, two small brothers (one of them was my father) set out by themselves on foot from their new home in south Texas, and when neighbors picked them up three miles from home, hundreds of miles from their goal, and asked them where they thought they were going, they answered confidently, "To Louisiana, to eat sugar cane," for they hadn't tasted sugar for months and remembered the happy times in my grandmother's cane fields there.*   1

Does anyone remember the excitement when for a few months we had rationed coffee? In my grandmother's day, in Texas, everybody seemed to remember that man who had a way of showing up with a dozen grains of real coffee in his hand, which he exchanged for a month's supply of corn meal. My grandmother parched a mixture of sweet potato and dried corn until it was black, ground it up and boiled it, because her family couldn't get over its yearning for a dark hot drink in the mornings. But she would never allow them to call it coffee. It was known as That Brew. Bread was a question, too. Wheat flour, during the period euphemistically described as Reconstruction, ran about $100 a barrel. Naturally my family ate corn bread, day in, day out, for years. Finally Hard Times eased up a little, and they had hot biscuits, nearly all they could eat, once a week for Sunday breakfast. My father never forgot the taste of those biscuits, the big, crusty tender kind made with buttermilk and soda, with melted butter and honey, every blessed Sunday that came. "They almost made a Christian of me," he said.†   2

My grandfather, a soldier, toward the end of the War was riding along one very cold morning, and he saw, out of all reason, a fine big thick slice of raw bacon rind lying beside the road. He dismounted, picked it up, dusted it off and made a hearty breakfast of it. "The best piece of bacon rind I ever ate in my life," said my grandfather. These little yarns are the first that come to mind out of hundreds; they were the merest surface ripples over limitless deeps of bitter memory. My elders all remained nobly unreconstructed to their last moments, and my feet rest firmly on this rock of their strength to this day.   3

* Paragraph 1: Why does the author capitalize "War"?

† Paragraph 2: Why, from the author's point of view, does she say that the period was "euphemistically" described as Reconstruction?

The woman who made That Brew and the soldier who ate the bacon rind had been bride and groom in a Kentucky wedding somewhere around 1850. Only a few years ago a cousin of mine showed me a letter from a lady then rising ninety-five who remembered that wedding as if it had been only yesterday. She was one of the flower girls, carrying a gilded basket of white roses and ferns, tied with white watered-silk ribbon. She couldn't remember whether the bride's skirt had been twenty-five feet or twenty-five yards around, but she inclined to the latter figure; it was of white satin brocade with slippers to match.   4

The flower girl was allowed a glimpse of the table set for the bridal banquet. There were silver branched candlesticks everywhere, each holding seven white candles, and a crystal chandelier holding fifty white candles, all lighted. There was a white lace tablecloth reaching to the floor all around, over white satin. The wedding cake was tall as the flower girl and of astonishing circumference, festooned all over with white sugar roses and green leaves. The room, she wrote, was a perfect bower of southern smilax and white dogwood. And there was butter. This is a bizarre note, but there was an enormous silver butter dish, *with feet* (italics mine), containing at least ten pounds of butter. The dish had cupids and some sort of fruit around the rim, and the butter was molded or carved, to resemble a set-piece of roses and lilies, every petal and leaf standing out sharply, natural as life. The flower girl, after the lapse of nearly a century, remembered no more than this, but I think it does well for a glimpse.   5

That butter. She couldn't get over it, and neither can I. It seems as late-Roman and decadent as anything ever thought up in Hollywood. Her memory came back with a rush when she thought of the food. All the children had their own table in a small parlor, and ate just what the grownups had: Kentucky ham, roast turkey, partridges in wine jelly, fried chicken, dove pie, half a dozen sweet and hot sauces, peach pickle, watermelon pickle and spiced mangoes. A dozen different fruits, four kinds of cake and at last a chilled custard in tall glasses with whipped cream capped by a brandied cherry. She lived to boast of it, and she lived along with other guests of that feast to eat corn pone and bacon fat, and yes, to be proud of that also. Why not? She was in the best of company, and quite a large gathering too.*   6

In my childhood we ate, my father remarked, ''as if there were no God.'' By then my grandmother, her brocaded wedding gown cut up and made over to the last scrap for a dozen later brides in the connection, had become such a famous cook it was mentioned in her funeral eulogies. There was nobody like her for getting up a party, for the idea of food was inseparably connected in her mind with social occasions of a delight-

* Paragraph 6: In sentence 2, why does the author say ''can I'' instead of ''could I''?

ful nature, and though she loved to celebrate birthdays and holidays, still any day was quite good enough to her. Several venerable old gentlemen, lifelong friends of my grandmother, sat down, pen in hand, after her death and out of their grateful recollection of her bountiful hospitality— their very words—wrote long accounts of her life and works for the local newspapers of their several communities, and each declared that at one time or another he had eaten the best dinner of his life at her table. The furnishings of her table were just what were left over from times past, good and bad; a mixture of thin old silver and bone-handled knives, delicate porcelain, treasured but not hoarded, and such crockery as she had been able to replace with; fine old linen worn thin and mended, and stout cotton napery with fringed borders; no silver candlesticks at all, and a pound of sweet butter with a bouquet of roses stamped upon it, in a plain dish—plain for the time; it was really a large opal-glass hen seated on a woven nest, rearing aloft her scarlet comb and beady eye.   7

Grandmother was by nature lavish, she loved leisure and calm, she loved luxury, she loved dress and adornment, she loved to sit and talk with friends or listen to music; she did not in the least like pinching or saving and mending and making things do, and she had no patience with the kind of slackness that tried to say second-best was best, or half good enough. But the evil turn of fortune in her life tapped the bottomless reserves of her character, and her life was truly heroic. She had no such romantic notion of herself. The long difficulties of her life she regarded as temporary, an unnatural interruption to her normal fate, which required simply firmness, a good deal of will-power and energy and the proper aims to reestablish finally once more. That no such change took place during her long life did not in the least disturb her theory. Though we had no money and no prospects of any, and were land-poor in the most typical way, we never really faced this fact as long as our grandmother lived because she would not hear of such a thing. We had been a good old family of solid wealth and property in Kentucky, Louisiana and Virginia, and we remained that in Texas, even though due to a temporary decline for the most honorable reasons, appearances were entirely to the contrary. This accounted for our fragmentary, but strangely useless and ornamental education, appropriate to our history and our station in life, neither of which could be in the least altered by the accident of straitened circumstances.*   8

Grandmother had been an unusually attractive young woman, and she carried herself with the graceful confidence of a natural charmer to her last day. Her mirror did not deceive her, she saw that she was old. Her youthful confidence became matriarchal authority, a little way of knowing best about almost everything, of relying upon her own experience for sole guide, and I think now she had earned her power fairly. Her bountiful

* Paragraph 8: In sentence 1, why does the author repeat the word "loved"?

hospitality represented only one of her victories of intelligence and feeling over the stubborn difficulties of life. Her mind and her instinct ran in flashes of perception, and she sometimes had an airy, sharp, impatient way of speaking to those who didn't keep up with her. She believed it was her duty to be a stern methodical disciplinarian, and made a point of training us as she had been trained even to forbidding us to cross our knees, or to touch the back of our chair when we sat, or to speak until we were spoken to: love's labors lost utterly, for she had brought up a houseful of the worst spoiled children in seven counties, and started in again hopefully with a long series of motherless grandchildren—for the daughters of that after-war generation did not survive so well as their mothers, they died young in great numbers, leaving young husbands and children—who were to be the worst spoiled of any. She never punished anyone until she was exasperated beyond all endurance, when she was apt to let fly with a lightning, long-armed slap at the most unexpected moments, usually quite unjustly and ineffectually.*   9

Truth was, when she had brought her eleven children into the world, she had had a natural expectation of at least as many servants to help her bring them up; her gifts were social, and she should never have had the care of children except in leisure, for then she was delightful, and communicated some of her graces to them, and gave them beautiful memories. We loved the smell of her face powder and the light orange-flower perfume she wore, the crinkled waves of her hair, the knot speared through with a small pointed Spanish comb. We leaned upon her knee, and sniffed in the sweetness of her essential being, we nuzzled her face and the little bit of lace at her collar, enchanted with her sweetness.   10

Her hands were long since ruined, but she was proud of her narrow feet with their high insteps, and liked to dress them in smooth black kid boots with small spool-shaped heels. When she went "abroad"—that is, shopping, calling, or to church—she wore her original mourning gowns, of stiff, dull, corded silks, made over and refurbished from time to time, and a sweeping crape veil that fell from a peaked cap over her face and to the hem of her skirt in the back. This mourning had begun for her husband, dead only twenty-five years, but it went on for him, and for her daughters and for grandchildren, and cousins, and then brothers and sisters, and, I suspect, for an old friend or so. In this garb, holding up her skirt in front with one black-gloved hand, she would walk with such flying lightness her grandchild would maintain a heated trot to keep pace with her.   11

She loved to have us say our prayers before bedtime in a cluster around her knees, and in our jealousy to be nearest, and to be first, we often fell fighting like a den of bear cubs, instead of christened children,

* Paragraph 9: In sentence 2, why is a comma more effective than a semicolon or period?

and she would have to come in among us like an animal trainer, the holy hour having gone quite literally to hell. "Birds in their little nests agree, and 'tis a shameful sight," she would remark on these occasions, but she never finished the rhyme, and for years I wondered why it was a shameful sight for little birds to agree, when Grandmother was rather severe with us about our quarreling. It was "vulgar," she said, and for her, that word connoted a peculiarly detestable form of immorality, that is to say, bad manners. Inappropriate conduct was bad manners, bad manners were bad morals, and bad morals led to bad manners, and there you were, ringed with fire, and no way out.   12

She was an individual being if ever I knew one, and yet she never did or said anything to make herself conspicuous; there are no strange stories to tell, no fantastic gestures. She rode horseback at a gallop until the year of her death, but it seemed only natural. Her sons had to restrain her from an engineering project, which seemed very simple to her and perhaps was really simple: she had wished to deflect the course of a small river which was encroaching on her land in Louisiana; she knew exactly how it should be done, and it would have made all the difference, she felt. She smoked cubeb cigarettes, for her throat, she would say, and add that she had always imagined she would enjoy the taste of tobacco. She and my father would sit down for a noggin of hot toddy together on cold evenings, or just a drop of good Bourbon before dinner because they enjoyed it. She could not endure to see a horse with its head strung up in a checkrein, and used to walk down a line of conveyances drawn up around the church, saying amiably to the dozing Negro drivers, "Good morning, Jerry; good morning, Uncle Squire," reaching up deftly and loosing the checkrein. The horses hung their heads and so did the drivers, and the reins stayed unfastened for that time, at any rate.   13

In a family full of willful eccentrics and headstrong characters and unpredictable histories, her presence was singularly free from peaks and edges and the kind of color that leaves a trail of family anecdotes. She left the lingering perfume and the airy shimmer of grace about her memory.*   14

* Paragraph 14: What does this paragraph mean?

The Whole Selection

1 What is the meaning of the title of the essay?
2 "These little yarns" and "merest surface ripples" (paragraph 3) describe examples used by Miss Porter. What purpose are the examples introduced up to this point meant to serve?
3 The stages in time are important for the descriptive effect the author hopes to achieve. How are the stages in time indirectly indicated here?

4 The introductory matter over, the essay concentrates on the description of a character—Grandmother. What is the dominant impression of her retained by the reader? Prove your point by a close examination of the details given to us about her.

5 Pick out any two paragraphs in which details are especially vivid and lively, pointing out what the details are and why they are especially vivid.

6 The details of the portrait of Grandmother are given to the reader in a casual fashion, not in a strict pattern of chronology. What reasons can you offer for this casual mode of organization?

THE INCOMING TIDE

ELIZABETH BOWEN

That Sunday, from six o'clock in the evening, it was a Viennese orchestra that played. The season was late for an outdoor concert; already leaves were drifting on to the grass stage—here and there one turned over, crepitating as though in the act of dying, and during the music some more fell.*   1

The open-air theatre, shelving below the level of the surrounding lawns, was walled by thickets and a few high trees; along the top ran a wattle fence with gates. Now the two gates stood open. The rows of chairs down the slope, facing the orchestra, still only filled up slowly. From here, from where it was being played at the base of this muffled hollow, the music could not travel far through the park—but hints of it that did escape were disturbing: from the mound, from the rose gardens, from the walks round the lakes, people were being slowly drawn to the theatre by the sensation that they were missing something. Many of them paused in the gateways doubtfully—all they had left behind was in sunshine, while this hollow which was the source of music was found to be also the source of dusk. War had made them idolise day and summer; night and autumn were enemies. And, at the start of the concert, this tarnished bosky theatre, in which no plays had been acted for some time, held a feeling of sequestration, of emptiness the music had not had time to fill. It was not completely in shadow—here and there blades of sunset crossed it, firing branches through which they travelled, and lay along ranks of chairs and faces and hands. Gnats quivered; cigarette smoke dissolved. But the light was so low, so theatrical and so yellow that it was evident it would soon be gone. The incoming tide was evening. Glass-clear darkness, in which each leaf was defined, already formed in the thicket behind the orchestra and was the other element of the stage.†   2

The Sunday had been brilliant, without a stain of cloud. Now, the burning turquoise sky of the afternoon began to gain in transparency as it lost colour: from above the trees round the theatre there stole away not only colour but time. Music—the waltzes, the marches, the gay overtures —now began to command this hourless place. The people lost their look of uncertainty. The heroic marches made them lift up their heads; recollections of opera moulded their faces into unconscious smiles, and during the waltzes women's eyes glittered with delicious tears about nothing. First note by note, drop by drop, then steadily, the music entered senses,

---

* Paragraph 1: What is the meaning of "crepitating"? Exactly how does it reinforce the metaphor of dying?

† Paragraph 2: What dominant impression do you get from the description of the open-air theater?

nerves and fancies that had been parched. What first was a mirage strengthened into a universe, for the shabby Londoners and the exiled foreigners sitting in this worn glade in the middle of Regent's park. This Sunday on which the sun set was the first Sunday of September 1942.* 3

Pairs of lovers, fatigued by their day alone with each other, were glad to enter this element not themselves: when their looks once more met, it was with refreshed love. Mothers tired by being mothers forgot their children as their children forgot them—one held her baby as though it had been a doll. Married couples who had sat down in apathetic closeness to one another could be seen to begin to draw a little apart, each recapturing some virginal inner dream. Such elderly people as had not been driven home by the disappearance of sun from the last chair fearlessly exposed their years to the dusk, in a lassitude they could have shown at no other time.   4

These were the English. As for the foreigners, some were so intimate with the music that you could feel them anticipate every note; some sat with eyes closed; others, as though aroused by some unbearable movement inside the breast, glanced behind them or quickly up at the sky. Incredulity, as when waking up from a deep sleep, appeared once or twice in faces. But in most of them, as they continued to sit and listen, stoicism only intensified.†   5

A proportion of the listeners were solitary; and, of the solitary, those who came every Sunday, by habit, could be told from those who had come this Sunday by chance. Surprise at having stumbled upon the music was written on the faces of first-timers. For many, chiefly, the concert was the solution of where to be: one felt eased by this place where something was going on. To be sitting packed among other people was better than walking about alone. At the last moment, this crowned the day with meaning. For these had been moments, heightening towards the end, when the Sunday's beauty—for those with no ambition to cherish, no friend to turn to, no love to contemplate—drove its lack of meaning into the heart.‡ 6

* Paragraph 3: Describe the distinct change of mood that comes about from turning away from the theater itself to a description of what is going on in the theater. Explain: "What first was a mirage strengthened into a universe." Of what importance to the essay is the date mentioned?

† Paragraphs 4 and 5: Is there some evidence of a calculated pattern in the presentation of the English from the "lovers" to the "elderly"? What do the English have in common? How do they differ from most of the foreigners?

‡ Paragraph 6: Why must the day be crowned with meaning? What is the "meaning" of the scene?

The Whole Selection

1 "Tone" may be defined as the attitude a writer has toward his material. How would you describe the tone of this essay?

2 Metaphor, as we have noticed before, is part of the essential statement of the writer, used to control or direct the attitude of the reader. Isolate at least four of the metaphors used by Miss Bowen (e.g., "The incoming tide was evening") and do the following:

a Show how the concrete term is used to signify the meaning of the situation—that is, how the transfer in meaning has taken place.

b Show what the elements of similarity and contrast in the metaphorical construction are.

c Show exactly how the metaphor directs or controls our attitude toward what it describes, explains, or illuminates.

3 The diction of the writer, especially his choice of connotative language, is important to descriptive writing. Is Miss Bowen's diction generally concrete or abstract, particular or general, lively or static? Cite examples.

4 What is the dominant impression of this piece of descriptive writing?

5 To which of the senses, if any, does Miss Bowen appeal especially?

6 The skilled descriptive writer does not allow adjectives alone to bear the whole burden of evoking the scene. Pick out some verbs and adverbs used by Miss Bowen to reveal the details of her scene.

THE DESERT

WILLIAM MAXWELL

In desert country the air is never still. You raise your eyes and see a wind-mill a hundred yards away, revolving in the sunlight, without any apparent beginning and for years to come without any end. It may seem to slow up and stop but that is only because it is getting ready to go round and round again, faster and faster, night and day, week in, week out. The end that is followed immediately by a beginning is neither end nor beginning. Whatever is alive must be continuous. There is no life that doesn't go on and on, even the life that is in water and in stones. Listen and you hear children's voices, a dog's soft padded steps, a man hammering, a man sharpening a scythe. Each of them is repeated, the same sound, starting and stopping like the windmill. 1

From where you are, the windmill makes no sound, and if you were blind would not be there. A man mowing grass must be accompanied by the sound of a lawn mower to be believed. If you have discovered him with the aid of a pair of binoculars then you have also discovered that reality is almost never perceived through one of the senses alone. With-draw the binoculars and where is the man mowing grass? You have to look to the mind for confirmation of his actuality, which may account for the inward look on the faces of the blind, the strained faces of the deaf who are forever recovering from impressions which have come upon them too suddenly with no warning sound. 2

. . .

The desert is the natural dwelling place not only of Arabs and Indians but also of people who can't speak when they want to and of those others who have nothing more to say, people who have stopped justifying and explaining, stopped trying to account for themselves or their actions, stopped hoping that someone will come along and love them and so make sense out of their lives. 3

There are things in the desert which aren't to be found anywhere else. You can see a hundred miles in every direction, when you step out of your front door, and at night the stars are even brighter than they are at sea. If you cannot find indoors what you should find, then go to the window and look at the mountains, revealed after two days of uncertainty, of no future beyond the foothills which lie in a circle around the town. If it is not actually cold, if you aren't obliged to hug the fire, then go outside, by all means, even though the air is nervous, and you hear wind in the poplars, a train, a school bell, a fly—all sounds building toward something which may not be good. For reassurance there is also a car horn, a spade striking hard ground, a dog barking, and an unidentifiable bird in the Chinese elm. For further comfort there is the gardener, an old Spaniard, squatting on his haunches near the house next door. He is cleaning out the winter's rubbish and rotting leaves from the fishpond. While you sit on your haunches watching him, he will catch, in a white enamel pan, the big goldfish and the five little ones that have as yet no color. Day after day he tends this garden for a woman who is always coming back but who never arrives. Patience is to be learned from him. His iris blooms, his roses fade, his potted pink geraniums stare out of the windows of the shut-up house. It is possible that he no longer believes in the woman's coming, but nevertheless, from time to time, he empties the goldfish pool and puts fresh water in it.   4

If the sound of somebody chopping wood draws you out of the front gate and into the empty lot across the road, you will find blue lupines growing and see blankets airing on a clothesline, and you can talk to the man who is adding a room onto his adobe house. A great deal is to be learned from him. Also from the man chopping wood, who knows even now that there is a thunderstorm coming over the mountains, brought on by the uneasy wind in the poplars.   5

If you go and live for awhile in desert country it is possible that you may encounter some Spanish boys, barefoot, wearing blue denim overalls. It is important that you who have moral standards but no word for addressing a stranger and conveying instantaneous approval and liking, no word to indicate a general warmth of heart; who sleep alone if you can and have lost all memory of a common table and go to tremendous lengths to keep your bones from mingling with the bones of other people— it is vitally important that you meet the little Spanish boys.   6

If you speak to them too abruptly they may run away, or they may even turn into statues; and how to give them back their freedom and release them from their fright is something that you alone can solve. One of them will have patches on the seat of his overalls, which have come down to him from many older brothers with some of their animal magic still left. When he is sent for water, his brothers are there to protect him. All through the day he wears their magic, until night when his brothers are with him actually, crosswise in the bed, or curled against him on a hard pallet on the floor.   7

One of the little Spanish boys will use expressions which were current in the time of Cervantes. Another will have a gray cotton sweat shirt with Popeye the Sailor on the back—the mark of the world and its cheapness upon him, innocent though he is of any world beyond this desert valley. And there will be another who is not innocent but born knowing the worst, though perhaps not where to find it. And two others will have Indians for ancestors and, for reasons that are hidden from them but urgent, will do things in a way that is different from the way that the others, the pure Spanish, the Mexicans, chose. Even the sleep of the little boys with Indian blood is different, being (in all probability) full of dancing and dreams which turn out to be prophecies.   8

The little Spanish boys have a word—*primo,* meaning cousin— which they use to convey their liking for strangers, their willingness to share the clothes on their back, the food on their table, their fire if they have one. This same uncritical love is offered frequently to goats, burros, dogs, and chickens, and it will be extended to you.   9

The Whole Selection

1 Maxwell tells us that "reality is almost never perceived through one of the senses alone." To which senses does he appeal especially in this description?

2 Paragraphs 6 through 9 *seem* to introduce a new subject. How are these paragraphs related to the previous five paragraphs?

3 What is the dominant impression of the whole essay?

4 In this selection there are almost no words that the average reader would not recognize on sight. Why is this kind of diction appropriate for the subject?

5 At times the author uses striking figurative language—e.g., "the air is nervous." Pick out at least three other examples of such language from the essay.

6 Find at least five examples of Maxwell's skill in using concrete nouns and suggestive active verbs—e.g., "his potted pink geraniums stare out of the windows of the shut-up house."

7 The author's emotional attitude toward the desert is particularly important for this essay. How would you describe his point of view?

"KNOXVILLE: SUMMER 1915"

JAMES AGEE

We are talking now of summer evenings in Knoxville, Tennessee in the time that I lived there so successfully disguised to myself as a child. It was a little bit mixed sort of block, fairly solidly lower middle class, with one or two juts apiece on either side of that. The houses corresponded: middle-sized gracefully fretted wood houses built in the late nineties and early nineteen hundreds, with small front and side and more spacious back yards, and trees in the yards, and porches. These were softwooded trees, poplars, tulip trees, cottonwoods. There were fences around one or two of the houses, but mainly the yards ran into each other with only now and then a low hedge that wasn't doing very well. There were few good friends among the grown people, and they were not poor enough for the other sort of intimate acquaintance, but everyone nodded and spoke, and even might talk short times, trivially, and at the two extremes of the general or the particular, and ordinarily nextdoor neighbors talked quite a bit when they happened to run into each other, and never paid calls. The men were mostly small businessmen, one or two very modestly executives, one or two worked with their hands, most of them clerical, and most of them between thirty and forty-five.   1

But it is of these evenings, I speak.   2

Supper was at six and was over by half past. There was still daylight, shining softly and with a tarnish, like the lining of a shell; and the carbon lamps lifted at the corners were on in the light, and the locusts were started, and the fire flies were out, and a few frogs were flopping in the dewy grass, by the time the fathers and the children came out. The children ran out first hell bent and yelling those names by which they were known; then the fathers sank out leisurely in crossed suspenders, their collars removed and their necks looking tall and shy. The mothers stayed back in the kitchen washing and drying, putting things away, recrossing their traceless footsteps like the lifetime journeys of bees, measuring out the dry cocoa for breakfast. When they came out they had taken off their aprons and their skirts were dampened and they sat in rockers on their porches quietly.   3

It is not of the games children play in the evening that I want to speak now, it is of a contemporaneous atmosphere that has little to do with them: that of the fathers of families, each in his space of lawn, his shirt fishlike pale in the unnatural light and his face nearly anonymous, hosing their lawns. The hoses were attached at spigots that stood out of the brick foundations of the houses. The nozzles were variously set but usually so there was a long sweet stream of spray, the nozzle wet in the hand, the water trickling the right forearm and the peeled-back cuff, and the water whishing out a long loose and low-curved cone, and so gentle a sound. First an insane noise of violence in the nozzle, then the still irregular sound of adjustment, then the smoothing into steadiness and a pitch as accurately tuned to the size and style of stream as any violin. So many qualities of sound out of one hose: so many choral differences out of those several hoses that were in earshot. Out of any one hose, the almost dead silence of the release, and the short still arch of the separate big drops, silent as a held breath, and the only noise the flattering noise on leaves and the slapped grass at the fall of each big drop. That, and the intense hiss with the intense stream; that, and that same intensity not growing less but growing more quiet and delicate with the turn of the nozzle, up to that extreme tender whisper when the water was just a wide bell of film. Chiefly, though, the hoses were set much alike, in a compromise between distance and tenderness of spray, (and quite surely a sense of art behind this compromise, and a quiet deep joy, too real to recognize itself), and the sounds therefore were pitched much alike; pointed by the snorting start of a new hose; decorated by some man playful with the nozzle; left empty, like God by the sparrow's fall, when any single one of them desists: and all, though near alike, of various pitch; and in this unison. These sweet pale streamings in the light lift out their pallors and their voices all together, mothers hushing their children, the hushing unnaturally prolonged, the men gentle and silent and each snail-like withdrawn into the quietude of what he singly is doing, the urination of huge children stood loosely military against an invisible wall, and gentle happy and peaceful, tasting the mean goodness of their living like the last of their suppers in their mouths; while the locusts carry on this noise of hoses on their much higher and sharper key. The noise of the locust is dry, and it seems not to be rasped or vibrated but urged from him as if through a small orifice by a breath that can never give out. Also there is never one locust but an illusion of at least a thousand. The noise of each locust is pitched in some classic locust range out of which none of them varies more than two full tones: and yet you seem to hear each locust discrete from all the rest, and there is a long, slow, pulse in their noise, like the scarcely defined arch of a long and high set bridge. They are all around in every tree, so that the noise seems to come from nowhere and everywhere at once, from the whole shell heaven, shivering in your flesh and teasing your eardrums, the boldest of all the sounds of night. And yet it is habitual to summer nights, and is of the great order of noises, like the noises of the sea and of the blood her precocious grandchild, which you realize you are hearing only when you catch yourself listening. Meantime from low in the dark, just outside the swaying horizons of the hoses, conveying always grass in the damp of dew and its strong green-black smear of smell, the regular yet spaced noises of the crickets, each a sweet cold silver noise threenoted, like the slipping each time of three matched links of a small chain. 4

But the men by now, one by one, have silenced their hoses and drained and coiled them. Now only two, and now only one, is left, and you see only ghostlike shirt with the sleeve garters, and sober mystery of his mild face like the lifted face of large cattle enquiring of your presence in a pitchdark pool of meadow; and now he too is gone; and it has become that time of evening when people sit on their porches, rocking gently and talking gently and watching the street and the standing up into their sphere of possession of the trees, of birds hung havens, hangars. People go by; things go by. A horse, drawing a buggy, breaking his hollow iron music on the asphalt; a loud auto; a quiet auto; people in pairs, not in a hurry, scuffling, switching their weight of aestival body, talking casually, the taste hovering over them of vanilla, strawberry, pasteboard and starched milk, the image upon them of lovers and horsemen, squared with clowns in hueless amber. A street car raising its iron moan; stopping, belling and starting; stertorous; rousing and raising again its iron increasing moan and swimming its gold windows and straw seats on past and past and past, the bleak spark crackling and cursing above it like a small malignant spirit set to dog its tracks; the iron whine rises on rising speed; still risen, faints; halts; the faint stinging bell; rises again, still fainter; fainting, lifting, lifts, faints forgone: forgotten. Now is the night one blue dew.

> Now is the night one blue dew, my father has drained, he has coiled
>   the hose.
> Low on the length of lawns, a frailing of fire who breathes.
> Content, silver, like peeps of light, each cricket makes his comment over
>   and over in the drowned grass.
> A cold toad thumpily flounders.
> Within the edges of damp shadows of side yards are hovering children
>   nearly sick with joy of fear, who watch the unguarding of a
>   telephone pole.
> Around white carbon corner lamps bugs of all sizes are lifted elliptic,
>   solar systems. Big hardshells bruise themselves, assailant: he
>   is fallen on his back, legs squiggling.
> Parents on porches: rock and rock: From damp strings morning glories:
>   hang their ancient faces.
> The dry and exalted noise of the locusts from all the air at once
>   enchants my eardrums.   5

On the rough wet grass of the back yard my father and mother have spread quilts. We all lie there, my mother, my father, my uncle, my aunt, and I too am lying there. First we were sitting up, then one of us lay down, and then we all lay down, on our stomachs, or on our sides, or on our backs, and they have kept on talking. They are not talking much, and the talk is quiet, of nothing in particular, of nothing at all in particular, of nothing at all. The stars are wide and alive, they seem each like a smile of great sweetness, and they seem very near. All my people are larger bodies than mine, quiet, with voices gentle and meaningless like the voices of sleeping birds. One is an artist, he is living at home. One is a musician, she is living at home. One is my mother who is good to me. One is my father who is good to me. By some chance, here they are, all on this earth; and who shall ever tell the sorrow of being on this earth, lying, on quilts, on the grass, in a summer evening, among the sounds of the night. May God bless my people, my uncle, my aunt, my mother, my good father, oh, remember them kindly in their time of trouble; and in the hour of their taking away.   6

　　　After a little I am taken in and put to bed. Sleep, soft smiling, draws me unto her: and those receive me, who quietly treat me, as one familiar and well-beloved in that home: but will not, oh, will not, not now, not ever; but will not ever tell me who I am.   7

The Whole Selection

1 What is the dominant impression of this selection? What details within the piece contribute to this impression?

2 Description achieves its results particularly by appealing to the senses of the reader in order to reach his imagination; but simply because the senses are called upon it does not necessarily mean, of course, that the intellect lies inoperative in the reader or in the writer. Examine paragraph 4 carefully. What sense is being appealed to especially?

3 Good description, like all good writing, depends upon effective diction, and description depends particularly upon the use of precise, specific, and vivid nouns and verbs. Evaluate the diction in this selection with relation to the effect for which the author is striving.

4 Is the poem concluding paragraph 5 an effective summary of the mood of the essay?

5 In paragraphs 4 through 6, observe how the rhythms of the prose, which are achieved by sentence structure and phrasing, suggest the specific dominant impression that the author wishes to give. Describe the rhythm of the prose, and try to determine how this rhythm achieves its effect (a difficult assignment).

6 As we have noted, description is seldom found by itself, more often being used to support some other form of discourse. This section is taken from an autobiographical novel, *A Death in the Family*. In this selection, what details suggest that an adult is looking back upon his boyhood experience?

7 Why does the author use the word "sorrow" in this excerpt from paragraph 6: ". . . and who shall ever tell the *sorrow* of being on this earth, lying, on quilts, on the grass, in a summer evening, among the sounds of the night."

8 What is the meaning of the final paragraph?

GENESIS

HERVEY ALLEN

In the beginning was the forest. God made it and no man knew the end of it. It was not new. It was old; ancient as the hills it covered. Those who first entered it saw it had been there since the beginning of habitable time. There were rivers in it and distant mountains; birds, beasts, and the mysterious villages of red men. The trees were vast, round, and countless; columns of the roof of heaven. The place beneath was endlessly aisled. There were green glades where the deer fed and looked at the buffalo; trails that went back into the animal time. There were valleys where the clouds lay and no man came there; caves where the wolves mated; peaks where the panther screamed.   1

But the forest itself was silent. It slept and dreamed of something in a perpetual gray-green shadow in the summer. The lightning flashed at evening and the thunder echo rolled. In the fall the leaves fell and the stars looked down through a roof of sticks. The snow sifted and glittered. Winds heavy with the silver breath of winter smoked on the mountains. The trees burgeoned. Red flashed into the green flame of spring. The gray-green shadow brooded in the forest again, gestating sunlight.   2

Birds, those free spirits of the weather, were the only beings who saw the spectacle entire. As the earth rocked, every spring and autumn their blood burned. They rose, trillions of them, feathered nations with innumerable tongues and various languages, and took to the air. Their nests and their love songs followed the tilting ecliptic like a pæan of time. They also sang the praises of the Almighty One with innocent, unthinking hearts. High in cold atmospheres, they beheld the grandeur and beauty of His thought.   3

Northward a necklace of great lakes glittered across the breast of the continent. Eastward the tabled plains of the Atlantic flashed lonely to the unbroken water rim. Not a sail gleamed. Only the steam clouds over the warm river in the ocean cliffed towering into heaven. The moon rose out of them at the full and looked at the sun setting beyond the Appalachians into a sea of western grass. Between lay the forest, green, gladed, unbroken, beautiful; riding the still waves of the long mountains, stretching from ice blink to palms.   4

The fingers of innumerable days trailed across the roof of the forest, while spring and autumn ran up and down it countless thousands of times. The stars shifted in their houses. Eastward over the waters the wings of gulls wheeled; gleamed and vanished; vanished and gleamed—prophetically. Until in the fullness of time something whiter glinted there; held the sunlight steadily; discovered the tracery of sails. Man-made thunder saluted the land.   5

Then harbors reflected the lights of ships' lanterns; the windows of gabled houses gleamed orange in the dusk. Broad plumes of smoke arose from capes and along the estuaries by day. Fire and steel axes ate the forest away, thinning it westward. Field patches and road scars began to show among the trees. The haze of wood smoke gathered over towns.   6

Generation after generation the ships kept coming. From one century into another the white man increased his town bases behind him. The tentacles and network of roads began reaching out for the hills. Vainly the silent stone-tipped arrows flitted from the forest at twilight. The flash and roar of musketry replied. Manitou and Jehovah wrestled in the valleys together—and the tasseled corn-god lost. Death like a mist out of lethal nowhere fell upon the red man until he vanished. The forefathers he left behind him slept in quiet mounds beside the east-running rivers. Only tobacco smoke lingered like a memorial incense scenting the breeze.   7

THE LANDING OF THE *NARCISSUS*

JOSEPH CONRAD

A week afterwards the *Narcissus* entered the chops of the Channel.   1

Under white wings she skimmed low over the blue sea like a great tired bird speeding to its nest. The clouds raced with her mastheads; they rose astern enormous and white, soared to the zenith, flew past, and falling down the wide curve of the sky, seemed to dash headlong into the sea—the clouds swifter than the ship, more free, but without a home. The coast to welcome her stepped out of space into the sunshine. The lofty headlands trod masterfully into the sea; the wide bays smiled in the light; the shadows of homeless clouds ran along the sunny plains, leaped over valleys, without a check darted up the hills, rolled down the slopes; and the sunshine pursued them with patches of running brightness. On the brows of dark cliffs white lighthouses shone in pillars of light. The Channel glittered like a blue mantle shot with gold and starred by the silver of the capping seas. The *Narcissus* rushed past the headlands and the bays. Outward-bound vessels crossed her track, lying over, and with their masts stripped for a slogging fight with the hard sou'wester. And, inshore, a string of smoking steamboats waddled, hugging the coast, like migrating and amphibious monsters, distrustful of the restless waves.   2

At night the headlands retreated, the bays advanced into one unbroken line of gloom. The lights of the earth mingled with the lights of heaven; and above the tossing lanterns of a trawling fleet a great lighthouse shone steadily, like an enormous riding light burning above a vessel of fabulous dimensions. Below its steady glow, the coast, stretching away straight and black, resembled the high side of an indestructible craft riding motionless upon the immortal and unresting sea. The dark land lay alone in the midst of waters, like a mighty ship bestarred with vigilant lights—a ship carrying the burden of millions of lives—a ship freighted with dross and with jewels, with gold and with steel. She towered up immense and strong, guarding priceless traditions and untold suffering, sheltering glorious memories and base forgetfulness, ignoble virtues and splendid transgressions. A great ship! For ages had the ocean battered in vain her enduring sides; she was there when the world was vaster and darker, when the sea was great and mysterious, and ready to surrender the prize of fame to audacious men. A ship mother of fleets and nations! The great flagship of the race; stronger than the storms! and anchored in the open sea.   3

The *Narcissus*, heeling over to off-shore gusts, rounded the South Foreland, passed through the Downs, and, in tow, entered the river. Shorn of the glory of her white wings, she wound obediently after the tug through the maze of invisible channels. As she passed them the red-painted light-vessels, swung at their moorings, seemed for an instant to sail with great speed in the rush of tide, and the next moment were left hopelessly behind. The big buoys on the tails of banks slipped past her sides very low, and, dropping in her wake, tugged at their chains like fierce watchdogs. The reach narrowed; from both sides the land approached the ship. She went steadily up the river. On the riverside slopes the houses appeared in groups—seemed to stream down the declivities at a run to see her pass, and, checked by the mud of the foreshore, crowded on the banks. Further on, the tall factory chimneys appeared in insolent bands and watched her go by, like a straggling crowd of slim giants, swaggering and upright under the black plummets of smoke, cavalierly aslant. She swept round the bends; an impure breeze shrieked a welcome between her stripped spars; and the land, closing in, stepped between the ship and the sea.   4

A low cloud hung before her—a great opalescent and tremulous cloud, that seemed to rise from the steaming brows of millions of men. Long drifts of smoky vapours soiled it with livid trails; it throbbed to the beat of millions of hearts, and from it came an immense and lamentable murmur—the murmur of millions of lips praying, cursing, sighing, jeering—the undying murmur of folly, regret, and hope exhaled by the crowds of the anxious earth. The *Narcissus* entered the cloud; the shadows deepened; on all sides there was the clang of iron, the sound of mighty blows, shrieks, yells. Black barges drifted stealthily on the murky stream. A mad jumble of begrimed walls loomed up vaguely in the smoke, bewildering and mournful, like a vision of disaster. The tugs backed and filled in the stream, to hold the ship steady at the dock-gates; from her bows two lines went through the air whistling, and struck at the land viciously, like a pair of snakes. A bridge broke in two before her, as if by enchantment; big hydraulic capstans began to turn all by themselves, as though animated by a mysterious and unholy spell. She moved through a narrow lane of water between two low walls of granite, and men with check-ropes in their hands kept pace with her, walking on the broad flagstones. A group waited impatiently on each side of the vanished bridge: rough heavy men in caps; sallow-faced men in high hats; two bareheaded women; ragged children, fascinated, and with wide eyes. A cart coming at a jerky trot pulled up sharply. One of the women screamed at the silent ship—"Hallo, Jack!" without looking at any one in particular, and all hands looked at her from the forecastle head.—"Stand clear! Stand clear of that rope!" cried the dockman, bending over stone posts. The crowd murmured, stamped where they stood.—"Let go your quarter-checks! Let go!" sang out a ruddy-faced old man on the quay. The ropes splashed heavily falling in the water, and the *Narcissus* entered the dock.   5

The stony shores ran away right and left in straight lines, enclosing a sombre and rectangular pool. Brick walls rose high above the water— soulless walls, staring through hundreds of windows as troubled and dull as the eyes of over-fed brutes. At their base monstrous iron cranes crouched, with chains hanging from their long necks, balancing cruel-looking hooks over the decks of lifeless ships. A noise of wheels rolling over stones, the thump of heavy things falling, the racket of feverish winches, the grinding of strained chains, floated on the air. Between high buildings the dust of all the continents soared in short flight; and a penetrating smell of perfumes and dirt, of spices and hides, of things costly and of things filthy, pervaded the space, made for it an atmosphere precious and disgusting. The *Narcissus* came gently into her berth; the shadows of soulless walls fell upon her, the dust of all the continents leaped upon her deck, and a swarm of strange men, clambering up her sides, took possession of her in the name of the sordid earth. She had ceased to live.   6

Suggestions for Writing

Listed below are several topics which lend themselves to the use of description in creating a dominant impression. In developing one of these topics, remember that you will be drawing upon the other modes of discourse as well.

1 Impressions of the city
2 The ideal relative (real or imagined)
3 "Another view of Father"
4 "A scene I hope to forget"
5 "The view from my room"
6 Five o'clock rush hour
7 "The place where I live"
8 Memories of the past
9 The sea
10 A view from the bridge
11 The neon jungle

5

WHAT HAPPENS NEXT_____

NARRATION

*We are all like Scheherazade's husband, in that we want to know what
happens next.*   E. M. Forster

"Once upon a time . . ." are the classic words that evoke for most of us the world of childhood. There was nothing we liked better than a story. Even after we were able to test our own personal, vivid, and real experiences, we still went on liking stories, because we discovered that our own experiences were usually limited and sometimes ordinary. Some of us, for instance, may remember a period of insatiable movie-going. Everyone has been charmed by "once upon a time," because that phrase excites our interest in a situation in which something is about to happen. Scheherazade was able to save her life, E. M. Forster notes, because she was inventive enough to escape her husband's sword by making him interested in what happened next in the thousand and one tales she told. Few writers have such demanding readers, but all writers of narrative hold the reader's attention in the same way.

The form of discourse called "narration" is nothing more than story-telling. If the story is a true one—if it is factual narrative—we can compare the facts and personalities in the story with their sources in life. In this case, the writer does not, or should not, invent things; he presents from his point of view the sequence of events and the people as they are, as Bernal Diaz del Castillo does in "The Storming of the Great Temple" (page 506). This factual incident can be seen from another perspective, as, indeed, William H. Prescott sees it (page 509); but the essential facts of the situation, used or unused in their totality, do not change. Thus, factual narrative presents facts that can be verified. Fictional narrative is what most of us think of when we hear the word "story"; we think of "story" in relation to our own progress from fairy tales through comics to the novel. What these narratives have in common is that they are all, in a sense, not true. Somebody "made them up." These stories are invented, and it is only by accident, usually, that we find exact counterparts in reality for the facts and persons we find in fiction. Fictional narrative depends upon reality, of course; the writer gets his observations and ideas from the real world. He cannot "make up" everything, although he may invent ways of combining his observations. Both factual narrative and fictional narrative, therefore, can be discussed under the general heading "narration," because both use the same patterns.

Narration is the kind of discourse that is concerned with *action*. Things must happen. A description of a scene, such as Elizabeth Bowen's "The Incoming Tide" (page 484), is not narration, because it is static. Description freezes a scene for us; narration gives us a moving picture, life in motion. Of course, this is only one aspect of narration. We may make motion pictures of the Grand Canyon or Yellowstone Park, and these are not narrative. A true narrative is concerned with *time* as well as with action. If something happens, it happens in time. Notice how important the time sequence is in both narrations of the Battle at Gettysburg. The writer may narrate what happens in terms of its chronology, presenting a moving picture of things in the order in which they happened. The writer may freely manipulate time, using foreshadowing or flashbacks, presenting the sequence of events in any order of his choice. Whatever his experimentation, he must have a beginning time, that which marks what happened before the events with which he deals. He must have a middle time, the time in which the happening takes place. And he must have an ending time, a terminal mark after which happenings are no longer recorded. The writer may "begin" as analytically as J. F. Powers does in "The Valiant Woman" (page 563). He may begin as casually as James Thurber in "The Night the Ghost Got In" (page 572).

The third, and probably most important, characteristic of a narrative is *significance*. The events presented within a time sequence must have some meaning. The causal connection between events is all-important. The narrative writer does not tell us *about* the events; he presents the events so realistically that we "see" the action for ourselves. Let us say that Bill has asked Jane to go to the freshman mixer and Jane has turned down his bid. When Bill tells his roommate Jack about this, he can simply say: "Jane has turned me down. She said she didn't like to dance, and, anyway, she was going to wash her hair that night. She also thinks that mixers are adolescent." His explanation is adequate; he has indicated her answer and the reasons for it—and this is an exposition. But suppose that Jack is the curious or sympathetic type and that before Bill can get a word out Jack says, "Tell me the whole story." Jack's eager prompting may encourage Bill to construct a small narrative: "Well, she was sitting at the table near the back door of the Union, and I think she pretended not to see that I was walking over. But I didn't care, because I'd made up my mind to ask her. She pretended she was reading and looked up kind of startled when I stopped at her table. 'Mind if I join you?' I said. . . ." And a story has begun. Jack will find out what happened next, when it happened, and the meaning of the happening for Bill.

In this brief example, an important ingredient appears—people. The actors in a narrative cause things to happen or have things happen to them. In factual narrative, the writer must take the people as they are. He uncovers the significance of the action by discovering why the people acted or reacted as they did within a sequence of events. He is free to interpret the actions and motivations of the characters within the limits of factual knowledge. Thus Robert Penn Warren (page 513) can highlight a certain quality in Malcolm X, but he cannot give him qualities that were not present in his character. In fictional narrative, the writer not only invents a sequence of events more or less corresponding to life but also invents characters. Of course, he cannot be irresponsible in his invention. The characters invented must fit the situation, or the situation must grow from the characters. Each character will act in a special way, "his way," in order to be believable. An invented character must become real enough to escape his creator; that is, once having invented his character, the author must be able to look at him with detachment and repose. In "The Valiant Woman," for instance, Mrs. Stover could not suddenly become a woman of exquisite tact and compassionate understanding.

Narrative, therefore, involves an action, the movement of life in a series of events within a terminated time sequence, all of which has significance. This significance is discovered by "seeing" the action as an experience, especially by understanding the people involved in it. It is impossible to define any one way in which the writer accomplishes this. There are as many ways as there are successful writers. A writer may be as casual as Fremantle (page 544) or as calculating as Nathaniel Hawthorne. The situation may be as simply domestic as that in "The Valiant Woman" or as panoramic as that in "The Storming of the Great Temple." The writer may concentrate on one characteristic, as Thurber does in his presentation of his grandfather, or he may give us the essence of the whole person's temperament through a single situation, as Eudora Welty does (page 557). In short, there are as many manners as there are successful writers.

This does not mean, however, that the reader cannot apply any tests to the manner of presentation. All narratives have a kind of general procedure in common. Actions do not occur in vacuums or fall from the sky; they arise from situations. The writer begins a narrative by making clear to the reader how the action on which he is concentrating arose in the first place. This beginning is called, technically, an "exposition"—nothing more or less than a dynamic, unstable situation that is capable of change. In Prescott's "The Storming of the Great Temple: A Historian's View," we meet Cortés in an unstable situation. He must get possession of the *teocalli*, but the numerical odds are against success. The middle section is known as the "complication," the heightening of specific changes or happenings. The conflict between the Aztecs and Cortés' party holds our attention as Cortés and his men battle from the base of the *teocalli* to the sanctuaries. The complication moves toward the culmination of the action, the moving portrayal of the victorious cavaliers tumbling Huitzilopochtli down the steps of the *teocalli*. The culmination of this dynamic series of events is called the "climax." The unstable situation must be stabilized; this is the function of the ending or the resolution. The cavaliers, having done their work, return to their own quarters in safety. Compare the last sentence of paragraph 1 with the final paragraph. The action ends because it has fulfilled itself, fulfilled the promise of the dynamic beginning. We have not been told *about* the action; we have *seen* what it is all about. This does not mean there are no problems left, that all speculation must cease. The narrative is complete only in the sense that the change implicit in the dynamic situation has come about.

FACTUAL NARRATIVE

Some of the most distinguished writing of factual narrative can be found in histories. Brilliant recorders of history, men like Parkman, Prescott, Fisk and Motley, most often have not been eye-witnesses; they have based their work on contemporary accounts. William Prescott's *Conquest of Mexico* was based on a variety of sources which gave him an excellent point of view for writing his monumental history. One of these sources was the work of Bernal Diaz del Castillo, a soldier with Cortés' army. Diaz was neither scholar nor professional writer. He was a literate man who wrote his chronicle to correct mistakes in previous records of the conquest. As an eye-witness, he felt that he could give to posterity a correct view of the scene and action. In a simple preface to the work he tells us: "That which I have myself seen and the fighting I have gone through, with the help of God, I will describe quite simply, as a fair eye-witness without twisting events one way or another. I am now an old man, over eighty-four years of age, and I have lost my sight and hearing, and, as luck would have it, I have gained nothing of value to leave to my children and descendants but this my true story, and they will presently find out what a wonderful story it is."

The following two excerpts deal with the storming of the great Mexican temple, the Cue of Huichilobos, the temple dedicated to the pagan gods. Cortés and his men had already captured Montezuma, the Mexican king. The Mexicans were driven to attack his quarters because of this violation of the peace. The great temple was situated near Cortés' quarters and the Mexicans were using it as a vantage point from which to molest the Spaniards. Diaz tells this exciting story as one who was a part of it. Prescott gives us the historian's point of view.

THE STORMING OF THE GREAT TEMPLE:
A SOLDIER'S VIEW

BERNAL DIAZ del CASTILLO

I do not know how to tell of the great squadrons of warriors who came to attack us that day in our quarters, not only in ten or twelve places, but in more than twenty, for we were distributed over them all and in many other places, and while we built up and fortified ourselves, as I have related, many other squadrons openly endeavoured to penetrate into our quarters, and neither with guns, crossbows nor muskets, nor with many charges and sword-thrusts could we force them back, for they said that not one of us should remain alive that day and they would sacrifice our hearts and blood to their gods, and would have enough to glut their appetites and hold feasts on our arms and legs, and would throw our bodies to the tigers, lions, vipers and snakes, which they kept caged, so that they might gorge on them, and for that reason they had ordered them not to be given food for the past two days. As for the gold we possessed, we would get little satisfaction from it or from all the cloths; and as for the Tlaxcalans who were with us, they said that they would place them in cages to fatten, and little by little they would offer their bodies in sacrifice; and, very tenderly, they said that we should give up to them their great Lord Montezuma, and they said other things. Night by night, in like manner, there were always many yells and whistles and showers of darts, stones and arrows.   1

As soon as dawn came, after commending ourselves to God, we sallied out from our quarters with our towers, with the cannon, muskets, and crossbows in advance, and the horsemen making charges, but, as I have stated, although we killed many of them it availed nothing towards making them turn their backs, indeed if they had fought bravely on the two previous days, they proved themselves far more vigorous and displayed much greater forces and squadrons on this day. Nevertheless, we determined, although it should cost the lives of all of us, to push on with our towers and engines as far as the great Cue of Huichilobos.   2

I will not relate at length the fights we had with them in a fortified house, nor will I tell how they wounded the horses, nor were the horses of any use to us, because although the horsemen charged the squadrons to break through them, so many arrows, darts and stones were hurled at them, that they, well protected by armour though they were, could not prevail against the enemy, and if they pursued and overtook them, the Mexicans promptly dropped for safety into the canals and lagoons where they had raised other walls against the horsemen, and many other Indians were stationed with very long lances to finish killing them. Thus it benefited us nothing to turn aside to burn or demolish a house, it was quite useless, for, as I have said, they all stood in the water, and between house and house there was a movable bridge, and to cross by swimming was very dangerous, for on the roofs they had such store of rocks and stones and such defences, that it was certain destruction to risk it. In addition to this, where we did set fire to some houses, a single house took a whole day to burn, and the houses did not catch fire one from the other; thus it was useless toil to risk our persons in the attempt, so we went towards the great Cue of their Idols. Then, all of a sudden, more than four thousand Mexicans ascended it,[1] not counting other Companies that were posted on it with long lances and stones and darts, and placed themselves on the defensive, and resisted our ascent for a good while, and neither the towers nor the cannon or crossbows, nor the muskets were of any avail, nor the horsemen, for, although they wished to charge, the whole of the courtyard was paved with very large flagstones, so that the horses lost their foothold, and the stones were so slippery that the horses fell. While from the steps of the lofty Cue they forbade our advance, we had so many enemies both on one side and the other that although our cannon shots carried off ten or fifteen of them and we slew many others by sword-thrusts and charges, so many men attacked us that we were not able to ascend the lofty Cue. However with great unanimity we persisted in the attack, and without taking the towers (for they were already destroyed) we made our way to the summit.   3

Here Cortés showed himself very much of a man, as he always was. Oh! what a fight and what a fierce battle it was that took place; it was a memorable thing to see us all streaming with blood and covered with wounds and others slain. It pleased our Lord that we reached the place where we used to keep the image of Our Lady, and we did not find it, and it appears, as we came to know, that the great Montezuma paid devotion to Her, and ordered the image to be preserved in safety.   4

We set fire to their Idols and a good part of the chamber with the Idols Huichilobos and Tezcatepuc was burned. On that occasion the Tlaxcalans helped us very greatly. After this was accomplished, while some of us were fighting and others kindling the fire, as I have related, oh! to see the priests who were stationed on this great Cue, and the three or four thousand Indians, all men of importance. While we descended, oh! how they made us tumble down six or even ten steps at a time! And so much more there is to tell of the other squadrons posted on the battlements and recesses of the great Cue discharging so many darts and arrows that we could face neither one group of squadrons nor the other. We resolved to

[1] This was the Great Teocalli of Tenochtitlan, quite close to the Spanish Quarters. Cortés says that five hundred Mexicans ascended the Teocalli itself to defend it.

return, with much toil and risk to ourselves, to our quarters, our castles being destroyed, all of us wounded and sixteen slain, with the Indians constantly pressing on us and other squadrons on our flanks.   5

However clearly I may tell all this, I can never fully explain it to any one who did not see us. So far, I have not spoken of what the Mexican squadrons did who kept on attacking our quarters while we were marching outside, and the great obstinacy and tenacity they displayed in forcing their way in.   6

In this battle, we captured two of the chief priests, whom Cortés ordered us to convey with great care.   7

Many times I have seen among the Mexicans and Tlaxcalans, paintings of this battle, and the ascent that we made of the great Cue, as they look upon it as a very heroic deed. And although in the pictures that they have made of it, they depict all of us as badly wounded and streaming with blood and many of us dead they considered it a great feat, this setting fire to the Cue, when so many warriors were guarding it both on the battlements and recesses, and many more Indians were below on the ground and the Courts were full of them and there were many more on the sides; and with our towers destroyed, how was it possible to scale it?   8

Let us stop talking about it and I will relate how with great labour we returned to our quarters and if many men were then following us, as many more were in our quarters, for they had already demolished some walls so as to gain an entry, but on our arrival they desisted. Nevertheless, during all the rest of the day they never ceased to discharge darts, stones and arrows, and during the night yells and stones and darts.   9

THE STORMING OF THE GREAT TEMPLE: A HISTORIAN'S VIEW

WILLIAM H. PRESCOTT

Opposite to the Spanish quarters, at only a few rods' distance, stood the great *teocalli* of Huitzilopochtli. This pyramidal mound, with the sanctuaries that crowned it, rising altogether to the height of near a hundred and fifty feet, afforded an elevated position that completely commanded the palace of Axayacatl, occupied by the Christians. A body of five or six hundred Mexicans, many of them nobles and warriors of the highest rank, had got possession of the *teocalli*, whence they discharged such a tempest of arrows on the garrison that no one could leave his defences for a moment without imminent danger; while the Mexicans, under shelter of the sanctuaries, were entirely covered from the fire of the besieged. It was obviously necessary to dislodge the enemy, if the Spaniards would remain longer in their quarters.

1

Cortés assigned this service to his chamberlain, Escobar, giving him a hundred men for the purpose, with orders to storm the *teocalli* and set fire to the sanctuaries. But that officer was thrice repulsed in the attempt, and, after the most desperate efforts, was obliged to return with considerable loss and without accomplishing his object.

2

Cortés, who saw the immediate necessity of carrying the place, determined to lead the storming party himself. He was then suffering much from the wound in his left hand, which had disabled it for the present. He made the arm serviceable, however, by fastening his buckler to it, and, thus crippled, sallied out at the head of three hundred chosen cavaliers and several thousand of his auxiliaries.

3

In the court-yard of the temple he found a numerous body of Indians prepared to dispute his passage. He briskly charged them; but the flat smooth stones of the pavement were so slippery that the horses lost their footing and many of them fell. Hastily dismounting, they sent back the animals to their quarters, and, renewing the assault, the Spaniards succeeded without much difficulty in dispersing the Indian warriors and opening a free passage for themselves to the *teocalli*. This building, as the reader may remember, was a huge pyramidal structure, about three hundred feet square at the base. A flight of stone steps on the outside, at one of the angles of the mound, led to a platform, or terraced walk, which passed round the building until it reached a similar flight of stairs directly over the preceding, that conducted to another landing as before. As there were five bodies or divisions of the *teocalli*, it became necessary to pass round its whole extent four times, or nearly a mile, in order to reach the

summit, which, it may be recollected, was an open area, crowned only by
the two sanctuaries dedicated to the Aztec deities.   4

Cortés, having cleared a way for the assault, sprang up the lower
stairway, followed by Alvarado, Sandoval, Ordaz, and the other gallant
cavaliers of his little band, leaving a file of arquebusiers and a strong
corps of Indian allies to hold the enemy in check at the foot of the monument. On the first landing, as well as on the several galleries above, and
on the summit, the Aztec warriors were drawn up to dispute his passage.
From their elevated position they showered down volleys of lighter missiles,
together with heavy stones, beams, and burning rafters, which, thundering
along the stairway, overturned the ascending Spaniards and carried desolation through their ranks. The more fortunate, eluding or springing over
these obstacles, succeeded in gaining the first terrace; where, throwing
themselves on their enemies, they compelled them, after a short resistance, to fall back. The assailants pressed on, effectually supported by a
brisk fire of the musketeers from below, which so much galled the Mexicans in their exposed situation that they were glad to take shelter on the
broad summit of the *teocalli*.   5

Cortés and his comrades were close upon their rear, and the two
parties soon found themselves face to face on this aerial battle-field, engaged in mortal combat in presence of the whole city, as well as of the
troops in the court-yard, who paused, as if by mutual consent, from their
own hostilities, gazing in silent expectation on the issue of those above.
The area, though somewhat smaller than the base of the *teocalli*, was large
enough to afford a fair field of fight for a thousand combatants. It was
paved with broad, flat stones. No impediment occurred over its surface,
except the huge sacrificial block, and the temples of stone which rose to
the height of forty feet, at the farther extremity of the arena. One of these
had been consecrated to the Cross. The other was still occupied by the
Mexican war-god. The Christian and the Aztec contended for their religions under the very shadow of their respective shrines; while the Indian
priests, running to and fro, with their hair wildly streaming over their
sable mantles, seemed hovering in mid-air, like so many demons of darkness urging on the work of slaughter!   6

The parties closed with the desperate fury of men who had no hope
but in victory. Quarter was neither asked nor given; and to fly was impossible. The edge of the area was unprotected by parapet or battlement.
The least slip would be fatal; and the combatants, as they struggled in
mortal agony, were sometimes seen to roll over the sheer sides of the
precipice together. Cortés himself is said to have had a narrow escape
from this dreadful fate. Two warriors, of strong, muscular frames, seized
on him, and were dragging him violently towards the brink of the pyramid.
Aware of their intention, he struggled with all his force, and, before they

could accomplish their purpose, succeeded in tearing himself from their grasp and hurling one of them over the walls with his own arm! The story is not improbable in itself, for Cortés was a man of uncommon agility and strength. It has been often repeated; but not by contemporary history.   7

The battle lasted with unintermitting fury for three hours. The number of the enemy was double that of the Christians; and it seemed as if it were a contest which must be determined by numbers and brute force, rather than by superior science. But it was not so. The invulnerable armor of the Spaniard, his sword of matchless temper, and his skill in the use of it, gave him advantages which far outweighed the odds of physical strength and numbers. After doing all that the courage of despair could enable men to do, resistance grew fainter and fainter on the side of the Aztecs. One after another they had fallen. Two or three priests only survived, to be led away in triumph by the victors. Every other combatant was stretched a corpse on the bloody arena, or had been hurled from the giddy heights. Yet the loss of the Spaniards was not inconsiderable. It amounted to forty-five of their best men; and nearly all the remainder were more or less injured in the desperate conflict.   8

The victorious cavaliers now rushed towards the sanctuaries. The lower story was of stone; the two upper were of wood. Penetrating into their recesses, they had the mortification to find the image of the Virgin and the cross removed. But in the other edifice they still beheld the grim figure of Huitzilopochtli, with his censer of smoking hearts, and the walls of his oratory reeking with gore,—not improbably of their own countrymen! With shouts of triumph the Christians tore the uncouth monster from his niche, and tumbled him, in the presence of the horror-stricken Aztecs, down the steps of the *teocalli*. They then set fire to the accursed building. The flames speedily ran up the slender towers, sending forth an ominous light over city, lake, and valley, to the remotest hut among the mountains. It was the funeral pyre of paganism, and proclaimed the fall of that sanguinary religion which had so long hung like a dark cloud over the fair regions of Anahuac![1] 9

Having accomplished this good work, the Spaniards descended the winding slopes of the *teocalli* with more free and buoyant step, as if conscious that the blessing of Heaven now rested on their arms. They passed through the dusky files of Indian warriors in the court-yard, too much dismayed by the appalling scenes they had witnessed to offer resistance, and reached their own quarters in safety.   10

[1] No achievement in the war struck more awe into the Mexicans than this storming of the great temple, in which the white men seemed to bid defiance equally to the powers of God and man. Hieroglyphical paintings minutely commemorating it were to be frequently found among the natives after the Conquest. The sensitive Captain Diaz intimates that those which he saw made full as much account of the wounds and losses of the Christians as the facts would warrant. (*Hist. de la Conquista, ubi supra.*) It was the only way in which the conquered could take their revenge.

The Two Selections

1 What evidence in their narratives indicates that Diaz is not a professional writer and that Prescott is?

2 Diaz tells us his story from the point of view of the first person. What are the advantages and limitations of this point of view? Contrast this point of view with that of the omniscient person used by Prescott.

3 In which excerpt do we find the exposition (or beginning) presented more fully? Why?

4 Indicate in each excerpt where, generally, the exposition ends and the complication ends.

5 Indicate where the climax occurs in each excerpt and show how it is built up to by the author.

6 In which version is more time devoted to the setting of the action? Why?

7 Do both versions tell us simply what happened, or can you detect that both (either) indicate(s) a certain attitude on the part of the author toward the happening which influences the reader?

8 Description in re-creating the scene or creating an atmosphere is especially important in some types of factual narrative. Point out two instances in each version of the use of description to make the action seem real to the reader.

9 The two versions seem to differ with respect to the difficulty of the return to the Spanish quarters. What is the effect of this difference on the ending of each excerpt?

10 In each version, what does the author stress most?
  a The immediate physical danger of the participants
  b The contrast between paganism and Christianity
  c The heroism of Cortés
  d The physical action itself

11 Diaz devotes a paragraph to paintings made of the battle by the Indians. Prescott puts such information in a footnote. What emotional effect did Diaz hope to achieve by the prominent mention of these paintings?

12 Which of the two writers emphasizes more forcefully the drama of the conflict?

MALCOLM X: MISSION AND MEANING

ROBERT PENN WARREN

James Farmer, lately the National Director of the Committee of Racial Equality, has called Malcolm X a "very simple man." Elijah Poole, better known to the Black Muslims as Muhammad and, indeed, as Allah, called him a "star gone astray." An editorial writer of the *Saturday Evening Post* put it: "If Malcolm X were not a Negro, his autobiography would be little more than a journal of abnormal psychology, the story of a burglar, dope pusher, addict and jailbird—with a family history of insanity—who acquires messianic delusions and sets forth to preach an upside-down religion of 'brotherly' hatred." Carl Rowan, a Negro, lately the director of the United States Information Service, substantially agreed with that editorial writer when he said, in an interview after Malcolm's assassination, that he was "an ex-convict, ex-dope peddler who became a racial fanatic." Another editorial writer, that of the *Daily Times* of Lagos, Nigeria, called him a martyr. 1

Malcolm X may have been, in varying perspectives, all these things. But he was also something else. He was a latter-day example of an old-fashioned type of American celebrated in grammar school readers, commencement addresses, and speeches at Rotary Club lunches—the man who "makes it," the man who, from humble origins and with meager education, converts, by will, intelligence, and sterling character, his liabilities into assets. Malcolm X was of that breed of Americans, autodidacts and homemade successes, that has included Benjamin Franklin, Abraham Lincoln, P. T. Barnum, Charles A. Edison, Booker T. Washington, Mark Twain, Henry Ford, and the Wright brothers. Malcolm X would look back on his beginnings and, in innocent joy, marvel at the distance he had come. 2

But in Malcolm X the old Horatio Alger story is crossed, as has often been the case, with another typical American story. America has been prodigally fruitful of hot-gospellers and prophets—from Dr. Graham and his bread, Amelia Bloomer and her bloomers, Emerson and the Oversoul, and Brigham Young, on to F.D.R. and the current Graham, Billy. Furthermore, to round out his American story and insure his fame, Malcolm X, like John Brown, Abraham Lincoln, Joseph Smith (the founder of Mormonism), and John Fitzgerald Kennedy, along with a host of lesser prophets, crowned his mission with martyrdom. Malcolm X fulfills, it would seem, all the requirements—success against odds, the role of prophet, and martyrdom—for inclusion in the American pantheon. 3

Malcolm Little, who was to become Malcolm X and El-Hajj Malik El-Shabazz, was born in Omaha, Nebraska, on May 19, 1925. All omens were right, and all his background. He was the seventh child of his father. One night during the pregnancy of his mother, hooded Ku Klux Klansmen, mounted and brandishing rifles and shotguns, surrounded the house, calling for the father to come out; the mother faced them down and persuaded them of the fact that her husband was not at home. The mother, a West Indian who looked white, was ashamed, not proud, of the white blood. The father, a Baptist preacher, was a militant follower of Marcus Garvey, and this was to lead to another attack on the Little home, in 1929, in Lansing, Michigan, this time by the Black Legion, which except for black robes was indistinguishable from the Klan; the house burned to the ground, while white police and firemen looked on. The memory of that night stayed with Malcolm from childhood—that and the pictures his father showed him of Marcus Garvey "riding in a fine car, a big black man dressed in a dazzling uniform with gold braid on it, and he was wearing a thrilling hat with tall plumes," and the Garveyite meetings at which his father presided and which always ended with the exhortation, "Up, you mighty race, you can accomplish what you will!" The people would chant these words after Malcolm's father.   4

To complete the picture of the preparation of the hero for his mission, his father, who had seen two brothers killed by white men and a third lynched, was found, one night, on a streetcar track, with skull crushed and body cut almost across. Negroes in Lansing—and the son all his life—believed that he had been attacked by white men, and then laid on the track. Malcolm always believed that he, too, would meet a violent death. When he first became aware of the long stalk, which was to end in gunfire in the Audubon Ballroom, Malcolm might accept it, then, as a fulfillment of old omens and intuitions.   5

In spite of the powerful image of the father, the pictures of Garvey in uniform, and the tales of black kings, Malcolm's early notion of Africa was still one "of naked savages, cannibals, monkeys and tigers and steaming jungles." He says that he never understood why. But that statement must be an example, in a form more bland than usual, of his irony, for a large part of his autobiography (*The Autobiography of Malcolm X*, with the assistance of Alex Haley, New York City: The Grove Press, 1966) is devoted to explaining *why*—that is, by the white man's "brain-washing"; and then explaining *how*, step by step, he came to the vision of another Africa, and of another self, different from the hustler, pimp, dope-addict, dope-pusher, burglar, and, by his own account, generally degraded and vice-ridden creature known as "Satin," who, in 1948, in Concord Prison, in Massachusetts, heard, in a letter from his brother Philbert, of the "natural religion for the black man." The religion was called the "Nation of Islam." 6

This autobiography is "told" to Alex Haley, a Negro, a retired twenty-year man of the Coast Guard turned journalist. From 1963 up to the assassination, Haley saw Malcolm for almost daily sessions when Malcolm was in New York, and sometimes accompanied him on his trips. Haley's account of this period, of how he slowly gained Malcolm's confidence and how Malcolm himself discovered the need to tell his story, is extremely interesting and, though presented as an Epilogue, is an integral part of the book; but the main narrative has the advantage of Malcolm's tone, his characteristic movement of mind, and his wit, for Haley has succeeded admirably in capturing these qualities, as can be checked by the recollection of Malcolm's TV appearances and conversation and by his taped speeches (*Malcolm X Speaks: Selected Speeches and Statements*, edited by George Breitman, New York: Merit Publishers, 1966).   7

The *Autobiography* and the speeches are an extraordinary record of an extraordinary man. They are, among other things, a record that may show a white man (or some Negroes, for Malcolm would say that many Negroes do not know the nature of their own experience) what it means to be a Negro in America, in this century, or at least what it so dramatically meant to one man of unusual intelligence and powerful personality. Being a Negro meant being "black"—even if black was no more than a metaphor for Malcolm, who was himself "marginy," a dull yellowish skin, pale enough to freckle, pale eyes, hair reddish-coppery. He had been "Detroit Red" in his hustling days.   8

To be black, metaphorically or literally, meant, according to Malcolm, to wear a badge of shame which was so mystically and deeply accepted that all the practical injustices the white world might visit upon the black would seem only a kind of inverted justice, necessary in the very nature of things, the working out of a curse. The black man had no history, no country, no identity; he was alienated in time and place; he lived in "self-hate," and being unable to accept "self," he therefore was willing to accept, supine or with random violence, his fate. This was the diagnosis of his own plight, as Malcolm learned it from the "Nation of Islam."   9

As for the cure, what he found was the doctrine of the Black Muslims. This involved a history of creation and a metaphysic which made the black man central and dominant, a secular history of kingly achievement in Africa. The divine and secular histories provided a justification for the acceptance of the black "self." In addition, the doctrine provided an understanding of the iniquity of the white man which would account for the black man's present lot and would, at the same time, mobilize an unquenchable hate against him. Total withdrawal from the white man and all his works was the path of virtue, until the day of Armageddon when he would be destroyed. Meanwhile, until the Chosen People had been relieved of the white man's presence, the black man was presented with a practical program of life: thrift, education, cleanliness, diet (no pork, for example, pork being a "nigger" food), abstemiousness (no alcohol or tobacco), manners and courtesy, puritanical morality and reverence for the home and Muslim womanhood—a general program of "wake up, clean up, and stand up." In fact, on the practical side, in spite of the hatred of the white man and contempt of his culture, the Black Muslim doctrine smuggled into the life of the Negro slum the very virtues which had made white middle-class America what it was—i.e., successful.   10

After Malcolm's death Dr. Kenneth B. Clark, the Negro psychologist and the author of an important book called *Dark Ghetto,* said that he had been "cut down at the point when he seemed on the verge of achieving the position of respectability he sought." In the midst of the gospel of violence and the repudiation of the white world, even in the Black Muslim phase, there appears now and then the note of yearning. In the *Autobiography* we find, for instance, this passage: "I was the invited speaker at the Harvard Law School Forum. I happened to glance through a window. Abruptly, I realized that I was looking in the direction of the apartment house that was my old burglary group's hideout. . . . And there I stood, the invited speaker, at Harvard."   11

Malcolm, still in prison, gave up pork and tobacco, and undertook a program of reading in the good library there available. He read in Plato, Aristotle, Schopenhauer, Kant, Nietzsche, and the "Oriental philosophers." He read and reread the Bible, and could match quotations with a Harvard Seminary student who conducted a class for prisoners. He studied *The Loom of Language,* by Frederick Bodmer, and memorized Grimm's Law. He read Durant's *Story of Civilization,* H. G. Wells' *Outline of History,* Herodotus, Fannie Kimball, *Uncle Tom's Cabin,* Gandhi, Gregor Mendel, pamphlets of the "Abolitionist Anti-Slavery Society of New England," and J. A. Rogers' *Sex and Race.* He was trying to find the black man's place— and his own—in history, trying, in other words, to document the doctrine of the Black Muslims. He wrote regularly to Muhammad to tell what he had found. While he was still in prison Malcolm also had a vision. He had written an appeal to Muhammad to reinstate his brother Reginald, suspended as a Muslim for "improper relations" with the secretary of the New York Temple. That night he spent in desperate prayer. The next night he woke up and saw a man sitting, there in the cell, in a chair by him. "He had on a dark suit, I remember. I could see him as plainly as I see anyone I look at. He wasn't black, and he wasn't white. He was light-brown-skinned, an Asiatic cast of countenance, and he had oily black hair. . . . I had no idea whatsoever who he was. He just sat there. Then suddenly as he had come, he was gone." The color of the man in the vision is an interesting fact. So is his immobility and silence.   12

When Malcolm Little came out of prison, he was Malcolm X, the "X," according to the practice of the Black Muslims, standing for the true name lost long ago in Africa to take the place of the false white name that had been forced on him. He had been reborn, and he now entered upon his mission. Soon he was an accredited minister of Muhammad, the official defender of the faith and the intellectual spokesman of the movement. His success, and especially the fact that he was invited to colleges, where Muhammad would never be invited, led to jealousy and, as Malcolm reports, contributed to his "silencing" as soon as a good justification appeared.   13

Malcolm X was not the only man drawn from the lower depths to be reborn in the Nation of Islam. It is generally admitted that the record of rehabilitation by the Black Muslims of dope-addicts, alcoholics, prostitutes, and criminals makes any other method seem a waste of time. They have, it would seem, found the nerve center that, once touched, can radically change both the values and the way of life for a number of Negroes in America; and it is important here to use the phrase "Negroes in America" with special emphasis, and no other locution, for those redeemed by the Black Muslims are those who have been only *in*, but not *of*, America, those without country, history, or identity. The Black Muslims have found, then, a principle that, if not of universal validity (or, in one perspective, isn't it? for white as well as for black?), at least involves a truth of considerable psychological importance. That truth is, indeed, shrouded in metaphysical mumbo-jumbo, political and economic absurdity, and some murderous delusions, but even these elements have a noteworthy symbolic relation to the central truth. It is reported that Martin Luther King, after seeing Malcolm X on TV, remarked: "When he starts talking about all that's been done to us, I get a twinge of hate, of identification with him. But hate is not the only effect." A man as intelligent, as cultivated, and as experienced as James Farmer has testified in his recent book *Freedom When?* that the Black Muslims and Malcolm X have had a very important impact on his own thinking and in helping to change his basic views of the Negro Revolution, especially on the question of "blackness" and on the nature of integration and the Negro's role in an open society.   14

If this is the case, then the story of Malcolm X assumes an added dimension. It shows the reader the world in which that truth can operate; that is, it shows the kind of alienation to which this truth is applicable. It shows, also, the human quality of the operation, a man in the process of trying to understand his plight, and to find salvation, by that truth. But there is another aspect to the *Autobiography*. Malcolm X was a man in motion, he was a seeker, and that motion led, in the end, away from orthodox Black Muslim doctrine. The doctrine had been, he said, a straitjacket. He was now in the process of stripping away, perhaps unconsciously, the mumbo-jumbo, the absurdities, and the murderous delusions. He was trying, as it were, to locate the truth that had saved him, and divest it of the irrelevancies. In the end, he might have come to regard the religion that, after his break with the Black Muslims, he had found in Mecca as an irrelevancy, too. Certainly, just before his death he could say that his "philosophy" was still changing. Perhaps what Mecca gave him, for the time being at least, was the respectability, the authority, of the established thing. But he might have finally found that authority in himself, for he could speak as a man whose very existence was witness to what he said. Something of that purely personal authority comes through in these books.   15

Malcolm X had, in his last phase, lost the mystique of blackness so important to the Black Muslims; he had seen the blue-eyed and fair-haired pilgrims in Mecca. He was no longer a separatist in the absolute sense of the Black Muslims. He had become enough of an integrationist to say: "I believe in recognizing every human being as a human being . . . and when you are dealing with humanity as a family, there's no question of integration or intermarriage. It's just one human being marrying another human being or one human being living around with another human being." And just before his death he had made a down-payment on a house, in Long Island, in a largely Jewish neighborhood. He no longer saw the white man as the "white devil"—metaphysically evil; and he was ready, grudgingly, not optimistically, and with a note of threat, to grant that there was in America a chance, a last chance, for a "bloodless revolution." He was ready to work with other Negro organizations, even those which he had most derided, to try to find common ground and solutions at a practical level.   16

Certain ideas were, however, carried over from the Black Muslim days. The question of "identity" remained, and the question of race pride and personal self-respect divested of chauvinism, and with this the notion of "wake up, clean up, and stand up," the notion of self-reliance, self-improvement, self-discipline. If he could say such things, which smacked of the discredited philosophy of Booker T. Washington, and which few other Civil Rights leaders would dare to utter, it was because he did so in the context of his intransigence vis-à-vis the white world and his radical indictment of white society. Even in the last phase, even if he believed in "recognizing every human being as a human being," and no longer took the white man to be metaphysically evil, his indictment of white society was still radical; unless that society could really be regenerated, the chance for the "bloodless revolution" was gone.   17

This radical indictment leads to what may be the greatest significance of Malcolm X, his symbolic role. He was the black man who looked the white man in the eye and forgave nothing. If the white man had turned away, in shame or indifference, from the awful "forgiveness" of a Martin Luther King, he still had to face the unforgiveness, with its shattering effect on his accustomed view of himself and with the terrifying discovery, as Malcolm's rage brought his own rage forth, of the ultimate of which he himself would, under pressure, be capable. To put it another way, Malcolm X let the white man see what, from a certain perspective, he, his history, and his culture looked like. It was possible to say that that perspective was not the only one, that it did not give the whole truth about the white man, his history, and his culture, but it was not possible to say that the perspective did not carry a truth, a truth that was not less, but more, true for being seen from the angle of "Small's Paradise" in Harlem or of the bedroom to which "Detroit Red," the "steerer," brought the "Ivy League fathers" to be ministered to by the big black girl, whose body had been greased to make it look "shinier and blacker" and whose Amazonian hand held a small plaited whip.   18

On the afternoon of Sunday, February 21, 1965, at a meeting of his struggling new Organization of Afro-American Unity, in the Audubon Ballroom, on West 166th Street, in Harlem, Malcolm X rose to speak and uttered the ritual greeting, "*Asalaikum,* brothers and sisters!" He was immediately cut down by shotgun and revolver fire from assassins waiting in the front of the audience. At 3:30 at the Columbia-Presbyterian Hospital, he was pronounced dead. Three men—Talmadge Thayer, Norman 3X (Brown), and Thomas 15X (Johnson)—were arrested in the case and tried for first-degree murder. Thayer denied Black Muslim connections, but Thomas 15X was identified as a member and Norman 3X as a lieutenant in the "Fruit of Islam"—the bodyguards of Elijah Muhammad. After deliberating for twenty hours a jury found them guilty, and all three were given life sentences.   19

What would have been Malcolm's role had he lived? Perhaps as some Negro leaders said shortly before his death, he had no real organization, and did not have the talent to create one. Perhaps his being in motion was only, as some held, a result of confusion of mind, a groping that could not be trusted to bring results. Perhaps, as James Farmer had put it, Malcolm, for all his talk, was not an activist; he had managed all along to be out of harm's way whenever harm was brewing, and he was afraid of the time when he "would have to chirp or get off the perch."   20

But perhaps the new phase of the Negro Revolution, with the violence of the great city slums, might have given him his great chance. He might have, at last, found himself in action. He might have found himself committed to blind violence, but on the other hand he might have had the power to control and canalize action and do something to reduce the danger of the Revolution's degenerating into random revolt. For, in spite of all the gospel of intransigence, Malcolm had always had a governing idea of a constructive role for the Negro, some notion of a society. After all, he had personal force, as no one who ever spent as little as ten minutes with him would have doubted: charisma, to use the fashionable word, and that to a degree possessed by no other leader except Martin Luther King. And he had one great asset which Martin Luther King does not have: he was from the lower depths and possessed the authority of one who had both suffered and conquered the depths.   21

Whatever the future might have held for him had he lived, his actual role was an important one, and in one sense the importance lay in his *being* rather than his *doing*. He was a man of passion, depth, and scale— and his personal story is a moving one. There is the long struggle. There is the sense of desperation and tightening entrapment as, in the last days, Malcolm recognized the dilemma developing in his situation. The "so-called moderate" Civil Rights leaders, he said, dodged him as "too militant," and the "so-called militants" dodged him as "too moderate." Haley reports that he once exclaimed "They won't let me turn the corner! I'm caught in a trap!" For there is a trap in the story, a real and lethal one. There is the gang of Black Muslims covering his every move in the Statler Hilton at Los Angeles, the mysterious Negro men who tried to get his room number at the Hilton in New York City, and the sinister telephone call to his room in the hotel the morning of his death. There is the bomb-ing of his house, and his despairing anger when the event was widely taken as a publicity stunt. There is his remark to Haley, as he asked to read the manuscript of his book for a last, unnecessary time: "I just want to read it one more time, because I don't expect to read it in finished form"— wanting, as it were, to get a last sense of the shape of his own life as he felt the trap closing. There is, as with a final accent of pathos, the letter by his six-year-old daughter Attilah (named for the Scourge of God), written just after his death: "Dear Daddy, I love you so. O dear, O dear, I wish you wasn't dead." But entrapment and pathos was not all. He had been bred to danger. When he stepped on the platform that Sunday after-noon, in the face of odds which he had more shrewdly estimated than anybody else, he had nerve, confidence, style. He made his last gesture.   22

As one reads the *Autobiography,* one feels that, whatever the his-torical importance of Malcolm Little, his story has permanence, that it has something of tragic intensity and meaning. One feels that it is an American story bound to be remembered, to lurk in the background of popular consciousness, to reappear some day in a novel, on the stage, or on the screen. No—the right medium might be the ballad. Malcolm was a figure out of the anonymous depth of the folk, and even now, in a slum bedroom or in the shadowy corner of some bar, fingers may be tentatively picking the box, and lips fumbling to frame the words that will mean, long after our present problems are resolved and forgotten, the final fame, and the final significance.   23

The Whole Selection

1 What is the precise function of the three introductory paragraphs?
2 The whole of the essay is calculated to reveal Malcolm's "greatest significance." What is it?
3 According to Warren, what did being black mean to Malcolm X? How was this concept related to his "greatest significance" for our culture?
4 Although Warren's essay is primarily intended to discuss the meaning of the life of Malcolm X, in order to do this he uses in part the narrative details of his subject's life. Point out these narrative elements in their chronological sequence. Even though Warren expects his reader to be familiar with Malcolm's life (and even to have read his autobiography), does he provide enough narrative details for the reader from which to draw the "meaning" of his life?
5 Explain what Warren means by the last two sentences of paragraph 12: "The color of the man in the vision is an interesting fact. So is his immobility and silence."

THE POOREST OF THE POOR

VED MEHTA

"Although throughout India there is a general opting-out of concern about the large problems of the poor by people with any means at all," one of the Ford Foundation planners tells me, "still, all over Calcutta, in a *busti* here and a *busti* there, a ward here and a ward there, volunteers and voluntary groups are doing welfare work. We did a study of a very poor section of the city that has a population of nearly a quarter of a million, and we found there were dispensaries, family-planning clinics, hospitals, coöperatives, primary and secondary schools, reading rooms, sports clubs, all run by private welfare groups. In fact, if it weren't for this volunteer work, the city might have collapsed long ago. But each religious, ethnic, or caste group tends to concentrate exclusively on its own poor. Muslims tend to work among Muslims, Gujaratis among Gujaratis, tanners among tanners. There are, it is true, a few groups that try to cut across the divisions and work throughout the city, yet, because the problem of poverty as a whole is so vast, even they end up having their own special concerns. For instance, the Bharat Savak Samaj works among the beggars and the Bengal Ladies' Union tries to rehabilitate prostitutes. Perhaps the most dreaded work is done by the Missionaries of Charity, who devote themselves to the lowest of the low. They devote themselves to those who are rejected by the rejected and despised by the despised. They work mostly with the lepers." A Calcutta friend, commenting on this part of the work of the Missionaries of Charity, says, "They attach special importance to their work among the lepers, perhaps because to all the rich of the world, if you really come down to it, all the poor of the world are, in a sense, lepers. The rich may give to the poor, may work among the poor, but they are really afraid to live with the poor." 1

The Missionaries of Charity is a Catholic congregation that was founded in 1948 by an Albanian-born nun, Mother Theresa. She is still its head, and one morning I go to meet her in the congregation's convent, which is on a narrow, unpaved lane just off Lower Circular Road. It is a small building enclosed by a high wall with an iron gate. Inside the gate is a courtyard. I am shown into a room, overlooking the courtyard, that serves as a parlor. It is furnished with a round wooden table, bearing a Bible and the *Catholic Directory of India,* and a few straight-backed wooden chairs, above which hang several framed photographs of clerical personages inscribed to the Missionaries of Charity. 2

Mother Theresa comes in. She is tiny and slim, but imposing. Her skin is ivory-colored, as if she had not been touched by the all-scorching Indian sun. Her face is creased with wrinkles, but she does not look elderly. Her eyes are small and gray-brown, her nose is strong, her lips are

thin, and, though her smile is quick, her expression is stern and purposeful. She is wearing a plain white cotton sari with blue edging and a high-
necked, long-sleeved blouse. On her, the traditional Indian dress seems
transformed into a practical uniform *cum* nun's habit. The sari has been
secured to her hair with ordinary straight pins and folded so that it looks
a little like a headdress, and its free end has been fastened at her shoulder
with a large safety pin, from which hangs a crucifix. "It's Christ's work we
are doing here in Calcutta," she says by way of greeting.   3

We sit down, and I ask Mother Theresa one or two general questions
about herself.   4

"There isn't much to tell," she says. "I was born in 1910. My father
was a shopkeeper, and I had a brother and a sister. I entered a Loreto convent when I was ten, and I came to Calcutta to teach in the convent here in
1929. I have been in Calcutta ever since. I feel completely Indian now. I
speak Bengali very well; my Hindi is not so good. But I would prefer it if
we didn't talk about me—if you've heard about one of the Missionaries of
Charity, you've heard about them all. I'd rather talk about our work, which
is God's work."   5

I ask her how the work got started.   6

"I found the vocation of charity here in Calcutta within the vocation
of religion," she says. "Even when I was teaching in the convent, I encouraged the senior girls in the sodality to go into the *bustis* and work
among the poor, but I really began this work after the Second World War,
when I saw a woman dying on the street outside Campbell Hospital. I
picked her up and took her to the hospital, but she was refused admission,
because she was poor. She died on the street. I knew then that I must
make a home for the dying—a resting place for people going to Heaven.
When God wants you to do something, He has His way of letting you know
it." She goes on to tell me that in 1948 the ecclesiastical authorities gave
her permission to form a congregation dedicated to relief work among "the
poorest of the poor." She began the work in a couple of small rooms in a
house in Moti Jheel Busti, establishing a school for orphan children in one
room and a Home for the Dying in the other. Soon afterward, she received
her first postulant as a Missionary of Charity, and soon after that she
found different quarters for the Home for the Dying, and expanded her
school for orphans into the second of the original rooms. "So, in time, the
congregation and its activities grew," Mother Theresa adds, and she
hands me a couple of leaflets about the work of the congregation today.
One leaflet, which is about the Home for the Dying, records:

> Mother says, "They have lived like animals, we help them to die like
> angels." Here is the story of one poor unfortunate woman who was
> brought in from the sewer. She was a beggar who had, apparently,
> overcome by hunger and fatigue, fallen into an open manhole. She lay
> there for five days barely alive and covered with maggots. As Mother

put her to bed and began gently cleaning her, whole areas of skin came off in her hand. The woman, half-unconscious, murmured, "Why are you doing this for me?" Mother replied, "For the love of God." This poor waif who probably never in her life had had loving hands tend her—looking at Mother, her soul in her eyes, faith in human nature restored—gave Mother a most beautiful smile and died. That is our reward—that we should make the last moments of the fellow being beautiful.   7

"In Calcutta, besides the Home for the Dying, we now have a children's home, sixteen schools, twenty-three Sunday schools, eight mobile clinics for lepers, seven mobile clinics for the poor in the *bustis,* a relief center for distributing food rations, and two convents for the sisters," Mother Theresa says. "Altogether, in Calcutta, we have fifty-nine centers for our work, and two hundred and eighty-five sisters, who come from all parts of India and from many other countries, too. We also have sisters doing work in twenty other Indian cities, but most of the sisters work here in Calcutta."   8

According to the rules of the congregation, Mother Theresa tells me, a candidate wishing to become a professed sister must display health of body and mind, the ability to acquire knowledge, common sense in abundance, and a cheerful disposition. Then, over a three-year period, she will be admitted as, in turn, an aspirant, to learn the nature of the work of charity; a postulant, to learn the rudiments of the religious life and to test her sense of vocation; and a novice, to continue the study of the religious life, to examine the vows of poverty, chastity, and obedience, and, under supervision, to work in the *bustis* among the poor. A member of the congregation must eat the same food as the poor and wear a plain white cotton sari with open sandals and a small crucifix; a dark-blue edging on the sari serves to distinguish a professed sister from a candidate. The prescribed language of the congregation is English, and the favorite ejaculation of the members is "Immaculate Heart of Mary! Cause of our joy! Pray for us!"   9

A bell now begins to chime in the distance, and files of nuns in white saris move across the courtyard outside. "They are going to the chapel," Mother Theresa says. "They are going to pray for one of our sisters who died this morning of rabies. She was a trained doctor, and six months ago, when she was working in one of our leper camps, a dog bit her. She didn't take the rabies injections, because the dog was just a puppy. It must have been her time to go to God." From the distance there now comes the sound of singing—of thin, high voices raised in the words of the Lord's Prayer. "I am thankful to say she died two days after the onset of the rabies. Five of us looked after her. We will all have to take injections. People who are bitten by rabid animals take about fourteen injections. We

had only indirect contact with the rabies, so we will have to take only seven
—it's not so bad."   10

Mother Theresa now prepares to visit some of the centers of the congregation. She invites me to accompany her, and asks for the ambulance,
explaining that she often travels in it, so that she can remove to the Home
for the Dying anyone she may see dying on the streets or in the *bustis*.   11

We take our places in the ambulance, beside the driver, and are
immediately surrounded by a throng of beggers—sick, emaciated, lame
—all with their open palms thrust forward. "Hey, *babu!*" and "Hey,
mataji!" and "Hey, *babu!*" they cry, in a dissonant jumble of voices.   12

I pass out the money in my pockets.   13

Mother Theresa, except for crossing herself, sits impassive. As the
ambulance pulls away, the beggars retreat and fall behind.   14

Mother Theresa tells me that her first stop will be at the Shishu
Bhavan ("children's home"), which houses nearly seventy children at present and has cared for over two thousand homeless children—orphaned,
abandoned, afflicted, or disabled—since it was opened, in 1955, nursing
them, teaching them, finding them foster parents, and arranging marriages
for them.   15

The ambulance stops at a crossing, and a thin, pale man comes up
to the window. "Mother, I want to find work," he says.   16

"I don't know of any jobs," she says. "I have already told you I
can't help you."   17

"Please, Mother . . ."   18

The ambulance moves away from him.   19

"He has five children," Mother Theresa says, after a moment. "He
has t.b., and he can't do heavy manual work. People who can't do such
work are the hardest to find jobs for. We are treating him at our t.b. clinic.
We can do nothing more."   20

At the next crossing, a small boy with a sad, wasted face appears at
the open window and extends his hands in appeal to her. She crosses herself, opens the door, picks him up, and takes him into the ambulance. "He
needs food," she tells me, "and at the Shishu Bhavan we distribute relief
rations."   21

The Shishu Bhavan, like the convent, has a high wall with an iron
gate leading to a courtyard. But here, pressing against the gate, is a crowd
of anxious-looking women, some of them old but most of them young, and
all of them dressed in faded cotton saris, carrying cotton bags, and holding
folded yellow cards.   22

Pulling the boy by the hand, Mother Theresa goes into the crowd of
women, shouting, in Bengali, "Form a line! Form a line! Everyone will get
her ration, but you have to form a line first."   23

The women do not budge, so Mother Theresa, coaxing and prodding them, lines them up herself. They begin moving into the courtyard, past a model of a grotto, and onto a veranda, where several sisters are working around a barrel of grain, a barrel of powdered milk, some large gunnysacks filled with more grain, and a stack of cartons marked "Non-Fat Dry Milk—Donated by the People of the United States of America." As the line of women moves along, one sister scoops up portions of grain with a measure and transfers them to the women's cotton bags, another sister measures portions of powdered milk into polyethylene bags and hands them out, and other sisters replenish the stores of grain and milk in the barrels from the gunnysacks and cartons, and check and punch the ration cards. A girl of about ten stares, unsmiling and without comprehension, at the face of her ration card, on which is printed:

> Catholic Relief Services
> NCWC
> Food for Peace
> A Free Gift from the People of America
> Distributed by the Missionaries of Charity   24

Mother Theresa, after she has seen the boy from the ambulance receive his ration, strides into a little room off the veranda, where about twenty babies lie on small pallets and in basketlike wicker cribs. A plain-looking Indian nun, who wears glasses and has the cheerful manner of a primary-school teacher, is occupied in tending the babies. She is Sister Lourdes.   25

"Oh, Karuna, you are crying," Sister Lourdes says, bending over a baby. "You always cry whenever there are visitors and my back is turned. Oh, your diaper is wet." Sister Lourdes changes Karuna's diaper and then makes the rounds of the room, checking the diapers of the other babies.   26

Mother Theresa, kneeling on the floor and clapping her hands, calls, "Shiggri, shiggri, shiggri" ("shiggri" is Bengali for "quickly"), and two little boys about eighteen months old toddle up to her. "Say good morning," she says to them.   27

They burble.   28

"Oh, here is a bright fellow with a big grin," she says, picking up a third little boy, who looks about three and is dressed only in shorts. "Naughty, naughty, naughty William. He smiles the whole time, does nothing else." Turning to me, she says, "A few months ago, no one thought William would live, but now he has been adopted by the Belgian Consul. That means he has a monthly stipend of twenty-five rupees, and he'll be able to go to an English-speaking boarding school." She straightens an overturned chair and sits William down on it. "There! Now, William, you look like a sahib in your chair."   29

Mother Theresa goes over to a crib, lifts the arm of a baby, and admires a gold bangle on the arm, saying, almost to herself, "What a nice present from a visitor!" She moves across to another crib. "Here is a little foundling who was left in the compound of a church in Howrah," she says, chucking him under the chin. She goes from crib to crib. "This is Helen. This is Angeline. This is Josephine. This is Patricia. This is Agnes. This is another Agnes. This is Krishna." She turns to me suddenly and says, "I must talk to the sisters here about the funeral of the sister who died, but we will meet in a few minutes." She leaves, telling Sister Lourdes to take me through the rest of the Shishu Bhavan.   30

Sister Lourdes calls another sister to take charge of the nursery, and leads me back to the veranda, which is now occupied by children just finishing their lunch. "Besides the nice little nursery room, we have here a nice dormitory room for the young children and a nice big dormitory room for the big girls," Sister Lourdes says. "The big boys we send to a little Boys' Town that the Catholic Church runs in Gangarampur. We use this veranda for meals because we are short of space."   31

Moving around among the children, she shoos them all into a room crowded with beds for their afternoon rest, but the children all stretch out on the bare floor—some under the beds, some in a small open area at the far end of the room.   32

"They like the floor because it's cooler," Sister Lourdes says, and she conducts me into the dormitory for older girls. Some of the girls are in their teens, and others seem to be in their late twenties or early thirties. Many of them are obviously pregnant.   33

A girl in a printed sari, who has a round, expressionless face and paralyzed legs, drags herself across the floor. "This is Philu," Sister Lourdes says. "She has been with us for six years. She lost the use of her legs after a bad case of typhoid."   34

Back in the ambulance, Mother Theresa tells me that she is now going to the house in Moti Jheel Busti where she first started her work, and where she still has the original school, to take measurements for a new blackboard. "Ordinarily, we don't have special buildings for schools now," she says. "During the good season, we hold our classes under the trees, and during the monsoon we meet wherever we can find shelter."   35

At Moti Jheel Busti, the ambulance stops at the stagnant pond, and immediately a crowd of children collects and starts following Mother Theresa, calling "Hey, Sister!" or "Hey, Mother!" or "Hey, *mataji*!" A few grownups join the train, shouting *"Jesu pranam!"* (Bengali for "Praise be to Jesus!").   36

A fair-skinned man intercepts Mother Theresa. "We Anglo-Indians are scattered all over this *busti*," he says in a stutter, wheezing and coughing. "We would all like to live together, Mother."   37

"Your old nonsense again," she says, and adds firmly, "Go to the

sister at the mobile clinic across the way and ask her for cortisone for
your asthma. Go along."   38

The man shuffles away, muttering to himself.   39

With children still following us, we go down a narrow street to a small
brick building, pass through a wooden gate with a cross on it, walk across
a courtyard, and enter a sad-looking old house. The school consists of two
dark rooms, which have peeling walls, rows of low wooden benches, two
crèches, and a few nursery pictures. As Mother Theresa is taking the
measurements for the blackboard, an old man, extremely drunk and wearing only a *dhoti*, appears from somewhere, kneels down, and clutches her
legs. "Please forgive me for drinking, Mother," the old man says.   40

"Stop drinking," Mother Theresa says, without interrupting her work.   41

"I can't."   42

"Then I can't forgive you."   43

Back in the ambulance, Mother Theresa tells me that we are now
going to the Home for the Dying, which is near the Kali Temple. "When
we wanted to move the Home for the Dying out of Moti Jheel Busti, we
made a request to the Calcutta Corporation for new quarters," she says.
"They gave us a *dharamshala* [a shelter for travellers] that used to serve
as the overnight hostel for pilgrims to the Kali Temple, and we moved
there in 1954. The *dharamshala* had two halls, and we made one of them
into a dormitory for dying male street cases and the other into a dormitory
for dying female street cases. Some street cases are brought to the Home
for the Dying when they are nearly dead, and we can't do anything about
them—many are dead within a few minutes. Some street cases are too
old, too crippled, or too far gone with t.b. ever to leave the Home for the
Dying, and we go on nursing them until they die. But some street cases
can be helped to recover, with calcium and vitamin injections. In fact, out
of eighteen thousand five hundred street cases we've admitted to the
Home for the Dying so far, about ten thousand have got well enough to
leave."   44

"Do you follow these up after they leave you?" I ask.   45

"We try to keep an eye on them if they are not well when they leave,"
she says. "Because many of them would rather live in the streets and beg
than stay in the Home for the Dying, they go as soon as they can get up.
But many of them come back to the Home for the Dying to die."   46

The Home for the Dying is a one-story yellow house off a typical
Indian crossroads crowded with shops and pavement stalls. Two Indian
sisters come out to greet Mother Theresa. One is short and plump, with a
round face, and is dressed in the sari with blue edging. She is Sister
Barbara. The other is thin, dark, and small, and is dressed in the plain
white sari. She is Sister Lillian. "Our sisters always work in pairs," Mother
Theresa says to me. "In emergencies, two heads and four hands are better
than one head and two hands."   47

The entrance to the yellow house is marked by a signboard reading "Corporation of Calcutta Nirmal Hriday Home for Dying Destitutes," and by an elaborate framed scroll headed "Holy Father's Message to Mother Theresa." Inside is a large, austere hall with an overpowering rancid smell. On each side of a long central aisle is a low platform extending the entire length of the hall. On the platforms and in the aisle are low beds, set so close together that there is very little space to move among them. They have no bedclothes, and consist of narrow metal frames with mattresses sheathed in polyethylene. Stretched out on the mattresses are men of all ages, and boys as well, some of them disfigured, all of them wrinkled and thin and motionless, their bodies mere forms, their eyes fixed in expressionless stares.   48

Sister Barbara, Sister Lillian, and Mother Theresa walk through the hall, stopping at one bed or another to take a pulse or to straighten a head or a limb and place it in a more restful position. Mother Theresa moves around quickly and is methodical. Sister Barbara always has something cheerful to say, and she talks fast. Sister Lillian follows shyly, seldom speaking, but smiling continuously. None of the men in the beds, however, seem to take notice or register recognition, except for one man, who soundlessly sits up as they approach. He seems to be in his thirties, with a strong-looking body, but he has the same expressionless eyes. He soon falls back on the mattress.   49

"The Corporation ambulances bring in people who collapse on the street—street cases so hopeless that hospitals won't take them," Sister Barbara tells me. "At present, we have sixty-eight male street cases and seventy-four female street cases here. They have no known relatives, no shelter, no food. Most are cases of starvation; for the last six years things have been very bad. No one has died so far today, but you can never tell—someone may die at any moment. We try to make them as comfortable as possible. We make the beds very low, so that they can't hurt themselves if they fall out. They are so helpless."   50

We have reached the end of the hall, where there is a passageway, with more beds in it, holding more men. This leads into another hall, which is crowded with women, most of them almost naked. Their bodies are gaunt and their eyes wild and demented. Some of the women are sitting upright on their beds; others are lying down, crying and moaning. One woman, who is completely naked, begins to scream, and Mother Theresa rushes over and covers her with a towel.   51

"Once they get this sick, they have no strength even to move, yet they can scream," Mother Theresa says.   52

Back in the ambulance, as we are driving to one of the congregation's leper camps, at Dhapa, Mother Theresa talks about criticisms that are occasionally made of the work done by the Missionaries of Charity. It is said that their staff is medically untrained, though the major part of their work is with the sick; that their efforts are often restricted to the most extreme and dramatic cases, though they might do more to alleviate suffering if they helped care for people with more hope of living; and, in particular, that their work at the Home for the Dying does little more than prolong misery, for even when the people admitted there are nursed back to health, they are turned out to the streets to face the old problems of starvation and filth. Of these criticisms, Mother Theresa says that although the Missionaries of Charity may not have extensive medical training, their work gives relief to those who would otherwise have no relief; that although their work at the moment may be restricted, they are always trying to widen its scope; and that although their work at the Home for the Dying may be concentrated on medical attention, they do try, whenever they can, to effect rehabilitation of the street cases who get better. "We minister to all those with whom we come in contact," she says. "We turn away no one —we always try to make room for one more person in our homes and camps. For when we feed a hungry person, we feed Christ, and when we clothe a naked baby, we clothe Christ, and when we give a home to the homeless, we are giving shelter to Christ. When we know the poor, we love them, and when we love them, we serve them. There are more people here in Calcutta now who care about the poor and serve them than there were when we started. Our work would be impossible without these people. We say in the morning, 'Today we have no food for relief,' and that day some-one will bring us food. It's wonderful how it comes. Just yesterday, a Brahman gentleman died. He loved mangoes, and his daughter brought us crates of beautiful mangoes, and every child in the Shishu Bhavan had a mango. Two weeks ago, a few Hindu ladies got together and cooked rice and curry, which they took to a leper camp and fed to the lepers. We need warm hearts that will love and loving hands that will work."   53

We reach Dhapa. Large vultures with long, thin legs glide overhead. From the refuse dump, a rough, untarred road goes alongside a slaughter-house, where emaciated buffaloes are now being herded through a gate. A few yards beyond the slaughterhouse is a dirty river, which seems to have no flow at all. We cross the river over a small bridge, get out of the ambulance, and pick our way among puddles and stones on the slimy, uneven bank.   54

"The lepers have to live wherever they can," Mother Theresa says. "In the marshes, under the trees—wherever they can find a place. So far, we have not had the means to build a colony for them, but we have a mobile clinic where they can come for medicine and treatment, and at least once a week we call at different places. We began our work for the lepers because, like the dying, they couldn't get help anywhere. Everyone shrank from them."   55

Leprosy, which is caused by *Mycobacterium leprae,* and which takes cutaneous, tubercular, and neural forms, has such manifestations as depigmentation, lesions, ulceration, nodules, thickening of tissue, mutilation, loss of sensation, loss of sight, and impairment of speech. It disfigures the face and hands especially, and through the ages has therefore been associated with so-called "leonine" faces and "claw" hands. It is not known exactly how the disease is contracted, how it is transmitted, why only human beings seem to be susceptible to it, or whether there is any cure for it—though it can sometimes be arrested through hygiene, isolation, and medication. What is known is that the disease is fostered by malnutrition, filth, and squalor. In recent years, thanks to improved standards of sanitation, leprosy has practically disappeared from the richer countries of the West, but in poorer countries, especially in areas of Africa and Asia, it is chronic for as much as ten per cent of the population. In fact, leprosy is now associated almost exclusively with dark-skinned, poor people living in tropical climates.   56

I ask Mother Theresa how many lepers there are in the Calcutta area.   57

"No one knows," she replies. "But some say two or three hundred thousand."   58

Ahead is the camp. It consists of rows of huts of stone or clay built wall to wall and with low red tile roofs, like the houses in the *bustis*. Between the rows of huts are muddy lanes. Cows, dogs, and chickens are everywhere. The place swarms with flies, and overhead are the vultures. Scores of men, women, and children are out in the open—standing outside doorways, lying on *charpoys* in front of the huts, or squatting on the ground in the shade of a few trees. Most of the people are missing fingers or toes; some have lesions at the mouth and no noses.   59

"Everything takes shelter here," Mother Theresa says to me. "We get rid of the dogs one day and more come the next."   60

"Salaam!" and "*Jesu pranam!*" the people call out to Mother Theresa as she moves around among them. She goes from hut to hut, greeting them by name and asking questions, listening, giving advice about medicine, about diet, about keeping cows tethered. "So the medicine has brought your fever down, Das," she says to a man who has lost all his fingers. "That's good. I see your children are doing well, too. That's good."   61

She tells me as we walk toward a hut, "One trouble with these camps is that very sick cases are mixed with not-so-sick cases, and so we rented this hut to isolate the very, very sick."   62

"What about all of you who work here?" I ask. "Isn't it dangerous for you?"   63

"Up to now, thank God, nothing," she says. "But we have to be ready."   64

We go into the hut, which is a few feet square. A line, on which wet cloths hang, is strung across the room. On the floor are two *charpoys* and a mattress sheathed in polyethylene, with three badly mutilated men lying on them.   65

The man on the mattress is sobbing. "No amount of medicine helps!" he cries out, in a heavy, constricted voice.   66

"The pain will go away," Mother Theresa says, bending over him and feeling his forehead. She helps a sister give him a morphine injection.   67

When we are outside again, she says to me, "In the early stages, the disease is not so painful, but people at his stage are in terrible pain."   68

When she has gone around to all the huts and has started back to the ambulance, those who can walk follow her, entreating, pleading, and crying for more medicine and more food. Mother Theresa, as she walks on, keeps talking to them, saying "Yes," and "Tomorrow," and "I will try." She crosses herself continually.   69

The Whole Selection

1 Mother Theresa says: "But I would prefer it if we didn't talk about me— if you've heard about one of the Missionaries of Charity, you've heard about them all. I'd rather talk about our work, which is God's work." Does the author follow her advice? In what ways is this a narrative of Mother Theresa? In what ways is this the story of their work? How does the author manage to do both?

2 What is the purpose of including the incident given in paragraphs 16 through 20?

3 What do we learn of Mother Theresa's character from her dialogue?

4 What do we learn of her character from the various incidents in which she is involved?

5 From a narrative point of view, is there any design to the arrangement of the principal incidents of the story:
   A. The distribution of food
   B. The visit to the Children's Home
   C. The measuring of the blackboard
   D. The visit to the Home for the Dying
   E. The visit to the leper camp

6 Point out at least four instances where description is used to make the reader "see" and "feel" the situation.

7 What is the effect of the author's use of the present tense, not usual in this form of narrative writing ("We sit down . . ." "I ask her . . ." "We go into the hut . . .")?

8 "Understatement" best describes Mehta's style. Why is it particularly apt for this narrative? Study the narrative carefully to determine what devices he uses to achieve understatement.

9 Comment on the final paragraph as an apt ending for the narrative.

Gettysburg was one of the crucial battles of the Civil War. It has been written of extensively. The two views presented here are among the finest contemporary accounts. First Lieut. Frank A. Haskell, the participant, was a young Wisconsin attorney, a Union officer who played a distinguished personal part in repelling General Pickett's charge. He wrote his account of the battle a few weeks later while still impressed with the fever of those memorable days. Eleven months later, now a colonel, he was killed at Cold Harbor. The observer, Lieut. Colonel James Fremantle of the Coldstream Guards, spent a leave from the British army traveling through the Confederacy. Fremantle journeyed to the Confederacy at the period of its highest morale, just before Gettysburg. Haskell's personal account as a participant should be read in the light of Fremantle's account as an observer. There is the further contrast of Haskell's seeing the battle from the Union point of view and Fremantle from the Confederate point of view.

THE BATTLE OF GETTYSBURG: THE PARTICIPANT

FRANK A. HASKELL

There was a pause between the acts, with the curtain down, soon to rise upon the great final act, and catastrophe of Gettysburg. We have passed by the left of the Second Division, coming from the First; when we crossed the crest the enemy was not in sight, and all was still—we walked slowly along in the rear of the troops, by the ridge cut off now from a view of the enemy in his position, and were returning to the spot where we had left our horses. General Gibbon had just said that he inclined to the belief that the enemy was falling back, and that the cannonade was only one of his noisy modes of covering the movement. I said that I thought that fifteen minutes would show that, by all his bowling, the Rebel did not mean retreat. We were near our horses when we noticed Brigadier General Hunt, Chief of Artillery of the Army, near Woodruff's Battery, swiftly moving about on horseback, and apparently in a rapid manner giving some orders about the guns.[1] Thought we, what could this mean? In a moment after-wards we met Captain Wessels and the orderlies who had our horses; they were on foot leading the horses. Captain Wessels was pale, and he said, excited: "General, they say the enemy's infantry is advancing." We sprang into our saddles, a score of bounds brought us upon the all-seeing crest. To say that men grew pale and held their breath at what we and they there saw, would not be true. Might not six thousand men be brave and without shade of fear, and yet, before a hostile eighteen thousand, armed, and not five minutes' march away, turn ashy white?   1

None on that crest now need be told that *the enemy is advancing.* Every eye could see his legions, an overwhelming resistless tide of an ocean of armed men sweeping upon us! Regiment after regiment and bri-gade after brigade move from the woods and rapidly take their places in the lines forming the assault. Pickett's proud division, with some additional troops, hold their right; Pettigrew's (Worth's)[2] their left. The first line at short interval is followed by a second, and that a third succeeds; and columns between support the lines. More than half a mile their front extends; more than a thousand yards the dull gray masses deploy, man touching man, rank pressing rank, and line suporting line. The red flags wave, their horsemen gallop up and down; the arms of eighteen thousand men, barrel and bayonet, gleam in the sun, a sloping forest of flashing steel. Right on they move, as with one soul, in perfect order, without im-pediment of ditch, or wall or stream, over ridge and slope, through orchard and meadow, and cornfield, magnificent, grim, irresistible.   2

All was orderly and still upon our crest; no noise and no confusion. The men had little need of commands, for the survivors of a dozen battles knew well enough what this array in front portended, and, already in their places, they would be prepared to act when the right time should come. The click of the locks as each man raised the hammer to feel with his fingers that the cap was on the nipple; the sharp jar as a musket touched

---

[1] Brig. Gen. Henry J. Hunt, Meade's very able chief of artillery, tried to have the Union batteries withhold their fire during this bombardment in order to be ready for the infantry assault which was bound to follow it, but he was overruled by Hancock, who felt that the Federal infantry would stand the pounding better if they saw their own guns firing in reply. As a result, most of the Second Corps batteries had exhausted their long-range ammunition by the time Lee's infantry began its advance, and had to wait until the Con-federates came into canister range—roughly, 250 yards—before they could effectively get into action. Hunt wrote afterward that if his plan had been followed the Federal artillery would have broken Pickett's charge before it ever reached the Union lines. It should be added that Union artillery north and south of Hancock's sector did conserve its ammunition and gave Pickett's men a cruel hammering during their long advance from Seminary Ridge.

[2] The left of the Confederate column of assault was composed of the division of Maj. Gen. Henry B. Heth. He had been wounded, and his troops were led in this charge by Brig. Gen. Johnston Pettigrew. Incidentally, Haskell slightly overestimates the number of men involved. In all, about 15,000 men participated in the Confederate attack.

a stone upon the wall when thrust in aiming over it, and the clicking of the iron axles as the guns were rolled up by hand a little further to the front, were quite all the sounds that could be heard. Cap-boxes were slid around to the front of the body; cartridge boxes opened, officers opened their pistol-holsters. Such preparations, little more was needed. The trefoil flags,[3] colors of the brigades and divisions moved to their places in rear; but along the lines in front the grand old ensign that first waved in battle at Saratoga in 1777, and which these people coming would rob of half its stars, stood up, and the west wind kissed it as the sergeants sloped its lance towards the enemy. I believe that not one above whom it then waved but blessed his God that he was loyal to it, and whose heart did not swell with pride towards it, as the emblem of the Republic before that treason's flaunting rag in front.   3

General Gibbon rode down the lines, cool and calm, and in an unim-passioned voice he said to the men, "Do not hurry, men, and fire too fast, let them come up close before you fire, and then aim low and steadily." The coolness of their General was reflected in the faces of his men. Five minutes has elapsed since first the enemy have emerged from the woods —no great space of time surely, if measured by the usual standard by which men estimate duration—but it was long enough for us to note and weigh some of the elements of mighty moment that surrounded us; the disparity of numbers between the assailants and the assailed; that few as were our numbers we could not be supported or reinforced until support would not be needed or would be too late; that upon the ability of the two trefoil divisions to hold the crest and repel the assault depended not only their own safety or destruction, but also the honor of the Army of the Potomac and defeat or victory at Gettysburg. Should these advancing men pierce our line and become the entering wedge, driven home, that would sever our army asunder, what hope would there be afterwards, and where the blood-earned fruits of yesterday? It was long enough for the Rebel storm to drift across more than half the space that had at first separated us. None, or all, of these considerations either depressed or elevated us. They might have done the former, had we been timid; the latter had we been confident and vain. But, we were there waiting, and ready to do our duty—that done, results could not dishonor us.   4

Our skirmishers open a spattering fire along the front, and, fighting, retire upon the main line—the first drops, the heralds of the storm, sound-ing on our windows. Then the thunders of our guns, first Arnold's then

---

[3] The Second Corps insigne—worn on the cap, in the Civil War, instead of on the shoulder, as in modern practice—was the trefoil, the same device that identifies the club suit in a deck of cards. Men of the Second Corps, who thought quite well of themselves, used to boast that "Clubs are trumps!" Flags and cap patches in the First Division were red, in the Second Division white, and in the Third Division blue.

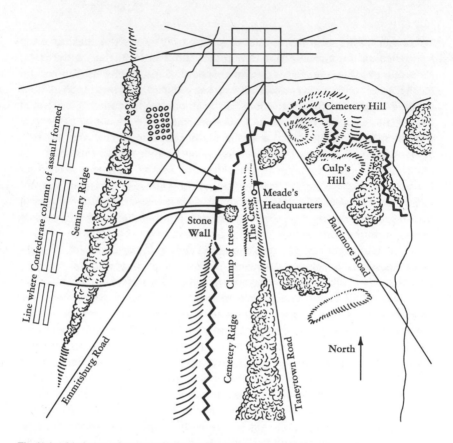

The Union Line along Cemetery Ridge on the afternoon of July 3.

The 15,000 Confederates in the attacking column formed on a broad front and consolidated into a powerful striking force as they crossed the Emmitsburg road and approached the stone wall, which was the part of the line where the blow fell. Driven from the wall at the points indicated by the arrows, some of the Unionists fell back a few yards to "the crest" mentioned by Haskell, and after a brief time drove the attackers back.

Cushing's and Woodruff's and the rest, shake and reverberate again through the air, and their sounding shells smite the enemy. The General said I had better go and tell General Meade of this advance. To gallop to General Meade's headquarters, to learn there that he had changed them to another part of the field, to dispatch to him by the Signal Corps in General Gibbon's name the message, "The enemy is advancing his infantry in force upon my front," and to be again upon the crest, were but the work of a minute. All our available guns are now active, and from the fire of shells, as the range grows shorter and shorter, they change to shrapnel, and from shrapnel to canister; but in spite of shells, and shrapnel and canister, without wavering or halt, the hardy lines of the enemy continue to move on. The Rebel guns make no reply to ours, and no charging shout rings out to-day, as is the Rebel wont; but the courage of these silent men amid our shots seems not to need the stimulus of other noise. The enemy's right flank sweeps near Stannard's bushy crest, and his concealed Vermonters rake it with a well-delivered fire of musketry. The gray lines do not halt or reply, but withdrawing a little from that extreme, they still move on.   5

And so across all that broad open ground they have come, nearer and nearer, nearly half the way, with our guns bellowing in their faces, until now a hundred yards, no more, divide our ready left from their advancing right. The eager men there are impatient to begin. Let them. First, Harrow's breastworks flame; then Hall's; then Webb's. As if our bullets were the fire coals that touched off their muskets, the enemy in front halts, and his countless level barrels blaze back upon us. The Second Division is struggling in battle. The rattling storm soon spreads to the right, and the blue trefoils are vieing with the white. All along each hostile front, a thousand yards, with narrowest space between, the volleys blaze and roll; as thick the sound as when a summer hail-storm pelts the city roofs; as thick the fire as when the incessant lightning fringes a summer cloud. When the Rebel infantry had opened fire our batteries soon became silent, and this without their fault, for they were foul by long previous use. They were the targets of the concentrated Rebel bullets, and some of them had expended all their canister. But they were not silent before Rorty was killed, Woodruff had fallen mortally wounded, and Cushing, firing almost his last canister, had dropped dead among his guns shot through the head by a bullet. The conflict is left to the infantry alone.   6

Unable to find my general when I had returned to the crest after transmitting his message to General Meade, and while riding in the search having witnessed the development of the fight, from the first fire upon the left by the main lines until all of the two divisions were furiously engaged, I gave up hunting as useless—I was convinced General Gibbon could not be on the field; I left him mounted; I could easily have found him now had he so remained—but now, save myself, there was not a mounted officer near the engaged lines—and was riding towards the right of the Second Division, with purpose to stop there, as the most eligible position to watch the further progress of the battle, there to be ready to take part according to my own notions whenever and wherever occasion was presented. The conflict was tremendous, but I had seen no wavering in all our line.   7

Wondering how long the Rebel ranks, deep though they were, could stand our sheltered volleys, I had come near my destination, when—great heaven! were my senses mad? The larger portion of Webb's brigade—my God, it was true—there by the group of trees and the angles of the wall, was breaking from the cover of their works, and, without orders or reason, with no hand lifted to check them, was falling back, a fear-stricken flock of confusion! The fate of Gettysburg hung upon a spider's single thread! A

great magnificent passion came on me at the instant, not one that over-
powers and confounds, but one that blanches the face and sublimes every
sense and faculty. My sword, that had always hung idle by my side, the
sign of rank only in every battle, I drew, bright and gleaming, the symbol
of command. Was that not a fit occasion, and these fugitives the men on
whom to try the temper of the Solinzen steel? All rules and proprieties
were forgotten; all considerations of person, and danger and safety
despised; for, as I met the tide of these rabbits, the damned red flags of
the rebellion began to thicken and flaunt along the wall they had just
deserted, and one was already wavering over one of the guns of the dead
Cushing. I ordered these men to "halt," and "face about" and "fire," and
they heard my voice and gathered my meaning, and obeyed my commands.
On some unpatriotic backs of those not quick of comprehension, the flat of
my sabre fell not lightly, and at its touch their love of country returned,
and, with a look at me as if I were the destroying angel, as I might have
become theirs, they again faced the enemy.[4] General Webb soon came to
my assistance. He was on foot, but he was active, and did all that one
could do to repair the breach, or to avert its calamity. The men that had
fallen back, facing the enemy, soon regained confidence in themselves, and
became steady.   8

This portion of the wall was lost to us, and the enemy had gained
the cover of the reverse side, where he now stormed with fire. But Webb's
men, with their bodies in part protected by the abruptness of the crest,
now sent back in the enemies' faces as fierce a storm. Some scores of
venturesome Rebels, that in their first push at the wall had dared to cross
at the further angle, and those that had desecrated Cushing's guns were
promptly shot down, and speedy death met him who should raise his body
to cross it again. At this point little could be seen of the enemy, by reason
of his cover and the smoke, except the flash of his muskets and his waving
flags. These red flags were accumulating at the wall every moment, and

---

[4] It was this part of Haskell's narrative that drew down upon him, years afterward, the
distilled wrath of the survivors of Webb's brigade——the Philadelphia Brigade, as it was
called, because its regiments had been recruited in and around Philadelphia. In a
pamphlet published in 1910 these survivors took after Haskell with all the fury of old
soldiers who feel that their good name has been impugned, and they produced one of the
most sprightly polemics in Civil War literature. They denied that they ever broke and
ran, denied that Haskell or anyone else had to rally them, and suggested that the men
Haskell took for Federal fugitives were actually disarmed Confederate captives making
their way to the Federal rear.
        It is probable that Haskell slightly overstated the extent of the rout. In his report on
Gettysburg, Hancock remarked that "when the enemy's line had nearly reached the stone
wall . . . the most of that part of Webb's brigade posted here abandoned their position,
but fortunately did not retreat entirely." Gibbon's report said that "Webb's line of three
small regiments was overwhelmed and driven back." Brig. Gen. Alexander S. Webb
reported that "the enemy advanced steadily to the fence, driving out a portion of the
71st Pennsylvania Volunteers." He added that "the 69th Pennsylvania Volunteers, and
most of the 71st Pennsylvania Volunteers, even after the enemy were in their rear, held
their position," and he concluded with the flat statement: "The conduct of this brigade
was most satisfactory. Officers and men did their whole duty."

they maddened us as the same color does the bull. Webb's men are falling fast, and he is among them to direct and to encourage; but, however well they may now do, with that walled enemy in front, with more than a dozen flags to Webb's three, it soon becomes apparent that in not many minutes they will be overpowered, or that there will be none alive for the enemy to overpower. Webb has but three regiments, all small, the 69th, 71st and 72d Pennsylvania—the 106th Pennsylvania, except two companies, is not here to-day—and he must have speedy assistance, or this crest will be lost.   9

Oh, where is Gibbon? where is Hancock?—some general—anybody with the power and the will to support that wasting, melting line? No general came, and no succor! I thought of Hays upon the right, but from the smoke and war along his front, it was evident that he had enough upon his hands, if he stayed the in-rolling tide of the Rebels there. Double-day upon the left was too far off and too slow, and on another occasion I had begged him to send his idle regiments to support another line battling with thrice its numbers, and this "Old Sumpter Hero" had declined.[5] At a last resort I resolved to see if Hall and Harrow could not send some of their commands to reinforce Webb. I galloped to the left in the execution of my purpose, and as I attained the rear of Hall's line, from the nature of the ground and the position of the enemy it was easy to discover the reason and the manner of this gathering of Rebel flags in front of Webb. The enemy, emboldened by his success in gaining our line by the group of trees and the angle of the wall, was concentrating all his right against and was further pressing that point. There was the stress of his assault; there would he drive his fiery wedge to split our line.   10

In front of Harrows' and Hall's Brigades he had been able to advance no nearer than when he first halted to deliver fire, and these commands had not yielded an inch. To effect the concentration before Webb, the enemy would march the regiment on his extreme right of each of his lines by the left flank to the rear of the troops, still halted and facing to the front, and so continuing to draw in his right, when they were all massed in the position desired, he would again face them to the front, and advance to the storming. This was the way he made the wall before Webb's line

[5] Haskell obviously had a low opinion of Maj. Gen. Abner Doubleday, who had been a member of the original garrison at Fort Sumter (which Haskell, like many others in that day, consistently misspelled "Sumpter"). His assertion that Doubleday on an earlier occasion had refused to send help may refer to the Battle of Antietam, in which Gibbon's brigade was very heavily engaged, with severe losses. In that fight Doubleday had succeeded to the command of the division in which Gibbon's brigade belonged, and Haskell seems to have blamed him for Gibbon's inability to get reinforcements. It might be noted that at Gettysburg, when Reynolds was killed, Doubleday took over command of the First Corps by right of seniority but that Meade refused to let him retain the command; while the battle was still being fought Meade detached Maj. Gen. John Newton from command of a division in the Sixth Corps and sent him over to replace Doubleday as head of the First Corps. The Hays Haskell mentions was Brig. Gen. Alexander Hays, commander of the 3rd division of the Second Corps.

blaze red with his battle flags, and such was the purpose there of his thick-crowding battalions.   11

Not a moment must be lost. Colonel Hall I found just in rear of his line, sword in hand, cool, vigilant, noting all that passed and directing the battle of his brigade. The fire was constantly diminishing now in his front, in the manner and by the movement of the enemy that I have mentioned, drifting to the right. "How is it going?" Colonel Hall asked me, as I rode up. "Well, but Webb is hotly pressed and must have support, or he will be overpowered. Can you assist him?" "Yes." "You cannot be too quick." "I will move my brigade at once." "Good." He gave the order, and in briefest time I saw five friendly colors hurrying to the aid of the imperilled three; and each color represented true, battle-tried men, that had not turned back from Rebel fire that day nor yesterday, though their ranks were sadly thinned. To Webb's brigade, pressed back as it had been from the wall, the distance was not great from Hall's right. The regiments marched by the right flank. Col. Hall superintended the movement in person. Col. Devereux coolly commanded the 19th Massachusetts. His major, Rice, had already been wounded and carried off. Lieut. Col. Macy, of the 20th Mass., had just had his left hand shot off, and so Capt. Abbott gallantly led over this fine regiment. The 42d New York followed their excellent Colonel Mallon. Lieut. Col. Steele, 7th Mich., had just been killed, and his regiment, and the handful of the 59th N. Y., followed their colors. The movement, as it did, attracting the enemy's fire, and executed in haste, as it must be, was difficult; but in reasonable time, and in order that is serviceable, if not regular, Hall's men are fighting gallantly side by side with Webb's before the all important point. I did not stop to see all this movement of Hall's, but from him I went at once further to the left, to the 1st brigade. Gen. Harrow I did not see, but his fighting men would answer my purpose as well.[6] The 19th Me., the 15th Mass., the 32d N. Y. and the shattered old thunderbolt, the 1st Minn.—poor Farrell was dying then upon the ground where he had fallen,—all men that I could find I took over to the right at the *double quick.*   12

As we were moving to, and near the other brigade of the division, from my position on horseback I could see that the enemy's right, under Hall's fire, was beginning to stagger and to break. "See," I said to the men, "See the *chivalry!* See the gray-backs run!" The men saw, and as they swept to their places by the side of Hall and opened fire, they roared, and this in a manner that said more plainly than words—for the deaf could have seen it in their faces, and the blind could have heard it in their voices—*the crest is safe!*   13

[6] Brig. Gen. William Harrow commanded the first brigade of Gibbon's division; when Gibbon took temporary command of the Second Corps—and later, when he was wounded —Harrow took over divisional command. If Haskell did not see Harrow, Harrow at least saw Haskell. In his report on the battle Harrow wrote that "Lieut. Haskell greatly distinguished himself by his constant exertion in the most exposed places."

The whole Division concentrated, and changes of position, and new phases, as well on our part as on that of the enemy, having as indicated occurred, for the purpose of showing the exact present posture of affairs, some further description is necessary. Before the 2d Division the enemy is massed, the main bulk of his force covered by the ground that slopes to his rear, with his front at the stone wall. Between his front and us extends the very apex of the crest. All there are left of the White Trefoil Division— yesterday morning there were three thousand eight hundred, this morning there were less than three thousand—at this moment there are somewhat over two thousand;—twelve regiments in three brigades are below or be- hind the crest, in such a position that by the exposure of the head and upper part of the body above the crest they can deliver their fire in the enemy's faces along the top of the wall. By reason of the disorganization incidental in Webb's brigade to his men's having broken and fallen back, as mentioned, in the two other brigades to their rapid and difficult change of position under fire, and in all the division in part to severe and con- tinuous battle, formation of companies and regiments in regular ranks is lost; but commands, companies, regiments and brigades are blended and intermixed—an irregular extended mass—men enough, if in order, to form a line of four or five ranks along the whole front of the division. The twelve flags of the regiments wave defiantly at intervals along the front; at the stone wall, at unequal distances from ours of forty, fifty or sixty yards, stream nearly double this number of the battle flags of the enemy. These changes accomplished on either side, and the concentration complete, although no cessation or abatement in the general din of conflict since the commencement had at any time been appreciable, now it was as if a new battle, deadlier, stormier than before, had sprung from the body of the old—a young Phoenix of combat, whose eyes stream lightning, shaking his arrowy wings over the yet glowing ashes of his progenitor.   14

The jostling, swaying lines on either side boil, and roar, and dash their flamy spray, two hostile billows of a fiery ocean. Thick flashes stream from the wall, thick volleys answer from the crest. No threats or expostula- tion now, only example and encouragement. All depths of passion are stirred, and all combatives fire, down to their deep foundations. Individual- ity is drowned in a sea of clamor, and timid men, breathing the breath of the multitude, are brave. The frequent dead and wounded lie where they stagger and fall—there is no humanity for them now, and none can be spared to care for them. The men do not cheer or shout; they growl, and over that uneasy sea, heard with the roar of musketry, sweeps the muttered thunder of a storm of growls. Webb, Hall, Devereux, Mallon, Abbott among the men where all are heroes, are doing deeds of note. Now the loyal wave rolls up as if it would over-leap its barrier, the crest. Pistols flash with the muskets. My "Forward to the wall" is answered by the Rebel counter- command, "Steady, men!" and the wave swings back. Again it surges, and

again it sinks. These men of Pennsylvania, on the soil of their own home-
steads, the first and only to flee the wall, must be the first to storm it.   15

"Major—, *lead* your men over the crest, they will follow." "By the
tactics I understand my place is in rear of the men." "Your pardon, sir; I
see *your* place is in rear of the men. I thought you were fit to lead." "Capt.
Sapler, come on with your men." "Let me first stop this fire in the rear, or
we shall be hit by our own men." "Never mind the fire in the rear; let us
take care of this in front first." "Sergeant, forward with your color. Let the
Rebels see it close to their eyes once before they die." The color sergeant
of the 72d Pa., grasping the stump of the severed lance in both his hands,
waved the flag above his head and rushed towards the wall. "Will you see
your color storm the wall alone?" One man only starts to follow. Almost
half way to the wall, down go color bearer and color to the ground—the
gallant sergeant is dead. The line springs—the crest of the solid ground
with a great roar heaves forward its maddened load, men, arms, smoke,
fire, a fighting mass. It rolls to the wall—flash meets flash, the wall is
crossed—a moment ensues of thrusts, yells, blows, shots, and undistin-
guishable conflict, followed by a shout universal that makes the welkin
ring again, and the last and bloodiest fight of the great battle of Gettysburg is ended and won.   16

Many things cannot be described by pen or pencil—such a fight is
one. Some hints and incidents may be given, but a description or picture
never. From what is told the imagination may for itself construct the scene;
otherwise he who never saw can have no adequate idea of what such a
battle is.   17

When the vortex of battle passion had subsided, hopes, fears, rage,
joy, of which the maddest and the noisiest was the last, and we were calm
enough to look about us, we saw that, as with us, the fight with the Third
Division was ended, and that in that division was a repetition of the scenes
immediately about us. In that moment the judgment almost refused to
credit the senses. Are these abject wretches about us, whom our men are
now disarming and driving together in flocks, the jaunty men of Pickett's
Division, whose steady lines and flashing arms but a few moments since
came sweeping up the slope to destroy us? Are these red cloths that our
men toss about in derision the "fiery Southern crosses," thrice ardent, the
battle flags of the rebellion that waved defiance at the wall? We know, but
so sudden has been the transition, we yet can scarce believe.   18

Just as the fight was over, and the first outburst of victory had a
little subsided, when all in front of the crest was noise and confusion—
prisoners being collected, small parties in pursuit of them far down into
the fields, flags waving, officers giving quick, sharp commands to their
men—I stood apart for a few moments upon the crest, by that group of
trees which ought to be historic forever, a spectator of the thrilling scene
around. Some few musket shots were still heard in the Third Division; and

the enemy's guns, almost silent since the advance of his infantry until the moment of his defeat, were dropping a few sullen shells among friend and foe upon the crest. Rebellion fosters such humanity. Near me, saddest sight of the many of such a field and not in keeping with all this noise, were mingled alone the thick dead of Maine and Minnesota, and Michigan and Massachusetts, and the Empire and Keystone States, who, not yet cold, with the blood still oozing from their death-wounds, had given their lives to the country upon that stormy field.   19

So mingled upon that crest let their honored graves be. Look with me about us. These dead have been avenged already. Where the long lines of the enemy's thousands so proudly advanced, see how thick the silent men of gray are scattered. It is not an hour since these legions were sweeping along so grandly; now sixteen hundred of that fiery mass are strewn among the trampled grass, dead as the clods they load; more than seven thousand, probably eight thousand, are wounded, some there with the dead, in our hands, some fugitive far towards the woods, among them Generals Pettigrew, Garnett, Kemper, and Armistead, the last three mortally, and the last one in our hands. "Tell General Hancock," he said to Lieutenant Mitchell, Hancock's aid-de-camp, to whom he handed his watch, "that I know I did my country a great wrong when I took up arms against her, for which I am sorry, but for which I cannot live to atone."[7] Four thousand, not wounded, are prisoners of war. More in number of the captured than the captors. Our men are still "gathering them in." Some hold up their hands or a handkerchief in sign of submission; some have hugged the ground to escape our bullets and so are taken; few made resistance after the first moment of our crossing the wall; some yield submissively with good grace, some with grim, dogged aspect, showing that but for the other alternative they could not submit to this. Colonels, and all less grades of officers, in the usual proportion are among them, and all are being stripped of their arms. Such of them as escaped wounds and capture are fleeing routed and panic stricken, and disappearing in the woods. Small arms, more thousands than we can count, are in our hands, scattered over the field. And these defiant battle-flags, some inscribed with "First Manassas," the numerous battles of the Peninsula, "Second Manassas," "South Mountain," "Sharpsburg" (our Antietam), "Fredericksburg," "Chancellorsville," and many more names, our men have, and are showing about, *over thirty of them.*   20

Such was really the closing scene of the grand drama of Gettysburg. 21

---

[7] Brig. Gen. Lewis A. Armistead, commanding a brigade in Pickett's division, had been a close friend of Hancock before the war, and the two exchanged emotional goodbyes at a farewell party at an army post in California in the spring of 1861, when Armistead and other Southern officers resigned their commissions in order to serve with the Confederacy. Armistead died among Cushing's guns at the point where Pickett's men briefly broke the Union line, and his last thought apparently was of Hancock, who commanded the troops he was attacking.

THE BATTLE OF GETTYSBURG: THE OBSERVER

JAMES FREMANTLE

1st July (Wednesday)—We did not leave our camp till noon, as nearly all General Hill's corps had to pass our quarters on its march towards Gettysburg. One division of Ewell's also had to join in a little beyond Greenwood, and Longstreet's corps had to bring up the rear.   1

During the morning I made the acquaintance of Colonel Walton, who used to command the well-known Washington Artillery, but he is now chief of artillery to Longstreet's *corps d'armée*. He is a big man, *ci-devant* auctioneer in New Orleans, and I understand he pines to return to his hammer.   2

Soon after starting we got into a pass in the South Mountain, a continuation, I believe, of the Blue Ridge range, which is broken by the Potomac at Harpers Ferry. The scenery through the pass is very fine. The first troops, alongside of whom we rode, belonged to Johnson's division of Ewell's corps. Among them I saw, for the first time, the celebrated "Stonewall" Brigade, formerly commanded by Jackson. In appearance the men differ little from other Confederate soldiers, except, perhaps, that the brigade contains more elderly men and fewer boys. All (except, I think, one regiment) are Virginians.   3

As they have nearly always been on detached duty, few of them knew General Longstreet, except by reputation. Numbers of them asked me whether the general in front was Longstreet; and when I answered in the affirmative, many would run on a hundred yards in order to take a good look at him. This I take to be an immense compliment from any soldier on a long march.   4

At 2 P. M. firing became distinctly audible in our front, but although it increased as we progressed, it did not seem to be very heavy.   5

A spy who was with us insisted upon there being "a pretty tidy bunch of *blue-bellies* in or near Gettysburg," and he declared that he was in their society three days ago.   6

After passing Johnson's division, we came up to a Florida brigade, which is now in Hill's corps; but as it had formerly served under Longstreet, the men knew him well. Some of them (after the General had passed) called out to their comrades, "Look out for work now, boys, for here's the old bulldog again."   7

At 3 P. M. we began to meet wounded men coming to the rear, and the number of these soon increased most rapidly, some hobbling alone, others on stretchers carried by the ambulance corps, and others in the ambulance wagons. Many of the latter were stripped nearly naked, and displayed very bad wounds. This spectacle, so revolting to a person unaccustomed to such sights, produced no impression whatever upon the advancing troops, who certainly go under fire with the most perfect non-chalance. They show no enthusiasm or excitement, but the most complete indifference. This is the effect of two years' almost uninterrupted fighting. 8

We now began to meet Yankee prisoners coming to the rear in considerable numbers. Many of them were wounded, but they seemed already to be on excellent terms with their captors, with whom they had commenced swapping canteens, tobacco, &c. Among them was a Pennsylvania colonel, a miserable object from a wound in his face. In answer to a question, I heard one of them remark, with a laugh, "We're pretty nigh whipped already." We next came to a Confederate soldier carrying a Yankee color, belonging, I think, to a Pennsylvania regiment, which he told us he had just captured. 9

At 4:30 P. M. we came in sight of Gettysburg, and joined General Lee and General Hill, who were on the top of one of the ridges which form the peculiar feature of the country round Gettysburg. We could see the enemy retreating up one of the opposite ridges, pursued by the Confederates with loud yells. The position into which the enemy had been driven was evidently a strong one. His right appeared to rest on a cemetery, on the top of a high ridge to the right of Gettysburg, as we looked at it. 10

General Hill now came up and told me he had been very unwell all day, and in fact he looks very delicate. He said he had had two of his divisions engaged, and had driven the enemy four miles into his present position, capturing a great many prisoners, some cannon, and some colors. He said, however, that the Yankees had fought with a determination unusual to them. He pointed out a railway cutting, in which they had made a good stand; also, a field in the center of which he had seen a man plant the regimental color, round which the regiment had fought for some time with much obstinacy, and when at last it was obliged to retreat, the color-bearer retired last of all, turning round every now and then to shake his fist, at the advancing Rebels. General Hill said he felt quite sorry when he saw this gallant Yankee meet his doom. 11

General Ewell had come up at 3:30, on the enemy's right (with part of his corps), and completed his discomfiture. General Reynolds, one of the best Yankee generals, was reported killed. Whilst we were talking, a message arrived from General Ewell, requesting Hill to press the enemy in the front, whilst he performed the same operation on his right. The pressure was accordingly applied in a mild degree, but the enemy were too strongly posted, and it was too late in the evening for a regular attack. 12

The town of Gettysburg was now occupied by Ewell, and was full of Yankee dead and wounded. I climbed up a tree in the most commanding place I could find, and could form a pretty good general idea of the enemy's position, although the tops of the ridges being covered with pine woods, it was very difficult to see anything of the troops concealed in them. 13

The firing ceased about dark, at which time I rode back with General

Longstreet and his staff to his headquarters at Cashtown, a little village eight miles from Gettysburg. At that time troops were pouring along the road, and were being marched towards the position they are to occupy tomorrow.   14

In the fight today nearly 6000 prisoners had been taken, and 10 guns. About 20,000 men must have been on the field on the Confederate side. The enemy had two *corps d'armée* engaged. All the prisoners belong, I think, to the 1st and 11th corps. This day's work is called a "brisk little scurry," and all anticipate a "big battle" tomorrow.   15

I observed that the artillerymen in charge of the horses dig themselves little holes like graves, throwing up the earth at the upper end. They ensconce themselves in these holes when under fire.   16

At supper this evening, General Longstreet spoke of the enemy's position as being "very formidable." He also said that they would doubtless intrench themselves strongly during the night. The staff officers spoke of the battle as a certainty, and the universal feeling in the army was one of profound contempt for an enemy whom they have beaten so constantly, and under so many disadvantages.   17

2d July (Thursday)—We all got up at 3:30 A. M., and breakfasted a little before daylight. Lawley insisted on riding, notwithstanding his illness. Captain ――― and I were in a dilemma for horses; but I was accommodated by Major Clark (of this staff), whilst the stout Austrian was mounted by Major Walton. The Austrian, in spite of the early hour, had shaved his cheeks and *ciréd* his mustaches as beautifully as if he was on parade at Vienna.   18

Colonel Sorrell, the Austrian, and I arrived at 5 A. M. at the same commanding position we were on yesterday, and I climbed up a tree in company with Captain Schreibert of the Prussian Army. Just below us were seated Generals Lee, Hill, Longstreet, and Hood, in consultation—the two latter assisting their deliberations by the truly American custom of *whittling* sticks. General Heth was also present; he was wounded in the head yesterday, and although not allowed to command his brigade, he insists upon coming to the field.   19

At 7 A. M. I rode over part of the ground with General Longstreet, and saw him disposing of M'Laws's division for today's fight. The enemy occupied a series of high ridges, the tops of which were covered with trees, but the intervening valleys between their ridges and ours were mostly open, and partly under cultivation. The cemetery was on their right, and their left appeared to rest upon a high rocky hill. The enemy's forces, which were now supposed to comprise nearly the whole Potomac army, were concentrated into a space apparently not more than a couple of miles in length. 20

The Confederates inclosed them in a sort of semicircle, and the extreme extent of our position must have been from five to six miles at least.

Ewell was on our left, his headquarters in a church (with a high cupola) at Gettsyburg; Hill in the center; and Longstreet on the right. Our ridges were also covered with pine woods at the tops, and generally on the rear slopes. 21

The artillery of both sides confronted each other at the edges of these belts of trees, the troops being completely hidden. The enemy was evidently intrenched, but the Southerners had not broken ground at all. A dead silence reigned till 4:45 P. M., and no one would have imagined that such masses of men and such a powerful artillery were about to commence the work of destruction at that hour. 22

Only two divisions of Longstreet were present today—M'Laws's and Hood's—Pickett being still in the rear. As the whole morning was evidently to be occupied in disposing the troops for the attack, I rode to the extreme right with Colonel Manning and Major Walton, where we ate quantities of cherries and got a feed of corn for our horses. We also bathed in a small stream, but not without some trepidation on my part, for we were almost beyond the lines, and were exposed to the enemy's cavalry. 23

At 1 P. M. I met a quantity of Yankee prisoners who had been picked up straggling. They told me they belonged to Sickles's corps (3d, I think), and had arrived from Emmetsburg during the night. About this time skirmishing began along part of the line, but not heavily. 24

At 2 P. M. General Longstreet advised me, if I wished to have a good view of the battle, to return to my tree of yesterday. I did so, and remained there with Lawley and Captain Schreibert during the rest of the afternoon. But until 4:45 P. M. all was profoundly still, and we began to doubt whether a fight was coming off today at all. 25

At that time, however, Longstreet suddenly commenced a heavy cannonade on the right. Ewell immediately took it up on the left. The enemy replied with at least equal fury, and in a few moments the firing along the whole line was as heavy as it is possible to conceive. A dense smoke arose for six miles. There was little wind to drive it away, and the air seemed full of shells—each of which appeared to have a different style of going, and to make a different noise from the others. The ordnance on both sides is of a very varied description. 26

Every now and then a caisson would blow up—if a Federal one, a Confederate yell would immediately follow. The Southern troops, when charging, or to express their delight, always yell in a manner peculiar to themselves. The Yankee cheer is much more like ours; but the Confederate officers declare that the Rebel yell has a particular merit, and always produces a salutary and useful effect upon their adversaries. A corps is sometimes spoken of as a "good yelling regiment." 27

As soon as the firing began, General Lee joined Hill just below our tree, and he remained there nearly all the time, looking through his field-glass—sometimes talking to Hill and sometimes to Colonel Long of his staff. But generally he sat quite alone on the stump of a tree. What I remarked especially was, that during the whole time the firing continued, he only sent one message, and only received one report. It is evidently his system to arrange the plan thoroughly with the three corps commanders, and then leave to them the duty of modifying and carrying it out to the best of their abilities.   28

When the cannonade was at its height, a Confederate band of music, between the cemetery and ourselves, began to play polkas and waltzes, which sounded very curious, accompanied by the hissing and bursting of the shells.   29

At 5:45 all became comparatively quiet on our left and in the cemetery; but volleys of musketry on the right told us that Longstreet's infantry were advancing, and the onward progress of the smoke showed that he was progressing favorably. About 6:30 there seemed to be a check, and even a slight retrograde movement. Soon after 7, General Lee got a report by signal from Longstreet to say "We are doing well."   30

A little before dark the firing dropped off in every direction, and soon ceased altogether. We then received intelligence that Longstreet had carried everything before him for some time, capturing several batteries, and driving the enemy from his positions; but when Hill's Florida brigade and some other troops gave way, he was forced to abandon a small portion of the ground he had won, together with all the captured guns, except three. His troops, however, bivouacked during the night on ground occupied by the enemy this morning.   31

Everyone deplores that Longstreet *will* expose himself in such a reckless manner. Today he led a Georgian regiment in a charge against a battery, hat in hand, and in front of everybody. General Barksdale was killed and Semmes mortally wounded; but the most serious loss was that of General Hood, who was badly wounded in the arm early in the day. I heard that his Texans are in despair. Lawley and I rode back to the General's camp, which had been moved to within a mile of the scene of action. Longstreet, however, with most of his staff, bivouacked on the field.   32

Major Fairfax arrived at about 10 P. M. in a very bad humor. He had under his charge about 1000 to 1500 Yankee prisoners who had been taken today; among them a general, whom I heard one of his men accusing of having been "so G—d d—d drunk that he had turned his guns upon his own men." But, on the other hand, the accuser was such a thundering blackguard, and proposed taking such a variety of oaths in order to escape from the U. S. Army, that he is not worthy of much credit. A large train of horses and mules, &c., arrived today, sent in by General Stuart, and captured, it is understood, by his cavalry, which had penetrated to within 6 miles of Washington.   33

3d July (Friday)—At 6 A. M. I rode to the field with Colonel Manning, and went over that portion of the ground which, after a fierce contest, had been won from the enemy yesterday evening. The dead were being buried, but great numbers were still lying about; also many mortally wounded, for whom nothing could be done. Amongst the latter were a number of Yankees dressed in bad imitations of the Zouave costume. They opened their glazed eyes, as I rode past, in a painfully imploring manner.   34

We joined Generals Lee and Longstreet's staff. They were reconnoitering and making preparations for renewing the attack. As we formed a pretty large party, we often drew upon ourselves the attention of the hostile sharpshooters, and were two or three times favored with a shell. One of these shells set a brick building on fire which was situated between the lines. This building was filled with wounded, principally Yankees, who, I am afraid, must have perished miserably in the flames. Colonel Sorrell had been slightly wounded yesterday, but still did duty. Major Walton's horse was killed, but there were no other casualties amongst my particular friends.   35

The plan of yesterday's attack seems to have been very simple—first a heavy cannonade all along the line, followed by an advance of Longstreet's two divisions and part of Hill's corps. In consequence of the enemy's having been driven back some distance, Longstreet's corps (part of it) was in a much more forward situation than yesterday. But the range of heights to be gained was still most formidable, and evidently strongly intrenched.   36

The distance between the Confederate guns and the Yankee position—i. e., between the woods crowning the opposite ridges—was at least a mile—quite open, gently undulating, and exposed to artillery the whole distance. This was the ground which had to be crossed in today's attack. Pickett's division, which had just come up, was to bear the brunt in Longstreet's attack, together with Heth and Pettigrew in Hill's corps. Pickett's division was a weak one (under 5000), owing to the absence of two brigades.   37

At noon all Longstreet's dispositions were made. His troops for attack were deployed into line, and lying down in the woods; his batteries were ready to open. The general then dismounted and went to sleep for a short time. The Austrian officer and I now rode off to get, if possible, into some commanding position from whence we could see the whole thing without being exposed to the tremendous fire which was about to commence. After riding about for half an hour without being able to discover so desirable a situation, we determined to make for the cupola, near Gettysburg, Ewell's headquarters. Just before we reached the entrance to the town, the cannonade opened with a fury which surpassed even that of yesterday.   38

Soon after passing through the toll gate at the entrance of Gettysburg, we found that we had got into a heavy cross fire; shells both Federal and Confederate passing over our heads with great frequency. At length two shrapnel shells burst quite close to us, and a ball from one of them hit the officer who was conducting us. We then turned round and changed our views with regard to the cupola—the fire of one side being bad enough, but preferable to that of both sides. A small boy of twelve years was riding with us at the time. This urchin took a diabolical interest in the bursting of the shells, and screamed with delight when he saw them take effect. I never saw this boy again, or found out who he was.   39

The road at Gettysburg was lined with Yankee dead, and as they had been killed on the 1st, the poor fellows had already begun to be very offensive. We then returned to the hill I was on yesterday. But finding that, to see the actual fighting, it was absolutely necessary to go into the thick of the thing, I determined to make my way to General Longstreet. It was then about 2:30. After passing General Lee and his staff, I rode on through the woods in the direction in which I had left Longstreet.   40

I soon began to meet many wounded men returning from the front. Many of them asked in piteous tones the way to a doctor or an ambulance. The further I got, the greater became the number of the wounded. At last I came to a perfect stream of them flocking through the woods in numbers as great as the crowd in Oxford Street in the middle of the day. Some were walking alone on crutches composed of two rifles, others were supported by men less badly wounded than themselves, and others were carried on stretchers by the ambulance corps; but in no case did I see a sound man helping the wounded to the rear, unless he carried the red badge of the ambulance corps. They were still under a heavy fire; the shells were continually bringing down great limbs of trees, and carrying further destruction amongst this melancholy procession.   41

I saw all this in much less time than it takes to write it, and although astonished to meet such vast numbers of wounded, I had not seen *enough* to give me any idea of the real extent of the mischief.   42

When I got close up to General Longstreet, I saw one of his regiments advancing through the woods in good order; so, thinking I was just in time to see the attack, I remarked to the General that "I wouldn't have missed this for anything." Longstreet was seated at the top of a snake fence at the edge of the wood, and looking perfectly calm and imperturbed. He replied, laughing, "The devil you wouldn't! I would like to have missed it very much; we've attacked and been repulsed: look there!"   43

For the first time I then had a view of the open space between the two positions, and saw it covered with Confederates slowly and sulkily returning towards us in small broken parties, under a heavy fire of artillery. But the fire where we were was not so bad as further to the rear: for although the air seemed alive with shell, yet the greater number burst behind us.   44

The General told me that Pickett's division had succeeded in carrying the enemy's position and capturing his guns, but after remaining there twenty minutes, it had been forced to retire, on the retreat of Heth and Pettigrew on its left. No person could have been more calm or self-possessed than General Longstreet under these trying circumstances, aggravated as they now were by the movements of the enemy, who began to show a strong disposition to advance. I could now thoroughly appreciate the term bulldog, which I had heard applied to him by the soldiers. Difficulties seem to make no other impression upon him than to make him a little more savage.   45

Major Walton was the only officer with him when I came up—all the rest had been put into the charge. In a few minutes Major Latrobe arrived on foot, carrying his saddle, having just had his horse killed. Colonel Sorrell was also in the same predicament, and Captain Goree's horse was wounded in the mouth.   46

The General was making the best arrangements in his power to resist the threatened advance, by advancing some artillery, rallying the stragglers, &c. I remember seeing a General (Pettigrew, I think it was) come up to him, and report that "he was unable to bring his men up again." Longstreet turned upon him and replied with some sarcasm: "Very well; never mind, then, General; just let them remain where they are: the enemy's going to advance, and will spare you the trouble."   47

He asked for something to drink. I gave him some rum out of my silver flask, which I begged he would keep in remembrance of the occasion; he smiled, and, to my great satisfaction, accepted the memorial. He then went off to give some orders to M'Laws's division. Soon afterwards I joined General Lee, who had in the meanwhile come to that part of the field on becoming aware of the disaster.   48

If Longstreet's conduct was admirable, that of General Lee was perfectly sublime. He was engaged in rallying and in encouraging the broken troops, and was riding about a little in front of the wood, quite alone—the whole of his staff being engaged in a similar manner further to the rear. His face, which is always placid and cheerful, did not show signs of the slightest disappointment, care, or annoyance; and he was addressing to every soldier he met a few words of encouragement, such as, "All this will come right in the end; we'll talk it over afterwards; but, in the meantime, all good men must rally. We want all good and true men just now," &c.   49

He spoke to all the wounded men that passed him, and the slightly wounded he exhorted "to bind up [their] hurts and take up a musket" in this emergency. Very few failed to answer his appeal, and I saw many badly wounded men take off their hats and cheer him. He said to me, "This has been a sad day for us, Colonel—a sad day; but we can't expect always to gain victories." He was also kind enough to advise me to get into some more sheltered position, as the shells were bursting round us with considerable frequency.   50

Notwithstanding the misfortune which had so suddenly befallen him, General Lee seemed to observe everything, however trivial. When a mounted officer began licking his horse for shying at the bursting of a shell, he called out, "Don't whip him, Captain; don't whip him. I've got just such another foolish horse myself, and whipping does no good." 51

I happened to see a man lying flat on his face in a small ditch, and I remarked that I didn't think he seemed dead; this drew General Lee's attention to the man, who commenced groaning dismally. Finding appeals to his patriotism of no avail, General Lee had him ignominiously set on his legs by some neighboring gunners. 52

I saw General Willcox (an officer who wears a short round jacket and a battered straw hat) come up to him, and explain, almost crying, the state of his brigade. General Lee immediately shook hands with him and said cheerfully, "Never mind, General, *all this has been* MY *fault*—it is *I* that have lost this fight, and you must help me out of it in the best way you can." 53

In this manner I saw General Lee encourage and reanimate his somewhat dispirited troops, and magnanimously take upon his own shoulders the whole weight of the repulse. It was impossible to look at him or to listen to him without feeling the strongest admiration, and I never saw any man fail him except the man in the ditch. 54

It is difficult to exaggerate the critical state of affairs as they appeared about this time. If the enemy or their general had shown any enterprise, there is no saying what might have happened. General Lee and his officers were evidently fully impressed with a sense of the situation; yet there was much less noise, fuss, or confusion of orders than at an ordinary field day. The men, as they were rallied in the wood, were brought up in detachments, and lay down quietly and cooly in the positions assigned to them. 55

We heard that Generals Garnett and Armistead were killed, and General Kemper mortally wounded; also, that Pickett's division had only one field officer unhurt. Nearly all this slaughter took place in an open space about one mile square, and within one hour. 56

At 6 P. M. we heard a long and continuous Yankee cheer, which we at first imagined was an indication of an advance; but it turned out to be their reception of a general officer, whom we saw riding down the line, followed by about thirty horsemen. Soon afterwards I rode to the extreme front, where there were four pieces of rifled cannon almost without any infantry support. To the nonwithdrawal of these guns is to be attributed the otherwise surprising inactivity of the enemy. 57

I was immediately surrounded by a sergeant and about half-a-dozen gunners, who seemed in excellent spirits and full of confidence, in spite of their exposed situation. The sergeant expressed his ardent hope that the

Yankees might have spirit enough to advance and receive the dose he had in readiness for them. They spoke in admiration of the advance of Pickett's division, and of the manner in which Pickett himself had led it. When they observed General Lee they said, "We've not lost confidence in the old man: this day's work won't do him no harm. 'Uncle Robert' will get us into Washington yet; you bet he will!" &c.   58

Whilst we were talking, the enemy's skirmishers began to advance slowly, and several ominous sounds in quick succession told us that we were attracting their attention, and that it was necessary to break up the conclave. I therefore turned round and took leave of these cheery and plucky gunners.   59

At 7 P. M., General Lee received a report that Johnson's division of Ewell's corps had been successful on the left, and had gained important advantages there. Firing entirely ceased in our front about this time; but we now heard some brisk musketry on our right, which I afterwards learned proceeded from Hood's Texans, who had managed to surround some enterprising Yankee cavalry, and were slaughtering them with great satisfaction. Only eighteen out of four hundred are said to have escaped.   60

At 7:30, all idea of a Yankee attack being over, I rode back to Moses's tent, and found that worthy commissary in very low spirits, all sorts of exaggerated rumors having reached him. On my way I met a great many wounded men, most anxious to inquire after Longstreet, who was reported killed; when I assured them he was quite well, they seemed to forget their own pain in the evident pleasure they felt in the safety of their chief. No words that I can use will adequately express the extraordinary patience and fortitude with which the wounded Confederates bore their sufferings.   61

I got something to eat with the doctors at 10 P. M., the first for fifteen hours.   62

I gave up my horse today to his owner, as from death and exhaustion the staff are almost without horses.   63

4th July (Saturday)—I was awoke at daylight by Moses complaining that his valuable trunk, containing much public money, had been stolen from our tent whilst we slept. After a search it was found in a wood hard by, broken open and minus the money. Dr. Barksdale had been robbed in the same manner exactly. This is evidently the work of those rascally stragglers, who shirk going under fire, plunder the natives, and will hereafter swagger as the heroes of Gettysburg.   64

Lawley, tho Austrian, and I walked up to the front about eight o'clock, and on our way we met General Longstreet, who was in a high state of amusement and good humor. A flag of truce had just come over from the enemy, and its bearer announced among other things that "General Longstreet was wounded, and a prisoner, but would be taken care of." General Longstreet sent back word that he was extremely grateful, but that, being neither wounded nor a prisoner, he was quite able to take care of himself. The iron endurance of General Longstreet is most extraordinary. He seems to require neither food nor sleep. Most of his staff now fall fast asleep directly they get off their horses, they are so exhausted from the last three days' work.   65

Whilst Lawley went to headquarters on business, I sat down and had a long talk with General Pendleton (the parson), chief of artillery. He told me the exact number of guns in action yesterday. He said that the universal opinion is in favor of the 12-pounder Napoleon guns as the best and simplest sort of ordnance for field purposes. Nearly all the artillery with this army has either been captured from the enemy or cast from old 6-pounders taken at the early part of the war.   66

At 10 A. M. Lawley returned from headquarters, bringing the news that the army is to commence moving in the direction of Virginia this evening. This step is imperative from want of ammunition. But it was hoped that the enemy might attack during the day, especially as this is the Fourth of July, and it was calculated that there was still ammunition for one day's fighting. The ordnance train had already commenced moving back towards Cashtown, and Ewell's immense train of plunder had been proceeding towards Hagerstown by the Fairfield road ever since an early hour this morning.   67

Johnson's division had evacuated during the night the position it had gained yesterday. It appears that for a time it was actually in possession of the cemetery, but had been forced to retire from thence from want of support by Pender's division, which had been retarded by that officer's wound. The whole of our left was therefore thrown back considerably.   68

At 1 P. M. the rain began to descend in torrents, and we took refuge in the hovel of an ignorant Pennsylvania boor. The cottage was full of soldiers, none of whom had the slighest idea of the contemplated retreat, and all were talking of Washington and Baltimore with the greatest confidence.   69

At 2 P. M. we walked to General Longstreet's camp, which had been removed to a place three miles distant, on the Fairfield road. General Longstreet talked to me for a long time about the battle. He said the mistake they had made was in not concentrating the army more, and in failing to make the attack yesterday with 30,000 men instead of 15,000.   70

The advance had been in three lines, and the troops of Hill's corps who gave way were young soldiers, who had never been under fire before. He thought the enemy would have attacked had the guns been withdrawn. Had they done so at that particular moment immediately after the repulse, it would have been awkward; but in that case he had given orders for the advance of Hood's division and M'Law's on the right. I think, after all, that General Meade was right not to advance—his men would never have stood the tremendous fire of artillery they would have been exposed to.   71

Rather over 7000 Yankees were captured during the three days; 3500 took the parole; the remainder were now being marched to Richmond, escorted by the remains of Pickett's division. It is impossible to avoid seeing that the cause of this check to the Confederates lies in the utter contempt felt for the enemy by all ranks.   72

Wagons, horses, mules, and cattle captured in Pennsylvania, the solid advantages of this campaign, have been passing slowly along this road (Fairfield) all day. Those taken by Ewell are particularly admired. So interminable was this train that it soon became evident that we should not be able to start till late at night. As soon as it became dark we all lay round a big fire, and I heard reports coming in from the different generals that the enemy was *retiring,* and had been doing so all day long. M'Laws reported nothing in his front but cavalry vedettes.   73

But this, of course, could make no difference to General Lee's plan: ammunition he must have—he had failed to capture it from the enemy (according to precedent); and as his communications with Virginia were intercepted, he was compelled to fall back towards Winchester, and draw his supplies from thence. General Milroy had kindly left an ample stock at that town when he made his precipitate exit some weeks ago. The army was also incumbered with an enormous wagon train, the spoils of Pennsylvania, which it is highly desirable to get safely over the Potomac.   74

Shortly after 9 P. M. the rain began to descend in torrents. Lawley and I luckily got into the doctor's covered buggy, and began to get slowly under way a little after midnight.   75

A VISIT OF CHARITY

EUDORA WELTY

It was mid-morning—a very cold, bright day. Holding a potted plant before her, a girl of fourteen jumped off the bus in front of the Old Ladies' Home, on the outskirts of town. She wore a red coat, and her straight yellow hair was hanging down loose from the pointed white cap all the little girls were wearing that year. She stopped for a moment beside one of the prickly dark shrubs with which the city had beautified the Home, and then proceeded slowly toward the building, which was of white-washed brick and reflected the winter sunlight like a block of ice. As she walked vaguely up the steps she shifted the small pot from hand to hand; then she had to set it down and remove her mittens before she could open the heavy door.   1

"I'm a Campfire Girl. . . . I have to pay a visit to some old lady," she told the nurse at the desk. This was a woman in a white uniform who looked as if she were cold; she had close-cut hair which stood up on the very top of her head exactly like a sea wave. Marian, the little girl, did not tell her that this visit would give her a minimum of only three points in her score.   2

"Acquainted with any of our residents?" asked the nurse. She lifted one eyebrow and spoke like a man.   3

"With any old ladies? No—but—that is, any of them will do," Marian stammered. With her free hand she pushed her hair behind her ears, as she did when it was time to study Science.   4

The nurse shrugged and rose. "You have a nice *multiflora cineraria* there," she remarked as she walked ahead down the hall of closed doors to pick out an old lady.   5

There was a loose, bulging linoleum on the floor. Marian felt as if she were walking on the waves, but the nurse paid no attention to it. There was a smell in the hall like the interior of a clock. Everything was silent until, behind one of the doors, an old lady of some kind cleared her throat like a sheep bleating. This decided the nurse. Stopping in her tracks, she

first extended her arm, bent her elbow, and leaned forward from the hips
—all to examine the watch strapped to her wrist; then she gave a loud
double-rap on the door.   6

"There are two in each room," the nurse remarked over her shoulder. 7

"Two what?" asked Marian without thinking. The sound like a
sheep's bleating almost made her turn around and run back.   8

One old woman was pulling the door open in short, gradual jerks,
and when she saw the nurse a strange smile forced her old face dangerously awry. Marian, suddenly propelled by the strong, impatient arm of
the nurse, saw next the side-face of another old woman, even older, who
was lying flat in bed with a cap on and a counterpane drawn up to her
chin.   9

"Visitor," said the nurse, and after one more shove she was off up
the hall.   10

Marian stood tongue-tied; both hands held the potted plant. The old
woman, still with that terrible, square smile (which was a smile of welcome) stamped on her bony face, was waiting. . . . Perhaps she said
something. The old woman in bed said nothing at all, and she did not
look around.   11

Suddenly Marian saw a hand, quick as a bird claw, reach up in the
air and pluck the white cap off her head. At the same time, another claw
to match drew her all the way into the room, and the next moment the
door closed behind her.   12

"My, my, my," said the old lady at her side.   13

Marian stood enclosed by a bed, a washstand and a chair; the tiny
room had altogether too much furniture. Everything smelled wet—even the
bare floor. She held onto the back of the chair, which was wicker and felt
soft and damp. Her heart beat more and more slowly, her hands got colder
and colder, and she could not hear whether the old women were saying
anything or not. She could not see them very clearly. How dark it was!
The window shade was down, and the only door was shut. Marian looked
at the ceiling. . . . It was like being caught in a robber's cave, just before
one was murdered.   14

"Did you come to be our little girl for a while?" the first robber
asked.   15

Then something was snatched from Marian's hand—the little potted
plant.   16

"Flowers!" screamed the old woman. She stood holding the pot in
an undecided way. "Pretty flowers," she added.   17

Then the old woman in bed cleared her throat and spoke. "They are
not pretty," she said, still without looking around, but very distinctly.   18

Marian suddenly pitched against the chair and sat down in it.   19

"Pretty flowers," the first old woman insisted. "Pretty—pretty. . . ." 20

Marian wished she had the little pot back for just a moment—she

had forgotten to look at the plant herself before giving it away. What did it
look like?   21

"Stinkweeds," said the old woman sharply. She had a bunchy white
forehead and red eyes like a sheep. Now she turned them toward Marian.
The fogginess seemed to rise in her throat again, and she bleated, "Who
—are—you?"   22

To her surprise, Marian could not remember her name. "I'm a Camp-
fire Girl," she said finally.   23

"Watch out for the germs," said the old woman like a sheep, not
addressing anyone.   24

"One came out last month to see us," said the first old woman.   25

A sheep or a germ? wondered Marian dreamily, holding onto the
chair.   26

"Did not!" cried the other old woman.   27

"Did so! Read to us out of the Bible, and we enjoyed it!" screamed
the first.   28

"Who enjoyed it!" said the woman in bed. Her mouth was unexpect-
edly small and sorrowful, like a pet's.   29

"We enjoyed it," insisted the other. "You enjoyed it—I enjoyed it."   30

"We all enjoyed it," said Marian, without realizing that she had said
a word.   31

The first old woman had just finished putting the potted plant high,
high on the top of the wardrobe, where it could hardly be seen from
below. Marian wondered how she had ever succeeded in placing it there,
how she could ever have reached so high.   32

"You mustn't pay any attention to old Addie," she now said to the
little girl. "She's ailing today."   33

"Will you shut your mouth?" said the woman in bed. "I am not."   34

"You're a story."   35

"I can't stay but a minute—really, I can't," said Marian suddenly.
She looked down at the wet floor and thought that if she were sick in here
they would have to let her go.   36

With much to-do the first old woman sat down in a rocking chair—
still another piece of furniture!—and began to rock. With the fingers of
one hand she touched a very dirty cameo pin on her chest. "What do you
do at school?" she asked.   37

"I don't know . . ." said Marian. She tried to think but she could not. 38

"Oh, but the flowers are beautiful," the old woman whispered. She
seemed to rock faster and faster; Marian did not see how anyone could
rock so fast.   39

"Ugly," said the woman in bed.   40

"If we bring flowers————" Marian began, and then fell silent. She
had almost said that if Campfire Girls brought flowers to the Old Ladies'
Home, the visit would count one extra point, and if they took a Bible with

them on the bus and read it to the old ladies, it counted double. But the old woman had not listened, anyway; she was rocking and watching the other one, who watched back from the bed.   41

"Poor Addie is ailing. She has to take medicine—see?" she said, pointing a horny finger at a row of bottles on the table, and rocking so high that her black comfort shoes lifted off the floor like a little child's.   42

"I am no more sick than you are," said the woman in bed.   43

"Oh yes you are!"   44

"I just got more sense than you have, that's all," said the other old woman, nodding her head.   45

"That's only the contrary way she talks when you all come," said the first old lady with sudden intimacy. She stopped the rocker with a neat pat of her feet and leaned toward Marian. Her hand reached over—it felt like a petunia leaf, clinging and just a little sticky.   46

"Will you hush! Will you hush!" cried the other one.   47

Marian leaned back rigidly in her chair.   48

"When I was a little girl like you, I went to school and all," said the old woman in the same intimate, menacing voice. "Not here—another town. . . ."   49

"Hush!" said the sick woman. "You never went to school. You never came and you never went. You never were anywhere—only here. You never were born! You don't know anything. Your head is empty, your heart and hands and your old black purse are all empty, even that little old box that you brought with you you brought empty—you showed it to me. And yet you talk, talk, talk, talk, talk all the time until I think I'm losing my mind. Who are you? You're a stranger—a perfect stranger! Don't you know you're a stranger? Is it possible that they have actually done a thing like this to anyone—sent them in a stranger to talk, and rock, and tell away her whole long rigmarole? Do they seriously suppose that I'll be able to keep it up, day in, day out, night in, night out, living in the same room with a terrible old woman—forever?"   50

Marian saw the old woman's eyes grow bright and turn toward her. This old woman was looking at her with despair and calculation in her face. Her small lips suddenly dropped apart, and exposed a half circle of false teeth with tan gums.   51

"Come here, I want to tell you something," she whispered. "Come here!"   52

Marian was trembling, and her heart nearly stopped beating altogether for a moment.   53

"Now, now, Addie," said the first old woman. "That's not polite. Do you know what's really the matter with old Addie today?" She, too, looked at Marian; one of her eyelids drooped low.   54

"The matter?" the child repeated stupidly. "What's the matter with her?" 55

"Why, she's mad because it's her birthday!" said the first old woman, beginning to rock again and giving a little crow as though she had answered her own riddle.   56

"It is not, it is not!" screamed the old woman in bed. "It is not my birthday, no one knows when that is but myself, and will you please be quiet and say nothing more, or I'll go straight out of my mind!" She turned her eyes toward Marian again, and presently she said in the soft, foggy voice, "When the worst comes to the worst, I ring this bell, and the nurse comes." One of her hands was drawn out from under the patched counterpane—a thin little hand with enormous black freckles. With a finger which would not hold still she pointed to a little bell on the table among the bottles.   57

"How old are you?" Marian breathed. Now she could see the old woman in bed very closely and plainly, and very abruptly, from all sides, as in dreams. She wondered about her—she wondered for a moment as though there was nothing else in the world to wonder about. It was the first time such a thing had happened to Marian.   58

"I won't tell!"   59

The old face on the pillow, where Marian was bending over it, slowly gathered and collapsed. Soft whimpers came out of the small open mouth. It was a sheep that she sounded like—a little lamb. Marian's face drew very close, the yellow hair hung forward.   60

"She's crying!" She turned a bright, burning face up to the first old woman.   61

"That's Addie for you," the old woman said spitefully.   62

Marian jumped up and moved toward the door. For the second time, the claw almost touched her hair, but it was not quick enough. The little girl put her cap on.   63

"Well, it was a real visit," said the old woman, following Marian through the doorway and all the way out into the hall. Then from behind she suddenly clutched the child with her sharp little fingers. In an affected, high-pitched whine she cried, "Oh, little girl, have you a penny to spare for a poor old woman that's not got anything of her own? We don't have a thing in the world—not a penny for candy—not a thing! Little girl, just a nickel—a penny————"   64

Marian pulled violently against the old hands for a moment before she was free. Then she ran down the hall, without looking behind her and without looking at the nurse, who was reading *Field & Stream* at her desk. The nurse, after another triple motion to consult her wrist watch, asked automatically the question put to visitors in all institutions: "Won't you stay and have dinner with *us*?"   65

Marian never replied. She pushed the heavy door open into the cold air and ran down the steps.   66

Under the prickly shrub she stopped and quickly, without being seen, retrieved a red apple she had hidden there.   67

Her yellow hair under the white cap, her scarlet coat, her bare knees all flashed in the sunlight as she ran to meet the big bus rocketing through the street.   68

"Wait for me!" she shouted. As though at an imperial command, the bus ground to a stop.   69

She jumped on and took a big bite out of the apple.   70

The Whole Selection

1 In a famous review of Hawthorne's *Twice-Told Tales*, a collection of short stories, Edgar Allan Poe formulated his often-quoted view of the structure of the short story. Analyze "A Visit of Charity" in light of the criteria implicit in the following paragraph from that review:

> A skillful artist has constructed a tale. He has not fashioned his thoughts to accommodate his incidents, but having deliberately conceived a certain *single effect* to be wrought, he then invents such incidents, he then combines such events, and discusses them in such tone as may best serve him in establishing this preconceived effect. If his very first sentence tends not to the outbringing of this effect, then in his very first step has he committed a blunder. In the whole composition there should be no word written of which the tendency, direct or indirect, is not to the one pre-established design. And by such means, with such care and skill, a picture is at length painted which leaves in the mind of him who contemplates it with a kindred art, a sense of the fullest satisfaction. The idea of the tale, its thesis, has been presented unblemished, because undisturbed—an end absolutely demanded, yet, in the novel, altogether unattainable.

2 Part of the short-story writer's problem is to get through the initial exposition quickly. How long does it take Miss Welty to set the scene and create the atmosphere?

3 What are the advantages or disadvantages of having the story told from the omniscient point of view rather than from the point of view of the first person?

4 In what ways is irony used in this story?

5 Is the resolution of the story accomplished with speed and finality? Why doesn't Miss Welty describe at greater length the effect of the action upon the girl after she leaves?

6 A color pattern, which is symbolic, can be discovered in the story. Show how various colors or suggestions of color are used to suggest or deepen the meaning of the story.

THE VALIANT WOMAN

J. F. POWERS

They had come to the dessert in a dinner that was a shambles. "Well, John," Father Nulty said, turning away from Mrs. Stoner and to Father Firman, long gone silent at his own table, "You've got the bishop coming for confirmations next week." 1

"Yes," Mrs. Stoner cut in, "and for dinner. And if he don't eat any more than he did last year————" 2

Father Firman, in a rare moment, faced it. "Mrs. Stoner, the bishop is not well. You know that." 3

"And after I fixed that fine dinner and all." Mrs. Stoner pouted in Father Nulty's direction. 4

"I wouldn't feel bad about it, Mrs. Stoner," Father Nulty said. "He never eats much anywhere." 5

"It's funny. And that new Mrs. Allers said he ate just fine when he was there," Mrs. Stoner argued, and then spit out, "but she's a damned liar!" 6

Father Nulty, unsettled but trying not to show it, said, "Who's Mrs. Allers?" 7

"She's at Holy Cross," Mrs. Stoner said. 8

"She's the housekeeper," Father Firman added, thinking Mrs. Stoner made it sound as though Mrs. Allers were the pastor there. 9

"I swear I don't know what to do about the dinner this year," Mrs. Stoner said. 10

Father Firman moaned. "Just do as you've always done, Mrs. Stoner." 11

"Huh! And have it all to throw out! Is that any way to do?" 12

"Is there any dessert?" Father Firman asked coldly. 13

Mrs. Stoner leaped up from the table and bolted into the kitchen, mumbling. She came back with a birthday cake. She plunged it in the center of the table. She found a big wooden match in her apron pocket and thrust it at Father Firman. 14

"I don't like this bishop," she said. "I never did. And the way he went and cut poor Ellen Kennedy out of Father Doolin's will!' 15

She went back into the kitchen. 16

"Didn't they talk a lot of filth about Doolin and the housekeeper?" Father Nulty asked. 17

"I should think they did," Father Firman said. "All because he took her to the movies on Sunday night. After he died and the bishop cut her out of the will, though I hear he gives her a pension privately, they talked about the bishop." 18

"I don't like this bishop at all," Mrs. Stoner said, appearing with a cake knife. "Bishop Doran—there was the man!"   19

"We know," Father Firman said. "All man and all priest."   20

"He did know real estate," Father Nulty said.   21

Father Firman struck the match.   22

"Not on the chair!" Mrs. Stoner cried, too late.   23

Father Firman set the candle burning—it was suspiciously large and yellow, like a blessed one, but he could not be sure. They watched the fluttering flame.   24

"I'm forgetting the lights!" Mrs. Stoner said, and got up to turn them off. She went into the kitchen again.   25

The priests had a moment of silence in the candlelight.   26

"Happy birthday, John," Father Nulty said softly. "Is it fifty-nine you are?"   27

"As if you didn't know, Frank," Father Firman said, "and you the same but one."   28

Father Nulty smiled, the old gold of his incisors shinning in the flickering light, his color whiter in the dark, and raised his glass of water, which would have been wine or better in the bygone days, and toasted Father Firman.   29

"Many of 'em, John."   30

"Blow it out," Mrs. Stoner said, returning to the room. She waited by the light switch for Father Firman to blow out the candle.   31

Mrs. Stoner, who ate no desserts, began to clear the dishes into the kitchen, and the priests, finishing their cake and coffee in a hurry, went to sit in the study.   32

Father Nulty offered a cigar.   33

"John?"   34

"My ulcers, Frank."   35

"Ah, well, you're better off." Father Nulty lit the cigar and crossed his long black legs. "Fish Frawley has got him a Filipino, John. Did you hear?"   36

Father Firman leaned forward, interested. "He got rid of the woman he had?"   37

"He did. It seems she snooped."   38

"Snooped, eh?"   39

"She did. And gossiped. Fish introduced two town boys to her, said, 'Would you think these boys were my nephews?' That's all, and the next week the paper had it that his two nephews were visiting him from Erie. After that, he let her believe he was going East to see his parents, though both are dead. The paper carried the story. Fish returned and made a sermon out of it. Then he got the Filipino."   40

Father Firman squirmed with pleasure in his chair.   41

"That's like Fish, Frank. He can do that." He stared at the tips of his fingers bleakly. "You could never get a Filipino to come to a place like this." 42

"Probably not," Father Nulty said. "Fish is pretty close to Minneapolis. Ah, say, do you remember the trick he played on us all in Marmion Hall!" 43

"That I'll not forget!" Father Firman's eyes remembered. "Getting up New Year's morning and finding the toilet seats all painted!" 44

"Happy Circumcision! Hah!" Father Nulty had a coughing fit. 45

When he had got himself together again, a mosquito came and sat on his wrist. He watched it a moment before bringing his heavy hand down. He raised his hand slowly, viewed the dead mosquito, and sent it spinning with a plunk of his middle finger. 46

"Only the female bites," he said. 47

"I didn't know that," Father Firman said. 48

"Ah, yes. . . ." 49

Mrs. Stoner entered the study and sat down with some sewing— Father Firman's black socks. 50

She smiled pleasantly at Father Nulty. "And what do you think of the atom bomb, Father?" 51

"Not much," Father Nulty said. 52

Mrs. Stoner had stopped smiling. Father Firman yawned. 53

Mrs. Stoner served up another: "Did you read about this communist convert, Father?" 54

"He's been in the Church before," Father Nulty said, "and so it's not a conversion, Mrs. Stoner." 55

"No? Well, I already got him down on my list of Monsignor's converts." 56

"It's better than a conversion, Mrs. Stoner, for there is more rejoicing in heaven over the return of . . . uh, he that was lost, Mrs. Stoner, is found." 57

"And that congresswoman, Father?" 58

"Yes. A convert—she." 59

"And Henry Ford's grandson, Father. I got him down." 60

"Yes, to be sure." 61

Father Firman yawned, this time audibly, and held his jaw. 62

"But he's one only by marriage, Father," Mrs. Stoner said. "I always say you got to watch those kind." 63

"Indeed you do, but a convert nonetheless, Mrs. Stoner. Remember, Cardinal Newman himself was one." 64

Mrs. Stoner was unimpressed. "I see where Henry Ford's making steering wheels out of soybeans, Father." 65

"I didn't see that." 66

"I read it in the *Reader's Digest* or some place."   67

"Yes, well. . . ." Father Nulty rose and held his hand out to Father
Firman. "John," he said. "It's been good."   68

"I heard Hirohito's next," Mrs. Stoner said, returning to converts.   69

"Let's wait and see, Mrs. Stoner," Father Nulty said.   70

The priests walked to the door.   71

"You know where I live, John."   72

"Yes. Come again, Frank. Good night."   73

Father Firman watched Father Nulty go down the walk to his car at
the curb. He hooked the screen door and turned off the porch light. He
hesitated at the foot of the stairs, suddenly moved to go to bed. But he
went back into the study.   74

"Phew!" Mrs. Stoner said. "I thought he'd never go. Here it is after
eight o'clock."   75

Father Firman sat down in his rocking chair. "I don't see him often,"
he said.   76

"I give up!" Mrs. Stoner exclaimed, flinging the holey socks upon the
horsehair sofa. "I'd swear you had a nail in your shoe."   77

"I told you I looked."   78

"Well you ought to look again. And cut your toenails, why don't you?
Haven't I got enough to do?"   79

Father Firman scratched in his coat pocket for a pill, found one,
swallowed it. He let his head sink back against the chair and closed his
eyes. He could hear her moving about the room, making the preparations;
and how he knew them—the fumbling in the drawer for a pencil with a
point, the rip of the page from his daily calendar, and finally the leg of the
card table sliding up against his leg.   80

He opened his eyes. She yanked the floor lamp alongside the table,
setting the bead fringe twinkling on the shade, and pulled up her chair on
the other side. She sat down and smiled at him for the first time that day.
Now she was happy.   81

She swept up the cards and began to shuffle with the abandoned
virtuosity of an old river-boat gambler, standing them on end, fanning
them out, whirling them through her fingers, dancing them halfway up
her arms, cracking the whip over them. At last they lay before him tamed
into a neat deck.   82

"Cut?"   83

"Go ahead," he said. She liked to go first.   84

She gave him her faint, avenging smile and drew a card, cast it aside
for another which he thought must be an ace from the way she clutched
it face down.   85

She was getting all the cards, as usual, and would have been invincible if she had possessed his restraint and if her cunning had been of a

higher order. He knew a few things about leading and lying back that she would never learn. Her strategy was attack, forever attack, with one baffling departure: she might sacrifice certain tricks as expendable if only she could have the last ones, the heartbreaking ones, if she could slap them down one after another, shatteringly.   86

She played for blood, no bones about it, but for her there was no other way: it was her nature, as it was the lion's and for this reason he found her ferocity pardonable, more a defect of the flesh, venial, while his own trouble was all in the will, mortal. He did not sweat and pray over each card as she must, but he did keep an eye out for reneging and demanded a cut now and then just to aggravate her, and he was always secretly hoping for aces.   87

With one card left in her hand, the telltale trick coming next, she delayed playing it, showing him first the smile, the preview of defeat. She laid it on the table—so! She held one more trump than he had reasoned possible. Had she palmed it from somewhere? No, she would not go that far; that would not be fair, was worse than reneging, which so easily and often happened accidentally, and she believed in being fair. Besides he had been watching her.   88

God smote the vines with hail, the sycamore trees with frost, and offered up the flocks to the lightning—but Mrs. Stoner! What a cross Father Firman had from God in Mrs. Stoner! There were other housekeepers as bad, no doubt, walking the rectories of the world, yes, but . . . yes. He could name one and maybe two priests who were worse off. One, maybe two. Cronin. His scraggly blonde of sixty—take her, with her everlasting banging on the grand piano, the gift of the pastor; her proud talk about the goiter operation at the Mayo Brothers', also a gift; her honking the parish Buick at passing strange priests because they were all in the game together. She was worse. She was something to keep the home fires burning. Yes sir. And Cronin said she was not a bad person really, but what was he? He was quite a freak himself.   89

For that matter, could anyone say that Mrs. Stoner was a bad person? No. He could not say it himself, and he was no freak. She had her points, Mrs. Stoner. She was clean. And though she cooked poorly, could not play the organ, would not take up the collection in an emergency, and went to card parties, and told all—even so, she was clean. She washed everything. Sometimes her underwear hung down beneath her dress like a paratrooper's pants, but it and everything she touched was clean. She washed constantly. She was clean.   90

She had her other points, to be sure—her faults, you might say. She snooped—no mistake about it—but it was not snooping for snooping's sake; she had a reason. She did other things, always with a reason. She overcharged on rosaries and prayer books, but that was for the sake of the poor. She censored the pamphlet rack, but that was to prevent scandal. She pried into the baptismal and matrimonial records, but there was no other way if Father was out, and in this way she once uncovered a bastard and flushed him out of the rectory, but that was the perverted decency of the times. She held her nose over bad marriages in the presence of the victims, but that was her sorrow and came from having her husband buried in a mine. And he had caught her telling a bewildered young couple that there was only one good reason for their wanting to enter into a mixed marriage—the child had to have a name, and that—that was what?   91

She hid his books, kept him from smoking, picked his friends (usually the pastors of her colleagues), bawled out people for calling after dark, had no humor, except at cards, and then it was grim, very grim, and she sat hatchetfaced every morning at Mass. But she went to Mass, which was all that kept the church from being empty some mornings. She did annoying things all day long. She said annoying things into the night. She said she had given him the best years of her life. Had she? Perhaps—for the miner had her only a year. It was too bad, sinfully bad, when he thought of it like that. But all talk of best years and life was nonsense. He had to consider the heart of the matter, the essence. The essence was that housekeepers were hard to get, harder to get than ushers, than willing workers, than organists, than secretaries—yes, harder to get than assistants or vocations.   92

And she was a *saver*—saved money, saved electricity, saved string, bags, sugar, saved—him. That's what she did. That's what she said she did, and she was right, in a way. In a way, she was usually right. In fact, she was always right—in a way. And you could never get a Filipino to come way out here and live. Not a young one anyway, and he had never seen an old one. Not a Filipino. They like to dress up and live.   93

Should he let it drop about Fish having one, just to throw a scare into her, let her know he was doing some thinking? No. It would be a perfect cue for the one about a man needing a woman to look after him. He was not up to that again, not tonight.   94

Now she was doing what she liked most of all. She was making a grand slam, playing it out card for card, though it was in the bag, prolonging what would have been cut short out of mercy in gentle company. Father Firman knew the agony of losing.   95

She slashed down the last card, a miserable deuce trump, and did in the hapless king of hearts he had been saving.   96

"Skunked you!"   97

She was awful in victory. Here was the bitter end of their long day together, the final murderous hour in which all they wanted to say—all he wouldn't and all she couldn't—came out in the cards. Whoever won at honeymoon won the day, slept on the other's scalp, and God alone had to help the loser.   98

"We've been at it long enough, Mrs. Stoner," he said, seeing her assembling the cards for another round.   99

"Had enough, huh!"   100

Father Firman grumbled something.   101

"No?"   102

"Yes."   103

She pulled the table away and left it against the wall for the next time. She went out of the study carrying the socks, content and clucking. He closed his eyes after her and began to get under way in the rocking chair, the nightly trip to nowhere. He could hear her brewing a cup of tea in the kitchen and conversing with the cat. She made her way up the stairs, carrying the tea, followed by the cat, purring.   104

He waited, rocking out to sea, until she would be sure to be through in the bathroom. Then he got up and locked the front door (she looked after the back door) and loosened his collar going upstairs.   105

In the bathroom he mixed a glass of antiseptic, always afraid of pyorrhea, and gargled to ward off pharyngitis.   106

When he turned on the light in his room, the moths and beetles began to batter against the screens, the lighter insects humming. . . .   107

Yes, and she had the guest room. How did she come to get that? Why wasn't she in the back room, in her proper place? He knew, if he cared to remember. The screen in the back room—it let in mosquitoes, and if it didn't do that she'd love to sleep back there, Father, looking out at the steeple and the blessed cross on top, Father, if it just weren't for the screen, Father. Very well, Mrs. Stoner, I'll get it fixed or fix it myself. Oh, could you now, Father? I could, Mrs. Stoner, and I will. In the meantime you take the guest room. Yes, Father, and thank you, Father, the house ringing with amenities then. Years ago, all that. She was a pie-faced girl then, not really a girl perhaps, but not too old to marry again. But she never had. In fact, he could not remember that she had even tried for a husband since coming to the rectory, but, of course, he could be wrong, not knowing how they went about it. God! God save us! Had she got her wires crossed and mistaken him all these years for *that*? *That!* Him! Suffering God! No. That was going too far. That was getting morbid. No. He must not think of that again, ever. No.   108

But just the same she had got the guest room and she had it yet. Well, did it matter? Nobody ever came to see him any more, nobody to stay overnight anyway, nobody to stay very long . . . not any more. He knew how they laughed at him. He had heard Frank humming all right— before he saw how serious and sad the situation was and took pity—

humming, "Wedding Bells Are Breaking Up That Old Gang of Mine." But then they'd always laughed at him for something—for not being an athlete, for wearing glasses, for having kidney trouble . . . and mail coming addressed to Rev. and Mrs. Stoner.   109

Removing his shirt, he bent over the table to read the volume left open from last night. He read, translating easily, "Eisdem licet cum illis . . . Clerics are allowed to reside only with women about whom there can be no suspicion, either because of a natural bond (as mother, sister, aunt) or of advanced age, combined in both cases with good repute."   110

Last night he had read it, and many nights before, each time as though this time to find what was missing, to find what obviously was not in the paragraph, his problem considered, a way out. She was not mother, not sister, not aunt, and *advanced* age was a relative term (why, she was younger than he was) and so, eureka, she did not meet the letter of the law—but, alas, how she fulfilled the spirit! And besides it would be a slimy way of handling it after all her years of service. He could not afford to pension her off, either.   111

He slammed the book shut. He slapped himself fiercely on the back, missing the wily mosquito and whirled to find it. He took a magazine and folded it into a swatter. Then he saw it—oh, the preternatural cunning of it!—poised in the beard of St. Joseph on the bookcase. He could not hit it there. He teased it away, wanting it to light on the wall, but it knew his thoughts and flew high away. He swung wildly, hoping to stun it, missed, swung back, catching St. Joseph across the neck. The statue fell to the floor and broke.   112

Mrs. Stoner was panting in the hall outside his door.   113

"What is it!"   114

"Mosquitoes!"   115

"What is it, Father? Are you hurt?"   116

"Mosquitoes—damn it! And only the female bites!"   117

Mrs. Stoner, after a moment, said, "Shame on you, Father. She needs the blood for her eggs."   118

He dropped the magazine and lunged at the mosquito with his bare hand.   119

She went back to her room, saying, "Pshaw, I thought it was burglars murdering you in your bed."   120

He lunged again.   121

The Whole Selection

1 How are we to interpret the sentence "Only the female bites" (paragraphs 47 and 117)? What are we to make of Mrs. Stoner's response (paragraph 118)?

2 The story is told from the point of view of a third person (*"They* had come to the dessert . . ."). Imagine its being told from the point of view of the first person, with Father Firman as narrator ("We came to the dessert . . ."). Compare the advantages and disadvantages of both points of view for this story.

3 Point out a few instances where description is used to give the reader a sense of the *presence* of the characters and of the theme.

4 What do we learn of the characters from their dialogue?

5 What is the purpose of introducing Father Nulty into the story?

6 Does Father Firman conclude that Mrs. Stoner's virtues outweigh her faults?

7 In what ways does the card-playing incident contribute to our knowledge of the characters and the theme of the story?

THE NIGHT THE GHOST GOT IN

JAMES THURBER

The ghost that got into our house on the night of November 17, 1915, raised such a hullabaloo of misunderstandings that I am sorry I didn't just let it keep on walking, and go to bed. Its advent caused my mother to throw a shoe through a window of the house next door and ended up with my grandfather shooting a patrolman. I am sorry, therefore, that I ever paid any attention to the footsteps.   1

They began about a quarter past one o'clock in the morning, a rhythmic, quick-cadenced walking around the dining-room table. My mother was asleep in one room upstairs, my brother Herman in another; grandfather was in the attic, in the old walnut bed, which, as you will remember, once fell on my father. I had just stepped out of the bathtub and was busily rubbing myself with a towel when I heard the steps. They were the steps of a man walking rapidly around the dining-room table downstairs. The light from the bathroom shone down the back steps, which dropped directly into the dining-room; I could see the faint shine of plates on the plate-rail; I couldn't see the table. The steps kept going round and round the table; at regular intervals a board creaked, when it was trod upon. I supposed at first that it was my father or my brother Roy, who had gone to Indianapolis but were expected home at any time. I suspected next that it was a burglar. It did not enter my mind until later that it was a ghost.   2

After the walking had gone on for perhaps three minutes, I tiptoed to Herman's room. "Psst!" I hissed, in the dark, shaking him. "Awp," he said, in the low, hopeless tone of a despondent beagle—he always half suspected that something would "get him" in the night. I told him who I was. "There's something downstairs!" I said. He got up and followed me to the head of the back staircase. We listened together. There was no sound. The steps had ceased. Herman looked at me in some alarm: I had only the bath towel around my waist. He wanted to go back to bed, but I gripped his arm. "There's something down there!" I said. Instantly the steps began again, circled the dining-room table like a man running, and started up the stairs toward us, heavily, two at a time. The light still shone palely down the stairs; we saw nothing coming, we only heard the steps. Herman rushed to his room and slammed the door. I slammed shut the door at the stairs top and held my knee against it. After a long minute, I slowly opened it again. There was nothing there. There was no sound. None of us ever heard the ghost again.   3

The slamming of the doors had aroused mother: she peered out of her room. "What on earth are you boys doing?" she demanded. Herman ventured out of his room. "Nothing," he said gruffly, but he was, in color,

a light green. "What was all that running around downstairs?" said
mother. So she had heard the steps, too! We just looked at her. "Bur-
glars!" she shouted, intuitively. I tried to quiet her by starting lightly
downstairs.   4
 "Come on, Herman," I said.   5
 "I'll stay with mother," he said. "She's all excited."   6
 I stepped back onto the landing.   7
 "Don't either of you go a step," said mother. "We'll call the police."
Since the phone was downstairs, I didn't see how we were going to call the
police—nor did I want the police—but mother made one of her quick,
incomparable decisions. She flung up a window of her bedroom which
faced the bedroom windows of the house of a neighbor, picked up a shoe,
and whammed it through a pane of glass across the narrow space that
separated the two houses. Glass tinkled into the bedroom occupied by a
retired engraver named Bodwell and his wife. Bodwell had been for some
years in a rather bad way and was subject to mild "attacks." Most everybody we knew or lived near had *some* kind of attacks.   8
 It was now about two o'clock of a moonless night; clouds hung black
and low. Bodwell was at the window in a minute, shouting, frothing a
little, shaking his fist. "We'll sell the house and go back to Peoria," we
could hear Mrs. Bodwell saying. It was some time before mother "got
through" to Bodwell. "Burglars!" she shouted. "Burglars in the house!"
Herman and I hadn't dared to tell her that it was not burglars but ghosts,
for she was even more afraid of ghosts than of burglars. Bodwell at first
thought that she meant there were burglars in his house, but finally he
quieted down and called the police for us over an extension phone by his
bed. After he had disappeared from the window, mother suddenly made as
if to throw another shoe, not because there was further need of it but, as
she later explained, because the thrill of heaving a shoe through a window
glass had enormously taken her fancy. I prevented her.   9
 The police were on hand in a commendably short time: a Ford sedan
full of them, two on motorcycles, and a patrol wagon with about eight in
it and a few reporters. They began banging at our front door. Flashlights
shot streaks of gleam up and down the walls, across the yard, down the
walk between our house and Bodwell's. "Open up!" cried a hoarse voice.
"We're men from Headquarters!" I wanted to go down and let them in,
since there they were, but mother wouldn't hear of it. "You haven't a
stitch on," she pointed out. "You'd catch your death." I wound the towel
around me again. Finally the cops put their shoulders to our big heavy
front door with its thick beveled glass and broke it in. I could hear a rending of wood and a splash of glass on the floor of the hall. Their lights
played all over the living-room and criss-crossed nervously in the dining-
room, stabbed into hallways, shot up the front stairs and finally up the

back. They caught me standing in my towel at the top. A heavy policeman bounded up the steps. "Who are you?" he demanded. "I live here," I said. "Well, whattsa matta, ya hot?" he asked. I was, as a matter of fact, cold; I went to my room and pulled on some trousers. On my way out, a cop stuck a gun into my ribs. "Whatta you doin' here?" he demanded. "I live here," I said.   10

The officer in charge reported to mother. "No sign of nobody, lady," he said. "Musta got away—what'd he look like?"   11

"There were two or three of them," mother said, "whooping and carrying on and slamming doors." "Funny," said the cop. "All ya windows and doors was locked on the inside tight as a tick."   12

Downstairs, we could hear the tromping of the other police. Police were all over the place; doors were yanked open, drawers were yanked open, windows were shot up and pulled down, furniture fell with dull thumps. A half-dozen policemen emerged out of the darkness of the front hallway upstairs. They began to ransack the floor; pulled beds away from walls, tore clothes off hooks in the closets, pulled suitcases and boxes off shelves. One of them found an old zither that Roy had won in a pool tournament. "Looky here, Joe," he said, strumming it with a big paw. The cop named Joe took it and turned it over. "What is it?" he asked me. "It's an old zither our guinea pig use to sleep on," I said. It was true that a pet guinea pig we once had would never sleep anywhere except on the zither, but I should never had said so. Joe and the other cop looked at me a long time. They put the zither back on a shelf.   13

"No sign o' nuthin'," said the cop who had first spoken to mother. "This guy," he explained to the others, jerking a thumb at me, "was nekked. The lady seems historical." They all nodded, but said nothing; just looked at me. In the small silence we all heard a creaking in the attic. Grandfather was turning over in bed. "What's 'at?" snapped Joe. Five or six cops sprang for the attic door before I could intervene or explain. I realized that it would be bad if they burst in on grandfather unannounced, or even announced. He was going through a phase in which he believed that General Meade's men, under steady hammering by Stonewall Jackson, were beginning to retreat and even desert.   14

When I got to the attic, things were pretty confused. Grandfather had evidently jumped to the conclusion that the police were deserters from Meade's army, trying to hide away in his attic. He bounded out of bed wearing a long flannel nightgown over long woolen underwear, a nightcap, and a leather jacket around his chest. The cops must have realized at once that the indignant white-haired old man belonged in the house, but they had no chance to say so. "Back, ye cowardly dogs!" roared grandfather. "Back t' the lines, ye goddam lily-livered cattle!" With that, he fetched the officer who found the zither a flat-handed smack alongside his head that sent him sprawling. The others beat a retreat, but not fast enough; grandfather grabbed Zither's gun from its holster and let fly. The report seemed to crack the rafters; smoke filled the attic. A cop cursed and shot his hand to his shoulder. Somehow, we all finally got downstairs again and locked the door against the old gentleman. He fired once or twice more in the darkness and then went back to bed. "That was grandfather," I explained to Joe, out of breath. "He thinks you're deserters." "I'll say he does," said Joe.   15

The cops were reluctant to leave without getting their hands on somebody besides grandfather; the night had been distinctly a defeat for them. Furthermore, they obviously didn't like the "layout"; something looked— and I can see their viewpoint—phony. They began to poke into things again. A reporter, a thin-faced, wispy man, came up to me. I had put on one of mother's blouses, not being able to find anything else. The reporter looked at me with mingled suspicion and interest. "Just what the hell is the real low-down here, Bud?" he asked. I decided to be frank with him. "We had ghosts," I said. He gazed at me a long time as if I were a slot machine into which he had, without results, dropped a nickel. Then he walked away. The cops followed him, the one grandfather shot holding his now-bandaged arm, cursing and blaspheming. "I'm gonna get my gun back from that old bird," said the zither-cop. "Yeh," said Joe. "You—and who else?" I told them I would bring it to the station house the next day.   16

"What was the matter with that one policeman?" mother asked, after they had gone. "Grandfather shot him," I said. "What for?" she demanded. I told her he was a deserter. "Of all things!" said mother. "He was such a nice-looking young man."   17

Grandfather was fresh as a daisy and full of jokes at breakfast next morning. We thought at first he had forgotten all about what had happened, but he hadn't. Over his third cup of coffee, he glared at Herman and me. "What was the idee of all them cops tarryhootin' round the house last night?" he demanded. He had us there.   18

MRS. BULLFROG

NATHANIEL HAWTHORNE

It makes me melancholy to see how like fools some very sensible people act in the matter of choosing wives. They perplex their judgments by a most undue attention to little niceties of personal appearance, habits, disposition, and other trifles which concern nobody but the lady herself. An unhappy gentleman, resolving to wed nothing short of perfection, keeps his heart and hand till both get so old and withered that no tolerable woman will accept them. Now this is the very height of absurdity. A kind Providence has so skilfully adapted sex to sex and the mass of individuals to each other, that, with certain obvious exceptions, any male and female may be moderately happy in the married state. The true rule is to ascertain that the match is fundamentally a good one, and then to take it for granted that all minor objections, should there be such, will vanish, if you let them alone. Only put yourself beyond hazard as to the real basis of matrimonial bliss, and it is scarcely to be imagined what miracles, in the way of recognizing smaller incongruities, connubial love will effect. $\qquad$ 1

For my own part I freely confess that, in my bachelorship, I was precisely such an over-curious simpleton as I now advise the reader not to be. My early habits had gifted me with a feminine sensibility and too exquisite refinement. I was the accomplished graduate of a dry-goods store, where, by dint of ministering to the whims of fine ladies, and suiting silken hose to delicate limbs, and handling satins, ribbons, chintzes, calicoes, tapes, gauze, and cambric needles, I grew up a very ladylike sort of a gentleman. It is not assuming too much to affirm that the ladies themselves were hardly so ladylike as Thomas Bullfrog. So painfully acute was my sense of female imperfection, and such varied excellence did I require in the woman who I could love, that there was an awful risk of my getting no wife at all, or of being driven to perpetrate matrimony with my own image in the looking-glass. Besides the fundamental principle already hinted at, I demanded the fresh bloom of youth, pearly teeth, glossy ringlets, and the whole list of lovely items, with the utmost delicacy of habits and sentiments, a silken texture of mind, and, above all, a virgin heart. In a word, if a young angel just from paradise, yet dressed in earthly fashion, had come and offered me her hand, it is by no means certain that I should have taken it. There was every chance of my becoming a most miserable old bachelor, when, by the best luck in the world, I made a journey into another state, and was smitten by, and smote again, and wooed, won, and married, the present Mrs. Bullfrog, all in the space of a fortnight. Owing to these extempore measures, I not only gave my bride credit for certain perfections which have not as yet come to light, but also

overlooked a few trifling defects, which, however, glimmered on my perception long before the close of the honeymoon. Yet, as there was no mistake
about the fundamental principle aforesaid, I soon learned, as will be seen,
to estimate Mrs. Bullfrog's deficiencies and superfluities at exactly their
proper value.   2

The same morning that Mrs. Bullfrog and I came together as a unit,
we took two seats in the stage-coach and began our journey towards my
place of business. There being no other passengers, we were as much
alone and as free to give vent to our raptures as if I had hired a hack for
the matrimonial jaunt. My bride looked charmingly in a green silk calash
and riding habit of pelisse cloth;[1] and whenever her red lips parted with a
smile, each tooth appeared like an inestimable pearl. Such was my passionate warmth that——we had rattled out of the village, gentle reader, and were
lonely as Adam and Eve in paradise——I plead guilty to no less freedom
than a kiss. The gentle eye of Mrs. Bullfrog scarcely rebuked me for the
profanation. Emboldened by her indulgence, I threw back the calash from
her polished brow, and suffered my fingers, white and delicate as her own,
to stray among those dark and glossy curls which realized my day-dreams
of rich hair.   3

"My love," said Mrs. Bullfrog tenderly, "you will disarrange my
curls."   4

"Oh, no, my sweet Laura!" replied I, still playing with the glossy
ringlet. "Even your fair hand could not manage a curl more delicately than
mine. I propose myself the pleasure of doing up your hair in papers every
evening at the same time with my own."   5

"Mr. Bullfrog," repeated she, "you must not disarrange my curls." 6

This was spoken in a more decided tone than I had happened to
hear, until then, from my gentlest of all gentle brides. At the same time
she put her hand and took mine prisoner; but merely drew it away from
the forbidden ringlet, and then immediately released it. Now, I am a
fidgety little man, and always love to have something in my fingers; so
that, being debarred from my wife's curls, I looked about me for any
other plaything. On the front seat of the coach there was one of those
small baskets in which travelling ladies who are too delicate to appear at a
public table generally carry a supply of gingerbread, biscuits and cheese,
cold ham, and other light refreshments, merely to sustain nature to the
journey's end. Such airy diet will sometimes keep them in pretty good flesh
for a week together. Laying hold of this same little basket, I thrust my
hand under the newspaper with which it was carefully covered.   7

"What's this, my dear?" cried I; for the black neck of a bottle had
popped out of the basket.   8

_____
[1] A calash is a large hood which is made on hoops so that it can be thrown back; a pelisse
is a long outer garment, often of silk.

"A bottle of Kalydor, Mr. Bullfrog," said my wife, coolly taking the
basket from my hands and replacing it on the front seat.   9

There was no possibility of doubting my wife's word; but I never
knew genuine Kalydor, such as I used for my own complexion, to smell so
much like cherry brandy. I was about to express my fears that the lotion
would injure her skin, when an accident occurred which threatened more
than a skin-deep injury. Our Jehu[2] had carelessly driven over a heap of
gravel and fairly capsized the coach, with the wheels in the air and our
heels where our heads should have been. What became of my wits I cannot
imagine; they have always had a perverse trick of deserting me just when
they were most needed; but so it chanced, that in the confusion of our
overthrow I quite forgot that there was a Mrs. Bullfrog in the world. Like
many men's wives, the good lady served her husband as a stepping-stone.
I had scrambled out of the coach and was instinctively settling my cravat,
when somebody brushed roughly by me, and I heard a smart thwack upon
the coachman's ear.   10

"Take that, you villain!" cried a strange, hoarse voice. "You have
ruined me, you blackguard! I shall never be the woman I have been!"   11

And then came a second thwack, aimed at the driver's other ear;
but which missed it, and hit him on the nose, causing a terrible effusion
of blood. Now, who or what fearful apparition was inflicting this punishment on the poor fellow remained an impenetrable mystery to me. The
blows were given by a person of grisly aspect, with a head almost bald,
and sunken cheeks—apparently of the feminine gender, though hardly to
be classed in the gentler sex. There being no teeth to modulate the voice,
it had a mumbled fierceness, not passionate but stern, which absolutely
made me quiver like calf's-foot jelly. Who could the phantom be? The most
awful circumstance of the affair is yet to be told: for this ogre, or whatever it was, had a riding habit like Mrs. Bullfrog's, and also a green silk
calash dangling down her back by the strings. In my terror and turmoil of
mind I could imagine nothing less than that the Old Nick, at the moment
of our overturn, had annihilated my wife and jumped into her petticoats.
This idea seemed the more probable, since I could nowhere perceive Mrs.
Bullfrog alive, nor, though I looked very sharply about the coach, could I
detect any traces of that beloved woman's dead body. There would have
been a comfort in giving her Christian burial.   12

"Come, sir, bestir yourself! Help this rascal to set up the coach,"
said the hobgoblin to me; then, with a terrific screech to three countrymen
at a distance, "Here, you fellows, ain't you ashamed to stand off when a
poor woman is in distress?"   13

The countrymen, instead of fleeing for their lives, came running at

[2] According to *II Kings* 9:20, Jehu "driveth furiously."

full speed, and laid hold of the topsy-turvy coach. I, also, though a small-sized man, went to work like a son of Anak.[3] The coachman, too, with the blood still streaming from his nose, tugged and toiled most manfully, dreading, doubtless, that the next blow might break his head. And yet, bemauled as the poor fellow had been, he seemed to glance at me with an eye of pity, as if my case were more deplorable than his. But I cherished a hope that all would turn out a dream, and seized the opportunity, as we raised the coach, to jam two of my fingers under the wheel, trusting that the pain would awaken me.   14

"Why, here we are, all to rights again!" exclaimed a sweet voice behind. "Thank you for your assistance, gentlemen. My dear Mr. Bullfrog, how you perspire! Do let me wipe your face. Don't take this little accident too much to heart, good driver. We ought to be thankful that none of our necks are broken."   15

"We might have spared one neck out of the three," muttered the driver, rubbing his ear and pulling his nose, to ascertain whether he had been cuffed or not. "Why, the woman's a witch!"   16

I fear that the reader will not believe, yet it is positively a fact, that there stood Mrs. Bullfrog, with her glossy ringlets curling on her brow, and two rows of orient pearls gleaming between her parted lips, which wore a most angelic smile. She had regained her riding habit and calash from the grisly phantom, and was, in all respects, the lovely woman who had been sitting by my side at the instant of our overturn. How she had happened to disappear, and who had supplied her place, and whence she did now return, were problems too knotty for me to solve. There stood my wife. That was the one thing certain among a heap of mysteries. Nothing remained but to help her into the coach, and plod on, through the journey of the day and the journey of life, as comfortably as we could. As the driver closed the door upon us, I heard him whisper to the three countrymen,— 17

"How do you suppose a fellow feels shut up in the cage with a she tiger?"   18

Of course this query could have no reference to my situation. Yet, unreasonable as it may appear, I confess that my feelings were not altogether so ecstatic as when I first called Mrs. Bullfrog mine. True, she was a sweet woman and an angel of a wife; but what if a Gorgon[4] should return, amid the transports of our connubial bliss, and take the angel's place. I recollected the tale of a fairy, who half the time was a beautiful woman and half the time a hideous monster. Had I taken that very fairy to be the wife of my bosom? While such whims and chimeras were flitting

---

[3] *Joshua* 11:21. The Anaks were giants.

[4] The Gorgons of classical mythology were three snaky-haired sisters so terrifying that they turned the beholder to stone. The most famous of the three is Medusa.

across my fancy, I began to look askance at Mrs. Bullfrog, almost expecting that the transformation would be wrought before my eyes.   19

To divert my mind, I took up the newspaper which had covered the little basket of refreshments, and which now lay at the bottom of the coach, blushing with a deep-red stain and emitting a potent spirituous fume from the contents of the broken bottle of Kalydor. The paper was two or three years old, but contained an article of several columns, in which I soon grew wonderfully interested. It was the report of a trial for breach of promise of marriage, giving the testimony in full, with fervid extracts from both the gentleman's and lady's amatory correspondence. The deserted damsel had personally appeared in court, and had borne energetic evidence to her lover's perfidy and the strength of her blighted affections. On the defendant's part there had been an attempt, though insufficiently sustained, to blast the plaintiff's character, and a plea, in mitigation of damages, on account of her unamiable temper. A horrible idea was suggested by the lady's name.   20

"Madam," said I, holding the newspaper before Mrs. Bullfrog's eyes, —and, though a small, delicate, and thin-visaged man, I feel assured that I looked very terrific,—"madam," repeated I through my shut teeth, "were you the plaintiff in this cause?"   21

"Oh, my dear Mr. Bullfrog," replied my wife sweetly, "I thought all the world knew that!"   22

"Horror! horror!" exclaimed I, sinking back on the seat.   23

Covering my face with both hands, I emitted a deep and death-like groan, as if my tormented soul were rending me asunder—I, the most exquisitely fastidious of men, and whose wife was to have been the most delicate and refined of women, with all the fresh dewdrops glittering on her virgin rosebud of a heart!   24

I thought of the glossy ringlets and pearly teeth; I thought of the Kalydor; I thought of the coachman's bruised ear and bloody nose; I thought of the tender love secrets which she had whispered to the judge and jury and a thousand tittering auditors,—and gave another groan! 25

"Mr. Bullfrog," said my wife.   26

As I made no reply, she gently took my hands within her own, removed them from my face, and fixed her eyes steadfastly on mine.   27

"Mr. Bullfrog," said she not unkindly, yet with all the decision of her strong character, "let me advise you to overcome this foolish weakness, and prove yourself, to the best of your ability, as good a husband as I will be a wife. You have discovered, perhaps, some little imperfections in your bride. Well, what did you expect? Women are not angels. If they were, they would go to heaven for husbands; or, at least, be more difficult in their choice on earth."   28

"But why conceal those imperfections?" interposed I tremulously. 29

"Now, my love, are not you a most unreasonable little man?" said Mrs. Bullfrog, patting me on the cheek. "Ought a woman to disclose her frailties earlier than the wedding day? Few husbands, I assure you, make the discovery in such good season, and still fewer complain that these trifles are concealed too long. Well, what a strange man you are! Poh! you are joking."   30

"But—the suit for breach of promise!" groaned I.   31

"Ah, and is that the rub?" exclaimed my wife. "Is it possible that you view that affair in an objectionable light? Mr. Bullfrog, I never could have dreamed it! Is it an objection that I have triumphantly defended myself against slander and vindicated my purity in a court of justice? Or do you complain because your wife has shown the proper spirit of a woman, and punished the villain who trifled with her affections?"   32

"But," persisted I, shrinking into a corner of the coach, however,— for I did not know precisely how much contradiction the proper spirit of a woman would endure,—"but, my love, would it not have been more dignified to treat the villain with the silent contempt he merited?"   33

"That is all very well, Mr. Bullfrog," said my wife slyly; "but, in that case, where would have been the five thousand dollars which are to stock your dry-goods store?"   34

"Mrs. Bullfrog, upon your honor," demanded I, as if my life hung upon her words, "is there no mistake about those five thousand dollars?" 35

"Upon my word and honor there is none," replied she. "The jury gave me every cent the rascal had; and I have kept it all for my dear Bullfrog."   36

"Then, thou dear woman," cried I, with an overwhelming gush of tenderness, "let me fold thee to my heart. The basis of matrimonial bliss is secure, and all thy little defects and frailties are forgiven. Nay, since the result has been so fortunate, I rejoice at the wrongs which drove thee to this blessed lawsuit. Happy Bullfrog that I am!"   37

Suggestions for Writing

1 After consulting your history book and other sources for details on the Battle of Waterloo (or any other battle), construct a narrative, as William H. Prescott did, emphasizing a single incident in a larger design.
2 From the point of view of the third person, write a narrative about any one of the following topics. You will not be able to say everything, so be selective in limiting your topic. Be sure to consult whatever sources are necessary to get the correct facts on which to build the narrative.
   a The Battle of the Bulge
   b Iwo Jima

c The *Monitor* and the *Merrimac*
d The sinking of the *Graf Spee*
e Pearl Harbor

3 A minor incident, narrated from the point of view of the first person, can often be used successfully in dramatizing something much larger, having broad human or social implications. Write an essay in which you are the center of such an action or incident (for example, meeting a stranger or a personal discovery). Try to allow the incident itself to reveal the larger issues as much as possible.

SOME ADDITIONAL PATTERNS

SPECIAL TYPES

There are certain types of writing that every college student is expected to master: the familiar essay and the book review. The ability to read the familiar essay and to write it with some competence is often regarded as a sign of the student's growing maturity. In some courses the student may be asked to write his reaction to a certain book or article that has some bearing on the subject matter being studied.

It is not easy to arrive at a tightly-knit definition of the familiar essay —perhaps because the type is so engaging and quixotic. But the study of enough familiar essays reveals certain characteristics. The writer of the familiar essay is himself noticeably prominent. Every piece of writing illustrates a writer standing behind it, so to speak, but in the familiar essay the presence of the writer is generally more prominent than in most other types of writing. The participants in a conversation deliberately use their personalities to engage each other's attention; each becomes highly conscious of the presence and personality of the other. The familiar essay is something like a conversation between a writer and a reader in which, for the duration of the essay, only the writer is speaking. It is, too, like a personal letter, in which the personality of the writer means everything to the reader, even though the essay is addressed to many people. The "I" is so important that we often characterize the personality of the writer from the essay that he writes. In his analysis of the familiar essay, Clifton Fadiman emphasizes the importance of the personality: "The familiar essayist invites me to rest in the shade of the perpendicular pronoun. His connection with me is a personal one, chancy and fragile, a friendship sustained only by a dozen paragraphs." When reading an essay of the familiar type, we feel that intimacy has been established with the author.

A second important characteristic of the familiar essay is its tone— the spirit, the temper, or the atmosphere of the essay. This accounts for the wide diversity of essays that can be included under this heading. A writer's special manner is readily seen in this type of writing. Of course, what a writer says is important; but what especially identifies the familiar essay is the manner of saying it. Carl Van Doren puts it this way: "If he has good matter, he *may* write a good essay; if he has a good manner, he probably *will* write a good essay." In reading the familiar essay, we should be alert to the writer's manner: we should try to identify, for instance, the casual charm of Christopher Fry, the wit and humor of Alexander Calandra, the reflective contemplation of John LaFarge, or the easy seriousness of Malcolm Muggeridge. Largely because the tone of such writing is important, we expect the familiar essayist to work by indirection, to be subtle instead of obvious. Also, we will not expect his essay to give us complete coverage of a subject in the same way that a more objective, impersonal account would. The writer's personal charm and valid eccentricity may serve as our best guide through whatever labyrinth he may construct.

Because the familiar essayist appeals to our general intelligence, he has a particular appeal for the reader in our day of specialization. Because he is himself a cultured man, he does not hesitate to discuss things in general or anything at all. He clearly warns us that his opinions are personal. His education and culture alert him to the general topics of human interest. He is probably not an authority on a given subject, as a specialist would be, but he is discriminating and perceptive and stimulating. David Daiches observes that such a writer "renders a very special service; he reminds us of the importance of general intelligence, demonstrating by the example of his own practice that the terms 'general' and 'intelligence' are not contradictory."

The review is another matter; it is not nearly so casual and informal. It does give us a personal reaction; but the reaction is one that should be measurable by standards common to many readers or by standards clearly identified by the writer for his reader. Joseph Wood Krutch contends that book reviewing is an art in itself. He insists on its completeness as a literary form. Thus, he establishes the three minimum tasks of the reviewer: (1) to describe the book, (2) to communicate something of its quality, and (3) to pass judgment upon it. There are other ways of describing the reviewer's function—by using, for instance, the three classic questions: (1) What was the writer's object? (2) How far did he succeed in accomplishing it? (3) Was it worth doing? After reading Kratch's "What Is a Good Review?" the reader should be able to discover the methods by which Irving Howe and W. H. Auden have written satisfactory reviews.

ENJOYING THE ACCIDENTAL

CHRISTOPHER FRY

When one or two unfortunate people tried to teach me to play the piano about forty years ago, I was particularly interested in what they called the accidentals—those notes of chromatic alteration which made all the difference to the simple notes of the octave. Indeed I invented a piece for the piano myself called "The Lovers' Quarrel," which was entirely composed of accidentals; at least I thought it was. And I was always very taken with the unexpected notes which occurred in a melody, or in a chord—notes I would never have anticipated, which nevertheless took their perfect place in the general harmony, as though they had flown in like birds and woken the whole landscape into receiving them.   1

Moments, like these unexpected notes, happen from time to time all through our lives. We receive them, and modulate our lives accordingly, either minutely or largely. Something happens; and, once it has happened, it seems an inevitable part of the mysterious organization of our existence. 2

Things we look forward to very much are sometimes a disappointment; or sometimes they can be, in the event, as good as expected; even, on occasion, better. But when something is unexpected as well as enjoyable, it calls up a special response in us, as though we had gained one more small foothold in a confusing world. There's a phrase we commonly use, "He started with surprise." I think the verb "to start," in that context, could fairly be given both its meanings. It may very well be that when we suddenly meet with the unexpected, we not only start with surprise, but start off fresh, in some small way or other. The accidental has made a chromatic alteration in us.   3

When I'm going to the seaside, I look forward to a number of certain, inevitable things. The sea will be there, the tide coming in or out, the air will be salt, the sand will be smooth underfoot and gritty in my sandwiches, the sea gulls will career and cry and walk about on their wet reflections. What I didn't anticipate, but saw last year, was a herd of cows ambulating, in an offhand way, across the sand until they reached the shallow foam, where they stood about like a lot of bored nursemaids. When I saw this, ocean and cows, the wide-open rolling water, and the inward, cud-chewing cows, both cows and sea appeared in a slightly different light. All they apparently had in common were the yellow sea foam and the foaming saliva dripping from the mouths of the cattle, but, even so, it was suddenly clear that the cows and the sea were expressions of the same world, like accidentals in a piece of music.   4

Soon after my wife and I had moved into an old house in Wales, a friend came to stay with us who had a particular fear of snakes. The garden was overgrown and ankle-high at the time, and whenever we walked about, our friend used to ask if we were sure there were no snakes. Of course we were sure; she might as well have asked if there were any crocodiles. Frogs and toads, certainly, I was glad to say, but no snakes. One morning when I was sitting with our friend in the kitchen, topping and tailing gooseberries, if I remember, my wife called me to join her in the drawing room. There, in the very centre of the yellow carpet, was a black snake. In point of fact, it was a slow-worm, a foot long; but by what accident it arrived there I shall never know, unless, in defiance of our lighthearted denials, it was there to say, "The world has, and will continue to have, snakes."   5

At another time, George Cole came to visit us. We were sitting round the fire talking, late at night—it was after midnight, I think—when he suddenly asked what was the hanging bell-shaped flower growing on the wall by the gate. I couldn't think what was there; nothing I had seen. The description he gave of it sounded like a fritillary, but a fritillary is a difficult flower to establish, even in the damp ground it likes, let alone in a dry stone wall. We got up from the fire, and went out into the night to search. A moon was shining, but not enough to see very clearly by, so we walked along the lane under the wall, striking matches, and there, by the spurt of a match, we found it: a purple freckled fritillary, growing alone on the top of the wall, an accidental, occurring against all the laws of its nature. The next morning it had gone—whether picked by some envious hand, or whether vanished with the moon, I don't know.   6

Before I was married I went, with my future wife, for a drive in the country. We had no map with us, and didn't trouble to think, or inquire, which way we were driving. After a time, we left the car by the road and walked across the heath to a circle of pine trees. From there we looked down across a valley. There were scarcely any houses to be seen. We looked at the two or three old roofs among the trees, and said to each other that this would be a valley to live in. But unless one had the money to buy a farm, there was no likelihood of that. We hadn't the money, but later we managed to take over, cheaply, the last few years of the lease of an old millhouse. It was arranged through a house agent, and we agreed to take the house before we had seen it. On the first morning there, we went for a walk. We walked around the millpond and up the hill; and when we reached the top we found we were standing in a circle of pine trees, the *same* circle of pine trees. When we stood there before, wishing to live in the valley, we had been looking down on the roof of the millhouse which was now our first home. It seemed to us an accidental wedding present of a quite remarkable kind.   7

The Whole Selection

1 What method of analysis is principally used to demonstrate that the accidental can be enjoyable?
2 Study the organization of the essay. Does one paragraph necessarily follow from another in a strictly logical way?
3 If Fry's purpose were to be strictly expository, what changes would have to be made in the essay, particularly in structure and style?
4 Describe the general tone, or attitude, of this essay.
5 Select from this essay for study three or four passages which have overtones of meaning—those which say a great deal more in a little space than they seem to say at first glance, e.g., ''The accidental has made a chromatic alteration in us.''

THE WEB OF CONFIDENCE

JOHN LaFARGE

Last year, toward the end of summer, I made a final visit to the old house in Newport that had been familiar to me since childhood. The last—and most devoted—occupant had passed on and been laid to rest. It was the final phase before the moment when the house's furnishings, books, pictures, "estate" of every kind would be duly and lovingly parcelled out and distributed among the heirs and friends. There was chill enough in the damp sea air to warrant filching some old newspapers and a few sticks out of the traditional wood closet and lighting up the old fireplace in the library, arranging kindling and pine splits in proper order, drawing a matchstick from the cloisonné-silver box on the gray stone mantelpiece, starting a bit of a blaze, and settling in the presumably eighth upholstered version of the easy chair for a few moments' solitude before the fire.   1

It is curious that fire, the most impermanent of all phenomena, is precisely that which (like the sea) shows no change, but is itself an endless thread of continuity through the years. (My very first recollection is of fire flickering in the stove.) This is one price we pay for our modern comfort. A mobile thermostat has taken the place of the glowing flames, at least here in the United States. We no longer experience the daily, intimate presence of fire as the center of our temperate-zone life. I am grateful to the thermostat, and have no yearning to exchange it for the log hearth. But it has no power to bind me to the past.   2

The flames flickered and the embers collapsed and crunched as they had flickered and crunched on winter nights when the sliding doors sealed off the big bay windows and the heavy red rep curtains shut out the northern drafts. As I watched the hearth I asked myself just what had happened during the years that had elapsed since a young artist and his wife and children moved into this house eighty-five years ago.   3

This moment was the very ultimate end of that subsequent long event, an event that left innumerable little tokens of remembrance in every corner of the old two-story frame house, tokens that none but myself could now read; that nobody in the future would ever know. The place where the big brothers hung their fishing-tackle, especially the fascinating silver mounted reel that you used when casting off Brenton's Point for rock bass. The triangular closet for carpenters' tools. The capacious drawers in the library bookcase for old letters and photographs. The child Saviour statue on the staircase and its companion upstairs. The pane of red glass a boy had installed in a closet wall, for developing photographs, and white-goateed Mr. Hammond, the perfect image of Uncle Sam, "Mr. Carpenter" per excellence, who had installed it. The cabinet housing the birds-egg

collection, and the series of cylindrical lacquer boxes that fitted so precisely. The silhouettes and miniatures of great-aunts and great-uncles and
cousins. The low window artfully constructed under the eaves so that the
lady of the house could spot possible visitors coming down the street, and
the three other eaves windows that followed it.   4

All was one great event, and that event was the fulfillment of a
divinely human institution, the life of one family: reflected finally in the
life of one person, who had entered the house as a child of four, and now
had bid goodbye to the house and to the world, at the age of eighty-nine.   5

That work had not been done perfectly, in entire peace. Temperaments had clashed with temperaments. Nonetheless the structure had
held firm, and the work was fulfilled and had ended in peace, for it was
worked in liberty. Other works, other enterprises, elsewhere, at home and
abroad, had sprung from it—new adventures, with trails of their own—
and were now continuing. With all stresses and strains, its faith—that
total perspective which, despite all hesitation it never lost—clung firmly
to the hard rock of the natural law. On all its shifting, movement and evolution, there was always an Absolute, a living Purpose behind it all, and a
living human Companionship beyond all individual families.   6

One humbling thought occurs to anyone who recalls the long story of
a family undertaking. None of this would have been possible had it not
grown in an atmosphere of confidence: of faith and friendship, given and
taken. What would all this venture have come to, had it not been for the
great web of interacting aid and companionship that embraced it?   7

Each item in the old house recalled some strand in that living web.
The book shelves recalled the school and college days, and the visits to the
library. The prayer books, the parish church and all its associations. The
china bowl in the hallway where formal summer-colony visitors left their
visiting cards—with one corner neatly bent, of course. The hundredfold
services, trade and professional, for the building and the dwellers therein:
including services rendered gratis in bitter, hard times, and in last ill-
nesses. The solitary gas lamp on the street which the city lit of evenings
and turned off at daylight, and the modern lamp that has taken its place.
The old coffee-mill telephone on the wall, now replaced with dial switch.
The tokens reminding of the glass-cutter, the roofer and tinsmith, the
furnace man and the plumber, the venerable, bearded gardener in the
pompous estate across the way, Mr. Jerry O'Connor, who let us raid his
patches of giant strawberries and commented on the annual but usually
becalmed August international yacht-races with the sardonic remark,
"There's nothing that can go any faster than it can go."   8

All of these, and a thousand other strands in the web of confidence,
near and far, that made ours and everybody else's family venture possible,
were but evanescent and relative. But as Ernest Hocking says, "the rela-

tive is present with the universal." Wherever, and to what extent, the free world's men and women of good will can meet and affirm that universal, just so far will they speak from strength, and not from the shifting ends of human passion.   9

The words of Ernest Hocking sum up much of what I wish to say: "The fallacy of identifying any given form of property law with Christianity has become a commonplace. But to infer from this that Christianity is indifferent to the functions of institutions would be an even graver fallacy. Institutions as they stand are structures of a positive law whose draperies are circumstantial, but whose backbone seeks absolute stability. If it can be maintained that the dignity of man, his freedom, and his development, require some form of property—yes, of private property as well as common property—and if it is true that Christianity demands such freedom as an aspect of the soul's dignity, and has been the original protagonist of this requirement in the growth of western institutions, then we must say that there is *something within the law* of property for which Christianity stands, and will always stand.   10

"Let us put the matter this way: in every social institution there are elements relative to the total internal balance of its particular society, and also elements of permanent validity. It is a current superstition that the relative, where it exists, excludes the absolute; the truth is that absolute and relative are commonly blended. And the presence of an absolute may be suspected even when its clean extraction long defies our efforts. If this is the traditional teaching on property, it is even more true of the family. There is such a thing as 'the Christian family'; it has something to do with that same Christian reverence for individual souls and their freedom, the equal dignity of man, woman, child, the consequent call for adult choice in this the most momentous human alliance, and for a one-to-one partnership. It is perhaps not too much to say that the 'Christian family' comes close to being an absolute, for Christianity a necessary consequence of its own universal precepts. For the family is the most direct embodiment of human love; and human love is, in its own complete self-consciousness, inseparable from the love of God. It is the natural context for a sacrament, inasmuch as it is by way of human love that the divine is most frequently and concretely discovered."[1]   11

Over those four-score years just such an institution had fulfilled itself, the central institution of our society. It was planted, it had grown, spread, fruited to maturity. However, my prevailing thought that late summer afternoon by the fire was not law nor institutions, but the memory of freedom and love. Not wilful freedom or a demonstrative love but nonetheless real. It was love in the true sense, a communication of deeds

---

[1] William Ernest Hocking, *The Coming World Civilization*, Harper & Brothers, New York, 1956, pp. 129–31.

rather than words. But being a love of deeds rather than of words, it took shape in the life of social institution, something permanent, something authentic and authoritative, something that continued to function, precisely because, in Dr. Hocking's language, the institution freely worked in a context of love.   12

I hadn't stacked much wood on the little fire, and soon only a few glowing embers were left, which I properly shielded with the fire-fender before leaving. The dusk had begun, and it was time to lock up and deliver the key next door. After all, there comes a point when what you see with the physical eye is as much a memory as that which you exhibit before the mind's vision. Nine-tenths of our meaningful vision is either anticipation or memory. But as the fire died down the thought occurred to me: should not the same factors, that united this individual family, be decisive in providing a basis, a condition of unity, for the great human family? After all, *this* particular family had never lived in a vacuum. At every stage of its long history, it was in association with countless other families, some now living, many others now passed away; and potentially, with families still to come. After all, the same elements are present in every case, diverse as they may seem to the outward eye: the same basic needs. If our home had been rich, like so many of the fabulously wealthy homes just around us; if we had lived on a great landed estate, we would perhaps have not felt how important for existence were our scant acre or two and the old slate-stone walls that bounded them. If we had been more tranquil and composed, we should not have appreciated what it was to overcome tensions and petty crises in our living. If we had been more lovable, we might not have found so much meaning in love.   13

The condition of one family is, after all, the condition of the world. There were elements in our faith; there were elements in our love, that we could not expect to share with all the entire world, much as we should have liked to do so. But there were elements in that faith and love, in those fundamental loyalties that unite all families, however great may be their variety of incidental differences—certain fundamental loyalties which the free world can unite in preserving and defending.   14

This was a house of peace, but nobody in those eighty-five years talked of peace, or of peace of mind. Nobody saw any particular reason why there should be peace of mind. But all were convinced of the things which in the long run do bring, alone bring, true peace of mind: not as an end sought in itself, but as the fruit which seasonably ripens on the tree of the Creator's law and the Creator's love. The path to peace is the path from the home family to the great world family of all mankind. But the world family, like the domestic family, is evanescent if based upon mere sentiment. For its concrete realization, it requires stable international institutions.   15

The Whole Selection

1 Trace the use of the metaphor of the web as an organizing device in the essay.
2 What are the exact parallels drawn between the "great world family" and the "home family"?
3 One of the characteristics of the familiar essay is its deliberate exploitation of the personality of the author within the essay, so that he almost becomes the subject of his writing. How would you describe the personality of LaFarge on the basis of this short selection?
4 Though written in a very personal, almost chatty tone, the essay makes a very serious point. What is it?

ANGELS ON A PIN

ALEXANDER CALANDRA

Some time ago, I received a call from a colleague who asked if I would be the referee on the grading of an examination question. He was about to give a student a zero for his answer to a physics question, while the student claimed he should receive a perfect score and would if the system were not set up against the student. The instructor and the student agreed to submit this to an impartial arbiter, and I was selected. 1

I went to my colleague's office and read the examination question: "Show how it is possible to determine the height of a tall building with the aid of a barometer." 2

The student had answered: "Take the barometer to the top of the building, attach a long rope to it, lower the barometer to the street, and then bring it up, measuring the length of the rope. The length of the rope is the height of the building." 3

I pointed out that the student really had a strong case for full credit, since he had answered the question completely and correctly. On the other hand, if full credit were given, it could well contribute to a high grade for the student in his physics course. A high grade is supposed to certify competence in physics, but the answer did not confirm this. I suggested that the student have another try at answering the question. I was not surprised that my colleague agreed, but I was surprised that the student did. 4

I gave the student six minutes to answer the question, with the warning that his answer should show some knowledge of physics. At the end of five minutes, he had not written anything. I asked if he wished to give up, but he said no. He had many answers to this problem; he was just thinking of the best one. I excused myself for interrupting him, and asked him to please go on. In the next minute, he dashed off his answer which read: 5

"Take the barometer to the top of the building and lean over the edge of the roof. Drop the barometer, timing its fall with a stopwatch. Then, using the formula $S=\frac{1}{2}at^2$, calculate the height of the building." 6

At this point, I asked my colleague if *he* would give up. He conceded, and I gave the student almost full credit. 7

In leaving my colleague's office, I recalled that the student had said he had other answers to the problem, so I asked him what they were. "Oh, yes," said the student. "There are many ways of getting the height of a tall building with the aid of a barometer. For example, you could take the barometer out on a sunny day and measure the height of the barometer, the length of its shadow, and the length of the shadow of the building, and by the use of a simple proportion, determine the height of the building." 8

"Fine," I said. "And the others?"   9

"Yes," said the student. "There is a very basic measurement method that you will like. In this method, you take the barometer and begin to walk up the stairs. As you climb the stairs, you mark off the length of the barometer along the wall. You then count the number of marks, and this will give you the height of the building in barometer units. A very direct method.   10

"Of course, if you want a more sophisticated method, you can tie the barometer to the end of a string, swing it as a pendulum, and determine the value of 'g' at the street level and at the top of the building. From the difference between the two values of 'g,' the height of the building can, in principle, be calculated."   11

Finally he concluded, there are many other ways of solving the problem. "Probably the best," he said, "is to take the barometer to the basement and knock on the superintendent's door. When the superintendent answers, you speak to him as follows: 'Mr. Superintendent, here I have a fine barometer. If you will tell me the height of this building, I will give you this barometer.' "   12

At this point, I asked the student if he really did not know the conventional answer to this question. He admitted that he did, but said that he was fed up with high school and college instructors trying to teach him how to think, to use the "scientific method," and to explore the deep inner logic of the subject in a pedantic way, as is often done in the new mathematics, rather than teaching him the structure of the subject. With this in mind, he decided to revive scholasticism as an academic lark to challenge the Sputnik-panicked classrooms of America.   13

MY TRUE LOVE HATH MY HEART

MALCOLM MUGGERIDGE

There is a story going around (it might even be true) of a donor who was lined up for a heart transplant operation. The recipient, however, at the last moment decided against having a transplant, and died; the putative donor was recently discharged from hospital. This certainly could happen. As everyone now knows, only a living heart can be transplanted, so the donor cannot be dead in the hitherto-accepted sense. Thus the fact must be faced that heart-transplanting amounts essentially to experimenting with human beings, as has hitherto (with the significant exception of the Nazis) been done only with animals—especially dogs. It is highly significant that the ice should have been broken for such experimentation in South Africa.   1

I raised this question on a television program with Dr. Christian Barnard himself. Why, I asked him, had the first heart-transplant operation been conducted in his hospital in Cape Town? Was it because the surgeons and equipment there were better than anywhere else? Or, as I believed, because the vile doctrine of apartheid, by reducing some human beings to the status of animals, devalued life itself, turning all our bodies into carcasses fit for experiment? The question was ill received. Dr. Barnard evaded it; the twenty or so distinguished doctors on the set with me barracked, and one of them got up to dissociate them all from my ill-chosen observations. Afterwards I was accused of bringing politics into a discussion about medicine and ethics. A number of letters I received in connection with the program were more understanding—one particularly, which related to a doctor who had worked in South Africa and then decamped because, as he put it, the prevailing attitude to the black African patients was veterinary rather than medical.   2

It is, indeed, the moral rather than the political implications of apartheid that make it so hateful. Politically speaking, it amounts to rule by a white oligarchy, who no doubt will in due course be succeeded by a black oligarchy, as has happened in all the former African dependencies. The world today is largely governed by entrenched oligarchies, whether party-machine men, money men, or communist apparatchiks. The replacement of one oligarchy by another can be exciting, and raise extravagant hopes, especially in the young, but when the dust has settled and the rhetoric spent itself there are the same old police, the same old prisons, and the same old cant. When the anarchists marched with their black flags in a procession in Paris led by party-line communists like Aragon, I remembered how Kropotkin had been given a state funeral in Leningrad when he died there in 1921. The procession passed the prison where his followers had already been incarcerated. Some of them were able to get their arms through the bars and salute his coffin, loaded with flowers, as it passed. It was the last anarchist demonstration ever to be permitted in the U.S.S.R.   3

How sinister that the South African achievement that has won esteem everywhere should be the very one that most exemplifies the true moral horror of apartheid! How disturbing that drawing attention to this should so enrage, not so much the upholders of apartheid, as those who ostensibly oppose it on the highest ethical grounds! The really terrible thing about apartheid is that it reduces the status of human souls, in Christian terms all equally dear to their creator and made in his image, to two categories—the driver and the driven. Seen so, their mortal shape deserves no particular respect. It can veritably be regarded as a collection of spare parts, to be sliced off and grafted on as required. In South Africa Dr. Barnard could try his hand without fear of serious opposition; in California and Texas—where the moral climate comes nearest to South Africa's—others followed suit. London came next, and soon, we may be sure, the knives will be out, and the quest for donors be on, all over the place. Then factory farming and the broiler house will loom up as our human lot and way of life.   4

The most ardent advocates of heart transplants are prepared to admit that there will never be enough donors in the foreseeable future for the operation to be available for more than a minute proportion of those who might benefit from it. This is even taking into account all that the roads offer on a sunny weekend—a fruitful source of spare organs, as could be gathered from an aside when they were on the prowl for a donor in Groote Schuur Hospital in Cape Town. For the moment, it was said, no one suitable had shown up, but over the weekend they might have better luck. Properly organized, the roads should yield quite a harvest of serviceable spare parts, in flesh as well as metal. Nothing wasted on our motorways this weekend! Moreover, the possibility is bound to come under consideration of using the organs of incurables to service productive citizens. After all, imbeciles have hearts and kidneys—often quite good ones. Since they cannot be fitted with new brains, why not put their organs to good use?   5

One wonders on what basis the fortunate recipients are to be chosen. Presumably, in America millionaires would have first call, followed by the luminaries of show business; in Russia, the party hierarchy, followed by spacemen and nuclear physicists. Fitting ex-President Eisenhower with a new heart was, it appears, at one point seriously considered. It was a pity, in a way, that his need for one did not coincide with Senator Robert Kennedy's assassination. Eisenhower with a Kennedy heart would have been a very powerful political combination. In this country one scarcely knows. Leaving aside the royal family, probably some weird protocol would prevail, with the Archbishop of Canterbury, the Lord Chief Justice, and other dignitaries heading the queue, and newspaper proprietors and property developers like Lord Thompson and Mr. Charles Clore able to jump it. 6

Another question I tried, without success, to raise with Dr. Barnard was that of the priorities involved. Can it be seriously maintained that the dedication of such rare skills and resources to protracting the life of a middle-aged Cape Town dentist for a few extra months or years can be justified in a continent where doctors and medical supplies are so woefully lacking? Doctors themselves have spoken out about this. Even in England, as we all know, patients sometimes have to wait an inordinate time for life-and-death operations, and hospital staff and accommodation are desperately short. Surely the resources tied up for heart transplants are out of all proportion to what has been, or may be, achieved in the way of advancing medicine's true aims—to heal the sick and alleviate suffering. So far the chief result of the transplants has been to advertise the transplanters in a highly distasteful and unprofessional manner, and to raise in sufferers from heart complaints, hopes that can never be realized. 7

I have in honesty to admit that I feel for this spare-part surgery—as I know others do—a deep, instinctive repugnance that is not capable of a wholly rational explanation. Such feelings, I am well aware, can be, and have been, dismissed as mere obscurantism and atavism. Yet the feeling of revulsion persists. It has to do with a sense that all creation pre-eminently deserves respect—the animals, the plants and trees and grass, the folds of the hills and the sweep of the plains, the very stones and soil, and especially man. That our present way of life is carrying us in the opposite direction—toward using creatures and crops and one another without respect; greedily, arrogantly bulldozing out whatever stands in our way, breeding weird animal grotesques for our meat, subordinating crops, fruits, the forests, and the springs, everything, to our purposes without reference to nature and its exigencies.   8

Somehow, to me, the heart transplants are part of this process: Man trying to grasp at some kind of crazy renewal of himself—of heart, of kidney, of liver. Toying with the notion, perhaps, deep in his unconscious, of reanimating his waning fertility. New ballocks in old crotches! (Did not Dr. Blaiberg, in proof of his new heart's efficacy, disclose that, three weeks after acquiring it, he was able to indulge in sexual intercourse? A miracle indeed!) Envisaging, even, a self-induced immortality. Living forever, like an old vintage car—each part replaceable, even the battery or headpiece, as it wears out. Man achieving everlasting life, not because his soul is immortal and belongs to eternity, but because his body can continue to exist in time till the end of time. What an immortality that would be! It recalls Swift's terrible account of the Struldbrugs, those melancholy creatures of the island of Luggnagg, who, unable to die, spent their days envying the dead.   9

Suggestions for Writing

1 The familiar essay often has had great success in dealing with the unusual, the strange, the "accidental." The writer of such an essay discovers his subject because he has a unique way of looking at things. In some degree, every person has this ability, since each of us is unique.
   a Faces in a railway station
   b Laughter in a theater
   c An unexpected ————
2 The familiar essay is often very successful in its use of "familiar" things. Some of the best have been written about the ordinary, the usual, even the trivial. There are no limits to the subject matter of this kind of writing, for the writer can make anything of interest to him interesting to the reader.
   a A trip to the attic
   b A family wedding
   c "Parents are also human"

WHAT IS A GOOD REVIEW?

JOSEPH WOOD KRUTCH

Of all literary forms the book review is the one most widely cultivated and least often esteemed. To many the very phrase "literary form" may smack of pretense when applied to a kind of writing which is usually so casual; and formlessness may, indeed, be the only form of many commentaries on books. Book reviewing can, nevertheless, become an art in itself and would be such more often if the ambitious reviewer would only devote himself to the cultivation of its particular excellences instead of attempting, as he so often does, to demonstrate his capacities by producing something "more than a mere review." The best review is not the one which is trying to be something else. It is not an independent essay on the subject of the book in hand and not an aesthetic discourse upon one of the literary genres. The best book review is the best review of the book in question, and the better it is the closer it sticks to its ostensible subject.   1

To say this is not to say that a good review is easy to write; in certain technical respects it is, indeed, the most difficult of all forms of literary criticism for the simple reason that in no other is the writer called upon to do so many things in so short a space. The critical essay, no matter how extended it may be, is not compelled to aim at any particular degree of completeness. It may—in fact it usually does—assume that the reader is sufficiently familiar with the work under discussion to make description unnecessary and it may also confine itself to whatever aspects of the subject the critic may choose.   2

But the book review as a literary form implies completeness; it has not really performed its function unless, to begin with, it puts the reader in possession of the facts upon which the criticism is based, and unless— no matter upon how small a scale—its consideration is complete. However penetrating a piece of writing may be, it is not a good review if it leaves the reader wondering what the book itself is like as a whole or if it is concerned with only some aspects of the book's quality.   3

I shall not pretend to say how large a proportion of the so-called reviews published in *The Nation* or anywhere else actually achieve the distinguishing characteristics of the book-review form, but a certain number of them do, and the sense of satisfactoriness which they give can always be traced to the fact that, whatever other qualities they may have, they accomplish the three minimum tasks of the book reviewer. They describe the book, they communicate something of its quality, and they pass a judgment upon it.   4

Each of these things is quite different from the others, but only the last is usually considered as carefully as it ought to be by either reader or writer. Adequate description implies a simple account of the scope and contents of the book; its presence guarantees that the reader will not be left wondering what, in the simplest terms, the book is about. "Communication of quality" implies, on the other hand, a miniature specimen of what is commonly called "impressionistic criticism"; it means that the reviewer must somehow manage to re-create in the mind of the reader some approximation of the reaction produced in his own mind by the book itself. And in however low esteem this form of criticism may be held as a be-all and end-all (Mr. Eliot calls it the result of a weak creative instinct rather than of a critical impulse), it is indispensable in a book review if that review is to perform the function it is supposed to perform, and if it is to become what it is supposed to be—namely, not merely an account of a book on the one hand or an independent piece of criticism on the other, but a brief critical essay which includes within itself all that is necessary to make the criticism comprehensible and significant.   5

Your "reviewer" often envies the more lofty "critic" because the critic is supposed to be read for his own sake while the reviewer must assume that the reader is attracted more by his interest in the book discussed than by the reviewer himself. For that very reason he is likely either to treat reviewing as a casual affair or to seek for an opportunity to write something else under the guise of a review. He might be happier himself and make his readers happier also if he would, instead, take the trouble to ask what a review ought to be and if he would examine his own work in the light of his conclusions. It is not easy to do within the space of a thousand words or less the three things enumerated. It is less easy still to combine the description, the impression, and the judgment into a whole which seems to be, not three things at least, but one.   6

How many reviewers of novels, for instance, seem to know how much of a particular story has to be told in order to provide a solid basis for the impression they intend to convey? And if it is decided that some part of the story must be told, how many know, as a story-teller must, whether the incidents are striking enough to come first or must be introduced with some comment which creates interest? Yet a first-rate review, despite its miniature scale, raises precisely the same problems as long narratives or expositions raise, and each must be solved as artfully if the review is to have such beauty of form as it is capable of. Doubtless the finest reviewer can hardly hope to have his art fully appreciated by the public. But there is every reason why he should respect it himself.   7

A REVIEW OF *MR. SAMMLER'S PLANET*

IRVING HOWE

From book to book, ornament and variations apart, Saul Bellow has really had one commanding subject: the derangements of the soul in the clutter of our cities, the poverty of a life deprived of order and measure. His work has in part continued the line of sensibility established by T. S. Eliot in *The Waste Land,* for in Chicago and New York one can ask as urgently as in London, "what branches grow out of this stony rubbish?" But Bellow has also diverged, in the more original portions of his work, from the Eliot line of sensibility, for he has come to feel that the once-liberating perceptions embodied in Eliot's great poem have, through the erosion of popularity, become clichés. Bellow now writes from a conviction that even today men can establish a self-ordering discipline which rests on a tentative-sardonic faith in the value of a life without faith. As he remarks in his latest and extremely brilliant novel *Mr. Sammler's Planet:*

> . . . people exaggerated the tragic accents of their condition. They stressed too hard the disintegrated assurances; what formerly was believed, trusted, was now bitterly circled in black irony. The rejected bourgeois black of stability thus translated. That too was improper, incorrect. People justifying idleness, silliness, shallowness, distemper, lust—turning former respectability inside out.   1

There is always a danger in the work of an urban novelist like Bellow that his books will turn into still another tiresome afterword to the literary talk about Angst and Alienation; but what has saved Bellow from that common fate has been his fierce insistence that, no matter how heavy the cloud of despair hanging over this (or any other) time, we can still find some pleasure in sociability and our bodies, or, at the least, still experience that root sense of obligation which the mere fact of being human imposes on us.   2

It is from such sentiments that Bellow moves into his latest book. More and more, in recent years, he has found himself cast as an adversary —not always openly, sometimes too cagily—of the dominant styles of our culture. Growing older, entering those hard years when one realizes that the middle of the journey is past, Bellow has not only become a master of his own special idiom, that verbal impasto which mixes demotic richness with mandarin eloquence, racy-tough street Jewishness with high-flown intellectual display; he has also found his place, no longer a dangling man, as person and writer, and set forth on a stubborn, uncertain quest for the cup of wisdom: that cup, if it exists at all, in which the veteran artist hopes to squeeze some essence of contemplation out of the wastes of experience.   3

For putting it so bluntly Bellow isn't likely to thank me, and indeed his characteristic strategy, at least until this new book, has been to protect his flanks through smoke screens of elaborate comic rhetoric. He has maintained two narrative voices signifying two world-outlooks, the first sententious and the second sardonic, yet with the declamations of the sententious voice never quite undone, and sometimes even slyly reinforced, by the thrusts of the sardonic voice. This has kept the reader on his toes, precisely where he belongs.   4

Mr. Sammler's Planet is set in a milieu that has become Bellow's own, a created province of the imagination quite as much as Wessex is Hardy's and Yoknapatawpha Faulkner's. The Upper West Side is a grimy place, at once unfit for human habitation and the scene of what must, I suppose, be called an advanced civilization. It is ugly, filthy, dangerous; it reeks with dog shit; its streets are crammed with the flotsam of society: winos, junkies, pushers, whores, grifters; yet here too are stately refugees, stuffy reformers, literary intellectuals, eager Puerto Ricans, and most of all, elderly Jews haunted by memories of sweatshops and concentration camps and no longer able to take life as incessant struggle. In this menagerie of integration, anomie, and good feeling, people still manage to live. 5

Bellow first immortalized this neighborhood in *Seize the Day*, but the Upper West Side in that great novella was mainly a bright-colored backdrop to a personal drama. In *Mr. Sammler's Planet,* however, the Upper West Side is more than setting, it becomes a tangible sign of the nature of our time. In the Upper West Side, as Bellow sees it, the continuities of ordinary living, by no means always a triumph but never to be sneered at, manage somehow to coexist with the raspy notional foolishness our culture casts off like smoke. The Upper West Side becomes transformed in Bellow's fiction into a principle of sorts, a mixture of health and sickness exemplifying our condition, and not merely through his great gift for evoking every street, every figure, every shade of light and dark, but still more through the saturation of his characters with the spirit of the place. On a smaller scale, Bellow does for the Upper West Side what Lawrence has done for the Midlands and Hardy for Dorset: a linkage of setting and figure so close that the two come to seem inseparable parts in a tradition of shared experience.   6

Mr. Sammler is a Polish Jew in his seventies. In his early years he had worked as a correspondent in London, which accounts for his old-fashioned liberal courtliness and values; later he escaped miraculously from a death convoy in the Nazi camps. Sated with experiences beyond absorption and reflections forever conjectural, Artur Sammler looks out upon America in the Sixties: its violence, its coarseness, its jabbery mindlessness, its sexual cult. He is not surprised, having lived in Europe after the first world war; he is alarmed, knowing that history can repeat itself.

Yet Sammler is not a polemicist, he is too canny for easy visions of apocalypse. Preparing for death, he knows the world is no longer his. He looks,
wonders, muses.   7

Sammlen means "to collect" in Yiddish, and Sammler, like all those
compulsive talkers, half-clown and half-philosopher, in Bellow's novels, is
a collector of experience, sometimes a tentative sorter of conclusions.
First of all his Sammlung consists of relatives, mostly female, the lot of
whom are presented by Bellow with wonderful vivacity and good-humored
tartness. Shula, Sammler's daughter, was saved by a Polish convent during
the holocaust and now is "almost always at Easter" a "week-long Catholic." Mercilessly devoted to the higher things in life, this amiable loon
believes her father is writing an inspired memoir of H. G. Wells. The complications of the plot, if there is a plot, devolve partly around Shula stealing an Indian scholar's manuscript because she thinks it will help her
daddy. Any day on Broadway, our garbaged Mortality Row, you can see
Shula between 72nd and 86th Streets:

> She turned up in a miniskirt of billiard-table green, revealing legs sen-
> sual in outline but without inner sensuality; at the waist a broad leather
> belt; over shoulders, bust, a coarse strong Guatemalan embroidered
> shirt; on her head a wig such as a female impersonator might put on
> at a convention of salesmen.   8

Next, Sammler's niece Margotte, also mad for culture but in a more
gemütlich Weimar way: a dumpy lady prepared to discuss Hannah Arendt's
theory of evil (or anyone else's theory about anything) all day long, while
looking helplessly for a piece of salami with which to make a sandwich.
And last, Angela, "one of those handsome, passionate, rich girls . . .
always an important social and human category," who is driving herself
crazy through sheer sexual concentration. The derangements of the first
two women are of earlier decades, Angela's of this very moment.   9

This cast, with several supporting players, is more than a bit mad yet
not at all insufferable. Human all too human, it is presented by Bellow with
an affectionate sardonic detail, and the incidents that pile up with seeming
casualness bring them into quick changes of relationship, all calculated to
set off Sammler's dilemmas and reflections. He detects a black pickpocket,
superbly elegant and powerful, working the Riverside bus; the pickpocket,
aware that he has been seen but not frightened, follows Sammler into an
apartment lobby; and there, as evidence of his superiority of being—quite
as if he'd been reading certain reviews—he exposes to Sammler his
formidable penis. It is an act of symbolism Sammler is prepared to understand, if not quite appreciate.   10

In another episode, again shot through with the fevers of our moment, Sammler accepts an invitation to lecture at Columbia about England during the Thirties:

> "Old Man! You quoted Orwell before."
> "Yes?"
> "You quoted him to say that British radicals were all protected by the Royal Navy? . . ."
> "Yes, I believe he did say that."
> "That's a lot of shit."
> Sammler could not speak.
> "Orwell was a fink. He was a sick counterrevolutionary. It's good he died when he did. And what you are saying is shit." Turning to the audience, extending violent arms and raising his palms like a Greek dancer, he said, "Why do you listen to this effete old shit? What has he got to tell you? His balls are dry. He's dead. He can't come."   11

Lively-odd figures, brilliantly managed incidents—but what does it all come to? That, until the very last paragraph, is the question one keeps asking about *Mr. Sammler's Planet.*   12

Perhaps there's an answer of sorts in the lectures and speeches, more in the style of *Herzog* than *Seize the Day*, that Bellow scatters through his pages? For whole sections the book moves into a genre somewhat like those conversations Thomas Love Peacock wrote in the nineteenth century, in which voices of varying refinement representing disembodied but fixed opinions are set up in an interplay of friction. There are readers who have always felt these portions of Bellow's novels to be digressive or pretentious, in any case lessening the immediate emotional impact of his work. I think such criticisms mainly—not always—ill-conceived, first because Bellow is a man of high intelligence so that his generalized commentary is intrinsically absorbing, and second because he has the rare gift of transforming dialectic into drama, casuistry into comedy, so that one is steadily aware of the close relationship between his discursive passages and the central narrative. Here is Sammler-Bellow ruminating about the culture of the Sixties:

> The labor of Puritanism now was ending. The dark santanic mills changing into light satanic mills. The reprobates converted into children of joy, the sexual ways of the seraglio and of the Congo bush adopted by the emancipated masses of New York. . . . Old Sammler with his screwy visions! He saw the increasing triumph of Enlightenment—Liberty, Fraternity, Equality, Adultery! . . . Dark romanticism now took hold. As old at least as the strange Orientalism of the Knights Templar, and since then filled up with Lady Stanhopes, Baudelaires, de Nervals, Stevensons, and Gauguins—those South-loving barbarians. Oh yes, the Templars. They had adored the Muslims. One hair from the head of a Saracen was more precious than the whole body of a Christian. Such crazy fervor! And now all the racism, all the strange erotic persuasions,

the tourism and local color, the exotics of it had broken up but the mental masses, inheriting everything in a debased state, had formed an idea of the corrupting disease of being white and of the healing power of black. The dreams of nineteenth-century poets polluted the psychic atmosphere of the great boroughs and suburbs of New York. Add to this the dangerous lunging staggering crazy violence of fanatics, and the trouble was very deep. Like many people who had seen the world collapse once, Mr. Sammler entertained the possibility it might collapse twice. He did not agree with refugee friends that this doom was inevitable, but liberal beliefs did not seem capable of self-defense, and you could smell decay. You could see the suicidal impulses of civilization pushing strongly.   13

Yet we are still dealing with fragments, episodes, set pieces: our most gifted novelist turning somersaults and negotiating leaps like Villella on a spree. Is that all? Are we not bound to expect some ultimate unity of action and theme, no matter how slyly achieved?   14

It is there, but so risky in execution that many readers, I suspect, will deny its presence. Throughout the book Sammler keeps returning to the hospital room of a friend, Dr. Arnold Elya Gruner, a rich and crafty man, sometime Mafia abortionist, soured father of Angela the handsome nymph, and yet, as we come to see, a decent man in quite commonplace ways. Elya had rescued Sammler and Shula after the war, had given them money with which to live: a not very costly, and if you wish, a *bourgeois* gesture. Sammler knows his faults, but knows too that in this ordinary man there are strengths and resources of a kind we must have if we are not to perish on this earth.   15

An old man implicated, despite his wish for detachment, in the lunacies of his daughter, the gabble of his niece, the suicidal thrust of Angela, the brutalities of the Columbia heckler, the threat of the pickpocket, and a host of other menacing fantasies and realities that rise out of the very pavements of the Upper West Side, Sammler all the while keeps yielding himself to the most fundamental themes of gravity: a man is dying, a man who has been good to me. He has shown himself responsible to me, I must be responsible to him. Gradually all the foolishness of Sammler's days, all the absurdity and ugliness of his encounters, all the brittleness and bravura of his thought, give way. There remains only the imperative of the human obligation. Standing over the dead body of his quite unremarkable friend, Sammler speaks the final words of the book:

He was aware that he must meet, and he did meet—through all the confusion and degraded clowning of this life through which we are speeding—he did meet the terms of his contract. The terms which, in his inmost heart, each man knows. As I know mine. As all know. For that is the truth of it—that we all know, God, that we know, that we know, we know, we know.   16

These lines, like all of Bellow's endings, constitute an overwhelming stroke. Carrying its truth as a precious cargo I yet find myself wondering whether Eliot, a writer of different persuasion, might not ask, "Yes, in our inmost hearts we know, or at least remember, but *how* do we know? Is it not through the memory of traditions lapsed and beliefs denied?" What Bellow might say in reply I would not presume to guess, but the strength of the position from which he would speak seems very clear to me. Of all the "American Jewish writers" of the last few decades Bellow is not merely the most gifted by far, but the most serious—and the most Jewish in his seriousness. In him alone, or almost alone, the tradition of immigrant Jewishness, minus the *Schmaltz* and *Schmutz* the decades have stuccoed onto it, survives with a stern dignity. Sammler speaking at the end is something like a resurrected voice: experience fades, explanations deceive, the iron law of life is the obligation we owe one another. The *Sammlung* is complete.   17

The Whole Selection

1 Comment on the function of paragraphs 1 through 4.
2 Does Howe satisfy the criteria for a good review as suggested by Joseph Wood Krutch in "What Is a Good Review" (page 601)?
3 What particular aspect of the novel (e.g., character, setting, theme) does Howe seem to emphasize in his analysis? Why?
4 Point out the specific passages of the review in which Howe makes his evaluation of the success of the novel.
5 Does Howe's use of quotations from the novel contribute anything to the review?
6 Of what use is the information which Howe gives us concerning the author of the novel?

CONCERNING THE UNPREDICTABLE

W. H. AUDEN

> In creation there is not only a Yes but also a No; not only a
> height but also an abyss; not only clarity but also obscurity;
> not only progress and continuation but also impediment and
> limitation . . . not only value but also worthlessness. . . . It
> is true that individual creatures and men experience these
> things in most unequal measure, their lots being assigned
> by a justice which is curious or very much concealed. Yet it
> is irrefutable that creation and creature are good even in the
> fact that all that is exists in this contrast and antithesis.
> —Karl Barth in "Church Dogmatics."

Rather oddly, I first heard of Dr. Loren Eiseley not in this country but in Oxford, where a student gave me a copy of "The Immense Journey," since which time I have eagerly read anything of his I could lay my hands on. His obvious ancestors, as both writers and thinkers, are Thoreau and Emerson, but he often reminds me of Ruskin, Richard Jefferies, W. H. Hudson, whom, I feel sure, he must have read, and of two writers, Novalis (a German) and Adalbert Stifter (an Austrian), whom perhaps he hasn't. But I wouldn't be sure. Some of the quotations in his latest book ("The Unexpected Universe," Harcourt, Brace & World) surprised me. I would not have expected someone who is an American and a scientist to have read such little-known literary works as the "Völuspá," James Thomson's "The City of Dreadful Night," and Charles Williams' play "Cranmer." [1]

I have one slight criticism of his literary style, which I will get over with at once. Like Ruskin, he can at times write sentences which I would call "woozy;" that is to say, too dependent upon some private symbolism of his own to be altogether comprehensible to others. For example:

> We refuse to consider that in the old eye of the hurricane we
> may be, and doubtless are, in aggregate, a slightly more diffuse and
> dangerous dragon of the primal morning that still enfolds us.

To this objection he has, I know, a crushing reply:

> One of Thoreau's wisest remarks is upon the demand scientific
> intellectuals sometimes make, that one must speak so as to be always
> understood. "Neither men," he says, "nor toadstools grow so." [2]

Dr. Eiseley happens to be an archeologist, an anthropologist, and a naturalist, but, if I have understood him rightly, the first point he wishes to make is that in order to be a scientist, an artist, a doctor, a lawyer, or what-have-you, one has first to be a human being. No member of any other species can have a special "field." One question his book raises is: "What differences have recent scientific discoveries, in physics, astronomy, biology, etc., made to man's conception, individually or collectively, of himself?" The answer is, I believe, very little.   3

We did not have to wait for Darwin to tell us that, as physical creatures, we are akin to other animals. Like them, we breathe, eat, digest, excrete, copulate, are viviparously born, and, whatever views we may have about an "afterlife," must certainly suffer physical death in this. Indeed, one result of urbanization has been that, despite what we now know about our ancestry, we feel far less akin and grateful to the animal kingdom than did primitive tribes, with their totem systems and animal folktales.   4

Speaking of the recognition of Odysseus by his dog Argos, Dr. Eiseley says:

> The magic that gleams an instant between Argos and Odysseus is both the recognition of diversity and the need for affection across the illusions of form. It is nature's cry to homeless, far-wandering, insatiable man: "Do not forget your brethren, nor the green wood from which you sprang. To do so is to invite disaster. . . . One does not meet oneself until one catches the reflection from an eye other than human."   5

Before Descartes, such a warning would have been unnecessary. On the other hand, nothing Darwin and the geneticists have to tell us can alter the fact that, as self-conscious beings who speak (that is to say, give Proper Names to other beings), who laugh, who pray, and who, as creators of history and culture, continue to change after our biological evolution is complete, we are unique among all the creatures we know of. All attempts to account for our behavior on the basis of our prehuman ancestors are myths, and usually invented to justify base behavior. As Karl Kraus wrote:

> When a man is treated like a beast, he says, "After all, I'm human." When he behaves like a beast, he says, "After all, I'm only human."   6

No; as Dr. Eiseley says, "There is no definition or description of man possible by reducing him to ape or tree-shrew. Once, it is true, the shrew contained him, but he is gone." Or, as G. K. Chesterton said, "If it is not true that a divine being fell, then one can only say that one of the animals went completely off its head."   7

What modern science has profoundly changed is our way of thinking about the non-human universe. We have always been aware that human beings are characters in a story in which we can know more or less what has happened but can never predict what is going to happen; what we never realized until recently is that the same is true of the universe. But, of course, its story is even more mysterious to us than our own. When we act, we do know something about our motives for action, but it is rarely possible for us to say why anything novel happens in the universe. All the same, I do not personally believe there is such a thing as a "random" event. "Unpredictable" is a factual description; "random" contains, without having the honesty to admit it, a philosophical bias typical of persons who have forgotten how to pray. Though he does use the term once, I don't think Dr. Eiseley believes in it, either:

> The earth's atmosphere of oxygen appears to be the product of a biological invention, photosynthesis, another random event that took place in Archeozoic times. That single "invention," for such it was, determined the entire nature of life on this planet, and there is no possibility at present of calling it preordained. Similarly, the stepped-up manipulation of chance, in the shape of both mutation and recombination of genetic factors, which is one result of the sexual mechanism, would have been unprophesiable.   8

I must now openly state my own bias and say that I do not believe in Chance; I believe in Providence and Miracles. If photosynthesis was invented by chance, then I can only say it was a damned lucky chance for us. If, biologically speaking, it is a "statistical impossibility" that I should be walking the earth instead of a million other possible people, I can only think of it as a miracle which I must do my best to deserve. Natural Selection as a negative force is comprehensible. It is obvious that a drastic change in the environment, like an Ice Age, will destroy a large number of species adapted to a warm climate. What I cannot swallow is the assertion that "chance" mutations can explain the fact that whenever an ecological niche is free, some species evolves to fit it, especially when one thinks how peculiar some such niches—the one occupied by the liver fluke, for example—can be. Dr. Eiseley quotes George Gaylord Simpson as saying:

> The association of unusual physical conditions with a crisis in evolution is not likely to be pure coincidence. Life and its environment are interdependent and evolve together.   9

Dr. Eiseley has excellent things to say about the myth of the Survival of the Fittest:

> A major portion of the world's story appears to be that of fumbling little creatures of seemingly no great potential, falling, like the helpless little girl Alice, down a rabbit hole or an unexpected crevice into some new and topsy-turvy realm. . . . The first land-walking fish was, by modern standards, an ungainly and inefficient vertebrate. Figura-

tively, he was a water failure who had managed to climb ashore on a continent where no vertebrates existed. In a time of crisis he had escaped his enemies. . . . The wet fish gasping in the harsh air on the shore, the warm-blooded mammal roving unchecked through the torpor of the reptilian night, the lizard-bird launching into a moment of ill-aimed flight, shatter all purely competitive assumptions. These singular events reveal escapes through the living screen, penetrated, one would have to say in retrospect, by the "overspecialized" and the seemingly "inefficient," the creatures driven to the wall.   10

The main theme of "The Unexpected Universe" is Man as the Quest Hero, the wanderer, the voyager, the seeker after adventure, knowledge, power, meaning, and righteousness. The Quest is dangerous (he may suffer shipwreck or ambush) and unpredictable (he never knows what will happen to him next). The Quest is not of his own choosing—often, in weariness, he wishes he had never set out on it—but is enjoined upon him by his nature as a human being:

> No longer, as with the animal, can the world be accepted as given. It has to be perceived and consciously thought about, abstracted, and considered. The moment one does so, one is outside of the natural; objects are each one surrounded with an aura radiating meaning to man alone.

> Mostly the animals understand their roles, but man, by comparison, seems troubled by a message that, it is often said, he cannot quite remember or has gotten wrong. . . . Bereft of instinct, he must search continually for meanings. . . . Man was a reader before he became a writer, a reader of what Coleridge once called the mighty alphabet of the universe.   11

For illustrations of his thesis, Dr. Eiseley begins with an imaginary voyage—Homer's epic the "Odyssey"—and goes on to two famous historical voyages, that of Captain Cook in the Resolution, during which he discovered not the Terra Incognita he was sent to find—a rich and habitable continent south and westward of South America—but what he described as "an inexpressibly horrid Antarctica," and Darwin's voyage in the Beagle, during which he found the data which led him to doubt the Fixity of Species. Lastly, Dr. Eiseley tells us many anecdotes from his own life voyage, and these are to me the most fascinating passages in the book. Of the "Odyssey" he says:

> Odysseus' passage through the haunted waters of the eastern Mediterranean symbolizes, at the start of the Western intellectual tradition, the sufferings that the universe and his own nature impose upon homeward-yearning man. In the restless atmosphere of today all the psychological elements of the Odyssey are present to excess: the driving will toward achievement, the technological cleverness crudely manifest

in the blinding of Cyclops, the fierce rejection of the sleepy Lotus Isles, the violence between man and man. Yet, significantly, the ancient hero cries out in desperation, "There is nothing worse for men than wandering."   12

Dr. Eiseley's autobiographical passages are, most of them, descriptions of numinous encounters—some joyful, some terrifying. After reading them, I get the impression of a wanderer who is often in danger of being shipwrecked on the shores of Dejection—it can hardly be an accident that three of his encounters take place in cemeteries—and a solitary who feels more easily at home with animals than with his fellow human beings. Aside from figures in his childhood, the human beings who have "messages" for him are all total strangers—someone tending a rubbish dump, a mysterious figure throwing stranded starfish back into the sea, a vagrant scientist with a horrid parasitic worm in a bottle, a girl in the Wild West with Neanderthal features. As a rule, though, his numinous encounters are with non-human objects—a spider, the eye of a dead octopus, his own shepherd dog, a starving jackrabbit, a young fox. It is also clear that he is a deeply compassionate man who, in his own words, "loves the lost ones, the failures of the world." It is typical of him that, on recovering consciousness after a bad fall, to find himself bleeding profusely, he should, quite unself-consciously, apologize to his now doomed blood cells— phagocytes and platelets—"Oh, don't go. I'm sorry, I've done for you." More importantly, he reveals himself as a man unusually well trained in the habit of prayer, by which I mean the habit of listening. The petitionary aspect of prayer is its most trivial because it is involuntary. We cannot help asking that our wishes may be granted, though all too many of them are like wishing that two and two may make five, and cannot and should not be granted. But the serious part of prayer begins when we have got our begging over with and listen for the Voice of what I would call the Holy Spirit, though if others prefer to say the Voice of Oz or the Dreamer or Conscience, I shan't quarrel, so long as they don't call it the Voice of the Super-Ego, for that "entity" can only tell us what we know already, whereas the Voice I am talking about always says something new and unpredictable—an unexpected demand, obedience to which involves a change of self, however painful.   13

At this point, a digression. Last September, I attended a symposium in Stockholm on "The Place of Value in a World of Fact." Most of those present were scientists, some of them very distinguished indeed. To my shock and amazement, they kept saying that what we need today is a set of *Ethical Axioms* (italics mine). I can only say that to me the phrase is gibberish. An axiom is stated in the indicative and addressed to the intellect. From one set of axioms one kind of mathematics will follow, from another set another, but it would be nonsense to call one of them "better" than the other. All ethical statements are addressed to the will, usually a reluctant will, and must therefore appear in the imperative. "Thou shalt love thy neighbor as thyself" and "A straight line is the shortest distance between two points" belong to two totally different realms of discourse.   14

But to return to Dr. Eiseley. As a rule, the Voice speaks to him not directly but through messengers who are unaware of the message they bear. In the following dream, however, he is spoken to without intermediaries:

> The dream was of a great blurred bear-like shape emerging from the snow against the window. It pounded on the glass and beckoned importunately toward the forest. I caught the urgency of a message as uncouth and indecipherable as the shape of its huge bearer in the snow. In the immense terror of my dream I struggled against the import of that message as I struggled also to resist the impatient pounding of the frost-enveloped beast at the window.
>
> Suddenly I lifted the telephone beside my bed, and through the receiver came a message as cryptic as the message from the snow, but far more miraculous in origin. For I knew intuitively, in the still snowfall of my dream, that the voice I heard, a long way off, was my own voice in childhood. Pure and sweet, incredibly refined and beautiful beyond the things of earth, yet somehow inexorable and not to be stayed, the voice was already terminating its message. "I am sorry to have troubled you," the clear faint syllables of the child persisted. They seemed to come across a thinning wire that lengthened far away into the years of my past. "I am sorry, I am sorry to have troubled you at all." The voice faded before I could speak. I was awake now, trembling in the cold.
>
>   15

I have said that I suspect Dr. Eiseley of being a melancholic. He recognizes that man is the only creature who speaks personally, works, and prays, but nowhere does he overtly say that man is the only creature who laughs. True laughter is not to be confused with the superior titter of the intellect, though we are capable, alas, of that, too: when we truly laugh, we laugh simultaneously *with* and *at*. True laughter (belly laughter) I would define as the spirit of Carnival.   16

Again a digression, on the meaning of Carnival as it was known in the Middle Ages and persisted in a few places, like Rome, where Goethe witnessed and described it in February of 1788. Carnival celebrates the unity of our human race as mortal creatures, who come into this world and depart from it without our consent, who must eat, drink, defecate, belch, and break wind in order to live, and procreate if our species is to survive. Our feelings about this are ambiguous. To us as individuals, it is a cause for rejoicing to know that we are not alone, that all of us, irrespec-

tive of age or sex or rank or talent, are in the same boat. As unique
persons, on the other hand, all of us are resentful that an exception cannot
be made in our own case. We oscillate between wishing we were unreflec-
tive animals and wishing we were disembodied spirits, for in either case
we should not be problematic to ourselves. The Carnival solution of this
ambiguity is to laugh, for laughter is simultaneously a protest and an acceptance. During Carnival, all social distinctions are suspended, even that
of sex. Young men dress up as girls, young girls as boys. The escape from
social personality is symbolized by the wearing of masks. The oddity of the
human animal expresses itself through the grotesque—false noses, huge
bellies and buttocks, farcical imitations of childbirth and copulation. The
protest element in laughter takes the form of mock aggression: people pelt
each other with small, harmless objects, draw cardboard daggers, and
abuse each other verbally, like the small boy Goethe heard screaming at
his father, *"Sia ammazzato il Signore Padre!"* Traditionally, Carnival, the
days of feasting and fun, immediately precedes Lent, the days of fasting
and prayer. In medieval carnivals, parodies of the rituals of the Church
were common, but what Lewis Carroll said of literary parody—"One can
only parody a poem one admires"—is true of all parody. One can only
blaspheme if one believes. The world of Laughter is much more closely
related to the world of Worship and Prayer than either is to the everyday,
secular world of Work, for both are worlds in which we are all equal, in the
first as individual members of our species, in the latter as unique persons.
In the world of Work, on the other hand, we are not and cannot be equal,
only diverse and interdependent: each of us, whether as scientist, artist,
cook, cab-driver, or whatever, has to do "our thing." So long as we
thought of Nature in polytheistic terms as the abode of gods, our efficiency
and success as workers were hampered by a false humility which tried to
make Nature responsible for us. But, according to Genesis, God made
Adam responsible for looking after the Garden of Eden on His behalf, and
it now seems as if He expects us to be responsible for the whole natural
universe, which means that, as workers, we have to regard the universe
etsi deus non daretur: God must be a hidden deity, veiled by His creation. 17

A satisfactory human life, individually or collectively, is possible only
if proper respect is paid to all three worlds. Without Prayer and Work, the
Carnival laughter turns ugly, the comic obscenities grubby and porno-
graphic, the mock aggression into real hatred and cruelty. (The hippies, it
appears to me, are trying to recover the sense of Carnival which is so
conspicuously absent in this age, but so long as they reject Work they are
unlikely to succeed.) Without Laughter and Work, Prayer turns Gnostic,
cranky, Pharisaic, while those who try to live by Work alone, without
Laughter or Prayer, turn into insane lovers of power, tyrants who would

enslave Nature to their immediate desires—an attempt which can only end
in utter catastrophe, shipwreck on the Isle of the Sirens.   18

Carnival in its traditional forms is not, I think, for Dr. Eiseley any
more than it is for me. Neither of us can enjoy crowds and loud noises.
But even introverted intellectuals can share the Carnival experience if
they are prepared to forget their dignity, as Dr. Eiseley did when he un-
expectedly encountered a fox cub:

> The creature was very young. He was alone in a dread universe.
> I crept on my knees around the prow and crouched beside him. It was a
> small fox pup from a den under the timbers who looked up at me.
> God knows what had become of his brothers and sisters. His parent
> must not have been home from hunting.
> He innocently selected what I think was a chicken bone from an
> untidy pile of splintered rubbish and shook it at me invitingly. There
> was a vast and playful humor in his face. . . . Here was the thing in
> the midst of the bones, the wide-eyed, innocent fox inviting me to play,
> with the innate courtesy of its two forepaws placed appealingly together,
> along with a mock shake of the head. The universe was swinging in
> some fantastic fashion around to present its face, and the face was so
> small that the universe itself was laughing.
> It was not a time for human dignity. It was a time only for the
> careful observance of amenities written behind the stars. Gravely I
> arranged my forepaws while the puppy whimpered with ill-concealed
> excitement. I drew the breath of a fox's den into my nostrils. On
> impulse, I picked up clumsily a whiter bone and shook it in teeth that
> had not entirely forgotten their original purpose. Round and round we
> tumbled for one ecstatic moment. . . . For just a moment I had held
> the universe at bay by the simple expedient of sitting on my haunches
> before a fox den and tumbling about with a chicken bone. It is the
> gravest, most meaningful act I shall ever accomplish, but, as Thoreau
> once remarked of some peculiar errand of his own, there is no use
> reporting it to the Royal Society.   19

Thank God, though, Dr. Eiseley has reported it to me. *Bravo!* say I. 20

The Whole Selection

1 What is the relationship of the quotation from Karl Barth at the beginning of the review to the review as a whole?

2 Although this is an essay-review in which the reviewer may be con-
cerned with an issue which transcends the book under scrutiny, does
Auden satisfy the three minimum tasks of the reviewer set forth by
Krutch in "What Is a Good Review"?

3 What do the two digressions (paragraph 14, and paragraphs 17 and
18), of a highly personal character, contribute to the review?

4 At what point in the review does Auden explain the central thesis of Eiseley's book? Why does he wait so long to make this statement?

5 What reasons does Auden present for his favorable judgment of the book?

6 A careful reviewer will always be sure to write so clearly that a reader will not confuse the reviewer's *opinion* of the book with the reviewer's report of what the author of the book says. In this review, cite a passage or passages illustrating such precision.

7 Check the accuracy of Auden's description of the content of Eiseley's book, as far as this can be done, by reference to the selection from Eiseley's book on page 88.

LOLITA

PAULINE KAEL

The ads asked "How did they ever make a movie of *Lolita* for persons over 18 years of age?" A few days later the question mark was moved, and the ads asked, "How did they ever make a movie of *Lolita*?" and after that, the caution: "for persons over 18 years of age." Either way, the suggestion was planted that the movie had "licked" the book, and that *Lolita* had been turned into the usual kind of sexy movie. The advertising has been slanted to the mass audience, so the art-house audience isn't going. A sizable part of the mass audience doesn't like the movie (their rejection is being interpreted as a vote for "wholesomeness," which according to *Variety* is about to stage a comeback) and the art-house audience is missing out on one of the few American films it might enjoy.   1

Recommend the film to friends and they reply, "Oh I've *had* it with *Lolita*." It turns out (now that *Lolita* can be purchased for fifty cents and so is in the category of ordinary popular books) that they never thought much of it; but even though they didn't really like the book, they don't want to see the movie because of all the changes that have been made in the book. (One person informed me that he wouldn't go to see the movie because he'd heard they'd turned it into a comedy.) Others had heard so much about the book, they thought reading it superfluous (they had as *good* as read it—they were *tired* of it); and if the book was too much talked about to necessitate a reading, surely going to the film was really *de trop*?   2

Besides, wasn't the girl who played Lolita practically a *matron?* The New York *Times* had said, "She looks to be a good seventeen," and the rest of the press seemed to concur in this peculiarly inexpert judgment. *Time* opened its review with "Wind up the Lolita doll and it goes to Hollywood and commits nymphanticide" and closed with "*Lolita* is the saddest and most important victim of the current reckless adaptation fad. . . ." In the *Observer* the premiere of the film was described under the heading "Lolita fiasco" and the writer concluded that the novel had been "turned into a film about this poor English guy who is being given the runaround by this sly young broad." In the *New Republic* Stanley Kauffmann wrote, "It is clear that Nabokov respects the novel. It is equally clear that he does not respect the film—at least as it is used in America. . . . He has given to films the *Lolita* that, presumably, he thinks the medium deserves. . . ." After all this, who would expect anything from the film?   3

The surprise of *Lolita* is how enjoyable it is: it's the first *new* American comedy since those great days in the forties when Preston Sturges recreated comedy with verbal slapstick. *Lolita* is black slapstick and at times it's so far out that you gasp as you laugh. An inspired Peter Sellers creates a new comic pattern—a crazy quilt of psychological, sociological commentary so "hip" it's surrealist. It doesn't cover everything: there are structural weaknesses, the film falls apart, and there's even a forced and humiliating attempt to "explain" the plot. But when the wit is galloping who's going to look a gift horse in the mouth? Critics, who feel decay in their bones.   4

The reviews are a comedy of gray matter. Doubts may have remained after Arthur Schlesinger, Jr.'s, ex cathedra judgment that *Lolita* is "willful, cynical and repellent. . . . It is not only inhuman; it is anti-human. I am reluctantly glad that it was made, but I trust it will have no imitators." Then, "for a learned and independent point of view, *Show* invited Dr. Reinhold Niebuhr, the renowned theologian, to a screening in New York and asked him for an appraisal." The higher primate discovered that "the theme of this triangular relationship exposes the unwholesome attitudes of mother, daughter, and lover to a mature observer." (Ripeness is all . . . but is it enough?) This mature observer does however find some "few saving moral insights"—though he thinks the film "obscures" them— such as "the lesson of Lolita's essential redemption in a happy marriage." (Had any *peripheral* redemptions lately?) If you're still hot on the trail of insights, don't overlook the *New Republic*'s steamy revelation that "the temper of the original might . . . have been tastefully preserved" if Humbert had narrated the film. "The general tone could have been: "Yes, this is what I did then and thought lovely. Dreadful, wasn't it? Still . . . it has its funny side, no?' " It has its funny side, oui, oui.   5

The movie adaptation tries something so far beyond the simple "narrator" that a number of the reviewers have complained: Bosley Crowther, who can always be counted on to miss the point, writes that "Mr. Kubrick inclines to dwell too long over scenes that have slight purpose, such as scenes in which Mr. Sellers does various comical impersonations as the sneaky villain who dogs Mr. Mason's trail." These scenes "that have slight purpose" are, of course, just what make *Lolita* new, these are the scenes that make it, for all its slackness of pace and clumsy editing, a more exciting comedy than the last American comedy, *Some Like It Hot*. Quilty, the success, the writer of scenarios and school plays, the policeman, the psychologist; Quilty the genius, the man whom Lolita loves, Humbert's brother and tormentor and parodist; Quilty the man of the world is a conception to talk about alongside Melville's *The Confidence Man*. "Are you with someone?" Humbert asks the policeman. And Quilty the policeman replies, "I'm not with someone. I'm with you."   6

The Quilty monologues are worked out almost like the routines of silent comedy—they not only carry the action forward, they comment on it, and this comment is the *new* action of the film. There has been much critical condescension toward Sellers, who's alleged to be an impersonator rather than an actor, a man with many masks but no character. Now Sellers does a turn with the critics' terms: his Quilty is a character employing masks, an actor with a merciless talent for impersonation. He is indeed "the sneaky villain who dogs Mr. Mason's trail"—and he digs up every bone that "Mr. Mason" ineptly tries to bury, and presents them to him. Humbert can conceal nothing. It is a little like the scene in Victor Sjostrom's magnificent *The Wind,* in which Lillian Gish digs a grave for the man she has murdered and then, from her window, watches in horror as the windstorm uncovers the body. But in *Lolita* our horror is split by laughter: Humbert has it coming—*not* because he's having "relations" with a minor, but because, in order to conceal his sexual predilections, he has put on the most obsequious and mealy-minded of masks. Like the homosexual professors who are rising fast in American academia because they are so cautious about protecting their unconventional sex lives that they can be trusted not to be troublesome to the college administrations on any important issues (a convoluted form of blackmail), Humbert is a worm and Quilty knows it.   7

Peter Sellers works with miserable physical equipment, yet he has somehow managed to turn his lumbering, wide-hipped body into an advantage by *acting* to perfection the man without physical assets. The soft, slow-moving, paper-pushing middle-class man is his special self-effacing type; and though only in his mid-thirties he all too easily incarnates sly, smug middle-aged man. Even his facial muscles are kept flaccid, so that he always looks weary, too tired and cynical for much of a response. The rather frightening strength of his Quilty (who has enormous—almost sinister—reserves of energy) is peculiarly effective just because of his ordinary, "normal" look. He does something that seems impossible: he makes unattractiveness magnetic.   8

Quilty—rightly, in terms of the film as distinguished from the novel—dominates *Lolita* (which could use much more of him) and James Mason's Humbert, who makes attractiveness tired and exhausted and impotent, is a remarkable counterpart. Quilty who doesn't care, who wins Lolita and throws her out, Quilty the homewrecker is a winner; Humbert, slavishly, painfully in love, absurdly suffering, the lover of the ages who degrades himself, who cares about nothing but Lolita, is the classic loser. Mason is better than (and different from) what almost anyone could have expected. Mason's career has been so mottled: a beautiful *Odd Man Out,* a dull Brutus, an uneven, often brilliant Norman Maine in *A Star Is Born,* a good Captain Nemo, and then in 1960 the beginnings of comic style as the English naval commander who pretends to have gone over to the Russians in *A Touch of Larceny.* And now, in *Lolita* he's really in command of a comic style: the handsome face gloats in a rotting smile. Mason seems to need someone strong to play against. He's very good in the scenes with Charlotte and with her friends, and especially good in the bathtub scene (which Niebuhr thinks "may arouse both the laughter and the distaste of the audience"—imagine being so drained of reactions that you have to be *aroused* to distaste!) but his scenes with Lolita, when he must dominate the action, fall rather flat.   9

Perhaps the reviewers have been finding so many faults with *Lolita* because this is such an easy way to show off some fake kind of erudition: even newspaper reviewers can demonstrate that they've read a book by complaining about how different the movie is from the novel. The movie *is* different but not *that* different, and if you can get over the reviewers' pre-occupation with the sacredness of the novel (they don't complain this much about Hollywood's changes in biblical stories) you'll probably find that even the characters that *are* different (Charlotte Haze, especially, who has become the culture-vulture rampant) are successful in terms of the film. Shelley Winters' Charlotte is a triumphant caricature, so overdone it recalls Blake's "You never know what is enough until you know what is more than enough."   10

Sue Lyon is perhaps a little less than enough—but not because she looks seventeen. (Have the reviewers looked at the schoolgirls of America lately? The classmates of my fourteen-year-old daughter are not merely nubile: some of them look badly used.) Rather it is because her role is insufficiently written. Sue Lyon herself is good (at times her face is amusingly suggestive of a miniature Elvis Presley) though physically too *young* to be convincing in her last scenes. (I don't mean that to sound paradoxical but merely descriptive.) Kubrick and company have been attacked most for the area in which they have been simply accurate: they could have done up Sue Lyon in childish schoolgirl clothes, but the facts of American life are that adolescents and even pre-adolescents wear nylons and make-up and two-piece strapless bathing suits and have *figures*.   11

Lolita isn't a consistently good movie but that's almost beside the point: excitement is sustained by a brilliant idea, a new variant on the classic chase theme—Quilty as Humbert's walking paranoia, the madness that chases Humbert and is chased by him, over what should be the delusionary landscape of the actual United States. This panoramic con-fusion of normal and mad that can be experienced traveling around the country is, unfortunately, lost: the film badly needs the towns and motels and highways of the U.S. It suffers not only from the genteel English land-scapes, but possibly also from the photographic style of Oswald Morris perhaps justly famous, but subtly wrong (and too tasteful) for *Lolita*. It may seem like a dreadfully "uncinematic" idea, but I rather wish that Kubrick, when he realized that he couldn't shoot in the U.S. (the reasons must have been economic) had experimented with stylized sets.   12

There *is* a paradox involved in the film *Lolita*. Stanley Kubrick shows talents in new areas (theme and dialogue and comedy), and is at his worst at what he's famous for. *The Killing* was a simple-minded suspense film about a racetrack robbery, but he structured it brilliantly with each facet shining in place; *Paths of Glory* was a simple-minded pacifist film, but he gave it nervous rhythm and a sense of urgency. *Lolita* is so clumsily structured that you begin to wonder what was shot and then cut out, why other pieces were left in, and whether the beginning was intended to be the end; and it is edited in so dilatory a fashion that after the first hour, almost every scene seems to go on too long. It's as if Kubrick lost his nerve. If he did, it's no wonder; the wonder is, that with all the pressures on American moviemakers—the pressures to evade, to conceal, to compromise, and to explain everything for the literal-minded—he had the nerve to transform this satire on the myths of love into the medium that has become consecrated to the myths. *Lolita* is a wilder comedy for being, now, family entertainment. Movie theaters belong to the same world as the highways and motels: in first-run theaters, "for persons over 18 years of age" does not mean that children are prohibited but simply that there are no reduced prices for children. In second-run neighborhood theaters, "for persons over 18 years of age" is amended by "unless accompanied by a member of the family." That befits the story of Humbert Humbert.   13

The Whole Selection

1 Although Krutch describes the three minimum tasks of a book reviewer, his criteria can easily be applied to a review of a film. Does Miss Kael satisfy Krutch's criteria for a good review?

2 Why are the comments of other critics introduced into the review?

3 Point out the specific language used by Miss Kael in characterizing some of the other critics.

4 Trace any one of the formal arguments (though written informally) in the review through its chain of reasoning.

5 Why does the review have such an argumentative tone?

6 Briefly summarize Miss Kael's evaluation of *Lolita* in your own words. Then provide specific evidence from the review to support your summary.

7 Is Miss Kael careful to distinguish *fact* from *opinion?* Point out a few instances in which fact and opinion are used which show whether Miss Kael has been careful or not.

8 Although Krutch's three minimum tasks of a book reviewer are easily applied to the review of a film, what problems, if any, does a film reviewer face that are different from those facing the reviewer of a book?

7

STYLE

For a man to write well, there are required three necessaries—to read the best authors, observe the best speakers, and much exercise of his own style.
                                                                Ben Jonson

In the essays in this section, a great master of English prose, an accomplished novelist, and a literary critic offer practical counsel on language and style. These writers discuss effective diction, style, and the elements of good style. All of them agree that good writing is based upon the principle of decorum: that is to say, good writing is the use of language appropriate to the purpose of the author and the thought that he seeks to express and communicate. These essays themselves are presented primarily for what the authors say and not so much for how they say it. But if we pause occasionally for a close look at the authors' prose, we will see that they generally practice what they preach. Although a full understanding of style can best be gained by firsthand study and practice in these matters, a careful reading of the following essays will give us a sound elementary understanding of style as far as it can be derived from the authority of others.

Both Walker Gibson and John Henry Newman are concerned with the problem of style, the personal accent in the use of the language of a given time within the appropriate standards of speech. Gibson's essay (page 627) suggests that modern prose style will tend to reflect the pluralistic and changing world of our time, and hence we should expect to find in that style a considerable mingling of formal and colloquial diction and a rhythm that is often as irregular as conversational prose, in which short sentences, even sentence fragments, appear frequently and "erratically" along with longer sentences. Gibson sees the changeful character of our times reflected in the modern lexicographer's reluctance to be "authoritative," for example, to label certain words as "standard," "colloquial," and "slang." No such label, he says, "is good for long in a culture as volatile" as ours. Newman's essay (page 635) stresses the inseparability of thought and speech. His definition of style as "a thinking out into language" is aimed against the artificial separation of thought from expression, a heresy as alive today as it was in Newman's time. Using a variety of the methods of analysis, he devotes the whole essay to a persuasive development of his definition. His organic view of style—it can never be "an addition from without"—is worthy of our most serious attention.

After reading Gibson's and Newman's discussions of style, we can profitably turn to Somerset Maugham's analysis of the characteristics of style (page 637). A novelist who is particularly distinguished for the smooth flow of his writing, Maugham emphasizes the strenuous effort that all good writing entails. His own prose is a reflection of the importance that he gives to decorum—being appropriate. His own experience of writing and rewriting should be a comfort and a warning to the less-practiced student of writing. Maugham asserts that "usage is the only test" for language, but does not advocate linguistic chaos. Instead, he is severe with people who write obscurely, accusing them of negligence, will-fulness, or ignorance. The three characteristics of style to which he devotes the major part of his essay—lucidity, simplicity, euphony—are universally recognized as the cures for obscurity and dullness of expres-sion.

Remembering Maugham's suggestion that writing cannot profit from too much theory or too much scolding, we think it best to refer the reader again to the essays in this section, hoping that he will balance a minimum of theory and scolding with "much exercise of *his own* style."

A NOTE ON STYLE AND THE LIMITS OF LANGUAGE

WALKER GIBSON

Questions about style can most usefully be approached if we think of a style as the expression of a personality. I do not mean at all that our words necessarily reveal what we are "really like." I do mean that every writer and talker, more or less consciously, chooses a role which he thinks appropriate to express for a given time and situation. The personality I am expressing in this written sentence is not the same as the one I orally express to my three-year-old who at this moment is bent on climbing onto my typewriter. For each of these two situations, I choose a different "voice," a different mask, in order to accomplish what I want accomplished. There is no point in asking here which of these voices is closer to the Real Me. What may be worth asking is this: what kinds of voices, in written prose, may be said to respond most sensitively and efficiently to the sort of contemporary world that this book has been describing?   1

First, let's be logical about it. Given the kind of dilemma with respect to knowledge and language that this book defines, what sort of style might we *expect* in our own time? What sort of speaking voice adopted by the writer, what mask, would be appropriate in a world where, as we have seen, the very nature of nature may be inexpressible? If we live in a pluralistic and fluxlike universe, what manner of word-man should we become in order to talk about it? Well, we might at least expect a man who knows his limits, who admits the inevitably subjective character of his wisdom. We might expect a man who knows that he has no right in a final sense to consider himself any wiser than the next fellow, including the one he is talking to. The appropriate tone, therefore, might be informal, a little tense and self-conscious perhaps, but genial as between equals. With our modern relativistic ideas about the impossibility of determining any "standard dialect" for expressing Truth in all its forms, we might expect the cautious writer to employ many dialects, to shift from formal to colloquial diction, to avoid the slightest hint of authoritarianism. The rhythm of his words will be an irregular, conversational rhythm—not the symmetrical periods of formal Victorian prose. Short sentences alternating erratically with longer sentences. Occasional sentence fragments. In sum we might expect a style rather like *this!*[1]   2

---

[1] A few of the writer's obvious attempts to echo a conversational tone in that paragraph can be quickly summarized. Contractions (let's). Colloquialisms (well . . . , the next fellow). Some very short sentences. Capitalization in an effort to place an ironical turn on a Big Fat Abstraction (Truth)—an effort that is of course much easier to accomplish with the actual voice. Italics (*expect*, like *this!*), again in mimicry of the way one speaks in conversation. And so on. The purpose of such devices, to compensate for the loss of oral intonation, is strictly speaking impossible to achieve. If only you were here I could say all this to you!

This style, indeed, is easily recognizable and can be discovered all around us in modern prose. Thirty years ago in a book called *Modern Prose Style*, Bonamy Dobrée described it much as we have done here. "Most of us have ceased to believe, except provisionally, in truths," he wrote, "and we feel that what is important is not so much truth as the way our minds move toward truth." The consequence is a kind of self-searching need for frankness and humility on the part of the writer. "The modern prose-writer, in returning to the rhythms of everyday speech, is trying to be more honest with himself than if he used, as is too wreckingly easy, the forms and terms already published as the expression of other people's minds." Finally, in a touching sentence, "In our present confusion our only hope is to be scrupulously honest with ourselves." That was written in 1933: since then the confusion has multiplied spectacularly, while our hopes of ever being "scrupulously honest" about anything look pretty dim. Still, the relation Dobrée made, between an intellectual difficulty and a style, is essentially the relation we are making here.   3

The trouble with it—and a reminder of the awful complexity of our subject—is that sometimes this proposition simply doesn't work. Some contemporary writers, sensitively aware of the limits of language, indeed conceding them explicitly, nevertheless write in a *style* that sounds like the wisdom of Moses, or like Winston Churchill. Far from echoing the rhythms of ordinary speech, they pontificate or chant in authoritarian rhythms the assertion that one cannot be authoritarian. We have a fine example of this paradox in the paragraph by Oppenheimer that I have so much admired:

> The problem of doing justice to the implicit, the imponderable, and the unknown is of course not unique to politics. It is always with us in science, it is with us in the most trivial of personal affairs, and it is one of the great problems of writing and of all forms of art. The means by which it is solved is sometimes called style. It is style which complements affirmation with limitation and with humility; it is style which makes it possible to act effectively, but not absolutely; it is style which, in the domain of foreign policy, enables us to find a harmony between the pursuit of ends essential to us and the regard for the views, the sensibilities, the aspirations of those to whom the problem may appear in another light; it is style which is the deference that action pays to uncertainty; it is above all style through which power defers to reason.

Oppenheimer uses a vocabulary, sentence structure, tone, and rhythm all highly structured and formalized; there is no unbending there. The theme of his discourse—that style is "the deference that action pays to uncertainty"—seems at odds with the *personality* we hear uttering this theme. That personality, because of the way the words are chosen and arranged, appears curiously self-confident, even dictatorial, with echoes perhaps of

Johnsonian prose, or Macaulay's elegant sentences. Thus the first sentence is built around a handsome triplet of alliterative abstractions ("the implicit, the imponderable, and the unknown"); the second sentence is built out of another triplet of nicely balanced clauses. The extraordinary final sentence approaches incantation in its parallel repetitions of structure. The "voice" we hear, remote indeed from ordinary conversation, seems to *know* even as it asserts its own humility. Different readers will explain all this in different ways: some will argue that the traditional manner lends sincerity and persuasiveness to the message, while others will be set off by what they consider a real discrepancy between matter and manner. We recall that the passage was taken from an address delivered at a formal occasion. I have heard Mr. Oppenheimer's platform manner described as "arrogant"; our stylistic observations might well account in part for such an impression. In any case it is clear that no easy formula—Dobrée's or anyone else's—is going to account for all the vagaries of modern prose.   4

Other writers in this collection will illustrate Dobrée's thesis with less embarrassment—that is, will show clear evidence of a "conversational" voice. Thus Muller

> Emerson remarked that it is a good thing, now and then, to take a look at the landscape from between one's legs. Although this stunt might seem pointless when things are already topsy-turvy, it can be the more helpful then. One may say that what this chaotic world needs first of all is *dis*sociation; by breaking up factitious alliances and oppositions, one may get at the deep uniformities. Or . . .

The simplicity of the diction in that first sentence, and the absurdity of the described action, support a familiar relation of equality between the speaking voice and the reader. There is no talking down; we all know who Emerson is. (Not "That great American Transcendentalist, Ralph Waldo Emerson. . . .") "Now and then," "stunt," "topsy-turvy" contribute the colloquial touch. The slightly awkward "then" at the end of the second sentence suggests that in this particular communication formal grace would be inappropriate. But with the third sentence the writer boldly shifts his tone as his diction becomes more polysyllabic and his sentence structure more complex. "Enough of geniality," he seems to say, "you must now follow me into a serious tangle." With this abruptness, Muller is perhaps "breaking up factitious alliances" *in his style,* so that his own prose both expresses and dramatizes the point he is making.   5

The trick, if that is what it is, of mingling formal and colloquial vocabulary can convey a kind of ironical thrust by the writer at his own pretensions. Thus he can have it both ways—make his great assertion and kid himself for his own gall. It is a device much employed in circles that are verbally sophisticated, including academic circles. Consider an extreme example, from a professor of Law at Chicago, here discussing a flexible approach to problems of judicial interpretation:

> But it leads to *good* rules of law and in the main toward flexible ones, so that most cases of a given type can come to be handled not only well but easily, and so that the odd case can normally come in also for a smidgeon of relief. The whole setup leads above all—a recognition of imperfection in language and in officer—to *on-going and unceasing judicial review of prior judicial decision* on the side of rule, tool, and technique. That, plus freedom and duty to do justice *with* the rules but *within* both them and their whole temper, that is the freedom, the leeway for own-contribution, the scope for the person, which the system offers.[2]

6

Here style and message work with a degree of co-operation: a call for unceasing flexibility in the operations of judicial review is expressed in an idiom that is itself almost wildly flexible. The speaker in this passage betrays the strains of an impassioned conversationalist, with his heavy reliance on italics and his interrupted sentence structures. We are button-holed. This is a technical discussion, and most of the vocabulary has to be fairly heavy, but we have "smidgeon" and "whole setup" to cut across the formality. We have even a jazzy bit of alliteration and rhyme—"rule, tool, and technique." The "recognition of imperfection in language," therefore, which is explicitly granted by the text, is implicitly conveyed as well by the unorthodox scramblings of language. Nobody has to like this style (many are simply irritated), but at least one can see what is going on, and why. 7

Or consider another extreme example, from a professor of English at Wisconsin, here discussing problems of usage:

> Bad, fair, good, better, best. Only the best is Correct. No busy man can be Correct. But his wife can. That's what women are for. That's why we have women to teach English and type our letters and go to church for us and discover for us that the English say 'Aren't I?' while we sinfully hunt golf-balls in the rough on Sunday and, when our partner finds two of them, ask 'Which is me?' (Webster: *colloq.*—Professor K of Harvard: I speak colloq myself, and sometimes I write it.) . . . Only a few of us today are aware of the other scales of English usage. It is our business to consciously know about their social utility.[3]

These sentences from a treatise on language admirably demonstrate that self-consciously unbuttoned informality which the subject nowadays seems to demand. To some, again, it will appear offensively "cute," idiosyncratic.

---

[2] From Karl N. Llewellyn, *The Common Law Tradition: Deciding Appeals*, Little, Brown, 1960.

[3] From Martin Joos, *The Five Clocks*. Copyright 1961 by Martin Joos.

Short sentences, some without predicates, surround one almost endless rambling sentence. The ironical capital in Correct (cf. Truth *supra*). Indifference to the rule that pronouns should have specific antecedents ("That's what women are for. That's why . . ."). Muddled number in using personal pronouns (we hunt golf-balls, our partner [sing.] finds, [we] ask 'Which is me?'). Deliberately split infinitive in the last sentence quoted, at a point in the utterance when a conventionally formal tone has begun to enter. We may anticipate, I am sure, a time when writers will endeavor to carefully split their infinitives, at whatever cost in awkwardness, just as writers of a former generation endeavored so elaborately to avoid the "error." All this should prove to at least be amusing.   8

To many readers, the style displayed by a Professor Llewellyn or a Professor Joos will seem undisciplined, vulgar, and chaotic. A sign of academic deterioration. A result of wild "permissiveness" in education and in society generally. But such readers will be missing the point. There is nothing indiscriminately permissive in this style, but the writers do accept and reject different kinds of language from those accepted and rejected by traditional stylists. They express different personalities. Without insisting on the merits of these particular passages, which are certainly debatable, it ought nevertheless to be clear that you do not write in this way simply by saying anything that occurs to you. The process of selection can be, indeed, *more* discriminating because the available supply of language and experience is larger. As this is being written, in the autumn of 1961, a mild flurry about such extensions of language is going on in the press, relating to the publication of a new edition of *Webster's New International Dictionary. The New York Times* has editorialized as follows:

> A passel of double-domes at the G. & C. Merriam Company joint in Springfield, Mass., have been confabbing and yakking for twenty-seven years—which is not intended to infer that they have not been doing plenty work—and now they have finalized Webster's Third New International Dictionary, Unabridged, a new edition of that swell and esteemed word book.
>
> Those who regard the foregoing paragraph as acceptable English prose will find that the new Webster's is just the dictionary for them. The words in that paragraph all are listed in the new work with no suggestion that they are anything but standard.
>
> Webster's has, it is apparent, surrendered to the permissive school that has been busily extending its beachhead on English instruction in the schools. This development is disastrous. . . .   9

The *Times* goes on to acknowledge "the lexical explosion that has showered us with so many words in recent years," and to congratulate the Dictionary for including 100,000 new words or new definitions. "These are improvements, but they cannot outweigh the fundamental fault." Webster's

has always been a "peerless authority on American English," and therefore its editors have "to some degree a public responsibility." "A new
start is needed."   10

There is, I think, something wrong about all this. If you are acknowledging a "lexical explosion," a language changing with accelerating rapid-
ity, then it seems rather difficult to insist at the same time on a "peerless
authority." The editors of the Dictionary may have fulfilled their public
responsibility by taking the only wise course—by including as many new
words and definitions as they could without making "authoritative" judgments about "standard," "colloquial," and "slang." This is not to say that
the modern writer ignores such distinctions; on the contrary he is sensitively aware of them as never before. But he knows, and the dictionary
editors know, that no such label is good for long in a culture as volatile as
this one. Yesterday's slang is today's standard, and the writer who remains
resonant to these shifts has at his disposal a huge and varicolored vocabulary for his art.   11

The reason we call that opening paragraph in the *Times* editorial "un-
acceptable English" is not that it contains slang. The reason is that it contains too many kinds of slang at once, without any awareness of their
differences. You do not say "passel of double-domes" unless you have
some good reason for juxtaposing terms from utterly distinct language
worlds. "Passel" is presumably of western-frontier origin and now has a
kind of weary whimsy about it, while "double-domes" is recent, cheaply
anti-intellectual, with a history something like "egghead" but without the
popular acceptance of "egghead." It is conceivable that these words could
be included in one sentence, but it would take more skill than the *Times*
man has employed. Of course the appearance of clumsiness was just what
served his purpose.   12

Meanwhile the writer who looks backward to "authority," who takes a
static view of Standard Language, is likely to sound like the "straight"
paragraphs of that editorial. The voice there is closer to a chiding or
dictatorial professor than were the voices of the actual professors quoted.
And when such a writer uses "modern" terms, he uses them in ways that
are long over-used before he gets to them—ways like "extending its beachhead on English instruction" or "lexical explosion that has showered us
with so many words." It is this sort of thing that is the true vulgarity in
our time.   13

Nevertheless our society remains generous with half-conscious concessions to the imperfections of its language. It may be, for example, that
the language of the beatniks, especially their oral conventions, could be
looked at in the light of such concessions. Consider just one curious symptom of jive-talk (now dated)—the suffix-plus-prefix *like*. "We came to this

big town like and all the streets were like crazy, man." This attempt at
rendering beat dialect is doubtless inaccurate but it should serve to make
the point. That point is that the beats have (deliberately?) modified or
qualified their nouns and adjectives by suggesting that they are not quite
accurate, not quite the way things are. "This big town like"—it is a one-
ended metaphor. Like what? We have a tenor but no vehicle, or is it a
vehicle without a tenor? I have been told that many beats are determinedly
antiverbal, preferring to listen to jazz while lying on beaches in Zenlike
silence. It fits. The skepticism about the validity of words that "like"
implies is a peculiarly twentieth-century skepticism, it seems to me,
though there may be analogies with other ages such as the seventeenth
century, when scientific developments encouraged similar self-scrutinies
and self-doubts. In any event the beats, in their crude and sloppy way of
course, have surrounded much of their language with a metaphorical blur
by using (among other things) the simple device of "like." They suggest,
with this blur, their conviction of the impossibility of anybody else's doing
any better with words. Only squares believe you can speak "precisely."   14

The complexities of experience do occasionally get faced one way or
another—if not with the beat's pose of inarticulateness, then with some
other pose that will serve to avoid the charge of *really knowing*. Modern
novelists adopt a "point of view" which is often no point of view at all, but
several points of view from which to indicate various inadequate interpretations of various fictitious characters. It is a technique that will show how
two novels as apparently unlike as *The Waves* and Faulkner's *As I Lay Dying*
belong after all to the same age. There is no narrator, no one of whom
the reader might conceivably say, "There! That's the author talking." The
technique is not new; there is *The Ring and the Book,* to mention one
example. But the difference is that when you read *The Ring and the Book,*
you feel how firmly and finally Browning is on Pompilia's "side," in spite
of his wonderful multiplicity throughout that great poem. Whereas in many
modern novels you scarcely know who is on anybody's side—you must
simply flow in the flux. Sometimes it is so lifelike you can hardly stand it.   15

And of course that road—the road of chaos chaotically expressing
chaos—is a dead end of imitative form where we end with a grunt, or
maybe a whimper. The very point is that language will never *say* our experience "as is," and recognizing this truth, we have immense freedom of
possibility to make, create, form what we can out of words or out of anything else. The most elaborate of villanelles is not much further removed
from Real Life than the latest Allen Ginsburg poem, or a slice of Mr.
Bloom's day. So write a villanelle if that will meet your need. But whatever
it is, there remains this simple blasphemy to be avoided, and that is the
blasphemy of ignoring the limits, of assuming that one's words do indeed

tell the reader what is going on. There is an important sense in which
nobody knows what he is talking about.   16
    I hope I do not except myself and everything uttered here.   17

The Whole Selection

1 Does the style which Gibson uses in paragraph 2 demonstrate the
definition of "style" which he gives in the first three sentences of
paragraph 1?
2 Note how different Gibson's style is in paragraph 4 from his style in
paragraph 2. What explanation can you give for this?
3 In paragraph 9, Gibson suggests that the styles of Professors Llewellyn
and Joos (see paragraphs 6 through 8) may have required considerable
discrimination in the linguistic choices evident in their writing, indeed
more discrimination than a traditional stylist need exercise. What does
Gibson find in the character of *Webster's New International Dictionary*
(now popularly known as "Webster's 3d") to support his suggestion
regarding the demands of the styles of Llewellyn and Joos?

STYLE

JOHN HENRY NEWMAN

Thought and speech are inseparable from each other. Matter and expression are parts of one: style is a thinking out into language. This is what I have been laying down, and this is literature; not *things,* not the verbal symbols of things; not on the other hand mere *words;* but thoughts expressed in language. Call to mind, Gentlemen, the meaning of the Greek word which expresses this special prerogative of man over the feeble intelligence of the inferior animals. It is called Logos: what does Logos mean? it stands both for *reason* and for *speech,* and it is difficult to say which it means more properly. It means both at once: Why? because really they cannot be divided,—because they are in a true sense one. When we can separate light and illumination, life and motion, the convex and the concave of a curve, then will it be possible for thought to tread speech under foot, and to hope to do without it—then will it be conceivable that the vigorous and fertile intellect should renounce its own double, its instrument of expression, and the channel of its speculations and emotions.   1

Critics should consider this view of the subject before they lay down such canons of taste as the writer[1] whose pages I have quoted. Such men as he is consider fine writing to be an *addition from without* to the matter treated of,—a sort of ornament superimposed, or a luxury indulged in, by those who have time and inclination for such vanities. They speak as if *one* man could do the thought, and *another* the style. We read in Persian travels of the way in which young gentlemen go to work in the East, when they would engage in correspondence with those who inspire them with hope or fear. They cannot write one sentence themselves; so they betake themselves to the professional letter-writer. They confide to him the object they have in view. They have a point to gain from a superior, a favour to ask, an evil to deprecate; they have to approach a man in power, or to make court to some beautiful lady. The professional man manufactures words for them, as they are wanted, as a stationer sells them paper, or a schoolmaster might cut their pens. Thought and word are, in their conception, two things, and thus there is a division of labour. The man of thought comes to the man of words; and the man of words, duly instructed in the thought, dips the pen of desire into the ink of devotedness and proceeds to spread it over the page of desolation. Then the nightingale of affection is heard to warble to the rose of loveliness, while the breeze of anxiety plays around the brow of expectation. This is what the Easterns are said to consider fine writing; and it seems pretty much the idea of the school of critics to whom I have been referring.   2

[1] Sterne, Sermon xlii.

another form of wilful obscurity that masquerades as aristocratic exclusiveness. The author wraps his meaning in mystery so that the vulgar shall not participate in it. His soul is a secret garden into which the elect may penetrate only after overcoming a number of perilous obstacles. But this kind of obscurity is not only pretentious; it is short-sighted. For time plays an odd trick. If the sense is meagre, time reduces it to a meaningless verbiage that no one thinks of reading. This is the fate that has befallen the lucubrations of those French writers who were seduced by the example of Guillaume Appollinaire. But occasionally it throws a sharp cold light on what had seemed profound and thus discloses the fact that these contortions of language disguised very commonplace notions. There are few of Mallarmé's poems now that are not clear; one cannot fail to notice that his thought singularly lacked originality. Some of his phrases were beautiful; the materials of his verse were the poetic platitudes of his day.   2

　　Simplicity is not such an obvious merit as lucidity. I have aimed at it because I have no gift for richness. Within limits I admire richness in others, though I find it difficult to digest in quantity. I can read one page of Ruskin with delight, but twenty only with weariness. The rolling period, the stately epithet, the noun rich in poetic associations, the subordinate clauses that give the sentence weight and magnificence, the grandeur like that of wave following wave in the open sea; there is no doubt that in all this there is something inspiring. Words thus strung together fall on the ear like music. The appeal is sensuous rather than intellectual, and the beauty of the sound leads you easily to conclude that you need not bother about the meaning. But words are tyrannical things, they exist for their meanings, and if you will not pay attention to these, you cannot pay attention at all. Your mind wanders. This kind of writing demands a subject that will suit it. It is surely out of place to write in the grand style of inconsiderable things. No one wrote in this manner with greater success than Sir Thomas Browne, but even he did not always escape this pitfall. In the last chapter of *Hydriotaphia* the matter, which is the destiny of man, wonderfully fits the baroque splendour of the language, and here the Norwich doctor produced a piece of prose that has never been surpassed in our literature; but when he describes the finding of his urns in the same splendid manner the effect (at least to my taste) is less happy. When a modern writer is grandiloquent to tell you whether or no a little trollop shall hop into bed with a commonplace young man you are right to be disgusted.   3

　　But if richness needs gifts with which everyone is not endowed, simplicity by no means comes by nature. To achieve it needs rigid discipline. So far as I know ours is the only language in which it has been found necessary to give a name to the piece of prose which is described as the purple patch; it would not have been necessary to do so unless it were characteristic. English prose is elaborate rather than simple. It was not always so. Nothing could be more racy, straightforward and alive than the prose of Shakespeare; but it must be remembered that this was dialogue written to be spoken. We do not know how he would have written if like Corneille he had composed prefaces to his plays. It may be that they would have been as euphuistic as the letters of Queen Elizabeth. But earlier prose, the prose of Sir Thomas More, for instance, is neither ponderous, flowery nor oratorical. It smacks of the English soil. To my mind King James's Bible has been a very harmful influence on English prose. I am not so stupid as to deny its great beauty. It is majestical. But the Bible is an oriental book. Its alien imagery has nothing to do with us. Those hyperboles, those luscious metaphors, are foreign to our genius. I cannot but think that not the least of the misfortunes that the Secession from Rome brought upon the spiritual life of our country is that this work for so long a period became the daily, and with many the only, reading of our people. Those rhythms, that powerful vocabulary, that grandiloquence, became part and parcel of the national sensibility. The plain, honest English speech was overwhelmed with ornament. Blunt Englishmen twisted their tongues to speak like Hebrew prophets. There was evidently something in the English temper to which this was congenial, perhaps a native lack of precision in thought, perhaps a naïve delight in fine words for their own sake, an innate eccentricity and love of embroidery. I do not know; but the fact remains that ever since, English prose has had to struggle against the tendency to luxuriance. When from time to time the spirit of the language has reasserted itself, as it did with Dryden and the writers of Queen Anne, it was only to be submerged once more by the pomposities of Gibbon and Dr. Johnson. When English prose recovered simplicity with Hazlitt, the Shelley of the letters and Charles Lamb at his best, it lost it again with De Quincey, Carlyle, Meredith and Walter Pater. It is obvious that the grand style is more striking than the plain. Indeed many people think that a style that does not attract notice is not style. They will admire Walter Pater's, but will read an essay by Matthew Arnold without giving a moment's attention to the elegance, distinction and sobriety with which he set down what he had to say.   4

The dictum that the style is the man is well known. It is one of those aphorisms that say too much to mean a great deal. Where is the man In Goethe, in his birdlike lyrics or in his clumsy prose? And Hazlitt? But I suppose that if a man has a confused mind he will write in a confused way, if his temper is capricious his prose will be fantastical, and if he has a quick, darting intelligence that is reminded by the matter in hand of a hundred things he will, unless he has great self-control, load his pages with metaphor and simile. There is a great difference between the magniloquence of the Jacobean writers, who were intoxicated with the new wealth that had lately been brought into the language, and the turgidity of Gibbon and Dr. Johnson, who were the victims of bad theories. I can read every word that Dr. Johnson wrote with delight, for he had good sense, charm and wit. No one could have written better if he had not wilfully set himself to write in the grand style. He knew good English when he saw it. No critic has praised Dryden's prose more aptly. He said of him that he appeared to have no art other than that of expressing with clearness what he thought with vigour. And one of his Lives he finished with the words: "Whoever wishes to attain an English style, familiar but not coarse, and elegant but not ostentatious, must give his days and nights to the volumes of Addison." But when he himself sat down to write it was with a very different aim. He mistook the orotund for the dignified. He had not the good breeding to see that simplicity and naturalness are the truest marks of distinction.

5

For to write good prose is an affair of good manners. It is, unlike verse, a civil art. Poetry is baroque. Baroque is tragic, massive and mystical. It is elemental. It demands depth and insight. I cannot but feel that the prose writers of the baroque period, the authors of King James's Bible, Sir Thomas Browne, Glanville, were poets who had lost their way. Prose is a rococo art. It needs taste rather than power, decorum rather than inspiration and vigour rather than grandeur. Form for the poet is the bit and the bridle without which (unless you are an acrobat) you cannot ride your horse; but for the writer of prose it is the chassis without which your car does not exist. It is not an accident that the best prose was written when rococo with its elegance and moderation at its birth attained its greatest excellence. For rococo was evolved when baroque had become declamatory and the world, tired of the stupendous, asked for restraint. It was the natural expression of persons who valued a civilized life. Humour, tolerance and horse sense made the great tragic issues that had preoccupied the first half of the seventeenth century seem excessive. The world was a more comfortable place to live in and perhaps for the first time in centuries the cultivated classes could sit back and enjoy their leisure. It has been said that good prose should resemble the conversation of a well-bred man. Conversation is only possible when men's minds are free from pressing anxieties. Their lives must be reasonably secure and they must have no grave concern about their souls. They must attach importance to the refinements of civilization. They must value courtesy, they must pay attention to their persons (and have we not also been told that good prose should be like the clothes of a well-dressed man, appropriate but unobtrusive?), they must fear to bore, they must be neither flippant nor solemn, but always apt; and they must look upon "enthusiasm" with a critical glance. This a soil very suitable for prose. It is not to be wondered at that it gave a fitting opportunity for the appearance of the best writer of prose that our modern world has seen, Voltaire. The writers of English, perhaps owing to the poetic nature of the language, have seldom reached the excellence that seems to have come so naturally to him. It is in so far as they have approached the ease, sobriety and precision of the great French masters that they are admirable.   6

Whether you ascribe importance to euphony, the last of the three characteristics that I mentioned, must depend on the sensitiveness of your ear. A great many readers, and many admirable writers, are devoid of this quality. Poets as we know have always made a great use of alliteration. They are persuaded that the repetition of a sound gives an effect of beauty. I do not think it does so in prose. It seems to me that in prose alliteration should be used only for a special reason; when used by accident it falls on the ear very disagreeably. But its accidental use is so common that one can only suppose that the sound of it is not universally offensive. Many writers without distress will put two rhyming words together, join a monstrous long adjective to a monstrous long noun, or between the end of one word and the beginning of another have a conjunction of consonants that almost breaks your jaw. These are trivial and obvious instances. I mention them only to prove that if careful writers can do such things it is only because they have no ear. Words have weight, sound and appearance; it is only by considering these that you can write a sentence that is good to look at and good to listen to.   7

I have read many books on English prose, but have found it hard to profit by them; for the most part they are vague, unduly theoretical, and often scolding. But you cannot say this of Fowler's *Dictionary of Modern English Usage*. It is a valuable work. I do not think anyone writes so well that he cannot learn much from it. It is lively reading. Fowler liked simplicity, straightforwardness and common sense. He had no patience with pretentiousness. He had a sound feeling that idiom was the backbone of a language and he was all for the racy phrase. He was no slavish admirer of logic and was willing enough to give usage right of way through the exact demesnes of grammar. English grammar is very difficult and few writers have avoided making mistakes in it. So heedful a writer as Henry James, for instance, on occasion wrote so ungrammatically that a schoolmaster, finding such errors in a schoolboy's essay, would be justly indignant. It is necessary to know grammar, and it is better to write grammatically than not, but it is well to remember that grammar is common speech formulated. Usage is the only test. I would prefer a phrase that was easy and unaffected to a phrase that was grammatical. One of the differences between French and English is that in French you can be grammatical with complete naturalness, but in English not invariably. It is a difficulty in writing English that the sound of the living voice dominates the look of the printed word. I have given the matter of style a great deal of thought and have taken great pains. I have written few pages that I feel I could not improve and far too many that I have left with dissatisfaction because, try as I would, I could do no better. I cannot say of myself what Johnson said of Pope: "He never passed a fault unamended by indifference, nor quitted it by despair." I do not write as I want to; I write as I can.   8

But Fowler had no ear. He did not see that simplicity may sometimes make concessions to euphony. I do not think a far-fetched, an archaic or even an affected word is out of place when it sounds better than the blunt, obvious one or when it gives a sentence a better balance. But, I hasten to add, though I think you may without misgiving make this concession to pleasant sound, I think you should make none to what may obscure your meaning. Anything is better than not to write clearly. There is nothing to be said against lucidity, and against simplicity only the possibility of dryness. This is a risk that is well worth taking when you reflect how much better it is to be bald than to wear a curly wig. But there is in euphony a danger that must be considered. It is very likely to be monotonous. When George Moore began to write, his style was poor; it gave you the impression that he wrote on wrapping paper with a blunt pencil. But he developed gradually a very musical English. He learnt to write sentences that fall away on the ear with a misty languor and it delighted him so much that he could never have enough of it. He did not escape monotony. It is like the sound of water lapping a shingly beach, so soothing that you presently cease to be sensible of it. It is so mellifluous that you hanker for some harshness, for an abrupt dissonance, that will interrupt the silky concord. I do not know how one can guard against this. I suppose the best chance is to have a more lively faculty of boredom than one's readers so that one is wearied before they are. One must always be on the watch for mannerisms and when certain cadences come too easily to the pen ask oneself whether they have not become mechanical. It is very hard to discover the exact point where the idiom one has formed to express oneself has lost its tang. As Dr. Johnson said: "He that has once studiously formed a style, rarely writes afterwards with complete ease." Admirably as I think Matthew Arnold's style was suited to his particular purposes, I must admit that his mannerisms are often irritating. His style was an instrument that he had forged once for all; it was not like the human hand capable of performing a variety of actions.   9

If you could write lucidly, simply, euphoniously and yet with liveliness you would write perfectly; you would write like Voltaire. And yet we know how fatal the pursuit of liveliness may be: it may result in the tiresome acrobatics of Meredith. Macaulay and Carlyle were in their different ways arresting; but at the heavy cost of naturalness. Their flashy effects distract the mind. They destroy their persuasiveness; you would not believe a man was very intent on ploughing a furrow if he carried a hoop with him and jumped through it at every other step. A good style should show no sign of effort. What is written should seem a happy accident. I think no one in France now writes more admirably than Colette, and such is the ease of her expression that you cannot bring yourself to believe that she takes any trouble over it. I am told that there are pianists who have a natural technique so that they can play in a manner that most executants can achieve only as the result of unremitting toil, and I am willing to believe that there are writers who are equally fortunate. Among them I was much inclined to place Colette. I asked her. I was exceedingly surprised to hear that she wrote everything over and over again. She told me that she would often spend a whole morning working upon a single page. But it does not matter how one gets the effect of ease. For my part, if I get it at all, it is only by strenuous effort. Nature seldom provides me with the word, the turn of phrase, that is appropriate without being far-fetched or common-place.   10

The Whole Selection

1 What are the causes of obscure writing, according to Maugham? Which of the kinds of obscurity discussed by him in paragarph 2 is most likely to be found in the writing of a beginner?

2 Can you find any "rolling period" (see paragraph 3) in Maugham's own writing here?

3 In paragraph 6, why does Maugham enclose "enthusiasm" in quotation marks?

4 Is Maugham's last sentence in paragraph 7, ending with a preposition, acceptable in current usage?

5 In paragraph 8, Maugham says that in English we cannot always "be grammatical with complete naturalness" and that the "sound of the living voice dominates the look of the printed word." Would you regard the third and fourth sentences of paragraph 5 in Maugham's own writing here as examples of the difficulty that he notes?

Absolute Phrase

A phrase, usually including a noun and participle, that modifies a main clause. Called "absolute," in the sense of "not being grammatically dependent," because—mistakenly—it has been regarded as having no grammatical relation to the rest of the sentence. E.g.: *"The car having left,* we remained at home."

Abstract Words

Name general qualities or classes rather than particulars or parts. E.g.: "beauty" and "liberty." Such words are indispensable for the advancement of knowledge and for the communication of serious ideas. One should avoid the overuse of such words, because the words are not specific in their appeal. **Concrete Words,** on the other hand, name particulars and specifics, things that can be seen and touched, thus appealing to the senses. E.g.: "geranium," "book," "dog."

Action

In narrative, the term used to describe the movement of events. The answer to the question, "What happened?"

Active Verb

The voice of the verb expressing action performed by its subject. E.g.: "We *went* to the bank." The subject is the doer of the action. E.g.: "Henry James *wrote Portrait of a Lady."* Contrast, e.g., *"Portrait of a Lady was written* by Henry James." See **Passive Verb.** The active verb form is preferred in most instances since it is more direct and forceful.

Ad Hominem

In argument, the fallacy that concerns itself with an attack upon the character of the man advancing the argument. In using it, we talk about a man's character, beliefs, etc., when these have nothing to do with the case. Of course, discussion of a man's character is permissible when it bears on the case being considered.

Alliteration

The recurrence of the same initial sound in words in close succession. More characteristic of poetry than of prose. E.g.: "What a tale of terror, now their turbulency tells!"

Allusive Style

A style characterized by allusions or references to things or persons. These references help to give the statements made richer meanings once the allusions are comprehended by the reader. E.g.: "We spent our vacation at Los Palmos, the *Eden* of the Atlantic."

Analogy
   See pages 371–372.

Antecedent
   The word or statement to which a pronoun refers. E.g.: "The *Johnstons* just bought *their house,* and now Bob wants to sell *it.*"

Argument
   See pages 367–372.

Assumption
   The taking of something for granted. The act of supposing something to be a fact or a truth. The thing taken for granted or supposed. E.g.: "It is assumed that both candidates have a real desire to serve the country." See page 431. Not to be confused with **Hypothesis, Theory,** or **Premise.**

Authority
   In argument, the use of a person or institution of established reputation in the subject under discussion as a type of evidence offered as proof. The tests for a given authority apear on page 458.

Auxiliary Verb
   A verb used to express distinctions of tense, mood, or voice or other aspects of another verb. E.g.: "I *am* going." "He *can* speak well." Some common auxiliary verbs are *be, do, have, can, may, shall, will.*

Balanced Sentence
   A sentence in which the clauses (or phrases) have identity or close correspondence of grammatical structure. E.g.: "I came, I saw, I conquered." See *Parallelism.*

Begging the Question
   In argument, a fallacy in which the writer assumes as truth something that needs proof. He may assume as true a proposition that merely states in equivalent terms the proposition to be proved. E.g.: "Since Jones has worked as Smith has, he should receive equal recognition." (If Smith's results have been superior, the fallacy is that industry should be rewarded no matter what the results are.) A related form of this fallacy is the "Vicious Circle"—arguing in a circle—which uses two propositions to prove each other in turn. E.g.: "The train is on time because its arrival agrees with my watch. My watch must be right because it agrees with the time of the train's coming in."

Book Review
   See pages 586, 601–602.

Cause and Effect
   See pages 259–261.

Central Purpose
   The guiding purpose of an individual piece of writing, to which all the elements of the composition should be directed. See **Thesis Statement.**

Characters
   In fictional narrative, the people who cause or are affected by the action. The author tries to present people as distinct characters by having them

act or talk in a certain way, by reporting what they do, by describing them. For a complete discussion of this subject, see E. M. Forster, *Aspects of the Novel,* Chapters III and IV.

Classification and Division
See pages 193–195.

Climax
In narrative, the culmination of a sequence of events. Often defined as the point of highest interest for the reader. Structurally, the part of a narrative in which things must go one way or the other. In the other forms of discourse, climax may be used to describe the culmination of an order arranged in increasing interest, intensity, or strength.

Coherence
In all discourse, the arrangement of unified parts into an apt pattern. A sentence has coherence when the parts of the sentence are arranged so that the reader is able to apprehend the same connection between the parts that the writer himself saw. A paragraph is coherent when the reader can go from one sentence to another without feeling an abrupt break. The whole composition is coherent when the reader can readily perceive the relationship between paragraph and paragraph and between one large section and another large section of the composition. Coherence is one of the three great principles underlying all composition. The other two are *Unity* and *Emphasis.*

Colloquial Language
Words or phrases (colloquialisms) acceptable in conversation and informal writing. The use of colloquial diction often gives a conversational tone to a piece of writing. Appropriate, for instance, in a personal letter, but sometimes inappropriate in an article intended for a learned journal. E.g.: "have a fit," meaning to grow very upset or perturbed.

Colon
That mark of punctuation (:) used to introduce certain materials, particularly a formal list or a series, a fairly long quotation, the body of a formal or business letter. It may also be used to introduce with emphasis a result, explanation, or example. E.g.: "He had one prominent virtue: generosity." For the same purpose, it may effectively introduce the second of two independent clauses. E.g.: "This was Brown's great year: he was graduated, married, and got his first job."

Common Ground
In argument, the starting point from which the contending parties begin to diverge. That which is accepted in the same way by the various sides of a controversy as a starting point. Not the same as an admitted issue. See *Issue.*

Comparison and Contrast
See pages 105–107.

Complex Sentence
A sentence that has a single main clause and one (or more) subordinate clause(s). E.g.: "When I see you again (subordinate), I will be a changed man (main)." The sentence type frequently used in sophisticated prose.

It is the subordinating conjunction ("when") that indicates the exact complex relationship between the two clauses. Thus, such conjunctions should be selected by the writer with great care.

Complication

That point of the narrative which flows from the *Exposition* or beginning of the action and issues in the *Climax* and *Resolution.* The entanglement of events that makes a climax and resolution necessary. The exposition, complication, climax, and resolution are really parts of a fluid action. The parts of a narrative are separated artificially for purposes of intelligent discussion.

Compound Sentence

A sentence containing two or more main or principal clauses, i.e., clauses of coordinate grammatical value. Usually these clauses are connected by a coordinating conjunction, such as "and," "but," "for," "or." E.g.: "There seem to be many ways to do this, *but* there is only one correct way." When a coordinating conjunction is not used, a compound sentence is usually punctuated with a semicolon. E.g.: "Such men are dangerous; they want power only."

Concrete Words

See *Abstract Words.*

Connotation

The association or atmosphere or suggestiveness of a word, rather than its precise *Denotation.* Thus, not the explicit or dictionary meaning, but the suggestive meaning developed from past use or from the context in present use. Compare, e.g.: "selective service," "conscription," "draft"; "lawyer," "attorney"; "home," "residence," "domicile." See *Denotation.*

Contrast (and Comparison)

See pages 105–107.

Decorum

In all writing, aptness. A general term that describes the fitness of the mode of expression with what is being expressed.

Deduction

See page 371.

Definition

Logical (or formal) and rhetorical (or extended), see pages 41–44.

Denotation

The explicit or dictionary meaning of a word as contrasted with the word's *Connotation.* Words of even the most ordinary denotation carry some connotation, e.g., "dog," "man," though, except in specific contexts, not so much as, e.g., "patriotism," "spy." Sometimes the connotative sense becomes so widely accepted that it may be regarded as almost denotative, e.g., "smell," "odor," "aroma." See *Connotation.*

Description

See pages 475–477.

Dialogue
A written conversation between two or more persons. The speech of each individual speaker is ordinarily presented as a separate paragraph, uses whatever punctuation the utterance itself demands, and is always enclosed within quotation marks. For examples, see any of the short stories in this anthology.

Diction
Choice of words or language used in a given situation. (The term also carries the sense—not used in this book—of articulation or pronunciation in speaking.) When good diction is used, the words chosen by the speaker or writer communicate his intention as specifically and fully as possible.

Differentia
See page 42.

Dominant Impression
See page 476.

Effect (and Cause)
See pages 259–261.

Elegant Variation
Variation in prose, including especially diction, simply for its own sake. Showy or pretentious writing. This is often referred to as "fine writing."

Emphasis
With **Unity** and **Coherence,** one of the great underlying principles of all rhetoric. Applies to the whole composition—paragraphs, sentences, and even phrases. Solves the question of the relative importance of the parts of the composition, the paragraph, or the sentence by making the important aspects seem important to the reader. Emphasis can be achieved in a variety of ways. (1) Position: The most emphatic position is the final one; the next most emphatic is the first one. (2) Subordination: In sentences, the less important idea generally is put in a subordinate clause, the more important idea in the main clause. (3) Active verb: Generally more emphatic than the passive form of the verb. (4) Alteration: A change of the normal subject-verb order of the English sentence calls attention to itself. (5) Repetition: One of the commonest and most obvious methods of achieving emphasis.

Enthymeme
See **Syllogism.**

Equivocation
Equivocal language is ambiguous in the sense that the true significance of what is said cannot be exactly determined. The deliberate use of such language with the intention of obscuring exact meaning.

Euphony
The pleasing or harmonius effect produced by the sounds of words or phrases. See Maugham's essay, page 637.

Evidence

Whatever is offered in argument to support the validity of the proposition. The result of valid evidence is proof. Facts and opinions are the commonest sources of evidence. See also pages 370–371.

Example

See pages 79–80.

Exposition

As a form of discourse, see pages 39–40.

Exposition

As used in *Narrative,* see page 503.

Fallacy

In argument, an error in the reasoning process, caused by ignorance or by intention. Some common fallacies are *Ad Hominem, Ignoring the Question,* and *Begging the Question.*

Familiar Essay

See pages 585–586.

Figurative Language

Commonly used figures of speech that create figurative language are *Metaphor, Simile, Personification, Hyperbole.* Figurative language helps to make writing more precise as well as more interesting. When using such language, the writer ignores the literal meaning of a word and bends the word to a new meaning. "Cool," used literally, describes a particular condition of the atmosphere. In being used, perhaps too extensively, to describe a particular kind of music, it has been bent to a new meaning. At times the new meaning of a word catches on and becomes one of the world's established meanings. Figurative language is an essential part of all discourse, oral and written.

Generalization (Absolute or Sweeping)

The tendency to generalize *without* sufficient attention to particulars. A common fault of much modern rhetoric. Either the writer does not have a sufficient number of instances or he ignores instances that would prove the contrary of his sweeping statement. E.g.: "All politicians are crooked."

General Words

The kind of diction (choice of words) that expresses general concepts or feelings. Apt in those cases and not to be avoided. Too often, however, the inexperienced writer, relying upon the first word that comes to mind, selects a general word where a specific and particular one would be better. Contrast the differences between fruit—apple; house—home, shack, mansion, bungalow; nice—discerning, pleasing, critical, over-refined, accurate, exact. See *Specific Words.*

Genus

See page 42.

Grammatical Structure

This means, with reference to the sentence, the grammatical pattern of the sentence—*Simple, Compound, Complex.*

History of the Question

The circumstances surrounding a proposition that explain why it is now being discussed, as well as information of past discussions of the same or a like proposition.

Hyperbole

A figure of speech that uses the technique of exaggeration in order to intensify through extravagance. Overuse of it in writing is to be avoided. E.g.: "He worked like a horse to get his book finished."

Hypothesis

A tentative supposition accepted for the time being to explain certain facts. Not to be confused with fact or *Theory.*

Ignoring the Question

In argument, a fallacy that avoids the point at issue by dealing with a different issue or by appealing to passion and prejudice in place of concentrating on the question at hand.

Induction

See page 371.

Intonation

Stress, rise and fall of pitch, and breaks or pauses in the speaking voice. Can sometimes be an aid to punctuation.

Inverted Order

A variation from the usual English word order in declarative statements for purposes of emphasis, it places the verb before its subject: "Then came the dawn." *Transposed Order,* as distinguished from inverted, places the object before the subject and verb: "Beethoven I have always liked." Such variations are to be used sparingly.

Irony

Verbal irony is saying one thing and meaning another, usually the opposite of what is said. E.g.: Antony's references in Shakespeare's *Julius Caesar* to Brutus as "an honorable man." Situational irony occurs when the outcome or result of an action is the opposite of what might have been expected from antecedent conditions or actions. E.g.: Julius Caesar, notable for his active character, meets his ruin through acts set in motion by Brutus, notable for his contemplative character.

Issue, Admitted and Crucial

See page 370.

Judgment

Any argument must be about a matter of judgment, the result of the operation of the understanding or reason to reach a decision based upon the mind's ability to discriminate and compare.

Levels of Usage

Language is divided into standard and substandard speech. Standard speech includes several levels: formal, informal, and colloquial. Formal speech, more often written than spoken, is used in restricted situations, such as reference works, dissertations, and commencement addresses.

Informal speech is the kind of language found in most good magazines, newspapers, and books and also in the conversations of well-educated people. Colloquial English is the basic conversational English of the educated person. No one of these levels is absolutely set off from the other. Substandard English includes illiterate speech, slang, and some localisms. Illiterate English, more spoken than written, is the conversational speech of the uneducated. Slang is the flashy invention of language for special circumstances. It seldom survives the reason for which it was invented. Localisms are expressions peculiar to a region or locality.

Linking Verb

Also called *Copula.* A verb that links or connects a subject with a predicate noun or predicate adjective. Most commonly used are forms of the verb "to be" and also of "appear," "become," "seem," "taste," "smell," "feel." E.g.: "She was his wife." "It appeared small." "The water feels good."

Loose Sentence

A sentence in which the main elements of meaning tend to appear towards the beginning rather than the end of the sentence. Of rhetorical, rather than grammatical, significance, it is exemplified most frequently in that kind of complex sentence in which the subordinate elements appear at the end rather than the beginning, an order that is normal in most written and oral English: "I voted for Smith because he was the most capable candidate." "Loose" in this context does not signify "weak" or "poor"; it should not be confused with "loose" as applied to a rambling whole composition or paragraph. See *Periodic Sentence.*

Main Clause

Sometimes called "independent clause." A group of words or a unit grammatically independent, upon which other clauses depend. E.g.: "Although he was a poor shot, *he continued to fire at the escaping prisoner.*"

Metaphor

A figure of speech, usually a comparison without the use of "like" or "as." A writer describes a thing as being what it is only similar to. E.g.: "The moon sleeps softly on the river bank." Metaphor is coming to be used by many critics as a term for the whole process of comparison by which all figures of speech are born.

Narrative, Factual

See pages 501–502.

Narrative, Fictional

See pages 501–502.

Narrative, Personal

See pages 3–4.

Non Sequitur

Literally, "it does not follow." In argument, a fallacy which consists in asserting a conclusion that does not follow from the premises because the conclusion contains material that is not supported by the premises. A simple *non sequitur* makes no attempt to show a cause-and-effect connection. E.g.: "Smith is a good neighbor and a fine father, so he ought to be elected to Congress." See *Post Hoc, Ergo Propter Hoc.*

Paradox

A statement that seems to be contradictory but is not, E.g.: "Never pray for what you most want; you might get it" (French proverb).

Paragraph

Generally, a group of sentences taken together and constituting a larger unit of thought. If a sentence can be said to express an idea, then a paragraph develops or elaborates the idea. One-sentence paragraphs, except for dialogue, are rarely used, except for purposes of emphasis or transition. The use of paragraphs allows the writer to develop his thesis through parts, that is, paragraphs of such size that each is easily grasped by the reader and the relation of one part to the rest of the parts and to the whole of the thesis is clear to the reader. A paragraph usually develops around a *Topic Sentence,* expressed or implied.

Parallelism

A rhetorical type of sentence structure in which coordinate ideas are expressed in a like manner or a like construction. A structure in which the grammatical elements are balanced one against the other. The ideas must be logically parallel if parallel structure is used. E.g.: "Nancy went home; Judith stayed here." Parallelism may apply to words, phrases, clauses, or sentences. E.g.: *"Swimming* and *hiking* are my favorite sports." See *Balanced Sentence.*

Partition

Another name for *Division.* See pages 193–195.

Passive Verb

A form of the voice of the verb in which the subject is being acted upon rather than doing the acting. Not to be preferred as a regular practice in the pattern of English sentences. E.g.: "The building was *seen* by me." See *Active Verb.*

Periodic Sentence

A sentence in which the main elements of meaning tend to appear towards the end rather than the beginning of the sentence. Of rhetorical, not grammatical significance, it is exemlified most frequently by the relatively long complex sentence, in which the main clause appears at the end of the sentence. Very often the more meaningful words or phrases are, for emphatic or dramatic effect, placed as close to the end of the clause as possible: "If the artist must have skill and invention, serenity and compassion, then a truly great artist was Leonardo." The periodic sentence, particularly in extended form, must be used sparingly and only functionally—that is, when the context calls for emphatic or dramatic effect. See *Loose Sentence.*

Personification

A figure of speech that gives animate, personal qualities to something nonanimate, nonpersonal: "Life weeps for its child, man." Used more in poetry than in prose.

Persuasion

See page 372.

Pleonasm

Redundancy; use of superfluous words: "I heard him with my ears." (May be used, but sparingly, for deliberate effects, as for emphasis: "I heard him with these very ears.") Distinguished from verboseness or wordiness, which mean simply the use of too many words.

Point of View

In narrative writing, Percy Lubbock's definition has come to be a classic: "The relation in which the narrator stands to the story." There are two basic points of view with many variations: (1) the omniscient point of view allows the author to stand outside of the story, knowing everything, being able to get inside the minds and hearts of the characters, playing God, as it were, to the universe; (2) the first person point of view has the story told by someone within the story who must see or be told everything he reports. Eudora Welty's "A Visit of Charity" (page 557) is told from the omniscient point of view; James Thurber's "The Night the Ghost Got In" (page 572) is told from the first person point of view. On point of view in *descriptive* writing, see page 477.

Post Hoc, Ergo Propter Hoc

Another form of the **Non Sequitur.** This fallacy consists in assuming that X is the cause of Y because X preceded Y in time. Time order is mistaken for a cause-and-effect relationship. E.g.: "Juvenile delinquency has grown since more young people have gone to high school." Going to high school is assumed to be the cause of juvenile delinquency.

Premise

See **Syllogism.**

Primary Intention

With respect to the forms of discourse, see page 39.

Process Analysis

See pages 149–151.

Proportion

A way of achieving emphasis in composition. Quite simply, the writer gives proportionally more space to more important ideas. The tail never wags the dog.

Proposition

As used in argument, see page 369.

Reasoning

In argument, the proof that results from thinking with a view toward arriving at a valid conclusion. The two forms are **Induction** and **Deduction.** See page 371.

Redundancy

See **Pleonasm.**

Refutation

In argument, the attempt to destroy the proofs of the opposition. Of its nature destructive rather than constructive. The three methods of *direct* refutation are these: (1) denial—simply denying the whole proposition and proving that the opposite is true; (2) retort—when the opposing argument is true, using it to support your own side; (3) distinction— accepting what is true in the opposing argument and rejecting what is false and then showing that the part accepted as true does not oppose your own proposition. The methods of *indirect* refutation are many: (1) reducing the opponent's argument to a logical absurdity by carrying it to its logical conclusion; (2) proving that the opposition contradicts itself or is ignorant of the facts; (3) facing the opponent with a dilemma, two or more alternatives: whichever is chosen proves the opposite position untenable; (4) using analogy, a similar argument based on other facts that turns out to be absurd; (5) building up more objections to the opposition's argument than can be mustered against your own.

Repetition

A rhetorical method of achieving emphasis. Simply repeating an idea, sometimes using the same words and phrases, sometimes altering the manner of expressing the same idea. One of the commonest and most obvious methods of securing emphasis. Used purposelessly, repetition is a weakness.

Resolution

In narrative, the term that describes the ending of the action. That which began terminates. Does not mean that all problems are resolved in the sense that everything is settled or cleared up. Those things, however, that were unstable in the exposition are now stabilized. As Elizabeth Bowen remarked, "We may get off the train, but the passengers on the train keep going."

Rhetoric

The art of expression through the medium of language. The use of the available means of effective expression in a given situation. The discovery, arrangement, and development of the means of expression.

Rhetorical Question

A statement in the form of a question. No immediate direct response is expected. A device used, especially orally, to hold the audience's attention, to emphasize a special point, or to indicate that a new turn in thought is to come. E.g.: "What would you have done?" "But was there any hope?"

Rhythm

In language, a recurring pattern of sounds involving balance and contrast, in English particularly distinguishable by more or less regularly contrasting unstressed and stressed syllables. Rhythm in prose can be observed or sensed but not so easily described. Much smooth-flowing English prose will tend to have a rising and falling effect, similar to what in verse would be an iambic or anapestic rhythm: an unstressed syllable rising to or followed by a stressed syllable or two unstressed syllables followed by a stressed syllable. It is a movement resulting very often from the very nature of our present language (e.g., articles—generally unstressed—followed by nouns—generally stressed; prepositions—generally unstressed—followed by nouns; the relative scarcity of inflectional endings). The rhythm of a given passage should be in keeping with the effect intended. The clipped, staccato effects of, for example, Hemingway may be much more effective for the intent of his works than a smooth-flowing line would be. Finally, rhythm in prose may also be achieved by units larger than syllables, by, for example, phrase structures, clause structures, and sentence structures presenting balance and contrast.

Semicolon

A mark of punctuation (;) signalling a separation much greater than the comma and almost as great as the period. (1) Used to separate main clauses not joined by a coordinate conjunction: "I came to the house; no one was at home." (2) Used to separate main clauses joined by a coordinate conjunction if the clauses contain smaller parts separated by commas, particularly if the clauses are long and involved: "These books, as I have already told you, are very important; and I will expect you, no matter what hapens, to treat them with care." (3) Used for clarity to separate other coordinate parts which themselves include commas or are rather long: see the second example under *Simple Sentence.* (4) Used between clauses joined by conjunctive adverbs, such as "nevertheless," "moreover," "however": "History is an interesting study; however, not all historians are interesting."

Sentence Structure

Sentences may be described or classified grammatically as simple, compound, or complex: see *Grammatical Structure.* Sentences or parts of sentences may be described for rhetorical purposes in terms of word, phrase, or clause order or balance or contrast: see *Balanced Sentence, Periodic Sentence, Parallelism.*

Setting

In narrative, the place where the action is revealed. Besides the actual physical setting—the room, the house, the city—the setting may include as well the atmosphere, the tone of the place. The environment, the *mise en scène,* the milieu.

Significance

In narrative. See page 503.

Simile

A figure of speech that compares two different or unlike things explicitly: "My love is like a red, red rose." See *Metaphor.*

Simple Sentence

Made up of one grammatically independent clause: "Brown went to the moon." The complexity of the modifying process can make the simple sentence in English seem very complicated: "There was room on the shelves for all of my records (some of little value); the literary, but popular, books; trinkets in abundance; and remembrances from many trips." See *Grammatical Structure.*

Slang

One of the levels of usage, usually substandard English. Greenough and Kittredge have defined it as "a peculiar kind of vagabond language always hanging on the outskirts of legitimate speech." It is commonly invented in order to give a unique or highly personal and immediate response to some situation calling forth a strong reaction. Usually harsh, violent, and ludicrous, it has strength, vitality, and color while alive. But it soon loses its currency because of overuse or because the situation that gave it birth has since disappeared. Some, of course, survives and becomes a part of colloquial and informal speech.

Species

See page 42.

Specific Words

In most circumstances in prose the writer chooses specific words for his expression, since specific words tend to be rich and colorful in their suggestiveness. Specific words refer to particular objects, actions, and attitudes. E.g.: "sombrero," "turban," "derby" are more specific than "hat." "Hat" is more specific than "headdress." See **General Words**.

Style

The personal accent of the writer in the use of language of a given time within the standards of speech. See pages 624–626.

Summary Paragraph

Often used by the writer within a long essay or in an essay on a complex subject to help the reader follow the explanation more carefully. At times a mere mechanical summary will do, but in most instances a summary paragraph should make an attempt to communicate emphatically the important material.

Syllogism

The typical form of all deductive reasoning. The relation between the predicate and subject of the proposition to be proved is established by comparing the known relations of each to a given third term, called the "middle term." This comparison is made in a series of three statements: (1) the first states the relation of the *predicate* to the middle term and is called the "major premise"; (2) the second states the relation of the *subject* to the middle term and is called the "minor premise"; (3) the third (the proved statement) brings the subject and predicate *together* and is called the "conclusion."

    (1) All men are mortal. (Major)
    (2) Stephen is a man. (Minor)
    (3) Stephen is mortal. (Conclusion)

There must be only three terms; each must occur twice. The middle term must appear in the major and minor premises but never in the conclusion. In writing, a syllogism is generally constructed by determining the proposition (conclusion), finding the reason for the proposition (minor premise), and stating this reason for the whole class to which the subject of the proposition belongs (major premise). In writing, also, the syllogism is often not stated in its complete form; sometimes one of the premises is omitted but "understood." Technically, this is called the **Enthymeme:** it is used more frequently because it helps to curtail the expression of commonplace statements.

Symbol

Something concrete that stands for something abstract, a visible sign for something invisible. The symbol, therefore, is made to take on a much larger meaning than it contains within itself. Writers use symbols habitually because the concrete is easier for the reader to apprehend than the abstract. A rose, for example, can be used as a symbol for youth or for beauty. The rose may, however, be used as a symbol for anything else, even for old age or ugliness, provided that the writer makes such use appropriate to his context.

Syntax

The arrangement or order of words in a sentence to show the words' relationships to each other.

Synthesis
The bringing together of parts to make a whole. See page 315.

Theory
A plausible and accepted general principle used to explain something. Hence, the general principles of any group of facts taken together. Not to be confused with *Hypothesis, Assumption.*

Thesis Statement
The brief statement of a topic limited to a specific and manageable area; summary of what the composition as a whole is about. See *Central Purpose.*

Tone
A term borrowed from music, not easily definable with respect to prose, but indispensable for analyzing it. It is the author's attitude toward his material or his audience. The dominating flavor or character of a piece of writing. Mood and temper are also used to describe this quality.

Topic Sentence
Also referred to as "topic thought" or "central thought." Used to describe the single sentence that summarizes the thought of a paragraph. May be expressed or implied. If expressed, it is often found as the first sentence of the paragraph or as the last sentence of the paragraph, since these are the emphatic positions.

Transitional Words and Phrases
Such expressions help the continuity of thought between sentences and paragraphs by linking what has gone before with what comes after. Take note of such words and phrases as the following in your reading and writing: "this," "that," "these," "those" (but be sure that these four are used with clear and precise reference), "on the contrary," "in the second place," "furthermore," "however," "a further reason."

Transposed Order
See *Inverted Order.*

Unity
Along with *Coherence* and *Emphasis,* one of the three great rhetorical principles. Applies to sentences, paragraphs, and whole compositions. Briefly, unity means the development of one idea or feeling at a time without a side trip into the development of a competing or intruding notion. Sentences, paragraphs, and whole compositions must have a point of focus that gives unity to what has been expressed. In short everything that belongs to the subject is present and accounted for and everything irrelevant is omitted. Unity, of course, must be judged in the final analysis by the writer's purpose in a given situation.

Usage
A living language is what it is because of the way it is used by the people who are supposed to be the most qualified users of language. Language is not legislated so much as it grows and is formed.

Word Play
Witty or clever exchange of words or play on words: "*Writing* between the lines" is a play on "*reading* between the lines."